PUBLIC LAW ADJUDICATION IN COMMON LAW SYSTEMS: PROCESS AND SUBSTANCE

This volume arises from the inaugural Public Law Conference hosted in September 2014 by the Centre for Public Law at the University of Cambridge, which brought together leading public lawyers from a number of common law jurisdictions. While those from such jurisdictions share background understandings, significant differences within the common law world create opportunities for valuable exchanges of ideas and debate.

This collection draws upon one of the principal sub-themes that emerged during the conference—namely, the way in which relationships and distinctions between the notions of 'process' and 'substance' play out in relation to and inform adjudication in public law cases. The essays contained in this volume address those issues from a variety of perspectives. While the bulk of the chapters consider topical issues in judicial review, either on common law or human rights grounds, or both, other chapters adopt more theoretical, historical, empirical or contextual approaches. Concluding chapters reflect generally on the papers in the collection and the value of facilitating cross-jurisdictional dialogue.

Public Law Adjudication in Common Law Systems

Process and Substance

John Bell, Mark Elliott, Jason NE Varuhas
and Philip Murray

• HART •
OXFORD • LONDON • NEW YORK • NEW DELHI • SYDNEY

HART PUBLISHING
Bloomsbury Publishing Plc
Kemp House, Chawley Park, Cumnor Hill, Oxford, OX2 9PH, UK

HART PUBLISHING, the Hart/Stag logo, BLOOMSBURY and the Diana logo are trademarks of Bloomsbury Publishing Plc
First published in Great Britain 2016

First published in hardback, 2016
Paperback edition, 2018

A catalogue record for this book is available from the British Library.

Library of Congress Cataloging-in-Publication Data

Names: Conference on the Law of Obligations (7th : 2014 : Hong Kong, China) | Robertson, Andrew, 1966– editor. | Tilbury, M. J. (Michael J.), editor.

Title: Divergences in private law / Edited by Andrew Robertson and Michael Tilbury.

Description: Hart Publishing, Oxford : 2016. | "Originally presented at the Seventh Biennial Conference on the Law of Obligations held in Hong Kong in July 2014"—ECIP galley. | Includes bibliographical references and index.

Identifiers: LCCN 2015038968 | ISBN 9781782256601 (hardback : alk. paper)

Subjects: LCSH: Obligations (Law)—Congresses. | Civil law—Congresses. | Common law—Congresses.

Classification: LCC K830.A6 D58 2016 | DDC 346—dc23 LC record available at http://lccn.loc.gov/2015038968

ISBN: PB: 978-1-50992-445-5
HB: 978-1-84946-991-3

Typeset by Compuscript Ltd, Shannon

Foreword

SIR JOHN LAWS

'Process and Substance in Public Law' is, I suppose, a dry enough title for a conference. It sounds like the sort of thing you would find in a seminar room on a quiet Thursday evening, attended by a few devoted specialists. But the colloquium at the Centre for Public Law in Cambridge, held under that name and sponsored by Hart Publishing in September 2014, was an international event with a remarkable range of speakers whose papers traversed a very varied legal landscape. The convenors sought contributions concentrating on the academic study of public law; in response distinguished speakers from a series of common law jurisdictions produced papers across a broad spectrum of theory and practice. The conference was attended by over 200 participants drawn from a wide variety of common law and other jurisdictions, including Australia, Canada, Hong Kong, Italy, Ireland, Japan, the Netherlands, New Zealand, Singapore, South Africa, the United Kingdom and the United States.

I will not attempt to summarise here the learning and perception of individual contributors: the editors have provided an admirable overview in the Introduction. Rather I will make three points. I may start with this observation from the commentary on the conference to be found on the Cambridge Law Faculty website:

> The intellectual case for a conference of this nature stems from the fact that common law systems are simultaneously similar to and different from one another. While those from common law jurisdictions all work from background understandings that have enough in common to facilitate fruitful engagement, significant differences between such systems open up opportunities for valuable exchanges of ideas and debate.

This is true. Each common law jurisdiction is enriched by the others. To be sure, the process demands a willingness among the judges to receive and respect the learning of other courts. In England and Wales, we are better at this than we once were. The process can only be enhanced by an academic conference such as this. To take just one example: Professor Kent Roach of the University of Toronto, in his chapter on 'Remedies for Laws that Violate Human Rights', has provided a conspectus of remedies for rights violations across common law jurisdictions whose purpose is to 'examine the variety of remedies available for legislation that may infringe human rights with a focus on how such remedies help define the respective roles of courts and legislatures'. To an English lawyer, his essay provides a fresh hinterland for the Human Rights Act 1998, and in particular the remedy of a declaration of incompatibility.

My second observation is related to the first. Enrichment from the legal materials of other jurisdictions is especially apt for the betterment of the common law, because of the common law's own distinctive methodology. I have described it elsewhere as a process of continuous self-correction.[1] The combination of precedent and innovation allows for an orderly development of principle, and the materials which may enrich the process are open-ended; there is no closed category of the sources of the common law. But the common law does not merely absorb external sources; it makes them its own. This is what has happened—is happening—with such concepts as proportionality, which we owe to Europe. The absorption of material from other common law jurisdictions is a yet more natural process.

So far I have said nothing that is specific to public law, the subject of the conference. My third comment is that this is an area in which there are particular benefits to be had from the fruits of such a conference. The reason is that although our public law has its roots in the ancient prerogative writs of certiorari, mandamus and prohibition, its modern development (say, from the 1960s and the seminal decisions of that era such as *Anisminic*) has been marked by the rapid evolution of principle (supercharged, so to speak, by the advent of law from Strasbourg and Luxembourg) in which academic lawyers have made signal contributions. Public lawyers in this jurisdiction, and no doubt others, will be very familiar with the frequent use made by the courts of such works as Sir William Wade's *Administrative Law* (now Wade and Forsyth). I remember a friend of mine at the commercial Bar telling me I was lucky to practise in public law: most of the great questions in mercantile law (other than fruits of statutes and treaties) had been settled by Lord Mansfield in the eighteenth century, or if not by him then by Scrutton, Bankes and Atkin LJJ in the 1920s, whereas in our field we were still making the common law. We are still making it; and the academics play a signal part. There is a lot of philosophy—moral and political philosophy—in public law. Its practitioners, certainly the judges, need the conceptual bricks and mortar which academic lawyers bring to the building of the law. The contributions to this conference provide many good instances. Professor Jerry Mashaw's piece on public reason is but one. I particularly enjoyed his example, from a *New Yorker* cartoon, of the view that 'to refuse to give reasons is to assert authority in a way that is fundamentally illegitimate':

> [A] small child is leaning forward from the backseat close to his driving father's ear. [The child is saying] 'Why aren't we there yet?' 'Why are you going so slow?' 'Why does Grandma live so far away?' And so on and on. At the bottom of the cartoon the caption gives the harassed father's response: 'Shut up, he explained'.

Here is a deep truth; public administrators, as well as public lawyers, should know this story.

This was a conference of very real value, for the depth and range of thought which its contributors brought to Cambridge. Its product—the contents of this book—will interest and stimulate thinking lawyers for a long time to come; an interest which will be renewed by the conference's successor. The intention is that it will become a biennial event, and preliminary plans are under way to hold the second conference at Cambridge in September 2016. Our public law will, of course, face new challenges between now and then; but, as always, it will build on what has gone before. Successive conferences of this kind will be a muscular contribution to the process.

[1] J Laws, *The Common Law Constitution* (Cambridge, Cambridge University Press, 2014) 9.

I have spoken of the worth of the conference, but not the pleasure of it. Conviviality is no less important than scholarship; sound learning and good fellowship enhance each other. This was a very convivial occasion. For that, and for much besides, the convenors and organisers at the Faculty of Law at Cambridge, as well of course as the participants, are much to be thanked.

Contents

Contributors

Mark Aronson is an Emeritus Professor of Law at the University of New South Wales, Australia. He has published widely in a number of areas, including civil and criminal procedure, the law of evidence, tort liability of public authorities and administrative law. His co-authored *Judicial Review of Administrative Action* (Sydney, Thomson Reuters, 2013) is currently in its fifth edition.

John Bell is Professor of Law at the University of Cambridge, a Fellow of Pembroke College, Cambridge, and a Fellow of the British Academy. He has particular research interests in relation to public law and the legal systems of continental European countries. He has published widely in these and other areas.

Varda Bondy is Senior Research Fellow at the University of Essex School of Law, and a co-founder of the United Kingdom Administrative Justice Institute, a national project funded by the Nuffield Foundation based at Essex. She practised as a legal aid lawyer for 15 years, specialising in housing and public law, before joining the Public Law Project where she was Director of Research until December 2013. Her Nuffield Foundation funded empirical research studies focused on various aspects of judicial review, including human rights, settlements. mediation and post-judgment impact. Her other research interests are ombudsmen and design of redress mechanisms.

Paul Daly is Associate Dean and Faculty Secretary at the Faculty of Law, University of Montreal. He is the author of *A Theory of Deference in Administrative Law: Basis, Application and Scope* (Cambridge, Cambridge University Press, 2012), numerous articles in leading peer-reviewed journals, and the award-winning blog, *Administrative Law Matters*.

Andrew Edgar is a Senior Lecturer in the Faculty of Law at the University of Sydney. He teaches administrative law in the undergraduate and JD programmes and environmental planning law in the postgraduate coursework programme. Andrew's research focuses on judicial review of public interest decisions, in particular, public participation in administrative decision-making processes and the law of standing.

Mark Elliott is Professor of Public Law at the University of Cambridge, a Fellow of St Catharine's College, Cambridge, and Legal Adviser to the House of Lords Select Committee on the Constitution. His recent books include *Public Law* (Oxford, Oxford University Press, 2014) (co-written with Robert Thomas), *The Cambridge Companion to Public Law* (Cambridge, Cambridge University Press, 2015) (co-edited with David Feldman) and *The Scope and Intensity of Substantive Review: Traversing Taggart's Rainbow* (Oxford, Hart Publishing, 2015) (co-edited with Hanna Wilberg).

David Feldman is the Rouse Ball Professor of English Law in the University of Cambridge, a Fellow of Downing College, Cambridge, and an Academic Associate of chambers at 39 Essex Street, London. He previously taught at the Universities of Bristol and Birmingham (where he was Dean of Law 1997–2000) and has held visiting positions at the Australian National University, the University of Melbourne, and the University of Nottingham. He was the first Legal Adviser to the UK Parliament's Joint Select Committee on Human Rights (2000–2004) and sat as an international Judge of the Constitutional Court of Bosnia and Herzegovina (2002–2010; a Vice-President 2006–2009). His research and writing have been predominantly in the field of public law, broadly defined, with a comparative flavour. He is a Fellow of the British Academy and a Queen's Counsel *honoris causa*, and served as President of the Society of Legal Scholars (2010–2011).

Christopher Forsyth is Professor of Public Law and Private International Law in the University of Cambridge. He is the author (with the late Sir William Wade) of *Administrative Law*, 11th edn (Oxford, Oxford University Press, 2014), an authoritative text relied upon by courts throughout the common law world. He is also the author of *Private International Law*, 5th edn (Cape Town, Juta, 2012), an authoritative text on South African private international law. He is an Honorary Professor in the University of Stellenbosch, a practising barrister and a Bencher of the Inner Temple.

Matthew Groves is a Professor in the Law Faculty of Monash University in Australia. His research is mainly in administrative law, particularly judicial review of administrative decisions, the requirements of fairness and the bias rule. Matthew's recent books include (with Mark Aronson) *Judicial Review of Administrative Action*, 5th edn (Sydney, Thomson Reuters, 2013) and (as editor) *Modern Australian Administrative Law* (Cambridge, Cambridge University Press, 2014).

Carol Harlow is Emeritus Professor of Law at the London School of Economics. Her research is focused on the liability of the state, accountability and more specifically accountability in the European Union. In 2013, she acted as Special Adviser to the House of Lords Select Committee on Inquiries. She is joint author with Richard Rawlings of *Law and Administration*, 3rd edn (Cambridge, Cambridge University Press, 2009) and *Process and Procedure in EU Administration* (Oxford, Hart Publishing, 2014). She is currently working on an edited collection of essays on EU Administrative Law. Carol is a Fellow of the British Academy and a Queen's Counsel *honoris causa*.

Mary Liston is an Assistant Professor at the Peter A Allard School of Law, University of British Columbia. Her research focuses on advanced and comparative public law, Canadian administrative law, Aboriginal administrative law, theories of the rule of law, and law and literature. Her work has been cited by the Supreme Court of Canada. She is a co-author along with Craig S Forcese, Adam Dodek, Philip Bryden, Peter Carver, Richard Haigh and Constance MacIntosh of *Public Law: Cases, Commentary and Analysis*, 3rd edn (Toronto, Emond Publishing, 2015). She is also a contributor to the leading casebook *Administrative Law in Context*, 2nd edn (Toronto, Emond Publishing, 2013).

Jerry L Mashaw is Sterling Professor of Law and Management at Yale University, where he teaches courses on administrative law, social welfare policy, regulation, legislation and the design of public institutions His award-winning books include *Bureaucratic Justice* (New Haven, CT, Yale University Press, 1983), *The Struggle for Auto Safety* (with David Harfst) (Cambridge, MA, Harvard University Press, 1990), *Greed, Chaos, and Governance: Using Public Choice to Improve Public Law* (New Haven, CT, Yale University Press, 1997) and *Creating the Administrative Constitution* (New Haven, CT, Yale University Press, 2013). He is a frequent contributor to legal and public policy journals and to newspapers and news magazines. Professor Mashaw is a founding member and past President of the National Academy of Social Insurance, a Fellow of the National Academy of Arts and Sciences, and was founding co-editor (with OE Williamson) of the *Journal of Law, Economics and Organization*.

Philip Murray was a Fellow in Law at St John's College, Cambridge and an Affiliated University Lecturer in the Faculty of Law at the University of Cambridge. He taught constitutional law, administrative law and Roman law, with a particular interest in the history of English judicial review. He was awarded the University of Cambridge's Yorke Prize for his doctoral thesis, 'Judicial Review for Jurisdictional Error of Law in Nineteenth-century Certiorari and Prohibition Proceedings'. Philip is now training for the priesthood at Westcott House, one of the Church of England's theological colleges.

Richard Rawlings is Professor of Public Law at University College London, having previously been Professor of Law at the London School of Economics. Rick has written widely in constitutional and administrative law, with works including *Process and Procedure in EU Administration* (with Carol Harlow) (Oxford, Hart Publishing, 2014), *Sovereignty and the Law* (jointly edited with Peter Leyland and Alison Young) (Oxford, Oxford University Press, 2013), *The Regulatory State: Constitutional Implications* (jointly edited with Dawn Oliver and Tony Prosser) (Oxford, Oxford University Press, 2010), *Devolution, Law-Making and the Constitution* (jointly edited with Robert Hazell) (Exeter, Imprint Academic, 2005), *Delineating Wales: Constitutional, Legal and Administrative Aspects of National Devolution* (Cardiff, University of Wales Press, 2003), *Law and Administration in Europe* (jointly edited with Paul Craig) (Oxford, Oxford University Press, 2003), *Pressure Through Law* (with Carol Harlow) (London, Routledge, 1992) and *Law and Administration*, 3rd edn (with Carol Harlow) (Cambridge, Cambridge University Press, 2009). Rick was elected Honorary Bencher of Middle Temple in 2009, and is a former Legal Adviser to the House of Lords Select Committee on the Constitution.

Kent Roach is a Professor of Law at the University of Toronto where he holds the Prichard-Wilson Chair of Law and Public Policy at the University of Toronto Faculty of Law, with cross-appointments in criminology and political science. In 2002 he was elected a Fellow of the Royal Society of Canada and in 2013, he won a Fellowship from the Pierre Trudeau Foundation for his academic and social contributions. Professor Roach's books include *Constitutional Remedies in Canada*, 2nd edn (Toronto, Canada Law Book, 2013) (winner of the 1997 Owen Prize),

Due Process and Victims' Rights: The New Law and Politics of Criminal Justice (Toronto, University of Toronto, 1999) (short-listed for the 1999 Donner Prize for best public policy book), *Brian Dickson: A Judge's Journey* (with Robert J Sharpe) (Toronto, University of Toronto Press, 2003) (winner of the 2004 JW Dafoe Prize) and *The 9/11 Effect* (Cambridge, Cambridge University Press, 2011) (winner of the Mundell Medal).

Alan Robertson was admitted to the New South Wales Bar from 1983 and practised nationally, mainly in public law including constitutional law, administrative law, revenue law and competition law. He was a part-time member of the Administrative Review Council from 1992 to 1997 and was appointed Senior Counsel in 1995. He became a judge of the Federal Court of Australia in 2011. He is a National Coordinating Judge of the Court's Administrative and Constitutional Law and Human Rights National Practice Area. He is also a Fellow of the Australian Academy of Law.

Cheryl Saunders is a Laureate Professor Emeritus at the University of Melbourne and founding Director of its Centre for Comparative Constitutional Studies. She works in the areas of Australian and comparative public law, on both of which she has written widely. She is a President Emeritus of the International Association of Constitutional Law and a former President of the Administrative Review Council of Australia. In 2005–06, she was the Arthur Goodhart Professor of Legal Science at the University of Cambridge. She is an Officer in the Order of Australia and a Chevalier de la Légion d'Honneur of France.

Maurice Sunkin is Professor of Public Law and Socio Legal Studies at the University of Essex. He is the General Editor of *Public Law* and an Associate Member of Landmark Chambers, London. His main research interests concern the use and effects of judicial review, administrative justice and the human rights implication of big data and new technologies. He is currently Director of the United Kingdom Administrative Justice Institute, a national project funded by the Nuffield Foundation based at Essex and Principal Investigation and Co-Director of an ESRC-funded project on human rights and big data. For the parliamentary session 2013–14 he served as Legal Adviser to the House of Lords Select Committee on the Constitution. He was a Trustee of the Public Law Project from 2000 to 2011.

Jason NE Varuhas is Associate Professor at the University of Melbourne, Associate Fellow of the Centre for Public Law, Faculty of Law, University of Cambridge, and Bye-Fellow of Christ's College, Cambridge. His research and teaching interests cross the public law-private law divide. His current research work includes major projects on 'mapping' public law and the 'socialisation' of private law. He has published on topics in private and public law in leading international journals, in a number of edited collections, and has several books forthcoming including his sole-authored monograph, *Damages and Human Rights* (Oxford, Hart Publishing), which stems from his doctoral work for which he won the Yorke Prize at the University of Cambridge. He is a founder and co-convenor of the biennial series of Public Law Conferences.

Greg Weeks is a Senior Lecturer in the Faculty of Law at the University of New South Wales, where he teaches the Administrative Law and Advanced Administrative Law courses. Greg's research interests are primarily related to judicial review and state liability and he has published a number of articles and book chapters in these fields. He has two books forthcoming in 2016. The first, which will be published by Hart Publishing, considers the remedies available when public authorities fail to adhere to their own soft law instruments. The second is the sixth edition of *Judicial Review of Administrative Action*, Australia's leading administrative law text, which Greg joins as a co-author alongside Mark Aronson and Matthew Groves.

Table of Cases

Australia

Canada

European Permanent Court of Arbitration

European Court of Human Rights

European Court of Justice

European General Court

New Zealand

South Africa

United Kingdom

United States of America

Table of Legislation

Australia

International Instruments

New Zealand

South Africa

United Kingdom

United States of America

1

Introduction

JOHN BELL, MARK ELLIOTT, JASON NE VARUHAS
AND PHILIP MURRAY

THE CONTRIBUTIONS TO this volume all originated as papers delivered at a major international conference that took place at the University of Cambridge in September 2014. The conference, entitled 'Process and Substance in Public Law', was the first in what is intended to be a series of international Public Law Conferences that will bring together common lawyers from a broad range of jurisdictions.

The intellectual case for such a series of conferences stems from the fact that common law systems are simultaneously similar to and different from one another. While those from common law jurisdictions thus all work from background understandings that have enough in common to facilitate fruitful engagement, significant differences between such systems open up opportunities for valuable exchanges of ideas and debate. These possibilities were realised at the conference; the exceptionally high quality of the papers was matched by the quality of the debate which they provoked, as participants grappled and engaged with points of contact and contrast between the many jurisdictions that were represented.

Our experience has been that there was significant demand for a conference concentrating on the academic study of public law. Following the issue of a call for papers, we received approximately 170 abstracts from scholars based across the common law world. The conference was attended by over 200 participants drawn from a wide variety of common law and other jurisdictions, including Australia, Canada, Hong Kong, Italy, Ireland, Japan, the Netherlands, New Zealand, Singapore, South Africa, the United Kingdom and the United States. The conference opened with an interview of Sir John Laws, a Lord Justice of Appeal in the England and Wales Court of Appeal, conducted by Cambridge's Professor David Feldman; the keynote address was given by Professor Jerry Mashaw of Yale University; and almost 50 papers were delivered by public law scholars representing many of the world's leading law schools.

The theme selected for the inaugural conference was intended to—and did—allow participants to contribute papers addressing a relatively broad range of cognate issues that are of both practical and theoretical importance to the study and development of contemporary public law. However, given the very large number of papers delivered at the conference itself, it was infeasible to produce an edited collection that included all or even most of the papers. Instead, in putting together this volume, we have sought to assemble a collection of pieces that relate both to one another and to one of the principal sub-themes that emerged from the conference, namely, the way in which relationships and distinctions between the notions of 'process' and 'substance' play out in relation to and inform adjudication in public law cases.

It is worth noting that not only has there been a lack of a regular conference forum for discussion of public law topics among common lawyers from different jurisdictions but, perhaps causally connected to this, there are surprisingly few edited collections which bring together common lawyers from different jurisdictions to address topics in public law, particularly outside the subfield of constitutional law. There are, in contrast, a reasonable number of jurisdiction-specific collections on public law topics and, for example, a very large number of collections addressing topics in EU public law and, increasingly, global administrative law. The contrast with private law is also stark: there has been a proliferation of collections comprised of papers by common lawyers from a range of jurisdictions, such as those collections that have flowed from the 'Obligations' series of conferences, and which have proven so successful. It is to be hoped that this collection and those stemming from future Public Law Conferences go some way towards filling this lacuna. Such collections are important for much the same reasons that underpin the series of conferences.

I. THE CHAPTERS

The chapters collected herein are all either comparative, or consider one jurisdiction with a view to distilling more general insights. All, in one way or another, engage with the theme of process and substance within the province of public law adjudication. Some chapters offer more theoretical insights, such as Jerry Mashaw's chapter exploring the trend towards conceptualising administrative law in terms of a 'public reason' rationale; Paul Daly's chapter elaborating a values-based framework for analysing administrative law; and Jason Varuhas' chapter, examining a public interest conception of public law, and charting its influence. The bulk of the chapters consider topical issues in judicial review, either on common law or human rights grounds, or both, such as the rise of substantive review, the interrelationship between 'procedural' and 'substantive' grounds, and remedies; this set includes chapters written by Mark Aronson, Christopher Forsyth, Matthew Groves and Greg Weeks, Andrew Edgar, Mary Liston, Justice Alan Robertson and Kent Roach. Two chapters—those by Philip Murray and Jason Varuhas—consider how procedure and substantive law have interacted historically in interesting ways in the field of judicial review. Two further chapters offer an important, wider contextual and empirical perspective, considering the impact of public law adjudication on government, and governmental responses to judicial decisions; these are written by Carol Harlow and Richard Rawlings, and Maurice Sunkin and Varda Bondy. We also asked Cheryl Saunders and David Feldman, both whom contributed to the closing sessions of the conference and who had served as members of its advisory board, to write shorter chapters, reflecting on the nature of contemporary public law scholarship in the light of the chapters collected herein and with particular reference to themes that had emerged during the conference.

In his chapter Jerry Mashaw argues that public reason is essential to a properly functioning democracy. But in a pluralist society, how do we give adequately reasoned justifications? One approach is to narrow the scope substantively of what might be considered 'reasonable' decisions. The other is to simply insist on procedural requirements and anything which results from a procedurally correct process is deemed to be legitimate. In administrative rationality, participation rights are secured through a requirement that the agency demonstrates that it has considered all relevant factors in coming to its determination and has provided justifications in a way that can be understood by participants. Mashaw identifies this approach both in US and EU approaches to decision-making. The justification for this approach is that it 'treats persons as rational moral agents who are entitled to evaluate and participate in the dialogue about official policies on the basis of reasoned discussion'. But there is a danger that this emphasis on giving reasons can slow down decision-making and the public good that results. Furthermore, the rejection of an applicant's claims are still liable to disappoint, however well reasoned and explained. Bureaucratic rationality may not be intended as a value statement on the applicant's worth to society, but is perceived as such. But that should not lead us to reject the benefits of administrative rationality, but continue to seek to make decisions that are both 'reasonable' and 'rational'.

Paul Daly's aim is to further our understanding of the field of administrative law as a whole, over time and across jurisdictions. To do this he develops a values-based framework for understanding administrative law. He argues that four values are immanent in core features of administrative law doctrine, and underpin judicial decision-making in the field. These values are the rule of law, good administration, democracy and the separation of powers. Daly also argues that we must take account of institutional considerations to ensure a full understanding of the field. Daly proceeds to examine how these stated values are reflected in and interact in the context of different administrative law doctrines, including bias, procedural fairness, substantive review and remedial discretion, concluding that 'judicial review of administrative action is a values-based enterprise'.

Jason Varuhas argues that in the wake of the procedural reforms of the late 1970s which established the judicial review procedure in English law, English courts sought to forge a distinctive system of public law based in the unifying idea that 'public law' is concerned with ensuring that public power is exercised for the common good and in accordance with axiomatic principles of good administration. This 'public interest' approach marked out public law's concerns as distinct from private law's concerns with promoting and protecting individual self-interested rights and interests. Since this formative era the public interest conception has been relied upon to guide legal development across various legal contexts, including emergent fields of public law such as human rights law. However, this has proven problematic. The public interest conception of public law was forged by reference to only one branch of contemporary public law, the common law of judicial review; this body of law formed the basis of the vast bulk of applications made via the public law procedure in the period during which the public interest conception was articulated. But public law has moved on. Contemporary public law is increasingly pluralistic in nature, addressing a range of issues and comprising a number of different subfields each marked by their own distinctive concerns. For example, while common law review continues to bear the hallmarks of the public interest approach, human rights law is, in contrast, necessarily concerned with protecting private rights and individual interests. Where the public interest conception has intruded beyond common law judicial review, into newer fields such as human rights law and review on EU grounds, it has often served to undermine the coherence of these branches of law and their distinctive functions. In Varuhas's view, contemporary public law has no inherent functional unity and it is a grave error to try to focus on protecting the public interest in all its branches to the detriment of other valuable functions.

Philip Murray's chapter continues the theme of the necessity of considering process and substance together in historical analysis of English law. His study of error of law shows the way in which we need to understand the procedural context in which substantive rules of law were developed. To focus on general principles of substantive administrative law, such as the reviewability of all errors of law, without understanding the procedural context in which judicial statements to this effect were pronounced potentially leads to an over-broad scope for judicial review. At the same time, argues Murray, the modern law is not constrained by earlier rules of procedure and we do need to develop substantive rules of law which are justified in their own right. Building modern administrative law on an apparent fidelity to judicial precedent is therefore, says Murray, disingenuous. Murray goes on to argue that the history of the distinction between jurisdictional and non-jurisdictional errors of law shows that the modern law has tried to use this device to expand judicial review when it was originally a device for limiting it. Murray concludes that doctrinal rules that have developed in one particular context can and do go on to have a separate life of their own outside that context, and that it is important that the new rules are properly grounded in principle, rather than simply based on an appeal to continuity of a precedent which is now operating outside its original context.

From history our focus moves to trends in contemporary public law adjudication across common law jurisdictions. Mark Aronson considers the growth of substantive review in Australia, contrasting and comparing these developments with concomitant changes in English judicial review. He charts the changes; new grounds have emerged, some explicitly substantive, others presented as procedural but substantive in nature. He considers how the changes reflect a changing sense of judicial review's 'mission', the change in orientation of review being less radical in Australia than England, given the influence of a constitutionally-entrenched separation of powers in the former. The chapter examines the underlying causes of these changes, including the impact of theory in a system traditionally sceptical of top-down thinking, legislative attempts to clamp down on review which backfired, judicialisation of tribunals, and the role of expanded reason-giving. Lastly, the chapter explores the possible consequences of this expansionist trend, including growth in judicial deference and discretion, the possibility that specific grounds of review might be swallowed by generalised grounds, as well as political and institutional ramifications.

Christopher Forsyth examines the relationship between process and substance in public law adjudication from a somewhat different perspective, and in the context of English law. His focus is on the process of reasoning by which judges decide public law cases, with particular reference to the recent (and, in Forsyth's view, alarming) tendency of the UK Supreme Court to elevate substantive but instinctive notions of fairness and justice above reliance on doctrine and conceptual reasoning. In particular, Forsyth draws attention to the way in which the distinction between jurisdictional and non-jurisdictional errors has, in English administrative law, been largely emptied of content, to be replaced, on the one hand, by judicial preparedness to intervene in certain matters by reference to ill-defined notions such as 'proportionate dispute resolution', and on the other hand, by the nakedly manipulated distinction between questions of fact and law. This, argues Forsyth, amounts to 'blasphemy against basics', robbing administrative law of its conceptual coherence, compromising legal certainty and risking the reduction of administrative law to a Tennysonian 'wilderness of single instances'.

As Matthew Groves and Greg Weeks note in their chapter, it is increasingly 'trite' to observe that Australia and England are embarked upon divergent paths in a number of crucial areas within the public law sphere. However, be that as it may, exploring the nature of those differences can be both illuminating in itself and also a way into better understanding the institutional distinctions that account for such differences in the first place. In this vein, Groves and Weeks consider, by reference to the relationship between process and substance in respect of the doctrine of legitimate expectation, the distinct ways in which the law has developed in this area in Australia and England. They note that the approaches adopted in those two jurisdictions differ from one another in striking ways, Australian courts having rejected the substantive notion of fairness upon which (some) English courts have fastened in developing the English variant of the legitimate expectation doctrine. Groves and Weeks go on to consider what might account for these contrasts, noting that while underlying differences of constitutional architecture and approach might go a long way towards understanding the contrasting jurisprudence of the Australian and English courts, those courts remain—helpfully and importantly, it is argued—in dialogue with one another.

Although Andrew Edgar's focus is more squarely on Australian law, his chapter also reflects a key difference between modern administrative law in England and Australia. The aim of Edgar's chapter is to explicate and examine the reasons that might animate Australian administrative law's ostensibly curious approach to judicial review of delegated legislation. He notes that while, in general, Australian courts (placing them increasingly at odds with their English counterparts) eschew relatively intrusive substantive review tools such as proportionality, that doctrine is to the fore when it comes to review in Australia of the lawfulness of secondary legislation. In contrast, notes Edgar, review of delegated legislation on procedural grounds is uncommon. In examining this apparent inversion of received (Australian) wisdom, Edgar argues (inter alia) that Australian courts' embrace of proportionality in this context can be accounted for by a combination of the perceived inaptness of process-oriented review of secondary legislation and the existence of constitutional concerns resulting from broad delegations of legislative authority to administrative bodies. Judging the status quo unsatisfactory, Edgar concludes by examining possible ways forward in this area.

Mary Liston provides an important Canadian perspective on the interrelationship between process and substance in contemporary public law, arguing that there has been a 'fusion' between procedure and substance in recent years in Canada. Accepting the importance of substantive conceptions of fairness as part of judicial review is an appropriate response to the 'real questions' which are being asked of administrators and on which the courts have to adjudicate. 'A political community committed to both democracy and legality will provide multiple routes for those affected by public power to demand fairness, to have input into the decision-making process, and to have quality reasons for those decisions', she argues. She identifies the way in which procedural requirements in aboriginal administrative law have not only enabled better participation, but also ensured respect for substantive fairness. Judicial decision-making established an institutional dialogue between judges and administrators which will encourage more reasonable decisions by the latter. Liston argues that legal frameworks make more transparent values of rights, social goods and social justice which are then taken on board in administrative frameworks. The emphasis is therefore on cooperation between the different fora for individual participation in the service of the public as a whole, rather than an antagonism between judiciary and the administrators.

Alan Robertson undertakes a detailed assessment of the nature of contemporary judicial review in Australia and England considering, as Liston has done for Canada, the interrelationship between process and substance across the field. Like a number of contributors in this volume, Robertson is firm in rejecting any bright line distinction between process and substance in public law. Through a thorough analysis of different aspects of judicial review (error of law review, procedural fairness, mandatory considerations and unreasonableness, amongst others), Robertson shows the distinction between procedure and substance to be an artificial mask, obfuscating the true qualitative nature of judicial review. At the same time, Robertson maintains that this qualitative review is not to be confused with merits review. While some distinctions drawn by administrative lawyers, like that between process and substance, might seem overly artificial, others, like the distinction between merits and legality, have a much deeper, constitutional significance.

Following on from chapters focused on trends in the substantive law of judicial review, Kent Roach's contribution reminds us of the dangers of paying inadequate attention to remedies when studying public law. He offers a thoughtful study of how different common law legal systems design remedies for the protection of human rights, ranging from the judicial strike-down of rights-infringing legislation, like in the United States, to the apparently weaker form of human rights protection under sections 3 and 4 of the UK Human Rights Act 1998. Roach's chapter illustrates that broad procedural categories, like the distinctions that are drawn between different human rights remedies, can hide the substantive reality of public law litigation. So supposedly strong forms of review, like that which occurs in the US Supreme Court under the auspices of the Bill of Rights, are shown to be substantively weaker when it is realised, for example, that many of the US Supreme Court's strike-downs are limited to the particular application of legislation in the particular case that comes before the Court. Contrariwise, apparently weaker forms of human rights protection, like the non-binding declaration of incompatibility used by British courts, are shown to be substantively stronger once it is appreciated that these remedies are used in a context of strong obedience by Parliament to the United Kingdom's international obligations, breach of which is implied by a declaration of incompatibility. At the same time as showing us that procedure can obfuscate substance, however, Roach highlights the necessary relationship that exists between process and substance. It is only with recourse to substantive constitutional norms that we can determine the most desirable form of procedure for protecting human rights—something Roach attempts admirably in the latter part of his chapter.

As they often have, Carol Harlow and Richard Rawlings offer us a wider perspective on public law adjudication often neglected in the generally court-focused literature on judicial review. Challenging the common view that courts control government and secure rights of citizens, but also arguably challenging characterisations of government as vulnerable or helpless in the face of an increasingly active domestic and supranational judiciary, they document numerous instances of government and Parliament responding to judgments or the prospect of unwelcome judgments through deliberately negative practices. Such practices may fall into one of two categories: 'striking back'—removing or minimising a judgment's effects after the event; or 'clamping down'—taking pre-emptive steps to protect governmental or public interests against future judicial interference by changing the rules of the public law game in restrictive fashion. They show these phenomena to be fundamental features of the working constitution, that they have been so for some time, and that there has been a high degree of continuity in the techniques adopted by government, even as the sources of the legal threats faced at Westminster have become more varied.

Similarly focused on the empirical realities of public law adjudication, Maurice Sunkin and Varda Bondy, with particular reference to recent initiatives to circumscribe access to judicial review in England, consider the extent to which judicial review aids—or, conversely, hinders—good government. They do so by challenging, through reliance upon detailed empirical studies, three assumptions which arguably underlie administrative antipathy to judicial review in England. Sunkin and Bondy argue that those assumptions—that there has been significant growth in the use of judicial review driven by claimants abusing the system; that judicial review necessarily impedes good administration; and that judicial review litigation is unlikely to provide effective redress to claimants—are ill-founded, and that the recent debate about judicial review in England has, as a result, been unfortunately skewed.

In her chapter, Cheryl Saunders reflects on the conference, the papers collected herein and trends in public law scholarship more generally from a comparative perspective. She notes that while neither this volume nor the conference from which it stems was explicitly comparative—in the sense that contributors were not required to adopt any systematic comparative approach—comparativism is nevertheless advanced and facilitated by the papers collected in this book. In this spirit, Saunders seeks to identify such points of public law related commonality as exist within the principal jurisdictions covered in this collection by examining the ways in which public law in those jurisdictions diverge. She goes on to note that such divergences notwithstanding, the common law remains more 'cohesive', and its constituent jurisdictions more 'interdependent', than might be supposed. Saunders concludes by arguing that these phenomena may be accounted for by broadly comparable trajectories of legal and political development in several key common law jurisdictions; the willingness of common law courts to facilitate jurisdictional cross-fertilisations; and an innate tendency of the common law towards what Saunders terms 'equilibrium'.

David Feldman offers three reflections on the directions of contemporary public law scholarship in the light of the conference and the papers collected in this volume. First, he argues some legal scholars have 'gone beyond rules, beyond rights, beyond even principles' and claimed that public law does or should require officials to give effect to 'values'. In his view this is a recipe for unconstrained moralism, a threat to legal predictability, and can render rigorous legal analysis impossible, thus squandering the distinctively valuable contribution that public lawyers can make in the study of public institutions. Secondly, there has been a shift of focus away from studying the important question of what public institutions should be allowed to do towards the second-order question of who should decide what institutions should be allowed to do. If we allow ourselves to become distracted in this way we may diminish our ability to limit the capacity of public actors to cause serious harm through unlawful acts, which is the principal goal of public law. Thirdly, Feldman offers a timely reminder that we ought to resist the temptation to allow our normative commitments to shape our approach to empirical analysis. In the province of comparative work this means acknowledging significant variations among different systems and 'not pretending that our preferred normative structure has some illusory universal normative force'.

II. ACKNOWLEDGEMENTS

In organising the conference from which this book arises and in subsequently putting this volume together, we have, inevitably, received assistance and support from a number of quarters. We are grateful to the group of doctoral students at the Faculty of Law in Cambridge—Chintan Chandrachud, Nikiforos Meletiadis, Ana Julia Mauricio, Laura Panades-Estruch, Barry Solaiman and Shona Wilson Stark—who served as our Conference Assistants in the run-up to and during the conference. We also thank the members of the Conference Advisory Board who offered helpful feedback and advice at key junctures in the planning of the conference. The members of the Board were: Professor David Feldman (Cambridge), Professor Carol Harlow (LSE), Professor Philip Joseph (Canterbury, New Zealand), Professor Susan Rose-Ackerman (Yale), Professor Robert Thomas (Manchester), Professor Adam Tomkins (Glasgow), Professor Mark Tushnet (Harvard) and Professor George Williams (UNSW). We are also grateful to all those at Hart Publishing, and specifically to Bill Asquith and Sinead Moloney, for their help and advice as we have produced this collection of essays.

Finally, and most particularly, we are greatly indebted to Richard Hart, who, as nearly every reader of this book will know, founded Hart Publishing. Richard was the Managing Director of Hart Publishing when the Public Law Conference Series was first conceived, and he had a significant role in the founding of the Series. The success of the first conference is thanks in no small measure to Hart Publishing's generous and continued support, and to Richard Hart's willingness to back the first of the Public Law Conferences. With the ongoing support of Hart Publishing it is our aim that the Public Law Series will quickly establish itself as a leading forum for debate and discussion of public law issues in the common law world. The enormously positive response to and feedback on the first Public Law Conference, and to the larger intellectual endeavour of which the inaugural conference forms only the starting-point, suggests that this aim is well on its way to being realised. It is hoped that this book conveys a sense of the richness and diversity of the papers delivered at the inaugural Public Law Conference, as well as a sense of the vibrancy of public law as an academic discipline today, of the fruitfulness of interjurisdictional dialogue within the common law world, and of what lies ahead as the Public Law Series of Conferences continues over the coming years. In this regard, we very much look forward to the second Public Law Conference, to be held in Cambridge in September 2016.

More information on the Public Law Conference, including video-recordings of the plenary sessions at the 2014 Conference, can be found at the conference website: www.publiclawconference.law.cam.ac.uk

2

Public Reason and Administrative Legitimacy

JERRY L MASHAW

I. INTRODUCTION

IN THIS CHAPTER, I want to make three principal arguments. First, I believe that public reason as theorised in political and moral philosophy is quite problematic. Although for the last several decades public reason has been almost the only game in town in political and moral philosophy when addressing the organisation of collective action, none of its variants are without serious difficulties.

Secondly, however, I want to argue that some such practice of public reasoning is crucially important to the maintenance of a functioning and acceptable conception of democracy and democratic citizenship in modern administrative states. This seems to be one of those cases in which an idea may work reasonably well in practice although it does not work very well in theory.

Thirdly, although I am arguing that some forms of public reasoning as a practice are necessary to the legitimation of collective action, and ubiquitous in the administrative regimes of advanced democracies, all is not well in practice. The forms of reasoning deployed in administrative governance are both procedurally demanding and substantively disappointing. Hence, public reason in practice tends to be simultaneously legitimating and delegitimating. This dual aspect of reasoning in practice presents a crucial challenge for the design of public institutions in the twenty-first century.

II. PUBLIC REASON AND ITS CRITICS

What might be called the 'public reason tradition', for there are many variants in the literature,[1] attempts to give an answer to how the authority of the state can be legitimated while simultaneously (1) respecting the liberty of those subjected to its commands, and (2) accepting the social fact of value pluralism. Theories of public

[1] J Quong, 'Public Reason' in EN Zalta (ed), *The Stanford Encyclopedia of Philosophy* (Summer 2013), available at plato.stanford.edu/archives/sum2013/entries/public-reason.

reason are motivated in part by the perceived inadequacy of theories of legitimacy based either on consent or on truth. The consent of the governed is certainly consistent with their liberty, but requiring consensus in pluralistic democracies yields anarchism as the appropriate form of governance. This position is philosophically respectable but operationally untenable. And, because we no longer believe that anyone has direct access to the true principles of moral conduct or political organisation, truth is also a non-starter. Public reason theories try to thread a middle ground between these positions while borrowing a bit from both. In general, public reason demands that moral or political principles be justifiable, or reasonably acceptable, to all those persons to whom the principles are meant to apply (including here constitutional arrangements, institutional architectures, rules of conduct, and so on). To put the matter bluntly, all public reason theories are directed at reconciling liberty and equality with authority by insisting that authority be justified by reasons that all could accept.[2]

The crux of the problem with public reason accounts, as numerous commentators have pointed out,[3] is that in all modern, large nation-states the heterogeneity of the population, combined with the value pluralism accepted by public reason theorists, virtually ensure that not every person would find any political principle justified. Indeed, if there were political principles that would be agreed to by all then the public reason account collapses into consent theory. To deal with this problem, public reason theorists have to relax the justification or acceptability requirement in some way. Two types of approaches dominate. One is substantive. The relevant constituency to whom justification must be given is restricted to those who are 'reasonable', that is, those susceptible to persuasion by the type of justifications that count as rational or as appropriate reasons in a particular variant of public reason theory. This, of course, requires giving some content to what is rational or reasonable. On most accounts this entails restricting argument to those sorts of principles that would be recognisable as the basic principles of a liberal democratic regime.[4] A similar but more procedural move involves imagining that everyone or almost everyone would accept the justification for a principle if they deliberated long enough and hard enough on the question.[5] In short, a process of legitimation that is meant to treat all persons as free and equal members of the polity must either exclude certain persons from concern or treat them as hypothetical persons rather than as the persons that they really are.

This, of course, is to paint with a very broad brush when constructing a portrait of a field in which both colour and composition can be very subtle indeed. Nevertheless, I believe it fair to say that public reason, as a philosophical theory,

[2] J Waldron, 'Theoretical Foundations of Liberalism' (1987) 37 *Philosophical Quarterly* 127; T Nagel, 'Moral Conflict in Political Legitimacy' (1987) 16 *Philosophy and Public Affairs* 215; J Quong, *Liberalism Without Perfectionism* (Oxford, Oxford University Press, 2011); G Gaus, *The Order of Public Reason* (New York, Cambridge University Press, 2011); K Vallier and R D'Agostino, 'Public Justification' in *Stanford Encyclopedia Online* (2013), available at plato.stanford.edu/entries/justification-public/.

[3] D Enoch, 'Against Public Reason', available at plato.stanford.edu/entries/public-reason.

[4] J Rawls, *Political Liberalism* (New York, Columbia University Press, 1993).

[5] *Gaus* (n 2).

has great difficulty living up to its stated aspirations, that is, to reconcile authority and liberty while remaining substantively neutral and procedurally inclusive. And yet, I also believe that giving operational content to something like a public reason approach is critically important to the legitimacy of modern states characterised by both democratic aspirations and a heavily administrative institutional structure.

III. WHY PUBLIC REASON IS NECESSARY

Asking 'Why?', that is, demanding an explanation, is a ubiquitous part of human social relations. According to Charles Tilly's view, the reason for reasons is entirely relational.[6] Reasons are given to negotiate, establish, repair, affirm or deny relationships. And, the type of relationship determines the types of reasons that are appropriate and therefore acceptable or persuasive. From this sociological perspective the types of reasons given in response to the 'Why?' question are a consequence both of the perception of the type of relationship that exists between the parties and of how the parties are attempting to shape that relationship for the future. The relationship of interest to democratic theorists, of course, is the relationship between officials who act with the force of law and those who are subject to their authority. Public reason theorists exclude certain sorts of relationships between officials and citizens because inconsistent with the conception of citizens as free and equal. Thus, for example, to refuse to give reasons is to assert authority in a way that is fundamentally illegitimate.

One of my favourite examples of the assertion of pure authority comes from a *New Yorker* cartoon in which a small child is leaning forward from the backseat close to his driving father's ear. The child's conversation must have been of a sort familiar to anyone who has taken a bored four-year-old on a car trip: 'Why aren't we there yet?' 'Why are you going so slow'? 'Why does Grandma live so far away?' And so on and on. At the bottom of the cartoon the caption gives the harassed father's response: 'Shut up, he explained'.

A less humorous example comes from the Book of Job. Job repeatedly asked God 'Why?', but the answers were of little use to him. In Carl Jung's famous interpretation,[7] Job gets answers that he cannot possible accept. His 'Why?' sounds in morality and justice while God's answer is in the wilfulness of the Old Testament, a will beyond human understanding.

It is this particular discourse of whyness, that between authority and subject or officials and citizens, that interests public reason theorists and that is the focus of this chapter. For these relationships aspire to be fundamentally different than those between parent and child or God and man. And for present purposes I want to concentrate on the particularly fraught relationship between administrative officials and citizens subject to their legally binding decisions.

[6] C Tilly, *Why?* (Princeton, NJ, Princeton University Press, 2006).

[7] CG Jung, *Answer to Job* (RFC Hall (trans), Princeton, NJ, Princeton University Press, 1973 [1958]).

In modern democracies the legitimation of administrative decision-making poses a continuing problem. The demands on contemporary governments ensure that much public policy-making will be in the hands of unelected officials carrying out programmes that are only vaguely defined by the legislation that empowers administrative action. At the supranational level, for example in the European Union, the connections between administrative action and electoral or 'aggregative' democracy are even more tenuous. And it is here, in the realms of administrative decision-making that legal requirements for reason giving are most prominent. The 'Why?' of the contemporary Job confronting contemporary secular authority often carries with it an enforceable right to justificatory reasons. And, here again, we might ask 'Why?'

Most explanations for this common practice tend to ignore the democratising character of public reason giving. Instead they echo the consequentialist explanations that are the hallmark of Tilley's relational account. For example, the right to reasons in my own particular field, American administrative law, is conventionally understood as parasitic on other rights, or on the necessities for effective judicial review or political oversight. For example, in its iconic statement of the demands of due process in individualised administrative adjudication, the US Supreme Court had this to say about reasons:

> Finally, the decision maker's conclusion … must rest solely on the legal rules and evidence adduced at the hearing. To demonstrate compliance with this elementary requirement, the decision maker should state the reasons for his determination and indicate the evidence he relied on.[8]

On this account, reason giving is meant to ensure that the constitutional hearing right is not a charade. The right to reasons is not a general right of citizenship. It is merely instrumental to the assurance of another legal right, the right to hearing.

In United States jurisprudence, reason giving is further rationalised as necessary to both facilitate and constrain judicial review. The judicial review provisions of the Federal Administrative Procedure Act (APA), for example, tell courts to set aside any administrative choice they find to be 'arbitrary, capricious, an abuse of discretion, or otherwise not in accordance with law'.[9] In another iconic case, *Citizens to Preserve Overton Park Inc v Volpe*, the Supreme Court explained that to determine whether the agency's action was or was not arbitrary 'the court must consider whether the decision was based on the consideration of the relevant factors and whether there has been a clear error of judgment'.[10] Rejecting the agency's reasons proffered in litigation affidavits as an inadequate basis for undertaking the required analysis, the Court concluded that reason giving is required contemporaneously with decision-making whenever an administrative decision may be subjected to judicial review.

In the United States this demand for reasons applies equally to general rules or regulations and to formal adjudications. The APA's laconic requirement that agencies

[8] *Goldberg v Kelley*, 397 US 254 (1970).

[9] 5 USC § 706.

[10] *Citizens to Preserve Overton Park Inc v Volpe*, 401 US 402 (1971).

provide 'a concise general statement of their basis and purpose' when issuing rules[11] has developed through judicial interpretation into a robust requirement of responsiveness to the 'why' questions raised by participants in the rule-making process. In an important early case, Judge Carl McGowan cautioned against an 'overly literal reading' of the APA's requirement of a 'concise general statement':

> These adjectives must be accommodated to the realities of judicial scrutiny, which do not contemplate that the Court itself will, by a laborious examination of the record, formulate in the first instance the significant issues faced by the Agency and articulate the rationale of the resolution. We do not expect the Agency to discuss every item of fact or opinion included in the submissions made to an informal rulemaking period. We do expect that, if the judicial review which Congress has thought it important to provide is to be meaningful, the 'concise general statement of ... basis and purpose' mandated by [the APA] will enable us to see what major issues of policy were ventilated by the informal proceedings and why the Agency reacted as it did.[12]

There is, of course, a certain synergy between the facilitation of judicial review and the reinforcement of parties' rights to participate in agency policy-making. In the rule-making process mandated for federal administrative agencies in the United States, any interested party may provide comments to the agency concerning its proposed rules. A judicial requirement that the agency demonstrate through published reasons that it considered the problems and issues raised in the rule-making process is in a practical sense a demand for responsiveness to the submissions of affected parties. It therefore reinforces their rights of participation as provided by the APA.

In addition, American courts use the reason-giving requirement as a shield against complaints that courts are taking over the policy-making processes of the government. As Judge McGowan suggested, the courts may not substitute their reasons for those of the agency or hypothesise what those reasons might have been. In United States administrative law, agency action is reversible if the reasons given are inadequate, even if the court believes that the agency may have reached the right conclusions.[13] The demand for reasons allows review of the policy choices for reasonableness while insulating the judiciary from the charge that it is engaging in inappropriate second-guessing of the political branches of government. The judicial demand for 'reasons' has become a legitimate procedural version of an otherwise illegitimate substantive demand for 'reasonableness' as judicially determined.

This proceduralisation of rationality—the conversion of the demand for non-arbitrariness into a demand for understandable reasons—transforms the question of whether the action is reasonable into a question of whether the agency has demonstrated a reasoning *process*. The demand for reasons, at least rhetorically, keeps the courts within their appropriate domain. That this 'restrained' judicial posture may nevertheless disable or impede regulatory activity is merely an unintended

[11] 5 USC § 553.
[12] *Auto Parts and Accessories Association v Boyd*, 407 F2d 330 (DC Cir 1968).
[13] *Securities and Exchange Commission v Chenery Corp*, 332 US 194 (1947).

consequence of the maintenance of the American understanding of the judiciary's role in the overall constitutional structure.[14]

The obligation of administrators to give reasons for decisions is also found in the European Code of Good Administrative Behaviour (ECGAB). According to article 18 of the ECGAB, reason giving applies to decisions 'which may adversely affect the rights or interests of a private person'. Although article 18 of the ECGAB seems to apply only to individualised adjudications, Article 253 of the Treaty establishing the European Community[15] requires:

> Regulations, directives and decisions adopted jointly by the European Parliament and the Council, and such acts adopted by the Council or the Commission, shall state the reasons on which they are based and shall refer to any proposals or opinions which were required to be obtained pursuant to this treaty.

As in the United States, both case law and scholarly writing justify reason-giving requirements in the EU on the need for judicial monitoring of institutional decisions and the facilitation of individual capacities to contest official determinations.[16] Commentators also emphasise that reason giving contributes to the general transparency of governmental action and to that degree to oversight and accountability of administrative actors to higher level officials and to the general public.[17]

Legal requirements for reason giving and their consequentialist basis in facilitating individual rights of defence and judicial monitoring are further echoed in the national law of EU Member States.[18]

Without trying to make a detailed comparison, it seems fair to say that the jurisprudence of US and EU courts have taken very similar approaches.[19] Like their American colleagues EU judges have also tended to proceduralise rationality. They demand more careful attention to articulation of the reasons for decisions where they are most within the technical expertise of administrators. The courts thus attempt to assure conformity to law without invading the technocratic policy space reserved for administrators.[20] In sum, in both American and European law the right to receive reasons is justified as a sort of derivative right. It facilitates individuals' decisions about whether to contest official determinations, protects the rights to individualised

[14] JL Mashaw and DL Harfst, 'Regulation and Legal Culture: The Case of Motor Vehicle Safety' (1987) 4 *Yale Journal on Regulation* 257.

[15] European Code of Good Administrative Behaviour (European Ombudsman, 2014), available at http://ec.europa.eu/transparency/code/_docs/code_en.pdf.

[16] K Kanska, 'Towards Administrative Human Rights in the EU: The Impact of the Charter of Fundamental Rights' (2004) 10 *European Law Journal* 296; B Vesterdorf, 'Transparency: Not Just a Vogue Word' (1999) 22 *Fordham International Law Journal* 902.

[17] ibid.

[18] L Millet, 'The Right to Good Administration in European Union Law' (2002) 47 *Public Law* 309; J Ponce, 'Good Administrative and Administrative Procedure' (2005) 12 *Indiana Journal of Global Legal Studies* 551; JM Joshua, 'The Right to be Heard in EEC Competition Procedures' (1991) 15 *Fordham International Law Journal* 16.

[19] M Shapiro, 'The Giving Reasons Requirement' (1992) *University of Chicago Legal Forum* 179; F Bignami, 'Creating European Rights: National Values and Supranational Interests' (2005) 11 *Columbia Journal of European Law* 241.

[20] J Schwarze, 'Judicial Review of European Administrative Procedure' (2004) 68 *Law and Contemporary Problems* 85.

adjudication, and promotes the monitoring activities of the judiciary and of political institutions. Reasons are also seen in both systems as having a special value in maintaining vigorous review along the contested boundary between law and policy. From this perspective the basic values of reason giving sound in political and legal accountability and the protection of individual rights. The reasons requirement is simply a crucially important means to those ends.

These instrumental accounts of reason giving are perhaps sufficient to make the case that this practice is of crucial importance in maintaining legal legitimacy in modern administrative states. However, I believe that there is more to reason giving as an aspect of good administration than is suggested by these instrumental accounts alone. There are clues that this may be true in the case law both in the European Union and the United States. As previously mentioned, Article 253 of the EC Treaty requires reasons for general acts even though there is no right to judicial review of all the general decisions in the European Union.[21] (And, at least some members of the US Supreme Court have believed that section 555(e) of the APA demands reasons in response to any petition to an administrative agency, even in cases where there is no right to hearing or to judicial review of the substance of the agency decision.)[22]

But what makes reason giving itself legitimating? I think the answer is to be found in the central concerns of public reason theories. For, in a pluralist polity where every individual is owed equal concern and respect, the fundamental ground for accepting law, or any official decision, as legitimate, is that reasons can be given why those subject to the law can understand its content as serving recognisable collective purposes.

To be sure, there is much disagreement and dispute about what public policies are preferable and which decisions affecting individual interests are justified. Interested parties disagree about the facts and about the values to be served by official actions. This is the moral pluralism that has bedevilled philosophical accounts of public reason. It would seem, nevertheless, as a practical matter, that a decision with which one disagrees can nevertheless be recognised as acceptable or legitimate because it is explicable as a plausible instance of rational collective action. Reason giving thus affirms the centrality of the individual in a democratic republic. It treats persons as rational moral agents who are entitled to evaluate and participate in the dialogue about official policies on the basis of reasoned discussion. It affirms the individual as a subject rather than an object of the law.

The instrumental grounds for reason giving the courts and commentators routinely provide are hardly unimportant. But, I am arguing that there is a deeper ground for reason giving in a democracy and therefore a reason for treating a right to reasons as a fundamental, rather than as a contingent or derivative, human right. Authority without reason is literally dehumanizing. It is, therefore, fundamentally at war with the promise of democracy, which is, after all, self-government.

If this is correct, viewing reason giving as a fundamental aspect of democratic governance has implications for the reach and strength of the right in a democratic

[21] 25/62 *Plaumann v European Commission* [1963] ECR 95, [1964] CMLR 29.

[22] *Heckler v Cheney*, 470 US 821, 841–42 (1985) (Marshall J concurring).

legal order, implications that I have developed elsewhere.[23] For now I want to turn to some issues of implementation or institutional design that bear on the legitimating power of reason giving in the administrative state. As I indicated at the beginning of this chapter, I believe that there is an important double effect of our current practices of reason giving—for reasons that count as good reasons for purposes of legal legitimation may yet be inadequate to fully satisfy the citizen's demands for explanation.

IV. TRIUMPH AND TRAGEDY OF ADMINISTRATIVE RATIONALITY

In talking about the development of reason-giving requirements I will use examples primarily from the system I know best, that is, the United States. But similar developments can be found elsewhere.[24] Indeed, I will narrow the discussion further to focus primarily on the growth of reason-giving requirements in rule-making.

The rapid development of the administrative state during the New Deal produced a strong conservative reaction against what Dean Roscoe Pound described as 'administrative absolutism'.[25] The Federal Administrative Procedure Act embodied this reaction. That statute's modest suggestion that agencies provide a 'concise general statement of the basis and purpose' for their regulations has over time developed into the requirement for comprehensive articulation of the factual basis, methodological presuppositions and statutory authority that justify any exercise in rule-making. As mentioned earlier, this demand for comprehensive instrumental rationality has, at the level of judicial review, been proceduralised into a judicial demand for exposure of a cogent reasoning process. While claiming not to second-guess the substance of agency judgments, American courts routinely reject what they term 'post hoc rationalisations',[26] use of untested facts outside the rule-making record,[27] and the invocation of undisclosed reservoirs of 'agency expertise'.[28] The rule-making process is made to some degree truly deliberative by demands for persuasive responses to cogent objections by outside parties.[29]

More specific regulatory statutes and executive orders have added a host of further analytic requirements to administrative rule-making functions. In addition to rationalising decisions in terms of their principal missions, agencies must routinely demonstrate that they have considered the environmental consequences of their actions; provide cost benefit analyses of regulatory alternatives; consider impacts on statutorily specified groups or entities; and assure objectors that, having canvassed

[23] JL Mashaw, 'Reasoned Administration: The European Union, the United States, and the Project of Democratic Governance' (2007) 76 *George Washington Law Review* 101.

[24] EF Jordao and S Rose Ackerman, 'Judicial Review of Executive Policymaking in Advanced Democracies: Beyond Rights Review' (2014) 66 *Administrative Law Review* 1.

[25] R Pound, 'Administrative Law: Its Growth, Procedure, and Significance' (1941) 7 *University of Pittsburgh Law Review* 269.

[26] *Citizens to Preserve Overton Park Inc v Volpe*, 401 US 402 (1971).

[27] *United States v Nova Scotia Food Products Corp*, 568 F2d 240 (2d Cir 1977).

[28] *Portland Cement Association v Ruckleshaus*, 486 F2d 375 (DC Cir 1973).

[29] *National Tire Dealers and Retreaders Association, Inc v Brinegar*, 491 F2d 31 (DC Cir 1974).

the universe of possible actions, they have chosen the least burdensome alternative to accomplish their statutorily specified ends.[30]

Similar stories can be told about other domains of administrative action. The so-called 'due process revolution', along with congressional attentiveness to the statutory provision of formal adjudicatory process, has dramatically increased the demand for transparently rational administrative adjudication. The triumph of reason has hardly been complete. I paint here again with a broad brush, leaving aside many qualifications and some counter-currents. Nevertheless, in general, the path of American administrative law has been the path of a progressive submission of power to reason. The promise of the administrative state as far back as the Progressive Era was to bring competence to politics. In some sense it is the institutional embodiment of the Enlightenment project to substitute reason for the authority of culture, tradition and heredity. 'Expertise' is no longer a protective shield to be worn like a sacred vestment. It is a capacity to be demonstrated by persuasive reason giving.

There are, indeed, downsides to this triumph of rationality. One serious practical concern is that multiple requirements for synoptic or comprehensive rationality, enforceable by well-resourced adversaries, can bring policy-making to a standstill. The demand for rationality can move from a concern for justification and legitimacy to an exercise in legal harassment. And, proceduralised rationality review in the hands of generalist judges can easily cross the line from rigorous concern for legality to ideological obstructionism.[31] 'Shut up, he explained' is not available to administrators. But, while a serious concern, this so-called 'ossification' of the administrative process is not the 'tragedy' on which I wish to focus attention.

I believe that the developments that I have described are indeed a triumph to be celebrated. Environmental regulations should not be based on myth, hunch or ideology; public benefits should not be awarded on the basis of inarticulate cultural premises. The vast discretion in the hands of modern administrators and administrative agencies should not be used as a mask for rule by decree.

Yet this triumph of legitimate, liberal administrative governance in a world full of dangerous alternatives has not yielded broad popular satisfaction. Since the 1980s 'reform' in much of the developed world has been in the direction of deregulation, devolution, the use of market mechanism and contracted out public services. 'Bureaucrat' is generally not a term of approbation, 'big government' is out of favour. Eurosceptics are not just nationalists: they question the legitimacy of technocratic rule, not just its location in Brussels.

Disappointment with administrative governance may, of course, have many causes. Rounding up the usual suspects, we might include at least the following. The displacement of blame for our frustration with bureaucratic encounters from the legislatures who over-promise and under-budget to the administrators who are the immediate cause of our disappointment. Pro-market ideology surely also plays a part in many

[30] WF Funk *et al* (eds), *Federal Administrative Procedure Source Book*, 4th edn (Chicago, IL, ABA Book Publishing, 2008).

[31] B Kraus and C Raso, 'Rational Boundaries for SEC Cost Benefit Analysis' (2013) 30 *Yale Journal on Regulation* 289.

countries, although a look at our collective practices suggests that we are ideological conservatives and operational liberals. Many of our demands on government are precisely for public bureaucrats to protect us from private ones. General post-modern scepticism of rationality itself conceivably plays a part. Yet again, our practices belie a strong commitment to a thorough-going post-modern sensibility. We recognise that our collective life must be managed, not merely interpreted.

While not denying that these usual suspects have some explanatory power, I want to suggest a problem that seems to lie at the heart of the project of rationality and reason giving in administrative states. My intuition is that the problem lies in too narrow a definition of rationality, too cramped a style of reason giving. Reason giving in the administrative state tends to treat us as people for whom reasons matter, but it often fails to attend to the range of reasons that we care about.

To structure this idea let me borrow, and misuse to some degree, categories about domains of reasons found in much of the work of Jürgen Habermas.[32] Habermas suggests that everyone operates in three broad domains of rational action: the material, the social and the personal. Rationality in these three domains functions quite differently. In the material world the claim is to truth; in the social realm the claim is about rightness or justice; and in the personal domain rational validity sounds in authenticity. The problem of state legitimacy, particularly administrative state legitimacy, may be its overcapacity to address truth claims combined with an undercapacity to address claims of justice and authenticity. While 'truth' may somewhat overstate the matter, our existing demands for reason giving insist that administrators demonstrate a purely instrumental rationality. They must explain, in short, why their actions satisfy the goals articulated by their governing statutes given the existing state of the world and the likely effects of the policies that they have chosen. Administrative reason giving takes the general form: 'If you want X (the statutory goal), given the current state of the world Y (as demonstrated in the record of the administrative proceeding), then we must adopt policy Z (which for highly technocratic reasons promises to produce the desired results)'.

Administrators whose decisions routinely survive judicial and political oversight are quite adept at providing these sorts of reasons. Yet, we also routinely confront rules that do not seem to fit our particular cases, that falsify our experience and challenge our conceptions of ourselves. In studying the processes for determining social security disability claims in the United States, I have discovered that claimants for benefits tend to be disappointed whether they win or lose. Half of those who apply for benefits have their claims denied on the ground that they can do some jobs available in the national economy. Very often these same persons have struggled for years to work despite serious impairments and advice from family members and physicians that they really should not work. Having finally decided to apply for disability benefits they are told that they were wrong. They may be a 'failed' worker, but

[32] A Brand, *The Force of Reason: An Introduction to Habermas' Theory of Communicative Action* (Sydney, Allen Unwin, 1990); D Ingram, *Habermas and the Dialectic of Reason* (New Haven, CT, Yale University Press, 1987); SK White, *The Recent Work of Jürgen Habermas: Reason, Justice and Modernity* (Cambridge, Cambridge University Press, 1988).

according to the Social Security Administration's rules they are not disabled. Insult is often added to injury by a further determination by a vocational rehabilitation service that the same claimant is too disabled to benefit from rehabilitation services that might get them back into the labour market.

Moreover, many successful claimants are unhappy with their favourable result because of the connotations that it entails. In order to receive income support that they needed they have been forced to accept a label 'disabled' that they fundamentally reject. The system demands an all or nothing result. Binary judgments can falsify a complex reality whether applicants experience a grant or a denial of their claims.

But, this example may be only to illustrate why addressing authenticity in the context of complex administrative programmes is an impossibility. The social security disability system must decide literally millions of claims each year. If this is to be done in a reasonably consistent way by thousands of adjudicators, 'rulishness' is the order of the day. Getting the balance right between rule-bound administration and individualised discretionary judgement presents almost intractable conundra for institutional designers.[33] And yet, that both winners and losers have the perception that their situations have been somehow falsified, or more mildly, not adequately attended to, has serious consequences for the perceived legitimacy of administrative action. It can easily yield a sense of being an object of social control, not an independent subject entitled to authentic respect and concern.

Deliberation about the rightness or justice of the rules themselves is often no more articulate than the administrative state's fumbling with issues of authenticity in adjudication. Administrators are not claiming to make value judgements; indeed, they largely deny that they are doing so. Yet, the technocratic analyses that appear in explanations of agency rules often seem simply to sweep value questions under the rug. Cost benefit analyses, for example, are done to determine whether, on some set of highly debatable assumptions, social welfare will go up because of the adoption of a rule. In the process, excruciatingly difficult questions concerning the value of human life—whether that value can be expressed in monetary terms, whether monetary valuations should be discounted if the life is to be saved at some future date, and so on—lie just below the surface of the analysis. To be sure, academic literature debates such questions endlessly, but administrators, perhaps for good reasons, believe that they must simply get on with their jobs. Participants in rule-making processes may question the rationality of these exercises in social cost accounting, but only within the confines of the professional norms that have developed to make the analytic exercise possible in the first place. Ultimate issues are side-stepped.

Once again we must ask what is to be done. Our democratic ideology suggests that administrators should be implementers, not Platonic guardians deciding questions of ultimate social value. I must confess that I have no good answers for how to deal with the missing discourses of reason, that is, reasons of justice and authenticity, in administrative implementation. It may simply be that these tensions among

[33] C Diver, 'The Optimal Precision of Administrative Rules' (1983) 65 *Yale Law Journal* 93.

the domains of rational action—the conflict inherent in our attempts to choose just ends, effectively manipulate the material world and live authentic lives—are inevitable and unresolvable. Perhaps we can do little better than to bracket these questions of social justice and individual authenticity when engaged in the instrumental business of implementing vague statutory directions.

Yet I fear that that path is dangerous. These disappointments with 'bureaucratic rationality' may cause us to devalue the triumphs of administrative rationality that have been won in Habermas' material domain. For strange as it may seem, administrative policy-making has moved some distance toward instantiating a working model of deliberative democracy that seems increasingly elusive in the presumptively democratic, but highly politicised, discourse of legislatures. Moreover, to fail to try to address these disappointments with the modern administrative state would deny some of our deepest aspirations. If we want to continue to understand ourselves as *Homo sapiens*, not just as *Homo oeconomicus*, we must attempt to broaden the domain of administrative reason, not abandon it as a failed idea. Public reason must, in John Rawls' terms, address what is 'reasonable' as well as what is 'rational'.[34] As we have seen, rationality can be proceduralised, addressing reasonableness probably cannot.

[34] J Rawls, *Political Liberalism* (New York, Columbia University Press, 1993).

3

Administrative Law: A Values-based Approach

PAUL DALY*

I. INTRODUCTION

I FOCUS IN this chapter on judicial review of administrative action, looking at the subject 'from the inside, trying to make sense of lawyers' reasons and arguments as they are actually presented and defended'.[1] Rather than starting from the constitutional basis of judicial review and working backwards to practice, I start by identifying the core values revealed by the practice of administrative law and then work forwards to analyse how they influence the shape and trajectory of the law.

I take this approach for pragmatic rather than philosophical reasons. Administrative law's topography has changed dramatically in recent decades; I am interested in understanding why that is and what further changes may await in the years to come.

My focus is on administrative law doctrine. I contend that administrative law in this sense is best understood by reference to several core values: the rule of law, good administration, democracy and separation of powers. I trace the contours of these values in section II. These values inform doctrinal choices that courts make in the areas of process, substance and remedial discretion, a body of law considered in section III.[2] I observe the values from a modern perspective, not out of philosophical dogmatism but because a modern understanding of the values coheres better with the development of administrative law. Throughout the process of writing, my practice has been reflective: the cases inform my understanding of administrative law values; and these values in turn inform my understanding of the cases. However, I do not suggest that administrative law values explain every single feature of the modern judicial review landscape. In section IV, I identify some institutional considerations that may also bear on judicial decisions and the development of administrative law.

Taking the time to discuss important areas of administrative law doctrine and determine whether judicial decisions are influenced by a set of values is a useful

* With thanks to Vincent-Alexandre Fournier and Mouhaimina Rebba for research assistance and the editors for valuable comments.

[1] TRS Allan, *The Sovereignty of Law: Freedom, Constitution and Common Law* (Oxford, Oxford University Press, 2013) 349.

[2] See also M Elliott, 'Judicial Review's Scope, Foundations and Purposes: Joining the Dots' (2012) *New Zealand Law Review* 75; D Feldman, 'Error of Law and Flawed Administrative Acts' (2014) 73 *CLJ* 275.

undertaking. Explaining doctrinal rules and outcomes in particular cases is valuable, all the more so if common themes can be traced across very different areas of administrative law. A values-based framework is capable of accommodating the development of doctrine over time, an urgent matter given the rapid growth in recent decades of the administrative state and legal constraints on administrative action. It may also help to account for convergence and divergence across the common law world: common law countries have (largely) a common heritage, one which they treat in different ways, but (generally) in a fashion that is comprehensible to all common lawyers, not just the natives of a particular jurisdiction.

This chapter is broad rather than deep, both in its treatment of administrative law values and of the jurisprudence. Where possible, I have concentrated on leading theorists and leading cases, with a view to providing a coherent account of the values I identify and the influence they have. I do not claim that each of the values identified lends itself to only one interpretation. On the contrary, they are liable to be understood differently by different jurists and to be given different weight in different contexts. Nonetheless, as my survey of cases demonstrates, they underlie much of the evolution—more hesitant, perhaps, in some places than in others—of modern administrative law. Even though overt or express judicial invocation of and reliance on these values is relatively rare, distilling shared themes from masses of decided cases is a familiar task for the common lawyer.

II. ADMINISTRATIVE LAW VALUES

Much like Ronald Dworkin's 'principles',[3] administrative law values[4] have weight which varies. In some situations, one of the values will prove more compelling than the others.[5] Often, each of the values can be accommodated, giving varying weight to each rather than treating any one value as determinative; that they overlap and interlock with one another facilitates this approach. As I will explain in more detail in section III, these features of administrative law values give them clarificatory and explanatory power: they help to clarify and explain areas of the law. They also have normative force, supporting decisions to adopt particular doctrines and decisions in particular cases, and providing benchmarks for criticism when judges fail to give effect to values, or give insufficient weight to values in particular contexts.

[3] See especially R Dworkin, *Taking Rights Seriously* (Cambridge, MA, Harvard University Press, 1977) 22–28, 94–100, 110–18, 123–30.

[4] See also P Cane, 'Theory and Values in Public Law' in P Craig and R Rawlings (eds), *Law and Administration in Europe: Essays for Carol Harlow* (Oxford, Oxford University Press, 2003) 3, 14–17; P Cane and L McDonald, *Principles of Administrative Law: Legal Regulation of Governance*, 2nd edn (Melbourne, Oxford University Press, 2012) ch 12; G Cartier, 'The *Baker* Effect: A New Interface Between the *Canadian Charter of Rights and Freedoms* and Administrative Law: The Case of Discretion' in D Dyzenhaus (ed), *The Unity of Public Law* (Oxford, Hart Publishing, 2004) 61; D Oliver, *Common Values and the Public-Private Divide* (London, Butterworths, 1999). For a critical take on the debate sparked by Cane's contribution, see M Loughlin, 'Theory and Values in Public Law: An Interpretation' [2005] *PL* 48.

[5] See, eg, Oliver, *Common Values* (n 4) 58.

They are a source, in short, of 'reasoned justification' for judicial review doctrines and decisions.[6] That is not to say that they explain every aspect of administrative law. Common law judges are not automatons, and administrative law is not a series of levers and pulleys that manufactures predictable products. As a result, deciding what administrative law values require in a particular context will ultimately call on judicial judgement.

Administrative law values are immanent in the law, found by interpreting existing legal materials. This task involves a process of interpretation which, because it is conducted from a jurist's perspective, focuses on what lawyers think the law *should* represent.[7] What proves to be in the materials will depend on who is looking and why: 'legal theorists and lawyers (both academic and practising) are necessarily concerned with moral and political values because determining what the law is on any particular topic *involves giving the best possible interpretation of relevant legal materials in the light of such values*'.[8]

Values are necessarily abstract and acquire 'their concrete meaning not only from their explicit treatment in case law (or other official sources of law) but also *from the way they are understood* by critics and commentators as well as ordinary citizens and public officials'.[9] The search for values involves a process of interpretation by jurists and judges who must resolve doctrinal controversies and concrete disputes between parties.[10]

For example, transparency is an important legal value. Judicial references to transparency, however, are a relatively modern phenomenon.[11] Yet it would be wrong to respond to an invocation of transparency as a legal value by stating that transparency was never explicitly relied upon by courts absent legislative authorisation. Although rights of access to records held by public bodies are a comparatively recent legislative development, the common law has long been hostile to secret justice: 'It is fundamental to our system of justice that, subject to certain established and limited exceptions, trials should be conducted and judgments given in public'.[12] Though its name is never mentioned, the value of *transparency* can thereby be observed. Doubtless, viewing older materials through a modern lens allows legal interpreters to see it more clearly. Nonetheless, it can plainly be said to be a value long present in the common law,[13] of which (to take one example) modern freedom of information provisions are an illustration, not the sole source. Moreover, once enacted

[6] P Craig, 'Ultra Vires and the Foundations of Judicial Review' (1998) 57 *CLJ* 63, 89.

[7] P Craig, 'Theory and Values in Public Law: A Response' in P Craig and R Rawlings (eds), *Law and Administration in Europe: Essays for Carol Harlow* (Oxford, Oxford University Press, 2003) 23, 24.

[8] Cane, 'Theory and Values in Public Law' (n 4) 11 (describing 'Dworkinian interpretivism') (emphasis added). See also A Beever and C Rickett, 'Interpretive Legal Theory and the Academic Lawyer' (2005) 68 *MLR* 320.

[9] Allan, *The Sovereignty of Law* (n 1) 334 (emphasis added).

[10] M Taggart, 'The Province of Administrative Law Determined?' in M Taggart (ed), *The Province of Administrative Law* (Oxford, Hart Publishing, 1997) 1, 6.

[11] See, eg, *R v Secretary of State for the Home Department, ex parte Doody* [1994] 1 AC 531, 561.

[12] *Bank Mellat v Her Majesty's Treasury (No 1)* [2013] UKSC 38, [81] (Lord Hope dissenting).

[13] See, eg *Scott v Scott* [1913] AC 417, 476 (Lord Shaw of Dunfermline).

such provisions fall to be interpreted against the backdrop of the common law's immanent values.[14]

It follows that values provide the motor for administrative law. Doctrine is dynamic. It 'changes according to current perceptions of what is required of the Courts in their distinctive judicial function'.[15] For example, doctrines relating to the right to reasons, error of fact and remedial discretion have been revolutionised or emerged in the last few decades. This is so because 'values are dynamic rather than static',[16] thereby providing an impetus for doctrinal reform. They are understood differently across space and time, varying in their breadth and weight from jurisdiction to jurisdiction and from generation to generation. Some judges will reject more expansive understandings of the values—and the number of such judges may be greater in some jurisdictions and some periods than others; indeed, present and future generations may consider the understandings of their forebears to be too expansive. Nevertheless, the understandings of administrative law values held by those who shape administrative law have, in my view, become more expansive, a point that can only be settled by examining the current legal landscape.

Interpretation of existing legal materials to identify the immanent values of administrative law will often shed light on the interpreter's political commitments.[17] Sometimes different constellations of values might arise depending on differing political commitments (eg libertarian versus liberal).[18] But these constellations must be drawn from the existing legal materials. And sometimes, political theory and legal doctrine will merge into one another, without values entering the picture at all. Cynics or sceptics might identify *judicial* values, preferences that judges have as to the way public administration should operate.[19] Paul Craig has argued persuasively that doctrines traceable to AV Dicey's constitutional theory are in fact based on a political theory of unitary democracy.[20] Political theory, in this instance, seeped more or less directly into legal doctrine. It remains the case, however, that for judges to avowedly take positions based on political theory is vanishingly rare and would be illegitimate: 'direct resort to abstract political theory' may well be 'deeply contentious' and take judges 'well beyond' their accepted role as 'interpreter[s] of existing law'.[21] The structure of adjudication, which requires personal interests to be 'converted' into legal claims, assists in maintaining this line between law and politics.[22] Thinking in terms of values, however, makes it easier to effectively identify 'political' decisions where judges rely on political preferences rather than values drawn from extant legal materials.

14 For a recent authority, see *Kennedy v Charity Commissioner* [2014] UKSC 20, [6].

15 *Thames Valley Electric Power Board v NZFP Pulp & Paper Ltd* [1994] 2 NZLR 641, 653 (Cooke P). See also *Doody* (n 11), 560 (Lord Mustill); *R v H* [2004] UKHL 3; *R v C* [2004] 2 AC 134, [11] (Lord Bingham of Cornhill).

16 Cane, 'Theory and Values in Public Law' (n 4) 17.

17 ibid 16; Craig, 'Theory and Values in Public Law: A Response' (n 7) 25.

18 ibid 34.

19 See, eg, D Feldman, 'Public Law Values in the House of Lords' (1990) 106 *LQR* 246; JAG Griffith, *The Politics of the Judiciary*, 5th edn (London, Fontana Press, 1997).

20 PP Craig, 'Dicey: Unitary, Self-correcting Democracy and Public Law' (1990) 106 *LQR* 105.

21 Allan, *The Sovereignty of Law* (n 1) 334.

22 LL Fuller, 'The Forms and Limits of Adjudication' (1978) 92 *Harvard Law Review* 353, 369.

A. The Rule of Law

My discussion of the rule of law as an administrative law value goes beyond the basic idea, 'common to all conceptions of the rule of law', that 'the exercise of all public power must be justified by law'.[23] I am interested in what the rule of law, as a value, or—in Jeffrey Jowell's apt phrase—'a principle of institutional morality'[24] requires in a modern liberal democracy with an administrative state. This, it might be said, is a substantive and not merely formal conception of the rule of law.[25]

As TRS Allan has elegantly written, 'The equal dignity of citizens, with its implications for fair treatment and respect for individual autonomy, is the basic premise of liberal constitutionalism, and accordingly the ultimate meaning of the rule of law'.[26] As a value in modern liberal democracies, then, the rule of law is concerned with the promotion of individual dignity and autonomy, on an equal basis.[27] Moreover, in terms of judicial review, 'the distinctively judicial public-law task ... is the protection of individual rights and interests against undue encroachment in the name of social interests'.[28] As an underlying value of administrative law, it urges judges to have regard to these considerations in fashioning doctrine and deciding individual cases.

B. Principles of Good Administration

Express judicial consideration of the principles of good administration[29] is rare. A notable exception is *R v Monopolies and Mergers Commission, ex parte Argyll Group*.[30] John Donaldson MR noted that '[g]ood public administration' has a number of concerns: 'substance rather than form'; 'the speed of decision'; 'a proper consideration of the public interest'; 'a proper consideration of the legitimate interests of individual citizens'; and 'decisiveness and finality'.[31] In very general terms, the

[23] J Laws, 'Wednesbury' in C Forsyth and I Hare (eds), *The Golden Metwand and the Crooked Cord: Essays on Public Law in Honour of Sir William Wade QC* (Oxford, Clarendon Press, 1998) 185, 192.

[24] J Jowell, 'The Rule of Law Today' in J Jowell, D Oliver and C O'Cinneide (eds), *The Changing Constitution*, 8th edn (Oxford, Oxford University Press, 2015) 11, 27.

[25] P Craig, 'Formal and Substantive Conceptions of the Rule of Law: An Analytical Framework' (1997) *PL* 467. In my view, a substantive conception of the rule of law better explains aspects of modern administrative law than does a formal conception. I recognise that some judges and jurists may be uncomfortable with a substantive conception. For this reason, my distinction between the rule of law and the principles of good administration, which overlap significantly with most formal conceptions of the rule of law, is a useful one to make. Those who do not endorse a substantive conception of the rule of law will generally endorse the principles of good administration discussed below.

[26] TRS Allan, *Constitutional Justice: A Liberal Theory of the Rule of Law* (Oxford, Oxford University Press, 2001) 2.

[27] T Bingham, *The Rule of Law* (London, Penguin Books, 2011) 55; D Dyzenhaus, 'The Politics of Deference: Judicial Review and Democracy' in M Taggart (ed), *The Province of Administrative Law* (Oxford, Hart Publishing, 1997) 279.

[28] Cane, 'Theory and Values in Public Law' (n 4) 15.

[29] It seems that the phrase was first introduced by DJ Galligan, 'Judicial Review and the Textbook Writers' (1982) 2 *OJLS* 257. Most writers have treated them as co-extensive with the existing grounds of judicial review. See, eg D Oliver, 'Is the Ultra Vires Rule the Basis of Judicial Review?' [1987] *PL* 543.

[30] *R v Monopolies and Mergers Commission, ex parte Argyll Group Plc* [1986] 2 All ER 257.

[31] ibid 266.

principles of good administration can be united under the heading of 'effectiveness'. Official decisions should be rational, in the sense that they should achieve the ends to which they are directed; policies should be consistent but open to change if required; and both decisions and policies should be transparent and capable of being complied with. The value of the principles of good administration, then, is that of effective policy-making and implementation.

Depending on the view taken of the rule of law, it overlaps to a significant degree with the principles of good administration, in two ways. First, in *The Morality of Law*, Lon Fuller identified 'principles of legality', 'eight kinds of legal excellence toward which a system of rules may strive'.[32] Roughly, these were that laws should be: general; published; not retroactive; understandable; not in contradiction with one another; possible to comply with; consistent; and possessing some congruence between the published rule and its administration.[33]

These are open to the objection, dutifully made by HLA Hart in a pungent review, that they are merely 'principles of good legal craftsmanship'.[34] Fuller himself recognised as much in his 'Reply to Critics'. Contrasting the enterprise of law with that of managerial direction of subordinates, he commented: 'Insofar as the principles of legality (or, perhaps I should say, their managerial analogues) are here applicable they are indeed "principles of efficacy"; they are instruments for the achievement of the superior's ends'.[35] For the purposes of describing the 'internal morality' of managerial direction on the part of government, Fuller dropped from his list generality, congruence and retrospectivity.[36] One can quibble with his decision to exclude congruence, which is surely an aid to the efficacy of regulation. But the general point should be clear. Some aspects of the rule of law can be described as principles of good administration.

Secondly, a concern for individual dignity and autonomy can be said to underpin the principles of good administration. Joseph Raz identified eight principles similar in nature to Fuller's, emphasised that they facilitate autonomy and protect individual freedom,[37] and went on to suggest that '[m]ore important than both these considerations is the fact that observance of the rule of law is necessary if the law is to respect human dignity'.[38]

However, there is a difference between the approach taken by Raz and that taken by Allan. For Raz, the principles of good administration further autonomy, liberty and dignity. Allan goes further. Autonomy and dignity, on his approach, require much more from judges: a commitment to the enforcement of fundamental rights, for example; and, in particular, attention to the justification of exercises of public power

[32] LL Fuller, *The Morality of Law*, rev edn (New Haven, CT, Yale University Press, 1969) 41.

[33] For a similar list, but a very different view of its legal and political import, see J Raz, 'The Rule of Law and Its Virtue' in J Raz (ed), *The Authority of Law*, 2nd edn (Oxford, Oxford University Press, 2009) 210. At the very least, those who reject a substantive conception of the rule of law would surely endorse the more formal conception that closely aligns with the principles of good administration.

[34] (1965) 78 *Harvard Law Review* 1281, 1285.

[35] Fuller, *The Morality of Law* (n 32) 209.

[36] ibid 214.

[37] Raz, 'The Rule of Law and Its Virtue' (n 33) 220.

[38] ibid 210–21.

in particular cases.[39] And yet, attention to the principles of good administration is necessary to round out Allan's approach to the rule of law, which aims to accommodate 'legitimate public purposes' and the 'common good'.[40] This opens the door to considerations of the more mundane principles of good administration. For one cannot know what constitutes the common good without considering the effectiveness of a government policy or decision. By definition, an illogical or irrational decision cannot further the common good or serve a legitimate public purpose. In Allan's rendering of the rule of law, these considerations are understandably secondary, but they are of independent importance, capable of guiding judicial decision-making by emphasising effectiveness of policy- and decision-making. Protection of individual interests can sometimes be good policy, but this will not inevitably be so, and the increasing importance accorded to individual dignity and autonomy by administrative law suggests a need to distinguish between the rule of law and the principles of good administration.

C. Democracy

At a most basic level, democracy requires that majority decisions to pass legislative measures ought to be respected (within constitutional limits). Where legislatures have passed laws, courts ought to pay attention to those laws. Courts, it is widely accepted, are under an obligation to give effect to legislative intent (however this may be discerned—a controversial question).[41] Accordingly, exercises of government power ought to have a basis in law and be true to the purposes for which they were granted.

As with the rule of law, the value of democracy is open to competing conceptions. In the modern Western world, democracy is a substantive concept, not a statistical one.[42] A process of simply counting voters' heads and legislators' hands is not sufficient unto the modern day. Democracy implies participation by all citizens in the formulation and debating of policy, inside and outside the tight confines of election campaigns.[43] Active citizens have voices and those voices should be heard in various forums designed to permit participation and deliberation.[44] As Dicey made clear, legislative authority is exercised by legislators aware that they must face re-election and that there are limits to the acceptable exercise of their powers.[45] Citizens, politicians and decision-makers should be allowed to interact in an ongoing process

39 Allan, *Constitutional Justice* (n 26) 9. See also D Dyzenhaus, 'Law as Justification: Etienne Mureinik's Conception of Legal Culture' (1998) 14 *South African Journal on Human Rights* 11.

40 Allan, *Constitutional Justice* (n 26) 17, 22.

41 See, eg, R Ekins, *The Nature of Legislative Intent* (Oxford, Oxford University Press, 2012).

42 R Dworkin, *Freedom's Law: The Moral Reading of the American Constitution* (New York, Oxford University Press, 1996).

43 See, eg, A Gutmann and D Thompson, *Democracy and Disagreement* (Cambridge, Belknap Press, 1996).

44 See, eg, S Breyer, *Active Liberty: Interpreting our Democratic Constitution* (New York, Alfred A Knopf, 2006).

45 AV Dicey, *Introduction to the Study of the Law of the Constitution*, 10th edn (London, Macmillan, 1959).

of elaboration of shared values,[46] a process that in federal systems takes place on multiple levels of governance. Although this conception of democracy fits more readily with the precepts of modern liberal democracy, it would be understandable if some judges were to feel more comfortable with a more limited conception focusing primarily or solely on giving effect to the law as written.

Democracy and the rule of law are intimately related: 'Our law's claim to legitimacy also rests on an appeal to moral values, many of which are imbedded in our constitutional structure'.[47] Effectiveness too underpins the values of the rule of law and democracy. Decisions that are ineffective because they are irrational or serve improper ends offend the value of the rule of law as much as they do the principles of good administration. And ineffective decisions sap the legitimacy of administrative decision-making structures established by legislative majorities.

D. Separation of Powers

It has been said that the concept of the separation of powers is 'infected with so much imprecision and inconsistency that it may be counted little more than a jumbled portmanteau of arguments for policies which ought to be supported or rejected on other grounds'.[48] Indeed, the modern administrative state has long since dispensed with rigid compliance with separation of powers: neat distinctions between legislative, executive and judicial functions have long since fallen out of favour.[49] Attention to the value of democracy requires no less, as it is legislatures that have created novel structures to address novel challenges and thereby 'deranged our three-branch legal theories'.[50]

Nonetheless, the concept of the separation of powers incarnates the idea of checks and balances, that 'foxes should not guard henhouses'.[51] That power ought not to be concentrated in one branch of government suggests the desirability of 'multiple mutually reinforcing forms and criteria of accountability'.[52] Accountability is a capacious concept,[53] but the core idea is that decision-makers should have to render an account of their actions to some external party: a higher-up, a court, the legislature, the market, civil society.

The affinity with other administrative law values is close. Attention to the separation of powers enhances the value of democracy by reminding unelected decision-makers of the need for caution in addressing matters that may better be left to

[46] D Dyzenhaus, 'Form and Substance in the Rule of Law: A Democratic Justification for Judicial Review?' in C Forsyth (ed), *Judicial Review and the Constitution* (Oxford, Hart Publishing, 2000) 141.

[47] *Reference Re Secession of Québec* [1998] 2 SCR 217, [67].

[48] G Marshall, *Constitutional Theory* (Oxford, Clarendon Press, 1971) 124.

[49] See generally, E Carolan, *The New Separation of Powers* (Oxford, Oxford University Press, 2009).

[50] *Federal Trade Commission v Ruberoid Co*, 343 US 470, 487 (1952) (Jackson J).

[51] CR Sunstein, *After the Rights Revolution: Re-conceiving the Regulatory State* (Cambridge, MA, Harvard University Press, 1990) 143.

[52] Cane, 'Theory and Values in Public Law' (n 4) 15.

[53] See generally, MD Dowdle, *Public Accountability: Designs, Dilemmas and Experiences* (Cambridge, Cambridge University Press, 2006).

elected representatives. Moreover, the role of the courts 'cannot be filled by the legislature or the executive: for in that case they or either of them would be judge in their own cause, with the ills of arbitrary government which that would entail'.[54] Separation of powers thus interlocks with the rule of law and principles of good administration by reducing the possibility of arbitrary official decision-making.

E. Conclusion

It is evident from the foregoing discussion that I reject a clear distinction between principle and policy; hence my preference for the term 'values'. Taking account of and giving effect to the value of the principles of good administration (and perhaps too the value of separation of powers) requires taking account of and giving effect to considerations of policy, understood as 'an improvement in some economic, political or social feature of the community'.[55] Judges do not have to determine whether the policies are good or bad, but they do have to form a view on the most efficacious means of fulfilling them. A distinction between principle and policy therefore entails a risk of confusion.[56]

III. VALUES AND DOCTRINAL RULES

Values can be identified at varying levels of abstraction. My choice of values aims to find a middle ground, between values abstract enough to cover the whole of the common law landscape[57] and those so specific that they cover only a small part of the modern administrative law map. Whether my choice is a fitting one or not depends on how effective the values I have identified are in explaining, clarifying and justifying the various doctrines discussed below. In this section, I will draw on various doctrines to demonstrate the close links between them and the underlying values I identified in the previous section. My survey of cases from around the common law world (past and present) demonstrates that the relationship between the values is a fluid, interdependent one.

A. Institutional Review: Bias

Different jurisdictions formulate the test for impartiality differently,[58] but as a general rule: where a decision-maker's participation in a decision would cause a reasonable apprehension of bias, she must recuse herself unless the party or parties concerned waive their right to object. Such is the importance of impartiality to the

[54] *R (Cart) v Upper Tribunal* [2010] 1 All ER 908, [37] (Laws LJ).
[55] R Dworkin, *Taking Rights Seriously* (Cambridge, Harvard University Press, 1977) 22.
[56] See also JA King, 'Institutional Approaches to Judicial Restraint' (2008) 28 *OJLS* 409, 416–19.
[57] Oliver, *Common Values* (n 4).
[58] See generally A Vermeule, 'Contra "Nemo Iudex in Sua Causa"' (2012) 122 *Yale LJ* 384.

legal system that the test operates in cases where bias might merely be perceived. Lord Hewart's formulation is well known: 'it is not merely of some importance but is of fundamental importance that justice should not only be done, but should manifestly and undoubtedly be seen to be done'.[59]

In part, the rule against bias is a device to serve the 'overriding public interest that there should be confidence in the integrity of the administration of justice',[60] a concern of good administration. However, it is plain that rule-of-law concerns underpin the operation of the bias test. Lord Hope of Craighead noted in *R v Bow Street Magistrates, ex parte Pinochet (No 2)* that the applicant was 'entitled to the judgment of an impartial and independent tribunal' on the question at issue.[61] In their comprehensive review of the cases on bias, an extremely strong bench of the Court of Appeal of England and Wales emphasised at the outset the personal interest of individuals in impartial decision-making, characterising the 'right' as 'fundamental', indeed, 'one of the most fundamental principles underlying the administration of justice'.[62]

That this individual interest may be waived, if 'clear and unequivocal' and 'made with full knowledge of all the facts relevant to the decision whether to waive or not' serves to emphasise the rule-of-law concerns underlying the rule against bias. Good administration may, moreover, intervene to ensure that the mere fact of an interest in the outcome of the litigation is not sufficient to require recusal.[63] '[P]ersonifying the reasonable man',[64] the reviewing court takes rule of law and good administration concerns into account in determining whether a decision-maker ought to have recused himself or herself.

Democracy is present too in the area of bias. In situations involving elected officials, the threshold for reasonable apprehension of bias is raised. Where the legislature has confided a discretionary power in an elected official or bodies of elected representatives, '[i]t would be naïve to suppose that Parliament can have meant Ministers to refrain from forming and expressing, even strongly, views' that they hold about questions submitted to them.[65] Municipal politicians, similarly, are not required to 'cast aside views on planning policy they will have formed when seeking election or when acting as councillors'.[66] The imperative of democracy demands that an applicant demonstrate that an elected official had a 'closed mind' in order to

[59] *R v Sussex Justices, ex parte McCarthy* [1924] 1 KB 256, 259. In the foundational case on direct interests in litigation, *Dimes v Proprietors of Grand Junction Canal* (1852) 3 HL Cas 759, it was the 'appearance of labouring under' a personal interest that grounded a finding of a reasonable apprehension of bias against the judge.

[60] *R v Gough* [1993] AC 646, 659. See similarly, *Gillies v Secretary of State for Work and Pensions* [2006] 1 All ER 731, [23].

[61] *R v Bow Street Magistrates, ex parte Pinochet (No 2)* [2000] 1 AC 119, 143.

[62] *Locabail (UK) Ltd v Bayfield Properties Ltd* [2000] IRLR 96, 98–99. This case involved judicial bias but the same doctrinal rules apply to administrative decision-makers, sometimes with modifications to take account of context.

[63] See, eg, *Ebner v Official Trustee in Bankruptcy* (2000) 176 ALR 643, [54].

[64] *Locabail* (n 62) 101.

[65] *CREEDNZ Inc v Governor General* [1981] 1 NZLR 172, 179 (Cooke P).

[66] *R (Lewis) v Persimmon Homes* [2008] LGR 781, 802 (Pill LJ). See also *Old St Boniface Residents' Association v Winnipeg (City)* [1990] 3 SCR 1170, 1192.

justify judicial intervention.[67] Good administration may further underpin the democratic imperative. Electing or appointing representatives to regulatory bodies may make those bodies more effective: 'No doubt many boards will operate more effectively with representation from all segments of society who are interested in [their] operations'.[68]

A super-added requirement of independence is inspired by separation of powers concerns. As has been said, 'One of the cornerstones of our legal system is the impartiality of the tribunals by which justice is administered'.[69] Independence and impartiality are 'closely linked', because independence 'is the structural or institutional framework which secures ... impartiality' and the appearance of impartiality.[70] The rule of law and good administration are subsequently secured by ensuring that external checks and balances are imposed on the exercise of administrative power.

B. Procedural Fairness

It has long been understood that the rules of procedural fairness 'are not engraved on tablets of stone'.[71] Accordingly, 'what the requirements of fairness demand ... depends on the character of the decision-making body, the kind of decision it has to make and the statutory or other framework in question'.[72] To translate 'character', 'kind' and 'framework' into the language of values: good administration, the rule of law (in terms of the relative impact on individuals of the decision) and democracy provide the context which allow reviewing courts to determine whether or not to impose procedural safeguards.[73]

Rule-of-law concerns are often dominant. After all, procedural fairness cases invariably involve a person (occasionally a legal person) who contends that his or her rights have been infringed, that they have been 'subjected to pains or penalties'.[74] And the more severe the pains and penalties, the greater the individual's claim to procedural protection: 'The more important the decision is to the lives of those affected and the greater its impact on that person or those persons, the more stringent the procedural protections that will be mandated'.[75]

The greater the effect, the greater the dignity interest served by according robust procedural rights. Recognition that '[i]n the modern state the decisions of

[67] See also *R v Amber Valley District Council, ex parte Jackson* [1985] 1 WLR 298; *Condron v National Assembly for Wales* [2007] LGR 87.

[68] *Newfoundland Telephone Co v Newfoundland (Board of Commissioners of Public Utilities)* [1992] 1 SCR 623, 635.

[69] *Pinochet (No 2)* (n 61), 140 (Lord Hope of Craighead).

[70] *Gillies v Secretary of State for Work and Pensions* [2006] 1 All ER 731, [38] (Baroness Hale).

[71] *Lloyd v McMahon* [1987] 1 AC 625, 702 (Lord Bridge of Harwich).

[72] ibid. See also *Morrissey v Brewer*, 408 US 471, 481 (1972); *R (L) v West London Mental Health NHS Trust* [2014] EWCA Civ 47.

[73] After the fashion of modern courts and commentators, I use the terms procedural fairness, procedural rights and duty of fairness interchangeably, to replace the older label 'natural justice'.

[74] *Selvarajan v Race Relations Board* [1976] 1 All ER 12, 19.

[75] *Baker v Canada (Minister of Citizenship and Immigration)* [1999] 2 SCR 817, [25].

administrative bodies can have a more immediate and profound impact on people's lives than the decisions of courts' has underpinned the expansion of procedural protections.[76] This concern for individual dignity and autonomy is underpinned by the substantive aspect of the value of democracy, which privileges participation by individuals when state action relevant to them is proposed. Good administration often supports these rule-of-law based claims, as when participatory rights would reduce the risk of error.[77]

Yet these individual procedural rights may be tempered by considerations of good administration: 'If there were too much elaboration of procedural safeguards, nothing could be done simply and quickly and cheaply'.[78] Indeed, '[a]t some point the benefit of an additional safeguard to the individual affected by the administrative action and to society in terms of increased assurance that the action is just, may be outweighed by the cost'.[79]

The right to reasons is a good example of creative tension,[80] one which, moreover, demonstrates the dynamic potential of values. Concern for individual dignity and autonomy suggests that a right to reasons ought to be recognised. 'Those affected may be more likely to feel they were treated fairly and appropriately if reasons are given',[81] 'thereby contributing to a more willing acceptance of the decision'[82] such that 'where the decision has important significance for the individual', reviewing courts ought to impose a duty on administrative decision-makers to give reasons: 'It would be unfair for a person subject to a decision … so critical to their future not to be told why the result was reached'.[83] Moreover, the provision of reasons would mean that the exercise of government power 'is less likely to be, *or to appear to be arbitrary*, if the decision maker formulates and provides reasons for his decision'.[84]

Good administration pulls in two ways. On the one hand, militating against a right to reasons are concerns of efficiency: 'increased cost and delay' and, perhaps 'a lack of candour' on the part of decision-makers.[85] On the other hand, reasons may lead to more accurate decision-making 'by ensuring that issues and reasoning are well articulated and, therefore, more carefully thought out'.[86]

Separation-of-powers concerns may also be relevant. Accordingly, the Irish Supreme Court recognised a right to reasons where the Minister's failure to provide any meant it was not possible for the individual 'to ascertain whether he has a

[76] *R v Higher Education Funding Council, ex parte Institute of Dental Surgery* [1994] 1 All ER 651, 667. See most notably, *Ridge v Baldwin* [1964] AC 40; *Goldberg v Kelly*, 397 US 254, 264 (1970).

[77] See, eg, *Nicholson v Haldimand-Norfolk Regional Board of Commissioners of Police* [1979] 1 SCR 311, 328. See also *May v Ferndale Institution* [2005] 3 SCR 809, [117]–[118]; *New Brunswick (Minister of Health and Community Services) v G (J)* [1999] 3 SCR 46, [72].

[78] *Pearlberg v Varty* [1972] 1 WLR 534, 547.

[79] *Mathews v Eldridge*, 424 US 319, 348 (1976). See also *Hannah v Larche*, 363 US 420 (1959).

[80] See generally, M Elliott, 'Has the Common Law Duty to Give Reasons Come of Age Yet?' [2011] *PL* 56.

[81] *Baker* (n 75) [39].

[82] *Taxquet v Belgium* (2012) 54 EHRR 26, [91].

[83] *Baker* (n 75) [43]. See also *Doody* (n 11) 565.

[84] *Public Service Board of New South Wales v Osmond* (1986) 63 ALR 559, 572 (Deane J) (emphasis added). See also TRS Allan, 'Procedural Fairness and the Duty of Respect' (1998) 18 *OJLS* 497.

[85] *Osmond* (n 84) 567 (Gibbs CJ).

[86] *Baker* (n 75) [39]. See also *Doody* (n 11) 563.

ground for applying for judicial review and, by extension, not possible for the courts effectively to exercise their power of judicial review'.[87] Similarly, in *R v Secretary of State for the Home Department, ex parte Doody*, Lord Mustill was concerned that an individual could not mount an 'effective attack' on a sentencing decision taken by the executive without reasons—'I think it important that there should be an effective means of detecting the kind of error which would entitle the court to intervene'[88]—a concern that outweighed any democracy-based concerns that the legislature had accorded the decision-maker an unfettered discretion. And in cases where an appeal has been provided for by statute, democracy concerns suggest that a duty to provide reasons is an uncontroversial corollary of the legislative decision to provide a means of appeal.[89] Attention to rule-of-law concerns, and the adoption of a new perspective on the principles of good administration and democracy, has led courts to insist ever-more that individuals have a right to receive reasons from administrative decision-makers.

Hovering over all content issues, save for situations in which a procedural right is constitutional in nature, is the prospect of legislative intervention. Democracy concerns mean that clear statutory language is predominant. Where procedural rights are excluded or compromised by express statutory language, values cannot come to the rescue. American courts, concerned in addition by good administration,[90] have warned courts 'against engrafting their own notions of proper procedures upon agencies entrusted with substantive functions by Congress'.[91] And in situations where the legislature has entrusted a decision-maker with a measure of discretion, reviewing courts must factor this legislative choice into the procedural fairness calculus.[92]

There are several categorical, values-based exclusions to the duty of fairness.[93] Most prominently,[94] legislative action has traditionally not been subject to the safeguards of procedural fairness. Where primary legislation is concerned, 'parliamentary tradition' and the doctrine of parliamentary sovereignty limit due process to the cut and thrust of parliamentary debate.[95] And it has regularly been said that, where administrative action takes legislative form, procedural fairness is excluded.[96]

[87] *Mallak v Minister for Justice, Equality and Law Reform* [2012] IESC 59, [65].

[88] *Doody* (n 11).

[89] See, eg, *Norton Tool Co v Tewson* [1973] 1 WLR 45; *Osmond* (n 84) 562.

[90] See, eg, *Federal Communications Commission v Schreiber*, 381 US 279, 290 (1965).

[91] *Vermont Yankee Nuclear Power Corp v Natural Resource Defense Council Inc*, 435 US 519, 525 (1978).

[92] See, eg, *Federal Communications Commission v Pottsville Broadcasting Co*, 309 US 134, 143 (1940); *Local Government Board v Arlidge* [1915] AC 120, 144 (Lord Parmoor); *Doody* (n 11) 561 (Lord Mustill).

[93] Whether the exclusions are truly categorical is doubtful. As Estey J unwittingly put it, in a decision which recognised (at 758) an exclusion in respect of an administrative decision of a legislative nature: 'It is *always* a question of construing the statutory scheme as a whole in order to see to what degree, if any, the legislator intended the principle to apply': *Attorney General of Canada v Inuit Tapirisat* [1980] 2 SCR 735, 755.

[94] Good administration rears its head in 'emergency' situations, allowing officials to abrogate procedural rights. See, eg, *Cardinal v Director of Kent Institution* [1985] 2 SCR 643, 655.

[95] *Authorson v Canada (Attorney General)* [2003] 2 SCR 40, [37].

[96] *Bates v Lord Hailsham* [1972] 3 All ER 1019, 1024.

Separation-of-powers and democratic concerns are most commonly invoked to justify this position.[97] Justificatory arguments have also been based on accountability to the legislature.[98] As Justice Holmes once put it, in such situations, individuals' 'rights are protected in the only way that they can be in a complex society, by their power, immediate or remote, over those who make the rule'.[99] Yet where action that is legislative in character touches a small number of people, rule-of-law concerns push reviewing courts to impose procedural protections.[100]

C. Substantive Review

In many jurisdictions it is now accepted that where an administrative decision-maker commits an error of law by interpreting a statute incorrectly, a reviewing court may intervene.[101] *Anisminic v Foreign Compensation Commission*[102] was a watershed case. A majority of the House of Lords held that an error in interpreting an Order in Council justified judicial intervention, even in the face of a privative clause. Concern for democracy was paramount. As Lord Pearce put it, administrative decision-makers must 'confine themselves within the powers specially committed to them on a true construction of the relevant Acts of Parliament'.[103] When courts intervene to keep an administrative decision-maker within boundaries established by legislation, this represents 'simply an enforcement of Parliament's mandate to the tribunal'.[104] That the 'very effectiveness' of statute should be ensured by judicial review[105] is underpinned by rule-of-law concerns: 'By acting in the absence of legal authority, the decision maker transgresses the principle of the rule of law'.[106]

Yet, as Lord Wilberforce acknowledged, determining the 'extent of the interpretatory power conferred upon the tribunal' should not be done with 'any necessary predisposition towards one that questions of law, or questions of construction, are necessarily for the courts'.[107] Accordingly, in those jurisdictions where deference to administrative decision-makers is embraced, a more subtle view is taken of democracy: 'Courts, while exercising their constitutional functions of judicial review, must be sensitive … to the necessity of avoiding undue interference with the discharge

[97] See *Inuit Tapirisat* (n 93) 754 for an argument based on 'practicality'. See similarly, *Bi-Metallic Investment Co v State Board of Equalization*, 239 US 441, 445 (1915).

[98] *Wilson v Esquimalt and Nanaimo Railway Company* [1922] 1 AC 202, 213.

[99] *State Board of Equalization* (n 97) 445.

[100] See, eg, *Londoner v Denver*, 210 US 373 (1908); *Homex Realty v Wyoming (Village)* [1980] 2 SCR 1011, 1031; *Bank Mellat* (n 12).

[101] I include several of the traditional grounds of review for abuse of discretion under this head: eg using a power for an improper purpose is ultimately a question of statutory interpretation. See, eg, *Padfield v Minister of Agriculture, Fisheries and Food* [1968] AC 997, 1034 (Lord Reid).

[102] *Anisminic Ltd v Foreign Compensation Commission* [1969] 2 AC 147.

[103] ibid 194. See similarly, ibid 207 (Lord Wilberforce).

[104] ibid 196. See similarly *R v Northumberland Compensation Appeal Tribunal, ex parte Shaw* [1952] 1 KB 338, 346.

[105] *Cart* (n 54) [38] (Laws LJ).

[106] *Dunsmuir v New Brunswick* [2008] 1 SCR 190, [29].

[107] *Anisminic* (n 102) 209.

of administrative functions in respect of the matters *delegated to administrative bodies by Parliament and legislatures*'.[108] Statutes are treated as relevant information which carve out a space for administrative decision-makers[109] or which inform the degree of deference courts ought to accord to administrative decision-makers.[110] The authority thereby granted is not absolute, and rule-of-law and good administration concerns ensure that the reasonableness of administrative decisions is policed by courts,[111] but democracy—the legislative choice to grant authority to administrative decision-makers—is respected.

Moreover, to defer to administrative decision-makers is to defer to expert bodies which can deal efficiently with complex issues, sometimes relying on input from interested parties. Such bodies can exercise their functions with 'cheapness, accessibility, freedom from technicality, expedition and expert knowledge of their particular subject'.[112] Both good administration and separation-of-powers concerns were expressed by the Supreme Court of the United States in its seminal *Chevron* decision: 'Judges are not experts in the field, and are not part of either political branch of the Government'.[113]

Competition between different conceptions of the values and between the values induces creative tension which may move the law in new directions.[114] Take factual error as an example. Common law courts have long been reluctant to recognise error of fact as a ground justifying judicial intervention.[115] Democracy seems to be the dominant concern here. Respect for the legislative choice to establish an administrative decision-maker counsels a restrained approach to matters falling within its bailiwick; the legislature has given responsibility for fact-finding to the administrative decision-maker, not the courts.[116]

Yet courts have become increasingly reluctant to keep their hands resolutely off cases of factual error. Good administration has been mentioned,[117] but the rule of law has been to the forefront. Lord Slynn of Hadley invoked rule-of-law concerns in *A v Criminal Injuries Compensation Board*,[118] a case in which the Board rejected a claim by an alleged rape victim without having had regard to an important medical report. He would have quashed the decision on the ground of unfairness: 'I do not

[108] *Dunsmuir* (n 106) [27] (emphasis added).

[109] It may be said, for example, that clear statutory language must be enforced because 'the court, as well as the agency, must give effect to the unambiguously expressed intent of Congress': *Chevron v Natural Resources Defense Council*, 467 US 837, 842–43 (1984). Within these boundaries, but only within these boundaries, the administrative decision-maker is free to choose between competing interpretations.

[110] PL Strauss, '"Deference" is Too Confusing: Let's Call Them "Chevron Space" and "Skidmore Weight"' (2012) 112 *Columbia Law Review* 1143.

[111] See, eg, *Dunsmuir* (n 106) [47].

[112] *Report of the Franks Committee on Administrative Tribunals and Enquiries*, Cmd 218 (1957) 9.

[113] *Chevron* (n 109) 865–66.

[114] There is some evidence that the English courts have begun to accept the deference argument. See, eg, *Jones v First Tier Tribunal* [2013] 2 AC 48.

[115] At least not expressly: see P Craig, *Administrative Law*, 7th edn (London, Sweet & Maxwell, 2012) 512; P Daly, 'Judicial Review of Factual Error in Ireland' (2008) 30 *Dublin University Law Journal* 187.

[116] See, eg, *R v Governor of Brixton Prison, ex parte Armah* [1968] AC 192, 234 (Lord Reid).

[117] See, eg, *Secretary of State for Education v Tameside Metropolitan Borough Council* [1977] AC 1014, 1030 (Scarman LJ).

[118] *A v Criminal Injuries Compensation Board* [1999] 2 AC 330.

think it possible to say here that justice was done or seen to be done'.[119] And in *E v Secretary of State for the Home Department*, Carnwath LJ justified the introduction of 'a separate ground of review' of error of fact 'on the principle of fairness'.[120] It is surely significant that *E* was a case involving an asylum seeker, as is true of many of the modern cases on factual error.[121] Error costs in this regime are extraordinarily high, as failed asylum seekers wrongly returned to their country of origin are at grave risk of physical danger. Concern for individual dignity and autonomy may well underpin the rapid rise of factual error.[122]

D. Remedial Discretion

John Donaldson MR was emphatic in his discussion of remedial discretion in *R v Monopolies and Mergers Commission, ex parte Argyll Group*: 'We have to approach our duties with a proper awareness of the needs of public administration'.[123] In *R v Chief Constable of the Thames Valley Police, ex parte Cotton*,[124] Bingham LJ set out six principles governing remedial discretion in public law cases. Several concerned good administration, for example, with respect to the idea that relief should not be granted where the decision-maker would have reached the same decision regardless of the error complained of, '[u]nless the subject of the decision has had an opportunity to put his case it may not be easy to know what case he could or would have put if he had had the chance'.[125] One principle overlapped good administration and the rule of law: 'It is generally desirable that decision-makers should be reasonably receptive to argument, and it would therefore be unfortunate if the complainant's position became weaker as the decision-maker's mind became more closed'.[126] Another was drawn from the rule of law: 'Where a decision-maker is under a duty to act fairly the subject of the decision may properly be said to have a right to be heard, and rights are not to be lightly denied'. One other principle was drawn from the separation of powers, invoking a danger of the court 'unconsciously stray[ing] from its proper province of reviewing the propriety of the decision-making process into the forbidden territory of evaluating the substantial merits of a decision'.[127]

In an elegant essay on remedial discretion, Peter Cane argued that remedial choices are influenced by the separation of powers. For example:

> when a body has the power to revise decisions of a decision maker who performs a different function from that performed by the reviser, so that the two bodies are not seen as belonging to the same decision-making hierarchy, it is much less appropriate that the reviser

119 ibid 347.
120 *E v Secretary of State for the Home Department* [2004] QB 1044, [63].
121 P Craig, 'Judicial Review, Appeal and Factual Error' [2004] *PL* 788.
122 It bears mentioning that the first case to suggest that exercises of discretion should in some circumstances be subject to 'anxious scrutiny' by reviewing courts was an immigration matter: *R v Secretary of State for the Home Department, ex parte Bugdaycay* [1987] AC 514, 531 (Lord Bridge of Harwich).
123 *Argyll* (n 30) 266.
124 *R v Chief Constable of the Thames Valley Police, ex parte Cotton* [1990] IRLR 344.
125 ibid 352.
126 ibid.
127 ibid.

> should have the power to make orders in substitution for decisions of the inferior decision maker.[128]

Yet, the principles of good administration also make a defiant appearance in Cane's essay. Lack of necessary 'qualifications, experience and competences' is an additional ground for restraint.[129]

Administrative law values have been woven into the area of remedies, which forms part of the fabric of administrative law doctrine, cut from the same cloth as the principles of institutional, procedural and substantive review. Judicial decisions when to issue a particular remedy may be guided by administrative law values. Consider the remedy of the mandatory order (*mandamus*), which has the effect of requiring a decision-maker to take a particular decision. Separation-of-powers and democracy concerns are evidently implicated, as the reviewing court must step into a pair of shoes that were set aside by the legislature for another body. Yet in some circumstances, rule-of-law and good administration concerns may point strongly in favour of issuing the remedy.

The applicant in *D'Errico v Canada (Attorney General)*[130] had suffered injuries in a car accident but was denied a disability pension, apparently on the basis that she had been taking yoga classes and working as a yoga instructor. Stratas JA quashed the decision and also made an order of *mandamus*. Quite properly, he noted that *mandamus* will only be issued in exceptional cases.[131] In determining that this case was exceptional, he focused on administrative law values. From a rule-of-law perspective, he emphasised the importance of the claimed benefit to the applicant and the deleterious effects of further delay. The benefits were 'meant to address a very serious condition, one that prevents the earning of meaningful income to sustain oneself', yet the applicant had been waiting eight years for resolution of her claim.[132] He then focused on good administration. Ordinarily, administrative decision-makers reach appropriate outcomes more quickly and efficiently than courts. But remitting a matter for further decision where the outcome is obvious would hurt good administration, not help it.[133] Democracy was not a pressing concern here: although the decision-maker had been designated by Parliament, it had not discharged its functions in a timely manner. And any separation-of-powers concerns about directing the decision-maker to reach a particular outcome were outweighed by the rule of law and good administration concerns.[134]

[128] P Cane, 'The Constitutional Basis of Judicial Remedies in Public Law' in P Leyland and T Woods (eds), *Administrative Law Facing the Future: Old Constraints and New Horizons* (London, Blackstone, 1997) 242, 246.

[129] ibid 247.

[130] *D'Errico v Canada (Attorney General)* 2014 FCA 95. See similarly *Canada (Public Safety and Emergency Preparedness) v LeBon* 2013 FCA 55.

[131] *D'Errico* (n 130) [17].

[132] ibid [19].

[133] See, eg, *Alberta (Information and Privacy Commissioner) v Alberta Teachers' Association* [2011] 3 SCR 654, [55].

[134] *D'Errico* (n 130) [21]. Multi-factor tests can mask the reality of the operation of administrative law values. It is refreshing that Stratas JA did not engage in a rote recitation of the lengthy and restrictive list of factors set out in the leading Canadian case on mandatory orders, *Apotex v Canada (Attorney General)* [1994] 3 SCR 1100.

Ordinarily, an applicant who can demonstrate that a decision was unlawful is entitled to relief: 'It is not for a court to deny that right and sense of justice on the basis of speculation as to what the result might have been had there been a hearing'.[135] Rule-of-law concerns are foremost in this analysis (though, reflecting the individual nature of rule-of-law concerns, breaches of procedural fairness can be 'cured' through internal appellate mechanisms that 'the parties should fairly be taken to have accepted when they joined the association').[136] Yet concerns of good administration counsel that, in some cases, courts should refuse to exercise their discretion to award a remedy. As Lord Wilberforce noted in *Malloch v Aberdeen Corporation*, there must be 'something of substance which has been lost by the failure. The court does not act in vain'.[137] An example is *Mobil Oil Canada Ltd v Canada-Newfoundland Offshore Petroleum Board*,[138] where although the applicant had established a breach of procedural fairness, the remedies sought were 'impractical'; compelling the decision-maker to reconsider its position would have been 'nonsensical' as it was 'bound in law' to reject the application because of the court's disposition of other aspects of the case.[139] In these 'exceptional' circumstances, Iacobucci J concluded, relief would be inappropriate.[140]

The tension between the rule of law, good administration and democracy is keenly felt in cases where the applicant did not take advantage of an alternative remedy. As a general matter, 'a remedy by way of judicial review is not to be made available where an alternative remedy exists'.[141] As Lord Templeman explained in *In re Preston*, a tax case, 'the remedy of the taxpayer lies in the appeal procedures' before bodies with 'wide knowledge and experience of fiscal law and practice' provided for by statute.[142] Good administration requires that judicial review processes 'should not be allowed to supplant the normal statutory appeal procedure' save in 'exceptional' circumstances.[143] Democracy plays a part too: 'When Parliament enacts a remedy with the clear intention that this should be pursued in place of judicial review, it is appropriate to have regard to the considerations giving rise to that intention'.[144]

Collateral attacks on administrative decisions also require reference to administrative law values. Good administration is rarely enhanced by collateral attacks on administrative decisions, as 'frequent and deliberate flouting of administrative processes could weaken the effectiveness of an agency by encouraging people to ignore its procedures'.[145] Nor is democracy, especially in cases where time limits or procedural restrictions have been imposed on access to judicial review,[146] because

[135] *Cardinal* (n 94) 661. See also *General Medical Council v Spackman* [1943] AC 627; *Annamunthodo v Oilfields Workers' Trade Union* [1961] AC 945.

[136] *Calvin v Carr* [1980] AC 574, 593.

[137] *Malloch v Aberdeen Corporation* [1971] 1 WLR 1579, 1595.

[138] *Mobil Oil Canada Ltd v Canada-Newfoundland Offshore Petroleum Board* [1994] 1 SCR 202.

[139] ibid 228.

[140] ibid.

[141] *Re Preston* [1985] 1 AC 835, 852.

[142] ibid 862.

[143] ibid.

[144] *R (G) v Immigration Appeal Tribunal* [2005] 1 WLR 1445, [20].

[145] *McKart v United States*, 395 US 185, 195 (1969).

[146] See, eg, *R v Wicks* [1998] AC 92.

collateral attacks frustrate 'the legislature's decision not to confer the power to hear an appeal from the administrative order on the court responsible for hearing the charge'.[147] Nevertheless, rule-of-law concerns require that collateral attacks be permissible in some instances. In *Boddington v British Transport Police*, a case involving a rail passenger who wished to contest the validity of a bye-law prohibiting smoking, the House of Lords permitted him to raise the invalidity of the bye-law as a defence to a criminal prosecution: 'It would be a fundamental departure from the rule of law if an individual were liable to conviction for contravention of some rule which is itself liable to be set aside by a court as unlawful'.[148] Democracy too may bolster these rule-of-law concerns in rare cases. So it was that where the Mayor of Toronto was threatened with the 'draconian' remedy of removal from office for a breach of conflict of interest legislation, a collateral attack on the underlying order was permissible.[149] And in some circumstances, good administration will not necessarily be undermined at all by permitting judicial review proceedings.[150]

In those fuzzy areas on either side of the public/private divide, similar issues regularly arise. Generally speaking, it would 'be contrary to public policy, and as such an abuse of the process of the court' to allow a person to attack by way of action an administrative decision because this would 'evade' provisions introduced 'for the protection of such authorities'.[151] Yet, if an individual seeks to assert private law rights against a public body, he or she will not be required to launch judicial review proceedings.[152] Where good administration and democracy would be undermined because the case involves 'a claim for judicial review with only a thin pretence to a private wrong', courts should use their inherent powers to prevent an inappropriate claim from proceeding.[153] Where no bright lines are apparent, resort to administrative law values becomes irresistible.

IV. INSTITUTIONAL CONSIDERATIONS

Administrative law is, for the most part, common law. A common law judge 'is not a knight-errant, roaming at will in pursuit of his own ideal of beauty or of goodness'.[154] In the common law tradition, judicial creativity is restrained by respect for precedent and the role of the legislature, and limited mostly to incremental change based primarily on legal principle; though judges in some jurisdictions will feel freer

[147] *R v Consolidated Maybrun Mines Ltd* [1998] 1 SCR 706, [24].

[148] *Boddington v British Transport Police* [1999] 2 AC 143, 154 (Lord Irvine of Lairg). See also *Wandsworth London Borough Council v Winder* [1985] AC 461.

[149] *Magder v Ford* 2013 ONSC 263, [58].

[150] See, eg, *Sackett v Environmental Protection Agency*, 132 S Ct 1367, 1374 (2012).

[151] *O'Reilly v Mackman* [1983] 2 AC 237, 285 (Lord Diplock). These protections include time limits and restrictions on discovery and disclosure.

[152] See, eg, *Roy v Kensington and Chelsea and Westminster Family Practitioner Committee* [1992] 1 AC 624, 628–29 (Lord Bridge of Harwich).

[153] *Canada (Attorney General) v TeleZone Inc* [2010] 3 SCR 585, [78].

[154] B Cardozo, *The Nature of the Judicial Process* (New Haven, CT, Yale University Press, 1921) 141.

to roam than their counterparts elsewhere. The importance of administrative law values should be understood in this light.

In addition, various institutional considerations may be invoked from time to time to supplement administrative law values. For example, remedial discretion can be invoked against misconduct to prevent the granting of relief 'even upon grounds otherwise legally sufficient, to applicants who in the matters before the Board have committed the fraud, trickery, and apparently perjury, found against the respondents here'.[155] Mischievous conduct by litigants should be sanctioned, not because of any particular administrative law value as such, but because litigants should not be tempted to use judicial machinery for purposes that are legally frivolous.

In this vein, it is worth also recalling Lord Lowry's comment on the public/private divide problem: 'there is much to be said in favour of the proposition that a court having jurisdiction ought to let a case be heard rather than entertain a debate concerning the form of the proceedings'.[156] It is plausible too that, sometimes, doctrinal rules will be chosen over doctrinal standards because the former are easier for courts to administer; for example, a bright-line rule disqualifying decision-makers from adjudicating on cases in which they have a financial interest may for institutional reasons be adjudged preferable to a standard.

Institutional considerations may also play a role complementary to that of administrative law values. *R (Cart) v Upper Tribunal*[157] is a case in point. Under the regime created by the Tribunals, Courts and Enforcement Act 2007, an individual may appeal to a First-tier Tribunal and thence to the Upper Tribunal. Sometimes, however, the Upper Tribunal will refuse to grant permission to appeal. If the Upper Tribunal's refusal is challenged, what criteria should a reviewing court apply in determining whether or not to grant a judicial review remedy? Baroness Hale of Richmond put the point bluntly: 'We all make mistakes … The question is, what machinery is necessary and proportionate to keep such mistakes to a minimum?'[158]

Several means of resolving this issue were proposed. First, the courts could carry on as before and review refusals for compliance with the general principles of administrative law. Yet this ran into a fundamental objection, the 'very fact' that Parliament had prescribed restrictive criteria for granting leave to appeal from the Upper Tribunal to the Court of Appeal 'destroys any possibility of an absolutist argument to the effect that the rule of law requires post-*Anisminic* unrestricted judicial review over all unappealable decisions of courts or tribunals of limited jurisdiction to ensure that they are not permitted, unsupervised by the higher courts, to commit errors of law'.[159] In short, the 'status, nature and role' accorded to the Upper Tribunal by Parliament had to be taken into account.[160] To this democratic concern could be

[155] *Cock v Labour Relations Board* (1960) 26 DLR (2d) 127, 129.
[156] *Roy* (n 152) 655.
[157] *R (Cart) v Upper Tribunal* [2012] 1 AC 663.
[158] ibid [38].
[159] ibid [99] (Lord Brown of Eaton-under-Heywood).
[160] ibid [123] (Lord Dyson).

added one of good administration: the tribunal structure gave 'several occasions' to individuals to scrutinise an adverse decision, which reduced the need for vigorous judicial oversight.[161] And also an institutional consideration: 'floodgates arguments ... cannot be ignored'.[162] Secondly, the courts could limit the grounds of review by reviving the distinction between jurisdictional errors (which would be reviewable) and non-jurisdictional errors (which would not be reviewable even in egregious cases). Rule-of-law concerns counselled against this, however, because it left open the possibility 'that serious errors of law affecting large numbers of people will go uncorrected'.[163]

Thirdly, the courts could adopt a set of limiting criteria, applying 'by analogy' the statutory criteria for permission to appeal from the Upper Tribunal to the Court of Appeal.[164] It was on this solution that the Supreme Court fastened, repeatedly invoking institutional considerations, most often in the guise of proportionality,[165] but also allied to administrative law values.[166] Indeed, institutional considerations appeared alongside the administrative law values of democracy and the rule of law in the following passage from the speech of Lord Phillips of Worth Matravers:[167]

> Where statute provides a structure under which a superior court or tribunal reviews decisions of an inferior court or tribunal, common law judicial review should be restricted so as to ensure, in the interest of making the best use of judicial resources, that this does not result in a duplication of judicial process that cannot be justified by the demands of the rule of law.

This approach was also said to safeguard both good administration, by resolving 'important point[s] of principle affecting large numbers of similar claims'; and the rule of law, by taking account of the 'compelling reasons presented by the extremity of the consequences for the individual'.[168] In summary, institutional considerations joined administrative law values in resolving the issue presented.

161 ibid [123] (Lord Dyson).

162 ibid [126] (Lord Dyson).

163 ibid [44] (Baroness Hale of Richmond). See also ibid [110] (Lord Dyson).

164 ibid [129] (Lord Dyson). See Tribunals, Courts and Enforcement Act 2007, s 13(6), which provides that permission shall not be granted unless: '(a) the proposed appeal would raise some important point of principle or practice; or (b) there is some other compelling reasons for the relevant appellate court to hear the appeal'.

165 See, eg, *Cart* (n 157) [41] (Baroness Hale of Richmond): 'There must be a limit to the resources which the legal system can devote to the task of trying to get the decision right in any individual case'. See also ibid [104] (Lord Clarke of Stone-cum-Ebony).

166 See, eg, ibid [100] (Lord Brown of Eaton-under-Heywood): 'The rule of law is weakened, not strengthened, if a disproportionate part of the courts' resources is devoted to finding a very occasional grain of wheat on a threshing floor full of chaff'.

167 ibid [89].

168 ibid [57] (Baroness Hale of Richmond).

V. CONCLUSION

It has become fashionable to say that administrative law has been 'reformed',[169] in particular by the taking of a more 'rights-based' approach inspired by the adoption across the Commonwealth of Bills of Rights.[170] A 'rights' revolution, however, cannot explain large swathes of administrative law doctrine.[171] Indeed, it takes little account of the expansion of judicial review in the twentieth century. It was precisely the limitation of the prerogative writs to *rights* that held judicial review back for so long.[172] It seems that judicial review of administrative action is a values-based enterprise. Its practice, and probably also its development, depends on the ongoing interaction between administrative law values—the rule of law, good administration, democracy and separation of powers—in the common law tradition.

[169] T Poole, 'The Reformation of English Administrative Law' (2009) 68 *CLJ* 142.

[170] See, eg, D Dyzenhaus, M Hunt and M Taggart, 'The Principle of Legality in Administrative Law: Internationalisation as Constitutionalisation' (2001) 1 *Oxford University Commonwealth Law Journal* 5.

[171] JNE Varuhas, 'The Reformation of English Administrative Law: "Rights", Rhetoric and Reality' (2013) 72 *CLJ* 369.

[172] *R v Electricity Commissioners, ex parte London Electricity Joint Committee Co* [1924] 1 KB 171; *R v Legislative Committee of the Church Assembly, ex parte Haynes-Smith* [1928] 1 KB 411.

4

The Public Interest Conception of Public Law: Its Procedural Origins and Substantive Implications

JASON NE VARUHAS*

I. INTRODUCTION

THE PROCEDURAL REFORMS of the late 1970s and early 1980s which established the judicial review procedure in English law might have had little effect. For some, such as Lord Wilberforce in the *Fleet Street Casuals* case, the procedural innovation was not a basis for altering the basic approach to adjudication of cases seeking the prerogative orders.[1] The reforms were procedural only and did not entail or necessitate any significant break from pre-existing substantive law, which notably eschewed any idea of a grand normative divide between public law and private law.[2] However, this approach, which would have maintained continuity, or at least maintained it in significant part, was destined to lose out. Other judges in this post-reform era, particularly Lord Diplock (described by Lord Scarman as the Castor to Wilberforce's Pollux),[3] Lord Donaldson and Lord Woolf saw the procedural innovation as an opportunity to eschew the Diceyan tradition that public law *is* private law by setting out to establish a discrete body of public law that was distinct from private law. Various developments over a critical 10 to 15-year period took this project forward, including the casting of the new procedural route as a 'public law' procedure; establishment and generalisation of public interest standing; entrenchment of a broad discretionary approach to procedural decisions, most

* I am grateful to John Allison, Mark Aronson, John Bell, Michael Dougan, Carol Harlow and Philip Murray for very helpful comments. I am also grateful to delegates at the 2014 Public Law Conference, where this paper was originally presented, for helpful comments and discussion. The usual disclaimers apply.

[1] *R v IRC, ex parte National Federation of Self-Employed and Small Businesses Ltd* [1982] AC 617.

[2] Some might claim that English law did at one time know a concept of public law, but even enthusiasts of a distinctive public law would accept that the last time that claim could have been made credibly was 250 years ago, and even that claim is disputed: M Loughlin, *Foundations of Public Law* (Oxford, Oxford University Press, 2010) 6; M Walters, 'Is Public Law Ordinary?' (2012) 75 *MLR* 894.

[3] Lord Scarman, 'Lord Diplock', *The Times*, 18 October 1985 ('For many years [Lord Diplock] and Lord Wilberforce were the Castor and Pollux of the legal firmament guiding the law through the troublesome seas of social and economic change which merged into the law through the channel of legislation').

significantly leave; formulation of general principles of public law geared towards ensuring public power was exercised for the public good and according to principles of good administration and which afforded administrators wide (at times extreme) scope to pursue what they considered to be in the public interest; articulation of a generalised discretion as to relief; and firm rejection of the availability of monetary relief. In this way a distinctive, integrated 'system' of public law emerged.

This chapter's core argument is that these developments and their substantive content were based in a particular conception of public law; that is, an idea of public law as concerned with the regulation of public power in the public interest and according to precepts of good administration. Private law was distinguished on the basis that its concern was enforcement of private, individual rights and protection of private interests. Identification of this public interest conception offers an important corrective to narratives of the development of modern English public law, specifically common law judicial review, which cast it as concerned principally with protection of (liberal, fundamental) individual rights, though challenging these narratives is not this chapter's main concern.[4]

One may speculate as to the importance of various contextual features which may have influenced the judges in adoption of the public interest conception. In particular, assertion of the importance of pursuit of the common good may be viewed as a judicial response to inculcation of public administration with free market values and the rise of public choice theory through the 1980s, while the assertion of a strict conceptual distinction between public and private arguably owes much to Lord Diplock's singular concern for conceptual and analytical purity; he also had experience of continental systems which maintained such divide and significant experience in government administration. What is clear, and does not require speculation, however, is that this idea of public law was secreted in the interstices of the procedural innovation; and so English legal history repeats itself.

The public interest conception of public law has been used and continues to be used as a normative idea to guide legal development in various contexts. Significantly, its influence is evident in facets of new and emergent bodies of public law doctrine. For example aspects of both the law under the Human Rights Act 1998 and review on EU grounds have been inculcated with a public interest ethos. However, this is problematic. The public interest conception of public law was forged by reference to only one branch of contemporary public law, the common law of judicial review; this body of law formed the basis of the vast bulk of applications made via the public law procedure in the period during which the public interest conception was articulated. But public law has moved on, and now comprises a range of different bodies of doctrine, while common law review has itself become more diverse, although the principal focus remains regulation of public power in the public interest. Where the public interest conception is used to guide development in fields other than common

[4] For example TRS Allan, *Law, Liberty and Justice: The Legal Foundations of British Constitutionalism* (Oxford, Clarendon, 1994); 'Dworkin and Dicey: The Rule of Law as Integrity' (1988) 8 *OJLS* 266. More generally see the work of the common law constitutionalist group of theorists, surveyed in T Poole, 'Back to the Future? Unearthing the Theory of Common Law Constitutionalism' (2003) 23 *OJLS* 435.

law review, the risk is that the distinctively valuable functions of these other fields are impeded, while the coherence of those bodies of doctrine may be distorted. I offer two examples of where this risk has become reality, both in the field of remedies: the approach to specific relief in review proceedings on EU grounds, and damages under the Human Rights Act 1998.

In order to avoid such negative consequences it is important that scholars, judges and practitioners look past the veneer of unity, fostered by a common procedure for public law claims, to the substance of contemporary public law which, like contemporary private law, is a diverse field of law composed of meaningfully distinct bodies of doctrine which each perform distinctively valuable functions, only one of which is regulating public power in the public interest. This involves eschewing reliance on any putative 'general' divide between public law and private law. For example, the idea that there is some sort of 'general functional separation between private law and public law'[5] is not only opaque, in that the nature of this divide is seldom articulated, but also fundamentally flawed. Different bodies of public law perform fundamentally distinct functions from other bodies of public law doctrine (some of which mirror the functions of bodies of law classified doctrinally as private law), just as the law of contract performs fundamentally distinct functions from the law of torts or the law of equity. If one is concerned with understanding and explaining the nature of contemporary English public law, then it is folly to speak of any general functional divide, and doing so is likely to lead to fuzzy thinking, incoherence and the warping of legal doctrine: such over-simplifications, while they may appear 'neat' or seem 'intuitive', should be repudiated.

II. PUBLIC INTEREST CONCEPTION

By amendments to the Rules of the Supreme Court in 1977 (taking effect in 1978) and again in the early 1980s, and enactment of the Supreme Court Act 1981, a new procedure to be known as the 'application for judicial review' was introduced into English law.[6] This change entailed provision for a *unified* procedure through which applications for the prerogative orders of certiorari, prohibition and mandamus *had* to be made; this was a break from the old as these orders were previously subject to procedures peculiar to each. A further novelty was that declarations and injunctions could be claimed via this procedure in tandem with the prerogative orders. Prior to the procedural innovation such remedies could not be claimed in tandem, injunctions and declarations being 'obtainable only in actions begun by writ or originating summons',[7] whereas applications for the prerogative orders were made according to

[5] D Nolan, 'Negligence and Human Rights Law: The Case for Separate Development' (2013) 76 *MLR* 286, 295.

[6] Rules of the Supreme Court (Amendment No 3) (SI 1977/1955), r 5; Rules of the Supreme Court (Amendment No 4) (SI 1980/2000), rr 2–7; Supreme Court Act 1981, ss 29–31. See now Civil Procedure Rules (SI 1998/3132), Pt 54; Senior Courts Act 1981, ss 29–31A.

[7] *O'Reilly v Mackman* [1983] 2 AC 237, 283.

different procedures, peculiar to the order claimed: 'a person seeking to challenge a decision had to make a choice of the remedy that he sought at the outset of the proceedings'.[8] According to the new unified procedure, an applicant would require leave of the court to apply, and would only be granted leave if they had 'sufficient interest in the matter to which the application relates'.[9] All applications had to be made promptly, and within a very short limitation period of three months (prior to reform the limitation period for certiorari, for example, was six months).[10] In cases of undue delay, the court could refuse leave or deny relief, if that delay 'would be likely to cause substantial hardship to, or substantially prejudice the rights of, any person or would be detrimental to good administration'.[11]

These changes were 'essentially procedural',[12] and did not, for example, 'create new remedies'[13] (although they did, to some degree, alter principles governing grant of particular types of relief)[14] nor did they, in themselves, alter or envision alteration of the substantive legal obligations of public authorities. As Lord Scarman said in the *Fleet Street Casuals* case, '[t]he new R.S.C., Ord. 53 is a procedural reform of great importance in the field of public law, but it does not—indeed, cannot—either extend or diminish the substantive law'.[15] The purpose of the reforms was, rather, to afford applicants procedural flexibility so that an applicant would not be denied relief solely because of procedural formalities.[16] In Lord Wilberforce's words, 'RSC Order 53 was, it is well known, introduced to simplify the procedure of applying for the relief formerly given by the prerogative writ or order—so the old technical rules no longer apply'.[17] Indeed, putting to the side the procedural changes themselves, the reforms could be said to have envisioned a high degree of continuity, reflected in core provisions such as section 29(1) of the 1981 Act: 'The High Court shall have jurisdiction to make orders of mandamus, prohibition and certiorari in those classes of cases in which it had power to do so immediately before the commencement of this Act'. As Lord Wilberforce put it, '[s]o far as the substantive law is concerned, it remained unchanged'.[18] Thus the reforms were not necessarily destined to lead to substantive legal change. But they did provide an *opportunity* for reform-minded judges to effect such change; for example, as we shall see, procedural unification had the potential to facilitate generalisation of rules and principles, for example governing standing, scope, leave, grounds and remedies, and moreover, generalisation according to a common set of normative concerns. Further, procedural features which distinguished review from ordinary procedure, such as the requirement for

[8] ibid.
[9] Rules of the Supreme Court (RSC) (SI 1965/1776), Order 53, r 3(7), as at 1 January 1978.
[10] ibid r 4(1).
[11] Supreme Court Act 1981, s 31(6), as enacted.
[12] *R v Panel on Take-Overs and Mergers, ex parte Datafin Plc* [1987] 1 QB 815, 821F.
[13] ibid.
[14] RSC, Order 53, r 1(2), as at 1 January 1978; Supreme Court Act 1981, s 31(2), as enacted.
[15] *IRC* (n 1) 647.
[16] ibid 647, and see 657.
[17] ibid 631.
[18] ibid 631.

leave, offered a foundation for conceptualising public law differently from private law more generally.

The opportunity was taken. As Freedland observes, there was a 'shared view that a developmental theory of public law as largely autonomous of private law could be constructed around the vigorous growth of judicial review',[19] while the judges themselves openly observed significant post-reform developments were in 'very substantial part' the product of 'judicial activism'.[20] By the mid-1980s a 'newly fledged' 'new-found' 'distinction between public and private law',[21] that was procedural (but not contemplated by the procedural reforms, and indeed undermined the policy the reforms were designed to give effect to, as we shall see) as well as substantive and normative, had become an entrenched, *iconic* feature of review jurisprudence. Courts came to recognise a 'system'[22] of public law, composed of generalised 'principles of public law'[23] and streamed via what had by this time been conceptualised as a 'public law procedure',[24] while the Master of the Rolls, Lord Donaldson, consistently referred to the High Court, in its reviewing capacity, as a 'new "public law court"'.[25] Of course, certain of these statements, such as Lord Donaldson's, may be criticised as inaccurate and hyperbolic. It was still the High Court, an ordinary court which also heard private law claims, which heard first-instance review applications, albeit via a distinctive procedure, while appeals were to the Court of Appeal and House of Lords—both general courts. Further, reliance on a general distinction between public law and private law was and remains open to all sorts of objections, including that it does not have an historical basis in English law; we are still to find any satisfactory conception of what it means for power to be 'public' absent any conception of the state; public law was—even at this time—surely not so narrow as to only be composed of the law streamed via review procedure; it ignores the longstanding, fundamental role of private law fields such as tort in disciplining exercise of governmental power and vindicating basic rights; while the distinction would often be invoked to determine legal questions without elaboration of the meaning of 'public law', leading to opaque, conclusory judicial reasoning. However, what the foregoing judicial statements offer is an insight into the judiciary's perception of change, and the 'project' they believed they were involved in. Further, it should be

[19] M Freedland, 'The Evolving Approach to the Public/Private Distinction in English Law' in M Freedland and JB Auby (eds), *The Public-Private Divide: Une Entente Assez Cordiale?* (Paris, Editions Panthéon-Assas, 2004) 111.

[20] H Woolf, 'The Role of the English Judiciary in Developing Public Law' (1986) 27 *William and Mary Law Review* 669, 669; *Council of Civil Service Unions (CCSU) v Minister for the Civil Service* [1985] AC 374, 414.

[21] *Gillick v West Norfolk and Wisbech Area Health Authority* [1986] AC 112, 178; *Datafin* (n 12) 845.

[22] eg *IRC* (n 1) 641, 644; *O'Reilly* (n 7) 279.

[23] eg *CCSU* (n 20) 407–8.

[24] eg *Cocks v Thanet District Council* [1983] 2 AC 286, 293; *O'Reilly* (n 7) 285 ('procedural public law').

[25] *R v Panel on Take-Overs and Mergers, ex parte Guinness Plc* [1990] 1 QB 146, 160; *R v Lancashire County Council, ex parte Huddleston* [1986] 2 All ER 941, 945; *R v Monopolies and Mergers Commission, ex parte Argyll* [1986] 1 WLR 763, 774; *R v Civil Service Appeal Board, ex parte Cunningham* [1992] ICR 816, 824.

reiterated that the aim of this section is the modest one of identifying the organising ideas underpinning change and the so-called system of public law.

Such developments, and judicial statements, were *radical* in a jurisdiction in which a fundamental principle of the rule of law, and defining feature of the legal system, was that public officers were subject to the same law as ordinary citizens, adjudicated in ordinary courts. It had only been in the mid-1960s that Mitchell had published his famous article analysing the reasons for the *absence* of a system of public law in England, and Lord Reid had observed that '[w]e do not have a developed system of administrative law'.[26] The marked deviation from traditional habits of thought was reflected in scepticism from leading judicial figures. For example, in the 1984 decision in *Davy*, Lord Wilberforce observed:[27]

> The expressions 'private law' and 'public law' have recently been imported into the law of England from countries which, unlike our own, have separate systems concerning public law and private law. No doubt they are convenient expressions for descriptive purposes. In this country they must be used with caution, for, typically, English law fastens, not upon principles but upon remedies. The principle remains intact that public authorities and public servants are, unless clearly exempted, answerable in the ordinary courts for wrongs done to individuals.

Parker LJ was another sceptic, saying of the expressions: 'There is in my view no particular merit in the terms and they are in any event imprecise'.[28] However, even sceptics, such as Lord Wilberforce, conceded: 'by an extension of remedies and a flexible procedure it can be said that something resembling a system of public law is being developed'.[29]

Symptomatic of the novelty of this assertion of a distinctive body of public law, scholarship on the idea of 'public law' blossomed. Some sought to make sense of the novel public law-private law distinction.[30] Others sought to understand the judicial conception of public law.[31] Others offered thorough-going critiques of the new-found distinction as one 'without definition', and considered these novelties through a critical, contextual lens, querying whether they were underpinned by bare, political concerns.[32] Others began to model public law (or administrative law), developing different models in the light of different political theories.[33] Later, powerful critiques focused on the problems of transplanting the idea of a separate system of public law from continental systems, given the absence within English law of an historical distinction between public law and private law, and contextual features which

[26] JDB Mitchell, 'The Causes and Effects of the Absence of a System of Public Law in the United Kingdom' [1965] *PL* 95; *Ridge v Baldwin* [1964] AC 40, 72.

[27] *Davy v Spelthorne Borough Council* [1984] AC 262, 276.

[28] *Bourgoin SA v Ministry of Agriculture, Fisheries and Food* [1986] QB 716, 788.

[29] *Davy* (n 27) 276.

[30] P Cane, 'Public Law and Private Law: A Study of the Analysis and Use of a Legal Concept' in J Eekalaar and J Bell (eds), *Oxford Essays in Jurisprudence*, 3rd series (Oxford, Clarendon, 1987).

[31] D Feldman, 'Public Law Values in the House of Lords' (1990) 106 *LQR* 246.

[32] C Harlow, '"Public" and "Private" Law: Definition Without Distinction' (1980) 43 *MLR* 241.

[33] M Loughlin, *Public Law and Political Theory* (Oxford, Oxford University Press, 1992); C Harlow and R Rawlings, *Law and Administration* (London, Weidenfeld and Nicolson, 1984).

characterised those continental jurisdictions and were conducive to the operation of separate systems of law.[34]

It is true that certain developments in this post-reform era built upon and even flowed naturally from pre-reform jurisprudence,[35] while there were some concerted attempts by reformist judges to explain novelties as the natural end-point of pre-reform developments (some attempts more plausible than others).[36] But, critically, it was only in this post-reform era that one could say plausibly, as the judges did, that an integrated *system* of 'public law' had been established, in the sense that a field of law emerged that was characterised by core features, procedural and substantive, which evinced a high degree of coherence, and were grounded in a unifying, normative idea of 'public law'. Of course, some, such as Lord Denning, had declared the existence of a 'developed system of administrative law' earlier.[37] But as Lord Woolf observed, Lord Denning's statement, made in 1971, was 'somewhat premature'—not least because judicial review was still spread across disparate types of application, each with its own peculiarities,[38] and further, because the theoretical foundations required for identification of a distinctive system had not been forged. However, as Lord Woolf observed, 'certainly by the beginning of the 1980s [it] could be said with confidence' that such a system had emerged.[39] In coming to this conclusion Lord Woolf rightly placed emphasis on the new system being grounded in a distinctive, organising idea of 'public law' as distinct from 'private law'.[40]

So, what was this idea of 'public law'? Despite the idea of 'public law' being invoked repeatedly in this era, routinely conditioning legal development in significant cases, it was not often elaborated upon. However, if one examines key developments during the post-reform period, as well as patterns in judicial dicta, the idea is readily discernible.

First, public law was not private law. Thus, for example, 'at the heart of the issues' in *Gouriet* lay 'the difference between private law and public law', and where one moves from private law to public law 'analogies may be deceptive and ... different principles apply';[41] *Maharaj* was 'concerned with public law, not private law',

[34] JWF Allison, *A Continental Distinction in the Common Law: A Historical and Comparative Perspective on English Public Law* (Oxford, Oxford University Press, 1996).

[35] I have in mind here important cases in the 1960s which expanded and took forward substantive law, including *Ridge* (n 26), *Anisminic Ltd v Foreign Compensation Commission* [1969] 2 AC 147, and *Padfield v Minister of Agriculture, Fisheries and Food* [1968] AC 997, as well as significant cases governing, for example, scope of application of the prerogative orders, such as *R v Criminal Injuries Compensation Board, ex parte Lain* [1967] 2 QB 864, which was relied on heavily in significant post-reform cases such as *CCSU* and *Datafin*.

[36] For example in *IRC* (n 1) Lord Diplock viewed his approach to standing as the natural end-point of what he saw as a process of gradual liberalisation and unification of standing criteria across the prerogative orders in the pre-reform era.

[37] *Breen v Amalgamated Engineering Union* [1971] 2 QB 175, 189.

[38] Lord Diplock, too, in 1974 had emphasised that *until the envisioned procedural reforms were enacted* 'we cannot claim to have a fully developed system of administrative law appropriate to the needs of our society in the last quarter of the twentieth century' ('Administrative Law: Judicial Review Reviewed' [1974] *CLJ* 233, 245).

[39] Woolf, 'The Role of the English Judiciary in Developing Public Law' (n 20) 669.

[40] ibid.

[41] *Gouriet v Union of Post Office Workers* [1978] AC 435, 496, 500.

liability not being 'in tort at all; it is a liability in the public law of the state';[42] *Hoffmann La Roche* did not concern 'an action to enforce a jus privatum' but rather one 'to enforce or to protect jus publicum', while certain 'concepts developed in the private law of contract [were] ill-adapted to the field of public law';[43] and *O'Reilly* established that 'an infringement of … rights in private law' would not be 'a proper subject for judicial review' which was reserved for 'rights that are entitled to protection in public law'.[44]

Secondly, whereas private law was conceptualised as individual-regarding, public law was public-regarding. Private law was concerned principally with enforcement of the *personal rights of individuals*, while public law was concerned with ensuring public power was exercised properly—that is, in accordance with precepts of *good administration*—for the good of the *public as a whole*, the principal concern and focus being with the qualities of the exercise of power itself. Within this public law paradigm private interests were seen as a potential corrupting force which could capture exercise of public power, so that it was not exercised for the benefit of all, as intended, but rather for the benefit of a select few.

A paradigmatic example of this conception of public power is Lord Diplock's explanation of the functions of the Law Society:[45]

> The purpose for which … statutory functions are vested in the [Law] Society and [its] Council is the protection of the public or, more specifically, that section of the public that may be in need of legal advice, assistance or representation. In exercising its statutory functions the duty of the Council is to act in what it believes to be the best interests of that section of the public, even in the event … that those public interests should conflict with the special interests of members of the Society or of members of the solicitors' profession as a whole.

Similarly in the *Fleet Street Casuals* case, Lord Scarman explained that the Inland Revenue Commissioners' statutory duties and discretionary powers were imposed and conferred not for the personal interests of specific individual taxpayers, but 'in the interest of good management', and that the Commissioners' duty of fairness in performance of their duties and exercise of their powers was 'a legal duty owed by the revenue to the general body of taxpayers' *as a collectivity*.[46] Breach of that duty would not be a private wrong (breach of an individual private right) but rather a 'public wrong'.[47] Indeed, pandering to personal interests would entail breach of a duty of public character: there must be 'no favourites'.[48]

In an article written in 1986 Lord Woolf clearly delineated public law and private law along these lines: he defined public law as 'the system which enforces the proper performance by public bodies of the duties which they owe to the public', whereas

[42] *Maharaj v Attorney-General of Trinidad and Tobago (No 2)* [1979] AC 385, 396, 399–400.

[43] *F Hoffmann La Roche & Co AG v Secretary of State for Trade and Industry* [1975] AC 295, 363, 366.

[44] *O'Reilly* (n 7) 284.

[45] *Swain v Law Society* [1983] 1 AC 598, 608.

[46] *IRC* (n 1) 651–53.

[47] ibid 651, 648.

[48] ibid 651.

private law is 'the system which protects the private rights of private individuals or the private rights of public bodies': 'The critical distinction arises out of the fact that it is the public as a whole, or in the case of local government the public in the locality, who are the beneficiaries of what is protected by public law and it is the individuals or bodies entitled to the rights who are the beneficiaries of the protection provided by private law'.[49] On this view, when the court intervenes in public law, it does so 'on behalf of the public'[50] or 'in defence of the citizenry'.[51]

Lord Donaldson, taking this view to the extreme, considered that courts and the administration should work together in a 'partnership' 'in the public interest':[52]

> the wider remedy of judicial review and the evolution of what is, in effect, a specialist administrative or public law court is a post-war development. This development has created a new relationship between the courts and those who derive their authority from the public law, one of partnership based on a common aim, namely the maintenance of the highest standards of public administration ... The courts, for their part, must and do respect the fact that it is not for them to intervene in the administrative field, unless there is a reason to inquire whether a particular authority has been successful in its endeavours.

Thirdly, within this conception of public law it was principally for the administrative decision-maker to determine what lay in the public interest, and the judicial role was necessarily a very limited one, geared towards guarding against clear abuses which marked patent deviation from the public goals for which power had been conferred or basic expectations of good administration. Whereas judges 'are equipped to find legal rights and administer, on well-known principles, discretionary remedies', 'decisions to be made as to the public interest are not such as courts are fitted or equipped to make'.[53] Importantly, protection of the public interest and maintaining standards of good administration were the basis of the review jurisdiction, but also the rationale for a restrained approach. Courts were weary of undermining, through overzealous judicial intervention, pursuit of the common good (as determined by the administration) and the administration's ability to perform its duties effectively, efficiently and vigorously.

Fourthly, a defining feature of a system of public law based in a public interest conception is 'a large discretionary content, which contributes to its value'.[54] The idea that 'the remedy of judicial review ... is a discretionary remedy' was repeated as dogma through the 1980s.[55] Broad judicial discretions, at different stages of the review process, particularly at the leave and remedial stages, but even, in some cases, in determining lawfulness, ensured review could be carefully regulated on a case-by-case basis. This ensured review did not operate to undermine (administrative pursuit of) the public interest, and the demands of good administration—the twin purposes it was, according to the prevailing conception of public law, constituted to promote.

[49] H Woolf, 'Public Law–Private Law: Why the Divide? A Personal View' [1986] *PL* 220, 221.
[50] *Guinness* (n 25) 193G.
[51] *Datafin* (n 12) 839.
[52] ibid 842; *Huddleston* (n 25) 945, and see also 947; *Cunningham* (n 25) 822–23.
[53] *Gouriet* (n 41) 482.
[54] *Guinness* (n 25) 177.
[55] *R v Hillingdon London Borough Council, ex parte Puhlhofer* [1986] AC 484, 518.

A. System Features

This section sketches some of the core features of the system of public law that emerged during the relevant era. The principal reason for undertaking this task is to make out the claim that these features are grounded in a public interest conception of public law, and in so doing to further elaborate that conception. In demonstrating that these features are so grounded, the claim that they can plausibly be said to comprise a 'system' is also established.

(i) A 'Public Law' Procedure

The Law Commission Report underpinning the procedural reforms rejected procedural exclusivity:[56]

> We are not in this report recommending ... that the new procedure ... should be exclusive in the sense that it would become the only way by which public law issues relating to the legality of the acts or omissions of persons or bodies could be decided; where such issues arise in ordinary actions or criminal proceedings they would not have to be referred to the Divisional Court but would continue to be dealt with as at present by the Court seized of the case.

In other words, as was the case prior to reform, the intention was that litigants would continue to have a choice whether to bring a claim alleging administrative unlawfulness via an application for review, or to proceed by action, for example by an action for a declaration of nullity or injunction, streamed via ordinary procedures. On the face of the new rules review was only *mandated* where an applicant sought one of the *prerogative orders*. Given this, it is not surprising that, as Lord Diplock observed in *O'Reilly*, 'Order 53 does not expressly provide that procedure by application for judicial review shall be the exclusive procedure available by which the remedy of declaration or injunction may be obtained for infringement of rights that are entitled to protection under public law'.[57]

It would therefore be rather surprising to someone unfamiliar with English public law to discover that Lord Diplock, in *O'Reilly*, his fellow Law Lords concurring, recognised a principle of exclusivity:[58]

> [I]t would in my view as a general rule be contrary to public policy, and as such an abuse of the process of the court, to permit a person seeking to establish that a decision of a public authority infringed rights to which he was entitled to protect under public law to proceed by way of an ordinary action and by this means to evade the provisions of Order 53 for the protection of such authorities.

As David Williams observed, this principle of exclusivity was 'entirely judge-made'.[59]

[56] *Report on Remedies in Administrative Law*, Law Com No 73 (1976) [34], [58].
[57] *O'Reilly* (n 7) 284.
[58] ibid 285.
[59] DGT Williams, 'Administrative Law in England: The Emergence of a New Remedy' (1986) 27 *William and Mary Law Review* 715, 716.

As is well known, the principle was not a success. Courts struggled to determine whether a dispute lay in the field of 'private law', so that it should proceed by ordinary procedure, or 'public law', so that it ought to proceed via review, given the historical absence of any such division in English law and the absence of any idea of the state. There may have been a background idea that public law is the area of law concerned with regulating public power in the public interest, against which legal development occurred, but the bounds and scope of that idea were amorphous. The result was sterile procedural litigation, fine line-drawing and, as judges observed, introduction of a new formalism into the law.[60] In this the principle, as Lord Wilberforce observed in *Davy*, undermined the very reason for reform: removal of procedural technicalities that operated to deprive worthy litigants of redress.[61] In turn, the courts gradually rowed back until procedural flexibility and common sense came to triumph over conceptual purity.[62]

Notwithstanding the sorry tale of the exclusivity principle, its recognition is of interest because it is illustrative of the judicial pursuit of a separate system of public law based in a public interest ethos.

In *O'Reilly* Lord Diplock stated the principle's rationale: litigants 'in the field of public law' should not be able to evade the 'safeguards [provided for by the review procedure and] imposed in the public interest against groundless, unmeritorious or tardy attacks upon the validity of decisions made by public authorities' by, for example, proceeding by an action for a declaration of nullity or injunction.[63] These safeguards included the leave requirement, a short limitation period, and a prescription that an application for leave must be accompanied by full, candid affidavits verifying the facts relied on by the applicant, not to mention a panoply of judicial discretions. On the other hand, the limitation periods for actions were longer, and discovery and interlocutory proceedings could be prolonged, so that proceedings would be lengthy even if allegations turned out to be baseless.[64] This would keep the defendant authority and others reliant on the challenged decision in suspense as to its validity—undermining the 'public interest in good administration'.[65] Thus, whereas '[w]hen individual rights are claimed'—in the realm of 'private law'—'there should not be a need for leave or a special time limit, nor should the relief be discretionary',[66] in public law the central concern is with preservation of the public interest, and individual interests, such as the applicant's interests in choice of procedure and access

[60] *Datafin* (n 12) 845.

[61] *Davy* (n 27) 276. Wade similarly observed that *O'Reilly* and its principle of exclusivity were 'a singularly unfortunate step back to the technicalities of a bygone age' ('Procedure and Prerogative in Public Law' (1985) 101 *LQR* 180, 187–88).

[62] *O'Reilly* was arguably the paradigm manifestation of what Lord Scarman described as 'perhaps' Lord Diplock's one 'weakness': 'excessive adherence to remorseless logic which he delighted to display, though he was neither philosopher nor logician by education', with others observing that 'his analytical genius occasionally went beyond ordinary practicalities' (n 3; 'The Late Lord Diplock' (1986) 7 *Singapore Law Review* 34, 35).

[63] *O'Reilly* (n 7) 282.

[64] ibid 284.

[65] ibid 280.

[66] *Roy v Kensington and Chelsea and Westminster Family Practitioner Committee* [1992] 1 AC 624, 654.

to court,[67] are subordinated to that concern. Further, although Lord Diplock[68] was at pains to stress that public law litigants would not be disadvantaged because the review procedure, following procedural reform, provided for discovery and cross-examination, the reality was—and proved to be (see below)—that discovery and cross-examination were hardly ever granted on review.[69] Indeed, while in one breath Lord Diplock emphasised that cross-examination was now available on review, in another he said it would be rare.[70] So, again, individual interests in procedural advantage were sacrificed for the sake of public interests in good administration.

Thus, the exclusivity principle was designed to effect a procedural cleaving of public law claims from private law claims, in the public interest. But it was also arguably designed to achieve a strict remedial separation between public and private law; remedies such as declarations and injunctions were 'private law' remedies and had no place in a system of 'public law', which was to be characterised by its own distinctive 'public law' remedies: the prerogative orders. Of course, while the principle could prevent a litigant from proceeding via an action for declaration or injunction, the procedural reforms had explicitly made these remedies available *within* review procedure. This threat to the conceptual purity of the new domain of 'public law' was met with attempts, in *O'Reilly* and its sister decision, *Cocks*, and later jurisprudence, to subordinate these remedies to the prerogative orders. (Of course, the elephant in the room in *O'Reilly* and *Cocks* was that damages, a paradigm 'private law' remedy, could also be claimed via review in tandem with prerogative orders.)

First, as we shall see below, the courts asserted an ultimate discretion to determine which remedy was appropriate on the facts.[71]

Secondly, the courts prioritised the prerogative orders. For example, in *O'Reilly* Lord Diplock emphasised that although the litigants had sought declarations, 'certiorari would unquestionably have been the more appropriate remedy' even though a declaration 'would achieve, though less directly, the same result'.[72] In *Cocks*, Lord Bridge was more prescriptive, observing that while nullification can be achieved 'if necessary' by declaration, 'certiorari to quash remains the primary and most appropriate remedy', observing that, following procedural unification, where an applicant sought to quash a decision there was no valid reason why it should not be via certiorari.[73]

Thirdly, in later cases we find the courts 'hitching' availability of declarations or injunctions to the availability of the prerogative orders. For example, Lord Scarman said in the *Fleet Street Casuals* case: 'For the two remedies (borrowed from the

[67] In contrast, Peter Pain J, the first instance judge, adopted a more orthodox approach to the question of procedural choice: it would be an 'abuse of language' to say that a litigant is abusing the process of the court 'because he exercises the choice in the way he thinks best in his own interest' (*O'Reilly* (n 7) 250).

[68] ibid 282.

[69] As observed by Woolf, 'Public Law–Private Law: Why the Divide?' (n 49) 229 in 1986: 'Although on an application for judicial review the court has power to order discovery and to hear oral evidence and to allow cross-examination, this does not normally take place unless the court otherwise orders. Discovery and cross-examination are of course normal in an ordinary action'.

[70] *O'Reilly* (n 7) 282.

[71] ibid 283H.

[72] ibid 274.

[73] *Cocks* (n 24) 295.

private law) are put in harness with the prerogative remedies. They may be granted only in circumstances in which one or other of the prerogative orders can issue'.[74] The text of Order 53 offered a basis for this approach, in that it made the circumstances in which prerogative orders could be issued a matter for the court to take into account in deciding whether to grant an injunction or declaration on review. However, it was only one factor in a list of non-exhaustive factors; it was the judges that reconceptualised these 'private law' remedies as 'public law' remedies.

It should be noted that although, as in *Cocks* and *O'Reilly*, there was some judicial animosity towards declaratory or injunctive relief within review, this wore off over time—at least in respect of declarations. The declaration became the judges' 'flexible friend'.[75] In particular, it could be used to declare unlawfulness, and therefore give effect to the public interest in government according to law, while leaving the impugned administrative action intact, thus ensuring the public interest in smooth administration was not compromised.[76]

More generally, the procedural cleaving of private law and public law claims, while not entirely successful, would give public law a distinct space, separate from private law, which allowed principles of public law to develop along their own trajectory in relative isolation from private law, and an idea of public law substantively distinct from private law to gain traction.

(ii) Standing

The *Fleet Street Casuals* case is the landmark case on standing of the post-reform era. It is significant for many reasons. For present purposes it is pertinent because underlying the divisions among the Law Lords were competing conceptions of public law.

Lords Wilberforce and Fraser favoured an approach to standing that maintained a degree of continuity with the past, eschewed discretion and, with Lord Roskill, would have maintained a model of standing closer to what might be described as a 'private law' model.

Lord Wilberforce maintained that the 'question of locus standi' should not be removed 'into the realm of pure discretion' but should be determined according to 'legal principles'.[77] While the procedural reforms had introduced a general standing criterion of 'sufficient interest' in place of the different tests that formerly attached to each of the prerogative orders,[78] Lord Wilberforce felt that 'the rule does not mean that the test is the same in all cases': 'reasoned authorities' should not be 'discard[ed]', while different rules could apply 'reflecting the different character of

[74] *IRC* (n 1) 648.

[75] C Harlow and R Rawlings, *Law and Administration*, 3rd edn (Cambridge, Cambridge University Press, 2009) 670.

[76] eg *Argyll* (n 25); *Datafin* (n 12) 840.

[77] *IRC* (n 1) 631, 646 (Lord Fraser); cf 658 (Lord Roskill).

[78] Although a degree of convergence was emerging: Law Commission, *Report on Remedies in Administrative Law* (n 56) [13].

the relief asked for'.[79] Thus, for example, as was traditionally the case, a 'stricter' rule could be applied to applications for mandamus compared to those for certiorari.[80]

The model of standing endorsed by the majority is close in nature to that which pertains in fields such as contract or tort: standing to sue is dependent on a personal right or interest. Thus, Lord Wilberforce would have denied standing in the *Fleet Street Casuals* case because the parent legislation did not provide for an express or implied 'right' for a third party to challenge the tax arrangements agreed between another taxpayer and the Revenue, while the applicant could not be said to have a 'direct' 'interest'.[81] The tax affairs of individual taxpayers were only the proper concern of those taxpayers and the Revenue: the relationship between individual taxpayer and Revenue was conceptualised as bipolar, marked by confidentiality and a degree of 'privity', with duties owed by the Revenue owed directly to that taxpayer,[82] ie the duties were personal and individualistic in nature. Given this conceptualisation of the relationship, third parties did not have a legitimate interest in the tax arrangements of other taxpayers, other than in exceptional cases.[83]

There is no evidence in the majority speeches of an idea of public law as distinct from private law. As in other fields of English law, such as tort, remedy is intertwined with right, and no one else other than the right-holder may bring a claim, while the Diceyan distaste for discretion is manifest. It is no surprise that Lord Wilberforce led this approach, given the scepticism he later expressed towards a novel conception of public law as distinct from private law, and his view, drawn from legal history, that English law fastens on remedies rather than categories of relationship such as state-person, person-thing or person-person.

Lords Diplock and Scarman took a rather different approach. In supporting a more 'liberal' approach they were in the minority. But it was their approach which would ultimately win out, and public interest standing rules would come to form a crucial component of the system of public law, grounded in a concern for the public interest.[84]

Each distinguished the approach that ought to prevail in 'public law' with that which they associated with 'private law'. In private law a plaintiff would need to show a 'legal right of his own was threatened or infringed'.[85] If such approach were taken to applications for remedies such as mandamus, the remedy 'would lose its public law character, being no more than a remedy for a private wrong'.[86] Private law is concerned with personal rights, public law is not, and the approach to standing ought logically to differ.

In stark contrast to Lord Wilberforce, both Lords Diplock and Scarman strongly emphasised that standing was a matter of discretion: the court had '*unfettered*

[79] *IRC* (n 1) 631, 646 (Lord Fraser); cf 656 (Lord Roskill).
[80] ibid 631.
[81] ibid 633, 646 (Lord Fraser).
[82] ibid 632 ('failed in its statutory duty *toward him*' (emphasis added)).
[83] ibid 633, 646–47 (Lord Fraser), 662–63 (Lord Roskill).
[84] See, eg, *Gillick* (n 21); *R v Secretary of State for Foreign and Commonwealth Affairs, ex parte World Development Movement Ltd* [1995] 1 WLR 386; *Walton v Scottish Ministers* [2012] UKSC 44.
[85] *IRC* (n 1) 639 (Lord Diplock), 649 (Lord Scarman).
[86] ibid 653 (Lord Scarman).

discretion to decide what in its own good judgment it considers to be "a sufficient interest" on the part of an applicant in the particular circumstances of the case'.[87] In this way the court could maintain maximal flexibility, using review as a precision instrument to intervene when required in the public interest.

Again in stark contrast to the majority, Lord Diplock stressed that pressure groups or publicly spirited individuals ought to be accorded standing where they could demonstrate a prima facie case of administrative unlawfulness.[88] *Any* taxpayer could bring a claim against the Revenue if they had an arguable case of administrative unlawfulness.[89] Whereas the majority opposed such a proposition on the basis that a third party should not be allowed to interfere in the 'private' relationship between taxpayer and Revenue, the principal concern for Lord Diplock was that the Revenue should not be permitted to exercise its powers for reasons extraneous to those for which they were conferred, thereby depriving the national exchequer; how the Revenue exercised its powers was a matter of public concern, that transcended the private concerns of individual taxpayers.[90] Similarly, it followed logically from Lord Scarman's characterisation of the Revenue's duty to act fairly as a *public* duty, owed to taxpayers *as a whole*, that standing should be afforded to an applicant who demonstrates a prima facie case of 'public wrong', regardless of whether they have a personal or direct interest in the matter under challenge.[91] For Lord Scarman the question was not so much one of who should be allowed standing but rather who should be prevented from accessing the court; he drew that category narrowly: 'busybodies, cranks, and other mischief makers'.[92]

In contrast to Lord Wilberforce, Lord Diplock considered the purpose of the procedural reforms to be to 'sweep away … procedural differences [among the orders] including, in particular, differences as to locus standi', and emphasised that older case law could not be relied upon as a safe guide as to the law.[93] For Lord Diplock, the father of the public law-private law divide, a unitary approach was arguably significant because it signalled a unified, integrated system of public law, as opposed to a field characterised by a mishmash of disparate types of claim. That he saw standing as fundamental to construction of a system of public law was explicit in his speech. To maintain divergent approaches to standing, and also to allow administrative unlawfulness to go unchecked because no individual right was affected by it, would be 'to reverse progress towards a comprehensive *system* of administrative law';[94] to prevent pressure groups and publicly-spirited individuals from bringing applications would leave a 'grave lacuna in our *system* of public law'.[95]

It is worth recording that the Law Commission Report, on which the procedural reforms were based, did not signal any intention that standing should be unified

[87] ibid 642 (Lord Diplock) (emphasis added); see also 653 (Lord Scarman).
[88] ibid 644.
[89] ibid 643.
[90] ibid 643–44.
[91] ibid 647–55.
[92] ibid 653.
[93] ibid 638, 640.
[94] ibid 641 (emphasis added).
[95] ibid 644 (emphasis added).

across different remedies, as Lord Diplock claimed. While the new procedural rules provided for a single test of 'sufficient interest' this followed from a desire not to be overly prescriptive and thereby constrain legal development.[96] Indeed, there seems to be an assumption that standing rules would continue to vary according to remedy: a 'formula' was needed 'which allows for further development of the requirement of standing by the courts *having regard to the relief which is sought*'.[97] Against this background it seems clear that the move to unification was the product of 'modern judicial policy',[98] albeit that the procedural changes offered the *opportunity* for implementation of such policy.

(iii) Other Procedural Aspects

Unlike ordinary proceedings, commenced by writ or summons, an applicant for judicial review required the leave of the court to proceed to full hearing. This was a feature of the prerogative remedies before procedural reform, as were many of the features discussed herein. However, it is worth observing how leave and the other procedural idiosyncrasies of review were characterised by the courts following procedural reform; in general these features supported a distinctive conception of public law as concerned with protection of the public interest and facilitation of good administration, and the courts strongly emphasised and asserted their discretionary control over review procedure.

The Law Commission, in the Report which underpinned procedural reform, considered the leave requirement should be retained as it provided an expeditious method for sifting out cases with no chance of success at little expense to both parties.[99] There was 'social value' in an applicant 'expeditiously and at small cost to himself [hearing] in public from the court that he has no legal case and the reasons for its refusal to give leave'.[100]

However, the courts, consonant with a public interest conception, rationalised leave quite differently. Leave was another discretionary precision instrument, which could be utilised to ensure protection of public interests in preservation of court resources and administrative certainty, and more generally to ensure that the administration was not unduly disrupted in its pursuit of the public good. For Lord Diplock, the purpose of leave was:

> to prevent the time of the court being wasted by busybodies with misguided or trivial complaints of administrative error, and to remove the uncertainty in which public officers and authorities might be left as to whether they could safely proceed with administrative action while proceedings for judicial review of it were actually pending even though misconceived.[101]

[96] Law Commission, *Report on Remedies in Administrative Law* (n 56) [48].
[97] ibid [48] (emphasis added).
[98] In the words of Lord Roskill: *IRC* (n 1) 658.
[99] Law Commission, *Report on Remedies in Administrative Law* (n 56) [37]–[38].
[100] ibid [38].
[101] *IRC* (n 1) 643 and see 630.

For the Master of the Rolls, 'limiting the number of cases in which leave to apply should be given' protected the 'public interest' in review proceedings proceeding 'very speedily'.[102]

Another core feature of the jurisprudence was strong emphasis upon review as a remedy of 'last resort', only to be available where alternative routes to redress, particularly statutory appeals, were unavailable, even if review would afford a more effectual, convenient or speedy remedy for the applicant.[103] This was 'a proposition of the utmost importance',[104] and it was repeated as mantra during the 1980s. Here too the public interest conception is lurking. In *Guinness*, Lloyd LJ said the rationale for the proposition 'is convenience, by which I mean not just the convenience of the court, but the public interest in abating litigation';[105] thus individuals may suffer detriment, say, because a statutory remedy will be less effectual, but this is required in the interests of the public. But, as was characteristic of review generally, the court could, 'in the exercise of its discretion', forgive failure to have recourse to alternative remedies and intervene if, for example, it identified clear administrative unlawfulness.[106] In other words, through exercise of its broad discretion the court could determine what best served the public interest: intervention to ensure proper exercise of power or preservation of court resources.

Administrative action is presumed valid—indeed, the courts were '*very willing* to assume that the authority has acted in accordance with law'—and it is for the applicant to rebut this and convince the court of 'his entitlement to relief'.[107] This presumption serves public interests in administrative certainty and citizen compliance with administrative actions. Further, it allows the administration to pursue public goals safe in the knowledge that the court's 'default setting' is non-intervention.

As we saw above, the procedural reforms included express provision for discovery and cross-examination on review, so that applicants for review were not disadvantaged relative to ordinary procedures; the Law Commission felt there should be express provision for discovery, etc, specifically because discovery and cross-examination were virtually unknown in applications for prerogative orders prior to reform. However, grant of each is subject to a 'wide discretion',[108] and in *O'Reilly* Lord Diplock indicated it would 'only be upon rare occasions that the interests of justice will require that leave be given for cross-examination of deponents on their affidavits'.[109] This contrasts with the practice in actions initiated by originating summons, where the same test—interests of justice—was applied but discretion was generally exercised in favour of discovery and cross-examination.

[102] *Guinness* (n 25) 177.

[103] *R v Chief Constable of Merseyside, ex parte Calveley* [1986] QB 424. Contrast the pre-reform approach in *R v Hillingdon London Borough Council, ex parte Royco Homes Ltd* [1974] QB 720, 729.

[104] *R v IRC, ex parte Preston* [1985] AC 835, 852, and see 862 (Lord Templeman); *R v Epping and Harlow General Commissioners, ex parte Goldstraw* [1983] 3 All ER 257, 262; *Guinness* (n 25) 178, 183, 184.

[105] *Guinness* (n 25) 184.

[106] *Calveley* (n 103) 433, 435.

[107] eg *Hoffmann* (n 43) 366; *Huddleston* (n 25) 945 (emphasis added); *R v Boundary Commission for England, ex parte Foot* [1983] QB 600, 634, 637.

[108] *IRC* (n 1) 638.

[109] *O'Reilly* (n 7) 282.

Why should cross-examination be rare? Lord Diplock explained that fact-finding is the preserve of the administration and not open to review; cross-examination may tempt judges to illegitimately substitute their own factual findings.[110] But also identifiable in Lord Diplock's speech is another reason: cross-examination would draw out proceedings, which in turn would, contrary to the interests of good administration, undermine speediness and administrative certainty, and also increase costs to the defendant and the court.[111] Discovery would have a similar effect. Lord Diplock described it as 'time-consuming',[112] while Lord Denning, in the Court of Appeal decision in *O'Reilly*, observed it will be 'rarely allowed' and 'kept within strict bounds' given it was liable to 'roam unchecked'.[113] In very rarely ordering cross-examination or discovery (despite the Law Commission's intention that both should be more freely available) the courts showed great faith in the candour of affidavits filed by the administration and formal statements of reasons, reflecting Lord Donaldson's idea of partnership and a high degree of trust between judiciary and administration.[114]

There is not space here to examine in depth the scope of judicial review during this era. As is well known, courts have struggled and largely failed to find a workable test for determining when 'public law principles' apply. However, what has largely been missed in commentary on this jurisprudence is the importance placed by the judiciary on the idea of public interest. For example, the Master of the Rolls' important judgment in *Datafin*, holding a body with no direct statutory or prerogative foundation but with responsibility for regulation of market activity subject to review, starts from the proposition that the body is 'intended to, and does, operate in the public interest'.[115] This was a 'field of our national life'[116] and courts should be able to intervene 'in defence of the citizenry'.[117]

(iv) Substantive Law

It is not possible here to offer a detailed account of substantive law as it developed in the relevant era. Instead I highlight several defining features of substantive law, which are illustrative of the move to establish a distinctive field of public law grounded in the public interest conception.

First, procedural unification provided the opportunity for unification of the substantive law governing grant of the prerogative orders around a corpus of generalised 'public law principles'. Importantly, substantive law would no longer be tied to the particular remedy sought. This would further mark public law out from private law fields such as tort or contract, in which remedy was and continues to be intimately

110 ibid.
111 ibid 284.
112 ibid 282.
113 ibid 257; *Huddleston* (n 25) 947.
114 *Huddleston* ibid.
115 *Datafin* (n 12) 827; *R v Jockey Club, ex parte RAM Racecourses Ltd* [1993] 2 All ER 853, 247E, 248E.
116 ibid 846.
117 ibid 839.

connected to right. Although there were a number of statements of these general principles,[118] the most famous is found in Lord Diplock's speech in *CCSU*:[119]

> Judicial review has I think developed to a stage today when without reiterating any analysis of the steps by which the development has come about,[120] one can conveniently classify under three heads the grounds upon which administrative action is subject to control by judicial review. The first ground I would call 'illegality', the second 'irrationality' and the third 'procedural propriety'.

As a sidenote, the reason for rebranding *Wednesbury* unreasonableness as 'irrationality' was that '"Reasonable" ... bears different meanings according to whether the context in which it is being used is that of private law or public law. To eliminate confusion'—and maintain the conceptual purity of the division between private law and public law and avoid judges being drawn into applying a reasonableness simpliciter standard—'it is best avoided in the latter'.[121]

Secondly, the starting point in public law cases was non-intervention. Judicial review was a supervisory 'long stop'[122] jurisdiction and something weighty was required to warrant judicial intervention. The reasons for this, reiterated through the 1980s, were reflective of the underlying conception of public law. What lies in the common good is for administrators, while courts ought not to impede administrative pursuit of the common good without good reason. Further, professional administrators know far more about administration than judges: courts repeatedly emphasised their trust in administrators to get matters right given their expertise and the need for understanding of the complexities and difficulties faced by authorities, this in turn counselling restraint:

> The judges who man the public law court are, or very soon will become, specialists *with a very real appreciation of the realities of public administration.* They know that the decision-making process can be *complex*. They know that it may often depend on the *expertise* of the decision-makers.[123]

Extreme examples of non-interventionism are found in the homelessness context, given the demands faced by public authorities, and in the context of financial regulation, given the apparently peculiar need for regulatory entities to act decisively and speedily in this context.[124] Thus, in *Puhlhofer*, concerning review of decisions under homelessness legislation, Lord Brightman, whose speech was brimming with sympathy for the challenges facing the defendant, held that review should be limited to the 'exceptional case'.[125] Where the decision was one as to the existence of a fact the court should not intervene 'save ... where it is *obvious* that the public

[118] eg *Preston* (n 104) 862; *Puhlhofer* (n 55) 518.
[119] *CCSU* (n 20) 410–11.
[120] For such reiteration see *O'Reilly* (n 7) 277 ff.
[121] *CCSU* (n 20) 409.
[122] *Guinness* (n 25) 177.
[123] *Huddleston* (n 25) 945 (emphasis added).
[124] Another classic example is in the field of macroeconomic decision-making (eg *R v Secretary of State for the Environment, ex parte Nottinghamshire County Council* [1986] AC 240), although extreme restraint seems more justifiable in this context than in those discussed in the text.
[125] *Puhlhofer* (n 55) 518.

body, consciously or unconsciously, are acting *perversely*'.[126] In cases concerning market regulatory bodies even lawfulness was transmuted into a matter of discretion, allowing courts maximal flexibility over intervention. Recognising an 'innominate ground', constituting 'an amalgam' of Lord Diplock's grounds in *CCSU*, Lord Donaldson in *Guinness* said that the 'ultimate question' in the case was 'whether something had gone wrong of a nature and degree which required the intervention of the court and, if so, what form that intervention should take'.[127] The court's role was 'a matter ... of discretion'[128] and it 'will regard its role as being one of last resort reserved for plain and obvious cases'.[129] In exercising this discretion 'great weight' would be given 'to the tribunal's view of what is fair' and the court 'will not lightly decide' it has acted unfairly, especially given the Panel was 'so distinguished and experienced'.[130] Importantly, one of the factors against intervention was the 'public interest in the panel getting on with, and being seen to get on with, its self-appointed task'.[131] And while aspects of the Panel's conduct were concerning and might engender 'a genuine sense of grievance' in those subject to the decision it was nonetheless important to 'stress' that the Panel should not be deterred 'from acting with all due expedition'.[132]

Thirdly, the way the grounds of and approach to review developed during this era reflects concerns to ensure power was exercised as it ought to be, for the public good, and that the manner of its exercise met basic standards of good administration.

It was considered axiomatic that public bodies were 'entrusted by Parliament with the exercise of powers *for the public good*'.[133] What decision lies in the public interest is ultimately for the primary decision-maker: 'Parliament has entrusted to the department or authority charged with the administration of the statute the exclusive right to determine the particular means within the limits laid down by the statute by which its [public] purpose can best be fulfilled'.[134] However, a fundamental aspect of ensuring power is exercised genuinely in the interests of the public is ensuring that its exercise is not captured by private interests or extraneous concerns. In other words, one of the principal functions of review is to ensure administrators do not go 'off the rails'[135] in exercise of their powers. From this premise it is a short step to the major grounds. Acting for improper purpose, considering extraneous concerns, or acting with bias are all ways in which administrators may deviate from the reasons why Parliament bestowed them with public power, so that administrators cannot be said to have genuinely exercised their powers for the common good. As Lord Templeman observed in *Preston*, it is an abuse of power to exercise or fail to exercise powers 'in

[126] ibid 517–18 (emphasis added).
[127] *Guinness* (n 25) 160.
[128] ibid 201.
[129] ibid 193.
[130] ibid 184.
[131] ibid 192.
[132] ibid 201.
[133] *HTV v Price Commission* [1976] ICR 170, 185 (emphasis added)
[134] *Home Office v Dorset Yacht Co Ltd* [1970] AC 1004, 1067.
[135] *Datafin* (n 12) 827.

order to achieve objectives which were not the objectives for which the powers had been conferred'.[136]

In terms of the substantive merits of the decision and reasoning offered in support of it, the 'emphatic language' of the *Wednesbury* test was relied on 'in order to drive home the message' that it is for the decision-maker to determine what lies in the public interest, and that there is wide scope for reasonable disagreement as to what lies in the common good, so even strong judicial disagreement with an administrative decision was not sufficient basis for intervention.[137] Only where the decision bordered on the absurd could it be said conclusively that there had been deviation from genuine pursuit of the public interest. The court's role was thus limited: to 'maintain a check on *excesses* in the exercise of discretion'.[138]

Apart from standing as a totem of non-intervention, Lord Brightman's statement in *Evans*, repeated as a mantra during the 1980s, signalled the other core concern of review, maintenance of basic standards of good administration: 'Judicial review is concerned, not with the decision, but with the decision-making process'.[139] The judges were not especially concerned with outcomes. But they were concerned to ensure robust processes were followed in determining outcomes. As Lord Donaldson said, the aim of review was 'maintenance of the highest standards of public administration' and the court should not intervene 'unless there is a reason to inquire whether a particular authority has been successful in its endeavours' in this respect.[140] Ensuring 'all relevant facts have been considered';[141] that the defendant has taken 'reasonable steps to acquaint [itself] with the relevant information to enable [it] to answer [the question] correctly';[142] acting without undue delay;[143] offering an explanation for a decision that might be difficult to understand otherwise and being responsive to the applicant;[144] ensuring all relevant concerns have been considered and irrelevant ones omitted from consideration; affording those who may be affected by a decision notice, consulting them or affording them an opportunity to be heard; decision-making unclouded by bias; and holding to representations or established practice,[145] are all basic expectations of good administrative practice, and make it more likely that decision-making processes will result in reliable outcomes.

Fourthly, rights, interests and/or expectations of individuals were a concern of judicial review. But this concern was subsidiary to the primary concern for the public interest and ensuring power was exercised properly, and the way individual interests were accounted for was moulded by these primary functions of review.

[136] *Preston* (n 104) 865.

[137] eg *R v Secretary of State for the Home Department, ex parte Brind* [1991] 1 AC 696, 765–66; *Foot* (n 107) 626.

[138] ibid (emphasis added).

[139] *R v Chief Constable of North Wales, ex parte Evans* [1982] 1 WLR 1155, 1173.

[140] *Huddleston* (n 25) 945.

[141] ibid 947.

[142] *Secretary of State for Education and Science v Tameside Metropolitan Borough Council* [1977] AC 1014, 1065.

[143] *Preston* (n 104) 853; *R v Governor of Durham Prison, ex parte Singh* [1984] 1 WLR 704.

[144] *Cunningham* (n 25).

[145] *Preston* (n 104) 866–67; *CCSU* (n 20) 401 (departure from established past practice could be 'unfair or inconsistent with good administration'); *Attorney-General of Hong Kong v Ng Yuen Shiu* [1983] 2 AC 629, 637D.

Where an individual's 'right to life', the 'most fundamental of all human rights', is at stake, the 'basis of the decision must surely call for the most anxious scrutiny'.[146] Such approach may sound strict but what this effectively amounted to was a requirement that the decision-maker consider the impact of her decision on the applicant's rights, and ask herself whether that impact is justifiable: '[i]f the Secretary of State has asked himself that question and answered it ... in the light of all relevant evidence, the court cannot interfere',[147] unless the balance struck by the decision-maker was perverse.[148] Thus, the extra burden on the decision-maker where basic rights were at stake was one to take them into account and consider the impact of her decision upon them. Beyond this the courts were very unlikely to interfere. In this light, the added obligations were imposed to facilitate good administration: if a decision-maker is to make a decision which could affect a basic right, they have an obligation to take that into account as a concern relevant to exercise of their public powers. The focus is the manner of the exercise of power itself, rather than securing actual protection or enforcement of the 'right'.

More generally any balancing of interests was quintessentially for the decision-maker. In *CCSU*, where the Minister denied individuals procedural fairness in the interests of national security, all the Law Lords demanded of the Minister was that she provide evidence that national security had indeed formed the basis of her decision. If such evidence was proffered 'the courts must accept that the claims of executive power must take precedence over those of the individual' and 'private rights must yield to the public interest'.[149] The unwillingness of the courts to intervene in a drastic denial of procedural fairness in turn illustrates the underlying conception of public law as a field concerned first and foremost with protection of the public. Similarly, in *Findlay*, Lord Scarman seemingly considered it unimaginable that the House would 'hamper, or even ... prevent, changes in [government] policy' to give effect to individual expectations formed on the basis of older policy: given 'the *importance of the public interest* in administration of parole I cannot think that Parliament intended the discretion to be restricted in this way'.[150]

Thus, as Woolf observed extra-judicially in 1986, an individual may, and often would, bring an application motivated by a desire to protect their private interests, but the applicant's subjective motivations did not reflect why the law allows them standing: he or she, like interest groups, or corporations that may be afforded standing, is afforded standing *on behalf of the public*, to enforce or seek proper performance of *public duties* in the *interests of the public*.[151]

[146] *R v Secretary of State for the Home Department, ex parte Bugdaycay* [1987] 1 AC 514, 531.

[147] ibid 532.

[148] *Brind* (n 137). Note that this development, and later developments (eg *R v Ministry of Defence, ex parte Smith* [1996] QB 517), were arguably due, at least in part, to supranational pressure to comply with the ECHR, but these concerns were integrated in a manner consonant with the conceptual structure and basic concerns of domestic 'public law'.

[149] *CCSU* (n 20) 406–7, 411, 413, 420.

[150] *In re Findlay* [1985] 1 AC 318, 338 (emphasis added).

[151] Woolf, 'Public Law–Private Law: Why the Divide?' (n 49).

(v) Remedies

There are at least three core features of a public interest conception of remedies: (i) remedies are discretionary; (ii) they may be denied in the public interest; (iii) they are limited to specific-type and declaratory relief.

The prerogative orders had been discretionary, and so too had the equitable remedies of declaration and injunction. This feature was strongly emphasised post-reform: the court has 'ultimate discretion'[152] whether to grant a remedy and may refuse relief 'notwithstanding that it holds and declares the decision to have been made ultra vires'.[153]

A core change post-procedural reform was assertion of 'a complete [judicial] discretion to select and grant the appropriate remedy'.[154] In other words, it did not really matter what remedy was sought by the applicant. If the court thought, in its discretion, that a remedy should be granted, it would then, in its further discretion, decide what remedy would be appropriate. Thus a procedural reform designed to guard against injustice to the applicant by allowing him or her the flexibility to choose among a range of remedies and change that choice through the course of proceedings[155] led to assertion of almost complete *judicial* control over remedies. Why? Because this allowed courts flexibility to ensure, on a case-by-case basis, preservation of public interests and minimum disruption to public administration. Assertion of judicial control again marked out 'public law' from some 'private law' fields within which it was for the litigant to elect his or her remedy, with the only question for the court being whether to grant the remedy claimed. One might link this difference to the different nature of the primary obligations in fields such as tort versus judicial review. In tort or contract, party autonomy is accepted given litigation concerns that litigant's individual, personal right, and (at least according to one way of thinking about rights) autonomy over decisions concerning the subject matter of the right is a core aspect of the right itself. In contrast, in public law the applicant is, in the eyes of the law, acting for the public good in seeking to ensure public power is exercised properly; and it may be that the public good is best served by a remedy different to that sought or no remedy. This difference also explains the apparent abrogation within review of the longstanding maxim, *ubi ius, ibi remedium*: public law does not concern 'rights' as traditionally understood in English law as individual, personal rights.

Remedial discretion proved a useful judicial tool to ensure public and administrative interests were protected where unlawfulness was proven: the court has 'ultimate discretion whether to set [decisions] aside and may refuse to do so in the public interest ... such decisions affect a very wide public which will not be parties to the dispute and ... their interests have to be taken into account as much as those of the immediate disputants'.[156]

[152] *Datafin* (n 12) 840.
[153] ibid.
[154] *IRC* (n 1) 647.
[155] Law Commission, *Report on Remedies in Administrative Law* (n 56) 19–20.
[156] *Datafin* (n 12) 840–41; see also *R v Dairy Produce Quota Tribunal for England and Wales, ex parte Caswell* [1990] 2 AC 738; *R v Stratford-on-Avon District Council, ex parte Jackson* [1985] 1 WLR 1319.

Argyll offers a paradigmatic example. In that case the Chairman of the Monopolies and Mergers Commission had acted alone, on the Commission's behalf, where there was no power for him to do so in the parent statute. In addressing remedies the Master of the Rolls said: 'We have to approach our duties with a proper awareness of the needs of public administration'.[157] He set out a non-exhaustive list of five 'concerns' or 'requirements' of good administration which bore on the question of remedy:[158]

(1) Substance over form: if the same administrative decision would have been and would still be reached if powers were exercised lawfully this tells against grant of relief.
(2) Speed: the retaking of administrative decisions causes administrative delay, which counsels against grant.
(3) Proper consideration of the public interest (as determined by the executive): in *Argyll*, the Minister ('the guardian of the public interest') consented to the Chairman's decision. This was a strong indicator that the Chairman's decision lay in the public interest, and should not be disturbed.
(4) The legitimate interests of citizens must be considered: but in judging the relevance of the interests, no matter how legitimate, regard has to be had to the goals of the administrative process concerned. If the individual's interests in bringing the review are at odds with the goals of the relevant administrative process, the latter are likely to trump, with relief denied.
(5) Decisiveness and finality, unless there are compelling reasons to the contrary: the core underlying concern here is administrative certainty. For example, in *Argyll*, it told against grant of a quashing order that the 'the financial public' would have already relied upon and made decisions on the basis of the Commission's decision. If other concerns are to trump such interests in good administration they must be compelling.

As one can see from this list and the outcome in *Argyll*—the decision was preserved—where the applicant's individual interests and rule-of-law concerns clash with the public interest, as determined by the executive, and administrative effectiveness and expeditiousness, the latter concerns will more likely prevail, especially where the public wrong was viewed by the court as 'technical' or 'merely procedural'.

In this era it became common for courts to preserve the status quo by refusing certiorari, but to declare impugned administrative action unlawful so that lessons could be learned for the future. Thus, review was, in a sense, an 'educative' exercise for the administration,[159] but one which should not disrupt administrative processes that had already run their course. In this way a balance was seemingly maintained between policing unlawfulness while ensuring minimal administrative disruption.

The third core feature of remedies is that they are limited to specific-type and declaratory relief and do not include damages. As Lord Bridge said in *Gillick*, 'the

157 *Argyll* (n 25) 774–75.
158 ibid.
159 eg *Datafin* (n 12) 842.

court's supervisory jurisdiction over the conduct of administrative authorities has been confined to ensuring that their actions or decisions were taken within the scope of the power which they purported to exercise or conversely to providing a remedy for an authority's failure to act or to decide in circumstances where some appropriate statutory action or decision was called for'.[160] Remedies are geared towards regulating and guiding public power so that it is exercised as it ought to be: for the common good and according to good administrative practice.

Damages are a 'private law' remedy and not available for breach of public duties. They would be out of place given they are concerned to remedy setbacks to interests personal to specific individuals pursuant to breach of personal rights, whereas the concern of public law is with public duties constituted to protect the public interest. Whereas in 'private law' the litigant may claim damages for loss suffered through breach of a 'duty owed specifically to him' and imposed 'for the benefit of private individuals to whom loss and damage is caused by breach of that duty',[161] in 'public law' only the 'remedy of judicial review is available to one who can establish a sufficient interest' and the concern is 'to have the law properly and fairly enforced and administered by a public authority in the performance of its *duties to the public at large*'.[162] Although the term 'public law right' was sometimes used in this era, 'a mere "right" to have the provisions of the law observed, shared as it is by every member of the public whether or not he is likely to suffer breach is … the antithesis of an 'individual' right … If the law gives him no remedy for … damage [suffered in consequence of breach of a duty] then he would not ordinarily be said to have any "individual right"'.[163] Reinforcing that damages should not be available for breaches of public law duties were concerns to ensure that 'a minister of the Crown should be able to discharge the duties of office expeditiously and fearlessly, a state of affairs which could hardly be achieved if acts done in good faith, but beyond powers, were to be actionable in damages'.[164]

Although the matter cannot be addressed in detail here, there are examples in private law fields of the influence of the public interest conception of public law, specifically in claims against public authorities. We find, for example, judicial reluctance to impose damages liability on public officials or entities based in concerns that pursuit of the common good could be undermined or skewed if private litigants could claim for personal loss suffered through exercise of public powers; imposition of liability could risk judges substituting their own views of how public powers should be exercised;[165] and/or public administration should not be impeded by fear of liability.[166] There are also instances of public authority liability being subordinated to public law concepts.[167]

[160] *Gillick* (n 21) 192.
[161] *Garden Cottage Foods Ltd v Milk Marketing Board* [1984] AC 130, 141.
[162] *Bourgoin* (n 28) 761 (emphasis added).
[163] ibid 761, 767.
[164] ibid 790.
[165] eg *Dorset Yacht* (n 134) 1067–68 (Lord Diplock).
[166] *Hill v Chief Constable of West Yorkshire* [1989] AC 53, 63.
[167] eg *Dorset Yacht* (n 134) 1068 ff (Lord Diplock).

III. LEGACY OF THE PUBLIC INTEREST CONCEPTION

Thus, from the late 1970s, and in the wake of procedural reform, a normative idea of 'public law' took hold in English law. This idea has proven hugely influential and been relied upon to guide legal development across fields doctrinally classified as 'public law', and has also demonstrated an imperialist quality, influencing legal development outside of public law, where public authorities are defendants.[168]

However, reliance on the idea can be problematic. Despite being framed as a conception of public law in general, the public interest conception was largely fashioned by reference to one field: common law judicial review, which formed the basis of the vast majority of claims streamed via review procedure during the public interest conception's formative era. This conception explains the core features of common law review during the time period examined above, and, in my opinion, common law review continues to bear the hallmarks of this conception today, and certainly cannot sensibly be explained without it.[169] From a normative perspective it also seems sensible that public law should include a field geared towards ensuring public power is exercised properly, albeit the degree of deference afforded to decision-makers in the formative era was, at times, extreme. However, public law today (and in the 1980s) quite clearly comprises a range of different bodies of doctrine. Where the public interest conception is used to guide development in fields other than common law review, the risk is that the distinctively valuable functions of those other fields are lost sight of and impeded, while their coherence may be distorted. I offer two examples of where this risk has become reality, both in the field of remedies: the approach to damages under the Human Rights Act (HRA) 1998, and the approach to specific-type relief in review proceedings on EU grounds. In turn, the story of the public interest conception is a tale of caution—against reliance upon a unitary conception of public law.

A. Damages Under the Human Rights Act 1998

Section 8 of the HRA 1998 provides that damages may be awarded for breach of enumerated rights. However, the Act's remedial provisions do not clearly prescribe a particular approach to damages, in large part leaving it to the courts to fashion the remedy. In the leading decision of *Anufrijeva* the Court of Appeal adopted an approach which bears all of the hallmarks of the public interest conception, the Court expressly extrapolating the approach to damages from that taken to remedies within common law review.[170] The House of Lords and Supreme Court later endorsed a

[168] eg *Financial Services Authority v Sinaloa Gold Plc* [2013] 2 AC 28 (addressing whether a public authority needs to proffer an undertaking as to damages in order to obtain a freezing order). For analysis see JNE Varuhas and PG Turner, 'Injunctions, Undertakings in Damages, and the Public-Private Divide' (2014) 130 *LQR* 33.

[169] See further JNE Varuhas, 'Against Unification' in H Wilberg and M Elliott (eds), *The Scope and Intensity of Substantive Review* (Oxford, Hart, 2015).

[170] *Anufrijeva v Southwark London Borough Council* [2004] QB 1124.

'mirror' approach, tying the approach to damages under the Act to the remedial practice of the European Court of Human Rights (ECtHR), but which, in practice, retained core aspects of a public interest approach.[171] Such approach is highly problematic. While the public interest approach to remedies is at one with core concerns of common law review, from which it has been sourced, it completely cuts against the core function of human rights law, which is not regulation of public duties in the public interest. Rather, human rights law performs the radically different function of strong protection and vindication of basic individual interests through creation of personal legal rights. By adopting a public interest approach to damages the courts have subordinated human rights law to pre-existing habits of public law thought utterly at odds with the distinctive nature of this novel field.

The approach in *Anufrijeva* is grounded in the idea that there is a fundamental remedial divide between public law and private law that should be maintained. Lord Woolf MR, for the Court, asserted that 'damages or compensation should play a different role in relation to claims in respect of public law rights from that which it plays in private law proceedings'.[172] This distinctive public law approach bears the three core features of a public interest approach to remedies. First, damages are subject to 'wide discretion'.[173] This was considered appropriate as most human rights claims would be brought via review procedure 'which has always been discretionary'.[174]

Secondly, damages may be denied and/or reduced below full compensation in the interests of 'the wider public': 'there is a balance to be drawn between the interests of the victim and those of the public as a whole'.[175] While the Court's decision drew attention to the negative effects that damages awards may have on public funds set aside to benefit the wider community and authorities' ability to perform their functions, little, if anything, was said of the negative effects of denying an individual damages for harm suffered pursuant to wrongful government action. By emphasising strongly that the power to award damages is a broad discretionary one, the court arrogates to itself the flexibility to deny relief where its grant would compromise the public interest.

The third core feature of the public interest approach is that the remedial focus is on declaratory and specific relief, and damages are not awarded. The second limb of this core feature is obviously difficult to sustain where Parliament has provided expressly for a damages remedy, but the courts have, in general, done their best to marginalise that remedy:[176] *Anufrijeva* 'downplays damages as a remedy in HRA cases'.[177] Lord Woolf stressed that in human rights cases what is of primary importance is bringing the authority's unlawful conduct to an end, with compensation of secondary, *if any*, importance; damages will thus play a 'less prominent role'

[171] *R (Greenfield) v Secretary of State for the Home Department* [2005] 1 WLR 673; *R (Faulkner) v Secretary of State for Justice* [2013] 2 AC 254.

[172] *Anufrijeva* (n 170) [54].

[173] ibid [56].

[174] ibid.

[175] ibid [56], [75]–[76].

[176] There are some exceptions: eg *Faulkner* (n 171) (although there was greater willingness to make awards in the specific context at issue in this case, awards made were exceptionally low).

[177] C Harlow, *State Liability: Tort Law and Beyond* (Oxford, Oxford University Press, 2004) 114.

for human rights violations compared to the role they play for 'breaches of private law obligations', and the remedial focus will be upon declaratory and specific-type relief, as in common law review.[178] In contrast to 'private law', damages will be a remedy of 'last resort' (language borrowed from common law review), being rarely awarded.[179] This is all of a piece with Lord Woolf's view, expressed extra-judicially in the 1980s—the heyday of the public interest conception—that in public law protection of the individual 'is incidental to the court's primary obligation, which is to stop the public body abusing its powers and the court does not so much establish the rights of the individual but confines the public body to performing its obligations and not exceeding its authority'.[180] By contrast, where private rights are at stake individual interests are afforded primacy: 'a claimant is invariably entitled, so far as money can achieve this, to be restored in the position he would have been in if he had not suffered the injury'.[181]

In addition to these three features, two more should be noted, which further illustrate the influence of the public interest conception. The Court in *Anufrijeva* held that human rights damages claims should be treated as 'public law' claims for procedural purposes, to be streamed through review procedure where possible, with all of its concomitant safeguards for public authorities, while the Administrative Court 'is well placed to take action expeditiously'.[182] Further, where appropriate, claims should be streamed through alternative routes such as the Parliamentary Ombudsman, in contrast to claims for damages based in private law rights which are quintessentially for courts.[183] At the forefront of the Court's thinking was the amount of money spent on the litigation in *Anufrijeva*, and what made the situation 'even more worrying' was that 'all the parties [were] funded out of public funds';[184] these concerns were reiterated by the Law Lords in *Greenfield*.[185]

Secondly, observations are sometimes made in the HRA damages jurisprudence that damages should be awarded if there is 'a need to encourage compliance by individual officials or classes of official'[186] or 'so that lessons can be learned'.[187] This suggests a distinctive conception of damages as a tool for ensuring public power is used as it ought to be into the future, consonant with traditional remedial concerns within common law review, and in particular the 'educative' conception of review mentioned above. On this view, damages are only likely to be awarded where the public goal of ensuring public power is properly exercised into the future would be served; in this way individual justice is subordinated to a concern with ensuring public power is exercised properly, to the benefit of all.

[178] *Anufrijeva* (n 170) [52]–[53].
[179] ibid [56].
[180] Woolf, 'Public Law–Private Law: Why the Divide?' (n 49) 227.
[181] *Anufrijeva* (n 170) [55].
[182] ibid [53], [79]–[81].
[183] ibid.
[184] ibid.
[185] *Greenfield* (n 171) [30].
[186] ibid [19].
[187] *A v Essex County Council* [2011] 1 AC 280, [118].

Anufrijeva 'shoehorns' human rights law into the public interest conception by adopting a remedial approach synonymous with a concern for proper performance of public duties in the public interest. It marginalises damages, prioritises traditional forms of relief, emphasises the central importance of the public interest, requires damages claims where possible to be streamed via a procedure which affords protection to authorities, while the approach to human rights damages is not to be compared with that in private law. In turn this maintains a strong remedial divide between public and private law, consonant with the conception of this divide developed during the 1980s: in private law the concern is protection of individual interests and the main remedy is naturally damages for personal losses, whereas in public law the concern is with the public good and relief is geared towards ensuring power is exercised as it ought to be and with preserving the public interest and administrative interests.

Before going on to explain the problems with this approach (which should be manifest), it is important to record that the now prevailing approach to HRA damages is the 'mirror' approach by which domestic courts seeks to replicate in domestic law the Strasbourg Court's practice of making compensatory awards.[188] The courts maintain this approach follows from section 8(4) of HRA 1998 which requires domestic courts to take into account the principles applied by the ECtHR in making awards in its own remedial jurisdiction under Article 41 of the European Convention on Human Rights. But given that provision only requires courts *to take into account* the *principles* (cf practice) applied by the ECtHR, such approach is not inevitable, while the approach suffers from other serious problems.[189] In any case, what is significant for present purposes is that alignment of the approach to HRA damages with the ECtHR's approach to just satisfaction *has the effect* of producing a domestic approach to human rights damages which is to a significant degree consonant with the approach favoured in *Anufrijeva* and the conception of public law which underlies that approach. Under Article 41, monetary relief is discretionary and marginal, the ECtHR often concludes that a finding of violation constitutes sufficient remedy in itself, while awards are very low by English standards. One might hypothesise that this mirror approach was a natural one for domestic courts to adopt as it gives effect to a pre-existing, domestic conception of public law, and maintains a pre-existing remedial divide in domestic law between public and private law.

So, for example, in *Greenfield*, in which the mirror approach was first established, Lord Bingham affirmed Lord Woolf's views in *Anufrijeva*, that damages will play a less prominent role under the HRA 1998 than in private law fields, and the principal concern in human rights cases will be to bring infringements to an end, with damages of secondary, if any, importance.[190] Lord Bingham supported these propositions by reference to 'the focus of the Convention' which 'is on the protection of human rights and not the award of compensation', and the ECtHR's practice, which

[188] *Greenfield* (n 171); *Faulkner* (n 171).

[189] JNE Varuhas, *Damages and Human Rights* (Oxford, Hart, 2016) ch V.

[190] *Greenfield* (n 171) [9].

follows from its focus, which entails the Court often holding that a finding of violation constitutes just satisfaction in itself.[191] In the subsequent case of *Dobson*, the Court of Appeal explicitly melded the mirror approach mandated by *Greenfield* and the 'public law' approach in *Anufrijeva*:

> The Convention serves principally public law aims; the principal objective is to declare any infringement and to put a stop to it. Compensation is ancillary and discretionary. The interests of the individual are part of the equation, but so are those of the wider public.[192]

Now, clearly, it is utterly implausible to maintain that the remedial practice of a supranational European court reflects a *sui generis* English conception of 'public law aims'; the ECtHR's approach to just satisfaction is explained by completely different concerns, such as its principal role as an international supervisory court being to set human rights standards across Europe rather than operate as a mechanism for affording individual redress, which is primarily for Member States.[193] But what the reasoning in *Dobson* and other cases renders explicit is the degree of synergy between an approach to damages based in the ECtHR's remedial practice—ie an approach that holds compensation to be a marginal, discretionary remedy—and a view that there is a significant normative difference between private law and public law in domestic law that ought to be reflected in distinct remedial approaches.

The problem with adoption of a public interest approach to human rights damages is it creates a fundamental mismatch between the functions of human rights law and the approach to remedies. The remedial approach is based in a conception of public law which holds that the principal function of public law is regulation of public duties in the public interest. But the function of human rights law is fundamentally distinct. It is concerned to ensure the strong protection of individual interests, in life, liberty, privacy, etc. The concern is protection of the individual, not of the public. If common law review ensures public power is exercised properly in the public interest, human rights law ensures strong protection of basic individual interests in the face of power so exercised.

The simplest way to illustrate the fundamental difference between common law review and human rights law, is to demonstrate how core features of the HRA action are similar to core features of actions in tort.[194] For example, negative obligations in human rights law closely mirror the structure of torts actionable per se, such as false imprisonment and battery, which similarly afford strong protection to basic individual interests: only those whose interests are wrongfully interfered with by the defendant's conduct may bring an action; the action may not be assigned as it is personal to the individual right-holder; these actions are actionable without proof of loss; liability is generally strict; the onus is on the defendant to justify an interference with protected interests; public interests are countervailing concerns rather

[191] ibid [4], [9].

[192] *Dobson v Thames Water Utilities Ltd* [2009] 3 All ER 319, [42]. See also *R (Sturnham) v Parole Board* [2012] 3 WLR 476, [15] ff; *DSD v Commissioner of Police of the Metropolis* [2015] EWCA Civ 646, [65]–[66].

[193] Varuhas, *Damages and Human Rights* (n 189) ch V.

[194] See further ibid chs II–III; JNE Varuhas, 'The Reformation of English Administrative Law? "Rights", Rhetoric and Reality' (2013) 72 *CLJ* 369, 398–402; Varuhas, 'Against Unification' (n 169).

than principal concerns; defences such as proportionality are construed narrowly; and only the weightiest countervailing interests may justify an interference, while specific relief is available to bring an ongoing wrong to an end, and damages are available to redress personal loss.

The two fields have further features in common. The House of Lords and Supreme Court consistently refer to rights under the HRA 1998 in a manner which indicates that they are personal to the particular claimants (rather than, say, public duties or free-standing standards of legality),[195] while in *Quila* it was stated expressly that 'decisions founded on human rights are essentially individual'; a determination of breach is a determination only in respect of that specific claimant's rights.[196] As in tort substantive questions, such as whether a risk was 'real and immediate' or 'reasonable steps' were taken in the context of the *Osman* duty, or whether interferences are proportionate, are determined objectively by the judiciary.[197] This follows from the nature of the claim as one of *individual right*; determination of questions of right is a quintessentially judicial rather than administrative function. Thus, in human rights law courts do not perform a secondary, reviewing function, and they, rather than the administrative decision-maker, have the final say over how any balance ought to be struck between interests: '[t]he court's function … is to decide for itself whether the decision was in accordance with Convention rights; it is not a purely reviewing function'; 'Under the HRA … the claimant would have a right to full merits review by the court, again on fact and law'.[198]

It is also important to observe that despite Lord Woolf's dicta in *Anufrijeva* human rights claims may now be brought via ordinary procedure and routinely are, alongside claims in tort, while the courts have gone so far as to hold that certain classes of human rights claims ought to be brought via ordinary procedure; in doing so the courts have emphasised commonalities between such claims and claims in tort.[199] Where they are brought via review procedure, restrictions on disclosure and cross-examination have been loosened so that, in significant respects, the procedure has the character of that which governs claims of individual right in private law, the courts again drawing analogies with tort.[200] Further, the courts have subsequently held the Ombudsman is not an alternative path for redress that must be exhausted

[195] These rights do not exist in the air but are 'the rights of the applicants', 'the Convention rights of these particular young people', 'his' or 'her' rights, 'the company's article 10 rights', 'individual's rights', 'the rights of designated persons': *R (Quila) v Secretary of State for the Home Department* [2012] 1 AC 621, [44], [61]; *Belfast City Council v Miss Behavin' Ltd* [2007] 1 WLR 1420, [12]–[13], [15] –[16], [20], [90]; *R (Begum) v Governors of Denbigh High School* [2007] 1 AC 100, [48], [59]; *Rabone v Pennine Care NHS Trust* [2012] 2 AC 72, [107]; *Tweed v Parades Commission for Northern Ireland* [2007] 1 AC 650, [5]; *R (Wilkinson) v Broadmoor Special Hospital Authority* [2002] 1 WLR 419, [61]–[62]; *Bank Mellat v Her Majesty's Treasury (No 2)* [2013] 3 WLR 179, [21] (substantive appeal).

[196] *Quila* (n 195) [59], [80].

[197] *Begum* (n 195) [29]–[30]; *Tweed* (n 195) [55]; *R (Williamson) v Secretary of State for Education and Employment* [2005] 2 AC 246, [51]; *Miss Behavin'* (n 195) [12]–[15], [31], [44]; *Denbigh* (n 195) [29]–[31]; *Huang v Secretary of State for the Home Department* [2007] 2 AC 167; *Quila* (n 195) [46], [61], [91]; *E v Chief Constable of the Royal Ulster Constabulary* [2009] 1 AC 536, [13], [52] ff; Varuhas 'Against Unification' (n 169).

[198] *Kennedy v Charity Commission* [2015] AC 455, [244].

[199] *Ruddy v Chief Constable of Strathclyde* [2012] UKSC 57; *Wilkinson* (n 195) [61]; *ID v Home Office* [2006] 1 WLR 1003, [105].

[200] *Tweed* (n 195); *Wilkinson* (n 195) [24]–[26], [56]–[59], [62].

before a damages claim may come to court,[201] given damages claims concern claims of legal right whereas the Ombudsman does not have jurisdiction over legal wrongs. Thus, the law governing procedure has evolved to reflect the distinctive nature of human rights law as a body of law based in individual rights.

Thus, the Court's critical mistake in *Anufrijeva* was in effect to adopt an approach to damages founded on a theory of public law which holds that public law is concerned with duties owed to the public and 'protection of the public', in a field that is specifically constituted to ensure the protection and vindication of fundamental individual rights and interests, and in this resembles the Court's stylised account of private law. Fundamentally different fields have been conflated under the umbrella of 'public law' with the consequence that the general remedial approach within common law review was inaptly read across to human rights law. The public interest approach to remedies may be apt in a field such as common law review, which is founded on a concern for preservation of the common good,[202] but it is out of place in a field specifically constituted to ensure protection of individual rights. As Feldman observes, the broad discretionary approach to damages under the HRA 1998 has been carried over from the traditional discretionary approach to remedies such as quashing orders at common law.[203] But that remedial approach is a remnant of the 'obligation-dominated days of public law' before 'rights' had a 'genuine place in English public law'.[204] Times have changed; 'public law' has moved on, and so must the remedial approach. But not only is the appending of a public interest approach to remedies to a field concerned with individual rights incoherent, such limp approach positively undermines the goals of human rights law. As I have argued elsewhere, the most appropriate model for damages in human rights law is that developed in common law fields of liability similarly concerned to afford strong protection to basic interests, such as torts actionable per se.[205] But to be alive to the clear link between these fields one must cast aside the conceptual yoke of the public law-private law divide.

B. Remedial Discretion for Breach of EU Environmental Directives

In *Walton* the applicant challenged the validity of schemes and orders made by the Scottish Ministers under the Roads (Scotland) Act 1984 enabling construction of a

[201] *K v Cornwall County Council* [2005] EWHC 1585, [11].

[202] Although such remedial approach may become inapt if the nature of that field were to become oriented increasingly towards individual rights, fundamental or otherwise: eg *Kennedy* (n 198); *Pham v Secretary of State for the Home Department* [2015] 1 WLR 1591; JNE Varuhas, 'Judicial Review at the Crossroads' (2015) 74 *CLJ* 215.

[203] D Feldman, 'Remedies for Violations of Convention Rights' in D Feldman (ed), *English Public Law* 2nd edn (Oxford, Oxford University Press, 2009) [19.08].

[204] ibid.

[205] Varuhas, *Damages and Human Rights* (n 189); JNE Varuhas, 'Damages: Private Law and the HRA: Never the Twain Shall Meet?' in D Hoffman (ed), *The Impact of the UK Human Rights Act on Private Law* (Cambridge, Cambridge University Press, 2011); JNE Varuhas, 'A Tort-Based Approach to Damages under the Human Rights Act 1998' (2009) 72 *MLR* 750. On the approach to damages within torts actionable per se, see JNE Varuhas, 'The Concept of "Vindication" in the Law of Torts: Rights, Interests and Damages' (2014) 34 *OJLS* 253.

new road network.[206] His principal argument, that Ministers had not undertaken public consultation on one element of the network as required by the Strategic Environment Assessment Directive (SEAD),[207] failed. However, the Supreme Court considered what approach should be taken to remedies if there had been a breach.

Lord Reed took a cautious approach, preferring to consider the matter in a case of actual breach. In contrast, Lord Carnwath propounded that the discretion to refuse relief within common law review applies equally to breaches of EU procedural norms, such as requirements in Directives such as the SEAD, for environmental impact assessments (EIAs) or public consultations where planned infrastructure projects pose environmental risks. In doing so he placed emphasis on *Argyll*, citing it for the proposition that the discretion 'may be important in maintaining the overall balance of public interest in appropriate cases'.[208] He also placed emphasis on Lord Hoffmann's speech in *Edwards*, which relied on considerations similar to those enunciated in *Argyll*.[209] These included that quashing would be 'pointless' (echoing the 'substance over form' concern in *Argyll*) and '[t]o this pointlessness must be added the waste of time and resources, both for the company and the Agency, of going through another process of application, consultation and decision' (echoing the concern in *Argyll* for disruption of administrative process and administrative certainty). For Lord Carnwath, where there was significant 'prejudice' to 'public and private interests' '[i]t would be extraordinary if … the court were precluded by principles of domestic or European law from weighing that prejudice in the [remedial] balance'.[210] It was important that interests protected by EIAs 'should be seen not in isolation, but rather in the context of the many other interests, public and private, which are in play in relation to a major [infrastructure] scheme'.[211] Further, assertion of remedial discretion was 'a necessary counterbalance' to wide standing rules, in order to maintain a proper balance of interests within the system of review.[212]

Lord Carnwath considered that had breach been found on the facts, considerations identified by defendant's counsel would have told overwhelmingly against relief, these considerations again echoing those invoked in *Argyll* and in common law review more generally.[213] They included the 'great public interest' in allowing the scheme to proceed, reflected in strong support for the scheme among large sections of the public and national and elected bodies, and lack of a legal challenge from environmental groups; in other words it was significant that those charged with preservation of the public interest or whose views serve as a litmus test for gauging what lies in the common good considered the scheme should go ahead. Set against this was the applicant's 'very attenuated' interests; as in *Argyll* the applicant's interests would be subordinated to the common good where they ran counter to it. Public interests in finality, certainty and preservation of public funds also loomed

[206] *Walton* (n 84).
[207] Strategic Environment Assessment Directive 2001/42/EC [2001] OJ L197/30 (SEAD).
[208] *Walton* (n 84) [103].
[209] ibid [130]; *R (Edwards) v Environment Agency* [2009] 1 All ER 57, [65].
[210] ibid [131].
[211] ibid [103].
[212] ibid [103].
[213] ibid [105], [114].

large: significant public monies had been spent on preparatory work, quashing would create uncertainty and blight, and impose significant burdens on those who had already participated in consultative processes as they would have to endure such processes over again.

Thus, quite clearly, the remedial approach associated with common law review, bearing all the hallmarks of the public interest conception, was read across to the remedial approach to breaches of EU law: a new area of law, drawn from the supranational plane, was subordinated to pre-existing, domestic habits of thinking.[214] This approach is problematic because it neglects the distinctiveness of the EU context generally, and specifically EU environmental law.

The relevant norms in EU law include the principle of cooperation in good faith, which holds that Member States must take all general or particular measures necessary to ensure compliance with EU law. The principle of procedural autonomy holds that the details of domestic procedure governing claims in EU law are for the Member State to determine, subject to the principles of equivalence (procedural rules should not be less favourable than those governing similar domestic situations) and effectiveness (procedural rules should not render impossible in practice or excessively difficult exercise of rights in EU law). It is a little tricky to predict how the application of domestic remedial discretion in EU cases would fare at Luxembourg. This is because the governing principles are all rather broad and the relative emphasis placed on each by the CJEU has varied over time and according to the specific legal context,[215] while the permissibility of the discretion may depend on how it is exercised in practice. However, those caveats notwithstanding, it is submitted that Lord Carnwath's approach is at least a precarious one because it ignores the distinctive concerns of environmental Directives and EU law more generally. Further, it might be one thing to hold remedies subject to a confined discretion to refuse relief if narrow grounds for refusal are proven but Lord Carnwath's judgment suggests a rather broad, unstructured discretion which could see remedies denied for a broad range of public interest reasons based on an open-ended balancing of factors.

It is difficult to interpret past European cases as providing a firm foundation for mainstreaming a general and broad remedial discretion. Lord Carnwath considered these cases, and found that they supported or did not tell against reading across the common law discretion to the EU context.[216] However, with respect, this conclusion is unsafe and a plain reading of the cases, particularly the most relevant decision from the CJEU Grand Chamber, tells strongly against such conclusion.

A core question is whether EU law *requires* or *generally requires* nullification of decisions taken in breach of EU environmental, procedural norms. It is difficult to derive a clear answer to this question from the earlier Chamber decision in

[214] Confirming this, see now *R (Champion) v North Norfolk District Council* [2015] UKSC 52.

[215] See the excellent analysis in M Dougan, 'The Vicissitudes of Life at the Coalface: Remedies and Procedures for Enforcing Union Law Before the National Courts' in P Craig and G de Búrca (eds), *The Evolution of EU Law* 2nd edn (Oxford, Oxford University Press, 2011).

[216] *Walton* (n 84) [134] ff.

Wells, which considered the issue of remedies for breach of the SEAD.[217] However, the more recent decision of the Grand Chamber in *Région Wallone* suggests that decisions taken in breach of SEAD should, as a matter of course, be nullified barring very exceptional, strictly confined circumstances.[218] The Grand Chamber held that 'courts before which actions are brought ... *must adopt*, on the basis of their national law, measures to suspend or annul a "plan" or "programme" adopted in breach of the obligation to carry out an environmental assessment'.[219] This follows from the duty of cooperation and the environmental context. The 'fundamental objective' of SEAD 'would be disregarded if national courts did not adopt in such actions brought before them, and subject to the limits of procedural autonomy, the measures, provided for by their national law, that are appropriate for preventing such a plan or programme, including projects to be realised under that programme, from being implemented' absent an EIA.[220] The approach to remedies is prescriptive: national courts *must* adopt whatever measures exist in their domestic law to suspend or annul a plan or programme adopted without the required EIA; such legally defective plans or programmes must be prevented from being implemented in the absence of an assessment, making use of the remedial tools that exist in domestic law to ensure prevention. What makes it especially clear that the Grand Chamber considered that nullification is generally required is that it thought it *exceptional* merely to allow domestic courts to briefly postpone, subject to strict conditions, annulment of an order made in breach of SEAD in unusual circumstances where immediate annulment would have caused the Member State to commit a separate breach of EU law, and postponement positively promoted the environmental goals of SEAD.[221] This is not suggestive of endorsement of a general discretion to refuse relief where the balance of interests tells against grant; it suggests annulment should ordinarily follow violation.

It is worth noting, in particular, that the Grand Chamber made a point of observing that the national court was not relying on 'economic grounds' to justify suspending annulment, but 'only ... the objective of protecting the environment, which constitutes one of the essential objectives of the European Union and is both fundamental and cross-cutting in nature'.[222] This is significant given Lord Carnwath's endorsement of the view that relief could be denied to protect public and private pecuniary interests in large infrastructure projects.

How does procedural autonomy bear on the matter? It is not clear from *Région Wallone* but working from the ruling that it would be exceptional to suspend

[217] C-201/02 *R (Wells) v Secretary of State for Transport, Local Government and the Regions* [2004] ECR I-723. See, eg, P Wennerås, *The Enforcement of EC Environmental Law* (Oxford, Oxford University Press, 2007) 132–34.

[218] C-41/11 *Inter-Environnement Wallonie ASBL v Région Wallone* [2012] 2 CMLR 21. Such prescriptive approach to remedies has also been taken in other contexts: eg C-213/89 *R v Secretary of State for Transport, ex parte Factortame Ltd* [1990] ECR I-2433 (interim relief); C-271/91 *Marshall v Southampton and South West Hampshire Health Authority (No 2)* [1993] ECR I-4367 (compensation and interest); C-326/96 *Levez v TH Jennings (Harlow Pools) Ltd* [1998] ECR I-7857 (compensation).

[219] *Région Wallone* (n 218) [46] (emphasis added), and see [AG31].

[220] ibid [47].

[221] ibid [58] ff.

[222] ibid [57].

annulment, and the general statements prescribing annulment as the ordinary response to breach, there are two possible readings. On the one hand, perhaps the Court considers a failure to annul will generally constitute breach of the effectiveness principle, and the scope for procedural autonomy in respect of remedies is narrowed in this context to the *form* of the remedy in domestic law (for example, in English law the remedy which would achieve annulment would be a quashing order, while prohibiting or mandatory orders would be the relevant remedies to prevent unlawful conduct);[223] this reading would not be a stretch given it is difficult to argue against the proposition that it 'strikes at the very essence of rights' and would render exercise of the rights 'impossible in practice'[224] for a court to refuse to require public consultation or an EIA where those are legal requirements but have not been fulfilled.[225] On the other hand, one may consider that the principle of procedural autonomy does not address remedies, but only the rules that govern the procedure by which claims are made, such as time limits or costs, for example, with remedies regulated differently.[226] Either way, *Région Wallone* suggests the scope for refusing relief altogether is exceptionally limited or non-existent.

A further indication of the precariousness of Lord Carnwath's approach is the CJEU emphasis on context in scrutinising remedial practices.[227] EU environmental Directives place heavy emphasis on public participation, environmental protection, a precautionary approach, sustainable development, and integration of environmental concerns into decision-making at the earliest possible stage. The CJEU repeatedly reiterates that the goal of such Directives is, as stated in the purpose clause of SEAD, 'to provide for a high level of protection of the environment', while protection of the environment is repeatedly said to be a fundamental goal of the EU order, finding reflection in Article 191 TFEU (ex Article 174 TEC).[228] This goal is also reflected in requirements in environmental Directives being interpreted stringently in accordance with their purpose of affording strong protection.[229] Requirements for consultation or EIAs are not 'merely' procedural, but of the very essence of such measures: the procedural requirements are the *outcomes*—'the fundamental objective'[230]—the Directives are passed to secure.[231] As Advocate-General Kokott said in *Région Wallone*, '[t]he right to an environmental assessment is not simply a formal step in the procedure but ... is intended to ensure that significant environmental effects of

[223] See ibid [AG34].

[224] C-246/96 *Maggorian v Eastern Health and Social Services Board* [1997] ECR I-7153, [44].

[225] This seems to be the implication in *Région Wallone* (n 218) [AG35].

[226] See the pre-*Wallone* discussion of this question in Wennerås, *Enforcement of EC Environmental Law* (n 217) ch 3; and see also Dougan, 'The Vicissitudes of Life at the Coalface' (n 215) 433–35.

[227] See generally Dougan, 'The Vicissitudes of Life at the Coalface' (n 215).

[228] eg C-240/83 *Procureur de la République v ADBHU* [1985] ECR 531, [13]; C-302/86 *European Commission v Denmark* [1988] ECR 4607, [8]; C-213/96 *Outokumpu Oy* [1998] ECR I–1777, [32]; C-176/03 *European Commission v Council* [2005] ECR I-7879, [41].

[229] See, eg, C-127/02 *Landelijke Vereniging tot Behoud van de Waddenzee v Staatssecretaris van Landbouw, Natuurbeheer en Visserij* [2004] ECR I-7405, eg [67]–[68]; C-567/10 *Inter-Environnement Bruxelles ASBL v Région de Bruxelles-Capitale* [2012] 2 CMLR 30, eg [28]–[30], [37], [41].

[230] *Région Wallone* (n 218) [40].

[231] More generally the CJEU has been willing to conceptualise procedural requirements as substantive in nature where this would promote the effectiveness of EU law and ensure fulfilment of the goals of a particular Directive: eg C-194/94 *CIA Security International SA v Signalson SA* [1996] ECR I-2201, [48].

implementing plans and programmes are taken into account during their preparation and before their adoption'.[232] Thus the procedural requirements are intimately connected to substantive goals. As the same Advocate-General has observed, 'it must be presumed that a measure subject to an assessment would be more favourable for the protection of the environment than the measure lacking that assessment',[233] while the SEAD's purpose clause states the aim of the Directive is to contribute to integration of environmental concerns into decision-making 'with a view to promoting sustainable development'.[234]

Given this backdrop, the CJEU would take a 'hard look' at a practice of refusing relief for breaches of requirements that go to the very heart of the EU regime for environmental protection. What matters is not, as Lord Carnwath appears to suggest, whether the balance of convenience is in the plan or programme going ahead unimpeded and undelayed or not, but whether environmental concerns have been properly taken into account in decision-making. The nature of the obligations in this field also rubs against the grain of the 'substance over form' or 'pointlessness' ideas that characterise remedial discretion at common law, and which could entail refusing relief where procedural unlawfulness is considered immaterial to final outcome.[235] Within the environmental context procedural guarantees *are* substantive. Furthermore, breach of 'procedural' obligations, such as conducting an EIA, will not uncommonly lead, *ipso facto*, to a breach of other obligations in the relevant Directive. For example, under the SEAD the relevant executive decision-maker is required to take into account, as mandatory relevant considerations, the EIA, and responses to it received during public consultation, in preparing the plan or programme, and before its adoption or submission to legislative procedure.[236] Further, they must, having produced the plan or programme, produce a statement summarising how environmental considerations have been integrated into the plan or programme and how the mandatory relevant considerations have been taken into account.[237] Obviously, if no assessment is produced in respect of a relevant plan or programme these obligations will also be violated. In other Directives the obligations that follow the assessment process are even more prescriptive. In the Habitats Directive, for example, national authorities may only agree upon a plan or project if they have 'ascertained that it will not adversely affect the integrity of the site concerned

[232] *Région Wallone* (n 218) [AG37].

[233] ibid [AG38].

[234] SEAD, art 1. Holder, in her book-length study of environmental assessment, concludes: 'My main finding is simple: environmental assessment is highly material to the outcome of a decision. This challenges the presentation of environmental assessment as an example of legal reflexivity, particularly that it operates as an indirect, abstract form of legal control because of its inherently procedural nature … environmental assessment is *not* entirely procedural. It has important substantive consequences, suggesting that the procedural–substantive dichotomy is not so clear as has been supposed' (*Environmental Assessment* (Oxford, Oxford University Press, 2006) 8).

[235] In any case it would surely be a rare case in which a court could conclude with any confidence that lack of an EIA in respect of a major infrastructure project would make no difference to the decision outcome, not least because an EIA is only legally required where it is established that the proposed project would be likely to have 'significant environmental effects' (SEAD, arts 1, 3).

[236] SEAD, art 8.

[237] SEAD, art 9.

and, if appropriate, after having obtained the opinion of the general public'.[238] If the procedural requirement of properly conducting an environmental assessment is not met, the national authorities will not have ascertained whether the plan or project will have such adverse impact, so that a condition-precedent to agreeing a plan or project will not have been met. Thus, even if one considers the requirement for the EIA itself to be merely procedural (which is untenable), a failure to produce one will lead to further, clearly substantive, violations.

In this light, the approach in the earlier House of Lords decision of *Berkeley* is more responsive to the EU environmental context.[239] The case concerned non-compliance with procedural norms in an environmental Directive. Their Lordships emphasised the duty of cooperation in Article 10 EC (now Article 4(3) TEU), which requires Member States to take all appropriate measures to ensure fulfilment of EU obligations, and held unless the violation was negligible the discretion to refuse relief altogether was virtually non-existent. Lord Bingham said: 'In the Community context, unless a violation is so negligible as to be truly de minimis and the prescribed procedure has in all essentials been followed, the discretion (if any exists) is narrower still [than that at common law]'.[240] This was reinforced by features of environmental Directives, such as strict conditions governing exemptions from procedural requirements, and the absence of any discretion for the Minister to waive requirements otherwise. Lord Hoffmann specifically stated that even where the result would have been the same but for the breach, relief should still generally be granted: 'A court is therefore not entitled retrospectively to dispense with the requirement of an EIA'; 'nothing less than substantial compliance with the Directive could enable the planning permission in this case to be upheld'.[241] In *Walton*, Lord Carnwath sought to distinguish *Berkeley* on various grounds. But the speeches clearly enunciate principles of general application, while the later decision in *Edwards*, which might be interpreted as a retreat from *Berkeley*, entailed no breach of EU law. More than this, they are consonant with the Grand Chamber judgment in *Région Wallone*, and with the distinctiveness of the environmental context.

More generally, the speeches in *Berkeley* are important because they bring into sharp focus the distinctiveness of the EU context relative to common law review more generally. EU law is characterised by a strong concern for ensuring supremacy and full effectiveness of EU law within the domestic order. Illustrative of this concern are, for example, those core doctrines regulating interaction between EU law and the domestic plane: direct effect, indirect effect, and imposition of state liability for failure to properly transpose a Directive. Provisions such as that relied upon in *Berkeley*, and others such as Article 47 of the EU Charter, which guarantees an effective remedy for breach of rights in EU law, reinforce this. Against this backdrop the idea of a broad discretion to dispense with core obligations in an EU Directive on the basis that requiring compliance would prejudice interests, such as economic interests, which it is clearly contemplated would be prejudiced by the relevant procedural

[238] Habitats Directive 92/43/EC [1992] OJ L206/7, art 6(3).

[239] *Berkeley v Secretary of State for the Environment* [2001] 2 AC 603.

[240] ibid 608.

[241] ibid 616.

requirements, runs against the grain. Rather, this background suggests, as recognised in *Berkeley* and *Wallone*, that quashing ought to be the standard response. To append a remedial discretion to review on EU grounds based in concerns distinct from those that characterise EU law is not only to introduce incoherence into the law, but to stymie the distinctive goals of EU law generally, and environmental Directives specifically.

It should be noted, for completeness, that in *Walton* there were indications that the discretion to refuse relief would be narrow: Lord Hope said that before relief could be denied there must be 'good grounds' for believing grant of relief would cause 'very great' prejudice to public interests.[242] However, such exhortations may not be observed in practice, especially in a discretionary context, and are open to interpretation. Indeed, there are myriad cases in which judges have emphasised the narrowness of the remedial discretion while denying relief;[243] the potential for this seems acute where economic and political interests in large infrastructure projects are set against an individual's complaint of procedural irregularity, as will nearly always be the case in the environmental context. In this respect, the facts of *Walton* are standard rather than exceptional, yet it is clear that if there had been a violation Lord Carnwath would have denied relief: nearly all of the concerns that told against relief in *Walton*, such as uncertainty and prejudice to the public interest in completion of projects, will be present in this class of case generally. Further, Lord Carnwath, in his own judgment, indicated the threshold for refusal may not be limited to cases of significant prejudice to the public interest, observing that relief will likely be withheld where the individual applicant suffers no significant prejudice, aligning the approach to relief with that in domestic law under planning statutes.[244] With respect, denying relief on the basis of whether an individual applicant happens to have personally suffered prejudice or not ignores the broader concerns of environmental Directives, ie environmental protection and integration of environmental concerns into decision-processes, which lie in the interests of all. This approach, if applied consistently, would hollow out procedural guarantees in environmental Directives, given that administrative action will be allowed to stand where the core purposes of Directives have been seriously undermined, yet the publically-spirited individual or non-governmental organisation who brought the application happens not to have suffered prejudice. Indeed, there will be many instances where proposed action threatens the environment but no person is individually prejudiced. This was one of the very reasons why the Supreme Court in *Walton* broadened standing, so that publically-spirited citizens could seek review even if they had not suffered individual prejudice.[245]

[242] *Walton* (n 84) [156].
[243] eg *Edwards* (n 209) [63]–[65]; *R (Hurley) v Secretary of State for Business Innovation and Skills* [2012] HRLR 13, [99]; *R (CPAG) v Secretary of State for Work and Pensions* [2012] EWHC 2579, [64]–[77]; *R (English Speaking Board (International) Ltd) v Secretary of State for the Home Department* [2011] EWHC 1788, [62]–[63]; *R v Lincolnshire County Council, ex parte Atkinson* (1996) 8 Admin LR 529, 550.
[244] *Walton* (n 84) [113], [133], [139]–[140].
[245] Ibid [94], [152].

Finally, the discretion to refuse relief at common law is a broad, unstructured one, and we know[246] that such discretions tend to be applied unpredictably and inconsistently. It ought to be recalled that the principle of certainty has application in assessing whether a remedial provision or practice renders application of EU law impossible or excessively difficult.[247] The CJEU has found, very recently, that a general judicial discretion in English law contravened the principle of certainty.[248] The warning signs are clear.

IV. CONCLUSIONS

In the years following the procedural reforms of the late 1970s, the English courts, led by reform-minded judges such as Lord Diplock and Lord Donaldson, forged a system of public law, based in a unifying idea of public law as concerned with ensuring public power was exercised for the common good and in accordance with axiomatic principles of good administration. This marked public law out as distinct from private law, the core concern of the latter being protection of personal, individual rights and interests. Core features of the system evinced this public interest conception of public law, including the principle of exclusivity, the approach to standing, facets of procedural law, substantive principles of public law, and the approach to remedies, while the system was characterised by broad judicial discretions, which enabled the judiciary to tailor judicial review to the demands of the public interest and effective administration on a case-by-case basis.

The public interest conception has been hugely influential since this formative era, and has been relied upon to guide legal development across that field of law categorised doctrinally as public law. This has proven problematic. The public interest conception was developed by reference to only one sub-field of public law, the common law of review. However, contemporary public law is composed of a plurality of meaningfully different fields of law, each of which performs distinctive functions: it is an error of the first order to maintain that contemporary public law has an inherent functional unity.

In contrast to the public-regarding nature of the public interest conception, human rights law has a strong individualist focus, while its principal function, of affording strong protection to and vindicating the importance of basic individual rights and interests, is much closer in nature to private law fields, such as tort. EU law evinces an integrationist rationale, the principal concern of core doctrines of EU law applied in domestic review proceedings being to ensure the supremacy and effectiveness of EU

[246] eg M Sunkin and AP Le Sueur, 'Applications for Judicial Review: the Requirement of Leave' [1992] *PL* 102; V Bondy and M Sunkin, 'Accessing Judicial Review?' [2008] *PL* 647 (both on the discretion as to permission on judicial review).

[247] C-312/93 *Peterbroeck Van Campenhout & Cie SCS v Belgium* [1995] ECR I-4599, [14].

[248] C-530/11 *European Commission v United Kingdom* [2014] 3 WLR 853 (regarding the judicial discretion as to protective costs orders). I am grateful to David Feldman for directing me to this case. See also C-406/08 *Uniplex (UK) Ltd v NHS Business Services Authority* [2010] 2 CMLR 47, [37]–[43] (judicial discretion in English law governing limitation period on judicial review incompatible with principle of certainty).

norms within municipal law, while different substantive fields of EU law have their own discrete concerns. Where the public interest conception has influenced legal development within these sub-fields, such as human rights law or EU environmental law, it has operated to undermine the coherence of these fields and stymie their distinctively valuable functions. For example, to adopt a public interest approach to remedies, developed by reference to an idea of public law concerned with protection of the collective good, within a field such as human rights law, which has a radically different function of affording strong protection to basic, individual personal rights and interests, is to spawn something akin to the mythical beast, Chimaera, described in Homer's *Illiad*: a monstrous, dangerous incongruity.

Ironically, principal lessons to be drawn from the emergence of the unitary public interest conception of public law are that there is no such thing as a unitary system of public law in contemporary English law, and that it is a grave error to seek to develop disparate fields which perform meaningfully different and distinctly valuable functions by reference to a unitary idea of public law.

5

Process, Substance and the History of Error of Law Review

PHILIP MURRAY*

I. INTRODUCTION

A. Process and Substance in Administrative Law

WRITING AT THE end of the nineteenth century, Sir Henry Maine observed that 'substantive law has at first the look of being gradually secreted in the interstices of procedure'.[1] In few areas of the common law can this better be seen than administrative law. Developed under the prerogative writs of certiorari, prohibition, mandamus and habeas corpus, each with their own highly technical procedures, administrative law has always demonstrated a close relationship between procedural rules and substantive legal doctrine.

All of this could have changed at the beginning of the twentieth century. The private law declaration was recognised as a possible remedy in judicial review,[2] in theory allowing for circumvention of the traditional prerogative writs and the technical procedural rules that had developed under them. However, as Jason Varuhas has explained in another part of this volume,[3] the courts very quickly held that special procedural requirements in judicial review, designed to protect public bodies from vexatious challenges, meant that those seeking declarations were required to bring their applications, just like any other judicial review applicant, through the special judicial review procedure enshrined in Order 53 of the Rules of the Supreme Court.[4] Any opportunity to disconnect judicial review doctrine from judicial review procedure was lost at that point.

* I am grateful to John Bell, Mark Elliott and David Feldman for their comments on earlier drafts of this chapter. I would also like to thank all those who participated in the session at the Public Law Conference in which this paper was presented: questions from Mark Aronson and Rebecca Williams were particularly insightful. All errors, however, remain my own.

[1] H Maine, *Dissertations on Early Law and Custom* (London, Murray, 1891) 389.

[2] *Dyson v Attorney General* [1911] 1 KB 410.

[3] Jason NE Varuhas, Chapter 4, 'The Public Interest Conception of Public Law: Its Procedural Origins and Substantive Implications'.

[4] *O'Reilly v Mackman* [1983] 2 AC 237. RSC Order 53 has now been replaced by Part 54 of the Civil Procedure Rules (CPR).

That being said, it would be disingenuous to say that the primary concern of today's administrative lawyer is with procedural technicalities, rather than substantive law. Just as private law in part came to be freed from its procedural base through the labours of legal treatise writers,[5] administrative law—thanks to the first administrative law textbook writers, Griffith and Street,[6] Wade[7] and de Smith[8]—has come to attain the same mature rationalisation. When we open up today's administrative law textbooks, we see a series of chapters on various 'grounds' of judicial review: error of law, fettering of discretion, *Wednesbury* unreasonableness, and so on. Substantive legal principles are the primary focus of the modern public lawyer, discussed with little reference to legal procedure. When remedies are discussed in administrative law textbooks, such discussion is to be found at the back of the textbook; remedies are considered as a stand-alone topic, to be treated separately from substantive law.[9]

While this rationalisation is to be welcomed for the clarity and maturity it has brought about in administrative law, there are also dangers with it. Administrative law did not develop as a wholly abstract entity: the principles of administrative law came out of cases decided under distinct legal remedies. Changes in procedural rules under these various remedies had a pronounced influence on the development of doctrine, and doctrinal principles developed in one remedial context could not automatically be transplanted into another. To separate process and substance in the history of administrative law is a fool's errand: the two are intimately connected, and attention to the former is crucial if the latter is to be properly understood.

B. Process and Substance in Error of Law Review

We can see the importance of the relationship between process and substance when it comes to judicial review for errors of law, that is, for errors committed by a decision-maker in his or her interpretation or application of legal rules. This chapter will use the history of error of law review to explore the relationship between process and substance in administrative law.

Historically, the primary mechanism for this form of judicial review was the prerogative writ of certiorari. The writ was originally used to review decisions whose formal record disclosed some error of law on its face. However, such records usually contained a very sparse amount of information, and it was often necessary to introduce external evidence, in the form of affidavits, in order to reveal the error of law a decision-maker had committed. In order to limit the circumstances in which such decisions could be challenged, the courts developed a procedural rule that only

[5] See DJ Ibbetson, 'Natural Law and Common Law' (2001) 5 *Edinburgh Law Review* 4, 4–7.

[6] J Griffith and H Street, *Principles of Administrative Law*, 1st edn (London, Pitman, 1952).

[7] HWR Wade, *Administrative Law*, 1st edn (Oxford, Clarendon Press, 1961).

[8] SA de Smith, *Judicial Review of Administrative Action*, 1st edn (London, Stevens, 1959).

[9] HWR Wade and CF Forsyth, *Administrative Law*, 11th edn (Oxford, Oxford University Press, 2014), chs 15 and 16; MC Elliott, *Beatson, Matthews and Elliott's Administrative Law*, 4th edn (Oxford, Oxford University Press, 2011), ch 13; PP Craig, *Administrative Law*, 7th edn (London, Sweet & Maxwell, 2012), ch 26.

where a decision-maker committed a 'jurisdictional' error of law could affidavits be introduced to found a certiorari challenge. The reviewability of an error of law thus depended on whether it could be said to relate to the jurisdiction of a decision-maker to make the decision concerned. The substantive distinction between jurisdictional and non-jurisdictional errors of law can thus be firmly connected with procedural rules concerned with the admissibility of affidavits in certiorari review proceedings: the doctrinal concept of jurisdiction determined the applicability of a procedural rule as to the availability of affidavit evidence. Indeed, as will be seen below, as the nineteenth century progressed, the procedural tail began to wag the substantive dog: the doctrine of jurisdiction itself came to be shaped in response to procedural concerns about the admission of affidavit evidence.[10]

As administrative law developed, the doctrinal distinction between jurisdictional and non-jurisdictional errors of law became, like the rest of administrative law doctrine, detached from its procedural base, serving as a stand-alone doctrinal device that determined the reviewability of administrative decisions. At the same time, commentators began to question the wisdom of the distinction, criticising it for being incoherent and unpredictable. It was said to be difficult, in abstract, to decide what sort of error would be considered 'jurisdictional', leading to what Gordon, writing in the first half of the twentieth century, called a 'wilderness of single instances'.[11] The downfall of the distinction began to look inevitable, and in *Anisminic Ltd v Foreign Compensation Commission*,[12] the House of Lords adopted a conceptualisation of jurisdiction that was so broad that the distinction between jurisdictional and non-jurisdictional errors of law was rendered meaningless.

With some irony, the downfall of that distinction has resulted in recent calls for its resurrection. It is increasingly being recognised that the *Anisminic* principle—that all errors of law are jurisdictional and thus reviewable—unduly limits the autonomy of decision-makers in many circumstances. It is also felt that the principle compounds the so-called 'domino effect' problem whereby invalid administrative acts can deprive subsequent administrative acts of validity.[13] One potential solution, it has been suggested, is to move away from the *Anisminic* approach, re-introducing the distinction between jurisdictional and non-jurisdictional errors of law in certain circumstances, so as to minimise instances of voidness in administrative decisions affected by an error of law, thus ultimately limiting judicial review.[14]

To assess these arguments properly we need to fully understand the history of error of law review, and specifically the volatile history of the doctrinal distinction between jurisdictional and non-jurisdictional errors of law. This history in

[10] P Murray, 'Escaping the Wilderness: *R v Bolton* and Judicial Review for Error of Law' [2016] *Cambridge Law Journal* (forthcoming).

[11] DM Gordon, 'The Relation of Facts to Jurisdiction' (1929) 45 *Law Quarterly Review* 458, 459.

[12] [1969] 2 AC 147.

[13] See CF Forsyth, '"The Metaphysics of Nullity": Invalidity, Conceptual Reasoning and the Rule of Law' in CF Forsyth and I Hare (eds), *The Golden Metwand and the Crooked Cord* (Oxford, Clarendon Press, 1998) 141–60.

[14] See CF Forsyth, 'The Rock and the Sand: Jurisdiction and Remedial Discretion' [2013] *Judicial Review* 360, especially at 377. See also DJ Feldman, 'Error of Law and Flawed Administrative Acts' [2014] *Cambridge Law Journal* 275. See also *R (Cart) v Upper Tribunal* [2011] QB 120 (DC and CA), discussed below.

turn raises a number of important questions. To what extent, for example, can the downfall of the distinction between jurisdictional and non-jurisdictional errors of law be linked to administrative law doctrine's disconnection from the procedural rules under which it was developed? Is it right to say that before *Anisminic* the distinction had become unworkable? To what extent should we take seriously the calls being made for the resurrection of a doctrine fashioned in a particular procedural context that does not necessarily exist today?

As well as offering a study on the history of error of law review, then, another aim of this chapter is to answer some of these questions. The focus of the chapter will be on the prerogative writ of certiorari, it being the remedy under which we see the distinction between jurisdictional and non-jurisdictional errors of law being most fully developed. The chapter will aim to explain the procedural rules that led to the development of the doctrinal distinction, and show how changes in legal procedure further shaped substantive law. At the same time, an evaluation of the substantive distinction itself will be offered, looking at whether Gordon and others were correct in saying that the distinction became unworkable in practice. The focus of this chapter will primarily be put on judicial review in the nineteenth century. This period has been relatively understudied, and yet is crucial to the formation of today's administrative law. At the same time, an eye will be kept on the broader historical picture, and in particular on the viability of emerging claims for a resurrection of the distinction between jurisdictional and non-jurisdictional errors of law. It is hoped that by rooting the distinction between jurisdictional and non-jurisdictional errors of law in its historical and procedural context, we will be better able to assess its suitability for modern administrative law.

II. DEVELOPMENT OF CERTIORARI TO QUASH

We turn then to the prerogative writ of certiorari, perhaps the most important remedy in the history of judicial review.[15] As mentioned above, the distinction between jurisdictional and non-jurisdictional errors of law was important under this writ because it determined when affidavit evidence could be introduced to challenge an administrative decision. In order to understand the procedural context in which the substantive distinction came to be applied, however, we need to begin with a brief history of the development of the writ of certiorari.

Certiorari was initially more of a tool for internal administrative management than it was a judicial remedy. In common use from around 1280,[16] the writ 'was the medieval equivalent of sending for the file':[17] it was used by the king simply to

[15] K Costello, 'The Writ of Certiorari and Review of Summary Criminal Convictions, 1660–1848' (2012) 128 *Law Quarterly Review* 443.

[16] SA de Smith, *Judicial Review of Administrative Action*, 1st edn (London, Stevens, 1959) 259.

[17] SFC Milsom, *Historical Foundations of the Common Law*, 2nd edn (London, Butterworths, 1981) 56. Earlier in his career, Milsom engaged in an admirable, and sadly unpublished, study of the medieval history of the writ: SFC Milsom, 'The Origins of Judicial Review in England: A Preliminary Study' (unpublished dissertation submitted for Prize Fellowship at Trinity College, Cambridge, and available in the College's Wren Library, 1948) 184–99.

demand information from his officials. Writs of certiorari issued mainly from the Court of King's Bench,[18] and their original purpose was to bring up the records of other courts of record, both superior and inferior, so that the King's Bench could be informed of the proceedings set down in the record, and so that the record could be used in other judicial proceedings. Review of the record—or of the decision enshrined by the record—was not the writ's primary purpose.

Over the course of time, however, the writ evolved into a remedy for the judicial review of judicial and administrative decisions. The most important part of this development occurred in the middle decades of the seventeenth century, from around 1630 to 1680. Between 1540 and 1600, a number of Acts of Parliament had conferred important powers on justices of the peace, enabling them to make various types of administrative order. During the course of the sixteenth century, justices came to take charge of the administration of the poor law, the maintenance of the bastardy regime, the regulation of relationships between masters and apprentices and other areas of public administration.[19] A majority of these powers were exercised at informal meetings of the justices, rather than in the more formal setting of the county quarter sessions.[20]

More importantly for the history of certiorari, at the same time justices came to be given extensive new powers to convict wrongdoers for minor ('summary') offences outside of quarter sessions at meetings that came to be known as 'petty sessions'.[21] It was this extension in justices' powers of summary conviction, rather than their accrual of extensive administrative powers, which necessitated judicial review in the King's Bench. Though justices' powers of summary conviction only related to minor offences, in theory they infringed the common law principle that a man could only be tried by a jury of his peers. It is no surprise, then, that both common law judges and legal commentators viewed such powers with 'deep suspicion'.[22] Paley, in his treatise on the subject, described summary proceedings as 'remarkably contrasted with the spirit of our primitive institutions'.[23] Burn's important handbook for justices of the peace was even more scathing.[24] Blackstone was perhaps the strongest critic of all.[25] These new powers thus posed serious constitutional problems, making it imperative that judicial review was extended so as to make their exercise as controllable as possible by the common law courts.

Finding a remedy that allowed for greater judicial supervision of these powers was, however, difficult. The ancient writ of error allowed for the review of justices'

[18] Though the writ, at least in its early history, would also issue from the Court of Chancery: WS Holdsworth, *A History of English Law*, 4th edn (London, Methuen & Co, 1927) vol 1, 228.

[19] EG Henderson, *Foundations of English Administrative Law: Certiorari and Mandamus in the Seventeenth Century* (Cambridge, MA, Harvard University Press, 1963) 93.

[20] JH Baker, *An Introduction to English Legal History*, 4th edn (London, Butterworths, 2002) 24–25.

[21] ibid 25 and 511. See also W Paley, *The Law and Practice of Summary Convictions*, 1st edn (London, Pheney & Sons, 1814) xxv–xxxii.

[22] Baker, *An Introduction to English Legal History* (n 20) 25, 511.

[23] Paley, *The Law and Practice of Summary Convictions* (n 21) xv.

[24] R Burn, *The Justice of the Peace and Parish Officer*, 21st edn (London, Strahan, 1810) vol 1, 553–54.

[25] W Blackstone, *Commentaries on the Laws of England*, 1st edn (Oxford, Clarendon Press, 1769) vol 4, 277–80.

decisions at quarter sessions, but would not apply to decisions made by the justices at petty sessions.[26] While a trespassory action might be available for petty sessions decisions where justices acted without jurisdiction, and where the enforcement of their decision constituted a trespass to the person or to goods,[27] *intra-jurisdictional* conduct of justices at petty sessions was free from judicial control. The writ of certiorari was adapted to fill this lacuna. It was sent to justices of the peace, calling upon them to send up their records to the King's Bench so that they might be 'certified'. To begin with, the King's Bench had a choice as to what it would do with the record once it arrived from the justices: the court could either quash the order on the basis of some error in the record,[28] or it could require the trial to be re-heard *de novo* before the bar of the court itself at Westminster. Over the later decades of the seventeenth century, however, the King's Bench slowly started to emphasise the use of the writ to quash a record rather than to secure a re-trial of the issue before the reviewing court, and by 1677 certiorari was being used exclusively for the quashing of convictions and also administrative decisions of justices of the peace.[29]

At around the same time, the writ also began to be used against other decision-makers. While the writ was still used primarily in the context of the decision-making powers of justices of the peace, it was soon extended to the commissioners of the sewers and then to a wider range of administrative bodies exercising statutory powers.[30] By the beginning of the eighteenth century, in a case concerning the College of Physicians, Holt CJ was able to say that it was 'a consequence of all jurisdiction to have their proceedings returned [to the King's Bench] by certiorari to be examined here'.[31]

It is out of this historical development that the distinction between jurisdictional and non-jurisdictional errors of law came to be fully rationalised. To understand this fully, however, we need to look at how evidence was used in certiorari proceedings before the King's Bench: as suggested at the beginning of this chapter, it was procedural rules concerning the admission of evidence that shaped the substantive principles of error of law review.

III. EVIDENCE IN CERTIORARI PROCEEDINGS

As we have just seen, it was the acquisition of new powers of criminal conviction by justices of the peace, along with the increase in their administrative powers, that

[26] A Rubinstein, *Jurisdiction and Illegality* (Oxford, Clarendon Press, 1965) 62–63.

[27] ibid 63–65.

[28] Technically this was a separate process: once a rule of court had been secured for a writ of certiorari, a separate rule would then be sought upon the return of the writ in order to have the record quashed. As certiorari developed, however, it came to be associated exclusively with the quashing of records: the writ would always be sought with an eye to quashing the decision.

[29] Henderson, *Foundations of English Administrative Law* (n 19) 109. For a more detailed study of this development see ibid ch 3.

[30] *Commins v Massam* (1642) TNA: PRO KB 29/291, m 39; Henderson, *Foundations of English Administrative Law* (n 19) 109.

[31] *Groenvelt v Burwell* (1700) 1 Ld Raym 454, 469. See also the *R v Inhabitants of Glamorganshire* (1700) 1 Salk 146, 1 Ld Raym 580.

led to the development of certiorari as a remedy for quashing decisions. In light of this, it might be thought that the drawing of distinctions between the different types of decision would be unnecessary: whether the decision being challenged was administrative or criminal in its nature, certiorari was equally available. Yet to think of criminal certiorari and administrative certiorari as representing identical proceedings would be mistaken. As a matter of practice at least, there were important differences between these two uses of the writ. This can be explained by the different ways in which evidence was used in these different contexts—differences of use which, in time, influenced the development of the distinction between jurisdictional and non-jurisdictional errors of law.

When it came to challenges to justices' summary convictions, very little evidence was needed to secure the writ of certiorari other than the record itself. This is because justices' summary convictions were recorded with a lot of factual detail, producing so-called 'speaking records' which disclosed most of the facts and legal reasoning that grounded the justices' conviction, and thus nearly all possible errors that a justice of the peace might commit.[32] Much of this review was technical and formalistic, the court looking for technical deficiencies in the way the substance of a decision was recorded.[33] However, from the start of the eighteenth century in this form of review, the King's Bench also began to look at the substance of the decision itself to see whether it disclosed some substantive error of law.[34] This came to be known as review for error of law on the face of the record. Save in cases where certiorari was displaced by Parliament by means of an ouster clause, in which case an error of law had to be jurisdictional if it were to be reviewed (such reasoning was long adopted before *Anisminic*),[35] it did not matter whether the error of law that was alleged was jurisdictional or non-jurisdictional: any error of law disclosed by the face of the record could lead to the record being quashed.

In contrast to justices' summary convictions, justices' administrative orders were much sparser in detail, disclosing far fewer errors on their face. A typical example can be seen in a case decided at the beginning of the nineteenth century, *R v Inhabitants of Great Marlow*.[36] In that case a decision of justices of the peace to appoint a certain person as a parish overseer was contested on the ground that the justices had previously made four valid appointments of overseers and thus could not, within the terms of section 3 of the Poor Relief Act 1743,[37] appoint any other overseer. We can see from the record of their decision that to argue that this error of law had

[32] S Anderson, 'Judicial Review' in W Cornish, S Anderson, R Cox *et al*, *The Oxford History of the Laws of England* (Oxford, Oxford University Press, 2010) vol 11, 490. A template example of such records can be found in Burn, *The Justice of the Peace and Parish Officer* (n 24) 555–59.

[33] Costello, 'The Writ of Certiorari and Review of Summary Criminal Convictions, 1660–1848' (n 15) 445–48.

[34] ibid 448–49.

[35] See Rubinstein, *Jurisdiction and Illegality* (n 26) 71–73. No-certiorari clauses were first held to be ineffective in the case of jurisdictional errors of law in the decision of the King's Bench in *R v Moreley* (1760) 2 Burr 1040.

[36] (1802) 2 East 244.

[37] Stat 17 Geo II, c 38.

been committed on the basis of the record alone would have been impossible. All the record said was this:

> Bucks. We two of His Majesty's justices of the peace in and for the said county one whereof is of the quorum, do hereby nominate and appoint James Field, being a substantial householder of the parish of Great Marlow in the said county to be one of the overseers of the poor of the said parish, according to the direction of the statute in that case made and provided.[38]

In order to advance their cases properly, applicants for certiorari in cases like *Great Marlow* had to go beyond the record, introducing affidavit evidence to flesh out the details of the case and show how the decision that was reached was affected by some error of law. From around the middle of the eighteenth century, the King's Bench started to allow affidavit evidence to be introduced.[39]

Crucially, however, the King's Bench did not allow affidavits to be admitted whenever the record needed to be supplemented with external evidence. While it had been perceived to be constitutionally necessary to make the review of justices' summary convictions as widely available as possible, this impetus was not felt in the context of justices' administrative orders, which did not infringe any principle as important as that of trial by jury. Furthermore, allowing the same scope of review in the administrative context as was allowed in the criminal context risked causing administrative chaos by rendering all proceedings leading to all administrative decisions vulnerable to re-examination through certiorari. The admissibility of affidavits was therefore limited. The circumstances by which affidavits could be admitted were the product of a compromise. On the one hand, the court recognised the importance of treating formal records as conclusive. On the other hand, it was recognised that the conclusive nature of records should not be allowed to formally enshrine decisions made in circumstances where a decision-maker had no legal power to act. Affidavits came to be admissible, therefore, only in circumstances where the alleged error of law related to the jurisdiction of the decision-maker.

The procedural rule that affidavits could be admitted to prove a jurisdictional error of law, therefore, contributed significantly to the development of the doctrinal distinction between jurisdictional and non-jurisdictional errors of law: it was the procedural rule that gave the doctrinal distinction practical relevance. In the context of administrative orders made by justices of the peace, and also those made by other administrative decision-makers, the distinction between jurisdictional and non-jurisdictional errors of law demarcated those decisions that were reviewable from those that were not. Only if an error of law could be described as jurisdictional could affidavit evidence be introduced to support the challenge; only if affidavit evidence could be introduced would the challenge stand any chance of success.

[38] TNA: PRO KB 16/23/1.

[39] Henderson, *Foundations of English Administrative Law* (n 19) 144; Rubinstein, *Jurisdiction and Illegality* (n 26) 70–71. This practice has been traced to the decisions of the King's Bench in *R v Wakefield* (1758) 1 Burr 485 and *R v Inhabitants of Hitcham* (1760) 1 Burr SC 589: LL Jaffe, 'Judicial Review: Constitutional and Jurisdictional Fact' (1957) 70 *Harvard Law Review* 953, 958 n 21.

The distinction between jurisdictional and non-jurisdictional errors of law was thus a control device for limiting the reviewability of administrative decisions: through their application of the distinction between jurisdictional and non-jurisdictional errors of law, the justices of the King's Bench could influence the admissibility of affidavit evidence, thus keeping the scope of judicial review under control. The precise conceptualisation of jurisdiction was therefore crucial to the availability of certiorari: the broader jurisdictional issues were defined, the more reviewable administrative decisions would be. It is this we must now consider as we turn from the procedural history of certiorari to the history of the substantive legal doctrine that developed under it.

IV. CERTIORARI, AFFIDAVITS AND THE CONCEPT OF JURISDICTION

Turning to the doctrine of jurisdiction, it is important to begin with the work of Amnon Rubinstein, whose monograph on the subject, written in 1965, offers an illuminating study of the history of error of law review. Rubinstein paints a picture of error of law review in which, during the course of the nineteenth and twentieth centuries, the courts moved from using a clearly articulated, narrowly defined conception of jurisdiction to one that was much broader and whose exact limits were hard to pin down.[40] Rubinstein laid the blame for this, in part, on the procedural rule that affidavits could only be introduced where a jurisdictional error of law was alleged. His argument was that the desirability—indeed, the necessity—of admitting affidavit evidence, and thus the need to phrase challenges in jurisdictional terms, led to a widening of the court's conceptualisation of jurisdiction. As more and more applicants sought to present the errors of law committed by decision-makers as jurisdictional (so as to admit affidavit evidence), pressure was increasingly put on the conceptualisation of jurisdiction adopted by the King's Bench: the more clearly wrong a decision presented to the King's Bench in fact was, the more tempting it would be to inflate artificially the conception of jurisdiction, allowing for review. The outcome of this development, Rubinstein claimed, was a shift in the court's conceptualisation of jurisdiction. While the courts, according to Rubinstein, began with a conception of jurisdiction which had 'limited meaning and clarity of principle',[41] their conception, by the end of the nineteenth century, was much broader, meaning that 'decisions of inferior [decision-makers] were not only reviewed by the superior courts but also partly reheard and retried by the latter'.[42]

Rubinstein's argument might seem, at first glance, to have a good deal of sense to it. It is certainly right that the concept of jurisdiction came under a lot of pressure precisely because there was a great need, given the sparse nature of administrative orders, to admit affidavit evidence, and because the concept of jurisdiction was the doctrinal gateway through which such evidence could be admitted. And yet, when we look at the case law concerning jurisdictional errors of law, the historical

[40] Rubinstein, *Jurisdiction and Illegality* (n 26) 71–73.
[41] ibid 70.
[42] ibid 71.

development of the court's conceptualisation of jurisdiction is very different to that described by Rubinstein. On a closer inspection of the case law it will be seen that rather than *broadening* the concept of jurisdiction, the King's Bench, during the course of the nineteenth century at least, came to adopt a narrower, more strictly defined conception of jurisdiction.

When looking at certiorari cases from the nineteenth century, a clear historical trajectory can be discerned. At the start of the nineteenth century, the conception of jurisdiction adopted by the King's Bench in certiorari cases was, on the whole, limited. However, little attention was paid to the precise limits of the concept of jurisdiction. From the 1840s onwards, however, the court started to articulate its conceptualisation of jurisdiction in much clearer terms. The conception that was adopted emphasised that once a decision-maker properly possessed jurisdiction, it could not then be lost by an erroneous decision made during the course of an administrative inquiry. Jurisdictional questions were identified as those that related to the subject matter or scope of an administrative inquiry, and were determinable at an inquiry's commencement. The adoption of this very limited conception of jurisdiction continued right through to the end of the nineteenth century.

It is important to be clear from that start precisely why it is argued that Rubinstein was wrong in his history of error of law review. In a sense, the conceptualisation of jurisdiction adopted by the King's Bench from the 1840s onwards was as limited as that which it adopted in the earlier period: the conception of 'limited meaning'[43] that Rubinstein noted. But it is suggested here that what Rubinstein failed to notice when constructing his history of error of law review was that, at least in certiorari proceedings, it was not until the 1840s that the 'limited meaning' of jurisdiction was accompanied with 'clarity of principle':[44] only then did the court begin expressly to articulate the conceptual language that *ensured* its conception of jurisdiction was limited. Until this shift in conceptual language, artificial inflation of the concept of jurisdiction in cases where more review might have been considered desirable was a real possibility. Only after the 1840s could this inflation be avoided. This explains the broader error in Rubinstein's history of jurisdiction: instead of a period in which the conception of jurisdiction adopted by the courts becomes wider and less strictly articulated, as Rubinstein alleged, we instead see the opposite phenomenon during the course of the nineteenth century, that is, a gradual restricting of the conceptual limits of jurisdiction over time.

A fuller account of this historical development will be provided elsewhere,[45] and need not be repeated here. The purpose of this chapter is not so much to chart this development in detail, but rather to assess the significance of the development for wider questions as to both the relationship between process and substance in administrative law and the continued utility of the distinction between jurisdictional and non-jurisdictional errors of law. Nonetheless, a couple of cases, decided either end of the nineteenth century, typify this historical development, and we can begin by considering them before going on to make a wider assessment of the law.

[43] ibid 70.
[44] ibid.
[45] Murray, 'Escaping the Wilderness' (n 10).

The first case is *R v Justices of the North Riding*,[46] decided by the King's Bench in 1827. In that case, justices of the peace had made an order allowing the accounts of the highway surveyors of a parish. Their decision was brought up to the King's Bench by a writ of certiorari, where it was sought to be quashed on the ground that the justices had not had jurisdiction to make their order. It was said that justices of the peace could only make such an order if the accounts had initially been submitted to a single justice of the peace, sitting at a special petty sessions hearing held for the purpose of considering such accounts. This was what the Highways Act 1773[47] required. It was therefore argued that the justices had committed a jurisdictional error of law by deciding to hear the case and to make the order concerned.

In the King's Bench, it was agreed that the order of the justices was invalid. Abbot CJ said:

> The statute certainly requires that the accounts shall be exhibited before one justice in such a manner as may enable him to exercise judgment upon them. The surveyor … neglected to take the assessments with him when he went before the justice, it was therefore impossible to ascertain whether the accounts were or were not correct. I think that sufficient was not done to satisfy the words of the statute, and that the allowance by the petty sessions was therefore invalid.[48]

Abbot CJ's judgment is characteristic of its time.[49] We are told that the justices' order was invalid because 'sufficient was not done to satisfy the words of the statute'. But little was said by Abbot CJ as to the precise borderline between jurisdictional and non-jurisdictional errors of law. It could be said that any error of law would lead to a decision-maker acting in a way that was insufficient to satisfy the words of the statute. What if an argument had been made that, substantively, the accounts of the surveyor should not have been allowed, and that the justices had acted without jurisdiction for that reason? Would the court have allowed certiorari to be brought on the basis of such an argument, if counsel could persuade them that allowing the accounts in such circumstances would mean sufficient had not been done to satisfy the statute? Abbot CJ's concern was clearly with the question of whether the justices of the peace had power to consider the accounts: his focus seems to have been on the commencement of an administrative inquiry, rather than on decisions made during the course of his inquiry. Abbot CJ was chiefly concerned with the simple question of whether the necessary preconditions for that inquiry existed, and there is no sense from his judgment that he would have countenanced substantive review of the merits of decisions made after the inquiry had properly commenced. Like most cases of this period, then, Abbot CJ seems to have favoured a limited approach to review. But in truth the doctrinal foundations of his judgment are so ambiguous that we cannot be sure how limited this approach really was.

[46] (1827) 6 B & C 152.

[47] Stat 13 Geo III, c 78.

[48] *R v Justices of the North Riding* (1827) 6 B & C 152, 153.

[49] See also *R v Allen* (1812) 15 East 333; *R v James* (1815) 2 M & S 321; *R v Walsall (Inhabitants)* (1818) 2 B & Ald 157; *R v Justices of Somersetshire* (1822) 1 Dow & Ry 443; *R v Commissioners of Sewers for Tower Hamlets* (1829) 9 B & C 517; *R v Justices of the North Riding* (1827) 6 B & C 152; *R v Justices of Denbighshire* (1830) 1 B & Ad 616; *R v Justices of Cambridgeshire* (1835) 4 A & E 111; *R v Justices of Cheshire* (1838) 8 A & E 398; *R v Justices of Lancashire* (1839) 11 A & E 144.

Following a decision of the Queen's Bench in 1841, however, the court began to adopt in certiorari proceedings a much more clearly articulated conception of jurisdiction. That decision was *R v Bolton*,[50] and it was crucially important because it expressly identified jurisdictional questions to be those concerned with the scope of an administrative inquiry: questions as to whether the subject matter of the decision the decision-maker was asked to make was one which fell within the range of his statutory powers. Importantly, jurisdictional questions were those that were addressed at the commencement of an administrator's decision-making process: once a decision-maker correctly determined that he had power to begin the decision-making process, nothing could happen during the course of the inquiry to deprive him of jurisdiction. Lord Denman CJ summarised this approach in *Bolton* when he said that 'jurisdiction does not depend on the truth or falsehood of the charge [laid before a decision-maker], but upon its nature: it is determinable on the commencement, not at the conclusion, of the inquiry'.[51]

From 1841 onwards, the approach to jurisdictional error of law set out in *Bolton* was universally adopted.[52] We can see this, for example, in our second case that typifies the history of nineteenth-century error of law review: *R v St Olave's Board of Works*, decided in 1857.[53] The Metropolis Management Act 1855[54] brought to an end the Commissioners of Improvement for Southwark. Under section 90 of the Act, the administrative staff of the Commissioners could apply to district boards of works for compensation for lost earnings caused by the abolition of the Commissioners. In the case at hand, a former clerk of the Commissioners had applied to the St Olave's Board of Works for compensation. His claim had been rejected, but the Metropolitan Board of Works allowed his appeal and awarded him compensation. The decision of the Metropolitan Board of Works to allow the appeal was challenged in the Queen's Bench by a writ of certiorari. Supported by detailed affidavits, it was argued that the Metropolitan Board of Works had acted without jurisdiction. Under section 214 of the 1855 Act, every 'officer' could, within six months of the Commissioners' abolition, make a claim for compensation from the district board of works. Any person making such a claim whose claim was refused by the district board could appeal to the Metropolitan Board of Works, which could award compensation to the claimant in the like manner as the district board was empowered to do if it appeared that it would be just to do so. Here it was argued that the order should be quashed on the ground that the clerk did not constitute an 'officer' of the Commissioners for the purposes of the statutory scheme. It was said that whether or not the clerk was an 'officer' was a question which conditioned the district board's jurisdiction, and thus also the jurisdiction of the Metropolitan Board.

[50] (1841) 1 QB 66.
[51] ibid 74.
[52] There are many such cases, but see, eg, *R v Arkwright* (1848) 12 QB 960; *R v Jarvis* (1854) 3 E & B 640; *R v Ratepayers of Northowram and Clayton* (1865) LR 1 QB 110; *R v Local Government Board* (1873) LR 8 QB 227; *R v Lee* (1876) 1 QBD 198; *R v Justices of the Central Criminal Court* (1886) 17 QB 598; *Ex parte Daisy Hopkins* (1891) 61 LJQB 240; *R v Lord Mayor of London, ex parte Boaler* [1893] 2 QB 146.
[53] (1857) 8 E & B 529.
[54] Stat 18 & 19 Vict, c 120.

In refusing the writ of certiorari, the majority of the justices of the Queen's Bench followed the conception of jurisdiction put forward in *R v Bolton*. Lord Campbell CJ commented that under 'well established principles' consistent with what the court had said in *Bolton*, the Metropolitan Board had jurisdiction: the sole criterion of the board's jurisdiction was an appeal being lodged from the district board.[55] This was a question to be addressed at the beginning of the inquiry, before the Metropolitan Board applied its mind to more substantive questions it was given statutory powers to determine. The question of whether the clerk was an 'officer', then, did not condition the jurisdiction of the board at all: it was not a question that the board had to determine before embarking upon its decision-making inquiry, but was rather 'the very point which on the appeal they were to inquire into'.[56]

The *North Riding* and *St Olave's* cases typify the pattern of the case law that we see unfolding throughout the nineteenth century. Until the decision of *R v Bolton* in 1841, the concept of jurisdiction was loosely articulated and at times suffered from a degree of ambiguity. Many cases in this period certainly evince a preference for limited review, holding that an erroneous exercise of power did not lead to a decision-maker acting outside his jurisdiction. But before 1841 jurisdiction was either not referred to expressly as a concept, or its limitations were not conceptualised in clear, unambiguous terms. In contrast, from the decision in *Bolton*, the admissibility of affidavits came to be grounded in a limited and clearly articulated conception of jurisdiction: jurisdiction was expressly said to be concerned with the scope of an administrative inquiry, to be assessed exclusively at the start of an inquiry and thus something which could not be lost by the wrong exercise of a prima facie validly conferred power.

All of this must cause us to re-assess Rubinstein's characterisation of the history of error of law review. Although affidavit evidence was clearly desirable, indeed necessary, in nineteenth-century certiorari challenges to administrative orders, it is by no means certain that the concept of jurisdiction was artificially expanded in error of law cases so that affidavits could be more readily introduced. In fact, the reverse seems to have been the case, with the King's Bench apparently favouring a limited approach to error of law review, and, from the decision in *R v Bolton* in 1841, tightening its conception of jurisdiction, explicitly putting forward one that was expressly limited and thus restricting the possibility even further of affidavits being introduced.

Rubinstein's argument that the introduction of affidavit evidence eventually led to the concept of jurisdiction losing its 'limited meaning and clarity of principle'[57] seems, therefore, to be misplaced. If we reflect on this history of the affidavit rule, however, this should not be too surprising. The procedural rule that affidavits could only be introduced where a jurisdictional error of law was alleged, it will be recalled, was the product of a compromise: a compromise between the desirability of reviewing administrative decisions and preventing an abundance of challenges to such decisions leading to administrative chaos. We have seen that the affidavit rule developed

[55] *St Olave's* (n 53) 533.

[56] ibid. See also Coleridge J at 533–34 and Wightman J at 534.

[57] Rubinstein, *Jurisdiction and Illegality* (n 26) 70.

as a control device, allowing certiorari in those cases where it was considered completely necessary (that is, where decisions were made without jurisdiction), while preventing certiorari from being too widely available. In light of this history, we should not be surprised to find a limited conception of jurisdiction being applied consistently through the nineteenth century. Once we change our way of seeing the affidavit rule, viewing it as a way of *limiting* review rather than, like Rubinstein, seeing it as a way of facilitating review, the history revealed by the case law makes a lot more sense.

Seeing the affidavit rule as a control device engineered to limit review also helps explain why exactly the conception of jurisdiction came to be more explicitly limited from *R v Bolton* onwards. As has been explained above, since the seventeenth century the principal ground on which summary convictions were reviewed was error of law—jurisdictional or not—on the face of the record.[58] On the whole it was unnecessary to have recourse to affidavit evidence and thus the conceptual distinction between jurisdictional and non-jurisdictional errors of law: records of summary convictions were much more detailed than their administrative counterparts, and thus many more errors were discoverable on their face. However, from the beginning of the nineteenth century Parliament made inroads into this form of review. Generous speaking records came to be supplanted by short-form convictions, mandated by statute,[59] which required only the smallest amounts of detail. As Lord Sumner came to say some years later in *R v Nat Bell Liquors Ltd*,[60] the effect of these statutory developments was that '[t]he face of the record "spoke" no longer: it was the inscrutable face of a sphinx'.[61]

It is these changes to the review of summary convictions, it is suggested, that better explains the decision in *R v Bolton* and the subsequent adoption of a precisely defined, limited conception of jurisdiction.[62] Under the statutory reforms to the summary conviction procedure, the Queen's Bench was limited in its oversight of summary convictions to those cases where a jurisdictional error of law was alleged. Now that review for error of law on the face of the record was no longer available, just like in certiorari review of administrative records, jurisdictional errors of law were the only legal errors that the court could review. The reforms manifested a preference instead for conclusive, localised review in the counties, rather than centralised review in Westminster, favouring statutory appeals to the quarter sessions as the primary means of redress. In order to prevent this new system of review being

[58] This form of review sat alongside other, less ideal forms of challenge, namely, appeal by case stated and trespassory proceedings. On the details of the case stated process, see Anderson, 'Judicial Review' (n 32) 488, 491–92. An important example of the use of ordinary trespassory proceedings to challenge administrative orders is *Brittain v Kinnaird* (1819) 1 Brod & Bing 432.

[59] See, eg, Summary Proceedings Act 1822 (Stat 3 Geo IV, c 23); Larceny Act 1827 (Stat 7 & 8 Geo IV, c 29), ss 71–73; Malicious Injuries to Property (England) Act 1827 (Stat 7 & 8 Geo IV, c 30), ss 37–39; Offences Against the Person Act 1828 (Stat 9 Geo IV, c 31), ss 35–36. The reforms were substantially enlarged by the so-called Jervis Acts of 1848: Indictable Offences Act 1848 (Stat 11 & 12 Vict, c 42), Summary Jurisdiction Act 1848 (Stat 11 & 12 Vict, c 43) and Justices Protection Act 1848 (Stat 11 & 12 Vict, c 44). See Anderson, 'Judicial Review' (n 32) 492; see also D Freestone and JC Richardson, 'The Making of English Criminal Law: Sir John Jervis and his Acts' [1980] *Criminal Law Review* 5.

[60] [1922] 2 AC 128 (PC).

[61] ibid 159.

[62] See generally Murray, 'Escaping the Wilderness' (n 10).

undermined, however, it was crucial for the Queen's Bench to tighten its conception of jurisdiction. New pressures came to be put on the distinction between jurisdictional and non-jurisdictional errors of law once affidavit-based certiorari became the only real way of securing superior-court oversight of justices' exercise of their summary powers. If the court had not consciously limited its conception of jurisdiction, protecting the relatively ambiguous conception it previously adopted from new pressures for inflation, then Parliament's intention in passing the statutory reforms would have been frustrated. Once adopted, this conception of jurisdiction became universal, being adopted in the administrative context as well as the criminal context.

From this overview of the nineteenth-century history of error of law review, then, we can begin to answer some of the questions raised at the start of this chapter. We have seen that the substantive distinction between jurisdictional and non-jurisdictional errors of law was very much shaped by developments in legal procedure. It was the overwhelming need for the review of administrative decisions, and thus for affidavits, that led to the development of the distinction as a control device for the limiting of review. And it was substantive changes to the summary conviction process that led to the tightening of the concept of jurisdiction in the 1840s. Aside from these conclusions that we might start to draw about the relationship between process and substance in administrative law, we have also seen, with regard to our substantive assessment of the distinction between jurisdictional and non-jurisdictional error of law, that the courts, throughout the nineteenth century, managed consistently to adopt a conception of jurisdiction that enshrined limited review: there is little sense from the case law of Gordon's wilderness of single instances. We might wonder, then, what caused the breakdown in the distinction between jurisdictional and non-jurisdictional errors of law. To answer this question, we need to look at developments in administrative law that occurred in the twentieth century. This will also raise more questions about the relationship between process and substance.

V. TWENTIETH-CENTURY DEVELOPMENTS IN ERROR OF LAW REVIEW

Given that by the end of the nineteenth century a clearly defined and limited conception of jurisdiction was being employed by the courts in certiorari proceedings for error of law, we might wonder why things went so supposedly awry over the course of the twentieth century. If a narrowly defined conception of jurisdiction could be employed so consistently throughout the nineteenth century, why was it that this conception came to be seen as untenable a century later? What was it that led to Gordon's wilderness of single instances, and to the eventual abandonment of the distinction between jurisdictional and non-jurisdictional errors of law?

To begin with, it should be noted that in a good number of judicial review cases at the beginning of the twentieth century, right up to the decision of the House of Lords in *Anisminic*, the limited conception of jurisdiction epitomised by the decision in *R v Bolton* continued to be adopted. At the beginning of the 1920s, Lord Sumner in the *Nat Bell* case[63] affirmed that the approach to jurisdiction adopted in *Bolton* had

[63] n 60.

'never been seriously disputed in England'.[64] And even as late as 1953, the orthodox understanding of the concept of jurisdiction could be described as the following:

> When the inferior tribunal has jurisdiction to decide a matter, it cannot (merely because it incidentally misconstrues a statute, or admits illegal evidence, or rejects legal evidence, or misdirects itself as to the weight of evidence, or convicts without evidence) be deemed to exceed or abuse its jurisdiction.[65]

For most of the twentieth century, jurisdictional errors of law were exclusively defined in narrow terms: errors of law would be considered jurisdictional only if they related to the scope of an administrative inquiry, and were determinable at its commencement.[66]

Nevertheless, as the twentieth century progressed, the size of the state increased to such an extent that the limited form of review enshrined by this conception of jurisdiction became untenable: the control device invented to limit review started to be thought of as too limiting. The welfare state created by the likes of the National Health Service Act 1946, the National Insurance Act 1946 and the National Assistance Act 1948 brought with it a whole host of statutory powers allowing for greater inroads to be made into the lives of a greater number of citizens. Increases in the number of administrative decisions and their invasiveness necessitated more judicial review.

From the 1950s, judicial review thus began to be reformed to meet the new needs of society. Initially, the courts tried to facilitate more judicial review by re-envisaging the doctrine of error of law on the face of the record. The doctrine was revived by Lord Denning in *R v Northumberland Compensation Appeal Tribunal, ex parte Shaw*,[67] a case which 'appeased, at least partially, the public demand for better justice in the welfare state'.[68] The courts expanded what was meant by 'the record': it was no longer understood to mean just the formal recording of the decision reached in a case, but covered all documents, and even oral evidence, pertaining to an administrative decision.[69] By extending the concept of the record, more errors of law could be put before the court in certiorari proceedings. And because it was unnecessary for an error of law on the face of the record to be labelled as jurisdictional before the decision it affected could be quashed, the courts were able to maintain the limited conception of jurisdiction that had been developed and refined during the nineteenth century. It was the courts' conception of what constituted a record which now served as the control device in certiorari proceedings.

The rediscovery of certiorari review for errors of law on the face of the record satisfied much of the perceived need for more extensive judicial review. It was particularly

[64] ibid 154.

[65] Halsbury and GT Simonds (eds), *Laws of England*, 3rd edn (London, Butterworths, 1953) vol II, 62.

[66] See, eg, *R (Limerick Corporation) v Local Government Board* [1922] 2 IR 76 (Court of Appeal in Southern Ireland) and *R v Justices of Weston-super-Mare, ex parte Barkers (Contractors) Ltd* [1944] 1 All ER 747 (King's Bench Division). A wider range of cases is discussed in Murray, 'Escaping the Wilderness' (n 10).

[67] [1952] 1 KB 338.

[68] Wade and Forsyth, *Administrative Law* (n 9) 226.

[69] *R v Medical Appeal Tribunal, ex parte Gilmore* [1957] 1 QB 574; *R v Chertsey Justices, ex parte Franks* [1961] 2 QB 152.

useful in the context of the various statutory tribunals created to administer the welfare state in the 1940s, from whose decisions there were few opportunities of appeal.[70] Yet Lord Denning's decision in *ex parte Shaw* was far from a panacea. The problem was that this form of review could only be secured through certiorari, and certiorari was not always an attractive remedy. Lord Denning himself, speaking extra-judicially a few years before *Shaw*, likened the use of certiorari in public law challenges to the use of 'the pick and shovel ... for the winning of coal'.[71] Certiorari and the other prerogative remedies were hampered by a number of procedural deficiencies: there was a six-month time limit for seeking them; permission was required to bring an application; disclosure of evidence could not be obtained from the opposing party, nor could interrogatories be served; cross-examination was seldom granted at hearings; and the prerogative remedies could not be sought alongside other remedies, such as damages.

These limitations meant that an alternative remedy was needed. The private law declaration, first recognised as a public law remedy in *Dyson v Attorney-General* in 1911,[72] became the preferred remedy for judicial review challenges. Declarations could be sought through a separate procedure free from the limitations which attached to the prerogative remedies, making it very desirable for those seeking to challenge administrative decisions. Although declarations were made available alongside the prerogative remedies in 1977, through the 'application for judicial review' introduced by Order 53 of the Rules of the Supreme Court,[73] the old procedural limitations attaching to the prerogative writs still applied when this procedure was followed. Up until 1983, however, applicants had a choice to proceed outside the formal judicial review procedure when seeking a declaration, being able instead to bring an ordinary private law action for a declaration.[74]

The increased use of declarations in public law resulted in a new emphasis being put on the substantive doctrinal distinction between jurisdictional and non-jurisdictional errors of law. Declarations, when granted, did not effect changes in the legal situation of those seeking the remedy. They were, unsurprisingly, merely declaratory: granting the remedy, the court simply declared the existing legal position of the parties to the litigation. Because of this, any error of law that founded the declaration had to be jurisdictional. If the error of law was not jurisdictional, then it would mean that the decision reached was still *intra vires*: declaring such would be pointless, and the person affected by the decision would still need to have recourse to certiorari, by which such a decision could be quashed, assuming the non-jurisdictional error of law was disclosed on the face of the record. It became crucial, then, for errors of law to be labelled as jurisdictional if a declaration was to be effective.

In twentieth-century declaration proceedings, therefore, the distinction between jurisdictional and non-jurisdictional errors of law was used significantly differently

[70] Wade and Forsyth, *Administrative Law* (n 9) 226.

[71] AT Denning, *Freedom Under the Law* (London, Stevens and Sons, 1949) 126.

[72] Cited above. See Anderson, 'Judicial Review' (n 32) 504–06. In 1911, the remedy was relatively recent: it was formally introduced only in 1983 in RSC Order 25, r 5.

[73] This was given statutory footing in Senior Courts Act 1981, s 31, and can now be found in CPR Part 54.

[74] cf *O'Reilly v Mackman* (n 4).

than in certiorari proceedings. It is important for us to be clear on exactly how the distinction was used differently. Originally, it will be recalled, the substantive distinction between jurisdictional and non-jurisdictional errors of law was developed in response to a procedural need for the admission of more affidavit evidence in certiorari proceedings: the distinction was the control device that limited judicial review. The role the distinction played in the middle of the twentieth century, however, was quite different. Unshackled from the procedural context in which it was developed, the distinction ceased being a control device designed to limit review, but instead became a doctrinal gateway through which further review was facilitated. With the increased popularity of the private law declaration as a remedy for judicial review, it became necessary for every error of law—indeed, for every breach of every principle of administrative law—to be characterised as leading a decision-maker outside his or her jurisdiction. This put a newfound pressure on the coherence of the concept of jurisdiction. When the distinction between jurisdictional and non-jurisdictional errors of law served as a control device limiting review, it was easy for the courts to maintain their limited conception of jurisdiction: the limited conception sat easily with the desire to restrict review. But once the distinction became the mechanism for effecting more review, then its conception was untenable: a conception that facilitated, rather than limited, review was needed. Viewed in this light, the inflation of jurisdiction seen in *Anisminic* (itself a case in which the remedy sought was a declaration) should be seen as inevitable.

From the twentieth-century history of error of law review, we can again see how changes in legal procedure have had a profound influence on legal doctrine. We have seen that the use of the distinction between jurisdictional and non-jurisdictional errors of law outside the context of certiorari proceedings ultimately caused it to lose its utility: the distinction, when employed in certiorari proceedings, became so inflated that it allowed for any form of review. This in turn raises interesting questions about the wisdom of calling for its reinstatement today, an issue that was particularly addressed by the Supreme Court in the recent decision in *R (Cart) v Upper Tribunal*.[75] This is what we will now consider.

VI. RE-EVALUATING THE DISTINCTION BETWEEN JURISDICTIONAL AND NON-JURISDICTIONAL ERRORS OF LAW

The real irony of the history painted above is that it was the necessity, in declaration proceedings, of labelling errors of law as jurisdictional that ultimately robbed the distinction between jurisdictional and non-jurisdictional errors of any utility. Given the gross inflation of the concept of jurisdiction that the use of declarations precipitated, practically all errors of law are now considered jurisdictional. What need is there, then, to pay heed to jurisdictional error of law's counterpart, non-jurisdictional error of law? Why speak of 'jurisdictional' error of law review at all, when we can just as easily speak solely of error of law review?

[75] *R (Cart) v Upper Tribunal* [2012] 1 AC 663.

As said above, the death of the distinction between jurisdictional and non-jurisdictional errors of law can be traced back to the *Anisminic* case. While judges and commentators argued over the exact consequences of *Anisminic* for over 20 years,[76] it came to be interpreted in the *Page* case[77] as providing that almost all errors committed by an administrative decision-maker in his or her interpretation of an Act of Parliament, or in his or her application of an Act of Parliament to the facts of a particular case, causes that decision-maker to act without jurisdiction. However, at the heart of *Page* was a contradiction. While Lord Browne-Wilkinson said that the effect of *Anisminic* was 'that in general any error of law made by an administrative tribunal or inferior court in reaching its decision can be quashed for error of law',[78] it was nonetheless recognised that where decision-makers commit an error in their interpretation of a specialised system of rules, rather than the general law of the land, then the distinction between jurisdictional and non-jurisdictional errors of law still pertains.[79] The decision of the Visitor of the University of Hull in *Page* was therefore held not to be quashable: the Visitor was interpreting the domestic statutes of the university, the distinction between jurisdictional and non-jurisdictional errors of law therefore still applied, and the error committed in this case was one that lay within his exclusive jurisdiction. So while *Page* might be treated as recognising *Anisminic*'s abolition of the distinction between jurisdictional and non-jurisdictional errors of law, it has as its *ratio decidendi* a recognition that the distinction still exists in certain circumstances. This has also been recognised where an administrative decision is made by an inferior court, at least in circumstances where the court's decision is protected from judicial review by an ouster clause.[80]

All this might be seen as minor instances of a broader uneasiness with the post-*Anisminic* approach to error of law review, which might be considered to give too little weight to interpretations of law made by expert, independent decision-makers. Given such uneasiness with *Anisminic*, the idea of a continued use of the historic distinction between jurisdictional and non-jurisdictional errors of law has regained interest. This was most recently explored in the *Cart* case.

The issue in *Cart* concerned the extent to which certain decisions of the Upper Tribunal could be judicially reviewed. The Upper Tribunal sits at the apex of the

[76] *Pearlman v Keepers and Governors of Harrow School* [1979] QB 56; *South East Asia Fire Bricks Sdn Bhd v Non-Metallic Mineral Products Manufacturing Employees Union* [1981] AC 363; *Re Racal Communications* [1981] AC 374; *O'Reilly v Mackman* (n 4). See also HWR Wade, 'Constitutional and Administrative Aspects of the *Anisminic* Case' (1969) 85 *Law Quarterly Review* 198, 209–12; SA de Smith, 'Judicial Review in Administrative Law: The Ever-open Door?' [1969] *Cambridge Law Journal* 161; BC Gould, '*Anisminic* and Jurisdictional Review' [1970] *Public Law* 358; DM Gordon, 'What Did the *Anisminic* Case Decide?' (1971) 34 *Modern Law Review* 1; K Diplock, 'Administrative Law: Judicial Review Unlocked' [1974] *Cambridge Law Journal* 233, 242–43; J Beatson, 'The Scope of Judicial Review for Error of Law' (1984) 4 *Oxford Journal of Legal Studies* 22, 31–33; I Hare, 'The Separation of Powers and Judicial Review for Error of Law' in CF Forsyth and I Hare (eds), *The Golden Metwand and the Crooked Cord* (Oxford, Clarendon Press, 1998) 113.

[77] *R v Lord President of the Privy Council, ex parte Page* [1993] AC 682.

[78] ibid 702.

[79] ibid 702–4.

[80] *Re Racal Communications Ltd* [1981] AC 374, 382–84 (Lord Diplock, *obiter*). While Lord Diplock seemed to resile from this view in *O'Reilly v Mackman* (n 4) 278, the exception was given some recognition by Lord Cooke in *R v Bedwelty Justices, ex parte Williams* [1997] AC 225, 233.

new tribunals system that was created by the Tribunals, Courts and Enforcement Act 2007. The ordinary route by which its decisions are challenged is through an appeal on a point of law to the Court of Appeal,[81] subject to permission being given by the Upper Tribunal or the Court of Appeal.[82] However, certain decisions of the Upper Tribunal are excluded from this appeal route, including decisions of the Upper Tribunal as to whether it will hear an appear from a lower tribunal.[83] In *Cart* itself, the Upper Tribunal had refused the claimant's appeal from a decision of the Social Security and Child Support Tribunal in a dispute between the claimant and the Child Support Agency as to how much child maintenance the claimant should pay to his ex-wife. Because the Upper Tribunal's decision not to hear an appeal was excluded from the ordinary appeal route, the claimant instead sought judicial review of the decision to refuse to hear the appeal on the ground that an error of law had been committed.

Both the Divisional Court and Court of Appeal recognised difficulties with applying the modern, post-*Anisminic* approach to error of law review in the case of the Upper Tribunal. The Upper Tribunal mirrored the High Court in many ways, being staffed in part by judges of the superior courts, and exercising a judicial review function alongside its appellate function. This, combined with its high degree of independence and expertise, meant that full-scale post-*Anisminic* error of law review was considered to be inappropriate: such an approach, which would always favour the reviewing court's interpretation of the law at the expense of the Upper Tribunal's interpretation, was considered to unduly threaten the Upper Tribunal's autonomy.[84] The solution for both Laws LJ in the Divisional Court and Sedley LJ in the Court of Appeal was to resurrect the pre-*Anisminic* distinction between jurisdictional and non-jurisdictional errors of law.[85] Sedley LJ said that there was 'a true jurisprudential difference between an error of law made in the course of an adjudication which a tribunal is authorised to conduct and the conducting of an adjudication without lawful authority'.[86] In order to maintain the autonomy of the Upper Tribunal, both Laws LJ and Sedley LJ thought it right to limit review to the former category of error. Jurisdictional errors of law were again identified by the traditional limited conception that had historically been applied by the courts: those concerned with the subject matter of an administrative inquiry, determinable at the inquiry's commencement. This small category of jurisdictional errors of law again sat alongside a much larger category of unreviewable non-jurisdictional errors. Again, the limited conception of jurisdiction came to be proposed as a control device for the restriction of judicial review.

In the Supreme Court, however, the method of limiting judicial review favoured by the Divisional Court and Court of Appeal was not followed. While it was recognised that the post-*Anisminic* approach to error of law review would come at too great a

[81] Tribunal, Courts and Enforcement Act 2007, s 13(1)–(2).

[82] ibid s 13(3)–(4).

[83] ibid s 13(8)(c).

[84] *Cart* (n 14) [99] (DC) (Laws LJ) and [36]–[37] (CA) (Sedley LJ).

[85] A similar approach had been adopted in the earlier case of *R (Sivasubramaniam) v Wandsworth County Court* [2003] 1 WLR 475.

[86] *Cart* (n 14) [36] (CA) (Seldey LJ).

cost to the efficiency, finality and autonomy of the system created by the Tribunals, Courts and Enforcement Act 2007,[87] the pre-*Anisminic* approach favoured by the lower courts was rejected as well. Lady Hale, giving the main judgment of the court, dismissed the pre-*Anisminic* approach for three reasons in particular. First, she felt that it could not be applied today because it was developed in a particular historical context. Lady Hale noted that before *Anisminic*, certiorari was available not just for jurisdictional error of law, but also to correct non-jurisdictional errors of law appearing on the face of the record.[88] To follow the approach of the lower courts in *Cart*, she said, would be to re-introduce 'a distinction which had become relevant for the most part only where judicial review was expressly excluded'.[89] While not stated explicitly, Lady Hale's argument seems to have been that the distinction was only really relevant in cases where judicial review was excluded by an ouster clause; otherwise, it did not pertain, given that review could also occur for errors appearing on the face of the record. Secondly, Lady Hale said that the distinction between jurisdictional and non-jurisdictional errors of law was capable of bearing 'many meanings ranging from the very wide to the very narrow'.[90] Such an amorphous concept, she said, led to many technicalities, and '[i]f the approach of the Court of Appeal … is maintained we may expect a return to some of the technicalities of the past'.[91] Thirdly, Lady Hale was uneasy about implying an intention on the part of Parliament to make the Upper Tribunal the ultimate interpreter of the law it was tasked with administering in the absence of an explicit statutory recognition that the Upper Tribunal was to be permitted to make mistakes of law.[92] The other justices of the Supreme Court agreed with Lady Hale's comments.[93]

Instead of adopting the lower courts' approach, the Supreme Court favoured limiting judicial review in accordance with the so-called second-tier appeals criteria, found in section 55 of the Access to Justice Act 1999.[94] These criteria determined the possibility of appeals from the Upper Tribunal to the ordinary courts,[95] and there was some precedent for their being used to limit judicial review.[96] Applying these criteria would mean that decisions of the Upper Tribunal that were excluded from the ordinary appeal route could be judicially reviewed only when they raised important points of principle or practice, or if there was some other compelling reason.

Following the foregoing analysis of the history of the distinction between jurisdictional and non-jurisdictional errors of law, there are a number of criticisms that can be made of the Supreme Court's approach, typified by the judgment of Lady Hale. This is especially so when it comes to Lady Hale's comments about the history of the distinction. The history outlined above makes it clear that certiorari review for jurisdictional error of law was not some minor phenomenon sitting alongside

[87] *Cart* (n 75) [47]–[51] (Lady Hale).
[88] ibid [40].
[89] ibid.
[90] ibid.
[91] ibid.
[92] ibid; see also [43].
[93] See especially Lord Dyson [111].
[94] ibid [52]–[56] (Lady Hale).
[95] Tribunal, Courts and Enforcement Act 2007, s 13(6).
[96] *R (Wiles) v Social Security Commissioner* [2010] EWCA Civ 258.

a much commoner review for errors of law disclosed on the face of the record, as Lady Hale suggests. The distinction between jurisdictional and non-jurisdictional errors of law was not just relevant in those cases where certiorari was expressly excluded by a statutory ouster clause. Instead, we have seen that in cases where certiorari review was sought for the quashing of an administrative order, jurisdictional error of law was practically the only ground on which review could meaningfully be sought, regardless of whether an ouster clause featured in the case or not. It was only if an error of law committed by a decision-maker was jurisdictional that affidavit evidence could be introduced; and, given the sparseness of administrative orders, it was only if affidavit evidence could be introduced that meaningful review could occur. Furthermore, as judicial review developed in the twentieth century, and the declaration came to take prominence as the primary remedy for effecting review, jurisdictional errors of law again became crucial because it was only if an error of law was jurisdictional that the decision could be described as ultra vires, and it was only if a decision was ultra vires that it made sense to seek a declaration. The distinction between jurisdictional and non-jurisdictional errors of law, in other words, lies at the heart of the entire modern history of administrative law; it is not some minor, anachronistic outlier.

It is this disregard for the historic importance of the distinction between jurisdictional and non-jurisdictional errors of law that explains the fundamental problem with the decision in *Cart*. That problem is the Supreme Court's eschewal of doctrine in favour of raw pragmatism. In orthodox theory, all principles of judicial review are conceptualised as delimiting the jurisdiction of administrative decision-makers. The effect of this is that every breach of every principle of judicial review leads to a decision being considered ultra vires, and can be declared as such in declaration proceedings, quashed in proceedings for a quashing order (as certiorari is now called) and acknowledged to be void *ab initio* when collaterally challenged. While this orthodox understanding of administrative law has had some detractors,[97] it continues to hold considerable sway in administrative law scholarship.[98] The Supreme Court's approach in *Cart*, however, considerably undermines this. It raises the possibility of a decision-maker making a decision that, in principle, is affected by a jurisdictional error of law, and thus void, while at the same time being completely unreviewable.[99]

[97] See especially Feldman, 'Error of Law and Flawed Administrative Acts' (n 14).

[98] Wade and Forsyth, *Administrative Law* (n 9) 27–28.

[99] There is some doubt over whether collateral challenge might be available in such circumstances. Following the recognition of the strong constitutional impetus for collateral challenge in *Boddington v British Transport Police* [1999] 2 AC 143, it might be thought that collateral challenge should be available in cases like *Cart*, in circumstances, for example, where one is prosecuted for disobeying an unreviewable decision of a tribunal. This view is put forward by Christopher F Forsyth, Chapter 7, '"Blasphemy Against Basics": Doctrine, Conceptual Reasoning and Certain Decisions of the UK Supreme Court'. Nonetheless, even after *Boddington*, the right to collateral challenge is not universal. In particular, there have been a number of cases where a defendant's request for collateral challenge has been refused on the ground that he or she was already involved in the decision-making process that led to the decision, in circumstances where the decision-making process was addressed to the defendant personally: *R v Wicks* [1998] AC 92; *DPP v T* [2007] 1 WLR 209. Collateral challenge of a non-reviewable or non-appealable tribunal decisions could be denied on this basis, for the same reasons set out in *Cart*: that Parliament, enacting the Tribunals, Courts and Enforcement Act 2007, intended to make the tribunal adjudication under the new tribunals system both authoritative and, in most cases, final.

The potential for conceptual confusion here is pronounced.[100] While it has always been recognised in administrative law that decisions that are, in principle, ultra vires might nonetheless continue to have a practical existence,[101] and resultant legal effects,[102] when unchallenged, *Cart* represents a significant step beyond this. Rather than passively allowing ultra vires decisions to stand because judicial review, for some reason, cannot be brought, *Cart* actively blocks judicial review from being brought for purely pragmatic reasons, such that ultra vires decisions continue to have a factual existence and possible legal effects.

It might, however, be argued that this messy result is the best that the Supreme Court could possibly have come up with. We have seen that the distinction between jurisdictional and non-jurisdictional errors of law came to dominate administrative law because of a particular procedural concern, namely, the desire to control the admission of affidavit evidence in certiorari proceedings, and we have seen that difficulties arose with the distinction once it was applied in a different procedural context. Of course, this was exactly the view put forward by Lady Hale, and supported by the other justices of the Supreme Court, in *Cart*. Lady Hale bemoaned the amorphous character of the concept of jurisdiction as received from the case law, with its many technicalities and fine distinctions.[103] This amorphousness, we have seen, came about once the distinction was removed from its original procedural context. What use, we might then ask, is the substantive distinction between jurisdictional and non-jurisdictional errors of law today, in an administrative law far removed from the procedural concerns for which it was specifically developed? Perhaps the distinction between jurisdictional and non-jurisdictional errors—of law, of fact, or of mixed law and fact—might in truth be said to have had its day.[104]

A careful reflection on the history of jurisdictional error of law review is needed here. So far, it has been asserted that we need to be very conscious of the relationship between process and substance in administrative law. But it is easy to be too conscious of this. It is doubtless true that the relationship between process and substance is important in English administrative law. It is not, however, wholly obvious why doctrinal rules that have developed in one particular context cannot, once their development is complete, go on to have a separate life of their own outside that context. Recalling Maine's comments about substantive law being 'secreted in the interstices of procedure',[105] might we not say that it is inherent in the very nature

[100] Just like in cases where the courts are asked to withhold a remedy against an administrative decision they have recognised as void. Such an approach was rejected strongly by the Supreme Court in *Ahmed v Her Majesty's Treasury (No 2)* [2010] 2 WLR 378. cf *R (Hurley and Moore) v Secretary of State for Business, Innovation and Skills* [2012] EWHC 201 (Admin).

[101] Wade described this as 'a general principle of legal relativity': HWR Wade, 'Unlawful Administrative Action: Void or Voidable?' (1967) 83 *Law Quarterly Review* 499, 512; (1968) 84 *Law Quarterly Review* 95. See also *F Hoffmann-La Roche and Co AG v Secretary of State for Trade and Industry* [1975] AC 295, 365–66 (Lord Diplock).

[102] As explained by Forsyth's 'second actor theory': Forsyth, '"The Metaphysics of Nullity"' (n 13).

[103] *Cart* (n 75) [40].

[104] We could, it might be said, accept the rejection of a distinction between jurisdictional and non-jurisdictional errors of *law* while at the same time allowing the distinction to apply with regard to other forms of error (eg errors of fact). But Lady Hale's comments in *Cart* seem to prevent this: her criticisms of the error of law case law are concerned with the concept of jurisdiction itself, thus amounting to a rejection of any continued use of a distinction between jurisdictional and non-jurisdictional error.

[105] Maine, *Dissertations on Early Law and Custom* (n 1).

of the common law that certain procedures give rise to substantive doctrine that goes on to have an independent life of its own? When questioning the viability of a substantive legal rule, then, it is better to be concerned not simply with the bare procedural context in which it was developed, but rather with the precise reason why the rule was developed: the procedural context of a rule can aid our understanding of its underlying reason, but is not exhaustive of it. It is only once we have a full understanding of the reason for a rule that was can properly decide what role the rule should play in our modern system of law.

If we apply this to the historical development of error of law review, it is clear that the significance of the distinction between jurisdictional and non-jurisdictional is not so much that it was necessary for the admission of affidavit evidence, but that it served as a control device, limiting judicial review. And it is equally clear that the problems encountered with jurisdictional errors of law in the middle of the last century stemmed not from any inherent defect in the concept of jurisdiction, nor from the use of the distinction between jurisdictional and non-jurisdictional errors of law beyond the procedural context in which it was first developed, but from the use of the distinction as a device for facilitating rather than limiting review. In other words, the problem was taking a substantive doctrine developed to solve one particular problem (the need to limit review) and using it in an attempt to solve another (the need for more review). The concept of jurisdiction, the case law shows us, is not simply a device for calibrating the scope of review, regardless of how intensive or detached one might wish that review to be. The concept, in its purest form, is inherently limited, and so best suited to *limiting* the scope of review. So, while using an inherently restrictive legal concept like jurisdiction to limit review makes sense, trying to persevere with that concept when limited review is no longer desirable causes problems.

Once viewed in this light, the historical picture painted above gives food for thought for today's administrative lawyer. It raises questions, for example, as to the continued use of the concept of jurisdiction as an organising principle for all of administrative law: we have seen that, where the concept of jurisdiction serves as the sole gateway to judicial review, it struggles to maintain its coherency of meaning, thus losing any real utility. More importantly, it raises questions as to the role the distinction between jurisdictional and non-jurisdictional errors of law might play today. With the limited, clearly articulated conception of jurisdiction that was adopted by the Queen's Bench from 1841 onwards (and, in a more ambiguous form, for many years before then), the substantive distinction between jurisdictional and non-jurisdictional errors of law did serve for over a century as a reliable and useful device for limiting judicial review. The history of error of law review thus provides significant fodder for those who have called for a resurrection of the distinction between jurisdictional and non-jurisdictional errors of law as a device for limiting review.[106] It shows us that, if put to its original use of limiting judicial review (as was sought to be done in *Cart*), the distinction might well be suitable for resurrection. The history of error of law review certainly supports the approach the Divisional

[106] See Feldman, 'Error of Law and Flawed Administrative Acts' (n 14) and Forsyth, '"The Metaphysics of Nullity"' (n 13).

Court and Court of Appeal favoured in *Cart*, undermining the somewhat simplistic account of administrative law's history adopted by the Supreme Court.

VII. CONCLUSION

At the beginning of this chapter, a number of questions were raised, both specifically about the historical development and continued utility of the substantive distinction between jurisdictional and non-jurisdictional errors of law, and also more generally about the interrelationship between process and substance in administrative law. It is hoped that, having discussed these issues in some depth, some ideas might have been distilled from the history of error of law review that are both interesting and pertinent for today's scholars of administrative law.

We have seen above that, while the distinction between jurisdictional and non-jurisdictional errors of law came about because of the particular procedural concern, under the prerogative writ of certiorari, as to the admission of affidavit evidence, it was not the use of the distinction outside that procedural context which caused its eventual decline. Instead, problems began to occur with the distinction when it came to be seen as a conceptual device for increasing the scope of review; originally, we have seen, it had the opposite function, namely, of limiting review. Calls for the resurrection of the distinction as a device for keeping the scope of judicial review under control, like in the lower courts in *Cart*, seem, then, far from misplaced. Rather than seeking to resurrect a distinction well passed its heyday and to apply it outside its proper context, those calling for the distinction between jurisdictional and non-jurisdictional errors of law to be given some substance are in truth calling for an approach that is both more reflective of administrative law's historical development, and more in keeping with the underlying rationale of the distinction. When too much pressure is put on the distinction, however, and it is used to facilitate more review, then there could be problems.

We have also seen that in order to have a full understanding of administrative law, it is necessary to be sensitive to the procedural contexts in which substantive rules developed. Equally, though, we have learnt that it is all too easy to be too sensitive, confining substantive doctrine to overly parochial contexts when it ought to be given a life of its own. The Supreme Court's condemnation of the distinction between jurisdictional and non-jurisdictional errors of law in *Cart* is just one example of this. While approaching administrative law doctrine with an eye to its procedural context is essential, it is equally important that we concentrate on the underlying motivation of the courts for the introduction of doctrine, rather than just purely on the procedural context in which it came about.

Administrative law serves as a strong example that stand-alone common law doctrine is the product of various procedural rules. It is important that all common law scholars peek into the interstices of procedure and root out the substantive law that they find therein. It is important too, however, that attention is paid to the historical development of law, both procedural and substantive. As this study has hopefully demonstrated, it is only if we fully understand the procedural context and historical development of legal rules and principles that we can properly assess their use in modern law.

6

The Growth of Substantive Review: The Changes, their Causes and their Consequences

MARK ARONSON*

I. INTRODUCTION

JUDICIAL REVIEW THESE days reaches to most corners of the administrative state. Its grounds for intervention have also grown, and it is one category of those grounds that forms the focus of this chapter. Originally narrow, judicial review's grounds concentrated for the most part on enforcing statutorily prescribed procedures, whilst staying well clear of substance. *Wednesbury* unreasonableness was exceptional for being overtly substantive, but its bar was set so high that it posed no real threat to the basic architecture of judicial review. Substantive review has now grown significantly, albeit more recently (and with considerably more hesitation) in Australia than England. My focus will be on Australia, using a select few English cases as comparators. Broadly, I want to look at the expansion of substantive review, its possible causes, its relationship to a changing sense of judicial review's 'mission', and its possible consequences.

For my purposes, courts engage in substantive review when they go beyond checking both that the administrators stayed within the four corners of their powers and mechanistically ticked all the requisite boxes, and also ask how well they performed their tasks (section II). *Wednesbury* unreasonableness used to be the only ground of review openly acknowledged to be substantive, but substantive review has expanded significantly. New grounds have emerged, some of them explicitly substantive, and some disguised as process (section III). One might expect an expansion of substantive review to produce an expanded theory of judicial review's overarching goals or functions, plus a feedback effect from broader theory to broadened bases for review. For constitutional reasons, however, Australia's mission creep has been more confined than England's, and certainly less reformist (section IV). In addition to the interactions between high theory and expansionism, there are other forces driving the growth of substantive review, but I will look at only three of these. One of them,

* I am grateful for the assistance, comments, and suggestions received from John Basten, Peter Cane, Carol Harlow, Matthew Groves, Grant Hooper, Philip Murray, Alan Robertson, Jason Varuhas and Greg Weeks.

ironically, is an unforeseen judicial reaction to Parliament's attempts to exclude substantive review of migration decisions (section V). Finally, I will speculate as to whether the growth of substantive review will affect the basic architecture of judicial review (section VI).

II. PROCESS, SUBSTANCE AND QUALITY

It is impossible to draw a hard-and-fast distinction between procedure and substance, and judicial review does not in fact claim to be organised around any such distinction. Nevertheless, there is a strong sense that judicial review's grounds were in some sense predominantly procedural until relatively recently. For my purposes, it suffices to say that a substantive ground of judicial review checks not on *whether* something was done, but on *how well* it was done; qualitative assessments are involved in substantive review.

I acknowledge that even that distinction has blurred edges, and one might well argue that the rules of procedural fairness are as much substantive as procedural. The courts have in recent times fallen back upon an increasingly demanding sense of fairness to impose more and more process requirements upon administrators. However, the central concern of this chapter is with the expansion of the substantive grounds of judicial review, and I will therefore confine my discussion of procedural fairness to such of its developments as have imposed substantive requirements disguised as procedural fairness, even though they are apparently entirely lacking in procedural content.

Speaking in the context of the judicial enforcement of substantive expectations, but in phraseology that was clearly pitched more broadly, Laws LJ said that the root principle of judicial review was the enforcement of the principles of good administration, principles which drew no distinction whatsoever between procedure and substance.[1] If (as I suspect) he is no expert in management theories or public administration, then he probably had in mind legal principles of morally defensible public administration, and most of these are in fact procedural. He has been quite clear that substantive review comes loaded with more deference, more judicial hesitancy, than process review.[2]

III. EXPANSION OF SUBSTANTIVE REVIEW

Australia has seen significant expansions in substantive review; some of them have been dressed up in procedural guise ('merits in drag' was the Kiwi term),[3] whilst

[1] *R (Nadarajah) v Secretary of State for the Home Department* [2005] EWCA Civ 1363, [69].

[2] *R v Secretary of State for Education and Employment, ex parte Begbie* [2000] 1 WLR 1115, 1130–31; *International Transport Roth GmbH v Secretary of State for the Home Department* [2003] QB 728, 767, [87].

[3] *Powerco Ltd v Commerce Commission* [2006] NZHC 662, [24], cited in *Real Estate and Business Agents Supervisory Board v Carey* [2010] WASCA 109, [58]; *LVR (WA) Pty Ltd v Administrative Appeals Tribunal* (2011) 55 AAR 518, [39]. *LVR*'s appellate reversal did not repeat the Kiwi term: (2012) 203 FCR 166.

others have been overtly substantive. We have in addition seen review on grounds that can only be described as holistic.

To emphasise the shift, I might start with Brennan J's once-canonical judgment in *Attorney General (NSW) v Quin*.[4] His Honour repeatedly emphasised that *Wednesbury* unreasonableness was Australia's only substantive ground of review, the only ground that inquired at some level into 'the merits'. It was an inquiry, however, that his Honour thought reserved for the truly exceptional cases involving only the plainest abuses of power, abuses that one could not imagine the legislature as having authorised.[5] One might argue that nothing much has changed since then, and that *Wednesbury* remains our only substantive review ground, even if its standard has now become more flexible and adaptable to context. However, that would be true only in the attenuated sense that the newer forays into substantive review can easily be rebranded as manifestations of unreasonableness review.

At perhaps a more fundamental level, the High Court has begun to depart from its previous adherence to a standardised list of rule-bound grounds that had moved very little over the years. The court declared in 2010 that the old lists are useful but not watertight: 'It is neither necessary, nor possible, to attempt to mark the metes and bounds of jurisdictional error'.[6] There is no 'rigid taxonomy'.[7]

This section will look at a number of these developments, starting with review for error of fact, for irrational reasoning, and for unreasonable outcomes—previously all firmly within 'the merits'. I will then look at two recent developments that masqueraded as review for want of procedural fairness, namely, review for misunderstanding the fundamentals of an applicant's case, and review for overlooking or forgetting the evidence. These latter developments link to a further development that might not be generic; it might apply only to specific tribunals. In these cases, there are sweeping statements that the tribunal hearing simply failed to answer to the statutory requirement of being a genuine ('meaningful' is the word sometimes used) 'review' or 'hearing'. Even the old 'relevancy' grounds have occasionally shifted from their traditionally narrow, 'tick-a-box' standard to something more substantive, although that is always said to be an exceptional product of interpreting particular governing statutes. And finally, there have been repeated suggestions of late that the High Court might be more receptive to proportionality review, perhaps in its own right, or as an example of unreasonableness.

A. Errors of Fact

If anything was quarantined from review, it was the decision-maker's findings of fact. This was probably the critical factor in making judicial review procedurally easy, fast and cheap—and, of course, substantively unsatisfying, especially when compared to tribunal appeals on the merits. There is typically very little contentious

[4] *Attorney General (NSW) v Quin* (1990) 170 CLR 1.

[5] ibid 36.

[6] *Kirk v Industrial Court (NSW)* (2010) 239 CLR 531, 573 (French CJ, Gummow, Hayne, Crennan, Kiefel and Bell JJ).

[7] ibid 574.

evidence in a judicial review matter, and even that is usually tendered in affidavit form with no cross-examination of deponents.

The most radical way of attacking the traditional restrictions upon fact review is to reject as untenable any distinction between errors of law and fact: all other manoeuvres are 'work-arounds'. And here, there is a significant split between the Australian and English cases. The Australian cases acknowledge the difficulties in distinguishing between errors of law and fact,[8] and also that no single test exists that is appropriate for all the different contexts in which lines need to be drawn.[9] However, they insist that the distinctions remain 'vital',[10] albeit not determinative.[11]

The English cases stand in stark contrast. Although the old distinctions between errors of law and fact have not entirely gone, one no longer sees claimants' judicial review challenges being subjected to any sustained analysis along those lines. Indeed, England's judicial review courts have started attacking the old distinctions between errors of law and fact head-on. *E v Secretary of State for the Home Department*[12] allowed review on condition that the parties could agree that the decision-maker was wrong about a critically important fact. In that circumstance, the court said that there would be substantive unfairness, which in turn would constitute error of law.[13] In *Jones v First Tier Tribunal*,[14] Lord Carnwath adopted a wholly pragmatic approach to the definition of error of law. As a matter of 'expediency' or 'policy',[15] he said that the Upper Tribunal, on appeals limited to points of law, could treat an error of fact by the tribunal beneath it as an error of law. In addition, he said that any further appeal (or judicial review) limited to errors of law should generally treat exactly the same error as one of fact, once again for reasons of expediency and policy. More recently, the Supreme Court approved of the Upper Tribunal giving non-binding 'guidance' judgments on frequently recurring questions of fact and procedure.[16]

One might start with a proposition that Australia has accepted for at least 50 years, namely, that a finding of material fact constitutes an error of law if there is absolutely *no* evidence to support it.[17] In Australian common law, errors of law

[8] See, eg, *Collector of Customs v Agfa-Gevaert Ltd* (1996) 186 CLR 389, 394; *Director of Public Prosecutions (Cth) v JM* (2013) 250 CLR 135, 157.

[9] Many statutory appeals, for example, are limited to 'law only'. Fine distinctions are drawn between statutes, depending on whether their appeal rights are limited to *points*, *questions*, or *errors* of law; or to *decisions* of, or *involving*, or *with respect*, to a *question* of law. See, eg, *Kostas v HIA Insurance Services Pty Ltd* (2010) 241 CLR 390, 417–18; M Aronson and M Groves, *Judicial Review of Administrative Action*, 5th edn (Sydney, Thomson Reuters, 2013) 196–97.

[10] *Collector of Customs v Agfa-Gevaert Ltd* (1996) 186 CLR 389, 394 (Brennan CJ, Dawson, Toohey, Gaudron and McHugh JJ).

[11] *Re Minister for Immigration and Multicultural Affairs, ex parte Applicant S20/2002* (2003) 198 ALR 59, [53]–[60].

[12] *E v Secretary of State for the Home Department* [2004] QB 1044. See C Forsyth and E Dring, 'The Final Frontier: The Emergence of Material Error of Fact as a Ground for Judicial Review' in C Forsyth, M Elliott, S Jhaveri, A Scully-Hill and M Ramsden (eds), *Effective Judicial Review: A Cornerstone of Good Governance* (Oxford, Oxford University Press, 2010).

[13] The Supreme Court cited *E* uncritically in *IA v Secretary of State for the Home Department* [2014] 1 WLR 384, [54].

[14] *Jones v First Tier Tribunal* [2013] 2 AC 48.

[15] ibid 64–65.

[16] *MN (Somalia) v Secretary of State for the Home Department* [2014] 1 WLR 2064.

[17] *Australian Broadcasting Tribunal v Bond* (1990) 170 CLR 321, 355–56.

are reviewable if jurisdictional, or (where certiorari is claimed) if they are apparent upon the face of the record.[18] 'No evidence' was at times stretched to 'no probative evidence', but that is now taken to mean no more than a requirement for fact-finding to have a rational basis.[19]

Then there is jurisdictional fact review, sometimes known in England as review for precedent or collateral fact.[20] This allows a completely *de novo* challenge to a decision, even to the extent of adducing fresh evidence. However, that type of review is available only where the court can construe the governing Act as stipulating that a certain fact's objective existence (or non-existence) is an absolute precondition to the validity of the ensuing decision.[21] In one case, for example, a major development application had to go through a process of widespread public consultation if it posed a potential threat to endangered species. The court construed the Act as leaving with the court the last word on whether such a threat was posed;[22] the result was to turn the court into a 'judicial ecologist'.[23] Such a construction leads to highly dysfunctional administrative outcomes; counsel frequently assert it, but thankfully are usually rebuffed.[24]

Over the last 10–15 years, the High Court has added more innovative (and to an extent, less defined) work-arounds to the mix. One of the most interesting developments was the recognition of review for serious irrationality or serious illogicality. Whilst not confined to reviewing errors of fact, that is where this approach does most of its work. It first appeared in a judgment written by only two judges.[25] A third judge joined them six months later,[26] but it took another six years before a High Court majority was able to confirm the existence of 'serious irrationality

[18] *Craig v South Australia* (1995) 184 CLR 163.

[19] See *Amaba Pty Ltd v Booth* [2010] NSWCA 344, [22]–[25]; *Rawson Finances Pty Ltd v Commissioner of Taxation* (2013) 296 ALR 307, [84]; *D'Amore v Independent Commission Against Corruption* (2013) 303 ALR 242, [235]. The Administrative Decisions (Judicial Review) Act 1977 (Cth) appears to extend the 'no evidence' ground to decisions based upon material errors of fact, but the cases have so read down the relevant provision as to make it useless. See *Curragh Queensland Mining Ltd v Daniel* (1992) 34 FCR 212; *Minister for Immigration and Multicultural Affairs v Rajamanikkam* (2002) 210 CLR 222. Reform has been suggested: Administrative Review Council, *Federal Judicial Review in Australia* , Report No 50 (2012) [7.68]–[7.78], available at www.arc.ag.gov.au. The Australian position has been misunderstood in England. See *R v Criminal Injuries Compensation Board, ex parte A* [1999] 2 AC 330, 344–45; *R (Alconbury Developments Ltd) v Secretary of State for the Environment, Transport and the Regions* [2003] 2 AC 295, 321; *E* (n 12) 1064–65.

[20] *R v Secretary of State for the Home Department, ex parte Khawaja* [1984] AC 74, 97, 99, 109; *R (A) v Croydon London Borough Council* [2009] 1 WLR 2557, 2567–68, 2574. *Croydon* said that whether someone is a child is jurisdictional for welfare purposes, but *R (AA) v Secretary of State for the Home Department* [2013] 1 WLR 2224 said that the same factual issue is not jurisdictional for immigration purposes.

[21] I will not examine the High Court's extension of the term 'jurisdictional fact' to cases where review is limited to the standard grounds applying to powers that are contingent upon the decision-maker's 'satisfaction' or 'opinion' of a fact's existence: *Minister for Immigration and Ethnic Affairs v Eshetu* (1999) 197 CLR 611, 651.

[22] *Timbarra Protection Coalition Inc v Ross River Mining NL* (1999) 46 NSWLR 55.

[23] *Nambucca Valley Conservation Association v Nambucca Shire Council* [2010] NSWLEC 38, [78] (Biscoe J).

[24] Aronson and Groves, *Judicial Review of Administrative Action* (n 9) 235–45.

[25] *Applicant S20* (n 11) [34], [37] (McHugh and Gummow JJ).

[26] *Minister for Immigration and Multicultural and Indigenous Affairs v SGLB* (2004) 207 ALR 12, [38] (Gummow and Hayne JJ).

or illogicality' as review grounds,[27] and that was in response to an attempt by government counsel[28] to talk them out of it altogether. Furthermore, the Federal Court views the High Court majority as having been split on whether a tribunal's seriously irrational reasoning matters if the same result could have been reached by rational reasoning. The issue was ventilated but not resolved in a matter before the Full Federal Court recently,[29] and the debate dropped from sight when the case got to the High Court.[30] The issue was the tribunal's acceptance of the possibility that an asylum claimant had committed serious, non-political crimes back in China. The High Court reversed, basically for 'error of law'. That was because the tribunal had placed too much emphasis on the claimant's many lies, none of which actually bore on his alleged crimes. The court said that the tribunal had failed to appreciate that the Act required something more than mere suspicion. But if that was an error of law, it could only have been because the tribunal's reliance on the man's lies was irrational.

Collectively, these inroads into the territory of fact-finding are certainly interesting, but it must be said that they have in practice made very little difference to the outcome of the great mass of cases. They have, however, introduced a real element of uncertainty, which will have its own consequences upon the conduct of respondents' cases.

B. Beyond *Wednesbury* Unreasonableness

Review for 'serious irrationality' has always been treated as an analogue of *Wednesbury* unreasonableness, and the subsequent relaxation of *Wednesbury*'s standard therefore flows through to the irrationality ground. Indeed, the only real advantage in coining this new ground was to distinguish it from *Wednesbury* unreasonableness, which was in those days not within the Federal Court's competence in migration matters. For roughly a decade, the migration legislation prevented the Federal Court from entertaining 'unreasonableness' challenges to migration decisions. However, the High Court devised a semantical loophole, by saying that irrationality was something different. 'Unreasonableness' tested the outcomes; 'irrationality' tested how these were reached. In essence, 'unreasonableness' was the old *Wednesbury*, but reserved for challenges to incredibly unreasonable choices made in the exercise of truly discretionary power; 'irrationality' applied to everything else.[31] The migration legislation no longer restricts unreasonableness challenges in the Federal and Federal Circuit Courts, and the High Court is understandably losing interest in distinguishing between the two grounds.[32]

27 *Minister for Immigration and Citizenship v SZMDS* (2010) 240 CLR 611.
28 Gageler SC, since appointed to the High Court.
29 *FTZK v Minister for Immigration and Citizenship* (2013) 211 FCR 158. See also *Minister for Immigration and Border Protection v SZSNW* [2014] FCAFC 145.
30 *FTZK v Minister for Immigration and Citizenship* (2014) 88 ALJR 754.
31 *Applicant S20* (n 11).
32 *Minister for Immigration and Citizenship v Li* (2013) 249 CLR 332, 371 (Gageler J).

Minister for Immigration and Citizenship v Li[33] seems to be the most important recent case, if only because its style is not just *non*-formalist—its whole approach is positively *anti*-formalist. That will drive some of us slightly mad, as we try to guess where the court might be going with some of its high-level abstractions, and how these will interact with the more familiar and precedent-bound grounds of review which judicial review pleaders can probably recite in their sleep. For the present, the cases have been emphasising *Li*'s context-dependent balancing of normative and functionality concerns.[34]

Ms Li had sought to upgrade to permanent residency on the basis of her skills as a professional cook, skills she maintained that she had acquired whilst working in Australia. Her skills base needed independent assessment and certification. It took her a long time to get the proper certificate. Through no fault of her own, the first was fraudulent, and the second was honest but in need of an amendment which took three months to obtain. Without giving any reason other than that she had had enough time, the tribunal had refused to wait for the amendment. The tribunal may have had good reasons for refusing an adjournment, but none was given.

The court published three different sets of reasons, each concluding that the refusal to adjourn invalidated the tribunal's decision, each identifying the tribunal's fatal flaw as failing to explain what it was that had counted against her application for postponement. The tribunal had neither identified any prejudice that an adjournment would occasion (either to itself or to the Department), nor indicated disagreement with her agent's view that there was a good basis for seeking a corrected skills assessment.

Each of the three judgments overturned the tribunal for unreasonableness in its refusal of an adjournment. Gageler J's approach was strikingly different from the others; his Honour was quite clear that he was not lowering the original *Wednesbury* standard,[35] a standard that I would paraphrase as 'lunatic'. The joint judgment of Hayne, Kiefel and Bell JJ was equally clear that reasonableness is a standard that varies between statutory contexts, sometimes excusing all but lunacy, sometimes not:[36]

> The legal standard of unreasonableness should not be considered as limited to what is in effect an irrational, if not bizarre, decision—which is to say one that is so unreasonable that no reasonable person could have arrived at it—nor should Lord Greene MR be taken to have limited unreasonableness in this way in his judgment in *Wednesbury*.

Their Honours emphasised that the whole purpose of a tribunal hearing was to provide appellants with a 'meaningful' opportunity to present their evidence and their arguments,[37] and that this was 'a substantive obligation'[38] which had been

[33] (2013) 249 CLR 332.
[34] Even though it preceded *Li*, the most influential judgment in this regard is that of Robertson J, in *Minister for Immigration and Citizenship v SZRKT* (2013) 212 FCR 99.
[35] *Li* (n 32) 377–78.
[36] ibid 364. That this has long been the position in English law was one of the few points of solid agreement amongst the seven judges in *Pham v Secretary of State for the Home Department* [2015] 1 WLR 1591.
[37] *Li* (n 32) 361–62.
[38] ibid 361.

denied for no apparent reason. The implication was clear: in the case of the tribunal, 'reasonableness' was to be analogised (albeit not equated) to the standard expected of judges exercising discretionary powers.[39]

French CJ thought that the tribunal's decision could also be struck down for breach of procedural fairness,[40] although the other judgments refrained from ruling on that ground in light of a statutory provision attempting to declare that the common law principles were not to be used to supplement the statute's own procedures. French CJ and the joint judgment hinted that had it been argued, proportionality review might have stood a good chance.[41] The Chief Justice also hinted that Ms Li's tribunal had acted not just unreasonably but irrationally;[42] the joint judgment appears to have taken the opposite position.[43]

There is a further sense in which the High Court's substantive review has been expanding, although it is too early to say whether these are new review grounds that are emerging, or just new ways of getting to some of the older and more familiar grounds such as breach of procedural fairness, unreasonableness, failure to take account of mandatory considerations, or even the newer ground of serious irrationality. A number of cases have emphasised the statutory duties imposed upon migration tribunals to *review* decisions, or to *invite* the affected person to attend a hearing and submit evidence and argument, or to *determine* or *hear* the appeal. Each of the words I have italicised seems to have been invested with a substantive content whose denial might in itself represent reviewable error. It is as if the court were saying (for example): 'That's not a *review*'.

There is also a sizeable body of Federal Court learning[44] (reflected in *Li*'s joint judgment)[45] that pivots from the migration tribunals' duties to *invite* appellants to attend their hearings. It is said that the invitation must surely be to attend *meaningful* hearings, with all of the substantive implications of engagement that that entails. In *Li* itself, French CJ and Gageler J referred repeatedly to the tribunal's *core functions*[46] and its *overriding duty to review*.[47] High Court judgments that have reasoned in this style[48] have generally built upon a recitation of the main features of the migration tribunals. These are that the tribunals are essentially adjudicative, albeit more inquisitorial than adversarial; that they are independent and impartial; that their hearings are *de novo*; that the Department sends its file, but does not attend the hearing; and that there is a duty to supply reasons, which must demonstrate a

[39] ibid 366–67, 376–77, analogising to *House v R* (1936) 55 CLR 499, which is still the leading case urging appellate restraint in overturning discretionary decisions of trial judges.

[40] *Li* (n 32) 346.

[41] ibid 352, 366.

[42] ibid 352.

[43] ibid 364.

[44] *Minister for Immigration and Multicultural and Indigenous Affairs v SCAR* (2003) 128 FCR 553; *Minister for Immigration and Citizenship v SZNVW* (2010) 183 FCR 575.

[45] *Li* (n 32) 361–62.

[46] ibid 342.

[47] ibid 371–72, 374.

[48] See *NAIS v Minister for Immigration and Multicultural and Indigenous Affairs* (2005) 228 CLR 470, 482–83, 526; *SZFDE v Minister for Immigration and Citizenship* (2007) 232 CLR 189, 205–6; *Saeed v Minister for Immigration and Citizenship* (2010) 241 CLR 252, 270; *Minister for Immigration and Citizenship v SZJSS* (2010) 243 CLR 164, 175; *Li* (n 32) 342–44, 361–62, 371–72, 374.

firm grasp of the facts and the law. These features have always been obvious, and are easily traced to the *minutiae* of the statute itself. What is new, however, is this sense of an holistic appraisal of whether the tribunal's conduct and decision answer the description of a proper 'invitation', 'hearing', 'appeal' or 'review'.

C. Proportionality Review

Proportionality review's more enthusiastic proponents[49] claim that its multi-staged structure is more disciplined than *Wednesbury* unreasonableness, giving it the advantage over *Wednesbury* of being 'more precise and more sophisticated',[50] with a 'structure' that prompts more 'rational' decision-making.[51] These claims might be doubted,[52] but proportionality is an established feature of review on EU grounds, and review for breach of the Human Rights Act 1998 (UK). With a bewildering array of possible meanings, the Supreme Court appears now to have accepted 'proportionality review' into the pantheon of judicial review more generally.[53]

Proportionality review means different things in different contexts,[54] but Australia already makes some allowance for proportionality review of the validity of bye-laws[55] and some federal law.[56] However, the High Court has yet to approve proportionality testing of administrative action more generally.[57]

Australia has no constitutionally entrenched Bill of Rights, and only two statutory Human Rights Charters, neither of them federal.[58] The High Court's decision in *Momcilovic v R*[59] ruled that judges exercising federal jurisdiction could not validly be given the task of declaring a statutory provision to be incompatible with a statutory Charter right, at least if that involves the judge in a proportionality assessment

[49] See, eg H Woolf, J Jowell, A Le Sueur, C Donnelly and I Hare, *De Smith's Judicial Review*, 7th edn (London, Sweet & Maxwell, 2013) 627–34; P Craig, *Administrative Law*, 7th edn (London, Sweet & Maxwell, 2012) [21-025]–[21-038].

[50] *R v Secretary of State for the Home Department, ex parte Daly* [2001] 2 AC 532, 547 (Lord Steyn).

[51] *Pham v Secretary of State for the Home Department* [2015] 1 WLR 1591, [95]–[96] (Lord Mance).

[52] See C Harlow and R Rawlings, *Law and Administration*, 3rd edn (Cambridge, Cambridge University Press, 2009) 106–7.

[53] Lord Mance appeared to support such a transition in *Kennedy v Charity Commission* [2014] 2 WLR 808, [54], but Lord Carnwath (at [246]) was less certain. Lords Carnwath, Mance, Clarke and Toulson left the matter open in *R (Sandiford) v Secretary of State for Foreign and Commonwealth Affairs* [2014] 1 WLR 2697, [66]. Conflicting understandings of the term were given in *Pham v Secretary of State for the Home Department* [2015] 1 WLR 1591, but all Justices seem to have accepted 'it' as a general ground.

[54] In *R (Cart) v Upper Tribunal* [2012] 1 AC 663, 683, for example, Lady Hale said that judicial review of the Upper Tribunal should be 'proportionate', meaning that the courts should not waste too much time and money checking the Tribunal's decisions for errors of law, which were unlikely to be plentiful or serious.

[55] See *Attorney General (South Australia) v Adelaide Corporation* (2013) 249 CLR 1.

[56] The principal debate is whether proportionality review applies to only two situations, namely, where the legislation impinges upon constitutionally-protected immunities or rights, and where the legislative head of power is purposive. See *Leask v Commonwealth* (1996) 187 CLR 579; *Theophanous v Commonwealth* (2006) 225 CLR 101; *Monis v R* (2013) 249 CLR 92.

[57] See *Sabet v Medical Practitioners Board (Vic)* (2008) 20 VR 414, 422–24; *Adelaide Corporation* (n 55) 37, 40–41; *Li* (n 32) 352, 366.

[58] Human Rights Act 2004 (ACT); Charter of Human Rights and Responsibilities Act 2006 (Vic).

[59] *Momcilovic v R* (2011) 245 CLR 1.

of whether the provision is a minimal and justifiable intrusion upon a Charter right. The political or policy element in that sort of proportionality balancing was part of the problem, and the political purpose or function of a declaration of incompatibility was the other big stumbling block. Although *Momcilovic* yields no clear rulings dealing entirely separately with each of those issues, it seems likely that federal legislation could validly set *some* proportionality constraints upon the administrative exercise of statutory powers. It might well be valid to entrust the courts with proportionality review in human rights matters, provided that the court's role is merely supervisory and focused on process, rather than entertaining a *de novo* consideration of the proportionality of a rights infraction.

D. Intellectual Engagement

Traditional accounts of procedural fairness maintain that its content is wholly procedural,[60] although a court's sense of substantive fairness is sometimes very close to the surface when it comes to setting the demands of procedural fairness for any particular context. Nevertheless, the traditional account keeps reappearing. It was a component, for example, of the High Court's emphatic rejection of England's decision to allow substantive enforcement of some legitimate expectations, a decision rationalised in various ways.[61]

Despite professing adherence to the traditional account, the High Court has extended the umbrella of procedural fairness to substantive territory. Tribunals now run the risk of breaching their procedural fairness obligations if they fail 'to respond to a substantial, clearly articulated argument relying on established facts'.[62] In practical terms, if they overlook or misunderstand a material element of a party's claim, they might be in breach of procedural fairness even though the party was afforded a full opportunity to appear and argue their case. Similarly, a tribunal that took ages to give a decision was held to have breached natural justice.[63] It had based its decision on an adverse assessment of the party's demeanour (and consequently, the party's credibility), and it appeared to have made no contemporaneous notes. The ruling was in one sense about procedure (the tribunal had impaired its capacity to assess the evidence), but it involved an assessment of the quality of the tribunal's reasoning process.

A similar picture of substance disguised as procedure emerges in the cases on review for failing to take relevant (and mandatory) considerations into account, and review for considering irrelevant (and prohibited) factors. For convenience, these may be called the 'relevancy' grounds of review. The traditional account of those grounds was that they were not concerned with weight; their sole job was to

[60] *Quin* (n 4) 22; *Leeth v Commonwealth* (1992) 174 CLR 455, 470.

[61] See *Re Minister for Immigration and Multicultural and Indigenous Affairs, ex parte Lam* (2003) 214 CLR 1, 21–22, rejecting *R v North and East Devon Health Authority, ex parte Coughlan* [2001] QB 213.

[62] *Dranichnikov v Minister for Immigration and Multicultural Affairs* (2003) 197 ALR 389, [24].

[63] *NAIS* (n 48) 526.

check *whether* the factors were considered, not whether they were given too much or too little weight. Where weight was the nub of the complaint, then *Wednesbury* unreasonableness used to be 'the preferred ground'.[64] It still is, in high theory, but review for serious irrationality is now a work-around, which can be deployed when the complaint is that the decision-maker did not 'really and genuinely' give consideration to the mandatory factor, or failed to engage in 'an active intellectual process',[65] or failed to give a mandatory factor 'proper, genuine and realistic' consideration.[66] It has even been suggested that none of these labels does anything more than describe different ways in which the government party can breach the requirements of procedural fairness.[67]

The Federal Court has recently used the relevancy grounds to strike down decisions whose authors failed either to notice or appreciate the basic thrust of a claimant's evidence, or at least an important aspect of that evidence. Previously, the court would have drawn a line of sorts between misunderstanding (or discounting) mere items of evidence, and misunderstanding a claim or integer of a claim. The court now acknowledges, however, that such distinctions cannot be dispositive (especially in light of the High Court's decision in *Li*),[68] and that the court has necessarily to make a qualitative assessment of the relative gravity of the tribunals' misunderstandings.[69] Proving such misunderstandings remains as difficult as ever, but the distinction between the relevancy grounds and merits review has become even more difficult.[70]

Full Federal Court decisions keep multiplying, and it is probably too early to assess where exactly that court is going. It does seem likely, however, that a new approach is emerging in its migration jurisdiction where the gist of the complaint is about the quality of a tribunal's fact-finding. At least in those cases, there is a noticeable lack of interest in the great mass of precedents with their fine-grained distinctions between the various review grounds. The Court's focus more recently has been on what lies behind the labels for the established review grounds, rather than whether a particular complaint might best be discussed under headings such as unreasonableness, serious irrationality or procedural fairness, for example.[71]

[64] *Minister for Aboriginal Affairs v Peko-Wallsend Ltd* (1986) 162 CLR 24, 41 (Mason J).

[65] *NAJT v Minister for Immigration and Multicultural and Indigenous Affairs* (2005) 147 FCR 51, 93 (Madgwick J); *Minister for Immigration and Citizenship v Khadgi* (2010) 190 FCR 248, 270 (Stone, Foster and Nicholas JJ).

[66] See *Minister for Immigration and Multicultural Affairs v Jia Legeng* (2001) 205 CLR 507, 540 (Gleeson CJ and Gummow J); *SZJSS* (n 48) 174–76.

[67] *SZRBA v Minister for Immigration and Border Protection* [2014] FCAFC 81, [24].

[68] *Li* (n 32).

[69] *SZRKT* (n 34)130; *Minister for Immigration and Border Protection v MZYTS* (2013) 136 ALD 547; *Minister for Immigration and Border Protection v SZSRS* (2014) 309 ALR 67; *Minister for Immigration and Border Protection v SZSSY* [2014] FCA 1144; *SZSNW* (n 29).

[70] See *Lo v Chief Commissioner of State Revenue* (2013) 85 NSWLR 86 (Basten JA).

[71] See, eg, *TCL Air Conditioner (Zhongshan) Co Ltd v Castel Electronics Pty Ltd* [2014] FCAFC 83; *Sullivan v Civil Aviation Safety Authority* [2014] FCAFC 93; *Minister for Immigration and Border Protection v CZBP* [2014] FCAFC 105.

IV. JUDICIAL REVIEW'S MISSION CREEP

A. Interpretivism

The expansion of judicial review's substantive grounds must affect how judges see their role. One might expect adjustments at the theoretical level to come in the first instance in arrears of the more practical redefinition of old grounds and formulation of new grounds. However, we might now see a feedback effect, with altered theory affecting the development of lower-level cases. If that is right, then shifts in judicial review's self-perception will be both cause and effect of the growth of substantive review.

Judicial review's mission is expanding, although its immediate task has never wavered; its grand role is to enforce the legal limits of and preconditions to the exercise of administrative power. Parliament can set those limits explicitly in the case of statutory power, but that happens surprisingly infrequently. There is an abundance of legislative rules directed to administrators, but there are very few instances of a governing Act actually telling us the consequences for judicial review of administrative breach of its rules. 'No invalidity' clauses are multiplying in migration legislation,[72] but they are exceptional elsewhere.

It follows that in most cases, the judicial review court has another job ahead of it after finding that the administrator breached a statutory requirement; it must then decide for itself whether to treat the error as harmless, or as invalidating the outcome. Although the courts in both Australia[73] and England[74] dress that up nowadays in terms of legislative purpose (that being 'a better test'[75] than the conclusory distinction between mandatory and directory rules), they are clearly doing more than merely enforcing the legal limits to administrative power—they are setting them.

This is not simply to make the obvious point that when the text is unclear, statutory interpretation is not a science. Rather, it is to highlight that there is often no relevant text whatsoever on one of the most critical issues of judicial review, namely, the consequences of breaching an Act.

The limits of textual meaning in administrative statutes provided much of the fuel for the so-called ultra vires debates in England, although their starting point (and a good one, too) was more typically that many judicial review grounds were entirely lacking in a textual basis in legislation. Judicial review of non-statutory government power or conduct provided extra fuel, because it could scarcely be either explained or justified in terms of effectuating legislative intent or meaning.

It is not my intention to enter the constitutional dimensions of the ultra vires debates.[76] The debates are relevant here only because of the creative ferment coinciding with (and possibly causally linked to) the frank recognition of the common

[72] See, eg, *Re Minister for Immigration and Multicultural Affairs, ex parte Palme* (2003) 216 CLR 212.

[73] *Project Blue Sky Inc v Australian Broadcasting Authority* (1998) 194 CLR 355, 388–90.

[74] *R v Soneji* [2006] 1 AC 340, 352–53; *R v Clarke* [2008] 1 WLR 338; *Public Prosecution Service v McKee* [2013] 1 WLR 1611; *R (Trail Riders Fellowship) v Dorset County Council* [2015] 1 WLR 1406, 1426, 1430–31.

[75] *Project Blue Sky* (n 73) 390 (McHugh, Gummow, Kirby and Hayne JJ).

[76] It suffices to refer to the essays in CF Forsyth (ed), *Judicial Review and the Constitution* (Oxford, Hart, 2000).

law provenance of almost all of judicial review's generic grounds of review—all, that is, that travel beyond a 'textual interpretation' of the relevant statute. In the field of statutory administrative power, even the 'interpretivists' (eventually describing themselves as adherents of a 'modified ultra vires' theory) acknowledged the fictional nature of imputing some of the review grounds to legislative intention, especially where (as in the case of privative clauses) the legislature and its judicial interpreters are so clearly at odds. The interpretivists advocate the imputation exercise as an interpretive methodology designed to respect legislative supremacy, rather than to identify the source of the review grounds.[77]

Australians are for the most part disengaged from the English debates, so far as these turned on the constitutional implications of striking a balance (if any) between, on the one hand, courts creating their own limits to statutory administrative power, and on the other hand, courts actually or constructively effectuating the intention (or meaning) of Parliament. It was always obvious that several of judicial review's generic review grounds came from the judges rather than legislative text. These include the requirements for procedural fairness, rationality and reasonableness, as well as the rules against bias, fraud and self-serving purpose. So long as these grounds remain reasonably stable, their imputation to legislative meaning (or intent) is no more remarkable than the imputation of the so-called principle of legality to legislation across many fields of law, and it poses no threat to legislative supremacy.

Operating under a written Constitution that separates the Commonwealth's judicial power from its legislative and executive branches, Australian courts were always likely to offer an interpretivist account of judicial review's generic grounds.[78] Speaking only in the context of procedural fairness governing the exercise of administrative powers conferred by statute, the High Court dismissed any need to refer to England's ultra vires debate between the common lawyers and the interpretivists. The court said that '[t]he principles and presumptions of statutory construction ... are part of the common law of Australia', and can be qualified or overridden by Interpretation Acts. It concluded that, in its view, the English debate therefore 'proceeds upon a false dichotomy and is unproductive'.[79]

B. Constitutional Considerations

The contrast between England's enthusiasm for, and Australia's lack of interest in, England's ultra vires debates is relevant to the way the judges of each country explain

[77] M Elliott, *The Constitutional Foundations of Judicial Review* (Oxford, Hart Publishing, 2001) ch 4.

[78] They were hardly likely to suggest that the common law modified legislative intent, and even less likely to treat the general run of judicial review grounds as constitutionally entrenched. I put to one side the possibility that some grounds might be entrenched. It has been suggested, for example, that Parliament cannot give advance authorisation for the administration to exercise its powers in bad faith: *Federal Commissioner of Taxation v Futuris Corporation Ltd* (2008) 237 CLR 146, 165.

[79] *Plaintiff S10/2011 v Minister for Immigration and Citizenship* (2012) 246 CLR 636, 666 (Gummow, Hayne, Crennan and Bell JJ). More generally, the High Court has tended to avoid overarching theory: M Aronson, 'Is the *ADJR Act* Hampering the Development of Australian Administrative Law?' (2004) 15 *Public Law Review* 202, 216–19; S Gageler, 'Impact of Migration Law on the Development of Australian Administrative Law' (2010) 17 *Australian Journal of Administrative Law* 92, 95.

judicial review's grounds. On a practical (if not constitutional) level, the common lawyers have the ascendancy in England, and it shows.

As far back as the mid-1980s, Lord Diplock organised England's grounds into three grand categories:[80]

— illegality (committed by misunderstanding the governing law); *and*
— irrationality (by which he meant *Wednesbury* unreasonableness); *and*
— procedural impropriety (by which he meant both breach of natural justice and breach of statutory rules of procedure).

I have italicised the conjunctions, because his Lordship was quite clear that his second category, and most of his third, had no connection to statutory interpretation. He added that his list was not closed, and he famously set the hares running with a suggestion that proportionality review might be the next cab off the common law rank.

Lord Diplock's message was obvious: the judges had written the larger part of the grounds, *and* were free to rewrite them according to their own, larger, conception of things. The same message has appeared ever since,[81] although different (and increasingly larger) abstractions have been offered: 'good administration';[82] 'abuse of power';[83] 'unfairness';[84] and the rule of law.[85] Laws LJ summed it up quite frankly:[86]

> The nature of the judicial review jurisdiction owned by the High Court has an elusive quality, because its limits are (generally) set by itself. In consequence, the distinction between a legal place where the jurisdiction cannot go, and a legal place where as a matter of discretion the High Court will not send it, is permeable: even unprincipled. Ultimately the court is simply concerned to give the jurisdiction the reach, or edge, which the rule of law requires.

The rule of law here is not just a background principle; it gives the judges direct licence to reshape judicial review; they become part of the policy design team. As Lord Phillips acknowledged, the judge's role is then to improve upon the statutes:[87]

> The administration of justice and upholding of the rule of law involves *a partnership* between Parliament and the judges. Parliament has to provide the resources needed for the administration of justice. The size and the jurisdiction of the judiciary is determined

[80] *Council of Civil Service Unions v Minister for the Civil Service* [1985] AC 374, 410–11.

[81] See, eg, *Cart* (n 54) 682–83 (Lady Hale): '[T]he scope of judicial review is an artefact of the common law whose object is to maintain the rule of law—that is, to ensure that, within the bounds of practical possibility, decisions are taken in accordance with the law, and in particular the law which Parliament has enacted, and not otherwise'.

[82] *Nadarajah* (n 1) [67]–[68]; *R (Lumba) v Secretary of State for the Home Department* [2012] 1 AC 245, 344–45.

[83] *R v Secretary of State for Education, ex parte Begbie* [2000] 1 WLR 1115, 1129; *Coughlan* (n 61) 242, 245.

[84] *Coughlan* (n 61) 245, 250; *R (Bancoult) v Secretary of State for Foreign and Commonwealth Affairs (No 2)* [2009] 1 AC 453, 513.

[85] *Cart* (n 54).

[86] *R (Cart) v Upper Tribunal* [2011] QB 120, 156.

[87] *Cart* (n 54) 698 (emphasis added). The 'partnership' model has a long history. Lord Donaldson MR maintained that the courts were in partnership with public agencies to advance good administration: *R v Lancashire County Council, ex parte Huddleston* [1986] 2 All ER 941, 945; *R v Panel on Take-overs and Mergers, ex parte Datafin Plc* [1987] 815, 842.

> by statute. Parliament has not sought to oust or fetter the common law powers of judicial review of the judges of the High Court and I hope that Parliament will never do so. It should be for the judges to decide whether the statutory provisions for the administration of justice adequately protect the rule of law and, by judicial review, to supplement these should it be necessary.

Despite acknowledging its often fictional character,[88] Australian courts still firmly adhere to the interpretivist account of non-text based statutory interpretation in general, and to the interpretivist account in judicial review in particular.[89] More importantly, the High Court theorises this as an 'expression'[90] or 'product'[91] of the 'interaction'[92] or 'relationship'[93] between the three branches of government. This has a limiting effect on the Australian judiciary's sense of the purpose of judicial review of administrative action.

There is a big gulf between Australia's inter-branch 'interactions' or 'relationships', on the one hand, and Lord Phillips' 'partnership', on the other. That gulf tends to be expressed at a high constitutional level, by reference to limitations on the judicial power that flow from the Constitution's separation of the federal judiciary from the legislative and executive branches. The High Court said in *Re Minister for Immigration and Multicultural and Indigenous Affairs, ex parte Lam*,[94] that constitutional considerations prevented courts exercising federal jurisdiction from following English moves[95] towards the enforcement of substantive legitimate expectations. Gleeson CJ's judgment in *Lam* rejected the idea that 'good administration' could be a ground of review in its own right.[96] Mike Taggart thought this 'bizarre', but he read it too broadly—as an assertion that 'administrative law is not about "good administration"'.[97] Of course, the courts recognise the need for efficient as well as fair administration: procedural fairness, for example, represents the balance between those competing tensions. 'Good administration', however, is for the executive branch to devise. Another judgment in *Lam* rejected 'abuse of power' as a standalone review ground; it is one of several rule of law values reflected in constitutional limitations upon both legislative and executive power, but those values do not constitute entrenched review grounds in their own right.[98] The same judgment said that the rule of law under the Constitution prevents the courts 'translating policy into statutory form or [engaging in] the executive function of administration'.[99]

88 *Quin* (n 4) 36 (Brennan J): 'In Australia, the modern development and expansion of the law of judicial review of administrative action have been achieved by an increasingly sophisticated exposition of implied limitations on the exercise or extent of statutory power'.

89 *Zheng v Cai* (2009) 239 CLR 446, 455; *Plaintiff S10* (n 79) 666.

90 *Zheng* (n 89) 455.

91 *Plaintiff S10* (n 79) 666.

92 ibid.

93 *Zheng* (n 89) 455.

94 *Lam* (n 61) 21–24.

95 *Coughlan* (n 61).

96 *Lam* (n 61) 12. Similarly, Gummow J said in *NAIS* (n 48) 477 that 'maladministration is not to be confused with the illegality which founds judicial review'.

97 M Taggart, '"Australian Exceptionalism" in Judicial Review' (2008) 36 *Federal Law Review* 1, 29.

98 *Lam* (n 61) 23 (McHugh and Gummow JJ).

99 ibid 25.

C. Between Principles and Rules

Lam's self-denying ordinances were admittedly vague, but that was appropriate given their constitutional foundation. Indecision about how far to push the boundaries of judicial review is usually best left to the normal common law processes of incremental change, rather than being elevated to the level of a constitutional debate.

Underlying *Lam*, however, was an almost palpable unease with any proposal to have review grounds propounded at a high degree of abstraction, particularly if those abstractions amounted to little else than contestable value judgements. High-level statements of value were acceptable, but only as usefully informing the content and application of more concrete review grounds; they could not be permitted to rise to the level of law itself. That accorded with Australia's long-held preference for small rules over abstract standards, a preference appearing not only in judicial review's case law, but also in its principal statutory codification. Depending on the rules of counting, the Administrative Decisions (Judicial Review) Act (ADJRA) 1977 (Cth) has at least 16 specific or particularised grounds of review,[100] plus two catch-all grounds whose use is almost impossible to detect. The catch-alls are 'otherwise contrary to law', and, almost incredibly, 'abuse of the power'.

Writing in 2008, Tom Poole characterised Australia's incrementalist, rule-bound approach as the devil, and England's broad-standard, normativist approach as the deep blue sea.[101] Poole implied that there had to be a middle ground. Australia's rules had a strong connection to precedent, but were in need of principles to guide their application and incrementalist development, whilst England's normativist standards needed anchoring in precedent and rules if they were to avoid the charge of conferring unfettered judicial discretion. One could always sift through the cases looking for earlier beginnings, but I have two main reasons for nominating the *Li* decision as Australia's first, unequivocal attempt to move to Poole's middle ground.

First, although all three of *Li*'s judgments affirmed their support for the interpretivist theory of judicial review, they no longer saw that as stopping at least some expansion of substantive review. Drawing on *Sharp v Wakefield*,[102] two of the three judgments referred very broadly to the 'rules of reason'.[103] The joint judgment dug further into the history books, and said that decisions cannot be 'arbitrary, vague and fanciful'.[104] French CJ declined to read the Act as excusing the tribunal 'from compliance with the criteria of lawfulness, fairness and rationality that lie at the heart of administrative justice', criteria found in the legislation and the common law.[105] To describe these sentiments as a shift in mission statement might be putting it too high. They are nevertheless consistent with (and perhaps a product of) the gradual acceptance of a greater degree of substantive review.

[100] Sixteen for 'decisions', and one more for failing or refusing to decide.

[101] T Poole, 'Between the Devil and the Deep Blue Sea: Administrative Law in an Age of Rights' in L Pearson, C Harlow, and M Taggart (eds), *Administrative Law in a Changing State: Essays in Honour of Mark Aronson* (Oxford, Hart Publishing, 2008).

[102] *Sharp v Wakefield* [1891] AC 173, 179.

[103] *Li* (n 32) 349–50 (French CJ), 363 (Hayne, Kiefel and Bell JJ).

[104] ibid 363 (Hayne, Kiefel and Bell JJ).

[105] ibid 344.

Secondly, *Li* reaffirmed a ruling given in 1999, dismissing an argument founded *directly* on an alleged breach of a series of statutory provisions about how the migration tribunals were to go about their business. The migration legislation has long required the migration tribunals to 'pursue the objective of providing a mechanism of review that is fair, just, economical, informal and quick'. It has also long required the tribunals to 'act according to substantial justice and the merits of the case', without being 'bound by technicalities, legal forms or rules of evidence'.[106] The essence of the court's 1999 decision[107] was to give those provisions no weight. They were said to be 'general exhortatory provisions',[108] intended to set the tribunals free from restrictions that apply to courts—they were 'facultative, not restrictive'.[109]

Fourteen years later, the *Li* decision repeated those conclusions, but with a marked difference of approach. All three of *Li*'s judgments said that these sort of highly generalised provisions give substance as to how the tribunal's powers or duties are to be exercised; in effect, they inform the more specific requirements found elsewhere in the Act. The result was to boost the chances of establishing what can only be described as a substantive breach of other (and largely procedural) provisions. For the joint judgment in particular, the tribunal's duty to exercise its procedural powers 'in a way that is fair and just'[110] actually amplified the standard common law requirement to act reasonably. It supplied the various powers and discretions of the tribunals with an overriding sense of purpose (in this case, to have a 'meaningful' review hearing),[111] and, it seems to have contributed to the conclusion that a migration tribunal's decision can be reviewable for unreasonableness even if it is not 'bizarre'[112] or lunatic in the original *Wednesbury* sense.

Li's use of a tribunal's statutory obligation to be fair and just is all the more striking because sections like that are not new. Some of them go back to the seventeenth century,[113] and a quick search of Austlii's legislation databases confirms that they are as common as dirt. It is therefore hard to believe that their presence in the migration legislation made anything more than a rhetorical difference. Statutory interpretation might have been used to *justify* *Li*'s shift towards substance, but it certainly failed to *explain* it.

V. SOME REASONS FOR EXPANSION

At this point, it might be worth considering three factors that appear to have contributed to the expansion of substantive review in Australia.

[106] It suffices to refer here to Migration Act 1958 (Cth), s 357A, whilst noting that the provisions here quoted are in template form, appearing also in other parts of the Act. A more recent amendment also required the tribunals to exercise their procedural powers conferred by a number of specific sections 'in a way that is fair and just', but it would be a distraction to relate here the back-story of that amendment.

[107] *Eshetu* (n 21).

[108] ibid 642 (Gummow J).

[109] ibid 628 (Gleeson CJ and McHugh J).

[110] Migration Act 1958 (Cth), s 357A(3).

[111] *Li* (n 32) 361–62.

[112] ibid 364.

[113] ibid 344 (French CJ).

A. Reasons Given for Challenged Decisions

First, there is a direct link between the expansion of substantive review, and the huge expansion of the procedural right to reasons for adverse administrative decisions. This is not just to make the obvious point that without access to reasons, there will be very little chance of inferring irrationality in the fact-finding or reasoning processes, for example, or for inferring that relevant and mandatory factors were given too little weight.

Despite all the ritual warnings against scrutinising statements of reasons 'with an eye keenly attuned to the perception of error',[114] courts engaged in judicial review are naturally disposed to reading statements of reasons, especially those made by tribunals, in much the same way as they read the reasons of a first instance judge. Gageler J acknowledged in the *Li* case that courts reviewing the exercise of 'judicial' discretions are fairly confident in their ability to spot unreasonableness. His Honour contrasted this with judicial review of 'administrative' discretions, which can be difficult, he said, where they are exercised by reference to 'opinion, policy or taste'.[115] In a telling passage, however, his Honour added:[116]

> There is no such practical difficulty in a court applying the test of *Wednesbury* unreasonableness to a refusal by the MRT [Migration Review Tribunal] to adjourn a review. The aspirations required to inform the performance of the MRT's duty to review—sufficiently captured in the repeated statutory references to what is fair and just—are aspirations at the core of the judicial function. The MRT is to some degree free from constraints otherwise applicable to courts of law, and a court must be careful not to draw too closely upon analogies in the conduct and determination of civil litigation. But a refusal by the MRT to adjourn a review will rarely, if ever, be legitimately affected by policies of which the court has no experience.

Tribunals and others who are bound to supply reasons know this, and put considerable effort into how they explain themselves. Indeed, one of the principal justifications for imposing a duty to supply reasons is its tendency to focus the administrator's mind, and induce more care and deliberation.[117] If that is a principal aim of a reasons regime, it is small wonder that substantive review has expanded.

The High Court refused some time ago to impose upon administrators a generalised common law duty to give reasons to those adversely affected by their decisions.[118] That ruling still stands,[119] although some decisions have chipped away at its edges.[120]

[114] *Minister for Immigration and Ethnic Affairs v Wu Shan Liang* (1996) 185 CLR 259, 272 (Brennan CJ, Toohey, McHugh and Gummow JJ) (internal reference omitted).

[115] *Li* (n 32) 377.

[116] ibid (internal quotation marks and references omitted).

[117] *Palme* (n 72) 242 (Kirby J).

[118] *Public Service Board (NSW) v Osmond* (1986) 159 CLR 656.

[119] *Wingfoot Australia Partners Pty Ltd v Kocak* (2013) 303 ALR 64, [43].

[120] See *Campbelltown City Council v Vegan* (2006) 67 NSWLR 372, 377, 396; *Sherlock v Lloyd* (2010) 27 VR 434, 437–39; *Watson v South Australia* (2010) 278 ALR 168, [115]–[144]; *Soliman v University of Technology, Sydney* (2012) 207 FCR 277, 290–92.

In Australia, however, express statutory duties to supply reasons apply to large swathes of decision-making by administrators, tribunals, and even Ministers. Sometimes, the reasons must accompany the decision itself, but the standard drafting template allows for decisions upon timely request after the relevant decision has been made. The English drift to the 'gisting' gerund is unknown.[121] Although some statutes allow statements of reasons to be 'brief', the standard template is considerably more demanding. For example, in the vast bulk of matters appealable to the Administrative Appeals Tribunal, or judicially reviewable in the Federal Court's codified judicial review jurisdiction, the putative challenger has a right to a written reasons statement that sets out the findings on material questions of fact, refers to the evidence or other material on which those findings were based, and gives the reasons for the decision.[122] That formula became so standard that the Interpretation Act adopted it for any Act that requires written reasons.[123] A failure to provide any or adequate reasons is at the very least a non-jurisdictional patent error of law amenable to certiorari and its statutory equivalents,[124] but it does not invalidate the underlying decision,[125] unless, perhaps, the reasons must be given with the decision itself.

The most commonly contested issue concerns the adequacy of a statement of reasons for a decision, and it appears that no single test is appropriate for all contexts.[126] There is currently considerable room for debate as to the requisite standard in different contexts and under different statutory formulas. However, whichever standard is used for testing the adequacy of a statement of reasons, the critical point for present purposes is that they are *all* qualitative. A requirement to give reasons can be policed as mere process in its own right; a requirement to give *adequate* reasons has the potential for facilitating substantive review, even if that be disguised as no more than enforcing the duty to *give* reasons.[127] That the expansion of substantive review coincides with the expansion of the supply of reasons is therefore no coincidence.

B. Judicialisation of Tribunals

In both Australia and England, the growth of tribunals over the last 50 or so years has been one of the most remarkable features of administrative law. Also remarkable has been a deliberate trend of modelling the tribunals upon the courts. Efforts have been made to staff the senior levels of the tribunals with legally qualified members, and to have judges as tribunal (and sometimes Divisional) heads. Steps are taken to protect the independence of tribunal members, who in their turn seek to avoid

[121] *Tariq v Home Office* [2012] 1 AC 452.

[122] Administrative Appeals Tribunal Act 1975 (Cth), s 28(1); Administrative Decisions (Judicial Review) Act 1977 (Cth), s 13(1).

[123] Acts Interpretation Act 1901 (Cth), s 25D.

[124] *Wingfoot* (n 119).

[125] *Palme* (n 72); *Soliman v University of Technology, Sydney* (2012) 207 FCR 277.

[126] *Wingfoot* (n 119) [44]–[46].

[127] M Shapiro, 'The Giving Reasons Requirement' [1992] *University of Chicago Legal Forum* 179, 184–85, 187–88.

ex parte contacts with government parties. Strictly speaking, the rules of evidence do not apply, but they cast an unmistakable shadow. Tribunal procedures are clearly cut-down versions of court procedures, and legally qualified advocates are usually welcomed, even though self-represented parties predominate on the non-government side in many areas. Tribunals structure and deliver their decisions as if they were judicial judgments, and these are published (along with headnotes) in series that differ not at all from regular law reporting series. Appeals on questions of law usually lie to the same courts as could take cognisance of the same issues by way of judicial review applications, and the feedback effects are obvious.

England was able to pursue the judicialisation model openly, because it has no entrenched separation of the judicial power.[128] Australia's separation of the federal judicial power requires that judicialisation be done covertly at the federal level, and the Administrative Appeals Tribunal (AAT) is a generalist tribunal that is necessarily restricted to handling disputes between government and subject. Australia's State constitutions have fewer restrictions, with the result that State generalist tribunals can handle disputes between subjects as well as disputes between subject and government.[129] Indeed, Victoria's generalist tribunal handles the bulk of civil disputes in trade and commerce in that State.[130] It is no surprise, therefore, that State generalist tribunals overtly model themselves on the 'regular' courts. They can even handle low-level disputes that would take the form of judicial review applications if heard in their Supreme Courts. England's Upper Tribunal has a similar judicial review jurisdiction.[131]

None of this is contentious, but it does pose a series of interesting questions to do with judicial review. In Australia, the old institutional dichotomy between administrators and tribunals, on the one hand, and inferior courts, on the other, is beginning to fray. The admonition to construe tribunals' statements of reasons more generously than those of inferior courts[132] remains canonical, but is obviously in tension with Gageler J's acknowledgment in *Li* that he felt more at home in scrutinising the reasons supplied by an adjudicative tribunal for its exercise of a function approximating a judicial function.[133] Indeed, one could make a good case for closer scrutiny of tribunals (especially those modelled after courts) than of administrators. After all, one reasonably expects so much more from judicialised tribunals.

In other words, I suspect that the increased judicialisation of tribunals might in Australia be contributing to the increase in substantive review, not just because judicialised tribunals have to give reasons, but also because the *whole point* of establishing merits review tribunals is to provide a greater degree of care than is typically

[128] The Tribunals, Courts and Enforcement Act 2007 (UK) created the First-tier Tribunal and the Upper Tribunal (s 3). These have extensive first instance and appellate jurisdictions. The judicial model is evident in their appointments, procedure and statutory protection of independence. The Upper Tribunal is a superior court of record, which was one of the main reasons for the decision in *R (Evans) v Attorney General* [2015] UKSC 21 to place severe restrictions upon the Attorney's statutory power to override that Tribunal's decision in a freedom of information matter.

[129] See *Kirk* (n 6) 573.

[130] K Bell, *One VCAT: President's Review of VCAT* (Melbourne, VCAT, 2009) 10.

[131] Tribunals, Courts and Enforcement Act 2007 (UK), s 15.

[132] *Wu Shan Liang* (n 114).

[133] Text to n 115 above.

provided at the first instance, bureaucratic level. If that is indeed the point, then surely the courts have good warrant for intensifying their substantive scrutiny, to make sure that the tribunals are doing what is substantively expected of them.

C. Legislative Restrictions that have Backfired

Given that the Commonwealth Parliament has tried various strategies since the early 1990s to restrict the tidal wave of migration litigation, it might seem peculiar to assign any blame to the Parliament for the expansion of substantive judicial review. That, however, has been one of the consequences of the legislative attacks on judicial review of migration decisions, particularly those involving claims for asylum. Legislative assaults have not only been repelled, but have backfired.[134] First, some background.

For almost 20 years now, the Parliament has been attempting to curtail judicial review of migration decisions. The Migration Reform Act (MRA) 1992 (Cth) was its first full-blooded attempt. The MRA 1992 attempted a trade-off: more tribunal review on the merits, in return for no judicial *appeals* on points of law (a radical departure from most tribunal models) and greatly reduced Federal Court competence in *judicial review*. The second part of that equation was to be achieved by preventing the Federal Court from entertaining some of the more substantive review grounds in migration matters. The Act had, in effect, two lists of judicial review grounds: those that were allowable in the Federal Court, and those that were not. The excluded grounds were procedural fairness, apprehended (but not actual) bias, failure to take relevant (and mandatory) considerations into account, bad faith short of fraud, unreasonableness and abuse of power. The Federal Court could use these grounds in non-migration matters, and the exclusions did not (and constitutionally could not) apply to matters commenced and heard in the High Court.

The MRA 1992 provided, in effect, that in the event of an overlap between the grounds thus excluded and the grounds specifically allowable in the Federal Court, the exclusions were to prevail. That put huge pressure on the High Court, which was flooded with fall-back applications in its untouchable original jurisdiction.[135] Lawyers had to do this to protect their clients against the risk of the Federal Court ruling that their grounds of claim fell within the exclusions, so for roughly a decade, claimants typically filed two challenges: the main one in the Federal Court, and the fall-back in the High Court. If the principal case failed, they would appeal to the High Court and at the same time, awaken the fall-back from its dormancy. The two matters would then be heard together.

[134] I am indebted to my PhD student, Grant Hooper, for some of the information and insights in this section.

[135] The situation was roundly condemned, but it took a long time before the Government backed down. See Australian Law Reform Commission, *The Judicial Power of the Commonwealth: A Review of the Judiciary Act 1903 and Related Legislation*, Report No 92 (2001) 116–20. The Commission's comments were extensive, despite the fact that its terms of reference disgracefully forbade it from making recommendations regarding judicial review of migration matters (117).

To its great credit, the High Court did not go into self-protection mode; it did not give restrictive interpretations of the grounds which only it could hear. It took on an astonishing number of claims that only it could hear.[136] However, it also cut back on the exclusionary provisions in two important respects, thus restoring considerable power to the Federal Court.

First, the High Court outflanked the *Wednesbury* exclusion by confining the scope of that ground, but in doing that, it set in train the drift to substantive review. True, *Wednesbury* unreasonableness was excluded, but the court said that the exclusion applied only to discretionary choices, not the newly minted grounds of 'serious irrationality' or 'serious illogicality', both of which were nested within two grounds[137] that remained allowable in the Federal Court.[138]

Secondly, in a commendable display of interpretive ingenuity, the court neutered the legislative attempt to exclude from the allowable grounds any challenges for taking irrelevant considerations into account, or for failing to take relevant considerations into account. It held that these exclusions applied only to limit the ground of 'improper exercise of power'; they left untouched two allowable grounds of error of law: no jurisdiction and unauthorised decision.[139] A subsequent Commonwealth Solicitor General (now a Justice of the High Court) wrote that this sounded the 'death knell' for the MRA 1992's focus on the allowable and excluded grounds of review.[140]

Starting in 2001, the Parliament changed tactics. First, it enacted a seemingly savage privative clause, but the High Court made short work of that, on an interpretive rather than a constitutional basis.[141] Secondly, the Act was amended to delete any mention of specifically allowable grounds, with the result that regardless of whether the matter was in the Federal Court or the High Court, all challenges had henceforth to allege jurisdictional error. Thirdly, the Parliament maintained its original goal (in the MRA 1992) of replacing the common law's flexible principles of procedural fairness with a statutory code of procedure, but it now adopted a different tactic, which was to use increasingly explicit statements that compliance with the statutory procedures would suffice to meet the requirements of procedural fairness.[142] Fourthly, the

[136] The year ending 30 June 2002 was the High Court's worst. Judicial review applications in the Court's original jurisdiction jumped to 300, up from 81 in the previous year. Of the 300 applications filed, 287 (ie 96%) were migration matters. The Court noted that a large back-log threatened to develop in migration matters, because so many could not be transferred down to the Federal Court: High Court of Australia, *Annual Report 2001–02* (2002) 9. The number of migration filings in the Court's original jurisdiction skyrocketed the following year to 2,105. However, one of the consequences of the Court's restrictive interpretation (in *Plaintiff S157/2002 v Commonwealth* (2003) 211 CLR 476) of the migration law's privative clause was that the Court could then (and did) transfer most of the migration matters down to the Federal Court. See High Court of Australia, *Annual Report 2002–03* (2002) 16.

[137] Namely, that the tribunal did not have jurisdiction to make the decision, and that the Act did not authorise the decision.

[138] See *Applicant S20* (n 11); *SGLB* (n 26). This summary used to be contentious, but the irrationality and illogicality grounds have now found acceptance: *SZMDS* (n 29).

[139] *Minister for Immigration and Multicultural Affairs v Yusuf* (2001) 206 CLR 323, 351–52.

[140] Gageler, 'Impact of Migration Law on the Development of Australian Administrative Law' (n 79) 101.

[141] *Plaintiff S157* (n 136).

[142] Migration Act 1958 (Cth), ss 51A, 97A, 118A, 127A, 306AG, 357A, 422B.

Minister is now explicitly free of the rules of natural justice when exercising a range of non-delegable powers in the public interest.[143]

So far as they applied to tribunal proceedings, the attempts to oust the common law's procedural fairness substantially failed,[144] and the Parliament subsequently capitulated in all but name.[145] Paradoxically, however, it was in the drawn-out course of that particular failure that the High Court started propounding its requirements that the tribunals engage intellectually with the applicant's case and evidence, and equally, that the tribunals allow applicants to engage with the material that was worrying the tribunal. As explained above, those requirements are quintessentially substantive.[146]

In essence, the court has outflanked the exclusion of the common law's principles of procedural fairness by reading some of the Act's procedural requirements as being 'informed' by the common law. Three procedural sections in particular have been used as bases for implying a requirement of substantive intellectual engagement. First, there is a section requiring the RRT to conduct a merits 'review' upon timely application.[147] Secondly, the court has used a section requiring that tribunal to warn the applicant of potentially adverse information, to ensure as far as reasonably practicable that the applicant understands the warning, and to invite comment.[148] Thirdly, the court has also used a section inviting the applicant's attendance at a hearing where he or she can give evidence, and present arguments.[149] In a strange twist, the common law's procedural fairness requirements have not just been smuggled into the Act's procedural requirements. They have become noticeably more substantive, and that development now applies to migration and non-migration contexts alike.

What had become a formulaic section also led to substantive consequences in rather surprising ways. The principal Act gave a time-honoured description of its tribunals as being free of technical legal rules, but added that they had to be 'fair, just, economical and quick', and 'act according to substantial justice and the merits of the case'.[150] Having initially treated this as if it were merely aspirational surplusage,[151] the court started treating it as generally indicative of the way the tribunals were to conduct themselves,[152] and then in *Li*, as noted above, the court said that these

[143] ibid ss 133A, 133C, 134A, 198AB, 198AD, 198AE, 500A, 501, 501A, 501BA.

[144] The legislative twists and turns are too complicated to pursue here. It must suffice to refer to *Re Minister for Immigration and Multicultural Affairs, ex parte Miah* (2001) 206 CLR 57; *Applicant NAFF of 2002 v Minister for Immigration and Multicultural and Indigenous Affairs* (2004) 221 CLR 1; *SAAP v Minister for Immigration and Multicultural and Indigenous Affairs* (2005) 228 CLR 294; *NAIS* (n 48); *SZBEL v Minister for Immigration and Multicultural and Indigenous Affairs* (2006) 228 CLR 152; *SZFDE* (n 48); *Minister for Immigration and Citizenship v SZIZO* (2009) 238 CLR 627.

[145] The Migration Act 1958 (Cth), s 422B, states that a range of procedural provisions represent 'an exhaustive statement of the requirements of the natural justice hearing rule in relation to the matters they deal with', but it then adds: 'In applying this Division, the Tribunal must act in a way that is fair and just'.

[146] See above, section III.D.

[147] Migration Act 1958 (Cth), s 414.

[148] ibid s 424A.

[149] ibid s 425.

[150] ibid s 420.

[151] *Eshetu* (n 21).

[152] *NAIS* (n 48) 523.

exhortatory provisions amplified the tribunals' duties to act reasonably, and to provide a 'meaningful' hearing.[153]

VI. POSSIBLE CONSEQUENCES OF EXPANDING SUBSTANTIVE REVIEW

A. 'Merits' are in Retreat

With every expansion of the grounds of judicial review, the courts have steadfastly maintained their denial of reviewing 'the merits' of a decision, but that could mean a number of things.[154] Most obviously, judicial review adheres to its refusal to remake the decision under review. In contrast to a court's powers in the resolution of statutory appeals, a court conducting judicial review has no warrant for taking the decision it thinks the administrator or tribunal should have made. At most, it must remit the matter for redetermination according to law. Aside from that consideration, it is apparent that 'the merits' is a term of 'beguiling simplicity'.[155]

It may have been largely intuitive, but we used to have a fair idea of what constituted the merits. They were the policies, outcomes and (above all) the facts, committed to the discretion or determination of the administrator. In so far as the governing Act left procedure undefined, that, too, was part of the merits, except that whatever the process, it had to be fair. The courts still speak of 'the merits' as judicial review's no-go area, but the concept itself has in one sense transformed from something with reasonably fixed components to a result—in this sense, the 'merits' are the left-overs from the court's scrutiny. This is most clear, perhaps, in the case of proportionality review, but it applies also to the other avenues for substantive review.

In a different sense, one might say that substantive review requires a 'consideration of the merits', but not 'a decision on the merits'.[156] However, that merely repeats the fundamental distinction between judicial appeals and judicial review: in the latter, the court cannot replace the administrator's decision with its own. One could view that as a remedial limitation of judicial review, rather than a substantive restriction upon the scope of a judicial review inquiry. We still have a sense of 'the merits' amounting to more than judicial review's left-overs (whether the applicant really was a refugee, genuinely homeless, unemployed or injured at work), but it has boiled down to the difference between review for correctness, and review for qualitative faults that leave room for reasonable minds to differ.

[153] Above nn 106–13.

[154] See *R (Lord Carlile) v Secretary of State for the Home Department* [2014] 1 WLR 1404 [30], [87], where Lord Sumption and Lady Hale thought it unhelpful to use the term.

[155] *D'Amore* (n 19) [232] (Basten JA). 'Blancmange-like quality' was Sir Anthony Mason's description: 'Judicial Review: Constitutional and Other Perspectives' (2000) 28 *Federal Law Review* 331, 333.

[156] P Daly, *A Theory of Deference in Administrative Law: Basis, Application and Scope* (Cambridge, Cambridge University Press, 2012) 140.

B. Judicial Discretion and Deference Expand

'Deference' was once a sensitive topic in English courts, conjuring up images of judicial servility to the executive branch.[157] Judicial dislike of the term is no longer universal, but 'weight' or 'respect' are safer terms,[158] and it remains the case that England forswears the need for any stand-alone deference 'doctrine'.[159] In Australia, the High Court was so emphatic in its rejection of America's '*Chevron* deference' to administrative determinations of the law that advocates would find it safer to use almost any other term, even where the issue is not statutory interpretation but an exercise of discretion, or administrative fact-finding.[160]

In effect, the courts of both countries have replaced North America's doctrinal commands for deference with something which is not just discretionary and flexible, but also occasional in the sense that it is not always present. When accorded, it amounts to a variable allowance for administrative or political judgement, either out of respect for the decision-maker's greater expertise or competence, or as a prudential exercise in self-restraint. As the grounds of review expanded further into substantive territory, it was inevitable that the courts would need something to stop review turning into full-scale *de novo* appeal. Perhaps not inevitable was that this would take the form of discretionary self-restraint, rather than a doctrinal rule.

Other manifestations of the rise of discretionary self-restraint on the part of the courts probably stem from factors other than simply the rise of substantive review. For example, the gradual relaxation of the requirements for standing to sue has brought in its train a recognition of the need to give greater consideration to third party and public interests when deciding whether to filter out challenges at the outset, and when deciding whether to deny relief even if the grounds of challenge have been made out.[161]

C. Will General Grounds Replace the Specific Generic Grounds?

For many years, the grounds of review were conceived narrowly, pleaded with care and particularity, and resistant to newcomers. In *Associated Provincial Picture*

[157] *R (ProLife Alliance) v British Broadcasting Corp* [2004] 1 AC 185, 240 (Lord Hoffmann); *A v Secretary of State for the Home Department* [2005] 2 AC 68, 155 (Lord Rodger).

[158] See *R (Lord Carlile) v Secretary of State for the Home Department* [2014] 3 WLR 1404 [150], [180], where Lord Kerr (in dissent) seemed to treat 'deference' as a question of the weight to be accorded to a government decision. Lord Sumption, however, said that at least in some circumstances, the term stands for nothing more than the fundamental principle that the courts do not replace the government's decision with their own: [22].

[159] See *R (SB) v Governors of Denbigh High School* [2007] 1 AC 100; *Huang v Secretary of State for the Home Department* [2007] 2 AC 167; *Belfast City Council v Miss Behavin' Ltd* [2007] 1 WLR 1420; *E v Chief Constable of the Royal Ulster Constabulary* [2009] 1 AC 536, 546, 560–61; *R (Quila) v Secretary of State for the Home Department* [2012] 1 AC 621, 643–44, 660; *AXA General Insurance Ltd v Lord Advocate (Scotland)* [2012] 1 AC 868, 907.

[160] *Enfield City Corporation v Development Assessment Commission* (2000) 199 CLR 135, 151–56; *NAIS* (n 48) 500; *SZMDS* (n 27) 621–22. Flick and Perram JJ put the word into parenthesis in *Jaffarie v Director General of Security* [2014] FCAFC 102, [48], and Edelman J suggested, in *Pilbara Infrastructure Pty Ltd v Economic Regulation Authority* [2014] WASC 346, [141]–[147], that 'judicial restraint' might be the most appropriate term.

[161] See, eg, *Walton v Scottish Ministers* 2012 SLT 1211, [103] (Lord Carnwath).

Houses Ltd v Wednesbury Corporation,[162] for example, Lord Greene MR said that a number of specific grounds could all be treated as manifestations of unreasonableness. Although the Master of the Rolls then added his famous tautological definition of unreasonableness, it is worth recalling that Professor de Smith's first edition, in 1959, was able to mount a credible argument against recognition of unreasonableness as a ground of review in its own right. He preferred that it be left as an evidentiary basis for inferring the presence of one or more of the established review grounds.[163] In his second edition, which appeared in 1968, de Smith was still defending his position, although he conceded that the courts had 'fluctuated' on whether to allow unreasonableness as an independent ground of challenge.[164]

I suspect that de Smith's 1959 defence of a restricted and mostly narrowly defined set of review grounds makes for easier reading in Australia than England. Whilst eventually admitting defeat in his stand against substantive review, de Smith's account of the procedural grounds readily acknowledged how often they overlapped, but insisted on their value as guides to what administrators should (or usually should not) do. Australian cases still tend to focus on the specific grounds, even though they acknowledge that in some cases, the grounds clearly overlap.[165] The discussion in section IV.C above noted how the *Li* decision spoke in general terms, such as 'the rules of reason',[166] or 'the criteria of lawfulness, fairness and rationality that lie at the heart of administrative justice'.[167] At the same time, however, no High Court case has ever gone as far as Lord Diplock's reductionist exercise, boiling the various review grounds down to three broad categories.[168] Nor would they ever join forces with Laws LJ to leverage directly from the rule of law,[169] or with Lord Philips to reshape deficient statutes.[170]

The Administrative Review Council (ARC) is the Commonwealth government's standing law reform body for administrative law. Both sides of politics now treat it with contempt, but its published research and consultation exercises should not be ignored. It recently considered two options for abolishing the long list of traditional review grounds in the ADJRA 1977. The first abolitionist option would have put nothing in place of the current list, leaving it to the common law to continue to develop and elaborate on the various ways of committing 'jurisdictional error'. The ARC rejected that option, arguing that the current list of grounds provides considerable assistance to practitioners and the public. It also noted that 'submissions to the

162 *Provincial Picture Houses Ltd v Wednesbury Corporation* [1948] 1 KB 223, 229–30.

163 SA de Smith, *Judicial Review of Administrative Action* (London, Stevens & Sons, 1959) 214: 'Unlike some foreign systems, English law has not adopted a general principle that the validity of administrative action is conditional upon its reasonableness'.

164 SA de Smith, *Judicial Review of Administrative Action*, 2nd edn (London, Stevens & Sons, 1968) 335.

165 *Kirk* (n 6) 574–75; *Li* (n 32) 350–51, 365–66.

166 *Li* (n 32) 349–50 (French CJ), 363 (Hayne, Kiefel and Bell JJ).

167 ibid 344 (French CJ).

168 *Council of Civil Service Unions* (n 80) 410–11; above, section IV.B.

169 *Cart* (n 86) 156.

170 *Cart* (n 54) 698.

Council overwhelmingly supported some form of codification'.[171] The ARC's second option was to replace the ADJRA 1977's admittedly lengthy list of grounds with a shorter Canadian list articulated at a higher level of generality.[172]

Australia's list runs for a page and a half, but the ARC chose to keep it, recommending only minor tweaking. The ARC thought that the current list gives more guidance, does not drive practitioners to the common law quite so often as the Canadian list, and has the same degree of flexibility for further developments. Only one submission had supported the Canadian option. The Law Council of Australia's submission proposed some clarifications, but:[173]

> argued that [Canada's] general grounds ... were 'too generic and vague'; would likely be sources of complexity and unpredictability; and distract from more pertinent issues with the ADJR Act.

Without knowing how it works in practice, it would be presumptuous to say that another country's approach is better or worse. What can be said, though, is that the High Court's recent excursions into slightly higher-level principles are welcome, indeed necessary. There is nothing wrong with having a long list of grounds, provided one has some sense not only of how they are to fit alongside each other, but also of how they might be applied and developed. And to have that sense, one needs some guiding principles.

The High Court used to have a quite visceral reaction to any suggestion of 'top down' theorising; its preference was for a 'bottom up' approach.[174] My point,[175] and Poole's,[176] is that one needs both, and the court seems to be edging towards that middle ground. Whilst retaining a list of specific grounds of review in *Kirk v Industrial Court (NSW)*,[177] it was at pains to emphasise that these are neither exhaustive nor self-explanatory.[178] Since the *Kirk* and *Li* decisions, the Federal Court seems to be saying that when it comes to review for serious errors of fact, the error's gravity might sometimes be more important than its label.[179] One might speculate as to whether this drift from specific labels to looser principles is another unintended result of the Migration Act's switch to 'jurisdictional error' after a decade of intense focus on tightly labelled review grounds.

[171] Administrative Review Council (n 19) [7.11].

[172] Namely, Federal Courts Act, RSC 1985, c F-7, s 18.1(4). See *Canada (Citizenship and Immigration) v Khosa* [2009] 1 SCR 339, [50].

[173] Administrative Review Council (n 19) [7.17].

[174] See, eg, *Lumbers v W Cook Builders Pty Ltd (In Liq)* (2008) 232 CLR 635, 662. See also S Gageler, 'The Underpinnings of Judicial Review of Administrative Action: Common Law or Constitution?' (2000) 28 *Federal Law Review* 303; B Selway, 'The Principle Behind Common Law Judicial Review of Administrative Action: The Search Continues' (2002) 30 *Federal Law Review* 217; K Mason, 'What is Wrong with Top-down Legal Reasoning?' (2004) 78 *Australian Law Journal* 574.

[175] M Aronson, 'Is the *ADJR Act* Hampering the Development of Australian Administrative Law?' (2004) 15 *Public Law Review* 202.

[176] Poole (n 101). See above, section IV.C.

[177] *Kirk* (n 6).

[178] ibid 573–74.

[179] See n 69.

D. Institutional and Political Consequences

Quoting Gareth Davies,[180] Lord Bingham said in the *Denbigh High School* case: 'The retreat to procedure is of course a way of avoiding difficult questions'.[181] The context was proportionality review under the Human Rights Act 1998 (UK), which might explain the notion of 'retreat'. In that context, and in contrast to the Canadian position,[182] England's judicial review courts theoretically decide for themselves where to strike the balance between public and individual interests. If the analysis were to stop there, the consequence would be a merger of substantive review and a full appeal on the merits of human rights claims. However, the theory is counterbalanced by the substantial respect, weight or deference usually accorded to the executive and legislative branches.[183] There are lively debates about the chances of proportionality review displacing *Wednesbury* unreasonableness in administrative law realms untouched by human rights.[184] However, none of the writers advocating displacement has also proposed that proportionality be assessed *de novo* in those other realms.

Even though substantive review is distinct from *de novo* merits appeal in all but one context, it is bound to impose a heavier burden upon the court than procedural review. It is true that the distinction between errors of law and fact is not as critical as it was in days gone by,[185] but there is nevertheless a large difference between review for '*no* evidence', and review for serious irrationality in deciding against the overwhelming weight of evidence. Setting the bar high for 'serious irrationality' might ease the burden, but the evidence still needs to be evaluated, and in any event, it has been shown that the High Court's decision in *Li* suggests that the bar will not always be set extremely high.

The courts have also to consider their own legitimacy when pushing the boundaries of substantive review. The closer they get not just to considering, but actually deciding, the merits, the more they imperil their own legitimacy. If one thing remains clear in this area, it is that the legislature gave the decisional role to a body other than the courts.

One must also consider the political consequences of extending substantive review. It comes as no surprise that many of the substantive developments these days occur in the context of migration litigation about asylum claims. Before the current wave of asylum claims, migration's most sensitive pressure point involved the deportation of criminal aliens at the end of their prison terms. Theoretically, the AAT has the power to disagree with lawful government policy, and even to frame its own policies.

180 G Davies, 'Banning the Jilbab' (2005) 1 *European Constitutional Law Review* 511, 517.

181 *Denbigh High School* (n 159) 116.

182 *Doré v Barreau du Québec* [2012] 1 SCR 395.

183 *R (Lord Carlile) v Secretary of State for the Home Department* [2014] 3 WLR 1404, [19]–[20], [30]–[31], [67], [88].

184 Those debates are made no easier by the semantical disagreements exhibited in *Pham v Secretary of State for the Home Department* [2015] 1 WLR 1591.

185 The Privy Council's decision in *R v Nat Bell Liquors Ltd* [1922] 2 AC 128, 151–52 represented the high point of a refusal to contemplate any form of fact review. The reasoning that *Nat Bell* had used to get to this result was rejected in *Kirk* (n 6) 569–71.

When he was the tribunal's first President, and in the context of criminal deportation, Brennan J warned against the tribunal exercising either of those powers. Underlying a number of seemingly neutral reasons, his Honour was evidently concerned not to provoke a legislative reaction against the fledgling tribunal.[186] Almost 35 years later, Lady Hale issued a similar warning of the political consequences of pushing English judicial review too far:[187]

> Had they [the judicial review courts] adopted the same restraint in asylum as in social security cases, it might not have been thought necessary to introduce the statutory review procedures. Ironically, therefore, the more troubling the context, the more necessary it has seemed to limit the availability of judicial review.

E. Piece-meal Imposition of a Tactical Burden of Proof

The spread of the duty to supply reasons is obviously one cause of the spread of substantive review, but it might also be seen as a consequence. There remain contexts not covered by a statutory duty to supply reasons with a decision or on demand shortly thereafter, but the courts have started to fill in those gaps in other ways. One Australian jurisdiction now says that it will order reasons following the issuance of originating process, even where the government party is under no statutory duty to supply reasons.[188] At the very least, this imposes a tactical burden of proof upon the government party. Others would see this development in more general (and important) terms, as further evidence of a shift to the so-called culture of justification. The argument is that the rule of law requires that governors give account to the governed for their use of force, and that giving account is necessary for the legitimacy of a democratic political order.[189]

It might be drawing a long bow to claim a linkage between the expansion of substantive review and a shift to a culture of justification.[190] What can be said, however,

[186] *Re Drake and Minister for Immigration and Ethnic Affairs (No 2)* (1979) 2 ALD 634, 644: 'The very independence of the Tribunal demands that it be apolitical; and the creation of its deportation jurisdiction is intended to improve the adjudicative rather than the policy aspects of deportation decisions'.

[187] *Cart* (n 54) 687.

[188] Uniform Civil Procedure Rules (NSW) (SI 2005/418), r 59.9. The West Australian Supreme Court tried to follow suit, but its new Rules aroused a political backlash, and they were disallowed in the Parliament: Joint Standing Committee on Delegated Legislation (WA Parl), *Supreme Court Amendment Rules 2013*, Report No 66 (2013).

[189] The literature started with E Mureinik, 'A Bridge to Nowhere? Introducing the Interim Bill of Rights' (1994) 10 *South African Journal on Human Rights* 31; D Dyzenhaus, 'Law as Justification: Etienne Mureinik's Conception of Legal Culture' (1998) 14 *South African Journal on Human Rights* 11. See also M Cohen-Eliya and I Porat, 'Proportionality and the Culture of Justification' (2011) 59 *American Journal of Comparative Law* 463. The High Court saw no point in exploring the concept in *Wingfoot* (n 119) [45] where the issue was whether a statement of reasons was sufficiently informative to satisfy a statutory duty to supply the decision-maker's opinion on a medical dispute.

[190] But see Daly, *A Theory of Deference in Administrative Law* (n 156) 184, where it is argued that 'a "culture of justification" is in fact hard-wired into unreasonableness'. In chapter 4, Daly analysed the leading cases from the apex courts of the United Kingdom, Canada and the United States. He concluded, in effect, that current practice already generates a tactical burden in the course of an 'unreasonableness' challenge, whenever the challenger establishes any one of a number of presumptive indicators of *Wednesbury* unreasonableness. Those indicators are: illogicality; disproportionality; inconsistency with statutory meaning, purpose, policy or value; and differential treatment of like cases or unexplained policy changes.

is that whether it be done by the occasional relaxation of *Wednesbury*'s 'lunacy' standard, or by any of the other and more recent strategies described above, substantive review is now *both* more possible, *and* less predictable, than ever before.

Government counsel had it easy back in *Wednesbury*'s day. They felt no embarrassment in refusing to supply reasons, and it required very little ingenuity to dreamup half-way rational hypotheses to repel most qualitative challenges. Respondents' counsel still get edgy about discovery applications, or proposals to cross-examine their deponents, but the current uncertainties about the availability and reach of substantive review must inevitably prompt them into presenting more reasoned justifications for challenged decisions. In most contexts, that will not rise to the level of reversing the legal burden of proof, but a tactical burden of proof can be very powerful.

The New South Wales Bar Association recently organised the publication in book form of 13 essays discussing both practical and theoretical problems for judicial review practitioners.[191] It is surely no coincidence that the book's longest chapter deals with the evidentiary issues that practitioners now face.[192]

VII. CONCLUSIONS

The old model of judicial review had a big advantage over the present arrangements—we knew where we were. The trouble was that nobody liked that place: its restrictions on who could enter; its requirements that entrants come bearing legal rights or interests in need of protection; its arcane remedial rules; its limited grounds for overturning administrative decision-making; and above all, its inability to replace a wrong decision with the right one.

The old model of judicial review had an appropriately narrow raison d'être, namely, to enforce the statutory limits to government power. England's judicial review, however, has now become markedly more substantive than Australia's, and its overall sense of mission in promoting the rule of law occasionally shows signs of translating directly into a ground of review in its own right. The Australian High Court is unlikely to follow suit, but it is placing noticeably less emphasis on the constitutional separation of the federal judicial power as a reason for resisting substantive review.

In both Australia and England, the judicial review courts remain unable at common law to replace a challenged decision with their own, preferred decision. That restriction serves only to emphasise that more important than any of the statutory reforms of judicial review was the proliferation of judicialised merits review tribunals. However, the emphasis on judicialised tribunals went hand-in-hand with the spread of statutory duties to supply reasons, and together, they appear to have contributed towards the expansion of substantive judicial review in Australia.

[191] N Williams (ed), *Key Issues in Judicial Review* (Sydney, Federation Press, 2014).

[192] N Williams and A Shearer, 'Evidence in Public Law Cases' in N Williams (ed), *Key Issues in Judicial Review* (Sydney, Federation Press, 2014).

The most surprising catalyst for that expansion, however, was the legislature's sustained attempt to rein in judicial review of the decisions of migration tribunals. Borrowing from the Act that invests the Federal Court with judicial review jurisdiction over most federal agencies, the Parliament set out a long list of allowable grounds of review, and a list that was almost as long of the grounds that the Federal Court was not to entertain in migration cases. Those two lists had unforeseen effects which continue to play out, even though the lists themselves survived in the Migration Act for only a decade. The governments'[193] overall aims had been abundantly clear. The goals were to replace the common law of procedural fairness with a statutory code; and to exclude review on substantive grounds, or on grounds where substance could be dressed up as process. For constitutional reasons, the disallowed grounds were still available in the High Court, and that court was predictably flooded with applications which it was unable to remit to lower courts. In the course of finding some loopholes in the exclusions, and in first resisting, and then outflanking, the attack on review for breach of procedural fairness, the High Court relaxed its previously unyielding opposition to substantive review, sometimes overtly, and sometimes in the guise of enforcing statutory or common law requirements for procedural fairness.

It is too early to say how far substantive review will be allowed to go, or how often it will produce a tangible difference to the outcome of judicial review applications. It is not too early to say, however, that the current state of uncertainty as to the scope for substantive review, and indeed, the unsettling effect that its expansion has had upon the previously stable catalogue of procedural review grounds, will combine to make life for respondents' counsel more difficult. Defending against process attacks is generally far less demanding than defending challenges to how much thought has gone into an administrative decision.

[193] The policy was bipartisan, and survived a change of government.

7

'Blasphemy Against Basics': Doctrine, Conceptual Reasoning and Certain Decisions of the UK Supreme Court

CHRISTOPHER FORSYTH

I. INVENTION OF THE COMMON LAW

SUPPOSE MINERVA J, a judge with preternatural abilities, wise beyond all telling, with unparalleled impartiality and unrivalled compassion rooted in her soul, finds herself administering justice, concentrating on judicial review cases, in a much elevated court—well above the Supreme Court in the judicial hierarchy. How would she, equipped with all these qualifications for office far beyond those of the ordinary mortal let alone judge, respond to the challenges of the task before her?

We may be sure that she would want to do justice. For each dispute before her she would analyse it more thoroughly than any mortal could and weigh the contending issues and arguments more finely than they had ever been weighed before; then she would pronounce which way the balance fell, confident that, according to her ideal of justice, justice had been done. Minerva J is so confident in her ability to discern justice that she is not concerned about law. She will discern where justice lies and judge accordingly.

But soon she will realise that this is not enough. First of all, she will be unable to decide every case. Time is too short; there are too many cases; and justice delayed is justice denied. Other judges in lower courts lacking her judgement and wisdom will have to decide most cases. And sensible individuals anxious to avoid litigation will want to know how to conduct themselves so as to achieve that end. How can her judgement and wisdom be made available to all?

So she starts to articulate in written judgments the principles upon which she decides her cases, so that her reasons can provide guidance to the other judges. Her wisdom and judgement, encapsulated in the *ratio decidendi* of her decisions, can thus escape the particular and apply generally. Here we see the invention of the common law: the secretion of rules that will guide other judges deciding future cases (and indeed other individuals seeking a guide to their conduct).

II. THE LAW AS THE JUDGE'S ONLY MASTER

Minerva J now comes to realise that she is also subject to these rules so developed. If she did not herself follow the rules which she had previously laid down they would fail in their task of providing guidance to others. Who would follow these rules if they knew that on appeal Minerva J had no obligation to follow them? It is vital that she follow her own rules or else an appeal to her would provide a permanent escape route from the law and uncertainty would reign. This should not surprise at all; it is the law. Minerva J like all judges beneath her has sworn an oath to 'do right to all manner of people after the laws and usages of this realm, without fear or favour, affection or ill will'.[1]

Naturally, Minerva J exemplifies judicial independence. She is independent of everyone and everything, except the law—which is her only master.[2] Naturally she does not have a superficial understanding of the law. In particular, she will use doctrine and juristic concepts to make sense of its complexities. She will link theory to practice.

She recognises, also, that the law needs to be developed to take account of changing needs. This is her task too but her fidelity to the law—founded in the oath—means that any changes that she introduces are interstitial and incremental and in accordance with recognised doctrine. The craft and the challenge of her office is to adapt the law to the challenges of today while staying within the overlapping constraints of the law and the constitution. Sometimes, of course, she finds it frustrating to proceed incrementally when she can see clearly that justice requires an immediate and broad reform. But the modern administrative law, extending the benison of the rule of law far into practically all exercise of public power, stands as eloquent testimony to what can be achieved by incremental reform. Whatever else might be the case, she does not make it up as she goes along.

III. WHAT ARE 'LIKE CASES'?

Minerva J does not articulate in terms her particular theory of justice but at the very least she believes that like cases should be treated alike. At first she believes that her judgments articulating rules to be followed by the judges in lower courts achieve this fundamental principle of justice. But now comes a disconcerting realisation: no case is identical to another; there always are nuances—and more than nuances—of difference everywhere. Two cases, for instance, may be alike except that in the second a public authority has made a promise to grant a certain boon or benefit to the other party. This might make a difference. Or it might in the circumstances be a legally irrelevant difference. So the crucial point becomes: which differences are

[1] The words cited come from the Promissory Oaths Act 1868, s 4.

[2] The phrase comes from H Hahlo and E Kahn, *The South African Legal System and its Background* (Juta, Cape Town, 1968) 39. But see to like effect Grundgesetz für die Bundesrepublik Deutschland, art 97(1): 'Die Richter sind unabhängig und nur dem Gesetze unterworfen' ['Judges are independent and subject only to the law'].

relevant? The principle of justice has to be that cases that are alike in all relevant characteristics should be treated alike.

Minerva J at first is inclined to respond to this realisation by the creation of more detailed rules specifying what is relevant and what is not relevant for the application of each rule. If only the rules were sufficiently detailed the lower court judges could apply them in an almost mechanical fashion; this would bring predictability and justice to the system.

Minerva J is attracted to certainty. She sees it as an essential for justice. Predictable and certain decisions are the proof that like cases are being treated alike and that the wisdom of her original judgments is tumbling down through the lower courts to the benefit of all. How, she wonders, can the principle of equality—another fundamental principle of justice she seeks to uphold—be upheld in a legal system unless one can predict what a like case will be and that it will be treated the same?

Minerva J's attraction to certainty flows from her deep understanding of the law. It is always difficult to predict which way Minerva J (or even the Supreme Court) will decide a case because every case that comes before such an elevated tribunal must be difficult in the sense that there must be something substantial to be said for each side. If this were not the case, the dispute should have been resolved at a much lower level and permission to appeal refused. Thus the observer, however perceptive, cannot reliably predict the outcome.

Minerva J naturally does not conclude from the fact that the outcome of every case that comes before her is uncertain, that certainty in the law is but 'a snare and a delusion'.[3] On the contrary, she is ever mindful of the need for her judgments to provide the guidance that ensures certainty in the administration of justice by lower courts, tribunals and officials.

IV. THE INEVITABILITY OF INJUSTICE

But now she becomes aware of a profound difficulty: the application of rules inevitably involves injustice. Notwithstanding Minerva's desire for justice it becomes clear that the application of rules, designed to extend justice, in fact leads to injustice. The difficulty is this: rules involve boundaries and the drawing of a clear boundary always leaves someone on the wrong side of the boundary. Take the rule that lays down that only persons over the age of 18 may vote in general elections.[4] The rule is clearly imposed as a result of a judgement by the legislature that generally persons younger than 18 lack the maturity to be involved in the democratic process. But, of course, there will be many people aged 17 or younger who are fully capable of playing their part as citizens but who are denied the franchise by the application of the rule. On the other hand, there are, alas, many of 19 or more years of age who are quite unsuitable to exercise the franchise. The certainty of applying a clear rule

[3] Hahlo and Kahn, *The South African Legal System and its Background* (n 2) 38, derived from Denman CJ in *O'Connell v R* (1844) 11 Clark and Finelly 351.

[4] Representation of the People Act 1983, s 1(1).

is bought at the expense of denying the franchise to some qualified candidates and granting it to some unsuitable ones. This is a problem with all boundaries. Faced with the complexity and muddle of human behaviour, the clarity of a rule introduces arbitrariness. Trade-offs have to be made. Some injustice to certain individuals must be tolerated so that there is justice for other individuals. Some injustice to individuals must be tolerated to achieve some greater public benefit.

How is Minerva to respond to this? She will surely reject the two extreme possible responses. The first of these would be to lay down ever more complicated rules in an attempt to achieve certainty and justice. But each new complexity would introduce more arbitrariness and justice would be diminished.

However, nor will she, at the other extreme, foreswear certainty and decide each case on its merits, deploying her preternatural ability to discern where justice lies in each case. She has already realised that this is no solution. But how will she come to terms with the inevitability of injustice?

V. MINERVA'S PREFERENCE FOR CERTAINTY

Minerva J will be looking for a *via media* between these two extremes that minimises injustice. Here perhaps is the heart of a challenge that often faces judges: finding a path that balances the injustice inevitably flowing from the application of a strict rule with the injustice born of the uncertainty created by attempting justice in every case. Minerva J may approach perfection in terms of her talents but she administers justice in a fallen world and must wrestle with imperfection.

A central argument of this chapter is that while Minerva would certainly not eschew justice as a goal, she would generally decide cases in a way that favoured certainty. She would generally favour 'bright line' rules rather than fuzzy rules. She warmly approves Laws LJ's judgment in *R (Tigere) v Secretary of State for Business, Innovation and Skills*.[5] This case concerned the eligibility of a prospective student for a student loan. The student did not qualify for support under the Education (Student Support) Regulations 2011 (SI 2011/1986) since, although a long-term resident in the United Kingdom, she was subject to immigration control having only discretionary leave to remain. The questions for the court were whether a disproportionate interference with her right to education was implied by treating her as ineligible simply on the ground of her immigration status, and whether there was unjustifiable discrimination by reference to the student's nationality or immigration status. Addressing these issues, Laws LJ said:

> [T]his is surely an area in which everyone, especially the affected student or students, needs to know where they are and, in the nature of things, to know it within what may be a relatively short timescale. The court cannot commit the system of student loans to the emergency of nice arguments about the impact of the ECHR case by case. The objection is not merely that such a system would be expensive and effectively unworkable. The law may no doubt take a strict or purist view about an objection of that kind. The real difficulty is that

[5] [2014] EWCA Civ 1216, [2014] HRLR 26. Now overruled by the Supreme Court ([2015] UKSC 57); concept of 'bright lines' discussed but not rejected in [37], [86].

> such a system would be uncertain and arbitrary. Some cases would be preferred over others on marginal grounds. Delays would occasion real hardship. Loss of confidence and even disrepute would, in consequence, dog the regime. So I have no doubt that a bright line rule is required or at least justified.[6]

This reasoning would apply with equal vigour to most administrative schemes. Minerva echos Laws LJ's scepticism over legal issues decided on a 'case by case' basis. While such an approach may secure justice for the individuals before the court, it promises injustice to others who, since the outcome of their case cannot be predicted, are bound to be drawn into damaging litigation as a result.

There are also some more straightforward reasons for the preference for certainty. In many cases practicality insists on certainty. This is so in relation to the rules of the road, entitlement to welfare benefits, liability to pay tax and in many other areas. Innumerable decisions have to be taken, they cannot all be reviewed by a judge and they have to be consistently reached. Clear law is the only option. Arbitrariness is these areas is not as important as clarity. Often when the law is clear individuals can act to mitigate the injustice to themselves.

Then the rule of law at its most fundamental requires rules fixed and announced in advance; in Lord Bingham's words '[q]uestions of legal right and liability should ordinarily be resolved by application of the law and not the exercise of discretion'.[7] This then is the mechanism that ensures that those subject to the law can confidently regulate their affairs conformably with the law. In judicial review, Minerva J's particular interest, this translates into the principle that public authorities have to show a strict legal pedigree for the power that they exercise. Thus the rules that determine the perimeter of power must be as clear as possible. The arbitrariness of the particular entailed by clear rules must be tolerated into order to avoid general administrative arbitrariness when administrators have no clear limits to their power. That is the path to authoritarianism, where action is upheld simply because it comes from an authority. Certainty, she realises, is not the only source of injustice.

But the reason why Minerva J tends to favour certainty is more subtle than these relatively obvious considerations. It relates to her conception of herself as an appellate judge. As such she is not concerned only with the resolution of the dispute between the parties before her but has wider concerns. She feels under a duty to use her office to provide guidance for lower judges. In part this is born of her realisation that because of her preternatural abilities she is best placed to provide that guidance. But in large part it is born of her recognition of her constitutional role.

The law is indeed her only master. Vital though the role of the appellate judge may be in developing the law, she remains subject to the law. In her search for justice she is not free to craft any solution that seems to her just. She must craft her decisions

[6] ibid [27]–[28].

[7] T Bingham, *The Rule of Law* (London, Allen Lane, 2010) 48. The phrase 'rules fixed and announced beforehand' comes from F Hayek, *The Road to Serfdom* (London, Routledge, 1944) 54: 'stripped of all technicalities this means that government in all its actions is bound by rules fixed and announced beforehand—rules which make it possible to foresee with fair certainty how the authority will use its coercive powers in given circumstances, and to plan one's individual affairs on the basis of this knowledge'. And see J Raz, 'The Rule of Law and its Virtue' (1977) 93 *Law Quarterly Review* 195.

according to the doctrine and learning of the past. The wisdom of the common law, beaten out on the anvil of argument, is then encapsulated in the reasoned judgment that cannot be ignored but must be followed. Given her ability to discern where justice lies this is a frustrating restriction on the quest for justice but Minerva J is wise as well as able and willingly accepts the supremacy of the law. With that, however, comes a fidelity to doctrine and a willingness to be castigated by the superficial critic as out of date and behind the times.

What this adds up to is that she is concerned with doctrine and conceptual analysis. Every time she takes a decision on purely pragmatic or policy grounds—which will sometimes be necessary—may be considered a failure. Development of the law is, of course, very important. The law is not static but changes continually—through legislation, of course, but also through changes made by the judges. But although, when developing the law, Minerva J is sometimes bold, she is always careful to found her rulings on the development of existing precedent and doctrine. And the best decisions of the past in which judges imposed the principles of the rule of law on the exercise of administrative discretion are deeply rooted in orthodox doctrine and its development rather than in pragmatic influences upon the judge.

The speech of Lord Reid in *Ridge v Baldwin*[8] (which concerned whether the rules of natural justice applied to the dismissal of a chief constable) is an exemplar of the approach adopted by Minerva J and is worthy of fuller consideration. Lord Reid commences by demonstrating 'an unbroken line of authority to the effect that an officer cannot lawfully be dismissed without first telling him what is alleged against him and hearing his defence or explanation'.[9] Then he turns to the difficulties 'introduced by statements in various fairly recent cases'.[10] One such case was *Nakkuda Ali v Jayaratne*,[11] which placed reliance on the proposition that before the prerogative writs would issue to a body—so raising the prospect of its decisions being quashed for lack of natural justice—'there must be superadded to that characteristic [that it determined rights] the further characteristic that the body has the duty to act judicially'.[12] This formed the basis of the proposition that while a judicial or quasi-judicial body engaged the rules of natural justice, a purely administrative one did not.

But Lord Reid shows that the 'superadded' requirement of a duty to act judicially was chimerical. It was 'impossible to reconcile with the earlier authorities' and the relevant part of the judgment in *Nakkuda Ali's* case 'was given under a serious misapprehension of the effect of the older authorities and therefore cannot

[8] [1964] AC 40.

[9] ibid 66. The cases cited start with *Bagg's Case* (1615) 11 Co Rep 93b.

[10] *Ridge* (n 8) 71.

[11] [1951] AC 66. The Pricy Council had held that a licensing authority was not acting judicially when it cancelled a licence and so did not have to act in accordance with natural justice.

[12] These words come from Lord Hewart CJ's judgment in *R v Legislative Committee of the Church Assembly, ex parte Haynes-Smith* [1928] 1 KB 411, 415, relying upon Atkin LJ in *R v Electricity Commissioners, ex parte London Electricity Joint Committee Co (1920) Ltd* [1924] 1 KB 171, 205, where the judge had said: 'Wherever any body of persons having legal authority to determine questions affecting the rights of subjects, and having the duty to act judicially, act in excess of their legal authority, they are subject to the controlling jurisdiction of the King's Bench Division exercised in these writs [of certiorari and prohibition]'.

be regarded as authoritative'.[13] Thus the writs would issue (or, putting it in more modern terms, the rules of natural justice would be engaged) if the decision simply affected the rights of subjects. So, in Lord Denning's phrase, *Ridge v Baldwin* 'scotched' the 'heresy' that the principles of natural justice only applied to judicial proceedings.[14] With that heresy scotched, the way was open for the development of the modern law of procedural justice.[15] But note the thoroughness with which Lord Reid distinguishes contrary precedent, corrects error and picks a sure way to justice while demonstrating his fidelity to law.

VI. JUDICIAL REVIEW OF THE UPPER TRIBUNAL: IS THE LAW THE MASTER IN THE SUPREME COURT?

Fortified by her understanding of her role, Minerva J now turns to consider some recent cases that have come before the Supreme Court. Here, in the first place, is an important decision, *R (Cart) v Upper Tribunal*, concerning the question of whether the Upper Tribunal is subject to judicial review.[16] A claimant had been refused permission by the Upper Tribunal to appeal to it from a decision of the First-tier Tribunal and sought judicial review of that refusal. Although there was, in many circumstances, a right of appeal to the Court of Appeal from a decision of the Upper Tribunal, this—the refusal of permission to appeal to the Upper Tribunal—was one of the occasions on which there was no right of appeal.[17] Any remedy would have to be by way of judicial review. But was the Upper Tribunal, by statute 'a superior court of record',[18] subject to judicial review?

Minerva J thinks she knows how this question should be approached. Since *Anisminic*[19] there had been growing support for the proposition that all errors of law of administrative bodies (including unreformed tribunals) were jurisdictional, so any error of law took the body outside its legal powers and rendered the decision in question liable to be quashed on judicial review. But as far as courts were concerned clear dicta from several House of Lords' decisions (most prominently *Racal*[20] and

[13] *Ridge* (n 8) 74.

[14] *R v Gaming Board for Great Britain, ex parte Benaim and Khaida* [1970] 2 QB 417, 430.

[15] For a fuller account see HWR Wade and CF Forsyth, *Administrative Law*, 11th edn (Oxford, Oxford University Press, 2014) 415–19.

[16] [2011] UKSC 28, [2012] 1 AC 663.

[17] Tribunals, Courts and Enforcement Act 2007, s 13(1) provides for an appeal to the Court of Appeal with permission of the Upper Tribunal or the Court of Appeal 'on any point of law arising from a decision made by the Upper Tribunal other than an excluded decision'. But s 13(8) provides that an 'excluded decision' includes 'any decision of the Upper Tribunal on an application under section 11(4)(b) (application for permission or leave to appeal [from a decision of the First-tier Tribunal])'. Thus did Parliament attempt to ensure that decisions of the Upper Tribunal refusing permission to appeal to the Court of Appeal, were not themselves subject to appeal: *interest reipublicae ut sit finis litium.*

[18] Tribunals, Courts and Enforcement Act 2007, s 3(1). At first instance (*R (Cart) v Upper Tribunal* [2009] EWHC 3052 (Admin), [2010] PTSR 824) Laws LJ rejected the proposition that the status of being a superior court of record was sufficient to exclude judicial review.

[19] *Anisminic Ltd v Foreign Compensation Commission* [1969] 2 AC 147.

[20] *Re Racal Communications Ltd* [1981] AC 374, 382–83.

Page,[21] which were not mentioned in the Supreme Court in *Cart*)[22] indicated that the position was different. It all depended upon the construction of the relevant statute. This was made clear by Lord Diplock in *Racal* where he said:

> In *Anisminic* this House was concerned only with administrative tribunals ... Nothing I say is intended to detract from the breadth of the scope of application to administrative tribunals of the principles laid down in that case. It is a legal landmark; it has made possible the rapid development in England of a rational and comprehensive system of administrative law on the foundation of the concept of *ultra vires*. It proceeds on the presumption that where parliament confers on an administrative tribunal or authority, as distinct from a court of law, power to decide particular questions defined by the Act conferring the power, parliament intends to confine that power to answering the question as *it* has been so defined: and if there has been any doubt as to what that question is, this is a matter for courts of law to resolve in fulfilment of their constitutional role as interpreters of the written law and expounders of the common law and rules of equity ... Parliament can, of course, if it so desires, confer upon administrative tribunals or authorities power to decide questions of law as well as questions of fact or of administrative policy; but this requires clear words, for the presumption is that where a decision-making power is conferred on a tribunal or authority that is not a court of law, parliament did not intend to do so ... But there is no similar presumption that where a decision-making power is conferred by statute upon a court of law, parliament did not intend to confer upon it power to decide questions of law as well as questions of fact. Whether it did or not and, in the case of inferior courts, what limits are imposed on the kinds of questions of law they are empowered to decide, depends upon the construction of the statute unencumbered by any such presumption.[23]

So a court deciding whether the Upper Tribunal was subject to judicial review should, if it were taking the existing law as its starting point, consider whether it was dealing with a court or an administrative body. The Upper Tribunal was, after all, by statute a court of record. And it is surely uncontroversial that the changes introduced by the Tribunals, Courts and Enforcement Act 2007 (eg the guarantee of judicial independence extended to tribunal members) meant that the tribunals were now a fully-fledged part of the judicial system.[24]

If the Upper Tribunal was a court then it might have been the intention of Parliament that some of the errors of law which the Upper Tribunal might make might be non-jurisdictional and so not subject to judicial review; or were all the errors of law made by the Upper Tribunal jurisdictional and so subject to judicial review?

This question would be the starting point in any inquiry into whether the Upper Tribunal was subject to judicial review. And this starting point is important because everyone else—the parties, their counsel, others involved in cases raising the same

[21] *R v Lord President of the Privy Council, ex parte Page* [1993] AC 682.

[22] Also not mentioned in the Supreme Court in *Cart* is the leading Privy Council decision on jurisdiction of *South East Asia Fire Bricks Sdn. Bhd v Non-Metallic Mineral Products Manufacturing Employees Union and Others* [1981] AC 363. Apart from *Anisminic*, the Supreme Court managed to overlook every modern House of Lords or Privy Council decision on jurisdiction!

[23] *Racal* (n 20) 382–83 (emphasis in original).

[24] See Wade and Forsyth, *Administrative Law* (n 15) 768 for discussion. The effect of the changes wrought by the 2007 Act was much discussed by the Supreme Court; see, eg, *Cart* (n 16) [54].

point, etc—would know that this was the starting point. If they have a common starting point they are more likely to arrive at the same destination. But this starting point at least requires the recognition of the possibility that some of those errors might be non-jurisdictional, ie that the pre-*Anisminic* distinction between jurisdictional and other errors still had some purchase.

The Supreme Court in *Cart*, however, rejected in terms any return to the pre-*Anisminic* law which, it said, would 'lead us back to the distinction between jurisdictional and other errors which was effectively abandoned [in that case]'.[25] There was in the relevant legislation:

> no clear and explicit recognition that the Upper Tribunal is to be permitted to make mistakes of law. Certain decisions are unappealable [such as the decision to refuse permission to appeal] and for the most part there are obvious practical reasons why this should be so. But this does not mean that the tribunal must always be permitted to make errors of law when making [such unappealable decisions].[26]

This implies that all errors of law by the Upper Tribunal are jurisdictional, ie any material error of law made by the tribunal renders its decision void (this is classic and unchallenged learning on the subject).[27] But the Supreme Court also made it clear that the Upper Tribunal would only rarely be subject to judicial review. How are these two propositions to be reconciled?

The judgments of the Supreme Court do not explain what the doctrinal basis of this restriction on the reach of judicial review was. In many situations the law allowed a right of appeal (with permission) to the Court of Appeal from the decisions of the Upper Tribunal 'on a point of law'. This would generally provide an adequate alternative remedy justifying the refusal of permission to apply for judicial review. But the proposition that an appeal or other alternative remedy may justify the refusal of permission does not limit the powers of the judicial review court. The refusal of permission because of an alternative remedy is a rule of practice not law. The jurisdiction of the High Court to grant judicial review, even in the face of an alternative remedy, is not in doubt.[28] If the alternative remedy is not 'equally convenient and effective'[29] judicial review may not be excluded by the availability of a right of appeal.

[25] *Cart* (n 16) [39]. The distinction was not abandoned in terms in *Anisnimic* and as far as courts were concerned had not been abandoned by subsequent cases.

[26] *Cart* (n 16) [40]. But this remark takes no account of the fact that the Upper Tribunal is made 'a superior court of record' and that the 2007 Act careful excluded the decision to refuse permission from the scope of any appeal. Did Parliament, notwithstanding these restrictions, intend to allow judicial review on the precise matters on which it had excluded appeal?

[27] See, eg, *Anisminic* (n 19); *Ridge* (n 8); *Crédit Suisse v Allerdale Borough Council* [1997] QB 306; *Boddington v British Transport Police* [1999] 2 AC 143, 158; *McLaughlin v Governor of the Cayman Islands* [2007] UKPC 50; and *HM Treasury v Ahmed (No 1)* [2010] UKSC 2, [2010] 2 AC 534 [177] and [187].

[28] Lord Phillips in *Cart* (n 16) [77]: 'The power of the High Court to conduct judicial review subsists alongside these statutory provisions for appeal. It is not, however, the practice of the Court to use this power where a satisfactory alternative remedy has been provided by Parliament. Where this is not the case the power of judicial review is a valuable safeguard of the rule of law. It is one which the judges guard jealously'.

[29] *R v Essex County Council, ex parte EB* [1997] ELR 327, 329 (McCullough J), discussed in Wade and Forsyth, *Administrative Law* (n 15) 605.

But this reasoning is not spelt out.[30] Instead the court restricts the availability of judicial review on pragmatic but not principled grounds. The court (in Baroness Hale's judgment) makes a profoundly pragmatic case (after a tour through the alternatives) that permission to apply for judicial review of the Upper Tribunal should only be granted when the stringent 'second tier appeal criteria', viz, whether judicial review 'would raise an important point of principle or practice; or … there is some other compelling reason for the Court of Appeal to hear it', were met. The Supreme Court thus, while establishing in principle the general availability of judicial review of the Upper Tribunal (because all errors of law are jurisdictional), has carved away so much of that principle that only rarely will judicial review lie against decisions of the Upper Tribunal.

Does *Cart* portend then the abandonment of jurisdiction as the organising principle of administrative law and its replacement by the court allowing judicial review on a discretionary basis when it is 'rational and proportionate' to do so (which would be a revolutionary change)? This may be inferred from Baroness Hales' dictum that now follows:

> [T]he scope of judicial review is an artefact of the common law whose object is to maintain the rule of law—that is to ensure that, within the bounds of practical possibility, decisions are taken in accordance with the law, and in particular the law which Parliament has enacted, and not otherwise. Both tribunals and the courts are there to do Parliament's bidding. But we all make mistakes. No-one is infallible. The question is, what machinery is necessary and proportionate to keep such mistakes to a minimum? In particular, should there be any jurisdiction in which mistakes of law are, either in theory or in practice, immune from scrutiny in the higher courts?[31]

As worthy as this outcome may be, the Court's path to it has sown uncertainty and conceptual confusion. Is the Supreme Court then to make decisions based upon pragmatism and practicality rather than doctrine and principle?

The consequences of the pragmatic approach are profound. The rejection of all distinctions between errors of law that go to jurisdiction and those that do not means that all courts[32] (except presumably the High Court as a court of unlimited jurisdiction) stray outside their jurisdiction when they make errors of law. It follows on classic principle, supported by innumerable decisions from the most authoritative courts, that any material error of law renders the decision void, ie legally non-existent.

Suppose then that the decision of a tribunal (perhaps that X repay a certain sum) is marred by an error of law. There is no possibility (as *Cart* teaches) of the error being non-jurisdictional, so the decision is void. Judicial review may be precluded either by an alternative remedy (eg a right of appeal) or non-compliance with the second-tier appeals criteria. But that is not the end of the story.

[30] The role of alternative remedies in preventing access to judicial review is mentioned by Lord Phillips in *Cart* (n 16) [77] and is perhaps implied in Baroness Hales' discussion in *Cart* of *R (Sivasubramaniam) v Wandsworth County Court* [2002] EWCA Civ 1738, [2003] 1 WLR 475.

[31] *Cart* (n 16) [31].

[32] After all, if the Upper Tribunal was subject to judicial review, then so too must other inferior courts yield to the same logic and be subject to judicial review.

When X is sued for payment he will be able to raise the invalidity of the decision collaterally as of right; and the house of cards will come tumbling down. The invalidity of the decision will be shown and the claim for payment will fail. This, presumably, was the kind of possibility Lord Diplock had in mind in *Racal* where he contemplated that courts might sometimes make non-jurisdictional errors of law. Where the error made is non-jurisdictional, the decision is not void and so cannot be raised collaterally.[33]

It can hardly be supposed that the courts would accept in practice that any material error of law by the Upper Tribunal rendered the decision of the tribunal void. But how would this obvious consequence of orthodoxy be avoided? Voidness itself might be abandoned. This would be contrary to the great weight of authority and the doctrinal reasons that justify the proposition that jurisdictional errors lead to voidness. But the Supreme Court in a *Cart*-like mood may abandon doctrine and precedent and set course across unknown waters in search of 'rationality and proportionality'. Alternatively, there might be a tendency to accept that any error of law rendered the decision void but then seek to use remedial discretion to avoid the logical consequences.

Minerva J would surely be dismayed by the Supreme Court's judgment in *Cart*. She would probably not have too much difficulty with the result of the case; she too believes that judicial review should be 'proportionate and rational'. But she surely also considers that in enacting the Tribunals, Courts and Enforcement Act 2007 Parliament intended that tribunals should emerge as a fully-fledged part of the judicial system. And this was surely fortified by the establishment of the Upper Tribunal as 'a superior court of record'. Parliament could hardly have been clearer that tribunals were, post-2007, part of the machinery of adjudication not administration and that consequently the *Racal* principle set out above was the starting point.

Moreover, she would be much dismayed by the abandonment of doctrine. Was the law of jurisdiction and all the learning and wisdom of the past to be set on one side with its place taken by the modern judge's estimate of what was 'proportionate'? Minerva J, as we have seen, specifically rejected deciding each case according to the judicial perception of justice but now she sees such judicial views taking the place of doctrine. The judges, even of the Supreme Court, should recognise the law as their master.

Minerva J favours doctrine and logic as providing the intellectual furniture that enables the law to be consistently applied. Thus, she is particularly dismayed by the Supreme Court's failure to face up to the consequences of the abandonment of doctrine. If there are no longer pre-*Anisminic* distinctions then any error of law leads to voidness. But for practical reasons most of those void decisions will have to be treated as valid. How is this to be justified and explained? It is surely not sufficient

[33] A non-jurisdictional error might be appealed (if statute provided an appeal) and, if the error of law appeared on the face of the record, it might be subject to judicial review on that ground (see Wade and Forsyth, *Administrative Law* (n 15) 224–26). But it would not be void and so could not be collaterally challenged.

to fall back on the judicial exercise of remedial discretion to avoid administrative chaos.[34]

VII. MALLEABLE BOUNDARY BETWEEN LAW AND FACT

Now here is another recent decision of the Supreme Court. It concerns whether the condition set by the statutory words is fulfilled—and whether this question is a 'hard edged' one that has to be got right for the decision-maker to stay within his jurisdiction (the 'correctness standard') or whether the condition is not in fact jurisdictional but is entrusted to the decision-maker (so that the courts apply a 'rationality standard'). This question arose in the context of the distinction between 'law' and 'fact'. This can be a difficult distinction to draw and judges facing such questions are sometimes tempted to manipulate the distinction between law (which, at least as far as administrative decision-makers are concerned, is always jurisdictional)[35] and fact (which may be non-jurisdictional and so need only comply with the 'rationality standard').

Of course, the distinction is often elusive. But in *Jones v First Tier Tribunal*,[36] now the leading decision in the Supreme Court on the topic, it was not really that difficult. The case concerned a tragic incident in which the driver of a lorry on a busy road swerved in an unsuccessful attempt to avoid an intending suicide who had jumped into his path. The lorry hit another vehicle causing very serious injury to its driver, Gareth Jones. Mr Jones applied to the Criminal Injuries Compensation Authority (CICA) for compensation. But compensation was only available if the injury was 'directly attributable to ... a crime of violence'.[37] The CICA declined to

[34] The answer, I argue elsewhere, to this problem of theoretical voidness but functionally voidability is resolved by the theory of the second actor in which the focus falls, not on the search for some characteristic of the invalid act that determines whether it is void or voidable, but upon the powers of the person (the second actor) who makes a decision in reliance upon the invalid act. The question being whether that person has power to act even if the first act is invalid. This approach to invalidity, which is discussed in full in Wade and Forsyth, *Administrative Law* (n 15) 254–26 and CF Forsyth, 'The Metaphysic of Nullity' in CF Forsyth and I Hare (eds), *The Golden Metwand and the Crooked Cord* (Oxford, Clarendon Press, 1998), has several times been approved by courts, including by the House of Lords in *Boddington* (n 27) 172 (Lord Steyn).

[35] I do not here discuss the subtle issues that arise when apparently jurisdictional questions are defined in the relevant statute in a way that leaves the evaluation of the question to the decision-maker. In such cases the decision-maker's assessment is upheld unless 'the decision is so aberrant that it cannot be classed as rational'. See *R v Monopolies and Mergers Commission, ex parte South Yorkshire Transport Ltd* [1993] 1 WLR 23, where the question was whether a particular area comprised a 'substantial part of the United Kingdom'. See further Wade and Forsyth, *Administrative Law* (n 15) 214–16.

[36] [2013] UKSC 19, [2013] 2 AC 48. The following account of *Jones* is based on the discussion of it in Wade and Forsyth, *Administrative Law* (n 15) 216–17.

[37] These words come from the Criminal Injuries Compensation Scheme 2012, clause 4. The 2012 Scheme is the one currently in force having been laid before Parliament under Criminal Injuries Compensation Act 1995, s 11(1). The 2012 Scheme has an Annex B: Crime of Violence which provides (omitting currently irrelevant words) in clause 2(1) that 'Subject to paragraph 3, a "crime of violence" is a crime which involves: (a) a physical attack; (b) any other act or omission of a violent nature which causes physical injury to a person; (c) a threat against a person, causing fear of immediate violence in circumstances which would cause a person of reasonable firmness to be put in such fear ... (2) An act or omission under sub-paragraph (1) will not constitute a crime of violence unless it is done either intentionally or

make an award, finding that Mr Jones was not the victim of 'a crime of violence'. The First-tier Tribunal agreed.[38] It was not satisfied that the intending suicide had the necessary intent to be guilty of an offence under section 20 (malicious wounding) of the Offences Against the Person Act 1861; and if the suicide was not guilty of the offence, there was no need to consider whether that offence was a 'crime of violence'. The Court of Appeal disagreed[39] and it was that decision that came on appeal to the Supreme Court. Lord Hope, for the majority, was clear: a section 20 offence was 'a crime of violence'. 'The words of the statute', he said, 'admit of only one answer. They speak for themselves ... The crime that section 20 defines will always amount to a crime of violence for the purposes of the scheme for compensation for criminal injury'.[40] Lord Hope is surely here laying down a proposition of law. But whether what the intending suicide *had done* amounted to a section 20 offence was a question of fact. The Supreme Court declined to interfere (as the Court of Appeal had done) with the First-tier Tribunal's finding of fact. This conclusion is in itself unexceptional. The point was crucial because the right of appeal only lay on 'a point of law'.

But what is noteworthy is how malleable the Supreme Court considered the distinction between law and fact to be. Lord Hope in the lead judgment said:

> it is primarily for the tribunals, not the appellate courts, to develop a consistent approach to these issues [of law and fact], bearing in mind that they are peculiarly well fitted to determine them. A pragmatic approach should be taken to the dividing line between law and fact, so that the expertise of tribunals at the first tier and that of the Upper Tribunal can be used to best effect. An appeal court should not venture too readily into this area by classifying issues as issues of law which are really best left for determination by the specialist appellate tribunals.[41]

This pragmatic approach to the distinction between law and fact is difficult to reconcile with the general thrust and purpose of the law of jurisdiction: to place objective limits on powers.[42] And if 'law' and 'fact' are to be manipulated by the courts to ensure the best use of the expertise of tribunals (as *Jones* suggests) on grounds that have nothing to do with law or fact, should we not call these two concepts Laurel and Hardy or Wallace and Gromit! Perhaps more realistically one might call them 'questions of correctness' and 'questions of rationality'.

But in truth there is a readily discernible difference between law and fact in many cases and *Jones* exemplifies this (even if the Court of Appeal made a mess of the distinction). Establishing the elements of the crime of malicious wounding is a question

recklessly. ... 4.(1) A crime of violence will not be considered to have been committed for the purposes of this Scheme if, in particular, an injury: (a) resulted from suicide or attempted suicide, unless the suicidal person acted with intent to cause injury to another person; (b) resulted from the use of a vehicle, unless the vehicle was used with intent to cause injury to a person'.

[38] As did the Upper Tribunal on judicial review.

[39] [2011] EWCA Civ 400, [2012] QB 345.

[40] *Jones* (n 36) [17]–[18].

[41] ibid [17]–[18]. See also Lord Carnwath [41] and [47]. See also Lord Hoffmann in *Serco Ltd v Lawson* [2006] UKHL 3, [2006] 1 All ER 823 [34], recognising 'policy' and 'expediency' as playing a part in determining the distinction between law and fact.

[42] See Wade and Forsyth, *Administrative Law* (n 15) 207.

of law, as is the question whether a section 20 offence is a 'crime of violence'.[43] Surely it would be intolerable in a society based on the rule of law if a section 20 offence was in some cases a crime of violence and in other cases not? However, whether what the intending suicide did, including in particular what was his intent at the time, amounted to a section 20 offence is a question of fact. There are, of course, difficult questions about 'law' and 'fact' far removed from the point in *Jones* of whether in that case an appeal 'on point of law' should lie.[44]

Minerva J is surely dismayed again by the abandonment of doctrine. In providing for the distinction between 'law' and 'fact' Parliament surely did not have in mind the kind of pragmatic distinction laid down in *Jones*. Surely 'law' must have something to do with norms (events from the *Sollen*) and 'fact' must have something to do with the real world (the *Sein*)? This neo-Kantian distinction is built upon the distinction between the realm of things that are, ie facts, and the realm of norms, things that ought to be. And in enacting that an appeal would lie only 'on a point of law' Parliament must have intended that the distinction between 'is' and 'ought' should determine whether an appeal was available. Given that the realm of law lies peculiarly within the expertise of the courts (to which the appeal lies) and that specialist tribunals may be expected to have specialist knowledge of the factual issues likely to arise, the distinction between 'law' and 'fact' in this context makes clear sense.[45]

Minerva J is surely also disappointed by how little guidance the Supreme Court gives to lower courts as to how the distinction is to be developed in the future. Consistency in the manipulation of the distinction is entrusted to the tribunals themselves, not the courts. But, in her view, it is an important aspect of an appellate court's role to provide guidance to the lower courts. Surely the Supreme Court should not abdicate and say to the tribunals: 'it is up to you'?

VIII. FINDING A HOOK

If Minerva J is concerned over what judges say in their judgments resolving cases through the exercise of pragmatic discretion rather than law, what they say in lectures off the bench can be even more disconcerting. Take Lord Carnwath's November 2013 lecture to the Constitutional and Administrative Law Bar Association, entitled 'From Judicial Outrage to Sliding Scales: Where Next for *Wednesbury*?'.[46] In the course

[43] There may be more difficult cases with offences which are not necessarily crimes of violence but only become so in certain circumstances. cf *Criminal Injuries Compensation Authority v First-Tier Tribunal (Social Entitlement Chamber)* [2014] EWCA Civ 65 [17] (relying on *R v Criminal Injuries Compensation Board, ex parte Webb* [1987] QB 74) finding that an offence contrary to Dangerous Dogs Act 1991, s 3(1) (having a dog dangerously out of control) was not a 'crime of violence', the reason being that that it was necessary to have regard to the nature of the crime rather than its consequences.

[44] For instance, where evaluative words are used; see Wade and Forsyth, *Administrative Law* (n 15) 214.

[45] This does not, of course, preclude appropriate respect being shown to the views of specialist tribunals that have great expertise in a particular area of law. But courts should have the last word on what is law.

[46] Available at www.supremecourt.uk/docs/speech-131112-lord-carnwath.pdf.

of an interesting lecture on the doctrinal developments in substantive review, he delivered himself of these words:

> In 19 years as a judge of administrative law cases I cannot remember ever deciding a case by simply asking myself whether an administrative decision was 'beyond the range of reasonable responses', still less whether it has caused me logical or moral outrage. Nor do I remember ever asking myself where it came on a sliding scale of intensity. My approach I suspect has been much closer to the characteristically pragmatic approach suggested by Lord Donaldson in 1988, by way of a rider to what Lord Diplock had said in CCSU: 'the ultimate question would, as always, be whether something had gone wrong of a nature and degree which required the intervention of the court and, if so, what form that intervention should take'. If the answer appears to be yes, then one looks for a legal hook to hang it on. And if there is none suitable, one may need to adapt one.

What is to be made of this? Did the mask slip and the judge reveal the truth? That in the judicial process doctrine (and law itself) is irrelevant to the decision? That what is crucial is whether the judge considers, from his internal sense of justice, that there should be intervention but he is not going to tell the observer why that is so? That the reasons given in his judgment are not the true reasons for his decision and so offer no guidance to the future? Is this not outrageous as a sketch of the judicial process?

Mark Elliott is quite right to comment on this passage that:

> Attempting to reduce substantive review to a catalogue of single instances, for all that it may bring the appearance of greater clarity and certainty to this area of administrative law, fails to grapple with the underlying need for a normative ordering of the values that warrant judicial protection. What is actually called for is a greater sense of the underlying principles and the theoretical framework in which they sit, not a retreat into pragmatism.[47]

Minerva J would doubtless agree.

IX. AN ALTERNATIVE VIEW: FIDELITY TO DOCTRINE

The cases just discussed show a distinct tendency to reject principle and conceptual reasoning—the bedrock of administrative law—in favour of the exercise of a judicial discretion in one way or another. If this approach were generally adopted, administrative law as hitherto known could, in theory, disappear to be replaced by the pragmatic wisdom of the Supreme Court.

But it should not be supposed that pragmatic discretion has been generally adopted by the Supreme Court. There are many cases in which the orthodox concepts that form the foundation of administrative law are applied in a straightforward way.

A clear example is the decision of the Supreme Court in *HM Treasury v Ahmed (No 2)*.[48] In this case the Treasury, purporting to act in terms of the United Nations

[47] M Elliott, 'Where Next for the *Wednesbury* Principle? A Brief Response to Lord Carnwath' (2013) *Public Law for Everyone*, available at http://publiclawforeveryone.com/2013/11/19/where-next-for-the-wednesbury-principle-a-brief-response-to-lord-carnwath/.

[48] [2010] UKSC 5, [2010] 2 AC 534. This case is discussed in depth in CF Forsyth, 'The Rock and the Sand' [2013] *Judicial Review* 360, from which this account is drawn.

Act 1946, section 1 (which provided that in order to implement Security Council Resolutions 'His Majesty may by Order in Council make such provision as appears to Him necessary or expedient for enabling those measures to be effectively applied') had made the Terrorism (United Nations Measures) Order 2006 (SI 2006/2657) and the Al-Qaida and Taliban (United Nations Measures) Order 2006 (SI 2006/2952). The Security Council Resolutions to which the Orders purported to give effect were designed to frustrate the financing and preparation of acts of terrorism. Thus the 'Orders provided for the freezing, without limit of time, of the funds, economic resources and financial services available to, among others, persons who had been designated. The effect of the Orders was to deprive those persons of all resources'.[49] The Terrorism Order and a crucial part of the Al-Qaida and Taliban Order were found to be invalid the first time the case came before the Supreme Court.[50] Lord Phillips consequently said that the orders were 'ultra vires and void'.[51]

The Treasury was understandably concerned by this result. The Treasury planned to (and did) introduce primary legislation to enable similar freezing orders to be lawfully imposed.[52] But what was to happen in the interim? Would the individuals suspected of involvement with terrorism have free access to their funds? Anxious to avoid this the Treasury approached the Supreme Court yet again and asked the Court, not to refuse relief in the Court's discretion, but simply to suspend the orders which it planned to make, viz appropriate declarations and quashing orders, for some weeks while the primary legislation was enacted.

But since the orders had already been found to be 'ultra vires and void' the question arises what effect a suspension would have. Lord Phillips said:

> The problem with a suspension in this case is, however, that the court's order, whenever it is made, will not alter the position in law. It will declare what that position is. It is true that it will also quash the [Terrorism Order] and part of the [Al-Qaida and Taliban Order], but these are provisions that are ultra vires and of no effect in law. The object of quashing them is to make it quite plain that this is the case. The effect of suspending the operation of the order of the court would be, or might be, to give the opposite impression. It would suggest that, during the period of suspension of the quashing orders, the provisions to be quashed would remain in force. Mr Swift [for the Treasury] acknowledged that it might give this impression. Indeed, he made it plain that this was the object of seeking the suspension … Mr Swift urged the court to suspend the operation of its judgment because of the effect that the suspension would have on the conduct of third parties. He submitted that the banks, in particular, would be unlikely to release frozen funds while the court's orders remained suspended. I comment that if suspension were to have this effect this would only be because the third parties wrongly believed that it affected their legal rights and obligations.[53]

The Treasury's belief that if the remedies were suspended, the banks would continue to obey the Orders that had been found void by the Supreme Court is disconcertingly

[49] *Ahmed (No 1)* (n 27) [4] (Lord Hope).

[50] ibid. The reasons for this need not now concern us. It suffices to say (as the headnote does): 'If the rule of law was to mean anything, decisions as to what was "necessary" or "expedient" for the purposes of s 1 could not be left to the uncontrolled judgment of the executive'.

[51] ibid [177] and [187].

[52] Terrorist Asset-Freezing etc Act 2010.

[53] *Ahmed (No 2)* (n 48) [4]–[5].

authoritarian. The executive expected obedience to an Order known to be invalid simply because it emanated from the Treasury and had the form of an Order in Council. No individual is obliged to obey an invalid order when it is known to be invalid. When the order is not known to be invalid, but an individual believes that it is, that individual may choose to run the risk that he is wrong and disobey the order. Prudence suggests that compliance while challenging is the correct course; but this is a rule of prudence not law.

Although the decision of the majority had consequences which many might consider deleterious[54] it is undeniable that the majority judgment followed logically from the jurisdictional basis of judicial review. Given that the orders were void, remedial discretion could not be used to breathe life into invalid orders. While the Court recognised that it had a remedial discretion it also held that the 'court should not lend itself to a procedure that is designed to obfuscate the effect of its judgment'.[55] This decision, with its deep fidelity to the law and the conceptual foundations of our subject, shows that pragmatic discretion has not been generally adopted as the Supreme Court's guiding principle in judicial review.

There is a further reason why such a development would be retrograde. In the electronic age where innumerable decisions are available at the click of a mouse the judge, practitioner or student is in constant danger of being overwhelmed. In these circumstances the importance of principle and conceptual analysis becomes more important. Adherence to fundamental principle in the analysis and assessment of cases is necessary in order to impose order upon the 'wilderness of single instances' that otherwise threatens. That order is essential to the great and abiding task of administrative law: the imposition of the rule of law onto the exercise of public power. And that great task is a principled undertaking or else it is nothing.

When all depends upon judicial discretion we enter that 'wilderness of single instances' where great uncertainty reigns. Professor Patrick Atiyah makes a similar point when he says that such judicial use of discretion 'can easily degenerate into complete "ad hockery", a casuistical methodology which eventually supplants the need for rigorous legal analysis and thought and replaces it with gut feeling and sentiment'.[56]

X. CONCLUDING REMARKS

Sir William Wade in a letter to Lord Cooke of Thornton (written as long ago as 12 March 1988) wrote of the academic wanting 'everything clear and sharp and logical and in accordance with principle' and of the judge, on the other hand, being

[54] As Lord Hope pointed out in *Ahmed (No 2)* (n 48) [13]–[14], it placed the United Kingdom 'in breach of its obligations under UN Security Council Resolution 1904/ 2009 … and under EC Regulation 881/2002' which required effect to be given to these designations in domestic law. And it meant that there was 'an increased risk of previously frozen funds being withdrawn from unfrozen bank accounts and diverted for terrorist purposes or being used as a conduit to this end'.

[55] *Ahmed (No 2)* (n 48) [8] (Lord Phillips).

[56] P Atiyah, *Pragmatism and Theory in English Law* (London, Stevens, 1987) 129.

resistant to being driven 'into a corner by ruthless logic and … compelled to decide contrary to what he wants'. While Sir William recognised that the judge's was 'a sound instinct for the administration of justice', he concluded: 'I am by my cloth obliged to protest when blurring becomes woolly thinking and blasphemy against basics'.[57]

This chapter has used the conceit of Minerva J to make a protest against the abandonment of doctrine and conceptual reasoning in favour of pragmatism and the discretion shown in some decisions of the Supreme Court. The reasons for the protest against such 'blasphemy against basics' have been set out in what has gone before but may be rehearsed here. It leads to great and deleterious uncertainty. It is of course true, for all the well-known reasons, that often the law cannot be known until the judges have spoken. Yet there is a profound difference between engaging in reasoned debate and analysis over what the law should be and being denied the conceptual tools to do so.[58] This chapter does not attempt to identify the 'implicit theory' that may underlie the pragmatism of the Supreme Court and which might tell us when the Supreme Court would abandon doctrine and principle (as in *Cart*)[59] and when it would apply it (as in *Ahmed (No 2)*). It simply calls for the consistent application of the law.

But this chapter ends on a broader point: the rejection of doctrine and conceptual reasoning has consequences for the legitimacy of the courts (and our subject) that few would welcome. There is much concern over the diversity of the judiciary (in the Supreme Court and elsewhere) with suggestions of a quota for women[60] (and logically, if there is concern over ethnicity, quotas for ethnic judges too).

But if doctrine has been abandoned and administrative law depends predominantly not on law but on the exercise of pragmatic discretion then the concern becomes not gender and ethnicity but broader questions of political representativeness. If the judiciary is to take important decisions on behalf of the whole polity on pragmatic rather than legal grounds, that polity may justifiably demand that the judiciary should be representative of it: not only in the sense that it should reflect society in terms of gender and ethnicity but that it should reflect society in terms of political opinion.

[57] The letter is quoted at greater length in Sir Jack Beatson's account of Sir William's life published in PJ Marshall (ed), *Proceedings of the British Academy*, vol 150, *Biographical Memoirs of Fellows, VI* (Oxford, Oxford University Press/British Academy, 2008) and reprinted in HWR Wade and CF Forsyth, *Administrative Law*, 10th edn (Oxford, Oxford University Press, 2009) app 5.

[58] Forsyth, 'The Metaphysic of Nullity' (n 34) 146.

[59] See Professor Atiyah's discussion in *Pragmatism and Theory in English Law* (n 56) 147–49. But he also says (at 159): 'we still lack an adequate theory to help explain when the courts will be innovative, and when conservative; when they will overrule old decisions … and when they will insist that change and reform is for the legislature. If there is indeed some implicit theory governing these matters (and some could say there is none) then it does seem to lie buried pretty deep'.

[60] See, eg, G Bindman and K Monaghan, 'Judicial Diversity Accelerating Change', available at http://ukscblog.com/wp-content/uploads/2014/11/Judicial-Diversity-Accelerating-Change.pdf. The report was drawn up at the request of the then Shadow Lord Chancellor. Meanwhile, s 63 of the Constitutional Reform 2005 Act (which directs that the Judicial Appointments Commission (JAC) make its recommendations on 'merit') is amended by the Crime and Courts Act 2013, sch 13, para 10, to permit the JAC, 'where two persons … of equal merit' are under consideration for appointment, to prefer 'one of them over the other for the purpose of increasing diversity'.

It is, one hopes, not too controversial to suggest that there may be a certain discrepancy between judicial opinion and public opinion in several important areas, for instance, that the judiciary is generally supportive of the judicial role in the protection of human rights while the public is significantly more sceptical. Such differences of opinion are inconsequential if the judiciary is simply deploying their special skill in the determination and application of the law. But if the judiciary must be defended not on the basis of their unique and especial expertise in the law but on the basis of their pragmatism, then a new world beckons: a world of confirmation hearings before standing committees of Parliament, penetrating scrutiny of the personal and political opinions of prospective judges and political controversy over the appointment of individuals.

8

The Legitimacy of Expectations About Fairness: Can Process and Substance be Untangled?

MATTHEW GROVES AND GREG WEEKS

I. INTRODUCTION

SEVERAL YEARS AGO, Tom Poole distinguished the judicial review doctrines of UK and Australian courts.[1] He identified quite different responses in the courts of each country to the spread of the 'jurisprudence of rights'. The Australian approach was hostile and used a formalism that harked back to earlier methods employed in Australian law before modern legislation and international jurisprudence presented great challenges.[2] The more open, fluid English approach had embraced and embedded considerations of rights. As with most comparative analyses, the comparisons were necessarily broad but there are many areas where the distinctions drawn by Poole ring true. One is the doctrine of legitimate expectations, where the formal (and constitutionally anchored) Australian approach has foreclosed the more open and rights-based English approach associated with *Coughlan*.[3]

English and Australian courts take strikingly different approaches to legitimate expectations. Australian courts have not only rejected the most well-known feature of the English conception of the doctrine—that substantive unfairness might be judicially remedied when an expectation is disappointed—they have rounded on the very language of the traditional procedural version of 'legitimate expectations'.[4] The reason given is that legitimate expectations no longer assist in determining who is

[1] T Poole, 'Between the Devil and the Deep Blue Sea: Administrative Law in an Age of Rights' in L Pearson, C Harlow and M Taggart (eds), *Administrative Law in a Changing State* (Oxford, Hart Publishing, 2008).

[2] Mainly the 'legalism' of Sir Owen Dixon, a long time Chief Justice of Australia; see J Goldsworthy, 'Australia: Devotion to Legalism' in J Goldsworthy (ed), *Interpreting Constitutions: A Comparative Study* (Oxford, Oxford University Press, 2006).

[3] *R v North and East Devon Health Authority, ex parte Coughlan* [2001] QB 213.

[4] *Plaintiff S10/2011 v Minister for Immigration and Citizenship* (2012) 246 CLR 636, [65] (Gummow, Hayne, Crennan and Bell JJ).

owed natural justice, which is now conceived broadly,[5] although judicial discomfort with the concept of legitimate expectations arose well before those developments.[6]

Until fairly recently, English law might have been thought to have reached a position that was a mirror image of the Australian one: it was almost the opposite of the Australian rejection of a substantive approach to fairness. The 'opposite image' came from the increasingly marginal position occupied by procedural concerns in English law, which appears to focus attention upon the rights of those affected by administrative processes.[7] Australian law had become unashamedly directed to procedural concerns at the expense of substantive issues. The UK Supreme Court signalled a change of emphasis in *Osborn*,[8] shifting attention from the requirements of the European Convention on Human Rights (ECHR) to the common law of natural justice. The Court's focus on the importance of a right *to* a hearing rather than any particular outcome *from* a hearing, may herald the return of process to English law.

This chapter explores the differing approaches of Australian and UK courts to the procedural and substantive application of legitimate expectations and more generally how and why legal systems embrace fairness. We take Poole's chapter as our starting point but do not share his expressed dissatisfaction with each of the opposing positions taken up by Australian and English law. For one thing, we argue that change to a substantive rather than merely procedural approach might yet prove a mixed blessing, at least if the Australian experience is any guide, but that experience also suggests that a procedural focus on fairness conceals deeper benefits. For another, we query the often assumed but infrequently analysed belief that there are inherent benefits to 'fairness'. To the extent that a debate about different conceptions of fairness was undertaken, and attendant criticisms of formalism (not unlike those made by Poole) were expressed, this first occurred much earlier in the law's development. We also consider the role of estoppel in both countries, one which led the public law doctrine of legitimate expectations to 'stand upon its own two feet' in England[9] but which in Australia never proceeded beyond the perennial state of doubt that public authorities can properly be held to their promises.

We conclude, in contrast to Poole and others, that there is not necessarily anything to regret about the fact that England and Australia have taken divergent paths on this and other legal issues. England has taken an approach which is still developing but with which English lawyers generally express a sense of satisfaction. Australia has taken an approach consistent with its own constitutional arrangements. Neither country need feel that the other has taken the wrong path. More than that,

[5] *Re Minister for Immigration and Multicultural and Indigenous Affairs; Ex parte Lam* (2003) 214 CLR 1, 16 (McHugh and Gummow JJ), 38 (Hayne J), 45–48 (Callinan J).

[6] G Weeks, 'Holding Government to its Word: Legitimate Expectations and Estoppels in Administrative Law' in M Groves (ed), *Modern Administrative Law in Australia: Concepts and Context* (Cambridge, Cambridge University Press, 2014) 227–28.

[7] In *R (Abdi and Nadarajah) v Secretary of State for the Home Department* [2005] EWCA Civ 1363, [69] Laws LJ invoked good administration as a requirement that 'takes its place alongside such rights as fair trial, and no punishment without law'. This locates administrative law requirements within a lexicon of fundamental rights.

[8] *Osborn v Parole Board* [2013] UKSC 61, [2014] AC 1115.

[9] *R v East Sussex County Council, ex parte Reprotech (Pebsham) Ltd* [2003] 1 WLR 348, 358 (Lord Hoffmann).

we argue that neither country should conclude that the choice of divergent paths justifies ignoring the jurisprudence of the other.

II. MODERN EXPANSION OF THE DUTY TO ACT FAIRLY

The reach of natural justice expanded steadily during the nineteenth century so that its requirements applied to decisions which affected property rights,[10] but also those dismissing people from public office,[11] or excluding them from professional associations and clubs.[12] Loughlin attributed much in these developments to the influence of individualism prevalent in Victorian England.[13] Such influences may have reflected the radical thinking of the time but the methodology of the courts did not. The courts took these expansionary steps in the classic common law incremental style and did so by use of another familiar feature of the common law in the form of the adjudicative method. Those decision-makers the courts found subject to the requirements of natural justice were also subject, in varying levels, to adjudicative procedures developed by and for the courts.

There was a retreat of sorts for much of the twentieth century as the 'duty to act judicially' became a restrictive requirement for the duty to observe the rules of natural justice.[14] That requirement arguably also reflected a reluctance of the courts to extend adjudicative procedures to other agencies and decision-makers.[15] Loughlin labelled the approach of the courts during this extended doctrinal slumber as an 'inactive formalist strategy'.[16] The inactivity was marked by the courts ceding the control they had claimed over administrative officials and their procedures, which was done through the formalism used to categorise and distinguish administrative and judicial functions.[17]

This period of retreat ended with *Ridge v Baldwin*,[18] when Lord Reid essentially revived nineteenth century developments in a judgment that signalled a new way

[10] The classic example is *Cooper v Wandsworth Board of Works* (1863) 14 CB (NS) 180.

[11] See, eg, *Willis v Gipps* (1846) 5 Moo PC 379 (PC);*Ex parte Ramshay* (1852) 18 QB 173. These cases can be traced to *Bagg's Case* (1615) 11 Co Rep 93b.

[12] See, eg, *Wood v Woad* [1874] LR 9 Ex 190; *Fisher v Keane* (1879) 11 Ch 353.

[13] M Loughlin, 'Procedural Fairness: A Study of the Crisis in Administrative Law Theory' (1978) 28 *University of Toronto Law Journal* 215, 218.

[14] Something largely traced to *R v Electricity Commissioners* [1924] 1 KB 171, 205 (Atkin LJ). Australian cases did not succumb to this change, at least not at the same time. See, eg, *Delta Properties Pty Ltd v Brisbane City Council* (1955) 95 CLR 11; *Commissioner of Police v Tanos* (1958) 98 CLR 383. The High Court of Australia finally followed the restrictive English approach in *Testro Bros Pty Ltd v Tait* (1963) 109 CLR 353, 362–63. That obedience ironically came *after* the English position had changed.

[15] Among the reasons offered was judicial recognition that an expansion of adjudicative procedures would hamper economic and political life during and between the World Wars: D Jabbari, 'Critical Theory in Administrative Law' (1994) 14 *Oxford Journal of Legal Studies* 189, 203.

[16] Loughlin, 'Procedural Fairness' (n 13) 221.

[17] The authors of *de Smith* argue that a similar approach is now achieved through the tests of 'public function' and justiciability: H Woolf *et al*, *de Smith's Judicial Review*, 7th edn (London, Sweet and Maxwell, 2013) 1048. That conclusion is difficult to reconcile with the broad approach those authors take to justiciability: ibid 19–28.

[18] [1964] AC 40. The High Court of Australia adopted this approach in *Banks v Transport Regulation Board (Vic)* (1968) 119 CLR 222.

forward despite being remarkably short on doctrinal guidance. The Privy Council gave some in *Durayappah v Fernando*,[19] when it suggested that whether natural justice applied would depend on the nature of the right affected by the decision, the breadth of the decision-maker's discretion or power and the impact of the decision. The presence of a legitimate expectation came to the fore within the first of the three '*Durayappah* factors' by providing a means to extend the reach of natural justice beyond decisions affecting rights and interests in a strict sense. Thus, the doctrine could encompass decisions within the realm of the so-called 'new property' of benefits which affected interests in the form of benefits such as social security and licences.[20]

While the rebirth of the old principles governing natural justice may have sat comfortably with the greater range of decisions that modern governments and their officials make, questions remained about whether adjudicative procedures should extend beyond the courts and whether the procedural and substantive conceptions of fairness could be separated, as the procedural focus courts seemed to presume was possible. During this time, distinct notions of 'fairness' or 'a duty to act fairly' (where, for some reason, the requirements of natural justice did not) developed not long before the legitimate expectation.

Mullan rejected suggestions that the (then) evolving doctrine of fairness would undermine administrative efficiency because it was neither coherent nor predictable. He argued that the new doctrine of fairness should be merged with the existing one of natural justice, so the courts could avoid replacing old problematic distinctions with newer ones. Combining the two would avoid the need to categorise different forms of fairness and allow the courts simply to ask: 'What procedural protections, if any, are necessary for this particular decision-making process?'.[21] Some criticised Mullan for underestimating the problems courts would face if they extended natural justice to less adjudicative processes and the difficulties in providing any real meaning to 'fairness' in these other contexts.[22] These criticisms did not answer another point raised by Mullan, which was that the emerging notion of fairness was vague and subjective. He argued:

> not only is this an almost inevitable concomitant of the development of the law on a case by case basis, but it is often said to be one of the major strengths of the common law in that it allows for a gradual assimilation of experience in relation to real life situations and provides an opportunity for the development of refinements. That is not possible in statutory law-making or, for that matter, in judicial decision-making which attempts to be the

[19] [1967] 2 AC 337, 349.

[20] This is famous terminology of C Reich, 'The New Property' (1964) 73 *Yale Law Journal* 733; C Reich, 'Individual Rights and Social Welfare: The Emerging Legal Issues' (1965) 74 *Yale Law Journal* 1245. An Australian perspective is given in I Holloway, 'Natural Justice and the New Property' (1999) 25 *Monash University Law Review* 85.

[21] D Mullan, 'Fairness: The New Natural Justice' (1975) 25 *University of Toronto Law Journal* 281, 315.

[22] See, eg, Loughlin, 'Procedural Fairness' (n 13). See also RA Macdonald, 'Judicial Review and Procedural Fairness in Administrative Law' (1980) 25 *McGill Law Journal* 520 and (1980) 26 *McGill Law Journal* 1. Beatson LJ was clearly mindful of these concerns in *R (L) v West London Mental Health NHS Trust* [2014] EWCA Civ 47.

> equivalent of a statute by laying down an immutable regime of rules for a whole area of law against the background of the facts of one particular case.[23]

Many of these concerns were forgotten as the requirements of natural justice quickly expanded to cover an increasing range of interests that might be affected by decision-makers outside the courts.[24] The central problems identified in earlier debates about fairness clearly remain. Beatson LJ recently cautioned that the possible problems of 'over-formalisation and judicialisation' of decision-making outside the courts cannot be solved 'simply by emphasising flexibility and context-sensitivity'.[25] He was concerned that too much reliance on the flexible nature of fairness might blur procedural and substantive fairness. Too much emphasis on the flexibility of fairness might create a new form of unfairness in:

> a modern version of Sir William Wade's nightmare of a Tennysonian 'wilderness of single instances' in which all the contextual factors will be relevant in considering what the requirements of procedural fairness are in a given situation without any factor or group of factors having decisive weight in shaping what is in practice required. The consequence may either risk obscuring the overarching principle or stating it at a level of generality which is not of use as a practical tool to decision-making. The result could be undue uncertainty and unpredictability. There is a need for simplified guidance which is practical and does not constitute either a procedural straitjacket, or 'safe harbour' for longstanding ways of doing things in a particular context, or operate with centripetal force towards adversarial adjudicative processes.[26]

Before we return to that issue, we raise a more recent but forgotten element of fairness: the very purpose of the doctrine.

III. REASONS FOR FAIRNESS

The purpose of natural justice is usually assumed rather than clearly explained. The benefits of fairness may seem obvious but they remain deeply contested, perhaps because a requirement of fairness that may benefit one person will usually burden another. The solution of the High Court of Australia has largely been to avoid any real examination of the benefits or arguments in favour of fairness.[27] That Court has taken a strong instrumental focus on the rare occasions it has touched on the underlying purpose of fairness.[28] That silence is all the more curious given the High Court's recent affirmation that natural justice was one of the fundamental common law principles protected by the principle of legality and therefore only able to

[23] Mullan, 'Fairness: The New Natural Justice' (n 21) 298.

[24] Beatson LJ has noted that many earlier cases expanding the reach of the principles of fairness applied or presumed a form of fairness that was diluted and less formal because it was applicable outside judicial or quasi-judicial decision-making: *R (L) v West London Mental Health NHS Trust* (n 22), [67].

[25] ibid [68].

[26] ibid [72].

[27] This surely reflects the High Court's longstanding refusal to settle upon a clear theoretical basis for natural justice. See Holloway, 'Natural Justice and the New Property' (n 20) 274–98.

[28] A strong example is *Lam* (n 5) [34]–[38] (Gleeson CJ), [105]–[106] (McHugh and Gummow JJ), [111], [122] (Hayne J) and [149] (Callinan J).

be displaced by legislation expressed with unmistakable clarity.[29] As with all other rights placed under the rubric of the principle of legality, the decision declaring the 'fundamental' status of natural justice protected the doctrine while saying nothing about its content or rationale.[30]

The failure of the High Court to address the purpose of fairness arguably reflects the wider absence of coherent theory underlying its modern judicial review principles,[31] but one can understand why the purpose of fairness remained neglected. After all, the key questions about fairness which occupied the courts for much of the latter part of the last century—namely, to which decision-makers and what decisions the requirements of natural justice applied—presumed the innate value of fairness.[32] Again, one can see why. If the basic tenet of fairness is to provide a fair and unbiased hearing, many benefits should naturally follow.[33] A fair hearing can provide a decision-maker with access to more or better material on which to base a decision, which is especially valuable if the decision turns on matters particular to the affected person.[34] A fair hearing can better enable decision-makers to appreciate the circumstances and concerns of the affected person, and the likely consequences of any decision.[35] The evidence and submissions supplied by the affected person may lead to more accurate decisions and better application of policy or relevant legal principles. The evaluation of that evidence and submissions can itself lead to more considered and better decisions.[36]

These benefits may all improve the accuracy or quality of the ultimate decision but benefits may extend beyond the decision itself. Providing a fair hearing should make it easier for those affected to understand and accept unfavourable decisions.[37] It should also avoid, or at least lessen, 'the subjective sense of injustice' people will likely feel after a hearing that was not fair.[38] Providing fair hearings should also

[29] *Saeed v Minister for Immigration and Citizenship* (2010) 241 CLR 252, [15].

[30] On such difficulties with the principle of legality, see D Meagher, 'The Common Law Principle of Legality in the Age of Rights' (2011) 35 *Melbourne University Law Review* 449.

[31] S Gageler, 'Impact of Migration Law on the Development of Australian Administrative Law' (2010) 17 *Australian Journal of Administrative Law* 92, 95.

[32] This assumption reflects the suggestion of Lord Millett that common law systems perceive procedural fairness as an end in itself, while civil law systems favour more utilitarian justifications: 'The Right to Good Administration in European Law' [2002] *Public Law* 309, 312–13.

[33] The beneficial role of fairness is assumed in legislative provisions which, for example, require tribunals to pursue procedures which are 'fair, just, economical, informal and quick'; see, eg, Administrative Appeals Tribunal Act 1975 (Cth), s 2A; Migration Act 1958 (Cth), ss 353, 420.

[34] This was a strong theme of *Osborn* (n 8) and *R (L) v West London Mental Health NHS Trust* (n 22).

[35] That is often because in many bureaucratic processes, the decision-maker and person affected have an ongoing relationship that both will want to maintain: PP Craig, *Administrative Law*, 7th edn (London, Sweet and Maxwell, 2012) 383.

[36] *Osborn* (n 8). *Dranichnikov v Minister for Immigration and Multicultural Affairs* (2003) 77 ALJR 1088 hinted that fairness can and should require decision-makers to undertake proper or genuine consideration of the evidence and submissions of those to whom the duty to observe the rules of fairness is owed, a question we leave aside.

[37] Known by psychologists as 'the fair process effect'. See K van den Bos, H Wilke and E Lind, 'When Do We Need Procedural Fairness? The Role of Trust in Authority' (1998) 75 *Journal of Personality and Social Psychology* 1449.

[38] *Secretary of State for the Home Department v AF (No 3)* [2009] UKHL 28, [2010] 2 AC 269, [72] (Lord Hoffmann). That sense of injustice (or lack of it) will also depend greatly on whether adequate reasons are given.

increase public confidence more generally in the administrative process and public decision-making. The fact that a hearing permits people to participate in the process leading to decisions which affect them can be regarded as a valuable benefit itself.[39] In some instances, such as consultation processes, a further benefit is 'reflective of the democratic principle at the heart of our society'.[40] Fairness can promote democratic values through its requirement that people who may be affected by decisions are given the chance to state their views.

Natural justice amounts essentially to a right that is important to the claimant—a chance to be heard, with notice of the issues, before an unbiased tribunal—that costs little or nothing to any other party (except time). Holding government to its promises does not fit this simple structure, at least where substantive legitimate expectations are concerned, since it is axiomatic that dividing public resources is a zero sum game.[41] A promise kept to one person will normally result in the removal or reduction of a benefit to one or more others. To use *Coughlan* as an example, honouring the promise that Ms Coughlan would have a home for life necessarily affected the authority's plans to open larger, modern care facilities that would cost less per patient and leave funds available for other healthcare. One should be careful not to ignore the fact that such decisions are heavily values-based and cannot be easily characterised as either 'good' or 'bad'.[42] It is interesting to note that, as with natural justice, courts do not usually articulate clearly the policy choices that underpin a preference for providing substantive enforcement of legitimate expectations or enforcing estoppels against exercises of statutory authority. It is perhaps even more interesting to speculate that, if this is because holding government to its word is thought, like natural justice, to be self-evidently 'good' by English courts, that assessment is not universally shared. Australian courts continue to insist upon decision-makers remaining within the limits of their jurisdiction and with unfettered discretion, regardless of what they have promised.[43] This divergence may simply recognise that binding government to its word is a more complex issue than natural justice and cannot therefore be assumed to be 'good' without greater analysis.

Australian courts have also eschewed the UK approach of requiring the executive to do as it has promised, taking the view that it is irrelevant whether the content of

[39] On the significance of participation, see PP Craig, *Public Law and Democracy in the United Kingdom and the United States of America* (Oxford, Clarendon Press, 1990) 116–36, 160–92; DJ Galligan, *Due Process and Fair Procedures: A Study of Administrative Procedures* (Oxford, Clarendon Press, 1996) ch 4; LB Solum, 'Procedural Justice' (2004) 78 *Southern California Law Review* 181, 273–304.

[40] *R (Mosley) v Haringey London Borough Council* [2014] UKSC 56, [2014] 1 WLR 3947, [24] (Lord Wilson).

[41] But there can be cost implications for officials to apply principles of fairness as required by the courts. In most instances, the cost is a minimal one but the courts occasionally acknowledge that fair processes will have *some* cost even if courts do not calculate it: *Canada (Attorney-General) v Mavi* [2011] 2 SCR 504, [40]. *Osborn* was unusual because its greater requirement of oral hearings led to considerably greater administrative costs. See the training and recruitment the Board explained were required by *Osborn*: [England] Parole Board, 'Update on the Fair for the Future Project' (2015), available at www.gov.uk/government/news/fair-for-the-future-update-march-2015.

[42] G Weeks, 'Estoppel and Public Authorities: Examining the Case for an Equitable Remedy' (2010) 4 *Journal of Equity* 247, 263–64.

[43] G Weeks, 'The Use and Enforcement of Soft Law by Australian Public Authorities' (2014) 42 *Federal Law Review* 181, 199.

that promise itself is judged by the court to be qualitatively good or bad. Australian courts rarely intervene in response to a decision which might be challenged in the United Kingdom by a legitimate expectation argument. When they have done so, it has been through the restrictive mechanism of the *Wednesbury* standard in its traditional form. That approach sits uneasily with the limited role Lord Woolf envisaged for *Wednesbury* in *Coughlan*,[44] that where a promise has been made of a substantive rather than a merely procedural benefit, the court must weigh the requirements of fairness against any reason behind a public body's change of policy.

Instrumental rationales justify procedural fairness in terms of its contribution in increasing the accuracy with which the criteria governing the decision are applied. Non-instrumental rationales give priority to other values, such as furthering participation, even at the expense of accuracy. The requirements of procedural fairness can usually be supported by both instrumental and non-instrumental justifications. Most theorists rely on a combination of both to justify the doctrine, but there has been considerable academic debate as to their relative importance and, in particular, whether observance of certain procedural requirements is necessary in order to show respect for persons affected regardless of whether that is likely to produce better outcomes.[45] Galligan favoured an approach that prioritises the instrumental role of procedures because:

> The general point is that fair treatment consists in being treated in accordance with authoritative standards what ever they be in each context ... Procedures are instruments to fair treatment; they are inherently neither fair nor unfair, but take on a quality of fairness to the degree that they are conducive to a person being treated properly according to authoritative standards and the values which ground such standards.[46]

By contrast, TRS Allan favoured a position closer to the 'dignitarian approach' of many American public law theorists,[47] which gives greater emphasis to the 'intrinsic' value of procedures.[48] Allan maintained that certain procedures may be required, in order to treat an affected person with respect, even though they do not promote better outcomes. Indeed, he suggested that the true purpose of procedures may extend, in an appropriate case, to enabling the legitimacy of authoritative standards to be contested and even facilitating repudiation of the applicable rules.[49]

The difference between these competing theoretical accounts has great significance to decisions about the appropriate reach of natural justice and the basis upon which the content of fairness is determined. Galligan observed that the position one takes within the range of possibilities between 'instrumentalist' and 'dignitarian' extremes 'will be based on the view one holds on much deeper issues about the very nature

[44] See the text accompanying n 98 below.

[45] See, eg, JL Mashaw, *Due Process in the Administrative State* (New Haven, CT, Yale University Press, 1985) chs 3–6; MD Bayles, *Procedural Justice: Allocating to Individuals* (Dordrecht, Kluwer Academic, 1990) ch 6; TRS Allan, 'Procedural Fairness and the Duty of Respect' (1998) 18 *Oxford Journal of Legal Studies* 497; Solum, 'Procedural Justice' (n 39).

[46] Galligan, *Due Process and Fair Procedures* (n 39) xviii.

[47] The most satisfactory of which remains Mashaw, *Due Process in the Administrative State* (n 45).

[48] Allan, 'Procedural Fairness and the Duty of Respect' (n 45). He expanded on this in TRS Allan, *Constitutional Justice: A Liberal Theory of the Rule of Law* (Oxford, Oxford University Press, 2001) 77–87.

[49] Allan, 'Procedural Fairness and the Duty of Respect' (n 45) 501.

of legal authority and the relationship between legal authority and deeper moral values'.[50] Craig argued that we should not assume that greater attention should be placed on:

> the general nature of the balancing process that operates within fairness. The extent, to which this should be viewed as a utilitarian calculus of some kind, or whether a more dignitarian approach should be pursued, is of considerable importance.[51]

That suggestion was prescient in light of *Osborn*,[52] where the Supreme Court considered when and why natural justice would require the board to provide prisoners seeking parole with an oral hearing rather than consider their case 'on the papers'. Lord Reed stressed a dignitarian basis for fairness:

> [J]ustice is intuitively understood to require procedure which pays due respect to persons whose rights are significantly affected by decisions taken in the exercise of administrative or judicial functions. Respect entails that such persons ought to be able to participate in the procedure by which the decision is made, provided they have something which is relevant to the decision to be taken.[53]

Lord Reed then quoted an article by Jeremy Waldron, which suggested there was no real difference in the core methods of judicial or administrative decision-makers. Each provides the same basic opportunity to people, namely, to present arguments and submissions, in answer to those provided by the other side, and to do so in an impartial and respectful hearing.[54] Lord Reed quoted only part of the passage in which Waldron explained the implications of the abstract details of a hearing. That entire passage, which deserves to be quoted in full, was as follows:

> These are abstract characteristics. But they are not arbitrary abstractions. They capture a deep and important sense associated foundationally with the idea of a legal system, that law is a mode of governing people that acknowledges that they have a view or perspective of their own to present on the application of the norm to their conduct and situation. Applying a norm to a human individual is not like deciding what to do about a rabid animal or a dilapidated house. It involves paying attention to a point of view and respecting the personality of the entity one is dealing with. As such it embodies a crucial dignitarian idea—respecting the dignity of those to whom the norms are applied as beings capable of explaining themselves.[55]

We would query whether judicial and administrative decision-makers can really be equated in this fashion. Lord Reed and Waldron both seemed to accept that consistent procedure and respectful treatment will generally amount to fairness. Perhaps so but there are many differences between administrative and judicial decision-making, particularly as the latter operates in judicial review. After all, the judicial role telescopes in judicial review and it is not simply a more refined version of the judicial role but it is also different to, and more limited than, that of administrative

[50] Galligan, *Due Process and Fair Procedures* (n 39) 82.
[51] Craig, *Administrative Law* (n 35) 383.
[52] *Osborn* (n 8).
[53] ibid [68].
[54] J Waldron, 'How Law Protects Dignity' (2012) 71 *Cambridge Law Journal* 200, 210.
[55] ibid, quoted in part in *Osborn* (n 8) [69].

decision-makers. It looks only at whether an exercise of power is affected by legal error. In the traditional expression, it asks whether decision-makers have exceeded their power. Given the difference in the central purposes of judicial and administrative decision-makers, it is not clear to us why it should be a problem that they apply different conceptions of fairness.

The reasoning used by Waldron has a long history in decisions affecting prisoners. It is evident in the more rights-sensitive approach to prison management of the late 1960s in the United States, which paid greater attention to procedural justice.[56] Lord Woolf raised similar issues in his inquiry into the devastating prison riots of 1990.[57] He suggested that fairer treatment of prisoners would influence how they viewed the prison system which, in turn, would enhance security and control by reducing the possibility that prisoners would vent their grievances with violence.[58] The legal and administrative changes which followed the Woolf Report introduced a discourse of legitimacy into prison administration that was slowly reflected in the law.[59]

In our view, the approach to fairness taken in *Osborn* is a more recent reflection of the anxieties that surfaced earlier in *AF*,[60] in which the House of Lords held that there was a minimum requirement of fairness which had to remain if a hearing were to be regarded as fair, even if providing that minimum level of fairness might not make a difference to the ultimate outcome of the proceeding.[61] *Osborn* explained important elements of that minimum requirement and why fairness could require a hearing or observance of particular procedures, even if they might not affect the substantive outcome. One was the affirmation of the courts' role in reviewing compliance for fairness. Lord Reed made clear that the function of a court was not merely to make the negative determination of whether the procedural choices of a decision-maker were reasonable, or rather avoided unreasonableness under the *Wednesbury* standard. It was instead to determine whether the procedure chosen was actually fair in a positive sense.[62] If a court is to gauge whether the procedure chosen by a decision-maker was fair rather than simply reasonable, the procedural discretion left to decision-makers is drastically reduced, and the scope of the court's legitimate inquiries concomitantly expanded. It is against this background that Lord Reed's meaning can be fully understood when he explained that the rule of law was fostered by fairness. Procedures which require officials to hear and consider what

[56] See D Fogel, *'We are the Living Proof…': The Justice Model of Corrections* (Cincinnati, OH, WH Anderson and Co, 1975); cf Lord Denning's shrill dismissal of the complaints of 'disgruntled prisoners' around this time: *Becker v Home Office* [1972] 2 QB 407, 418.

[57] The Woolf Report noted a 'recurring theme' in the evidence of prisoners was 'that their actions were a response to the manner in which they were treated … they felt a lack of justice': *Prison Disturbances, April 1990: Report of an Inquiry by the Rt Hon Lord Justice Woolf and His Honour Judge Stephen Tumin*, Cmnd 1456 (1991) [14.437].

[58] ibid [9.24].

[59] JR Sparks and AE Bottoms, 'Legitimacy and Order in Prisons' (1995) 46 *British Journal of Sociology* 45. On the remarkable evolution of prisoners' rights in this time, see M Loughlin and P Quinn, 'Prisons, Rules and Courts: A Study in Administrative Law' (1993) 56 *Modern Law Review* 497.

[60] *AF (No 3)* (n 38).

[61] See PP Craig, 'Perspectives on Process: Common Law, Statutory and Political' [2010] *Public Law* 275; A Kavanagh, 'Special Advocates, Control Orders and the Right to a Fair Trial' (2010) 73 *Modern Law Review* 836.

[62] *Osborn* (n 8) [65].

those affected by their decisions had to say would 'promote congruence between the actions of decision-makers and the law which should govern their actions'.[63]

Lord Reed identified the very participation of those affected as another indicator of fairness, since:

> the purpose of holding an oral hearing is not only to assist in its decision-making, but also to reflect the prisoner's legitimate interest in being able to participate in a decision with important implications for him, where he has something useful to contribute.[64]

Lord Reed held that these and the other purposes of fairness he identified were distinct from the question of whether a prisoner should be released or transferred because the Parole Board might have to consider other issues, such as the prisoner's overall progress.[65] He reasoned that whether an oral hearing is required to satisfy a prisoner's right to a fair hearing:

> does not depend on his establishing that his application for release or transfer stands any particular chance of success: that approach would not allow for the possibility that an oral hearing may be necessary in order for the prisoner to have a fair opportunity of establishing his prospects of success, and thus involves circular reasoning.[66]

This approach contrasts starkly with the leading Australian case, in which the High Court marginalised the applicant's legitimate expectation and stressed the relevance of a different possible outcome rather than outright success, with an approach to fairness that is superficially simple but devoid of principle.[67] In *Lam*, the High Court considered the effect of an apparent promise of administrative officials that they would not make a final decision on the possible deportation of Mr Lam until they had spoken to the carer of his children. The officials did not do so before making an adverse decision. The High Court held the failure to honour this assurance did not make the process unfair because it made no difference to Mr Lam's case.[68] The Court saw little purpose in a claim that failing to honour the assurance had disappointed a legitimate expectation. Any expectation might illuminate the content of the requirements of fairness but would not determine whether those requirements had actually been met.[69] The influential judgment of Gleeson CJ stressed that any legitimate expectation should not become more than a means to the end of fairness:

> Fairness is not an abstract concept. It is essentially practical. Whether one talks in terms of procedural fairness or natural justice, the concern of the law is to avoid practical injustice.[70]

This move from theoretical questions to practical consequences led Gleeson CJ to focus on the effect of decision-makers' conduct. On this view, it was the *effect* of

63 ibid [71].
64 ibid [82].
65 ibid [84].
66 ibid [88].
67 See M Groves, 'Unincorporated Treaties and Expectations: The Rise and Fall of *Teoh* in Australia' (2010) 12 *Judicial Review* 323.
68 *Lam* (n 5) 12–14 (Gleeson CJ), 34–35 (McHugh and Gummow JJ), 38–39 (Hayne J), 48–49 (Callinan J).
69 ibid 9, 12–13 (Gleeson CJ), 27–28, 34 (McHugh and Gummow JJ), 35–37 (Hayne J), 48–49 (Callinan J).
70 ibid 14.

what decision-makers did (or failed to do) that mattered, not what they had done (or failed to do) because:

> what must be demonstrated is unfairness, not merely departure from a representation. Not every departure from a stated intention necessarily involves unfairness, even if it defeats an expectation ... In a context such as the present, where there is already an obligation to extend procedural fairness, the creation of an expectation may bear upon the practical content of that obligation. But it does not supplant the obligation. The ultimate question remains whether there has been unfairness; not whether an expectation has been disappointed.[71]

This approach is unashamedly functional. It does not take clear account of normative principles such as the rule of law, participation or dignitarian ideals, nor does it necessarily reject them. Perhaps it reflects the remarkable reluctance of the High Court of Australia to talk openly about the principles that might underpin even its most central public law concepts.[72]

One consequence of that reluctance has arisen in the question of whether a breach of fairness might simply be technical or would have made no difference (and, therefore, should not attract relief). The approach of Gleeson CJ implicitly accepts the possibility of a merely technical breach by requiring applicants to demonstrate practical unfairness. This possibility has much support in Australian law,[73] but has long been doubted in England.[74] The best known example is the reminder of Megarry J that the law is:

> strewn with examples of open and shut cases which, somehow, were not; of unanswerable charges which, in the event, were completely answered; of inexplicable conduct which was fully explained; of fixed and unalterable determinations that, by discussion, suffered a change.[75]

Bingham LJ later reached a similar position, though for different reasons. He rejected the possibility that there might be purely technical breaches of the requirement to provide fairness (which made no difference to the outcome of the case) because it obscured the simpler, more important question of whether a procedure was fair or unfair. His Lordship explained that, since courts are concerned as much with substance as procedure, they could and should accept the notion of a technical or inconsequential form of unfairness.[76] In *AF*, Lord Phillips also rejected any distinction between a fair procedure and one that produced a fair result, noting that the object of procedure is to ensure, so far as possible, that the *outcome* of the process accords with the law.[77]

[71] ibid 12–13.

[72] See Gageler, 'Impact of Migration Law on the Development of Australian Administrative Law' (n 31) 105.

[73] *Stead v State Government Insurance Commission* (1986) 161 CLR 141.

[74] There are many older English cases to the contrary, eg *Malloch v Aberdeen Corporation* [1971] 1 WLR 1578. These have been consigned to history by *AF (No 3)* (n 38) [61]–[63] (Lord Phillips).

[75] *John v Rees* [1970] Ch 345, 402.

[76] *R v Chief Constable of the Thames Valley Police, ex parte Cotton* [1990] IRLR 344, 350–51.

[77] *AF (No 3)* (n 38) [60]. See *Osborn* (n 8) [67]–[68].

Interestingly, Gleeson CJ applied similar reasoning in Australia, but came to the opposite conclusion.[78] It is striking that this approach demonstrates that, like Lord Bingham, he was looking only at the question of whether a certain procedure was fair or unfair. However, he did so by looking at what *practical* unfairness the claimant suffered. In other words, the Australian approach encapsulated by Gleeson CJ in *Lam*, in contrast to Lord Phillips' speech in *AF*, allows for the possibility that an unfair procedure (in the sense of failing to adhere to a representation) need not necessarily lead to an unfair result. Whether the English approach will be significantly altered by recent amendments to the Senior Courts Act 1981 is not yet clear. Those changes require English courts to refuse relief 'if it appears to the court to be highly likely that the outcome for the applicant would not have been substantially different if the conduct complained of had not occurred'.[79] This new requirement is superficially similar to the approach of Gleeson CJ in *Lam* but it is not limited to claims of a denial of natural justice. The application of such a requirement to other grounds of review may not be easy. Another difficulty of the requirement is that it need not be applied if the court considers there are 'reasons of exceptional public interest' for it to do otherwise.[80] Whether and why that criterion might differ from established principles governing the grant of leave or the discretionary refusal of relief is equally unclear.

Lam also stands for the point that any unfairness created by a procedural representation could be remedied either by fulfilling it (for example, allowing a claimant to be heard on whether the promised steps should be taken) or by simply giving notice to the claimant that the representation will not now be met.[81] The difference between the UK and Australian approaches may be one of form rather than substance: each surely involves some judicial assessment of the overall fairness of the process, whether tacit or explicit. Gleeson CJ's more backward-looking assessment requires a largely unspoken judgement of whether the alleged unfairness was arguable in light of the entire process but surely then requires some assessment of the outcome that followed the process. Lords Bingham and Phillips may have simply conflated the two more openly.

IV. EXPECTATIONS, ESTOPPEL AND FAIRNESS

After *Ridge v Baldwin*,[82] the focus of many cases fell to the 'threshold question' of whether natural justice applied. The answer usually depended on whether the courts could identify a particular reason why it should. The existence of a legitimate expectation was commonly invoked as a reason in cases where public officials created or maintained some form of expectation. The classic example was where the holder of

[78] *Lam* (n 5) [25]. See also the passage quoted at n 71 above.

[79] Senior Courts Act 1981 (UK), s 31(2A) (refusal of relief at substantive hearing) and s 31(3D) (refusal of relief in application for leave). These amendments were introduced by the Criminal Justice and Courts Act 2015 (UK). We thank Rick Rawlings for alerting us to this provision.

[80] Senior Courts Act 1981 (UK), s 31(2B), (3E).

[81] *Lam* (n 5) [36] (Gleeson CJ).

[82] *Ridge v Baldwin* (n 18).

a visa, licence or permit would argue its existence created an *expectation* they would enjoy the benefit for a stated time and that this would not change without notice and a chance to argue why the benefit should not be removed.[83] Thus, there were two important procedural benefits of legitimate expectations: the rights to notice and to be heard.[84]

Legitimate expectations came to be invoked in four main categories:[85]

— where people had relied upon a policy or norm of general application but were then subjected to a different rule or policy;
— where a policy or norm of general application existed and continued but was not applied to the case at hand;[86]
— where an individual received a promise or representation which was not honoured because of a later change to a policy or norm of wider application;[87] and
— where an individual received a promise or representation which was subsequently dishonoured, not because of a general change in policy but because the decision-maker changed its mind in that instance.[88]

Key questions about the doctrine remained. One was whether an expectation needed to be reasonable,[89] thereby providing an apparently objective quality that was thought to provide a useful limit, by precluding the recognition of unrealistic or inappropriate expectations. Another was whether the expectation should be assessed on subjective or objective terms. In other words, who should assess whether it was reasonable to recognise and enforce the expectation? A related issue was whether a claimant should be required to demonstrate his or her reliance on the expectation and that it had caused detriment. While detrimental reliance is essential to establishing an estoppel,[90] many legitimate expectation cases accepted that the doctrine could still be invoked even if its claimant could not prove reliance on the relevant representation, or detriment in consequence of that reliance.[91] In the terms employed

[83] Support for the utility of legitimate expectations in Australia, never unanimous and now deeply unfashionable, has focused on such cases, principally *FAI Insurances Ltd v Winneke* (1982) 151 CLR 342.

[84] P Tate, 'The Coherence of "Legitimate Expectations" and the Foundations of Natural Justice' (1988) 14 *Monash Law Review* 15. Regarding English law during this same time, see *R (Abdi and Nadarajah) v Secretary of State for the Home Department* [2005] EWCA Civ 1363, [49].

[85] A taxonomy taken from Craig, *Administrative Law* (n 35) 679–80. On closer inspection, the third category includes most examples from the first and the fourth category is another variation of the third.

[86] *Council of Civil Service Unions v Minister for the Civil Service* [1985] 1 AC 374 (natural justice arguments accepted but claim failed for other reasons); *R v Home Secretary, ex parte Khan* [1984] 1 WLR 1337 (claim succeeded); *Haoucher v Minister for Immigration and Ethnic Affairs* (1990) 169 CLR 648 (claim succeeded).

[87] *Attorney-General (NSW) v Quin* (1990) 170 CLR 1 (claim failed); *Hamble Fisheries* [1995] 2 All ER 714 (claim succeeded).

[88] *R v Inland Revenue Commissioners, ex parte Preston* [1985] AC 835 (claim succeeded); *Paponette v Attorney-General of Trinidad and Tobago* [2012] 1 AC 1 (claim succeeded).

[89] See, eg, *Attorney-General of Hong Kong v Ng Yuen Shiu* [1983] 2 AC 629, 636; *Minister of State for Immigration and Ethnic Affairs v Teoh* (1995) 183 CLR 273, 291 (Mason CJ and Deane J), 314 (McHugh J).

[90] Weeks, 'Estoppel and Public Authorities' (n 42) 254.

[91] See, eg, *R v Secretary of State for the Home Department, ex parte Begbie* [2000] 1 WLR 1115, 1124. By contrast, Lord Woolf stated, without anything by way of factual support, that Ms Coughlan had relied on the relevant representation and thereby avoided dealing with issues of detriment: *Coughlan* (n 3) 247.

in estoppel cases, this position allowed claimants to bind public authorities to a mere promise.[92] The inconsistency of this position becomes apparent once it is recalled that several formative English cases on legitimate expectations drew clear analogies between grants of power under statute and the performance of contracts.[93]

Another difficulty was the extent to which the legitimate expectation might extend to determining actual outcomes, as opposed to procedural requirements. If a legitimate expectation is of a substantive outcome (an *actual* advantage or benefit), it differs from an expectation of a *procedural* outcome. A substantive legitimate expectation usually arises in two scenarios: first, when people who enjoy a benefit or advantage argue that they expect it to continue.[94] Enforcement of such expectations effectively precludes or greatly limits officials from exercising their powers in a way that removes or limits the expected benefit. The second scenario is when people who do not yet enjoy a benefit or advantage argue a rightful expectation of its grant.[95] In such cases, the expectation can effectively compel decision-makers to grant what is expected.

Coughlan marked a decisive English acceptance of the substantive enforcement of legitimate expectations (or substantive unfairness), but key elements of that doctrine had been hinted at years earlier when the House of Lords used a blend of private law estoppel and public law fairness to determine the obligations of tax officials in *Preston*.[96] The Lords concluded that the statutory obligation of tax officials to act 'fairly' could sometimes prevent them acting in a manner that broadly equated to a breach of contract or to making a representation that would give rise to an estoppel if the tax authority were a private actor. If the tax officials had acted unfairly according to these principles influenced by estoppel, their decision would constitute an abuse of power.[97] Curiously, *Preston* did not rely on fairness as a concept, which implies a distinction between natural justice and fairness. If so, it becomes a small doctrinal step to recognise a ground of substantive unfairness distinct from procedural unfairness.

The doctrine was entirely refashioned in *Coughlan*, when the Court of Appeal held that there can be situations in which expectations generated by promises or representations made by public authorities must be fulfilled. The substantive legitimate expectation, foreshadowed in *Preston* as a form of abuse of power, and the move away from the merely procedural legitimate expectation, were each strongly pronounced. The Court of Appeal used a three-fold taxonomy of promises, representations and legitimate expectations that could arise from public or official action. These categories were mainly used to distinguish the different questions that each sort of expectation might pose to a court rather than to explain the content of the expectations.

92 *R v Board of Inland Revenue, ex parte MFK Underwriting Agencies Ltd* [1990] 1 WLR 1545, 1569–70 (Bingham LJ).

93 *HTV Ltd v Price Commission* [1976] ICR 170; *Preston* (n 88) 866–67 (Lord Templeman); cf *Minister for Immigration and Ethnic Affairs v Kurtovic* (1990) 21 FCR 193, 220 (Gummow J).

94 *Coughlan* (n 3); cf *Kurtovic* (n 93).

95 *R (Patel) v General Medical Council* [2013] 1 WLR 2801; cf *Lam* (n 5).

96 *Preston* (n 88).

97 ibid 866; cf *Lam* (n 5) 23 (McHugh and Gummow JJ).

The first category was the 'previous policy or other representations' that the government would only be required to 'bear in mind ... giving [them] the weight it thinks right but no more, before deciding whether to change course'.[98] The court would only overturn a decision relating to such expectations if it was satisfied that it was unreasonable on the *Wednesbury* standard.

The second category was of expectations in which an official 'promise or practice induces a legitimate expectation ... [such as] being consulted before a particular decision is taken'.[99] In these instances the court would require consultation with those affected, in accordance with the expectation, after which the promisee could be disappointed as to his or her preferred substantive outcome if the decision was lawful and supported by appropriate reasons. Neither category is novel. The first requires a court to apply the various grounds of review that fall within the scope of rationality. The same is true for the second category, with perhaps additional need to observe the requirements of procedural fairness as the circumstances of the case require. Both categories essentially represent a procedural standard and highlight how a court can examine the process of decision-making. If *Coughlan* had decided no more than this, it would have been entirely uncontroversial.[100]

However, the Court of Appeal identified a different and clearly radical third category of expectation, which arose:

> [w]here the court considers that a lawful promise or practice has induced a legitimate expectation of a *benefit which is substantive*, not simply procedural ... [T]he court will in a proper case decide whether to frustrate the expectation is so unfair that to take a new and different course will amount to an abuse of power. Here, once the legitimacy of the expectation is established, the court will have the task of weighing the requirements of fairness against any overriding interest relied upon for the change of policy.[101]

The Court of Appeal made clear that this category arose when public officials had created an expectation of a substantive benefit and then acted contrary to that expectation. The court could find such conduct to be an unlawful abuse of power. The Court of Appeal accepted that the lawfulness of any attempt to renege on a promise, or change the policy upon which an expectation was based, depended on whether the court was satisfied there was an 'overriding' reason to do so. The court made clear that this balancing of individual and more general public interests, which would determine whether the public interest could override a personal one, would take account of the fairness of the outcome.[102]

One of the many difficulties in this reasoning was the lack of principle to determine when or why an exercise of power may become an 'abuse'. Does the fact that an administrative decision, which may benefit many individuals who are not parties to proceedings for judicial review, bears heavily (or even disproportionately) upon a certain individual necessarily mean that it constitutes an abuse of the decision-maker's power? A question which follows logically is who should decide whether

[98] *Coughlan* (n 3) 241.
[99] ibid 242.
[100] M Groves, 'Substantive Legitimate Expectations in Australian Administrative Law' (2008) 32 *Melbourne University Law Review* 470, 478.
[101] *Coughlan* (n 3) 242 (emphasis in original).
[102] ibid [71].

an exercise of power amounts to an abuse of that power? In Australia, these are seen as considerations of policy and considerable scope is given to decision-makers, particularly those whose powers are granted under statute. In theory, the courts do no more than decide whether a decision-maker's power has been exceeded by considering whether the decision-maker has committed a jurisdictional error, usually for breach of an established ground of review. As with abuse of power, the label of jurisdictional error is a cloak that enables courts to cast a vague, malleable doctrine over decisions. Casting the cloak distracts attention from the variable, often policy based, reasoning used by the courts.

The Court of Appeal in *Coughlan* did not address these issues but simply held that it falls to a court to decide whether an abuse of power has occurred and 'whether the consequent frustration of the individual's expectation is so unfair as to be a misuse of … power'.[103] The principle within this approach is not readily apparent. Another difficulty was the tendency of cases within *Coughlan*'s third category to limit the ability of governments to adjust and remake policies and like statements as circumstances might require.[104] The Court of Appeal accepted that government and its officials could change their policies and sometimes not honour statements that had been made, but held that the freedom to do so would often be limited by notions of abuse of power. Within the confines of that principle, the Court reasoned that limiting the freedom of government to change its mind or break its word:

> recognises the primacy of the public authority both in administration and in policy development, but it insists, where these functions come into tension, upon the adjudicative role of the court to ensure fairness to the individual.[105]

As much as the result of *Coughlan* itself, this statement indicates clearly that a judicial inquiry into 'fairness' is weighted heavily in favour of the individual claimant and against the more abstract interests of the public generally.

The difficulties within *Coughlan* were implicitly acknowledged by the many subsequent cases which relied upon substantive unfairness while also seeking to modify or better explain the doctrine. The first was decided just a month later.[106] In *Begbie*, Laws LJ made the first of several valiant attempts to fashion a stronger doctrinal foundation for the substantive enforcement of legitimate expectations in the more general notion of abuse of power, which he saw as 'the root concept which governs and conditions our general principles of public law'.[107] According to this view, the controversial point of *Coughlan* was not whether the concept of substantive enforcement of legitimate expectations ought to be accepted but how the concept should

[103] *Coughlan* (n 3) [82]. The failure directly to address or weigh such issues mirrors that of the natural justice cases where judgments about cost implications are rarely made explicit. The United States is an exception because decisions about due process rights can consider 'cost/benefit' and other issues: *Mathews v Eldridge*, 424 US 319, 334–35 (1976); *Bowen v City of New York*, 476 US 467, 483–85 (1986). This approach provides a methodology to courts and an invitation to the parties to lead evidence to inform that methodology.

[104] See *Quin* (n 87).

[105] *Coughlan* (n 3) [70].

[106] *Begbie* (n 91).

[107] ibid 1129. This echoed his previous argument from Sir John Laws, 'Public Law and Employment: Abuse of Power' [1997] *Public Law* 455.

be articulated within the wider rubric of abuse of power.[108] Laws LJ also doubted the adoption in *Coughlan* of different approaches to the review of each category of expectation. *Coughlan* held that some expectations were amenable to review for irrationality/unreasonableness, while the final (novel) category was amenable to review with a context sensitive consideration of fairness. Laws LJ reasoned that these principles of review possessed overlapping qualities and 'each is a spectrum, not a single point, and they shade into one another'.[109]

A differently constituted Court of Appeal in *Bibi*[110] acknowledged the clear tension between the 'administrative and democratic gains in preserving for the authority the possibility in the future of coming to different conclusions' about decisions and the 'value in holding authorities to promises which they have made, thus upholding responsible public administration and allowing people to plan their lives sensibly'.[111] Put differently, what compelling reason would cause a court to give primacy to the need of public authorities to respond to changing circumstances over the desire of individuals to plan ahead based on their expectation of how a public authority will act?[112]

Laws LJ adopted a more detailed but essentially similar approach in *Nadarajah and Abdi*,[113] in which he conceded that notions of abuse of power alone would not explain a great deal. He returned to the general principle that underpinned the legitimate expectation cases, namely, that a public authority that made or adopted a promise representing how it would act was required to follow that promise or practice unless there was a compelling reason otherwise. He accepted that this legal obligation was 'grounded in fairness' but lay in a much deeper 'requirement of good administration, by which public bodies ought to deal straightforwardly and consistently with the public'.[114] He explained:

> The principle that good administration requires public authorities to be held to their promises would be undermined if the law did not insist that any failure or refusal to comply is objectively justified as a proportionate measure in the circumstances.[115]

These more normative justifications distract attention from the fact that legitimate expectations are generally formed based on representations which amount in effect to rules of some form. The enforcement of legitimate expectations might therefore be

[108] *Begbie* (n 91) 1129–30.

[109] ibid 1130.

[110] *R (Bibi) v Newham London Borough Council* [2002] 1 WLR 237.

[111] ibid [24]. The Court also made clear that officials could not simply fail to consider the nature and consequences of any relevant expectation, as seemed to occur in the case at hand: [49]–[51]. This approach might be seen to make the substantive expectation a mandatory consideration, whereas *Coughlan* proceeded on the assumption that expectations could and should be considered.

[112] ibid [24].

[113] *R (Abdi and Nadarajah) v Secretary of State for the Home Department* [2005] EWCA Civ 1363. The judgment of Laws LJ was effusively praised by Lord Phillips in *R (Lumba) v Secretary of State for the Home Department* [2012] 1 AC 245, 344 [311].

[114] *Nadarajah and Abdi* (n 113), [68]. By contrast, Gleeson CJ noted that the judicial review jurisdiction under s 75(v) of the Australian Constitution 'does not exist for the purpose of enabling the judicial branch of government to impose upon the executive branch its ideas of good administration': *Lam* (n 5) [32].

[115] *Nadarajah and Abdi* (n 113) [68].

seen to provide a consistent and appropriate way of requiring governments and its officials to abide by their own rules.[116] This rule-based account is said to overcome questions about the rigour of legitimate expectations in its identification of a coherent rule-based foundation. In our view, that argument is flawed both in its presumption of the very legitimacy of the expectations it seeks to investigate and its failure adequately to explain the regular cases in which English courts decline to enforce expectations. Furthermore, the problems inherent in enforcing 'soft' rules of any sort from which the rule-maker seeks to depart are significant.[117]

The fact is that, while the substantive unfairness doctrine, as it now operates in England, might favour claimants able to point to some evidence of unfairness in their case, it is nonetheless premised on weighing that unfairness against the possibility of an 'overriding' public benefit. Substantive unfairness is not made out by simply establishing the breach of a rule, whether soft or hard. A similar result follows if one relies on the dignitarian rationale favoured in *Osborn*.[118] The main reason is not simply because Lord Reed appeared to draw a connection between dignitarian ideals and the very procedural issues of participation but that the notion of respectful treatment of an individual which underpins the dignitarian ideal cannot add anything more to the balancing exercise that substantive expectations are said to require. If anything, the use of a dignitarian focus could make the identification or adjudication over the validity of an expectation an even more one-sided affair, by leaving little room for the views of the authority that generated any claimed expectation.

A wooden house can be demolished when it ages but if the owner wishes to save the structure it can sometimes be 'restumped', thereby placing a useful structure on new, more solid, foundations. Many cases appear to want to keep the house built in *Coughlan*, but realise it has shaky foundations.[119] The need to restump *Coughlan* may have been shaped by the impending realisation that estoppel, from which many early legitimate expectation cases drew, was nearing its end in public law. That step was formally taken in the *Reprotech* case,[120] when the House of Lords signalled that any connection that had existed between the two was at an end. Lord Hoffmann, with whom the other Lords agreed, cited *Coughlan* to acknowledge the clear 'analogy between a private law estoppel and the public law concept of a legitimate expectation created by a public authority, the denial of which may amount to an abuse of power'[121] but concluded that it was 'no more than an analogy' because, in crafting

[116] This position is taken in F Ahmed and A Perry, 'The Coherence of the Doctrine of Legitimate Expectations' (2014) 73 *Cambridge Law Journal* 61.

[117] Weeks, 'The Use and Enforcement of Soft Law by Australian Public Authorities' (n 43).

[118] See the quote from *Osborn* at n 53 above.

[119] The same may be true in other areas of public law, such as in cases suggesting the importance of the common law rather than human rights legislation or European laws or conventions to decide rights issues: see, eg, *Osborn* (n 8) [57] and *Kennedy v Charity Commission* [2014] UKSC 20, [2014] 2 WLR 808, [46]. The judicial reliance on the common law basis means that many modern public law cases would remain on a secure foundation if there was legislation to repeal or refashion the Human Rights Act 1998. A referendum on the membership of the EU is likely, given the current English political climate, to occur sooner rather than later. See Lady Hale's comments in 'UK Constitutionalism on the March?' [2014] *Judicial Review* 201, 208.

[120] *R v East Sussex County Council, ex parte Reprotech (Pebsham) Ltd* [2003] 1 WLR 348.

[121] ibid [34].

remedies against public authorities, courts 'have to take into account the interests of the general public which the authority exists to promote' as well as rights protected under the Human Rights Act 1998.[122] Lord Hoffmann went on to state that 'public law has already absorbed whatever is useful from the moral values which underlie the private law concept of estoppel and the time has come for it to stand upon its own two feet'.[123]

This quite decisive severance of public and private law is notable on several counts. First, the use of estoppel in legitimate expectation cases was always inexact and was never properly regarded as more than analogous to the public law doctrine,[124] which explained why those cases did not demand that the applicant demonstrate detrimental reliance on the representation. If the differences between estoppel and its loose parallel in public law had accommodated such differences, there seems no clear reason why the two areas had to be more formally separated.

Secondly, estoppel is typically based on a case sensitive consideration of the issues affecting the two parties which cannot include the wider elements of public interest that are present in many, perhaps even most, public law proceedings. While the discretionary nature of relief is common to the equitable doctrine of estoppel and judicial review remedies,[125] very different considerations guide the respective exercises of discretion.

A third reason is because the equity created by an estoppel need not always be fulfilled by holding the representor to the substance of his or her representation. Where the 'minimum equity' required to achieve justice in the circumstances does not require that the estoppel be enforced, equitable compensation may be available as an alternative remedy.[126]

V. REJECTION OF ESTOPPEL IN AUSTRALIAN PUBLIC LAW

Although English courts severed the doctrinal connection between estoppel and public law, it is useful to note that no such connection ever took root in Australian law. Australian courts have long held that rules of estoppel should not and cannot apply to public officials in the exercise of statutory powers or discretions which are peculiarly public or governmental.[127] This long established principle was reiterated in *Kurtovic*,[128] which had many similarities to *Coughlan*, although the circumstances of the claimant and the nature of the representation made to him were very different. Mr Kurtovic was a non-citizen and had served a long prison sentence when the Minister ordered his deportation. After Mr Kurtovic successfully appealed this decision, the Minister wrote to him and warned that he would reconsider the issue if

[122] ibid.
[123] ibid [35].
[124] cf *Bellinz v Commissioner of Taxation* (1998) 84 FCR 154, 164.
[125] *Commonwealth v Verwayen* (1990) 170 CLR 394, 454 (Dawson J).
[126] Weeks, 'Estoppel and Public Authorities' (n 42) 276–82.
[127] *Maritime Electric Co Ltd v General Dairies Ltd* [1937] AC 610; *Southend-on-Sea Corporation v Hodgson (Wickford) Ltd* [1962] 1 QB 416.
[128] *Kurtovic* (n 93).

Kurtovic was convicted of more crimes. Kurtovic took this to mean that, if he stayed out of trouble, he would not be deported. The Minister later decided to deport Mr Kurtovic after being alerted to 'concerns' raised by his parole officials, even though Mr Kurtovic had not committed more crimes.

The Full Court of the Federal Court noted that the circumstances of the case had not changed significantly,[129] but rejected arguments that Minister's earlier letter estopped him from making the second deportation order. It held that letter did not contain an utterly clear promise but reasoned that, even if it had, such a promise would have impermissibly fettered the Minister's statutory power.[130] Gummow J, with whom Neaves and Ryan JJ agreed on this issue, reasoned that the distinct character of public powers and the rationale of the non-fettering rule, were strong reasons to reject the application of estoppel to public powers.[131] This reasoning remains orthodox in Australian law,[132] although neither *Kurtovic* nor the judgment of Mason CJ in *Quin*[133] went so far as to say that estoppel can *never* be raised to prevent the performance of a statutory duty or hinder the exercise of a statutory discretion.

Gummow J strongly rejected arguments that the decision was substantively unfair. That argument drew from suggestions of Lord Denning MR in *Laker Airways Ltd v Department of Trade*[134] that, although the Crown could not normally be estopped in the exercise of public power 'even though this may work some injustice or unfairness to a private individual', that would not be so when the Crown was not:

> properly exercising its powers, but is misusing them; and it does misuse them if it exercises them in circumstances which work injustice or unfairness to the individual without any countervailing benefit for the public.[135]

Gummow J saw 'two fatal objections' to this possibility that enabled the court to detect injustice or unfairness to the individual 'by some process of "judicial balancing" between public and private interests'.[136] They were:

> First the question of where the balance lies between competing public and private interests in the exercise of a statutory discretion goes to the merits of the case, and is one for the decision-maker, not the courts, to resolve. Secondly, a conclusion that a representation or decision is *ultra vires* ordinarily will preclude its effectiveness. An *ultra vires* representation is not a mere factor in favour of which the scales of judicial balancing might be allowed to swing, but peremptorily forecloses such deliberation.[137]

[129] ibid 196 (Neaves J), 201 (Ryan J), 208–14 (Gummow J). The Court held Mr Kurtovic was denied natural justice by the failure to provide notice of and a chance to respond to the information from parole officials: 197 (Neaves J), 205 (Ryan J), 222–24 (Gummow J).

[130] ibid 196 (Neaves J), 201 (Ryan J), 207 (Gummow J).

[131] ibid 210 (Gummow J).

[132] Sir Anthony Mason, 'Estoppel in Administrative Law' in M Groves (ed), *Law and Government in Australia* (Sydney, Federation Press, 2005).

[133] *Quin* (n 87) 18.

[134] [1977] QB 643.

[135] ibid 707.

[136] *Kurtovic* (n 93) 221.

[137] ibid 221.

This rejection of estoppel also effectively precludes substantive unfairness, whether in the form of the test adopted in *Coughlan* or by weighing different factors where a claimant argues for an estoppel to be enforced, because it clearly amounts to merits review.

Mason CJ appeared to take a contrary position in *Quin* when he suggested a possible exception to the principle that estoppel was not available against public authorities in respect of exercise of their discretionary powers. His Honour explained that, despite his acceptance of this general principle, he did:

> not deny the availability of estoppel against the Executive, arising from conduct amounting to a representation, when holding the Executive to its representation does not significantly hinder the exercise of the discretion in the public interest. And, as the public interest necessarily comprehends an element of justice to the individual, one cannot exclude the possibility that the courts might in some situations grant relief on the basis that a refusal to hold the Executive to a representation by means of estoppel will occasion greater harm to the public interest by causing grave injustice to the individual who acts on the representation than any detriment to that interest that will arise from holding the Executive to its representation and thus narrowing the exercise of the discretion.[138]

It is notable that, regardless of what Mason CJ in fact said in this judgment, *Quin* (like *Kurtovic*) has for over two decades been treated as precluding the enforcement of an estoppel over the exercise of public powers or discretions.[139]

VI. CONCLUSION

After a period of time, it becomes trite to observe that the United Kingdom and Australia have followed different paths on issues such as public law estoppel and legitimate expectations without seeking to explain why that should be so. Part of the reason is inevitably constitutional. While Mike Taggart rightly urged Australians to remember that their written Constitution 'is not a conversation stopper',[140] it must also be acknowledged that it is the nature of written constitutions to limit the scope of courts to decide matters as they consider most fair,[141] especially in the absence of a judicially enforceable bill of rights in Australia's federal jurisdiction. The divergent views in Australia and the United Kingdom on the consequence of public authorities breaking their promises might be considered to have their source in Australia's constitutionally mandated separation of powers. As a result, where English courts have looked to the disadvantage suffered by people to whom government has failed to keep its word, Australian courts have focused instead on their incapacity to compel government decision-makers either to act contrary to statute or to fetter their discretion.[142]

[138] *Quin* (n 87) 18–19.

[139] Weeks, 'Estoppel and Public Authorities' (n 42) 254.

[140] M Taggart, '"Australian Exceptionalism" in Judicial Review' (2008) 36 *Federal Law Review* 1, 11.

[141] J Boughey and G Weeks, '"Officers of the Commonwealth" in the Private Sector: Can the High Court Review Outsourced Exercises of Power?' (2013) 36 *University of New South Wales Law Journal* 316.

[142] Significantly, they do so relying on UK jurisprudence: *Maritime Electric* (n 127); *Southend-on-Sea* (n 127).

However, as important as this constitutional element is, we believe that there is greater complexity to the division between English and Australian approaches than it reflects alone. This is in part to do with differing conceptions about fairness: the extent of the duty to be fair, the content of that duty and the rationale behind being fair at all. Much might be explained by differences in approach that fall short of differences in doctrine. Alternatively, identification of the same key issue—for example, which courts must look only at the fairness of a certain procedure rather than the manner of its breach—can lead different courts in different directions. Lord Bingham concluded that unfairness could never be ignored on the basis that it was inconsequential;[143] Gleeson CJ concluded that the absence of fairness must equate to the presence of practical injustice, or there will have been no unfairness.[144]

What follows from this is that the differences in approach between Australia and the United Kingdom are significant, perhaps even profound, but are not in the final analysis definitive. There are compelling constitutional reasons for courts in each jurisdiction to decide matters regarding legitimate expectations as they do and UK courts can scarcely avoid applying a rights-based analysis any more than Australian courts can ignore the Australian Constitution. However, the dialogue between the two countries remains and has been beneficial to developing the law. It is noteworthy and oddly pleasing that the High Court devoted so much of its judgment in *Lam* to refuting *Coughlan* even though the applicant had not mentioned *Coughlan* at all. While the Court of Appeal did not directly influence the result in *Lam*, the thinking of the High Court had certainly been affected by developments in the United Kingdom. Nobody need feel defensive about this, since it proves that neither Australia nor the United Kingdom is truly isolated from each other or the rest of the common law world.

[143] *Ex parte Cotton* (n 76) 350–51.
[144] *Lam* (n 5) [37].

9

Judicial Review of Delegated Legislation: Why Favour Substantive Review over Procedural Review?

ANDREW EDGAR*

I. INTRODUCTION

PROPORTIONALITY REVIEW OF delegated legislation has been accepted in Australia since the 1930s.[1] In this form of review the courts assess delegated legislation for whether it could reasonably have been adopted as a means for achieving the ends of the relevant statutory power. This has recently been confirmed by the High Court in *Attorney-General (SA) v Corporation of the City of Adelaide*.[2] This confirmation of proportionality review prompts a question regarding the kinds of challenge to delegated legislation that can be made under Australian law. The question is why proportionality, an intensive form of substantive review, is an available ground of judicial review of delegated legislation while procedural review is effectively excluded.

Procedural review of delegated legislation is uncommon in Australia for two reasons. The first relates to the statutes that establish general controls on rule-making, such as the Legislative Instruments Act 2003 (Cth) in Australia and the Statutory Instruments Act 1946 in the United Kingdom. I will refer to such statutes as 'general rule-making legislation' to distinguish them from enabling statutes that authorise the making of particular pieces of delegation legislation. General rule-making legislation in Australia commonly includes public consultation provisions but in a manner that makes consultation discretionary or unenforceable. Secondly, procedural fairness in Australia does not extend to decisions that affect the public generally,[3] as is the case for delegated legislation.[4]

* Thanks to Mark Aronson, Rayner Thwaites and Mark Elliott for their comments on an earlier draft. Of course, all errors and omissions are my own.

[1] *Williams v City of Melbourne* [1933] HCA 56, (1933) 49 CLR 142, 155; D Pearce and S Argument, *Delegated Legislation in Australia*, 4th edn (Chatswood, LexisNexis Butterworths, 2012) 339.

[2] [2013] HCA 3, (2013) 249 CLR 1, [56] (French CJ), [117] (Hayne J, Bell J agreeing), [199]–[201] (Crennan and Kiefel JJ).

[3] *Kioa v West* [1985] HCA 81, (1985) 159 CLR 550, 582, 584 (Mason J), 619–20 (Brennan J), 632 (Deane J).

[4] *Re Gosling* [1943] NSWStRp 20, (1943) 43 SR (NSW) 312, 318.

The emphasis on substantive review over procedural review inverts the norm of judicial review of administrative action that courts focus generally on matters of process rather than substance.[5] This chapter focuses on the reasons in Australian law for the effective exclusion of judicial review on procedural grounds and the acceptance of intense review on substantive grounds. The answers that I come to can be outlined for introductory purposes as follows. First, the public consultation provisions that are included in general Australian rule-making legislation have been designed to exclude judicial review for lack of public consultation and for poor public consultation practices. The reasons for designing the public consultation provisions in this manner are, however, either unclear or questionable (examined in section III.A). Secondly, procedural fairness doctrine, as understood in the landmark case *Kioa v West*,[6] is based on an outdated conception of judicial review of administrative decisions that have political significance or polycentric characteristics (examined in section III.B). Thirdly, substantive review, particularly in the form of proportionality review, is necessary for review of delegated legislation due to constitutional concerns about broad delegations of rule-making power (examined in section IV). Following on from the analysis of each of these forms of review, section V suggests some options for correcting this imbalance between procedural and substantive forms of review of delegated legislation in Australian law.

While the chapter focuses on Australian law it is worthwhile briefly highlighting some similarities and differences between Australian law and the law in related Commonwealth countries regarding review of delegated legislation on procedural and substantive grounds. On procedural grounds Australian law is similar to these countries. In the United Kingdom,[7] Canada[8] and New Zealand,[9] public consultation provisions are not included in general rule-making legislation—consultation is instead regulated according to unenforceable, informal policies or due to consultation provisions in sector-specific legislation. Similarly, procedural fairness does not generally extend in these countries to the making of delegated legislation,

[5] David Dyzenhaus and Evan Fox-Decent, 'Rethinking the Process/Substance Distinction: *Baker v Canada*' (2001) 51 *University of Toronto Law Journal* 193, 195; Robin Creyke and John McMillan 'Judicial Review Outcomes: An Empirical Study' (2004) 11 *Australian Journal of Administrative Law* 82, 97; Mark Elliott, 'Legitimate Expectations: Procedure, Substance, Policy and Proportionality' (2006) 65 *Cambridge Law Journal* 254, 255. See also Mark Aronson, 'Process, Quality and Variable Standards: Responding to an Agent Provocateur' in David Dyzenhaus, Murray Hunt and Grant Huscroft, *A Simple Common Lawyer: Essays in Honour of Michael Taggart* (Oxford, Hart Publishing, 2009) 5, 7–10.

[6] *Kioa* (n 3).

[7] Statutory Instruments Act 1946. Note, however, that consultation is required for Legislative Reform Orders under the Legislative and Regulatory Reform Act 2006, s 13. See also P Craig, *Administrative Law*, 7th edn (London, Sweet and Maxwell, 2012) 449–56; P Cane, *Administrative Law*, 5th edn (Oxford, Oxford University Press, 2011) 106–13.

[8] Statutory Instruments Act 1985. See JM Keyes, *Executive Legislation*, 2nd edn (Markham Ontario, Lexis Nexis, 2010) 198–99; G Heckman, G Van Harten and DJ Mullan, *Administrative Law: Cases, Text and Materials*, 6th edn (Toronto, Emond Montgomery Publications, 2010) 652–53; A Green, 'Regulations and Rule Making: The Dilemma of Delegation' in CM Flood and L Sossin, *Administrative Law in Context*, 2nd edn (Toronto, Emond Montgomery Publications, 2013) 125, 142–43.

[9] Legislation Act 2012. Note, however, that consultation is required by s 51 of that Act for the incorporation of material by reference into an instrument with legislative effect. See also R Carter, J McHerron and R Malone, *Subordinate Legislation in New Zealand* (Wellington, Lexis Nexis, 2013) 72–73, 98, 238; PA Joseph, *Constitutional and Administrative Law in New Zealand*, 4th edn (Wellington, Thomson, 2014) 1107–8.

although it may where the delegated legislation is directed to a particular person or a legitimate expectation is established.[10] On the other hand, substantive review has traditionally been available for review of delegated legislation on the ground of unreasonableness[11] and in recent years in these countries has extended to proportionality review in human rights-based challenges.[12] The major difference between Australian law and related countries is that substantive review has been extended in Australian law to proportionality review for delegated legislation without the support of human rights law.

II. REVIEW OF DELEGATED LEGISLATION: LEGITIMACY QUESTIONS

It is worthwhile starting with two distinctions that divide matters that are legitimate for courts to review from matters that are more controversial and require a more restricted form of review.

The first is the process/substance distinction. While the legitimacy of judicial review on procedural grounds is commonly accepted,[13] review on substantive grounds such as unreasonableness or proportionality raises concerns. These substantive grounds raise questions for the legitimacy of judicial review because they can relate to social and economic policy issues that have been allocated to the administrator for their assessment and decision. The issues that have to be resolved are suited to the expertise of that administrator and the processes by which they are informed.[14] Substantive forms of review are not excluded for these reasons but they are more controversial and are commonly subject to measures designed to restrict intrusion by the courts on the evaluative judgements that are allocated to the administrator. On the other hand, judicial review on procedural grounds raises fewer questions because there is less

[10] For England, see *R (Moseley) v London Borough of Haringey* [2014] UKSC 56, [2014] PTSR 1317 [35]–[39] (Lord Reed), cf [24] (Lord Wilson); *Bank Mellat v Her Majesty's Treasury (No 2)* [2013] UKSC 39, [2014] AC 700 [44]–[46] (Lord Sumption); *Bates v Lord Hailsham of St Marylebone* [1972] 1 WLR 1373, 1378; Lord Woolf *et al*, *De Smith's Judicial Review*, 7th edn (London, Sweet and Maxwell, 2013) 399–400. For Canada, see *Inuit Tapirisat of Canada v Canada (Attorney-General)* [1980] 2 SCR 735; Keyes, *Executive Legislation* (n 8) 209–12, 217–19; Green, 'Regulations and Rule Making' (n 8) 141–42. For New Zealand, see Joseph, *Constitutional and Administrative Law in New Zealand* (n 9) 1108–10; Carter *et al*, *Subordinate Legislation in New Zealand* (n 9) 239.

[11] See Craig, *Administrative Law* (n 7) 459–60. There seems to be reluctance in Canada and New Zealand to review delegated legislation on the unreasonableness ground except in the context of review of municipal bye-laws: Keyes, *Executive Legislation* (n 8) 259–60; Joseph, *Constitutional and Administrative Law in New Zealand* (n 9) 1135–39.

[12] See, eg, in England *R (Quila) v Secretary of State for the Home Department* [2011] UKSC 45, [2012] 1 AC 621. For Canada see *Doré v Barreau du Québec* 2012 SCC 12, [2012] 1 SCR 395, [37]; *Alberta v Hutterian Brethren of Wilson Colony* 2009 SCC 37, [2009] 2 SCR 567. For New Zealand, see *Schubert v Wanganui District Council* [2011] NZAR 233 and C Geiringer, 'Sources of Resistance to Proportionality Review of Administrative Power under the New Zealand Bill of Rights Act' (2013) 11 *New Zealand Journal of Public and International Law* 123, 137–38.

[13] See, eg, J Jowell, 'Of Vires and Vacuums: The Constitutional Context of Judicial Review' [1999] *Public Law* 448, 450–52; A Tomkins, 'The Role of the Courts in the Political Constitution' (2010) 60 *University of Toronto Law Journal* 1, 6; M Aronson and M Groves, *Judicial Review of Administrative Action*, 5th edn (Sydney, Lawbook Co, 2013) 19.

[14] Jowell, 'Of Vires and Vacuums' (n 13) 454.

risk of judges affecting such judgements and the issues that arise are often thought to be suited to judges' experience.[15]

There are further legitimacy questions in Australian law that are related to the process/substance distinction. A particular concern relates to the legitimacy of delegated legislation in a jurisdiction with a written constitution that separates legislative, judicial and executive functions. Rule-making by the executive under powers delegated by Parliament is, at least in a prima facie sense, inconsistent with the distribution of powers in the Commonwealth Constitution. This was recognised by Dixon J in the primary Australian case on the constitutionality of such powers, *Victorian Stevedoring and General Contracting Co Pty Ltd and Meakes v Dignan*, and led him to say that delegated legislation made according to general rule-making powers may be treated as 'lacking the independent and unqualified authority which is an attribute of true legislative power'.[16] As we will see in section IV such concerns have been said to justify extended review of the substance of delegated legislation, in the form of proportionality review.

However this use of proportionality review as a solution to the problematic legitimacy of delegated legislation raises a question: would not it be better for concerns about the legitimacy of delegated legislation to be addressed by establishing enforceable procedures that facilitate public discussion and debate prior to delegated legislation being made? Such procedures would reduce the concerns about the legitimacy of delegated legislation by ensuring that the rule-maker is informed by members of the public in relation to the technical detail of the proposed rule and the values on which it is based. Moreover, enforcing such procedures would provide a more legitimate form of engagement by the courts with delegated legislation than substantive review, according to accepted norms of judicial review.

The second distinction that is relevant to examining the legitimacy of judicial review of delegated legislation is between harms to individual interests and harms to public interests. Review of decisions that harm individual, personal interests is commonly accepted as being the traditional area of judicial review of administrative action.[17] This is most apparent within Australian case law regarding standing[18] and procedural fairness.[19] Restricting judicial review to challenges that seek to protect against personal harms is designed to disable the courts from interfering with governmental policy.[20] Historically, decisions affecting the public generally could only be challenged by the Attorney-General, by way of a relator action, or when the

[15] ibid 451–52; Tomkins, 'The Role of the Courts in the Political Constitution' (n 13) 6.

[16] (1931) 46 CLR 73, 102.

[17] See, eg, Sir Gerard Brennan, 'The Purpose and Scope of Judicial Review' in M Taggart (ed), *Judicial Review of Administrative Action in the 1980s: Problems and Prospects* (Auckland, Oxford University Press, 1986) 18, 23, 35; C Harlow, 'A Special Relationship?: American Influences on Judicial Review in England' in Ian Loveland (ed), *A Special Relationship?: American Influences on Public Law in the UK* (Oxford, Clarendon Press, 1995) 79, 83.

[18] See, eg, *Onus v Alcoa of Australia Ltd* [1981] HCA 50, (1981) 149 CLR 27, 74 (Brennan J).

[19] See, eg, *Kioa* (n 3) 582, 584 (Mason J), 619–20 (Brennan J), 632 (Deane J).

[20] JL Mashaw, *Creating the Administrative Constitution: The Lost One Hundred Years of American Administrative Law* (New Haven, CT, Yale University Press, 2012) 305. See also M Taggart, 'Reinventing Administrative Law' in N Bamforth and P Leyland (eds), *Public Law in a Multi-Layered Constitution* (Oxford, Hart Publishing, 2003) 311, 312–13.

applicant has been subject to special damage or has a special interest.[21] It is only with the liberalisation of standing laws that challenging administrative decisions that affect the public generally has become more common, and then more so in the United Kingdom[22] than in Australia.

The process/substance and individual/public distinctions highlight the unusual nature of the case law that has developed for judicial review of delegated legislation. The case law guides a plaintiff to the most controversial area of judicial review: review of public interest decisions on substantive grounds. The unusual nature of this can be seen by contrasting two historically significant decisions of the High Court of Australia. In the landmark Australian case on procedural fairness *Kioa v West*,[23] Justice Mason illustrated the exclusion of procedural fairness for decisions affecting the public generally by way of an example of a council's decision regarding rates to be paid by local landowners. He said that 'a decision to impose a rate or a decision to impose a general charge for services rendered to ratepayers, each of which indirectly affects the rights, interests or expectations of citizens generally does not attract this duty to act fairly'.[24] He then quoted Jacobs J in *Salemi v MacKellar (No 2)*[25] who said that these decisions are understood by courts to be 'policy' or 'political' decisions.[26] Yet 13 years prior to *Kioa v West*, the High Court in *Parramatta City Council v Pestell* applied *Wednesbury* unreasonableness (for the first time)[27] to invalidate precisely such a decision.[28]

III. PROCEDURAL REVIEW

Why then is judicial review of delegated legislation on procedural grounds effectively excluded while substantive review is accepted? The reasons for the exclusion of review on procedural grounds are hard to find and those reasons that can be found turn out to be unsatisfactory.

A. Statutory Procedures

It is convenient to examine why Australian rule-making legislation commonly makes its consultation provisions discretionary and unenforceable by seeking the

[21] *Australian Conservation Foundation v Commonwealth* [1980] HCA 53, (1980) 146 CLR 493, 526.

[22] See, eg, *R v Inspectorate of Pollution, ex parte Greenpeace (No 2)* [1994] 4 All ER 329 and *R v Secretary of State for Foreign and Commonwealth Affairs, ex parte World Development Movement Ltd* [1995] 1 WLR 386.

[23] *Kioa* (n 3).

[24] ibid 584.

[25] [1977] HCA 26, (1977) 137 CLR 396.

[26] *Kioa* (n 3) 584.

[27] Searches on Westlaw and AUSTLII reveal brief references to *Wednesbury* unreasonableness in earlier cases: *Election Importing Company Proprietary Ltd v Courtice* [1949] HCA 20, (1949) 80 CLR 657, 664; *Ex parte Howells; Re McCulloch* [1949] NSWStRp 12; (1949) 49 SR (NSW) 238, 241.

[28] [1972] HCA 59, (1972) 128 CLR 305, 327.

answer at the national level rather than for the states and territories.[29] The current Commonwealth legislation, the Legislative Instruments Act 2003 (Cth), was the result of a 15-year process, starting with an inquiry by the Administrative Review Council in August 1989 and finishing with the commencement of the Act in early 2005. Prior to the 2003 Act there was no general, legal requirement for public consultation—it was required only by sector-specific legislation.[30]

The relevant provisions of the Legislative Instruments Act 2003 (Cth) make it clear that public consultation is discretionary and unenforceable. Section 17 states that 'the rule-maker must be satisfied that any consultation that is considered by the rule-maker to be appropriate and that is reasonably practicable to undertake, has been undertaken'. The reference to the administrator's 'satisfaction' in this provision is an example of a form of drafting referred to by the Administrative Review Council as 'tailoring' a statutory provision to minimise the prospect of a successful judicial review challenge to an administrator's application of it.[31] Section 17 supplements this by making consultation dependent on the rule-maker's sense of 'appropriateness' and 'reasonable practicability'. Such terminology can also be understood as a drafting technique designed to make judicial review difficult. They are matters of preference and opinion which make it hard for a court to identify a remediable error.[32] Section 19 of the Legislative Instruments Act 2003 (Cth) confirms these attempts to make public consultation unenforceable by stating that the 'fact that consultation does not occur does not affect the validity or enforceability of a legislative instrument'. The intention of these provisions is clear: public consultation is facilitated but there should be no judicial review for failure to carry it out.[33]

This does not mean that there is no accountability for lack of public consultation. There is an alternative accountability mechanism but its effectiveness is questionable. The Senate Standing Committee on Regulations and Ordinances reviews delegated legislation for whether it is 'in accordance with the statute'.[34] The Committee can review delegated legislation for compliance with section 26 of the Legislative Instruments Act, which requires an explanatory statement to be provided with a legislative instrument that includes a description of any consultation that has been carried out or, if there has been none, includes an explanation as to why that is the case.[35] However, if no consultation has been held and the agency has not provided

[29] The States have a range of provisions for public consultation in their rule-making legislation. New South Wales and Tasmania have similar provisions to the Commonwealth legislation, the Legislative Instruments Act 2003 (Cth) (Subordinate Legislation Act 1989 (NSW), ss 5(2), 6, 9; Subordinate Legislation Act 1992 (Tas), ss 5–6, 10). The Victorian provisions have apparently mandatory language (Subordinate Legislation Act 1994 (Vic), ss 6, 11, 12C) and other States have no consultation requirements (Legislative Standards Act 1992 (Q); Subordinate Legislation Act 1978 (SA); Interpretation Act 1984 (WA), Pt VI).

[30] Administrative Review Council, *Rule Making by Commonwealth Agencies*, Report No 35 (1992) 27–28.

[31] Administrative Review Council, *The Scope of Judicial Review*, Report No 47 (2006) 22–24.

[32] Woolf *et al*, *De Smith's Judicial Review* (n 10) 22–23; *Buck v Bavone* [1976] HCA 24, (1976) 135 CLR 110, 118–19.

[33] Whether or not such provisions succeed in achieving this objective is a different question: see Administrative Review Council, *The Scope of Judicial Review* (n 31) 20. See also L McDonald, 'The Entrenched Minimum Provision of Judicial Review and the Rule of Law' (2010) 21 *Public Law Review* 14.

[34] Commonwealth Senate, Standing Orders, Order 23(3)(a).

[35] Legislative Instruments Act 2003 (Cth), s 26(1A)(d), (e).

an explanation, all the Committee can do is request the agency or the particular Minister to provide an explanation—it cannot require an agency to undertake a consultation process. The accountability for lack of consultation is therefore minimal. Moreover, the Senate Committee has criticised agencies and departments for their 'cursory, generic, and unhelpful' explanation of consultation processes.[36]

Why then were the consultation provisions included in the Legislative Instruments Act designed to be discretionary and unenforceable? There was no intention for them to be that way at the start of the reform process. The Administrative Review Council, in its report on rule-making published in 1992, recommended that consultation should be mandatory.[37] This was initially accepted by both of the major political parties. When in government in the 1990s each of them prepared Bills that included detailed and apparently mandatory public consultation provisions.[38] However, in 2003 both parties supported the Bill that was enacted with the discretionary consultation provisions.[39]

The reasons for including discretionary consultation provisions in the 2003 Act were not clearly stated. The provisions were referred to in the parliamentary debates as an improvement on the past that could be monitored and reviewed.[40] The Attorney-General insisted in Parliament that the risk of litigation be minimised. In response to an amendment to the Bill that was unsuccessfully proposed by one of the minor parties and would have made the consultation provisions enforceable, the Attorney-General stated that the amendment 'creates the risk that the validity of the legislative instrument may be challenged on the basis that appropriate consultation was not undertaken'.[41] This indicates that the government was seeking to avoid including consultation requirements that enable supervision by the courts; however, it does not explain why that should be the case.

The push for discretionary, unenforceable consultation provisions seems to have come from a non-political source: the government agencies that would be required to administer such provisions. The opposition spokesperson stated in the Senate debates that the agencies had successfully lobbied the government to replace the mandatory consultation provisions in the previous Bills with discretionary provisions that were ultimately included in the 2003 Act.[42] This point has also been made in reports on rule-making by the Commonwealth government.[43] It seems that the discretionary consultation provisions were therefore included due to resistance to mandatory provisions by government departments and agencies. Although the

[36] Commonwealth Senate Regulations and Ordinances Committee, *Consultation under the Legislative Instruments Act 2003, Interim Report*, Report No 113 (2007) 6–7.

[37] Administrative Review Council, *Rule Making by Commonwealth Agencies* (n 30) 35.

[38] Legislative Instruments Bill 1994 (Cth), Pt 3; Legislative Instruments Bill 1996 (Cth), Pt 3.

[39] Commonwealth Senate, *Parliamentary Debates*, 4 December 2003, 19192–19193 (Senator Troeth, Senator Ludwig).

[40] Commonwealth Senate, *Parliamentary Debates*, 9 September 2003, 14641 (Senator Campbell); Commonwealth Senate, *Parliamentary Debates*, 2 December 2003, 18625–18626 (Senator Ludwig).

[41] Commonwealth House of Representatives, *Parliamentary Debates*, 3 December 2003, 23648–23649 (Mr Ruddock—Attorney-General).

[42] Commonwealth Senate, *Parliamentary Debates*, 2 December 2003, 18626 (Senator Ludwig).

[43] See Administrative Review Council, *Rule Making by Commonwealth Agencies* (n 30) 31, 33; David Borthwick and Robert Milliner, *Independent Review of the Australian Government's Regulatory Impact Analysis Process* (20 April 2012) 52–53.

departments' and agencies' particular concerns with public consultation were not referred to in the parliamentary debates, it seems likely that they related to additional costs and delays as they had raised these concerns in an earlier inquiry.[44]

It is worthwhile briefly considering such concerns about costs and delay. They arise because public consultation processes delay decision-making due to the time taken to give notice, provide a period for making submissions and for submissions to be considered. There is also the potential for litigation to enforce statutory consultation requirements which would involve delays and cost. These are, however, consequences of much of administrative decision-making and the accountability mechanisms that are aligned with it. The important question is whether the additional time and expenditure associated with public consultation outweigh the benefits that it provides, such as ensuring that the draft rule, and the information on which the government has relied, are exposed to the public and commented on, criticised, and potentially revised prior to the rule being made. If these benefits are recognised as a primary legitimating measure for delegated legislation in a democracy, then concerns about costs and delay would be regarded as something to be mitigated rather than a reason for making consultation provisions unenforceable.[45]

The reason for not having enforceable public consultation provisions at the Commonwealth level is therefore either not clear or is based on concerns that are questionable. Yet the consequence in terms of litigation concerning the administration of the provisions is apparent. Searches of the Westlaw and AUSTLII databases reveal that since the Legislative Instruments Act 2003 (Cth) commenced in 2005 there have been no cases raising issues regarding breach of the consultation provisions of the Act. That does not mean that there are no concerns about how consultation processes are administered by Commonwealth agencies. As we have seen, concerns have been expressed by the Senate Committee that reviews regulations.[46] Concerns have also been raised by business and public interest groups about the lack of public consultation for regulations and the tokenistic manner in which they are administered when they have been carried out.[47]

B. Procedural Fairness

Why then is the making of delegated legislation in Australia not subject to review on the ground of procedural fairness? The first case that is commonly referred to is a decision of the New South Wales Supreme Court in the 1940s, *Re Gosling*.[48] The reasoning in that case was influenced by the functional approach to procedural fairness of the time. Chief Justice Jordan referred to procedural fairness applying

[44] Administrative Review Council, *Rule Making by Commonwealth Agencies* (n 30) 33.

[45] See also Craig, *Administrative Law* (n 7) 453–54.

[46] Commonwealth Senate Regulations and Ordinances Committee, *Interim Report* (n 36) 6–7.

[47] Productivity Commission, *Regulatory Impact Analysis: Benchmarking* (November 2012) 222; Borthwick and Milliner, *Independent Review of the Australian Government's Regulatory Impact Analysis Process* (n 43) 52.

[48] *Gosling* (n 4) 318. See also Pearce and Argument, *Delegated Legislation in Australia* (n 1) 186; Aronson and Groves, *Judicial Review of Administrative Action* (n 13) 429.

to judicial and administrative decisions 'in the nature of a *lis inter partes*', but not to the exercise of rule-making powers granted by statute.[49] The High Court's decision in *Kioa v West*[50] in the 1980s is the accepted current source of principles that exclude procedural fairness for the making of delegated legislation. *Kioa v West* established that a broad range of decisions require procedural fairness and confirms that it is very difficult for it to be excluded by legislation. It does, however, set an important limit: procedural fairness does not apply to decisions that affect the public generally.[51] This necessarily excludes procedural fairness for the making of delegated legislation.

The exclusion of procedural fairness is explained in *Kioa v West* on the basis of the individual/public distinction. The judges were clear that for procedural fairness to apply the decision has to affect an individual in a very personal, direct manner, particularly regarding, as Mason J stated, 'personal liberty, status, preservation of livelihood and reputation, as well as ... proprietary rights and interests'.[52] On the other hand, the judges were also clear that procedural fairness is not required for decisions that affect the public generally. Justice Mason quoted Jacobs J in *Salemi v MacKellar (No 2)*[53] that procedural fairness does not apply to decisions that affect individuals as 'members of the public or a class of the public'.[54] Brennan J stated that it is unlikely that the legislature would intend that procedural fairness is required when the 'interests of all members of the public are affected in the same way by the exercise of such a power'.[55] For procedural fairness to apply, his Honour said the decision should 'single out' individuals in a manner that is different to the way the interests of the public are affected.[56]

Why make such a distinction between decisions that affect individuals and decisions that affect the public? The reasons for it are difficult to find in the reasoning of the judges in *Kioa v West*. As we will see, the primary reason turns out to be a concern regarding non-justiciability. However, the conception of non-justiciability that is drawn on is rather outdated. Moroever, practical concerns that arise with an extension of procedural fairness to decisions that affect the public generally can be resolved through adapting the form of procedure to suit such decisions.

The judges in *Kioa v West* gave the following reasons for the distinction. Brennan J relied on English precedent, *Bates v Lord Hailsham of St Marylebone*,[57] for the exclusion of delegated legislation and discussed harmonising the interests that engage procedural fairness with the interests that satisfy standing requirements.[58]

[49] *Gosling* (n 4) 318. See also the criticism of this aspect of *Re Gosling* in *Bread Manufacturers of New South Wales v Evans* [1981] HCA 69, (1981) 180 CLR 404, 415–17 (Gibbs CJ) and M Taggart, 'From "Parliamentary Powers" to Privatization: The Chequered History of Delegated Legislation in the Twentieth Century' (2005) 55 *University of Toronto Law Journal* 575, 602.

[50] [1985] HCA 81, (1985) 159 CLR 550.

[51] *Kioa* (n 3) 582, 584 (Mason J), 619–20 (Brennan J), 632 (Deane J).

[52] ibid 582 (Mason J).

[53] [1977] HCA 26, (1977) 137 CLR 396.

[54] *Kioa* (n 3) 584 (Mason J), 632 (Deane J); *Salemi* (n 25) 452 (Jacobs J).

[55] *Kioa* (n 3) 620.

[56] ibid 620.

[57] *Bates* (n 10) 1378.

[58] *Kioa* (n 3) 620–21.

Justice Mason, on the other hand, seemed to suggest that decisions that affect the public generally are non-justiciable. This can be seen in his quote from Jacobs J in *Salemi v MacKellar (No 2)* that a decision affecting the public is 'truly a "policy" or "political" decision [that] *is not subject to judicial review*'.[59] The italicised words of the sentence suggest that decisions affecting the public should be non-justiciable in a general sense, not merely excluded from the requirements of procedural fairness.

There is a reason to doubt whether Mason J meant to suggest in *Kioa v West* that such decisions are non-justiciable by quoting *Salemi v MacKellar (No 2)*. Justice Mason was at the forefront of High Court judges who narrowed down the traditional breadth of non-justiciability principles by applying judicial review to Cabinet decisions and decisions of representatives of the Crown.[60] However, tracing Justice Mason's reference in *Kioa v West* to *Salemi v MacKellar (No 2)* does lead one eventually to non-justiciability. In his judgment in *Salemi v MacKellar (No 2)* Justice Jacobs provided no explanation to support his statement that decisions that affect the public generally should be excluded from procedural fairness. He merely referred in that case to his earlier judgment in *Mutton v Ku-ring-gai Municipal Council*[61] when he was President of the New South Wales Court of Appeal.[62] The *Mutton* case squarely related to non-justiciability.

Mutton involved a challenge to a local council resolution regarding classification of particular roads to regulate their use by trucks. The plaintiff was concerned that there would be an increase in the number of trucks using the road on which he lived.[63] The council's decision had polycentric characteristics as any restriction on trucks using the plaintiff's road would result in the trucks using other roads, thus disturbing a different set of residents.[64] The council's solution was to lift restrictions on the use of the plaintiff's road by trucks, increase policing of that road, and gain the agreement of truck companies to use the road only between 8 am and 6 pm.[65] The plaintiff brought proceedings claiming that the council failed to consider the initial residential classification of his road.[66] However, Jacobs J regarded the council's resolution as being non-justiciable as it involved an 'indeterminate number of considerations, political, social, and economic' that could not be adequately reviewed by courts.[67] *Mutton v Ku-ring-gai Municipal Council* is therefore best understood as concerning non-justiciability on the basis of the challenged decision being polycentric.

There are two problems with relying on *Mutton* as providing authority for decisions that affect the public being political or policy decisions for which procedural

[59] ibid 584 (Mason J) (emphasis added); *Salemi* (n 25) 452 (Jacobs J). See also *Bread Manufacturers* (n 49) 416–17 (Gibbs J).

[60] See *FAI Insurances Ltd v Winneke* [1982] HCA 26, (1982) 151 CLR 342 and *R v Toohey; Ex Parte Northern Land Council* [1981] HCA 74, (1981) 151 CLR 170. Thanks to Mark Aronson for pointing this out to me.

[61] [1973] 1 NSWLR 233.

[62] *Salemi* (n 25) 452.

[63] *Mutton* (n 61) 235–36.

[64] ibid 237–38.

[65] ibid 238.

[66] ibid 239.

[67] ibid 240–43.

fairness should be excluded. The first is the obvious point that procedural fairness was not raised in the case; it was instead concerned with whether there had been a failure to consider a relevant matter. Moreover, there seems to have been no problem regarding participation in the council's decision. Residents of the affected streets had made submissions and lodged a petition to the relevant council indicating that there had been an informal public consultation process.[68]

The second problem is that the understanding of non-justiciability in the *Mutton* case is outdated. Since the 1970s when the *Mutton* case was decided, the case law on non-justiciability has changed from being a comprehensive exclusion of judicial review for particular kinds of decision, to the courts managing review of such decisions by careful attention to the limits built into the various grounds of review and conducting judicial review in a deferential manner.[69] The result is that the reasoning in *Mutton v Ku-ring-gai Municipal Council*, and by extension *Kioa v West*, that policy considerations in an administrative decision or polycentricity are reasons for non-justiciability, are unlikely to be accepted any longer. Instead, such characteristics of a decision require the applicant to frame the challenge in a manner that can be managed by the courts through the recognised grounds of judicial review. Moreover, and as pointed out in section II above, policy and polycentric characteristics of administrative decisions may raise concerns with regard to substantive review but are not necessarily problematic for procedural grounds of review such as procedural fairness. Therefore, the rationale provided by Mason J in *Kioa v West* when traced through *Salemi v MacKellar (No 2)* to *Mutton v Ku-ring-gai Municipal Council* seems to apply an outdated concept of non-justiciability to the procedural fairness threshold principle.

It therefore seems that any current reason for excluding procedural fairness for decisions that affect the public generally should have a different basis. The most likely would be the practical reasons that have been raised to support exclusion of procedural fairness for delegated legislation. Such reasons have been helpfully collected (and challenged) by Professor Craven in his influential article, 'Legislative Action by Subordinate Authorities and the Requirement of a Fair Hearing'.[70] The most significant practical concern relates to the procedural fairness requirement to provide adverse information to individuals affected by a decision and enable them an opportunity to respond to it. The concern is that this would be unmanageable for decisions that affect many people. In the words of Mason P in *Minister for Local Government v South Sydney City Council*, there is a risk of 'an infinite regression of counter-disputation' if all adverse information has to be disclosed to each affected person throughout the decision-making process.[71] Professor Craven has a response

[68] ibid 237–38.

[69] See C Finn, 'The Justiciability of Administrative Decisions: A Redundant Concept?'(2002) 30 *Federal Law Review* 239; E Campbell and M Groves, 'Polycentricity in Administrative Decision-Making' in M Groves (ed), *Law and Government in Australia* (Sydney, Federation Press, 2005) 213, 239; P Daly, 'Justiciability and the "Political Question" Doctrine' [2010] *Public Law* 160, 166–68; Aronson and Groves, *Judicial Review of Administrative Action* (n 13) 116; Woolf *et al*, *De Smith's Judicial Review* (n 10) 21.

[70] (1988) 16 *Melbourne University Law Review* 569.

[71] [2002] NSWCA 288, (2002) 55 NSWLR 381, [267].

to this concern with which I agree. It is that a different type of 'hearing' is required, a form of public consultation that does not require notice to particular individuals of adverse information and an opportunity to be heard in relation to each issue.[72] While there may be some doubts about judicial review of public consultation processes, those concerns relate to review of particular aspects of consultation processes, such as reviewing the responsiveness of the decision-maker to the submissions lodged and whether public consultation should extend to non-statutory, policy decisions,[73] rather than whether the courts should supervise such processes at all.

In summary then, the answer to why procedural fairness does not extend to decisions that affect the public generally is not fully explained in the primary case, *Kioa v West*. On investigation it seems to relate to non-justiciability in a manner that does not equate well with developments that have occurred since the 1980s when *Kioa v West* was decided. Therefore, when we add the exclusion of procedural fairness for delegated legislation to the discretionary nature of public consultation provisions in Australian rule-making legislation, the result is that there is very little scope for judicial review of the processes for making delegated legislation.

IV. SUBSTANTIVE REVIEW

A. *Williams* Proportionality Test

When we move to examining judicial review of delegated legislation on substantive grounds it can be seen that concerns about the legitimacy of judicial review are less apparent. As explained in the introduction to this chapter, Australian courts have accepted that they can review delegated legislation for whether it is proportionate to the objects of the relevant legislation. This has in the past been regarded as the only administrative law context in which proportionality is accepted in Australia,[74] although the High Court recently suggested in *Minister for Immigration and Citizenship v Li*[75] that proportionality may be adopted as part of unreasonableness review and proportionality review has been applied in cases dealing with State human rights legislation.[76]

The proportionality test that was recently confirmed by the High Court in *Attorney-General (SA) v Corporation of the City of Adelaide*[77] comes from Justice

[72] Craven, 'Legislative Action by Subordinate Authorities and the Requirement of a Fair Hearing' (n 70) 593.

[73] See A Edgar, 'Judicial Review of Public Consultation Processes: A Safeguard Against Tokenism?' (2013) 24 *Public Law Review* 209, 220–22; A Edgar, 'Procedural Fairness for Decisions Affecting the Public Generally: A Radical Step Towards Public Consultation?' (2014) 33 *University of Tasmania Law Review* 56, 78.

[74] *Bruce v Cole* [1998] NSWSC 260, (1998) 45 NSWLR 163, 185 (Spigelman CJ). It is, however, fairly commonly used in Australian constitutional law: see S Kiefel, 'Proportionality: A Rule of Reason' (2012) 23 *Public Law Review* 85.

[75] [2013] HCA 18, (2013) 249 CLR 332 [30] (French CJ), [73]–[74] (Hayne, Kiefel and Bell JJ).

[76] See, eg, *Kerrison v Melbourne City Council* [2014] FCAFC 130, [234]–[242].

[77] *Attorney-General (SA) v Corporation of the City of Adelaide* (n 2) [56] (French CJ), [117] (Hayne J), [199] (Crennan and Kiefel JJ).

Dixon's judgment in a decision of the High Court in the 1930s, *Williams v City of Melbourne*.[78] Justice Dixon stated in the *Williams* case:

> The true nature and purpose of the [statutory] power must be determined, and it must often be necessary to examine the operation of the by-law in the local circumstances to which it is intended to apply. Notwithstanding that ex facie there seemed a sufficient connection between the subject of the power and that of the by-law, the true character of the by-law may then appear to be such that *it could not reasonably have been adopted as a means of attaining the ends of the power*. In such a case the by-law will be invalid, not because it is inexpedient or misguided, but because it is not a real exercise of the power (Compare *Widgee Shire Council v Bonney* (1907) 4 CLR 977, 982, 986).[79]

The emphasised words make it apparent that proportionality review is to be employed, requiring an assessment of the reasonableness of the delegated legislation for achieving the purpose of the rule-making power in the relevant Act.

The *Williams* test is a rudimentary form of proportionality review, one that lacks the features of modern proportionality tests. Modern proportionality tests divide the assessment into a series of sub-questions such as whether the particular measure is rationally connected to the desired legislative objective, whether it impairs a relevant right or interest no more than is necessary to achieve the objective, and whether it strikes a fair balance between the gains to be achieved and the restrictions on relevant rights and interests.[80] Much of what is included in modern proportionality tests is contained within the reference to reasonableness in the *Williams* principle in the emphasised part of the above quote.

The first feature implied in the reference to reasonableness is the rights and interests that are to be protected. The bye-laws that were challenged in *Williams* regulated the movement of cattle through the streets of Melbourne. Justice Dixon examined the bye-laws as to whether they were a reasonable means for achieving the statutory objective of 'safety, convenience and proper facility of traffic'.[81] This involved assessing whether they were an overly broad suppression of traders' freedom of movement on public streets.[82] This is an unlikely candidate for the rights and fundamental interests that are usually protected by proportionality tests. Other cases that have employed the *Williams* proportionality test have concerned interests that would be regarded as fundamental, such as religious speech[83] and property,[84] however they have also extended beyond this to matters such as commercial fishing operations,[85] and an appointment to an agency.[86] The *Williams* proportionality test is therefore not expressly or impliedly limited to protecting fundamental rights and freedoms. The reference point for assessing the reasonableness of the delegated legislation for

[78] *Williams* (n 1).
[79] ibid 155 (emphasis added).
[80] See M Elliott, *Beatson, Matthews and Elliott's Administrative Law*, 4th edn (Oxford, Oxford University Press, 2011) 252–53; Craig, *Administrative Law* (n 7) 657.
[81] *Williams* (n 1) 156.
[82] ibid 156.
[83] *Attorney-General (SA) v Corporation of the City of Adelaide* (n 2).
[84] *South Australia v Tanner* [1989] HCA 3, (1989) 166 CLR 161.
[85] *Minister of State for Resources v Dover Fisheries Pty Ltd* [1993] FCA 366, (1993) 43 FCR 565.
[86] *Vanstone v Clark* [2005] FCAFC 189, (2005) 147 FCR 299.

achieving the ends of the regulation-making power is therefore vague and in practice likely to relate to the impact of the regulation on the applicant's particular interests.

Secondly, the reference in the *Williams* proportionality test to the reasonableness of the delegated legislation for achieving the statutory objectives implies rather than states that the relevant interest at stake is to be impaired in the most minimal manner available. This is included in English proportionality tests as being whether the means adopted 'are no more than is necessary to accomplish the objective'[87] and is an accepted aspect of proportionality assessments in Australian constitutional law.[88] The High Court in the recent *City of Adelaide* case accepted that minimal impairment could be relevant when applying the *Williams* proportionality test[89] but some of the judges nevertheless expressed concerns. Chief Justice French was concerned that it would involve courts 'second guessing the merits' and that courts may not have institutional competence to make such comparative judgments.[90] Justice Hayne J referred to less restrictive means as being peripheral to determining whether the delegated legislation is sufficiently connected to the regulation-making power in the Act.[91] The result is that a minimal impairment assessment now seems to be a relevant consideration for applying the *Williams* proportionality test, although there is some ambivalence about it.

The rudimentary nature of the *Williams* test and its over-reliance on reasonableness are likely to lead to uncertainty and inconsistency of application. This is apparent in the *City of Adelaide* case where three different approaches were taken to proportionality and the *Williams* test in the different judgments. Chief Justice French regarded proportionality as a 'class of criteria' for determining the validity of delegated legislation by reference to 'rational relationships between purpose and means, and the interaction of competing legal rules and principles'.[92] This suggests an assessment of whether the delegated legislation is rationally connected to the purpose of the rule-making power and whether there is a fair balance between the delegated legislation and other accepted interests and principles. Hayne J, on the other hand, referred to the *Williams* test but did not use the term 'proportionality' and focused on the sufficiency of the connection with the rule-making power in the Act.[93] This is really a question of the consistency of the delegated legislation with the objective disclosed in the relevant Act—an approach that avoids the aspects of the test that do most of the work in a proportionality assessment. Crennan and Kiefel JJ referred to the *Williams* proportionality test but did not apply it. They instead carried out the proportionality assessment according to principles that have developed in Australian constitutional law.[94] The fact that the judges in the *City of Adelaide*

[87] *De Freitas v Ministry of Agriculture* [1999] 1 AC 69, 80; *R (Daly) v Secretary of State for the Home Department* [2001] UKHL 26, [2001] 2 AC 532, [27]; *Bank Mellat* (n 10) [20].

[88] *Unions NSW v New South Wales* [2013] HCA 58, (2013) 88 ALJR 227, [44].

[89] *Attorney-General (SA) v Corporation of the City of Adelaide* (n 2) [65] (French CJ), [120]–[121] (Hayne J), [206]–[207] (Crennan and Kiefel JJ).

[90] ibid [65].

[91] ibid [120]–[121].

[92] ibid [55].

[93] ibid [117]–[118].

[94] ibid [198]–[201].

case took disparate approaches suggests that there is doubt about the form and operation of Justice Dixon's test.

For these reasons, the *Williams* test should be regarded as rudimentary. The question that we can now turn to is: How does the test compare to other forms of substantive review, in particular the ground of *Wednesbury* unreasonableness and the forms of unreasonableness utilised for review of delegated legislation prior to the *Williams* case? The answer to that question, that it is a more intense form of review, raises a second question: Why extend substantive review in this context beyond unreasonableness?

It is clear that the proportionality test in *Williams* calibrates substantive review in a different manner to *Wednesbury* unreasonableness. The proportionality test is commonly understood to establish a relatively intense form of review: a form that enables greater judicial scrutiny of the scope and operation of delegated legislation than related types of substantive review.[95] It does not require the delegated legislation to be 'absurd' or involve 'something overwhelming' and therefore does not include the form of deference built into *Wednesbury* unreasonableness.[96] In recent years, Australian courts have for the most part accepted the deference in *Wednesbury* unreasonableness, influenced by Justice Brennan's statement in *Attorney-General (NSW) v Quin* that the scope for judicial intervention on this ground is 'extremely confined' in order for the court to avoid dealing with the merits of the administrator's decision.[97] Relative to *Wednesbury* unreasonableness understood in this manner,[98] Justice Dixon's proportionality test in *Williams* involves an intense form of review. The court's assessment of the rule-maker's method for achieving the statutory object and its effect on other judicially recognised values and interests involves a close review of the evaluative judgments made by the administrator.

Justice Dixon's reasoning in *Williams* is also quite different from the earlier cases concerning unreasonableness review of delegated legislation, *Kruse v Johnson*,[99] *Slattery v Naylor*[100] and *Widgee Shire Council v Bonney*.[101] While those cases used terminology similar to proportionality such as 'capricious' and 'oppressive',[102] they also emphasised, as in *Wednesbury*, that courts should apply the ground in a deferential manner, as seen by statements such as that courts 'ought to be slow to condemn' delegated legislation,[103] should intervene only in 'some very extreme' circumstances,[104] and that 'it is very difficult to make a successful attack on a by-law

[95] ibid [56] (French CJ); *Tanner* (n 84) 175 (Brennan J); P Bayne, 'Reasonableness, Proportionality and Delegated Legislation' (1993) 67 *Australian Law Journal* 448, 448–49.

[96] *Associated Provincial Picture Houses, Ltd v Wednesbury Corporation* [1948] 1 KB 223, 229–30.

[97] [1990] HCA 21, (1990) 170 CLR 1, 36.

[98] It must be recognised, however, that some of the judges of the High Court recently criticised the deference included in *Wednesbury* unreasonableness in *Minister for Immigration and Citizenship v Li*, and suggested it may be dropped from the court's assessment: *Li* (n 75) [68] (Hayne, Kiefel and Bell JJ), cf [106]–[113] (Gageler J).

[99] [1898] 2 QB 91.

[100] (1888) 13 App Cas 446.

[101] [1907] HCA 11, (1907) 4 CLR 977.

[102] *Kruse* (n 99) 99–100 (Lord Russell of Killowen CJ); *Slattery* (n 100) 458 and *Widgee* (n 101) 986 (Isaacs J). See also *Williams* (n 1) 150 (Starke J).

[103] *Kruse* (n 99) 99 (Lord Russell of Killowen CJ).

[104] *Slattery* (n 100) 458.

on this ground'.[105] Such views are absent from Justice Dixon's judgment in *Williams*. Moreover, in *Widgee Shire Council v Bonney*, Chief Justice Griffiths CJ seemed to reject proportionality review by referring to 'expediency'[106] as not being for the court.[107] Justice Dixon in the passage from *Williams* quoted above refers to expediency but obscures the significance it had in the earlier cases as a limitation on review of delegated legislation.

There is a second aspect of Dixon J's judgment in *Williams* that involves a break from the early cases: there is no reference to the institutional characteristics of the rule-maker in his judgment. In the three earlier cases the judges emphasised that the institutional characteristics of the rule-maker should be taken into account by the court. The judges referred to the relevance of the rule-maker's expertise, whether they are elected and required to use processes for engaging the public when making the particular rule, and whether there is a mechanism for review of the particular rule by Parliament or other supervisory institution.[108] The inclusion of such considerations is designed to encourage restraint in the court's assessment of the reasonableness of the delegated legislation as it emphasises the suitability of the rule-maker for balancing the factors that are relevant when making rules. The lack of reference to such matters in Justice Dixon's judgment in *Williams* suggests he thought that they are not of great significance when the review ground is proportionality.[109]

Therefore, when proportionality was introduced by Dixon J in *Williams* it was intended to be a more intensive form of review than was contemplated by the courts in the earlier review of delegated legislation cases, *Kruse v Johnson*, *Slattery v Naylor* and *Widgee Shire Council v Bonney*. In those cases, substantive review was accepted but balanced by factors designed to encourage judicial restraint and to steer courts away from reviewing the merits of the challenged rule. The recent decision of the High Court in *Attorney-General (SA) v Corporation of the City of Adelaide* suggests that some judges would prefer to bring back some form of deference. For example, French CJ referred to proportionality review in *Williams* as being a 'high threshold test'[110] and Hayne J referred to the courts not examining the 'expediency' of the delegated legislation as one of the 'fundamental points' that 'must not be obscured'.[111] While such terminology may be questioned for being too general for the subtle task of apportioning deference to primary decision-makers in proportionality review, the comments also highlight the unease of some current judges with the intensive nature of the proportionality review in the *Williams* test.

[105] *Widgee* (n 101) 982.

[106] 'Expedient' is commonly given more than one meaning in dictionaries. It is referred to in terms of means/ends reasoning similar to proportionality but also more generally along the lines of desirable in the circumstances. For example, the Oxford English Dictionary refers to, 'Conducive to advantage in general, or to a definite purpose; fit, proper, or suitable to the circumstances of the case'.

[107] *Widgee* (n 101) 982–83.

[108] *Kruse* (n 99) 97–99 (Lord Russell of Killowen CJ); *Slattery* (n 100) 453. See also *Widgee* (n 101) 985 (Isaacs J) and Pearce and Argument, *Delegated Legislation in Australia* (n 1) 332–33.

[109] In the recent High Court decision, *Attorney-General (SA) v Corporation of the City of Adelaide*, there was some reference to such institutional considerations but they did not play a substantial role in the reasoning: (n 2) [118] (Hayne J); see also [65] (French CJ).

[110] ibid [56]–[60], [64].

[111] ibid [117].

The *Williams* proportionality test therefore raises a number of concerns. The first is what I have referred to as its rudimentary nature. Too much in the *Williams* test is contained within the reference to whether the delegated legislation could *reasonably* have been adopted as a means for achieving the ends of the power.[112] There is no express reference to the particular norms that are to be protected according to the proportionality test, no reference to minimal impairment, or an express reference to balancing individual and public interests. Accordingly, it appears to modern eyes to be an under-developed form of proportionality review. The second concern relates to its potential intensity. There is no reference in Justice Dixon's judgment in *Williams* to the deference considerations that apply in related forms of substantive review. This has raised uncertainty as to whether deference is to be factored into the proportionality assessment and, if so, the form of deference that is appropriate.

B. *Williams* Proportionality: A Constitutional Rationale

Why then was judicial review extended to enable substantive review of delegated legislation according to the *Williams* proportionality test? While Justice Dixon provided no indication of the rationale of the test in *Williams*, it was explained decades later by Brennan J in *South Australia v Tanner*[113] in a manner that provides a justification for intensive substantive review of delegated legislation. To be clear, Justice Brennan dissented in *South Australia v Tanner*, however his explanation of *Williams* is worth considering due to his great influence on Australian administrative law,[114] and because it links the proportionality test to broader questions of Australian public law.

Justice Brennan started his reasoning in the *Tanner* case by contrasting the way courts review the consistency of legislation with the Commonwealth Constitution and the consistency of delegated legislation with an empowering Act. He stated that the liberal approach taken by courts to interpreting the legislative powers included in the Commonwealth Constitution should not be adopted for interpreting statutory rule-making powers. This was because:

> Parliament is the organ of government in which legislative power is vested and Parliament should not be held to have delegated to another repository more power than is clearly denoted by the words it has used. In my opinion, a delegation of legislative power should be narrowly construed unless the Parliament has, by express provision or necessary intendment, revealed a contrary intention.[115]

While Brennan J recognised in *South Australia v Tanner* that the courts in the early cases, such as *Kruse v Johnson*, exercised restraint in order to avoid dealing with the expediency of the delegated legislation under review, he referred to Justice Dixon's proportionality test in *Williams* as the 'foundation of the modern approach' to such

[112] *Williams* (n 1) 155.

[113] *Tanner* (n 84).

[114] See, eg, R Creyke and P Keyzer (eds), *The Brennan Legacy: Blowing the Winds of Legal Orthodoxy* (Sydney, Federation Press, 2002).

[115] *Tanner* (n 84) 173–74.

review.[116] Justice Brennan suggested that the more intense form of review may have been prompted by the publication four years prior to the *Williams* case of Lord Hewart's *The New Despotism*,[117] which had raised the 'spectre of unexaminable executive power'.[118] We may take from this that the rationale of the proportionality test in *Williams* is that an intense form of judicial review is required as a response to Parliament granting the executive a function that raises constitutional concerns.

This acceptance of proportionality review should be recognised to be an unusual position for an Australian judge to take, particularly given that Justice Brennan is known for emphasising the restraints that should be adopted when applying unreasonableness review in the *Wednesbury* sense. For example, in his commonly quoted judgment in *Attorney-General (NSW) v Quin* he referred to administrators having to 'balance the interests of the public at large and the interests of minority groups or individuals'—a task that is within the merits of the administrative decision and is beyond the institutional competence of courts.[119] Justice Brennan added that if judicial review were to extend to such balancing and assessment of the merits of the decision, a court 'would put its own legitimacy at risk'.[120]

Justice Brennan's judgment in *Attorney-General (NSW) v Quin* is difficult to square with his support for proportionality review in *South Australia v Tanner*. Proportionality review necessarily involves balancing public interests with the interests of individuals and minority groups. The reasonableness of the delegated legislation's achievement of the statutory purposes is assessed by the extent of its impact on individual and minority group interests (albeit expressed as fundamental values). Understood in this way, there is an apparent contradiction between Justice Brennan's judgments in *Attorney-General (NSW) v Quin* and *South Australia v Tanner*. The judgment in the latter case pushes past the boundaries established in *Attorney-General (NSW) v Quin*, putting at risk the courts' legitimacy but justified by the constitutional factors operating in the background.

The proportionality test in *Williams* should therefore be understood to have involved a conscious step towards intensive substantive review of delegated legislation, a step explained by Justice Brennan by reference to concerns about broad rule-making powers being granted to administrators. This reason for adopting proportionality review is different in Australia from the reasons for its use in related Commonwealth countries. When proportionality review is used to review delegated legislation in these countries, it is mostly due to their adoption of human rights laws which apply to all forms of administrative decision-making.[121] The different starting point in Australian law tends to confirm the commonly made point that

[116] ibid 175.

[117] (London, Benn, 1929).

[118] *Tanner* (n 84) 175.

[119] [1990] HCA 21, (1990) 170 CLR 1, 37.

[120] ibid 38.

[121] Note, however, that the New Zealand academic literature indicates that the landmark case in that jurisdiction for review of bye-laws involves a version of proportionality review: D Knight, 'Brothels, Bylaws, Prostitutes and Proportionality' [2005] *New Zealand Law Journal* 423, 425; Joseph, *Constitutional and Administrative Law in New Zealand* (n 9) 1137–39; Carter *et al*, *Subordinate Legislation in New Zealand* (n 9) 300.

proportionality is a form of legal reasoning that has been adopted in numerous different legal contexts.[122]

V. OPTIONS FOR CORRECTING THE IMBALANCE

We have seen that in Australian law review of delegated legislation on substantive grounds is heavily favoured over review on procedural grounds and that this inverts the judicial review norm by which procedural review is regarded as a more legitimate form of review of administrative decision-making than substantive review. We have also seen that while extended substantive review of delegated legislation has a rationale based on constitutional concerns, the reasons in Australian law for lack of procedural review are either unclear or questionable. The imbalance between the forms of review is particularly pronounced in Australia but it is not inconsistent with related countries. As explained in the introduction to the chapter, procedural fairness does not generally extend in comparable countries to the making of delegated legislation and there are commonly no general, enforceable statutory procedures for making delegated legislation but, on the other hand, delegated legislation is subject to substantive review in the form of unreasonableness review and proportionality review according to human rights law.

What then are the options for achieving a better balance between substantive and procedural review of delegated legislation? At this stage there is sufficient space to provide only an outline of possible options for correcting this imbalance. The options that I want to focus on can be understood as being direct and indirect ways of adding procedural review into the forms of review that are available for delegated legislation. Direct procedural review by enforceable consultation provisions or extending procedural fairness is preferable for numerous reasons. First, direct procedural review does not raise the legitimacy concerns that occur for substantive review. They draw the attention of the courts away from the core of the evaluative judgements made by administrators and their preferred outcome.[123] Secondly, these forms of review directly address the legitimacy concerns with delegated legislation made according to broad powers with minimal parliamentary involvement. Imposing enforceable procedural requirements ensures that proposed delegated legislation can be debated publicly prior to being made. They establish legal requirements directed to ensuring that administrators are informed by the individuals and groups with interests related to the norms that are to be protected. Thirdly, direct forms of procedural review address the common problems occurring in public consultation processes: that inadequate information is included in a public notice, that submissions may not be considered, etc.

[122] Kiefel, 'Proportionality: A Rule of Reason' (n 74) 85–86; Aronson and Groves, *Judicial Review of Administrative Action* (n 13) 376; Craig, *Administrative Law* (n 7) 641; Joseph, *Constitutional and Administrative Law in New Zealand* (n 9) 1011.

[123] Jowell, 'Of Vires and Vacuums' (n 13) 451; A Kavanagh, 'Reasoning about Proportionality under the Human Rights Act 1998: Outcomes, Substance and Process' (2014) 130 *Law Quarterly Review* 235, 247.

However, direct forms of procedural review raise a number of questions. Should such review be enabled by legislative reforms that make statutory public consultation provisions enforceable or by courts broadening the scope of procedural fairness?[124] Would imposing such processes be so impractical, costly and time-consuming that it is best avoided or are these concerns manageable and in any case merely a price that should be paid in a democracy?[125] Is there such dissatisfaction with delegated legislation and the processes by which it is made for courts or Parliaments to consider reforms are necessary? Professor Cane states that there is a lack of any real dissatisfaction with rule-making processes in Britain,[126] but as stated in section III.A above, concerns have been recently expressed in Australia.[127]

The aim of this chapter is not to answer such questions. Rather, the contribution that I hope to make is to suggest a further dimension to the questions and debates about whether enforceable procedural requirements should be imposed on the making of delegated legislation. It is that the questionable legitimacy of delegating broad rule-making powers may be better addressed by extending procedural grounds of judicial review rather than by extending substantive review according to the *Williams* proportionality test. This involves recognising, as stated by Mark Aronson,[128] that the main concerns with broad delegations of rule-making powers relate to the lack of democratic legitimacy of such rules when made according to processes that exclude public, political discussion. Enforceable public consultation procedures can help to supplement the reduced involvement of Parliaments in the making of delegated legislation. They enable public debate of proposed rules and the potential for officials to respond by tightening the rule to avoid unintended and unnecessary harms to relevant interests.

A further difficulty with the direct process review options, however, is that there seems little indication that such changes are likely in the short to medium term. The limits of procedural fairness are very well established in Australia and there does not seem to be any indication that general rule-making legislation will be amended to make consultation provisions enforceable. This leads to consideration of indirect procedural review as a possible option, one that would involve a narrower change in the law.

The indirect option would involve introducing a form of deference into the *Williams* proportionality test that focuses on the processes used by the rule-maker. Instead of deference being informed by general concepts such as 'something overwhelming' as in *Wednesbury* unreasonableness, or being a 'high threshold test' as referred to by French CJ in the *City of Adelaide* case,[129] the courts could adopt more modern forms of deference such as those that focus on the decision-maker's expertise

[124] See *R (BAPIO Action Ltd) v Secretary of State for the Home Department* [2007] EWCA Civ 1139, [46] (Sedley LJ), [58] (Maurice Kay LJ); Edgar, 'Procedural Fairness for Decisions Affecting the Public Generally' (n 73).

[125] Craig, *Administrative Law* (n 7) 453–54. See also Green, 'Regulations and Rule Making' (n 8) 139.

[126] Cane, *Administrative Law* (n 7) 111–12.

[127] See text to n 47.

[128] M Aronson, 'The Great Depression, this Depression, and Administrative Law' (2009) 37 *Federal Law Review* 165, 174–76.

[129] *Attorney-General (SA) v Corporation of the City of Adelaide* (n 2) [56]–[60], [64].

and democratic accountability. More relevantly, it should also be possible for courts to adjust the intensity of its proportionality review according to whether the rule-maker has utilised processes to engage individuals and groups with interests that are relevant to the rule that has been made.[130] In order to clarify how I think this could operate I will contrast it with related approaches to deference.

The first is the form of deference adopted in the early review of delegated legislation cases such as *Kruse v Johnson*. The deference in those cases focuses the court's attention on the 'checks and safeguards' included in the relevant Act, such as (and as was relevant in those cases) a requirement to give public notice of the delegated legislation in order for the rule-maker to elicit 'public opinion'.[131] The difficulty with this process-based form of deference is that it does not provide sufficient guidance for the current circumstances in Australia where public consultation provisions are included in general rule-making legislation in a discretionary, unenforceable manner, or the circumstances in other jurisdictions where public consultation principles are included in informal policy documents. Such unenforceable provisions and principles cannot realistically be regarded as 'checks and safeguards' in themselves as there is no effective accountability if they are not used. However, if a public consultation process in accordance with these provisions and principles has in fact been carried out in the making of the challenged delegated legislation, there would be a good reason I think for courts to take this into account in their proportionality assessment.[132]

The second form of deference that can provide a useful contrast is a form of deference that is utilised in UK human rights cases. Its primary significance is that it has a case-specific focus, although, as is explained in the next paragraph, it has an important difference to the form of deference that I want to suggest as an option. In the *Denbigh High School* case Lord Bingham gave weight to the administrator's judgement when there was evidence of their engagement with the relevant human right in the process leading to the making of the challenged decision.[133] Baroness Hale captured this form of deference well in *Belfast City Council v Miss Behavin' Ltd*, as being that if the decision-maker provides evidence of such engagement the court would 'find it hard to upset the balance' struck by the administrator; however, if there is no indication of such engagement, the court has 'no alternative but to strike the balance for itself'.[134] The point that I want to draw from this approach to deference is that the courts make an assessment of the deliberations carried out by the administrator in coming to the decision being challenged in order to inform the intensity of its proportionality assessment.

There are, however, difficulties with the form of deference in the UK human rights cases for our purposes. The judges in the human rights cases focus on the administrator's consideration of the relevant right rather than whether a consultation process

130 See M Hunt, 'Against Bifurcation' in D Dyzenhaus, M Hunt and G Huscroft (eds), *A Simple Common Lawyer: Essays in Honour of Michael Taggart* (Oxford, Hart Publishing, 2009) 99, 114.

131 *Kruse* (n 99) 98–99. See also *Slattery* (n 100) 453; *Widgee* (n 101) 984–95 (Isaacs J).

132 See also Hunt, 'Against Bifurcation' (n 130) 116.

133 See, eg, *R (Begum) v Headteacher and Governors of Denbigh High School* [2006] UKHL 15, [2007] 1 AC 100, [31], [34]; Kavanagh, 'Reasoning about Proportionality under the Human Rights Act 1998' (n 123) 248.

134 [2007] UKHL 19, [2007] 1 WLR 1420, [37].

was carried out. For this kind of case-specific deference to be relevant in our context, it would need to be redirected to the procedural steps leading to delegated legislation being made, rather than the reasoning process.[135] To adapt Baroness Hale's language: the court would find it hard to upset the balance struck by the administrator if they have relied on expertise, are subject to political forms of accountability and have carried out a consultation process but, if not, the court would have no alternative but to strike the balance for itself.

If the imbalance between procedural and substantive review were to be broken down in Australia by varying the intensity of review according to modern reasons for deference, such as expertise, political accountability, and most relevantly whether a consultative process was used in making the regulation being challenged, the discretionary public consultation provisions that are included in legislation such as the Legislative Instruments Act 2003 (Cth) would take on particular significance. A court could give weight in carrying out its proportionality review to evidence of the use of such provisions to engage members of the public on the purposes to be achieved by the proposed rule and whether it achieves that objective in a manner that involves minimal impairment of fundamental interests. This would help to add deference into the analysis in particular cases and provide an incentive to administrators to use the provisions of the Legislative Instruments Act to engage interested members of the public in the rule-making process.

While factoring process considerations into substantive review in this way could help to reduce the imbalance between procedural and substantive review of delegated legislation, it would not, I think, be the preferable option. More direct forms of procedural review are preferable because they not only ensure that a consultation process has been held, they also enable review of the elements of a public consultation, such as the content of the public notice, the adequacy of the period in which members of the public can make submissions, and that such submissions are considered. More generally, direct procedural review also raises fewer concerns about the legitimacy of judicial review than substantive review, even with modern forms of deference factored into the analysis.

VI. CONCLUSION

Australian judicial review is therefore imbalanced in its utilisation of procedural and substantive review of delegated legislation. While this imbalance is pronounced in Australian law, we have also seen that it is not so different from the available forms of review in related Commonwealth countries. The lack of procedural review is due to unwillingness to establish enforceable procedures in rule-making legislation and the limits of procedural fairness. For substantive review, on the other hand, there are constitutional concerns in Australia regarding broad delegations of rule-making powers that have driven the acceptance of proportionality review. The Australian

[135] Kavanagh, 'Reasoning about Proportionality under the Human Rights Act 1998' (n 123) 246–49.

case law is, I think, right to raise the broad delegation of rule-making authority as a problem but it is questionable whether proportionality review, particularly in the form expressed in *Williams*, is the appropriate answer to it. The better solution suggested in this chapter is to enable some form of process-based review of delegated legislation. While a form of deference could possibly be factored into the *Williams* test that gives weight to the processes used by the administrator to engage individuals and groups with relevant interests, the preferable option would be to enable direct forms of procedural review.

10

Transubstantiation in Canadian Public Law: Processing Substance and Instantiating Process

MARY LISTON*

I. INTRODUCTION

CANADIAN PUBLIC LAW blurs process and substance, a result confirming the prevailing view that this dichotomy ought never to be conceived as a simplistic bright-line distinction. Recent developments have created more than just a blurring but, rather, a strong linking or even fusion of the two. This chapter probes the implications of these developments in public law. Section II briefly presents the historic and jurisprudential distinction between process and substance and assesses its current legal import. Here I argue that judicially created analytic frameworks could assist by bringing a process-substance problem to the surface and constraining its potentially pernicious effects. Section III grounds this initial discussion in Canadian public law by showing how the distinction generally appears in judicial review of procedures in administrative law. The decisional framework employed in procedural fairness is examined. Sections IV and V turn to two significant new developments in Canadian public law. Section IV considers how the duty to consult and accommodate in public law completely fuses process and substance. Aboriginal administrative law currently provides the most vibrant and dynamic jurisprudential example of the conceptual puzzles that the distinction raises and its decisional framework exemplifies many of the tensions discussed in the chapter as a whole. Section V examines the new Canadian approach to the substantive review of discretionary decisions and how the current decisional framework may fall short in terms of rights protection. The chapter concludes that the 'transubstantiation' of process and substance is conceptually and legally desirable due to the cross-fertilisation of rule of law and democratic norms in public law, and that improved decisional frameworks could fruitfully assist in this cross-fertilisation.

* I am grateful to John Bell, Mark Elliott, Philip Murray and Jason Varuhas for their constructive and incisive feedback. I would also like to thank the chair and co-presenters at the 2014 Public Law Conference where this chapter was originally presented, Cora Hoexter, Anashri Pillay and Tom Hickman, and audience members for helpful insights.

II. SIGNIFYING PROBLEMS: PROCESS VERSUS SUBSTANCE IN GENERAL JURISPRUDENCE AND IN PUBLIC LAW

A. Two Conventional Approaches to the Separation of Process and Substance and Why they don't Work

The distinction between process and substance was never as conceptually bright-line as traditional jurisprudence would have it.[1] The difficulty of rendering a clear distinction has long been noted, despite the fact that law schools continue to teach as if the dichotomy remains crystal clear.[2] Even the strongest defender of the distinction—Jeremy Bentham—conceded that neither could conceptually exist without the other. He may, however, have firmly agreed with Thomas Hobbes that any suggestion that the two might be fused or co-exist in legal doctrines and analytic frameworks would amount to utter nonsense not unlike that absurd religious claptrap called transubstantiation.[3]

Traditional jurisprudence therefore relegates matters that affect the existence, extent or enforceability of rights and duties of the parties to a legal action as substance, not procedure. Procedure would then encompass all matters relating to the fairness or efficiency of the litigation and the evidentiary process (such as facts, judgments and evidentiary rules). Alternatively, a second traditional approach relegates issues concerning the manner and means needed to access courts, the availability of remedies, and matters relating to justiciability as procedure. But fuzzy boundaries rapidly arise.

Regarding the first approach—historically understood as a practical allocation—we quickly come to an imprecise demarcation when the distinction is broadly considered from an institutional and systemic perspective. We value procedural law in and of itself because it conforms to the ideal of the rule of law (ie a norm-governed process). The ideal of the rule of law animates our collective hope that we can value, uphold and legitimise a certain procedure because it is more likely to lead to a just

[1] See the discussion concerning the division between substance and procedure (or 'adjective' law), arguably created by Jeremy Bentham and criticised by John Austin in A Kocourek, 'Substance and Procedure' (1941) 10 *Fordham Law Review* 157.

[2] Kocourek, 'Substance and Procedure' (n 1) 160–62 canvassed older jurisprudence proposing various 'solutions' to the conceptual problem by: (1) suggesting that procedural rules are wholly equivalent to substance (John W Salmond); or (2) subsuming process entirely into substance (Charles Frederic Chamberlayne); or (3) offering the notion of a penumbra or 'twilight zone' between process and substance (Walter Wheeler Cook in his seminal 1933 *Yale Law Journal* article entitled '"Substance" and "Procedure" in the Conflict of Laws'). Kocourek, 'Substance and Procedure' (n 1) 164 recharacterised the problem by suggesting the use of 'telic rights' instead of substance, and 'instrumental rights' instead of procedure, with the result that: '"Telic" rights are those abstract rights whose realisation is effected by the concrete application, directly or indirectly, of "instrumental" rights'.

[3] He writes: 'And words whereby we conceive nothing but the sound, are those we call *Absurd* … and *Non-sense.* And therefore if a man should talk to me of a *round Quadrangle*; or *accidents of Bread in Cheese*; or *Immaterial Substances* … but are taken up, and learned by rote from the Schooles, as *hypostatical, transubstantiate, consubstantiate, eternal-Now*, and the like canting of Schoole-men'. R Tuck (ed), *Leviathan* (Cambridge, Cambridge University Press, 2002) I.V, 19 at 35.

outcome.[4] This potentially just outcome is partly legitimated because it is the product of a fair procedure.[5] The connection between procedure and substance as a matter of procedural justice, in turn, validates the institution of the judiciary and its associated legal practices. Substance and process are therefore inextricably entangled as a matter of procedural justice and just institutions.[6]

The second approach encompasses several discrete points of fusion between process and substance. Standing and other justiciability doctrines, for example, procedurally regulate the initial stages of engaging the judicial process for accessing rights and enforcing duties. But, they also contain a significant element of substance because they affect the ultimate result.[7] Alexander Bickel noted that when a court declines to hear a case on its merits, and provides little explanation, it indirectly validates the government's action as a matter of substance.[8] Moreover, by obtaining standing, a person is recognised as having legal status and a potentially valid legal claim requiring judicial resolution. The litigant gains a substantive right of access to a further protected right or enforceable duty. Standing is therefore an end in itself as a form of legal status, but also entails the recognition that one's claim is justiciable and one can therefore make use of the available procedures to vindicate the right or enforce the duty. Standing further validates the courts as the appropriate forum in which to hear the legal matter, thereby confirming their jurisdiction. In the way that many process and substance issues seem nested within each other, jurisdiction itself is also a further matter of substance (ie the lawful and legitimate exercise of judicial power) *and* also of procedure (ie the process used to structure a court's discretionary control over its own processes).[9]

To take another example, remedies combine process and substance because the substance of remedial principles is closely connected to the procedures of the particular court in which they are applied and because of their close connections with procedural doctrines of standing and justiciability.[10] Without standing and a justiciable

[4] See O Malcai and R Levine-Schnur, 'Which Came First, the Procedure or the Substance? Justificational Priority and the Substance-Procedure Distinction' (2014) 34 *Oxford Journal of Legal Studies* 1. See also André Nollkaemper discussing the contemporary view in international criminal law that procedure does not merely enforce substance, but represents its own values that are not merely instrumental: A Nollkaemper, 'International Adjudication of Global Public Goods: The Intersection of Substance and Procedure' (2012) 23 *European Journal of International Law* 769, 782.

[5] Lawrence Solum argues that a complex view of the relationship between procedure and substance appreciates the 'ineliminable and inherent entanglement' between them. He suggests that the real work of procedure is to 'provide particular action-guiding legal norms' across all areas of law for individuals and public actors: 'Procedural Justice' (2004) 78 *Southern California Law Review* 181, 224–25, 320.

[6] See Rawls' conception of just institutions on this point: J Rawls, *Political Liberalism* (New York, Columbia University Press, 1993) 72.

[7] Malcai and Levine-Schnur, 'Which Came First, the Procedure or the Substance?' (n 4) 7.

[8] A Bickel, *The Least Dangerous Branch: The Supreme Court at the Bar of Politics* (New Haven, CT and London, Yale University Press, 1986) 69.

[9] See *R v Inland Revenue Commissioners, ex parte National Federation of Self Employed and Small Businesses Ltd* [1982] AC 617, where the House of Lords rejected the possibility of determining standing without reference to the substance of the claim for judicial review.

[10] Nollkaemper, 'International Adjudication of Global Public Goods' (n 4) 775. Michael Risinger cites Bentham for the view that the availability of remedies for a violation of a right is part of substantive law. See M Risinger, '"Substance" and "Procedure" Revisited (with Some Afterthoughts on the Constitutional Problems of "Irrebuttable Presumptions")' (1983) 30 *UCLA Law Review* 189, 191.

claim, a complainant cannot use procedures to access a remedy. And, finally, procedure may also include (if broadly construed) matters of interpretation and rules originating in the democratic process, both of which are often labelled substance.[11]

Contemporary legal scholars emphasise that the consequences of the process/substance distinction are complex. Some consequences are concrete and relate only to the specific parties in the case, while others are more general and concern the operation of the overall legal system in terms of fairness, efficiency or justice.[12] A difficulty arises, then, when we try to define the scope of the outcome of the legal process. A narrow view of a legal matter will see the consequences—and the process-substance dichotomy—differently than a broader scope that may engage considerations of jurisdiction and just institutions. At its broadest, the distinction orients us towards and grounds a conception of judicial review and its appropriate contours as expressed in the principle of the rule of law, the principle of legality, the doctrine of the separation of powers and the institutional demands of deference.[13]

We therefore must confront a legal characterisation puzzle inevitably involving judicial interpretation and issue framing.[14] A formalistic approach will wish to see issues 'naturally' belonging to a particular category differentiated by form and function.[15] Over time, these distinctions, if regularly applied and followed, will become a recognisable jurisprudential pattern with set expectations. This process in law possesses some similarity with how 'genres' are used to classify literary texts and other artistic works. Established authorities will rely on prior characterisations of the distinction, such as the two approaches outlined above, however, different institutions and areas of law contain the possibility of upsetting past characterisations and generating different legal consequences. A legal issue or rule might be characterised as procedural for one purpose, substantive for another, or even both at the same time. Does this blurring raise the Hobbesian view that we are talking about a legal absurdity? The answer is again no, but for a different reason than the categorisation problem just discussed.

B. A Pragmatic and Functional Approach to the Distinction

Many legal scholars who acknowledge the intractable nature of the categorisation problem also concede that the legal distinction provides tactical and functional import in the management of legal disputes. Blurred therefore does not mean muddled and muddy and it becomes incumbent on courts to develop methods that help them navigate this difficult terrain, while exhibiting transparency in the methods that

[11] Malcai and Levine-Schnur, 'Which Came First, the Procedure or the Substance?' (n 4) 9.

[12] ibid 12.

[13] D Dyzenhaus and E Fox-Decent, 'Rethinking the Process/Substance Distinction: *Baker v Canada*' (2001) 51 *University of Toronto Law Journal* 193, 196.

[14] On categorisation in law generally, see AG Amsterdam and J Bruner, *Minding the Law* (Cambridge, MA and London, Harvard University Press, 2002) ch 2.

[15] See K Petroski, 'Statutory Genres: Substance, Procedure, Jurisdiction' (2012) 44 *Loyola University Chicago Law Journal* 189, 240–43.

they themselves devise. Judges must therefore strive to faithfully apply the artificial reason and common law methods of reckoning that make use of logic, proportionality, principles of equity and justice.

In their article on the process-substance dichotomy, public law scholars David Dyzenhaus and Evan Fox-Decent suggest that the process/substance distinction is fraught with difficulty partly because the term 'substance' is itself ambiguous.[16] Dyzenhaus and Fox-Decent raise the tantalising suggestion that the traditional dichotomy is completely illusory—it is substance all the way down—but ultimately reject this conclusion.[17] They instead argue that the distinction is not likely to disappear any time soon, that it does functionally serve to demarcate jurisdictional issues between other branches and the judiciary, and that it involves a necessary complication that points toward a defensible conception of judicial review in a democratic legal order. According to them, substance designates a legal area where judges are less likely to intervene, thereby engaging the principle of deference within a conception of the separation of powers. Substance serves as a criterion to legitimate the activity of judicial review or its denial. 'Process', on the other hand, indicates areas that the judiciary considers itself to be constitutionally charged with or deems itself capable of supervising.

Traditionally in public law, judges left substance to the legislature and the executive while nominating themselves the guardians of procedure.[18] Since the late 1970s and early 1980s in Canadian administrative law, the dichotomy has tracked the changes from the traditional 'Diceyan' model of the judiciary with monopoly over adjudication, law interpretation and supervision through a correctness standard in administrative law (for both procedure and substance) to a more respectful judiciary that ought to exhibit 'deference as respect'[19] towards the legislative and executive branches.

We can see this interplay at work in Canadian administrative law. Reviewing courts examine administrative procedures for fairness, but elements of procedure also act as justifying norms for the review of substance. The key link here (which will be discussed more fully in section III) is the provision of reasons. Reasons may be required as part of the content of procedural fairness. But substantive review (ie judicial review of the decision or policy) also relies on reasons. The outcome of the decision may be justified as reasonable if the result stems from fair procedures and intelligible reasons. Here, the legal dichotomy relies on an underlying philosophical distinction between procedural and substantive norms, but reasons simultaneously embody both types of norms. In Canadian administrative law (similar to administrative law in other common law countries), the process-substance distinction therefore indicates two avenues to access judicial review, as well as at least two

[16] Dyzenhaus and Fox-Decent, 'Rethinking the Process/Substance Distinction' (n 13) 195.

[17] ibid 196.

[18] ibid 195.

[19] D Dyzenhaus, 'The Politics of Deference: Judicial Review and Democracy' in M Taggart (ed), *The Province of Administrative Law* (Oxford, Hart Publishing, 1997) 279, 286 is the source for the idea of 'deference as respect'. The Supreme Court of Canada has cited this article, from whence the phrase comes, in several landmark cases.

justificatory grounds for judicial deference to another branch of government: (1) the recognition of fair procedure; and (2) the recognition of sound decision-making or policy application.

Moreover, the process-substance dichotomy also engages questions of jurisdiction in public law, resolution of which in some respects operates in a manner akin to a conflict of laws.[20] In a conflict of laws matter where an inter-state legal dispute involves both domestic and foreign law, the law of the forum governs matters of procedure, and matters of substance are governed by a choice of law rule that could privilege either domestic or foreign law. In Canadian administration law, a presumption of reasonableness has emerged in reasonableness review. This strong presumption of deference applies to *all* administrative decision-makers operating within their home statute in terms of process, interpretation and substance.[21] At judicial review, procedure is generally governed by judge-made common law, while substance is largely informed by the statutory objectives and norms applied by administrative actors (subject to common law judicial constraints on the scope of decision-making). In substantive review, the administrative decision-maker's authority is generally viewed robustly, but judges can use common law principles to shape the exercise of discretion,[22] to confirm or reject interpretive choices,[23] to conclude that a decision does not exhibit rationality or proportionality,[24] and to reject unreasonable outcomes.[25] In sum, the (rebuttable) presumption of reasonableness automatically privileges the interpretations and conclusions regarding substance, but also often the procedures used, by administrative decision-makers thereby averting institutional conflict.

Dyzenhaus and Fox-Decent argue that, despite its inherent ambiguity, the notion of 'substance' can serve a variety of functions including: (1) facilitating access to the remedy when process serves to deny a particular outcome because substance indicates the possibility of a right to a particular outcome; (2) indicating which body can define the content of procedural fairness thereby legitimating the actions used by an administrative body to render a decision; (3) pointing to the form and content of procedural fairness when the statute leaves that determination to the administrative body and its judgement about the weight of factors that it uses; (4) supplying the justification requirement in procedural fairness, usually met by the provision

[20] See Nollkaemper, 'International Adjudication of Global Public Goods' (n 4) on this point where he discusses how questions of jurisdiction are treated either as questions of substance or procedure depending on the territory, on the context, and also on the particular area of law.

[21] *Agraira v Canada (Public Safety and Emergency Preparedness)* [2013] 2 SCR 559 (presumption applies to all administrative actors, not just adjudicative tribunals, and includes Ministers and other statutory delegates).

[22] *Mission Institution v Khela* 2014 SCC 24 (procedures involving discretionary choices may be owed deference by a reviewing court).

[23] *McLean v British Columbia (Securities Commission)* [2013] 3 SCR 895, 2013 SCC 67 (administrative decision-makers have the 'interpretive upper hand' in their home statute).

[24] *Loyola High School v Quebec (Attorney General)* 2015 SCC 12 (reasonableness review requires proportionality and the Minister must exercise discretion to advance the freedom of religion enjoyed by a Catholic high school).

[25] *Canada (Attorney General) v PHS Community Services Society* [2011] 3 SCR 134, 2011 SCC 44 ('*Insite*') (the Minister's decision not to grant an exemption for a provincial safe injection facility was arbitrary in substance and disproportionate in its effects).

of reasons, which blurs into the substance or reasonableness of the decision; and (5) indicating political morality, understood in a conception of fairness, which informs legal conceptions of procedural fairness.[26]

C. Good Principles and Proper Methods

Instead of striving for a clear a priori distinction between process and substance, then, contemporary thinking suggests that judges, lawyers and administrative decision-makers develop decisional frameworks and other higher-order legal rules that operate as a cognitive process to bring these kinds of process-substance problems to the surface of legal thought and judgement.[27] While a comprehensive discussion of cognitive or analytic frameworks is not possible in this chapter, several insights from this growing literature are highly relevant.

A key text from cognitive science is *Thinking, Fast and Slow* by Daniel Kahneman, a book that illustrates the inescapable effects that experience, assumption, values, emotions and unconscious biases have on our ability to think clearly and come to 'right reason'.[28] According to Kahneman, our mind is a dual-process model that contains two interactive modes of thinking, both of which produce the 'thinking I'. System 1 is like the operation of automatic pilot, operating quickly and continuously with little effort and producing intuitive, unconscious thought. It is impressionistic, metaphorical, associative, and cannot be switched off. It 'authors' our thought without us even being aware of its activity. System 2 is slower, deliberative and more effortful, requiring our attention when it is operative. It is associated with agency, choice, concentration and complex computations and so is considered more rational.[29] System 1 controls most of our actions and generates a 'narrative' that allows us to make sense of the world we encounter. It enables us to perform the thousands of daily complex tasks we need to do, but unconsciously and often automatically. It is, however, prone to common reasoning errors because of its associative nature and its mode of 'jumping to conclusions'. System 2 kicks into gear when System 1 is challenged and it can oversee and correct System 1, but only if pushed to do so, because it is lazy.

This relatively recent research on human cognition contains valuable insights for law. Foremost is the fact that when decision-makers (either individual persons or professional decision-makers) approach the decision-making process, they unavoidably bring background influences and values with them, not all of which they are aware about.[30] Judges form ideas and beliefs about issues and people by drawing on their previous experiences, both personal and professional. Such expert

[26] Dyzenhaus and Fox-Decent, 'Rethinking the Process/Substance Distinction' (n 13) 195–96. This links back to the understanding of fairness in Rawls' theory of justice.

[27] This kind of jurisprudential resolution is one that even Hobbes might approve: 'The first cause of Absurd conclusions I ascribe to the want of Method'. See Tuck, *Leviathan* (n 3) 35.

[28] D Kahneman, *Thinking, Fast and Slow* (Toronto, Anchor Canada, 2013).

[29] See ibid chs 1–3 for further elaboration.

[30] For elaboration on these points, see ibid chs 4–5.

intuition, Kahneman suggests, can be reliable if a field requires skills to discern and an environment that is sufficiently regular to be predictable.[31] Law and legal reasoning can satisfy these requirements, and this fit is often expressed in the concept of 'common sense' deliberation.[32] Nevertheless, these regularities do not necessarily arise to a robust statistical level of the kind typical of poker playing, medicine, stocks and athletics.

Instead of pretending that a completely objective judgment is achievable, judges should mitigate arbitrariness by using thinking techniques that encourage them to be 'mindful'.[33] These techniques can stimulate and support System 2 modes of thinking. Common techniques include being open to new information in order to check conclusions and avoid overconfidence, taking into account more than one perspective in order to counter tunnel vision,[34] and creating new categories to (re)sort information. These techniques may help us to understand how we make errors in choices and judgement. They make us aware of the role of our emotions in deliberation and direct us to analyse how our internal narrative framing affects beliefs, choices and assessment of facts or evidence.[35]

These analytic frameworks cannot resolve the problem of characterisation but, instead, guide thinking so that choices can become more consciously made, more transparent, and ideally accompanied by reasons explaining why a particular categorical choice or generic distinction has been made. This is important when we realise that characterisation is not just performed for a practical purpose, but has sometimes profound normative consequences. With a framework in place, a court can either develop further or re-visit prior characterisations made by legislatures, parties, lawyers, lower courts and administrative decision-makers. Attention therefore shifts from a focus on once-and-for-all fixing the difference between substance and process to a necessary examination of how well these frameworks and their accompanying interpretive methodologies are working.

This section has argued that the process/substance distinction, while tenable, is fraught with tensions and must be viewed as shifting and complex. Substance

[31] See ibid ch 6.

[32] Insights from cognitive science animate the legal literature on jury deliberation, procedural problems resulting in miscarriages of justice, judicial biases involving stereotypes, and promoting empathy in judicial decision-making. See SA Bandes, 'Remorse and Demeanor in the Courtroom: Cognitive Science and the Evaluation of Contrition' (2013) *DePaul Legal Studies*, Research Paper No 14-05, available at http://ssrn.com/abstract=2363326; N Negowetti, 'Judicial Decisionmaking, Empathy, and the Limits of Perception' (2012) *Valparaiso University Legal Studies*, Research Paper No 12-15, available at http://ssrn.com/abstract=2164325; DL Martin, 'Lessons about Justice from the Laboratory of Wrongful Convictions: Tunnel Vision, the Construction of Guilt, and Informer Evidence' (2001–02) 70 *University of Missouri-Kansas City Law Review* 847; M Nussbaum, *Upheavals of Thought: The Intelligence of Emotions* (Cambridge, Cambridge University Press, 2001).

[33] The literature on 'mindfulness' zeroes in on the contextualised nature of thinking or judging, rather than empirical models of the brain. See J Nedelsky, 'Receptivity and Judgment' (2011) 4 *Ethics and Global Politics* 231; J Nedelsky, *Law's Relations* (New York, Oxford University Press, 2011).

[34] Nedelsky's work on reflective judgement focuses on overcoming cognitive biases like tunnel vision. Nedelsky claims that mindfulness is an imaginative act of contextualised thinking that leads the rational agent to challenge her own subjectivity by broadening her frame of reference. Contrast this with Martha Nussbaum's work on empathy and judgement where she describes empathy as 'an imaginative reconstruction of another person's experience' that does not require us to align our interests with that of another person. Nussbaum, *Upheavals of Thought* (n 32) 302.

[35] See Kahneman, *Thinking, Fast and Slow* (n 28) ch 34.

informs process and process legitimises substance, ultimately providing the justificatory grounds for judicial review as a set of institutional practices and normative choices. The answer lies in becoming aware of how and why a legal matter is characterised as one or the other and what results from that. Not all doctrinal areas make use of decisional frameworks that aim to bring substantive-procedural characterisation matters into sharper focus. Canadian administrative law, however, does.

The chapter now turns to three recent examples of this blurring of substance and procedure and the three frameworks that have been created to assist: procedural fairness, the duty to consult and accommodate, and substantive review of discretionary decisions.

III. CROSS-FERTILISATION OF PROCESS AND SUBSTANCE: PROCEDURAL FAIRNESS AS THE FIRST FAULT-LINE

Section II briefly examined how the process-substance connection already exists in public law generally and administrative law in particular. It probed how the distinction is used to, among other functions, establish jurisdiction thereby legitimising judicial review. When the process-substance distinction is raised, one can readily discern the presence of fault-lines or stressors in the jurisprudential terrain. These stressors create high anxiety in appellate judges who see the implications of the distinction and know that a particular stressor can quickly and easily crack open the 'Pandora's Box of legality'.[36] This section first presents the current framework used to determine the content of procedural fairness in Canadian administrative law. It then turns to the three main stressors in procedural fairness—legitimate expectations, weight and reasons—stressors that resonate in developments that the next two sections consider.

A. *Baker* Framework for Determining the Content of Procedural Fairness

In Canadian administrative law, a reviewing court asks one overarching question to determine the content of the duty of fairness for review of the procedures used by an administrative decision-maker: Was the procedure used in this case fair considering all of the circumstances? To answer this question, a court employs what is now termed the '*Baker* framework'—an analytic, decisional framework of the kind identified in section II.[37] When considering and applying the framework, the reviewing court must find a balance among an open list of factors and principles that include:

(1) the nature of the decision and the process followed;
(2) the nature of the statutory scheme and the terms of review;
(3) the importance of the decision to the individual(s) affected;

[36] Evan Fox-Decent uses this term to describe the judicial anxiety arising from the realisation that procedural fairness has substantive implications. See E Fox-Decent, *Sovereignty's Promise: The State as Fiduciary* (New York, Oxford University Press, 2011), 189–90.

[37] *Baker v Canada (Minister of Citizenship and Immigration)* [1999] 2 SCR 817, [21]–[28].

(4) the legitimate expectations of the persons challenging the decision;
(5) the need to respect agency expertise in determining and following its own procedures.

Despite strong judicial statements that no one factor takes priority over the other, four of these factors 'pull' a reviewing court closer to or further away from deference, minimal intrusion and a sole focus on process: 1, 3, 4 and 5. I have used the phrase 'pull' to indicate that some factors may carry more 'weight' in the context of a particular case, though they may appear neutral initially. A reviewing court accords weight to a particular factor that, in turn, may pull the judges towards greater scrutiny and intrusion. Factors 3 and 4 indicate elements that most clearly blur the process/substance distinction and move what is generally conceived solely as review of procedures towards review on substantive fairness grounds.[38]

B. How the Framework Blurs Process and Substance

Regarding Factor 1 (the nature of the decision and the process followed) less deference or more scrutiny will be demanded if, for example, the nature of the decision is closer to the judicial process or if a right of appeal exists. Most courts take the traditional view that tribunals are not owed ample deference on procedural fairness matters and that the standard of fairness is a rigorous one akin to correctness. More deference, however, may be appropriate when the enabling statute delegates broad discretion to make procedural choices to the decision-maker. The result is a lessening intensity in the standard of review for procedures, from a stricter standard akin to correctness towards a fairness standard that reflects respect for agency expertise (or Factor 5). In other words, Factors 1, 2 and 5 can combine to produce a posture that mirrors the reasonableness standard used in substantive review.[39] The Supreme Court of Canada in the *Khela* decision best expressed this contextually deferential stance using the words 'margin of deference' to the administrative decision-maker (in this case a Commissioner or Warden of a prison) who employed a procedure that required the exercise of discretion (in this case, withholding information from the prisoner).[40] More deference will be accorded if the nature of the decision is polycentric in substance (ie involving many parties) or if it involves complex considerations regarding the public good. More deference will therefore be shown to an administrative body that is acting 'legislatively' or in complex policy matters rather than 'judicially'—terms that are both synonyms for substance and process,

[38] For commentary on the concept of substantive fairness in Australian and New Zealand administrative law, see K Stern, 'Substantive Fairness in UK and Australian Law' (2007) 29 *Australian Bar Review* 266 and DR Knight, 'Simple, Fair, and Discretionary Administrative Law' (2012) 2 *Victoria University of Wellington Law Review* 34.

[39] For academic commentary on the possibility of fusing procedural and substantive review in this way, see P Daly, 'Canada's Bi-Polar Administrative Law: Time for Fusion' (2014) 40 *Queen's Law Journal* 213.

[40] *Khela* (n 22) [89]. The concept of 'substantive fairness' as a fusion of process and substance appears to be on the horizon in Canadian procedural fairness, but it is unclear whether or not it has any legs.

respectively.[41] Cases that fall at the legislative end may be viewed as near non-justiciable or highly inappropriate for judicial review.

More content will also be required if the decision involves a strong individual right and the decision is very important to the individual (eg matters concerning livelihood, personal security, reputation, and so on).[42] The *Baker* framework is a balancing exercise implicitly guided by the principle of proportionality. Factor 3 implicitly compels judges to engage in a mini-balancing or proportionality exercise since the substance of the individual right must be weighed relative to the other factors that may compete. In practice, the content of procedural fairness varies mostly depending on the strength of Factor 3—the right, interest or privilege being weighted as more or less important against the other variables. This mini-proportionality review within procedural fairness calls into play concerns about the limits of judicial review, parliamentary supremacy and legislative intent. Canadian administrative law wavers between adhering to legislative intent, primarily through statutory communications about process requirements, and engaging in judicial creativity by augmenting content on common law grounds. As Paul Craig argues, the 'reality was that a general presumption of legislative intent had to be framed in abstract terms, to the effect that Parliament believed in justness between citizen and government and that this generated a general legislative intent that statutes should comply with the precepts of public law developed by the common law courts over time, subject to any special legislative intervention'.[43] The *Baker* framework has brought into focus, but not really at the surface, demands for 'process legitimacy' that blur the process-substance distinction in judicial decisions.[44]

In some cases, the weight given to a particular factor will be the same as the initial decision-maker, but in others the court may re-determine weight explicitly or implicitly and the re-weighting may have substantive remedial effects. When Factor 1 is more substantive (that is, more legislative or discretionary or broadly policy-oriented) then Factor 3's weight may be quite curtailed or even eliminated. But when Factor 3 is strong, and the remedy is that the decision is sent back for reconsideration, the practical effect may be that the decision-maker has before them only one possible outcome, and process blurs into substance again. This was the result in the *Baker* case. The administrative official had to reconsider the original decision to deny Mavis Baker an exemption to apply for permanent resident status on humanitarian and compassionate grounds by taking into greater account the best interests of her Canadian-born children. Only two possibilities therefore remained for that office: to approve or deny the exemption. The exemption was approved.

[41] For a discussion of so-called legislative decisions, see G Huscroft, 'From Natural Justice to Fairness: Thresholds, Content, and the Role of Judicial Review' in C Flood and L Sossin (eds), *Administrative Law in Context*, 2nd edn (Toronto, Emond Montgomery, 2013). Cabinet and ministerial decisions, for example, may be exempt from the common law duty of fairness if they are characterised as broad policy decisions or appear legislative in form (eg an Order in Council).

[42] Note, however, that procedural fairness protects not just rights, but also privileges and interests. See *Cardinal v Director of Kent Institution* [1985] 2 SCR 643, 653.

[43] PP Craig, 'The Nature of Reasonableness Review' (2013) 66 *Current Legal Problems* 131, 160.

[44] Fox-Decent, *Sovereignty's Promise* (n 36) 189 discusses how the majority in the *Knight* case amplified the content of procedural fairness using, in part, the principle of legitimacy.

As a result of this case, greater substance—weightier principles and additional values—were simultaneously imported into the process of judicial review as well as the decision-making procedure used by immigration officials. In many cases, a procedural remedy like reconsideration (certiorari combined with mandamus) will have a substantive result because the decision-maker will be so constrained by the court's reasoning and final determination that only one option will be before her: using an improved process to render the same decision as the court.

Factor 4 distinguishes Canada from some other common law jurisdictions, like England and Wales and South Africa.[45] Canadian jurisprudence explicitly and repeatedly states that legitimate expectations confers *only* procedural protection and is available only if government conduct includes an overt promise, representation, undertaking or regular practice.[46] If Canada had substantive legitimate expectations, instead of only procedural, then Factor 4 would have the potential to exert greater pull. To date, Canadian courts have shown no willingness to revisit the jurisprudential ousting of substantive legitimate expectations in administrative law.[47] This denial of substantive legitimate expectations makes the *Baker* framework appear more 'procedural' than 'substantive,' but this is a false conclusion for several reasons.

C. Three 'Stressors': Weight, Legitimate Expectations and Reasons

First, as discussed above, the mini-proportionality exercise required by Factor 3 blurs process and substance by requiring reviewing courts to weigh the five factors and balance them against each other. Secondly, and briefly adverted to above, the denial of substantive legitimate expectations makes the *Baker* framework appear more procedural than substantive, but this is a false conclusion overall and one that is subject to no jurisprudential change around legitimate expectations. It may only be a matter of time, and with the right case, that Canadian public law reverses the bright line it has drawn between procedural and substantive legitimate expectations and follows the lead established by courts in South Africa and the United Kingdom.[48] Thirdly, and as discussed in section II, the duty to give reasons further erodes the distinction between process and substance in judicial review.

[45] See C Hoexter, 'The Enforcement of Official Promises in South African Law: Process, Substance and the Constitutional Court', paper given at the 2014 Public Law Conference, Faculty of Law, University of Cambridge; G Weeks and M Groves, 'The Legitimacy of Expectations about Fairness: Can Process and Substance be Untangled?', paper prepared for the 2014 Public Law Conference, Faculty of Law, University of Cambridge; CF Forsyth, 'Legitimate Expectations Revisited', ALBA Summer Conference, 29 May 2011, available at www.adminlaw.org.uk/library/publications.php; A Perry and F Ahmed, 'The Coherence of the Doctrine of Legitimate Expectations' [2014] *Cambridge Law Journal* 61.

[46] See *Canada (Attorney-General) v Mavi* [2011] 2 SCR 504, [68].

[47] Even in English law, many legitimate expectations cases concern only procedure. Substantive legitimate expectations provide protection from actions a court *may* conclude are an abuse of public power to disappoint. See Laws LJ in *Niazi v Secretary of State* [2008] EWCA 755, [41]–[42].

[48] The Supreme Court has recently made more use of the mandamus remedy to order Ministers to exercise their discretion in specific ways in both the *Insite* (n 25) and *Loyola* (n 24) cases. It may be that this kind of move toward more intrusive remedies may have an effect on legitimate expectations as courts move away from the doctrine of improper fettering of discretion and overcome their reticence about substantive expectations.

Canadian scholars have long noted the connection between dignity interests, legitimacy and the common law reasons requirement. In an early analysis of *Baker*, David Mullan stated that the Supreme Court came 'close to trading in "fairness" as a substantive and not purely procedural concept … Indeed, it serves to further emphasize that there is no bright line between procedural and substantive review'.[49] Very quickly, the reasons requirement became a problem for judicial review. Litigation around the quality or adequacy of reasons further stressed the distinction since it was not clear if poorly executed reasons constituted only a procedural flaw or were properly a matter for substantive review as the reasoning undermined the reasonableness of the decision.

The Supreme Court recognised the possibility that a severe fault-line around the reasons requirement could completely collapse the distinction between process and substance and moved quickly to shore it up in the *Newfoundland Nurses* case.[50] In this case, the Court confirmed that inadequate reasons are indeed not reviewed under procedural fairness but, rather, through reasonableness review. The only question regarding reasons in review for procedural fairness is: are reasons required by the common law or not? All other questions regarding adequacy, in form or content, should be dealt in substantive review. By relegating the adequacy of reasons to substantive review, the court was also able to re-affirm its own jurisdiction. Procedural fairness review could continue to treat the absence of reasons with more judicial scrutiny since procedural fairness is akin to correctness review in Canadian administrative law. The Court therefore affirmed its traditional guardianship and checking of administrative procedures. The Court then bolstered its more deferential stance in substantive review by affirming that the adequacy of reasons is a matter for reasonableness—not correctness—review. By making this move, the Court forestalled another potential stressor—the collapsing of the distinction between reasonableness review and review of the merits of the decision—by removing the possibility of using the most intrusive standard, correctness, to get at the merits through the reasons that were offered or could be offered to support a decision.[51]

Legitimate expectations, weight and reasons are three stressors for the process/substance distinction in procedural fairness. While the Supreme Court has worked hard to protect common law procedural review from these stressors, their disruptive potential has come to the fore in a related, but novel, area of law: the duty to consult and accommodate in Aboriginal administrative law.

[49] D Mullan, '*Baker v Canada (Minister of Citizenship & Immigration)*: A Defining Moment in Canadian Administrative Law' (1999) 7 *Reid's Administrative Law* 145, 151.

[50] *Newfoundland and Labrador Nurses' Union v Newfoundland and Labrador (Treasury Board)* 2011 SCC 62, [2011] 3 SCR 708 ('*Newfoundland Nurses*').

[51] In English law, the absence of reasons may be challenged as procedurally unfair or as substantively unreasonable. See T Endicott, *Administrative Law*, 2nd edn (New York, Oxford University Press, 2011) 186–215. This chapter cannot address the recent Canadian case law where courts have 'coopered up' reasons 'which could be offered' by statutory delegates when the original reasons are deficient or sometimes non-existent.

IV. EXPECTING LEGITIMACY: THE DUTY TO CONSULT AND ACCOMMODATE AS THE SECOND FAULT-LINE

This section analyses the process/substance distinction in what is now called Aboriginal administrative law in Canada. Aboriginal law is a distinct area of public law and involves constitutional, common law, statutory law, international law and, increasingly, Indigenous customary law. In keeping with the overall historical development of Aboriginal law in Canada, the duty to consult and accommodate differs significantly from other forms of consultation and accommodation in public law such as those found in labour and human rights law. Instead, it is a sui generis blend of administrative and constitutional law. This is because the source of the various duties differs, originating in the early sovereign-to-sovereign relations between the British Crown and Indigenous peoples. The roots of Aboriginal public law therefore predate the establishment in 1867 of the positive legal authority that Confederation represents in Canada.

A. Honour of the Crown as the Guiding Principle for Process and Substance

The Royal Proclamation of 1763[52] constitutes one fundamental source of the Crown's legal relations with Indigenous peoples in North America. Key promises from the Royal Proclamation include the Crown's overall obligation to protect Indigenous rights from settler encroachment, the guarantee that Indigenous peoples should be able to access a legal system in order to benefit from good governance, and the promise to resolve disputes equitably through a judiciary committed to the rule of law. The Royal Proclamation has been interpreted as one key source for the fiduciary nature of the constitutional relationship between the Crown and Indigenous peoples.[53] It is also a source for the resulting principle of the honour of the Crown, which the Supreme Court of Canada describes this way in the landmark *Haida Nation* case:

> Put simply, Canada's Aboriginal peoples were here when Europeans came, and were never conquered. Many bands reconciled their claims with the sovereignty of the Crown through negotiated treaties. Others, notably in British Columbia, have yet to do so. The potential rights embedded in these claims are protected by s. 35 of the Constitution Act, 1982. The honour of the Crown requires that these rights be determined, recognized and respected. This, in turn, requires the Crown, acting honourably, to participate in processes of negotiation. While this process continues, the honour of the Crown may require it to consult and, where indicated, accommodate Aboriginal interests.[54]

[52] Royal Proclamation 1763 (UK), reprinted RSC 1985, App II, No 1.

[53] Two key cases explain the source and nature of the fiduciary relationship: *Guerin v R* [1984] 2 SCR 335 and *R v Sparrow* [1996] 3 SCR 101. The fiduciary relationship is rooted in the concept of Aboriginal title, which pre-exists the assertion of Crown sovereignty in Canada, and entails the requirement, outlined above, that Aboriginal interests in land may be alienated only by surrendering the land to the Crown so as to prevent exploitation from third parties such as settlers.

[54] *Haida Nation v British Columbia (Minister of Forests)* [2004] 3 SCR 511, [25].

These promises, and the subsequent understanding of the Crown-Aboriginal fiduciary relationship, informs section 35(1) of the Constitution Act 1982, the provision which constitutionally guarantees Aboriginal rights.[55]

The duty to consult and accommodate acts as a sub-principle of the principle of the honour of the Crown. It can arise in four contexts: historical treaties, comprehensive modern land claims agreements, proved Aboriginal rights and title, and unproved Aboriginal rights and title. The duty rests on both federal and provincial governments and their agents, representatives and/or delegated authorities.[56] The duty will therefore also engage decisions made by administrative actors and tribunals.[57] The duty primarily regulates the relations among Indigenous peoples, the executive branch and the courts.

My main interest is with the most vulnerable area: unproved rights and interests. Though not fully grounded in the fiduciary nature of the principle of the honour of the Crown—because the interests and rights have not yet been recognised (unlike section 35 rights)—the duty nevertheless entails that government action which negatively affects an unproved Indigenous right and deprives the community of their benefits, real or potential, will be found inconsistent with this principle and will require protection from the courts. Otherwise, the integrity of the constitutional order would be at risk because the judiciary would be permitting the Crown to run roughshod over potentially weighty, but unproved, minority rights, and the judiciary's legitimacy, in turn, would be imperilled. Recognised Indigenous rights possess independent force or presumptive weight that ought to be given priority in government decision-making implicating broad policy or economic considerations, and the need to balance these with other competing rights and interest.[58] Unrecognised rights and interests do not carry this same weight, but may become recognised and hence are vulnerable in the transition stages to full recognition. Importantly then, *Haida Nation* provides a framework for preventing the abuse of claimed Indigenous rights in the early stages before they achieve full status in Canadian law.

These types of Indigenous rights cases often involve profound uncertainty about the nature of the right. Moreover, the implementation process for fulfilling the duty is complex due to multiple stakeholders in the affected community and many non-legal variables, including economic, political, cultural and social factors. The judicial approach to Crown-Aboriginal relations that the *Haida Nation* framework represents also relieves the judiciary from a variety of remedial dilemmas, including

[55] Constitution Act 1982, s 35(1) reads: 'The existing aboriginal and treaty rights of the aboriginal peoples of Canada are hereby recognized and affirmed'. The provision has been interpreted to mean that existing Aboriginal rights ought not to be diminished due to the effects of colonisation.

[56] The Crown can delegate some procedural aspects to private actors such as industry partners, and they must properly perform that delegated power: *Haida Nation* (n 54) [53].

[57] Tribunals empowered to consider questions of law and whose decisions affect potential Aboriginal interests and rights must also satisfy the duty. See *Rio Tinto Alcan Inc v Carrier Sekani Tribal Council* 2010 SCC 43.

[58] Where an existing constitutionally-protected Aboriginal right is affected, the Crown must grant it priority both in the process used to allocate resources and in the actual resulting allocation. See *R v Gladstone* [1996] 2 SCR 723.

imposing interlocutory injunctions on government or private action, and also forestall ongoing supervision by the courts. In many respects, the substantive remedial tail waived the procedural rights dog in the original case and this problem—how far should courts go to protect Indigenous rights?—plagues the case law. This result confirms the two problems that Lawrence Solum suggests procedural justice must face: (1) to provide accurate outcomes at a reasonable cost; and (2) to address the deeper problem of working out shared goals when a consensus about these goals may not exist.[59]

B. Framework for the Duty to Consult and Accommodate

Similar to common law procedural fairness, the duty to consult and accommodate in Aboriginal administrative law works with a higher-order, decisional framework—but it is much more complicated than the *Baker* framework and even further instantiates process and substance. The legal framework that crystallised in the *Haida Nation* case has two functions. First, it aims to guide negotiations between Indigenous and non-Indigenous governments when established Indigenous rights and interests are affected by non-Indigenous decision-makers at both the federal and provincial levels of government. Secondly, it aims to prevent the abuse of Indigenous rights and interests in the stages *before* they obtain full legal recognition.

The framework for the duty to consult and accommodate contains two parts: (1) consultation, which is largely, though not wholly, procedural in nature; and (2) accommodation, which is mainly substantive, but is also procedural. The procedural components of the duty to consult mirror those commonly found in the duty of fairness in administrative law but, because of the constitutional nature of the Indigenous right or interest, the content of the norm does differ and, unlike common law procedural fairness, involves specific reciprocal duties on both the Crown and Indigenous peoples.

The *Haida Nation* framework is premised on an ideal model of stages and steps that a government should follow if it wishes to fulfil the duty satisfactorily. Four stages are contemplated, each with its own set of steps that need to be implemented: (1) Stage 1 examines the Crown's real or constructive knowledge; (2) Stage 2 involves a spectrum approach to determining the scope of the duty that rests on the Crown; (3) Stage 3 determines if consultation obligations have been met or are required; (4) Stage 4 considers whether or not accommodation is required and, if it is, what is its content. Each stage is accompanied by the standard of review a court will use to examine the decision when it is challenged at that particular time in the framework. Table 10.1 sets out the framework.

[59] Solum, 'Procedural Justice' (n 5) 320.

Table 10.1: Framework for the duty to consult and accommodate

	Stage 0	Stage 1	Stage 2	Stage 3	Stage 4
Steps	Crown engages in high-level strategic decision-making in various policy areas.	Crown has knowledge (real or constructive) of a potential Aboriginal right or title.	Crown determines scope of duty by engaging in a 'spectrum' analysis.	Crown consults with affected parties (consultation need only be *adequate*).	Accommodation (*may* be required).
Sub-steps		Step 1 of Stage 1 'The trigger' of Crown knowledge. Step 2 of Stage 1 Crown decides to act. Step 3 of Stage 1 Crown knows of potential adverse effect from its decision to act.	Crown engages in the *first mini-proportionality analysis* by balancing the strength of the Aboriginal claim with other variables such as the potential impact on the right/interest and/or public interest. If the claim is strong, then deep consultation and maximum responsiveness is required; the opposite, if not.	Crown needs to identify relevant parties.	Crown balances competing interests in a *second mini-proportionality analysis* and must demonstrate that Aboriginal interests were considered usually through the provision of reasons. Stage 4 may require modification of decision or policy to minimise impact on Aboriginal peoples.
Standard of review	No review of Crown discretion at this stage.	*Reasonableness*	*Correctness* for strength of claim and severity of impact. Unless decision involves a large degree of factual determination, then *reasonableness*.	*Reasonableness/fairness* regarding adequacy of process of consultation.	*Reasonableness or correctness* regarding adequacy of accommodation required. *Reasonableness* regarding outcomes and balancing of interests.

Ideally, the duty to consult and accommodate permits courts to oversee the executive branch to check the wide-ranging power of the Crown, chiefly by eliminating broad or unstructured discretion.[60] A reviewing court will accord a margin of appreciation to the process used and the policy choices made by the Crown in either of the two proportionality analyses indicated in Table 10.1. A reviewing court will ask whether or not consultation was reasonably adequate given the circumstances. In order to answer this question, the reviewing court will need to look at whether the process used was meaningful in proportion to the seriousness of the harm. It should also examine whether the Crown's practice of informing itself and consulting affected parties was in good faith. Lastly, the reviewing court considers whether or not a reasonable balance was struck between Indigenous and other interests/values in its final decision, including whether or not the outcome is reasonably accommodating of the prioritised Indigenous interests. The standard of review 'toggles' according to the particular stage, with case law confirming that correctness is the norm for the question of law concerning the strength of the claim but with reasonableness as the preferred standard for other components of the duty. Notably, as Table 10.1 indicates, reasonableness and fairness are often fused when scrutiny turns to the adequacy of the consultation process indicating a tangled movement towards substantive procedural fairness in this jurisprudence.

In this area of public law, the duty to consult and accommodate completely fuses process and substance. Process, however, routinely works to undermine substance because of judges' desire to avoid the underlying issues of emergent Indigenous sovereignty, development of self-government as a more complex form of Canadian federalism, and demands for a post-colonial relationship. Though never fully addressed in consultation cases—indeed, the conundrum of sovereignty is often submerged even in Aboriginal title cases—the duty must manage conflicts arising from the existence of multiple communities whose claims contradict the unilateral assertion of Crown sovereignty originally made by the British sovereign. In this area, then, the two major 'stressors' are relations between sovereigns and polycentricity.

The duty, however, is plagued by key structural weaknesses, including the burden of knowledge on under-resourced Indigenous groups to specify alleged infringements as well as potential harms; the problem of inadequate notice to affected Indigenous communities; the presence of too much Crown discretion; judicial deference; and inadequate accommodation. The weakness that I want to focus on is accommodation since accommodation is the final stage of a process (consultation), but is also a substantive end in itself and therefore fuses the distinction.

C. How the Two Stressors Create a Sub-optimal Fusion of Process and Substance

At judicial review, *Haida Nation* advises judges to focus '*not on the outcome*, but on the process of consultation and accommodation'.[61] These instructions, at odds

[60] The Crown's fiduciary obligation facilitates judicial 'supervision of the high degree of discretionary control gradually assumed by the Crown over the lives of aboriginal peoples': *Wewaykum Indian Band v Canada* [2002] 4 SCR 245, [79].

[61] *Haida Nation* (n 54) [63] (emphasis added).

with how the standard of review works in administrative law in general, seem to indicate strongly that those procedural violations, rather than unreasonable outcomes, will first trigger a remedy. Conventional administrative law remedies, such as remitting an unsatisfactory consultative case back to the original decision-maker to engage in further consultation (process), or to reconsider some of the factors that led to the original unreasonable decision (substance), often leave a vacuum given the breadth of Crown discretion, potential for unilateral arbitrary behaviour, or lack of capacity. Conventional remedies regularly result in the under-enforcement of Indigenous rights through the duty to consult and accommodate. The two major stressors—relations between sovereigns and polycentricity—account for both legal complexity and sub-optimal enforcement.

We can see that the envisaged process demands that government decision-makers make efforts to understand the interests that are asserted by Indigenous claimants and to assess the potential harms that Indigenous communities perceive government action might cause. This awareness, however, does not always translate into substantial accommodation, whereby action is barred or policy is markedly modified.[62] What kinds of actions will be inconsistent with the Crown's duty? Again, it is up to the decision-maker to determine as a matter of discretionary judgement the intensity of the effects of infringement, resulting in both a skewed process and a potentially arbitrary outcome. The process selected by the government decision-maker could fail and thereby never attend to the need for accommodation because it did not allow for the kind of knowledge that is essential for the assessment of the impact and harm. The decisional framework of the duty seemingly aims to correct for this possibility, but anxieties about substance often mean that this potential is not realised.

André Nollkaemper argues that the procedures employed to guide and shape substantive law themselves reflect normative choices and our assessment of these choices depends on 'whom we want to entrust with making them'.[63] Aboriginal administrative law illustrates a collective action problem when public values, which require recognition and enforcement, are weakened. These values are 'public goods' requiring protection in the name of individual cases and the larger public interest. If government decision-makers do not consult properly, they will inevitably fail to accommodate properly, and the process/substance connection will function sub-optimally. Nollkaemper further writes that: 'Procedures, and the voices that can be heard through procedure, are part of the process for identifying what a public good is, how to interpret it and how to strike balances when it comes to conflict with other public goods'.[64] We need to know if those claimants who are making use of legal procedures and framing legal arguments see their own understanding of values and public goods reflected back in administrative and judicial decisions. The substantive political issues of recognition and representation and the corresponding existential problems of Indigenous loyalty, voice and exit anxiously percolate throughout these cases.

[62] For an illustration of judicial conflict about substantive accommodation, see *West Moberly First Nations v British Columbia (Chief Inspector of Mines)* 2011 BCCA 247, [163]–[165]. In this decision, the reviewing court folded substantive accommodation back into a future consultative process.

[63] Nollkaemper, 'International Adjudication of Global Public Goods' (n 4) 772.

[64] ibid 781.

The process/substance problem is further exacerbated when multiple parties and decision-makers are involved—as is often the case in this polycentric area where a case may involve several Aboriginal groups, more than one government decision-maker, industry third parties and/or interest groups. Nollkaemper, citing examples from international law, calls the kinds of complex public goods prevalent in these cases 'aggregate-effort' goods and includes cases involving climate change and nuclear weapons as examples.[65] The uncertainty posed by the unproved rights and interests, combined with the polycentric nature of the cases, invites a high degree of deference from reviewing courts. Indeed, these cases appear at the 'legislative end' of the spectrum of decisions that a reviewing court may or may not review. Though this chapter does not consider claims that common law procedural fairness should be extended to address citizens' demands for greater democratic participation in government or regulatory decision-making, it does, however, suggest that Indigenous participatory rights should be increased to overcome the prohibition against interfering in policy-oriented or 'legislative' decisions.[66]

Courts are increasingly grappling with these aggregate and competing public goods and disagreement exists over the question of which substantive values procedural rules should serve. Courts may also not be fully attentive to, or not wish to address, the balance of power. Procedural fairness and lack of substantive equality between the parties may pull the judge in different directions. As Thomas Main argues, procedures are 'an instrument of power that can, in a very practical sense, generate or undermine substantive rights'.[67] A paradox emerges whereby a court may seek to preserve 'the value of an intermediate good [which] may undermine its contribution to the final public good'.[68] The intermediate good that the courts are protecting is the legitimacy of judicial review. Courts are of course a good worth protecting, but their approach to the duty to consult and accommodate undermines a final public good, such as the protection of Aboriginal rights (from the perspective of Indigenous peoples) and reconciliation (from the perspective of the larger Canadian public interest which also includes Indigenous peoples). No easy solution exists for this problem, but the application of the current framework prevents examination of the implicit choices judges make in order to skirt the 'big questions'.[69] I suspect that if Canadian jurisprudence acknowledged the presence of substantive fairness and substantive legitimate expectations in procedural fairness, then the fairness of

[65] ibid 778.

[66] The possibilities for cross-fertilisation, however, are strong. For an argument that the common law may legitimately extend participatory rights, see G Cartier, 'Procedural Fairness in Legislative Functions: The End of Judicial Abstinence?' (2003) 53 *University of Toronto Law Journal* 217.

[67] TO Main, 'The Procedural Foundation of Substantive Law' (2010) 87 *Washington University Law Review* 801, 802.

[68] Nollkaemper, 'International Adjudication of Global Public Goods' (n 4) 783.

[69] Jenny Martinez reconsiders process and substance in the US 'War on Terror' decisions, examining five procedural strategies judges use to avoid substance: (1) procedure as avoidance; (2) process as merely signalling substantive issues; (3) process as substance; (4) substance as disguised process; and (5) process as housekeeping where values like accuracy and efficiency drive the decisions. All of these strategies are evident in the Canadian jurisprudence on the duty to consult and accommodate. See JS Martinez, 'Process and Substance in the "War on Terror"' (2008) 108 *Columbia Law Review* 1013.

consultative procedures and accommodations might be made more transparent and rigorous.[70]

Looking at the duty to consult and accommodate from the perspective of process and substance in procedural fairness discussed in section III, the differing roles accorded to legitimate expectations is manifest. If we understand a legitimate expectation simply as an expectation that deserves judicial protection based on a government promise, representation or practice then it initially seems akin to but less onerous than the fiduciary duty that underpins state-Aboriginal legal relations. But jurisprudence from England (and Wales) suggests that substantive legitimate expectations can play as weighty a role as the fiduciary duty does in Aboriginal administrative law. In the leading English case on substantive fairness, *Coughlan*,[71] the Court of Appeal explained the different forms of protection available for expectations: (1) the government must give appropriate weight to the previous policy or other representation and, if it does, the courts will review on a highly deferential standard; (2) if the promise or practice induces a legitimate expectation of, eg being consulted, courts will then require that outcome unless there is an overriding reason to deny it; and (3) if a legitimate expectation is established, and the benefit is substantive rather than procedural, a reviewing court will weigh whether frustrating the expectation is so unfair as to amount to an abuse of power.[72] In *Coughlan*, the promise to Mrs Coughlan of a home for life was very important and the financial consequences of holding the authority to account were minimal, so the court decided in her favour.

In more recent cases, however, the English courts have moved away from this categorised approach toward one where proportionality is the appropriate test, subject to deference since substantive unfairness is a ground that does not generally justify judicial review. Once an applicant establishes the legitimacy of the expectation, the relevant authority must identify any overriding interest on which it relies to justify frustration of the expectation. The courts will then step in to weigh the requirements of fairness against the overriding interest(s) and demand objective justification that the measures used were proportionate in the circumstances.[73] Deference will be shown when the authority proves, through evidence and/or reasons, that its refusal or failure to honour the expectation was justified in the public interest and that it had carefully considered both the substance of the issue and fairness concerns as

[70] Lorne Sossin discusses judicial tactics similar to those identified by Martinez, tactics he terms 'prudential proceduralism'. He also considers creatively designed procedures, such as the frameworks discussed in this chapter, where courts manage substantive issues through procedural means. See L Sossin, 'The McLachlin Court and the Promise of Procedural Justice' in DA Wright and AM Dodek (eds), *Public Law at the McLachlin Court: The First Decade* (Toronto, Irwin Law, 2011) 58.

[71] *R v North and East Devon Health Authority, ex parte Coughlan* [2001] QB 231 (CA).

[72] See Endicott, *Administrative Law* (n 51) 289–95.

[73] For a recent statement of the test for substantive legitimate expectations, see the Privy Council decision *Paponette v Attorney General of Trinidad and Tobago* [2010] UKPC 32, [49]. For a discussion of proportionality, reasons and legitimate expectations as a highly relevant factor, see Lord Dyson's decision at [36]–[42]. This is consistent with earlier cases such as *R v Department of Education and Employment, ex parte Begbie* [2000] 1 WLR 1115 and *R (Abdi and Nadarajah) v Home Secretary* [2005] EWCA Civ 1363, both cases where expectations received no protection.

highly relevant factors in its decision-making process. Proportionality, again, is key and provides the mechanism to link, join or fuse process and substance.

Canadian judicial direction to focus on process at the expense of outcome is at odds with contemporary constitutional and administrative law. The Canadian Charter of Rights and Freedoms, section 1[74] balancing exercise employed under the *Oakes* test, for example, explicitly incorporates into the analysis the outcome under step 2. The framework for the *Oakes* test has two steps, the second with three sub-steps: (1) there must be a pressing and substantial objective; (2) the means to achieve it must be proportional; (2a) the means must be rationally connected to the objective; (2b) there must be minimal impairment of rights; and (2c) there must be proportionality between the infringement and objective.[75] Moreover, it shifts the burden to the government to justify the consequences so that they are consistent with both upholding constitutional rights and permitting their limitation when such limits further legitimate democratic goals. Similarly, under reasonableness review in administrative law, as well as under the new *Doré*[76] framework for assessing discretionary decisions that implicate Charter values (discussed further below), the court may invalidate a decision on the basis of the *unreasonableness of the outcome*, as well as the process of articulating the reasons supporting the outcome. Procedural rules implement substantive law to produce quality outcomes as measured by norms embedded in substantive law and the decision-maker's own reasons.[77] But, in the duty to consult, we see that process undermines substantive legality, legitimacy and the recognition of potential rights.

If we hold institutional comity in mind, it is not a breach of that doctrine to hold an authority to account for decisions and choices to which it has committed itself, unless it provides reasons indicating legitimate grounds to support a change of mind. Following Timothy Endicott, then, a continuum of different kinds of expectations might exist attracting greater or lesser substantive content. Legitimate expectations could range from the largely minimal, as in current procedural fairness, to the more maximal, as in current Aboriginal administrative law.[78] In either case, this component fuses process and substance to explicitly acknowledge the role of substantive fairness. Duty to consult cases that involve unproved interests and rights raise real concerns about abuses of power. If we agree with Timothy Endicott that '[i]t can be procedurally unfair to disappoint an expectation without a hearing, and it can be substantively unfair to disappoint an expectation. And then the decision is unlawful if it is procedurally unfair, or it is so unfair in substance that it is an abuse of power',[79] then the duty to consult and accommodate and procedural fairness share a

[74] Section 1 reads: 'The *Canadian Charter of Rights and Freedoms* guarantees the rights and freedoms set out in it subject only to such reasonable limits prescribed by law as can be demonstrably justified in a free and democratic society'. See Canadian Charter of Rights and Freedoms, Part I of the Constitution Act 1982, being Schedule B to the Canada Act 1982 (UK).

[75] *R v Oakes* [1986] 1 SCR 103.

[76] *Doré v Barreau du Québec* 2012 SCC 12, 1 SCR 395.

[77] Nollkaemper, 'International Adjudication of Global Public Goods' (n 4) 779.

[78] For a provocative philosophical argument that the state should be considered a fiduciary of its entire political community, see Fox-Decent, *Sovereignty's Promise* (n 36).

[79] Endicott, *Administrative Law* (n 51) 295.

similar problem wrought by the process/substance distinction: further jurisprudential development of substantive (un)fairness, better reason-giving and explicit proportionality analyses within their respective decisional frameworks. Greater attention to outcomes may result in the minimisation of infringements on unproved but strong Aboriginal rights; the lessening of impact of activity on Indigenous land so that it does not disrupt Indigenous use and occupation (especially given the requirement of prioritisation); and go some distance to accommodating Indigenous peoples' preferred mode of exercising their rights as part of self-governance.

V. CONSUBSTANTIATING PROCESS AND SUBSTANCE: REVIEW OF DISCRETIONARY DECISIONS AS THE THIRD FAULT-LINE

The analogous legal frameworks employed in administrative and constitutional law have developed (or are developing) proportionality analyses that protect fundamental rights and values, permit justified limitations through the provision of adequate reasons, and exhibit deference where appropriate. These frameworks permit reviewing courts to assess the legitimacy of the substance and the outcomes which limit or harm important rights and values. Section III showed how analysis is bifurcated in procedural fairness since the presence of reasons is a question for procedure while the adequacy of reasons is a question for substantive review. Section IV illustrated how the duty to consult and accommodate shares these features, but does not always succeeded in justifying the limitations or fully attend to the consequential harmful effects of the decision, despite employing two mini-proportionality analyses and insisting that the decision-maker correctly assess the strength of the claim and the severity of the impact (potentially, but only if outcomes are considered).

In the 2012 Supreme Court of Canada decision, *Doré*, the Supreme Court overturned the past methodological approach that was used in previous jurisprudence to review discretionary decisions involving Charter interests and values. The Supreme Court confirmed that the old orthodox approach used to review whether or not a law justifiably infringes a right or freedom—the *Oakes* test—should not replace administrative law review of discretionary decisions. *Doré* affirmed that an administrative decision-maker must not disproportionately and unreasonably limit a Charter right or value when exercising a statutory discretion.

A. Framework for the Standard of Review Involving Discretionary Decisions

In exercising discretion, the decision-maker should first identify the relevant statutory objectives as well as the values pertinent to that statutory context.[80] Once identified, the decision-maker then engages in a balancing exercise that involves weighing the relevant statutory objectives and the Charter values. The decision-maker needs to consider how Charter values will best be protected in light of the statutory scheme. This involves engaging in a proportionality analysis that balances the severity of the

[80] *Doré* (n 76) [55].

interference (if any) with the importance of the statutory objectives.[81] The decisional framework used by courts to review the resulting decision on substantive grounds (the standard of review framework) contains four factors:

(1) Look to past jurisprudence to see how the particular category of question was addressed—*if satisfactorily*—regarding level of deference owed.[82]
(2) If not satisfactory, contextually analyse using the modern purposive approach to statutory interpretation involving four factors:
    (a) the presence or absence of a privative clause;
    (b) the purpose of the tribunal as determined by interpretation of enabling legislation;
    (c) the nature of the question at issue;
    (d) the expertise of the tribunal.[83]

A reviewing court will exhibit deference to a decision-maker's decision that is the result of this balancing exercise.[84] The appropriate standard of review for discretionary decisions that implicate Charter values is reasonableness contextually applied.[85] Since the *Dunsmuir*[86] case, and with a recent fundamental qualification, reasonableness has so far been confirmed as the presumptive standard for reviewing administrative decisions in administrative law when: (1) a specialised or expert tribunal; (2) interpreting its enabling or home statute; (3) on a question of fact or mixed fact and law; (4) or having the jurisdiction to consider questions of law; (5) or exercising broad statutory discretion; (6) correctly applies all legal principles or tests; (7) to construct an interpretation of its statutory powers that falls within the range of possible acceptable interpretations; (8) resulting in a decision that demonstrates justification, transparency and intelligibility; (9) and produces a reasonable outcome which is defensible in respect of the facts and law. Should the tribunal satisfy all of these conditions, the reviewing court must find the decision reasonable. So far, correctness review has been relegated to the margins, but not ruled out.[87] Following *Dunsmuir*, the proportionality test will be satisfied if the measure falls within a range of possible, acceptable outcomes and is explained by reasons exhibiting justification, transparency and intelligibility. The principle of deference informs this exercise, as a reviewing court must recognise that, when the nature of the decision is

[81] ibid [57].

[82] Note that the case law has not yet sorted out how and when precedent will control.

[83] Note that a privative clause and agency expertise generally receive enough weight to attract the deferential reasonableness standard either alone or in concert, whereas a question of law should only attract a correctness standard if it is a question of general law outside of specialised areas of expertise and of central importance to the legal system as a whole.

[84] *Doré* (n 76) [57]. Reasonableness review is not 'a single, rigid Procrustean standard of decontextualized review' but, rather, encompasses a range of degrees of deference based on the circumstances of the case. See *Canada (Citizenship and Immigration) v Khosa* 2009 SCC 12, 1 SCR 339, [59].

[85] ibid [56].

[86] *Dunsmuir v New Brunswick* 2008 SCC 9, [2008] 1 SCR 190, [47].

[87] See JM Evans, 'Triumph of Reasonableness: But How Much Does It Really Matter?' (2014) 27 *Canadian Journal of Administrative Law and Practice* 101.

discretionary, polycentric and involves balancing competing considerations, micro-managing by courts should be eschewed.[88]

Entrenched fundamental values are recognised as having deontological weight, but it is permissible to limit these values if the limitation is proportionate, accompanied by a legally structured justification, and the harmful effects minimal. In Canadian constitutional law, this methodology is embedded in the *Oakes* test that pragmatically combines deontological and consequentialist considerations. We have seen part of this common law methodology in both procedural review and the duty to consult and accommodate. Recent administrative law cases therefore indicate that the post-Charter cross-fertilisation of Canadian administrative and constitutional law continues.[89] But, as Dyzenhaus and Fox-Decent claim:

> To generalize that methodology in the common law of judicial review is undeniably to reform administrative law. Elements that were part of administrative law, but not central to it, move to centre stage. Talk of unfettered discretion and jurisdictional talk become gradually obsolete as they are replaced by talk of structures of justification. No hard and fast distinction between process and substance is available, as recognition grows of the inevitable substantive implications of process as well as of the fact that the justification for having process at all is in some sense substantive.[90]

As discussed above, the movement of reasons into substantive review confirms this view because reasons have now taken centre stage in Canadian administrative law.

B. Comparing Current Frameworks for Process and Substance

But the modern reform of Canadian administrative law clearly needs to continue. To that end, I want to engage in a synthetic thought experiment using the framework from procedural fairness and that from substantive review, at the same time keeping in mind the fault-line around substantive fairness that the duty to consult and accommodate discloses. Table 10.2 compares the two frameworks used in reviewing procedures and substance.[91]

[88] *Doré* (n 76) [51].

[89] See E Fox-Decent, 'The Charter and Administrative Law: Cross-Fertilization or Inconstancy' in C Flood and L Sossin (eds), *Administrative Law in Context: A New Casebook*, 2nd edn (Toronto, Emond-Montgomery, 2013).

[90] Dyzenhaus and Fox-Decent, 'Rethinking the Process/Substance Distinction' (n 13) 238.

[91] In Table 10.2, italics indicate a factor unique to that particular framework. Underline indicates guidance from the jurisprudence but which is not formally part of the framework.

Table 10.2: Comparison of the Baker framework with the framework used in substantive review

What is similar and what is not	Baker five-factor framework for determining the level of procedural fairness	Standard of review decisional framework (formerly pragmatic and functional analysis)
Overlap	Nature of the decision (and the process followed). May involve interpretation or discretion regarding procedures.	Nature of the question: law, fact, mixed fact and law, or discretion.
Unique	—	*Privative clause.*
Overlap	Nature of the statutory scheme and the terms of review. Weight of home statute.	Language/purpose of the provision and within the Act as a whole. Weight of home statute.
Overlap (when dicta included)	Importance of the decision to the individual(s) affected.	*Decisions must reflect the 'fundamental importance' of Charter values.*
Unique	*Legitimate expectations of the person(s) challenging the decision.*	—
Overlap	Respect agency expertise in determining and following own procedures particularly with respect to its home statute.	Expertise of the tribunal particularly with respect to its home statute.
Role of reasons	May be required by the common law.	Reasons must demonstrate justification, transparency and intelligibility.
Consequentialism	Defensible outcome in respect of facts and law.	Reasonable outcome in respect of facts and law.

When placed side-by-side like this, the overlap is striking. The nature of question, the statutory scheme, the weight of fundamental values along with the concurrent demand for proportionality, the requirements of deference in the acknowledgement of expertise, and the role of reasons in terms of justifying the outcome are all shared between the two frameworks. The key differences are: the role given to a privative clause as a different ground for deference in substantive review; legitimate expectations as a separate factor in procedural fairness; and the bifurcation of reasons between procedure (providing reasons) and substance (examining reasons for reasonableness and rationality in the decision under review). As discussed above, Canadian administrative law currently burbles with tensions and overlaps between process and substance and this juxtaposition of the two frameworks underscores a vital question: Does the distinction between process and substance in administrative law have any continued salience given that the two frameworks used in judicial review markedly overlap and could potentially be combined? Furthermore, what might the implications be for Charter review and the *Oakes* test? Could one simple overarching test in public law be constructed that takes into account rights, legislative intent and the principles of deference, legality and proportionality?

C. Hypothesising One Universal, Overarching Framework for Public Law

If, as I have suggested above, Canadian law embraced substantive fairness, acknowledged more transparently the need to identify and specify the content of fundamental values explicitly in proportionality analyses, and conceded that reasons consubstantiate substance and process, we might re-imagine a court reviewing process and substance using a unified framework.[92] This framework and its animating questions might look like the 'macro review' framework set out in Table 10.3.[93]

Table 10.3: Over-arching framework when distinction is removed

Question asked	Framework element
What is being challenged?	Nature of the decision and/or the process followed.
What guidance does the statute provide?	Nature of the statutory scheme, terms of review and purpose of the provision. Note that the framework subsumes the private clause into the statutory scheme but gives it heavy weight instead.
What are the animating principles and values in the home statute as well as those identified by the person who is challenging the decision?	Identify the fundamental values implicated in the case as a whole.
How much deference is owed?	Respect agency expertise in procedures and in interpretation of the law under the home statute.
Are the reasons adequate?	Demonstrate justification, transparency and intelligibility appropriate to the context.
Is the outcome reasonable?	Outcome/effects of limit are proportionate.

My intent here, however, is not prescriptive. Major renovation of the current frameworks used for procedural fairness and substantive review seems highly unlikely in Canadian public law right now. The point is that if courts acknowledged the process/substance connection—rather than merely distinction—the decisional framework used for judicial review in administrative law might be simplified by being shared between the two domains. Weighting factors would move into the spotlight, fairness would be assessed substantively and contextually, attention to outcomes would be more robust, and courts could finally explicitly recognise that agency expertise includes interpretation and not just procedure. Deference would be grounded in these considerations combined with a transparent examination of the values brought to the case from the statute, the common law and the parties. Reasons

[92] It is difficult to fit the complex framework developed under the duty to consult and accommodate into these simpler frameworks. This begs two questions: (1) should the duty to consult and accommodate framework be simplified?; or (2) should the other frameworks be complexified?

[93] I thank Jason Varuhas for suggesting this characterisation of the proffered framework.

would identify harms and would explain the rationale for upholding, expanding or denying individual rights and the exercise of government power. In this manner, the principle of deference could therefore embody the connection between procedural and substantive norms and, in turn, structure the scope of judicial review.

In short, acknowledgement of the process/substance connection would affect the Canadian model of judicial review. It would ground deference differently and move it closer to the 'deference as respect' ideal where administrative decision-makers are recognised as expert partners, though not co-equals, in coordinate construction of the constitutional order.[94]

VI. CONCLUSION: RITES OF TRANSUBSTANTIATING PROCESS AND SUBSTANCE

The previous section concluded that process and substance are connected—indeed, even transubstantiated in administrative law—but my argument also concedes that the terms continue to serve functional and descriptive purposes in practice. The reality of many features of the law is not just the co-existence of these attributes, but their necessary and reciprocal intermingling. Acknowledging the reality of the connection should lead not just to the creation of higher-order decisional frameworks but also to the better and more transparent application of these frameworks. In other words, the focus is on better and best practices. Accepting the existence of substantive fairness in the doctrine of legitimate expectations would be one example of a better practice within a best practice framework. As both Geneviève Cartier and David Mullan contend, ridding ourselves of pernicious and formalistic effects of the process/substance distinction in administrative law permits the 'real questions' to be asked and demands that public officials and judges provide 'real answers' in their decisions.[95]

This conclusion is also based a consideration of the importance of fundamental values whose content and reach are being currently worked out in Canadian public law. These fault-lines have had beneficial effect. They suggest that the Canadian practice of judicial review now rests on substantive ideals or values and that judges use these substantive criteria as guidance and for justification. These values include democracy, dignity, equality, autonomy and human rights.[96] Or, as L'Heureux-Dubé J

[94] Similarly, Craig, 'The Nature of Reasonableness Review' (n 43) 163 when writing about proportionality and reasonableness review states: 'Suffice it to say for the present that a condition precedent to reasoned deliberation as to how the balancing should be conducted is open and honest recognition that it is being undertaken'.

[95] G Cartier, 'The Doctrine of Legitimate Expectations' in G Huscroft and M Taggart (eds), *Inside and Outside Canadian Administrative Law* (Toronto, University of Toronto Press, 2006) 186–87. She is citing the seminal article by David Mullan, 'Fairness: The New Natural Justice?' (1975) *University of Toronto Law Journal* 281.

[96] Dawn Oliver identifies five overarching systemic values: autonomy, dignity, respect, status and security: see D Oliver, 'The Underlying Values of Public and Private Law' in M Taggart (ed), *The Province of Administrative Law* (Oxford, Hart Publishing, 1997). Paul Daly identifies four 'core' values, namely, the rule of law, good administration, democracy and the separation of powers: see Paul Daly, Chapter 3, 'Administrative Law: A Values-Based Approach'.

writes in the *Baker* decision: 'discretionary decisions will generally be given considerable respect ... discretion must be exercised in accordance with the boundaries imposed in the statute, the principles of the rule of law, the principles of administrative law, the fundamental values of Canadian society, and the principles of the Charter'.[97]

A political community committed to both democracy and legality will provide multiple routes for those affected by public power to demand fairness, to have input into the decision-making process, and to have quality reasons for those decisions. These considerations constrain public power under the rule of law, but they also enable members to participate as members of a democracy, as rights holders, and as claims-makers. The reasons requirement furthers accountability, but it also provides the bases for public justification and judicial deference to administrative decisions. Of the three areas canvassed, Aboriginal administrative law shows the potential for greater democratic content, despite its current flaws. The procedural nature of the duty to consult and accommodate for Aboriginal communities as emerging constitutional partners means that democratic participatory rights are heightened and the decision-maker may be required to change her mind in order to avoid substantive unfairness. This duty stands as a touchstone for emerging substantive content on consultation, participation and accommodation in other areas of public law.

These ideals, however, place enormous stress on both the traditional 'Diceyan' and quintessential American model of judicial review. The stress is mitigated, but not removed, by the provision of reasons. Reasons place a burden and an advantage: the burden rests on the decision-maker to justify their decision according to fundamental values, but the advantage shifts in judicial review because judges must look to the justification given for the outcome, not just the outcome itself. In administrative law, this means that correctness review is presumptively foreclosed and, when the judge disagrees with both the reasoning and the outcome, she must herself engage with the decision and provide her own justification for a different result. Moreover, there are many ways for other branches to respond to judicial decisions in administrative law. This creates a more responsive, transparent and accountable relationship between the judiciary and other institutional actors, an ideal that in Canada is called 'institutional dialogue'.[98] Just as importantly, an institutional dialogue which permits a fruitful connection between process and substance can also buttress and generate 'dialogue rights' and relations among individuals, groups and decision-makers that go beyond the content of more conventional duties and rights.[99]

Both democracy and the rule of law justify the creation of institutional mechanisms for citizens and affected persons to prevent or challenge the abuse of power by public officials. As we have seen, the rule of law supports the creation of procedures that treat individuals fairly when their rights, interests and privileges are

[97] *Baker* (n 37) [56].

[98] For an overview of the various models of institutional dialogue, including Canada's, see S Gardbaum, 'Reassessing the New Commonwealth Model of Constitutionalism' (2010) 8 *International Journal of Constitutional Law* 167.

[99] See PP Craig, 'Process and Substance in Judicial Review' in G Huscroft and M Taggart (eds), *Inside and Outside Canadian Administrative Law* (Toronto, University of Toronto Press, 2006) 176.

affected in public decision-making. The rule of law also supports judicial review of administrative decisions on their merits and greater access to the courts through the expansion of standing and intervener status. The hope here is that judicial deliberation will lead to better and more reasonable decision-making processes and policy outcomes. A participatory democracy will create conduits for direct participation in decision-making and greater accountability through both legal and public oversight. Deliberative practices such as reason-giving support the creation of open processes for public reasoning and debate and may lead to more justifiable public policies. At their best, these practices show how 'our shared sense of justice is compatible with a plurality of reasonable comprehensive doctrines' inherent in a liberal-democratic culture.[100] Contemporary governance therefore offers a range of institutional possibilities for public participation on democracy and rule of law grounds.[101] From my examination of recent developments in administrative law, I look to the larger democratic potential of public law to better realise the connection between procedural fairness and substantive public law values for all affected persons, citizens or not, in a liberal democracy.[102] As most modern political theorists contend, the modern state in pluralist conditions fundamentally depends on the working out of substantive values through institutional practices that contribute to procedural legitimacy in public institutions.[103]

The legal frameworks examined here should, and in some cases do, amount to practices of discourse that, when properly engaged, are reflexive in nature and compel claimants and decision-makers to become more transparent about their background suppositions concerning rights, goods and conceptions of justice. These frameworks disclose the reciprocal relationship between process and substance. I have argued that the relationship between process and substance contains the further promise of our ability to bootstrap the reciprocal relationship 'between government and citizen with respect to the observance of rules',[104] standards and now fundamental values in Canadian liberal-democracy.

[100] J Gledhill, 'Procedure in Substance and Substance in Procedure: Reframing the Rawls-Habermas Debate' in JG Finlayson and F Freyenhagen (eds), *Habermas and Rawls: Disputing the Political* (Routledge, New York, 2011).

[101] R Bellamy, 'The Republic of Reasons: Public Reasoning, Depoliticization, and Non-Domination' in S Besson and JL Martí (eds), *Legal Republicanism: National and International Perspectives* (New York, Oxford University Press, 2009).

[102] Rawls' theory would specify content. In contrast, Jürgen Habermas argues that a legal procedural morality is one where law 'has rid itself of all specific normative contents ... [and which have been] sublimated into a procedure for the justification of possible normative contents'. See J Habermas, 'Law and Morality' in *The Tanner Lectures on Human Values* (Kenneth Baynes (trans), 1986) 247, available at http://tannerlectures.utah.edu/_documents/a-to-z/h/habermas88.pdf.

[103] Habermas privileges democratic procedures, while Rawls' a priori constraining principles entail that courts play a vital role in creating guidelines for what counts as admissible reasons. Through practices of public reason, the hope is that we can reconcile ourselves to the unreconcilable: our social world and its multiplicity of incompatible or overlapping comprehensive doctrines. See J Rawls, *Political Liberalism* (New York, Columbia University Press, 1993) lviii.

[104] L Fuller, *The Morality of Law*, rev edn (New Haven, CT and London, Yale University Press, 1969) 39. See James Boyle on the unresolved tensions concerning form, process and substance in Fuller's work: 'Legal Realism and the Social Contract: Fuller's Public Jurisprudence of Form, Private Jurisprudence of Substance' (1993) 78 *Cornell Law Review* 371.

11

Is Judicial Review Qualitative?

ALAN ROBERTSON

I. INTRODUCTION

THE ARGUMENT IN this chapter is that in judicial review there is in practice no clear division between process and substance: in each the courts must and do make qualitative judgements in relation to the particular exercise of administrative power. This may be expected to increase owing to the 'increasingly sophisticated exposition of implied limitations on the extent or the exercise of statutory power'.[1] Properly understood, the qualitative judgements made in relation to process are no different from those made on so-called substantive review. I therefore question the usefulness of the analysis by reference to process or substance. The common question on judicial review does not depend on that divide but on whether something has gone wrong in a legal sense of such gravity that the decision-maker has not performed the (usually statutory) task given to them. Even where courts make qualitative judgements on judicial review, that is to be distinguished from merits review.

First, I explain the jurisdictional basis of the greatest number of *federal* judicial review cases in Australia. I then summarise 'jurisdictional error' in Australia, which remains a fundamental concept.[2] I also state shortly my understanding of what 'process' and 'substance' in public law mean. I next attempt to identify the 'merits' from which the courts are so often adjured to stay away. I then turn to the central part of the chapter, which is an examination of the extent to which judicial review is qualitative. I examine, in particular: natural justice/procedural fairness; relevant (mandatory) and irrelevant (prohibited) considerations; and legal unreasonableness in the exercise of an administrative discretionary power. I also look at cases where

[1] *Attorney-General for New South Wales v Quin* (1990) 170 CLR 1, 36 (Brennan J).

[2] Jurisdictional error may also be relevant to state judicial review. By virtue of *Kirk v Industrial Court (NSW)* [2010] HCA 1, (2010) 239 CLR 531, [55] (French CJ, Gummow, Hayne, Crennan, Kiefel and Bell JJ) it is not within the legislative competence of a state legislature to 'strip the Supreme Court of the State of its authority to confine inferior courts [and tribunals] within the limits of their jurisdiction by granting relief on the ground of jurisdictional error'. See also *South Australia v Totani* [2010] HCA 39, (2010) 242 CLR 1, [26] (French CJ), [128] (Gummow J), [193] (Hayne J), [268] (Heydon J), [415] (Crennan and Bell JJ); *Public Service Association of South Australia Inc v Industrial Relations Commission of South Australia* [2012] HCA 25, (2012) 249 CLR 398, [60] and *Wingfoot Australia Partners Pty Ltd v Kocak* [2013] HCA 43, (2013) 303 ALR 64, [26].

error of fact may found a conclusion of jurisdictional error. As will be seen, I link process and substance by reference to what courts do in examining what the person or body exercising administrative power has done in the particular case in order to demonstrate that the court on judicial review will often examine the quality of the exercise of the administrative power. I seek to show that judicial review of the exercise of administrative power on both process grounds and on so-called substantive grounds may each involve qualitative judgements by the court.

I refer to power rather than to decisions because administrative action is the exercise of power. This is not a new idea: in 1962 Professor Wade identified 'the great problem as we now see it: how far is power to be controlled by law?'[3]

I observe that in federations, perhaps especially in Australia, there is a long history of review of legislation for validity under the Constitution, where the courts stay away from the wisdom, or merits, of the legislation while characterising the law by reference to the rights and liabilities it creates, imposes or affects.

II. PERSPECTIVE

It may assist in understanding the international differences in judicial review of administrative power, and my perspective, if I begin by setting out what may be reviewable error under section 75(v) of the Australian Constitution, limiting my discussion to those errors which amount to 'jurisdictional error'. Most federal administrative law cases are brought, directly or indirectly, under this provision which states that 'In all matters … in which a writ of Mandamus or prohibition or an injunction is sought against an officer of the Commonwealth … the High Court shall have original jurisdiction'.

An authoritative statement is to be found in *Minister for Immigration and Multicultural Affairs v Yusuf*,[4] where McHugh, Gummow and Hayne JJ said:

> It is necessary, however, to understand what is meant by 'jurisdictional error' under the general law and the consequences that follow from a decision-maker making such an error. As was said in *Craig v South Australia* [(1995) 184 CLR 163 at 179] if an administrative tribunal (like the Tribunal):
>
>> 'falls into an error of law' which causes it to identify a wrong issue, to ask itself a wrong question, to ignore relevant material, to rely on irrelevant material or, at least in some circumstances, to make an erroneous finding or to reach a mistaken conclusion, and the tribunal's exercise or purported exercise of power is thereby affected, it exceeds its authority or powers. Such an error of law is jurisdictional error which will invalidate any order or decision of the tribunal which reflects it.
>
> 'Jurisdictional error' can thus be seen to embrace a number of different kinds of error, the list of which, in the passage cited from *Craig*, is not exhaustive [*cf Re Refugee Review Tribunal, ex parte Aala* (2000) 204 CLR 82]. Those different kinds of error may well overlap. The circumstances of a particular case may permit more than one characterisation of the

[3] HWR Wade, 'Law, Opinion, and Administration' (1962) 78 *Law Quarterly Review* 188, 189.

[4] *Minister for Immigration and Multicultural Affairs v Yusuf* [2001] HCA 30, (2001) 206 CLR 323.

> error identified, for example, as the decision-maker both asking the wrong question and ignoring relevant material. What is important, however, is that identifying a wrong issue, asking a wrong question, ignoring relevant material or relying on irrelevant material in a way that affects the exercise of power is to make an error of law. Further, doing so results in the decision-maker exceeding the authority or powers given by the relevant statute. In other words, if an error of those types is made, the decision-maker did not have authority to make the decision that was made; he or she did not have jurisdiction to make it. Nothing in the Act suggests that the Tribunal is given authority to authoritatively determine questions of law or to make a decision otherwise than in accordance with the law [*Craig* (1995) 184 CLR 163 at 179].[5]

The similarity in concept between jurisdictional error and ultra vires[6] is apparent: each concerns a failure to comply with common law or statutory requirements for a legally effective exercise of administrative power. A major difference between Australia and England in this respect is that Australian law requires a court to decide whether an error of law, once identified, constitutes jurisdictional error whereas in England and Wales in general any error of law made by an administrative tribunal or inferior court in reaching its decision can be quashed for error of law.[7]

III. ESSENCE OF COMMON LAW JUDICIAL REVIEW

It is not possible to define jurisdictional error, although it may be described. It is a conclusion born of an evaluation by the court, expressed as a legal conclusion, of what is said to have gone wrong in a legal sense. In *Kirk v Industrial Court (NSW)*,[8] the High Court repeated[9] that it is important to recognise that the reasoning in *Craig v South Australia*[10] was not to be seen as providing a rigid taxonomy of jurisdictional error. The three examples given in further explanation of the ambit of jurisdictional error by an inferior court were just that—examples. They were not to be taken as marking the boundaries of the relevant field.[11]

Given that the subject of this chapter is administrative law, I put aside jurisdictional error by bodies exercising judicial power so as to concentrate on the exercise of administrative power.

Once it is accepted that an error going to jurisdiction is not limited to the threshold, the embarking on the exercise of administrative power, and once it is borne in mind that jurisdictional error is now most often to be seen in a failure (often constructive) of the decision-maker to carry out his or her task laid down by the

[5] ibid [82].

[6] See *R v Lord President of the Privy Council, ex parte Page* [1993] AC 682, 701–02 (Lord Browne-Wilkinson).

[7] cf *Kirk v Industrial Court (NSW)* [2010] HCA 1, (2010) 239 CLR 531, [65] and *Page* (n 6) 702 (Lord Browne-Wilkinson). See also *R (Cart) v Upper Tribunal* [2011] UKSC 28, [2012] 1 AC 663 where the Supreme Court appears to have adopted a different and differential approach in relation to errors of law in cases coming from the Upper Tribunal.

[8] ibid.

[9] See the passage from *Yusuf* (n 4) set out above (text to n 5).

[10] *Craig v South Australia* (1995) 184 CLR 163.

[11] *Kirk* (n 7) [73].

common law or by statute (as construed by the court), then the essential questions become:

(i) What is the task that the Parliament has given to the decision-maker, including procedural imperatives? The answer to that often-difficult question is to be found in construing the statute.

(ii) What is said, in broad terms, to have gone wrong in a legal sense, whether by way of misconstruction of a statute or other error, including error in fact-finding? This will have been shaped, but perhaps no more than shaped, by the available 'grounds' for judicial review. It is, I think, to put things back to front to begin analysis with the grounds.

(iii) Has anything gone wrong, the judge having at the forefront of his or her mind that, except in the case of a claimed misconstruction of a legal text, or a jurisdictional fact, the power to decide is vested in the decision-maker and not in the court?

(iv) If anything has gone wrong in a legal sense, then assess the gravity of the error (*Kirk v Industrial Court (NSW)*):[12] is what has gone wrong of such significance to the statutory task that the person exercising the administrative power has not embarked on the prescribed task (for example, a jurisdictional fact does not exist) or has departed from the task so that the person has not carried out or completed his or her task?

There may be no error in the person exercising the power embarking on the statutory task but what has happened thereafter may be affected by such serious error so as to mean that the jurisdiction or power has not been exercised. Denial of procedural fairness in the course of a hearing is an obvious example.

Gravity of error, as referred to in *Kirk*, does not, in my view, mean only that the error must be material, but relates to the quality of the error as going to the root of the exercise of the power: the terms of the power and the conditions on which it may be exercised.

As I have indicated above, the position is, I think, different in England. Speaking generally, the elision of error of law and jurisdictional error may mean that the analysis would stop at the third of the points I have set out above.[13] Similarly, there seems to be less emphasis in England from time to time on a claimed error being assessed by reference to the statute in question. In my opinion, the approach in each jurisdiction is open to criticism, at least in hard cases, because of the lack of predictability of the result. To ask in England whether something has gone wrong of a nature and degree that warrants judicial intervention, or in Australia whether the error is of such significance to the statutory task that the person exercising the administrative power has not embarked on or has departed from the prescribed task so as not to carry it out, does not provide certainty. Different judges may arrive

[12] ibid [64].

[13] See *R v Panel on Take-Overs and Mergers, ex parte Guinness plc* [1990] 1 QB 146, 160 (Lord Donaldson of Lymington MR): 'the ultimate question would, as always, be whether something had gone wrong of a nature and degree which required the intervention of the court and, if so, what form that intervention should take'.

at different conclusions. They are less likely to do so where the touchstone is, for example, material error of law, as under section 5 of the Administrative Decisions (Judicial Review) (AD(JR)) Act 1977 (Commonwealth).

The matter is to be tested against the usual form of relief: what appeared to be an exercise of power was made without authority of the statute and is not therefore legally effective. So-called 'grounds' help to organise types of error, but the grounds or categories of error overlap and should be seen as guides to the resolution of the ultimate question. There is no formula. The grounds are not causes of action.

I refer to a judgment I gave in 2013 in *Minister for Immigration and Citizenship v SZRKT*.[14] The Refugee Review Tribunal, an administrative body established by statute and with statutory duties and functions, found the visa applicant's claim to have studied Persian was implausible and this was important to its general finding that it did not believe the visa applicant. However, in the materials before the Tribunal was an academic transcript apparently showing the visa applicant had studied Persian. The Tribunal did not refer to the academic transcript during the hearing or in its reasons for decision. Having found the visa applicant was not a credible witness, the Tribunal concluded that there was no evidence to support his claim to be a refugee. I considered the legal consequences of the finding that the Tribunal had given no consideration to the academic transcript as follows:

> In my opinion, recent High Court authority shows that this is a case specific inquiry and it is not one which should be analysed by reference to fixed categories or formulas, to the effect that a decision within a category or formula is always or is never affected by jurisdictional error: compare *Universal Camera Corporation v National Labor Relations Board* 340 US 474 (1951) at 489 per Frankfurter J, delivering the opinion of the Supreme Court. Useful for analysis though categories or formulas are, they should be seen as servants rather than masters. To proceed otherwise in the area of jurisdictional error is to look for more precision than the nature of the subject admits. In each case what the decision-maker has decided must be analysed in detail in order to arrive at the correct description of conclusion, 'jurisdictional error'.
>
> It is not, in my opinion, the case that a finding in relation to credit may never found a conclusion of jurisdictional error, particularly where a finding on credit on an objectively minor matter of fact is the basis for a tribunal's rejection of the entirety of an applicant's evidence and the entirety of the applicant's claim.
>
> …
>
> [M]erely to ignore 'relevant material' does not establish jurisdictional error. This is consistent with proper limits on judicial review so that fact-finding is a matter for the tribunal of fact while the Court is concerned with whether the tribunal has acted so as to warrant the conclusion that it was not performing the task conferred on it by the legislation.[15]

[14] *Minister for Immigration and Citizenship v SZRKT* [2013] FCA 317, (2013) 212 FCR 99, [77]–[78], [97]–[98].

[15] The analysis may well be different in England where *E v Secretary of State for the Home Department* [2004] EWCA Civ 49, [2004] QB 1044, 1071, establishes that 'a mistake of fact giving rise to unfairness is a separate head of challenge in an appeal on a point of law, at least in those statutory contexts where the parties share an interest in co-operating to achieve the correct result'. The 'ordinary requirements for a finding of unfairness are … First, there must have been a mistake as to an existing fact, including a

> While accepting that ignoring material relevant only to fact-finding does not of itself found jurisdictional error, is it the case, as contended for by the Minister, that to be 'relevant' it must be possible to see, in effect *a priori*, that the material is in terms part of the claim to be a refugee? Is it only that which, in the present statutory context, adequately delineates and demonstrates the 'gravity of the error' referred to by Professor Jaffe in his article 'Judicial Review: Constitutional and Jurisdictional Fact' (1957) 70 *Harvard Law Review* 953 at 963 ... In my opinion the answer to the questions I have posed is 'No' because otherwise the identification of jurisdictional error would put out of account the actual course of decision-making by the Tribunal and would proceed impermissibly by reference to categories or formulas. Although ultimately it is the claim which the *Migration Act* requires to be considered, there are many ways, actual or constructive, of failing to consider the claim.[16]

The necessary focus on the actual course of decision-making by the tribunal and the diminution in importance of categories or formulas means, in many cases, that the court on judicial review must evaluate, qualitatively, the actual course of decision-making by the person on whom the administrative power is conferred.

IV. CONCEPTS

Next, I set out my understanding of what is 'process' and what is 'substance' in administrative law. 'Process' in this connection is the means by which the power is exercised, including ordinary error of law, as opposed to the content or 'substance' of the exercise of power itself.

It may be accepted that (for Australia) judicial review is not so much about the outcome of the exercise of administrative power, but the process by which that outcome was achieved. It is said that the grounds almost invariably go to the process of exercising the power, not the outcome. The commonly stated exception is *Wednesbury* unreasonableness.[17] The classic exposition in Australia is by Brennan J in *Attorney-General for New South Wales v Quin*, who said:

> The essential warrant for judicial intervention is the declaration and enforcing of the law affecting the extent and exercise of power: that is the characteristic duty of the judicature as the third branch of government ... The duty and jurisdiction of the court to review administrative action do not go beyond the declaration and enforcing of the law which determines the limits and governs the exercise of the repository's power. If, in so doing, the court avoids administrative injustice or error, so be it; but the court has no jurisdiction simply to cure administrative injustice or error ...

mistake as to the availability of evidence on a particular matter. Secondly, the fact or evidence must have been "established", in the sense that it was uncontentious and objectively verifiable. Thirdly, the appellant (or his advisers) must not have been responsible for the mistake. Fourthly, the mistake must have played a material (not necessarily decisive) part in the tribunal's reasoning'.

[16] Special leave to appeal refused: transcript of proceedings in *Minister for Immigration and Citizenship v SZRKT* [2013] HCATrans 251 (11 October 2013). The decision has been cited with approval by full courts in *Minister for Immigration and Border Protection v MZYTS* [2013] FCAFC 114, (2013) 136 ALD 547, [68]–[70] and in *Minister for Immigration and Border Protection v SZSRS* [2014] FCAFC 16, (2014) 309 ALR 67, especially [52] for the proposition that the distinction between claims and evidence might be a useful tool of analysis but is not itself the fundamental question. The fundamental question is the importance of the material to the exercise of the tribunal's function and the seriousness of the error.

[17] *Associated Provincial Picture Houses Ltd v Wednesbury Corporation* [1948] 1 KB 223.

> The consequence is that the scope of judicial review must be defined not in terms of the protection of individual interests but in terms of the extent of power and the legality of its exercise …
>
> There is one limitation, '*Wednesbury* unreasonableness' …[18]

Nevertheless, it is an oversimplification to say that because the grounds of judicial review are about the process of the exercise of the power, the substance of the exercise (leaving aside the distracting word 'merits' which I consider further below) is irrelevant. I also omit here but mention later what may flow from substantive relief, for example *R v North and East Devon Health Authority, ex parte Coughlan*,[19] which is not followed in Australia.

My contention is that, at least in cases of any complexity, judicial review does involve a qualitative assessment and is qualitative. What has been done by the person who has exercised the administrative power must, on judicial review, be considered and evaluated and that evaluation involves a qualitative assessment of what was done. Indeed it has been said that the development by the courts of techniques for reviewing the quality of decision-making has been a fundamental doctrinal shift central to administrative law's development during the twentieth century and occurring primarily after the Second World War.[20] But this judicial review is not for the purpose of the judge considering whether or not he or she agrees with the decision and whether it is correct in that sense. Merits review and judicial review overlap but each type of review is conducted for a different purpose.

The major differences between judicial review and merits review, in my opinion, are as follows. First, what is subject to assessment by the court is most often limited to the particular power, because other powers available to the person exercising the primary power are not available to the court. Further the court is generally limited to reviewing the manner of exercise of power under review and to the material before the person who has exercised the power. Secondly, the legislature has not vested in the court the power directly to decide the ultimate outcome so that the court is not concerned with what ultimately is the correct or preferable decision. Likewise the court is not concerned with good administration of or in itself. However, I contend that qualitative assessment by the court links judicial review of both process and substance. Put differently, the conceptual division between process and substance may tend to disguise what goes on in judicial review. Conversely, I question whether

[18] *Attorney-General for New South Wales v Quin* (1990) 170 CLR 1, 35–36. The position in England may well be different, particularly in its adoption of proportionality analysis. To the extent that 'reasonableness' cases in England stray into outcome-oriented review they show qualitative judicial review by the courts but also demonstrate the divergence between the law of England and Australia in this respect. *R (Litvinenko) v Secretary of State for the Home Department* [2014] EWHC 194 (Admin) provides a recent example.

[19] *R v North and East Devon Health Authority, ex parte Coughlan* [2001] QB 213.

[20] G Airo-Farulla, 'Rationality and Judicial Review of Administrative Action' (2000) 24 *Melbourne University Law Review* 543, 552, citing I Yeats, 'Findings of Fact: The Role of the Courts' in G Richardson and H Genn (eds), *Administrative Law and Government Action* (Oxford, Clarendon Press, 1994) 131, 133.

what happens in judicial review when *Wednesbury* unreasonableness is deployed is accurately described as substantive review.

The difference is essentially the purpose for which, and thus the perspective from which, the primary exercise of power is being examined, rather than process or substance, except when it comes to remedy. It would be quite incorrect, in my experience, to characterise what a judge does on judicial review as involving the question: 'do I think this is the correct or preferable decision?' As illustrated by *FTZK v Minister for Immigration and Border Protection*,[21] which I consider further below, in the circumstances of that case the claim that the tribunal had committed a jurisdictional error warranting the issue of constitutional writs did not involve an examination of the correctness of the findings of fact made by the tribunal but did involve a consideration of whether those findings disclosed that the tribunal did not respond to the question it was required to ask in order to perform its task.

In addition, although, as I have said above, in judicial review the facts are not at large, being in most cases limited to the material before the person exercising the primary power,[22] they must be understood in order to understand what the exercise of the power has been, without divorcing the substance of what was decided from how (the process by which) it was decided. In *Reid v Secretary of State for Scotland*, Lord Clyde said:

> But while the evidence may have to be explored in order to see if the decision is vitiated by such legal deficiencies it is perfectly clear that in a case of review, as distinct from an ordinary appeal, the court may not set about forming its own preferred view of the evidence.[23]

I am also drawing a distinction here between the mental process involved in reviewing the primary exercise of power and the different, although evaluative, task of construing the legislation, as clearly explained by Lord Reid in *Padfield v Minister of Agriculture, Fisheries and Food*.[24]

I next state my understanding of 'merits'. What are the merits from which the judicial arm must stay away?

This is a distinction which is blurred at the edges. Indeed, Santow JA said in *Greyhound Racing Authority (NSW) v Bragg*[25] 'the merits' is that diminishing field left after permissible judicial review. Stephen Gageler described the merits as 'the residue of administrative decision-making that in any given case lies beyond any question of legality'.[26] Sir Anthony Mason has written, in comparing judicial and merits review:

> I agree with Professor Cane ['Merits Review and Judicial Review: The AAT as Trojan Horse' (2000) 28 *Federal Law Review* 213] that the difference is not as great as it is often

[21] *FTZK v Minister for Immigration and Border Protection* [2014] HCA 26, (2014) 310 ALR 1.

[22] It would appear that the courts in England admit more frequently than do the courts in Australia evidence that was not before the primary decision-maker. This would seem to be so in light of the broader availability on judicial review in England of a mistake of fact giving rise to unfairness as a separate head of challenge in an appeal on a point of law, following *E v Secretary of State for the Home Department* [2004] EWCA Civ 49, [2004] QB 1044.

[23] *Reid v Secretary of State for Scotland* [1999] 2 AC 512, 541–42.

[24] *Padfield v Minister of Agriculture, Fisheries and Food* [1968] AC 997, 1030.

[25] *Greyhound Racing Authority (NSW) v Bragg* [2003] NSWCA 388, [46].

[26] S Gageler, 'The Legitimate Scope of Judicial Review' (2001) 21 *Australian Bar Review* 279, 280.

> represented to be but the difference is still significant. The comparison is hampered by the blancmange-like quality of the expression 'merits review'. For the most part, it is used in the sense of review that includes, but goes beyond, what is comprehended in review for legality. The distinction between judicial review and merits review assumes that the content of review for legality is not co-extensive with the scope of potential review; in other words, the grounds of judicial review for legality do not include review on the basis that the decision-maker, though making no error of law, arrived at a decision which, though not unreasonable, falls short of the correct or preferable outcome.
>
> …
>
> The difference between judicial review and appeal is well recognised. In an appeal, the tribunal can substitute its opinion of what is a correct (or preferable) outcome on the material before it for that of the decision-maker; in judicial review, the court cannot do that. The difference is a central element of recent High Court judgments, and of English judgments of high authority as well.[27]

The term 'merits' has a 'beguiling simplicity'.[28]

The search for a clear line of demarcation is perhaps explained, first, by the statutory history in Australia, particularly the enactment of the Administrative Appeals Tribunal Act 1975 (Commonwealth), establishing what is called a 'merits review system' in a tribunal; secondly, by the early cases on that Tribunal's powers and functions, particularly *Drake v Minister for Immigration and Ethnic Affairs*[29] and *Collector of Customs (NSW) v Brian Lawlor Automotive Pty Ltd*;[30] and by the later enactment of the AD(JR) Act 1977, dealing with judicial review, not limited to jurisdictional error, primarily in the Federal Court; and thirdly, against the background of the separation of executive power and judicial power required by the Constitution.[31]

Rather than seeking to identify the merits as opposed to the lawfulness of the exercise of power in question, perhaps the better enquiry is to emphasise the distinguishable and distinct processes: merits review, on the one hand, and judicial review, on the other.

First, in merits review the facts need to be found and evaluated and this involves choice. Where the matter turns on evaluation of, and choice between, competing views of the facts by the person exercising administrative power there is likely to be

27 A Mason, 'Judicial Review: A View from Constitutional and other Perspectives' (2000) 28 *Federal Law Review* 331, 333–34 (citations omitted).

28 *D'Amore v Independent Commission Against Corruption* [2013] NSWCA 187, (2013) 303 ALR 242, [232] (Basten JA).

29 *Drake v Minister for Immigration and Ethnic Affairs* (1979) 24 ALR 577, 589, establishing that the question for the determination of the tribunal was not whether the decision which the decision-maker made was the correct or preferable one on the material before him but that the question for the determination of the tribunal was whether that decision was the correct or preferable one on the material before the tribunal.

30 *Collector of Customs (NSW) v Brian Lawlor Automotive Pty Ltd* (1979) 41 FLR 338, (1979) 24 ALR 307, establishing that the tribunal had power to review a decision although the decision under review was not taken by the administrator in a legally effective way, either because there was no relevant power at all or because the official acted ultra vires the power conferred.

31 In England these relationships are of course less definite. This may go some way towards explaining the differing approaches between England and Australia to whether, first, any error of law constitutes jurisdictional error and, secondly, the extent to which errors of fact may constitute reviewable error.

'mere' fact-finding,[32] in respect of which no legal error could be successfully maintained on judicial review.[33] In contrast, in judicial review it is necessary to understand the facts and, often, the fact-finding process of the person who has exercised the power in order to understand and judge the claims of legal error.

Secondly, in merits review the making of the correct or preferable decision is a defining characteristic. Where there is a legally available alternative then to select one over the other, whether or not accurately described as 'policy', is plainly a matter of merits, but, in my view, the same analysis applies where, upon an evaluation of the facts, only one decision, described after the conclusion has been reached as the correct decision, is available. In each case what happens is accurately described as choice.[34]

Thus, choices are at the heart of merits review and, on judicial review, the court must understand the choices but must do no more than decide whether the choice that was made was legally available. I do not, of course, contend that there are no choices made by a court on judicial review but they are different in kind and subject matter and chiefly flow from statutory construction and from evaluating the reasons of the person exercising the administrative power, in light of the material before that person.

There is also a clear distinction between the 'place' of primary decision-making and judicial review. The merits may be seen as the outcome of primary decision-making, what is described in Australia as the 'correct or preferable'[35] decision on the material before the primary decision-maker. And most often that will be the final decision. Where there is merits review the same description will apply. On the other hand, judicial review is review of the process of primary decision-making and of the legality of the primary exercise of administrative power.

This is reflected in the normal form of order on successful judicial review, at least in Australia, which is to set aside the decision or exercise of power and to remit the matter to the person in whom the primary power is vested for further consideration or determination 'according to law', which includes the court's reasons.

[32] See *R v Hillingdon London Borough Council, ex parte Puhlhofer* [1986] 1 AC 484, 518 (Lord Brightman) and *Waterford v Commonwealth* (1987) 163 CLR 54, 77 (Brennan J), referred to below.

[33] A 'jurisdictional fact' stands outside this analysis since, by definition, it is the court's task finally to decide whether or not a jurisdictional fact, which may be a complex of elements, exists: see *Corporation of the City of Enfield v Development Assessment Commission* [2000] HCA 5, (2000) 199 CLR 135, [28] (Gleeson CJ, Gummow, Kirby and Hayne JJ). cf *R v Monopolies and Mergers Commission, ex parte South Yorkshire Transport Ltd* [1993] 1 WLR 23, 32 where the House of Lords identified as a jurisdictional fact the statutory condition 'the supply of services of that description … in a substantial part of the United Kingdom' but, having construed those words to establish the criterion, held that the criterion so established was itself so imprecise that different decision-makers might reach differing conclusions when applying it to the facts of a given case and therefore that the court was entitled to substitute its own opinion for that of the person to whom the decision had been entrusted only if the decision was so aberrant that it could not be classed as rational.

[34] See Jaffe's description of discretion as the power of the administrator to make a choice from among two or more legally valid solutions: LL Jaffe, *Judicial Control of Administrative Action*, abridged student edn (Boston, Little, Brown & Company, 1965) 586.

[35] *Drake* (n 29): the question for the determination of the Administrative Appeals Tribunal was whether the decision was the 'correct or preferable one' on the material before the tribunal.

Generally, it is where only one answer would be available on remitter, or the parties consent, that the court will dispose of the matter finally. In matters of procedural fairness most often there will be 'more than one answer' as the court will have looked only at procedure.[36] The position may well be different if a fixed time limit for making the original decision has expired.

In Australia, the merits do not include questions of statutory interpretation, even where those questions are contestable, which many of them are. The limited exception is where the meaning of a word or words is said to involve a question of fact only. I return to this below. In other words, the courts on judicial review decide whether the meaning given to the statute by the primary decision-maker was right or wrong. There is no deference on questions of statutory interpretation.[37] This contrasts with the position in the United States[38] and in Canada.[39]

Chief Justice French, writing extra-judicially, has recently said that '[a] better distinction might be drawn by using the terms "factual merits review" and "legal merits review"'.[40] The former is a power to reconsider decisions, the latter is to police the limits of the power to decide.[41]

I have referred above to the classic exposition on the limits of judicial review by Brennan J in *Attorney-General for New South Wales v Quin*[42] but note that his Honour said 'The merits of administrative action, *to the extent that they can be distinguished from legality*, are for the repository of the relevant power and, subject to political control, for the repository alone'.[43]

As may be seen, I prefer the description 'consideration of the merits but not a decision on the merits'[44] and I resist the proposition that the distinction between merits review and judicial review reduces to the fact that on judicial review the court does not substitute its decision. As explained above, I emphasise the distinguishable and distinct processes involved in merits review, on the one hand, and judicial review, on the other.

[36] Contrast the enforceable expectation of a substantive benefit as a species of procedural fairness under the law in England: *Coughlan* (n 19).

[37] *Enfield* (n 33).

[38] *Chevron USA Inc v Natural Resources Defense Council Inc*, 467 US 837, 842–44 (1984).

[39] See *Canada (Attorney-General) v Public Service Alliance of Canada* [1991] 1 SCR 614, 644; *Nor-Man Regional Health Authority Inc v Manitoba Association of Health Care Professionals* [2011] 3 SCR 616, [36], [38], [40]. Deference on a question of statutory construction is, in my view, different to construing a statutory word or phrase as having a width or imprecision on the application of which minds may reasonably differ so as to give rise largely to a question of fact. In such a case the court on judicial review should intervene only where the decision is not reasonably open: *South Yorkshire Transport* (n 33) 32; *Vetter v Lake Macquarie City Council* [2001] HCA 12, (2001) 202 CLR 439, [24] (Gleeson CJ, Gummow and Callinan JJ).

[40] RS French, 'Administrative Law in Australia: Themes and Values Revisited' in M Groves (ed), *Modern Administrative Law in Australia: Concepts and Context* (Melbourne, Cambridge University Press, 2014) 24, 34.

[41] See P Cane and L McDonald, *Principles of Administrative Law: Legal Regulation of Governance*, 2nd edn (Melbourne, Oxford University Press, 2012) 225.

[42] *Quin* (n 18).

[43] ibid 36 (emphasis added). Approved in *Enfield* (n 33), [44].

[44] P Daly, *A Theory of Deference in Administrative Law: Basis, Application and Scope* (Cambridge, Cambridge University Press, 2012) 140.

I next turn to consider categories of judicial review. As will have been seen, I have not accepted for present purposes Mark Aronson's division between review grounds that deal with process, in which he includes errors of law, and other grounds, such as *Wednesbury* unreasonableness, which turn on the quality of the decision.[45] My starting point is that there is no bright line in the present context between process and substance. Secondly, and more importantly, my proposition is that both process review and substantive review are qualitative but in neither case in the sense of the court undertaking merits review.

V. CATEGORIES

A. Natural Justice/Procedural Fairness

To 'process' is conventionally allocated procedural fairness, particularly an opportunity to be heard. But on judicial review this may often be a qualitative exercise. Procedural fairness may extend to the quality of the hearing, such as frequent interjections by a tribunal member in relation to the credibility of the claims[46] or, where there was an interpreter, the quality of translation or interpretation before a tribunal.[47] The High Court has held that a decision of the Refugee Review Tribunal was procedurally unfair where the Tribunal made demeanour-based findings against the appellants in circumstances where four and a half years elapsed between the observation of the demeanour and the making of the findings. Chief Justice Gleeson said that a procedure that depended significantly upon the tribunal's assessment of individuals may become an unfair procedure if, by reason of some default on the part of the tribunal, there was a real and substantial risk that the tribunal's capacity to make such an assessment was impaired.[48]

Those are perhaps obvious cases where a qualitative assessment is involved in deciding whether or not there has been a denial of natural justice or procedural fairness.

Less obviously, except in the now rare cases where the issue is whether natural justice or procedural fairness applies at all, the issue is the content of natural justice in the circumstances of the particular case. The court works out what the applicant

[45] M Aronson, 'Process, Quality, and Variable Standards: Responding to an *Agent Provocateur*' in D Dyzenhaus, M Hunt and G Huscroft (eds), *A Simple Common Lawyer: Essays in Honour of Michael Taggart* (Oxford, Hart Publishing, 2009) 5, 9–10. As will appear, I do not accept that because certain grounds are more readily seen as objective, the review by the court does not involve a qualitative assessment of the decision-making and of the decision.

[46] *SZRUI v Minister for Immigration, Multicultural Affairs and Citizenship* [2013] FCAFC 80.

[47] *SZRMQ v Minister for Immigration and Border Protection* [2013] FCAFC 142, (2013) 219 FCR 212.

[48] *NAIS v Minister for Immigration and Multicultural and Indigenous Affairs* [2005] HCA 77, (2005) 228 CLR 470, [9]. Callinan and Heydon JJ said ([172]) that unfairness could spring not only from a denial of an opportunity to present a case, but from denial of an opportunity to consider it. A way in which the tribunal could disable itself from giving consideration to the presentation of a case arose where it permitted so much time to pass that it could no longer assess the evidence offered. Kirby J ([105]) agreed.

knew to be in issue and what the steps or stages of the exercise of the power were, in order to answer whether what happened was unfair, in a practical sense,[49] as a matter of process. And in so doing, it is inevitable that the court assesses the quality of the exercise of the power and, although focused on process, does so in light of what was done or decided: the substance.

Importantly, I would not regard what I have just described as an intrusion into the merits. This is despite the suggestion in *Re Minister for Immigration and Multicultural and Indigenous Affairs, ex parte Lam* that the quality of the exercise of the power and the merits of the outcome are intertwined. There McHugh and Gummow JJ said:

> The notion of 'abuse of power' applied in *Coughlan* [[2001] QB 213] appears to be concerned with the judicial supervision of administrative decision-making by the application of certain minimum standards now identified by the English common law. These standards fix upon the quality of the decision-making and thus the merits of the outcome. As was indicated in *Coughlan* itself, this represents an attempted assimilation into the English common law of doctrines derived from European civilian systems.[50]

But their Honours were probably there considering substantive procedural fairness, that is, procedural fairness having a substantive result, as seen in *R v North and East Devon Health Authority, ex parte Coughlan*.[51]

Another basis on which the courts are involved in qualitative assessment in dealing with a claim of denial of natural justice arises because the applicant for judicial review is not limited, in terms of evidence in the court, to material which was before the primary decision-maker. *Ridge v Baldwin* provides an example.[52] At the trial of the action the appellant gave evidence that after his arrest the Town Clerk told him he had been suspended under or in accordance with police regulations and the appellant's recollection as to this was not challenged in cross-examination. In complementary reasoning, the Supreme Court said in *R (Osborn) v Parole Board*[53] that the courts below were wrong to adopt the approach that the reviewing court should decide the question of the Parole Board's fairness as if it were reviewing a matter of judgement on *Wednesbury* grounds. The court must determine for itself whether a fair procedure was followed: its function was not merely to review the reasonableness of the decision-maker's judgement of what fairness required.

Turning to the bias limb of natural justice, in Australia a claim of reasonable apprehension of bias depends on a qualitative assessment of what was said and done against the legal test 'whether a fair-minded lay observer might reasonably apprehend that the [decision-maker] might not bring an impartial and unprejudiced mind to the resolution of the question the [decision-maker] is required to decide'.[54]

[49] See *Re Minister for Immigration and Multicultural and Indigenous Affairs, ex parte Lam* [2003] HCA 6, (2003) 214 CLR 1.

[50] ibid [73].

[51] *Coughlan* (n 19).

[52] *Ridge v Baldwin* [1964] AC 40, 107–08 (Lord Morris).

[53] *R (Osborn) v Parole Board* [2013] UKSC 61, [2014] AC 1115, [65] (Lord Reed, with whom Lord Neuberger, Baroness Hale, Lord Kerr and Lord Clarke agreed).

[54] *Johnson v Johnson* [2000] HCA 48, (2000) 201 CLR 488, [11].

The same assessment would have to be made in applying the English test: 'The court *must first ascertain all the circumstances which have a bearing on the suggestion* that the judge was biased. It must then ask whether those circumstances would lead a fair-minded and informed observer to conclude that there was a real possibility, or a real danger, the two being the same, that the tribunal was biased'.[55] The ground is available on judicial review of an administrative decision.[56] An extreme illustration of qualitative review for bias is provided by *Sun v Minister for Immigration and Ethnic Affairs*,[57] where, *Wednesbury* unreasonableness not being available but actual bias being available as a ground of judicial review under the Migration Act, it was held that to err in relation to the facts 'so many times and in such ways, and each time against the appellant' showed that the tribunal member considered the case from a preconceived opinion and a fixed position so adverse to him that he could not obtain a fair hearing.

While therefore it is true that on judicial review for an alleged denial of natural justice or procedural fairness the courts are reviewing the process by which a power has been exercised, the judicial review itself is qualitative. Perhaps this is implicit in what Lord Mustill said: 'What fairness demands is dependent on the context of the decision, and this is to be taken into account in all its aspects'.[58]

B. Relevant and Irrelevant Considerations

I now consider two other grounds of judicial review, which are often a more or less well-disguised appeal to the merits. They are, first, whether a mandatory or relevant consideration was not taken into account and, secondly, whether a prohibited or irrelevant consideration was taken into account by the person who has exercised the primary power.

The latest edition of *De Smith's Judicial Review* speaks of unreasonable process which 'focuses upon the quality of reasoning underlying or supporting the decision; upon the weight placed upon the factors taken into account on the way to reaching the decision; upon the way the decision is justified'.[59] The authors refer in this context to 'the factors taken into account by the decision-maker on the way to making the decision; the evidence by which the decision was influenced or the quality of it[s] justification'.[60] Nevertheless the authors state that 'the question of what is a relevant or material consideration is a question of law, whereas the question of what weight to be given to it is a matter for the decision-maker', subject to the decision being held to be unreasonable.[61]

[55] *Porter v Magill* [2001] UKHL 67, [2002] 2 AC 357, [102]–[103] (Lord Hope), citing *Re Medicaments and Related Classes of Goods (No 2)* [2001] 1 WLR 700, 727 (emphasis added).
[56] *Laws v Australian Broadcasting Tribunal* (1990) 170 CLR 70.
[57] *Sun v Minister for Immigration and Ethnic Affairs* (1997) 81 FCR 71, 133–34.
[58] *R v Secretary of State for the Home Department, ex parte Doody* [1994] 1 AC 531, 560.
[59] H Woolf *et al, De Smith's Judicial Review*, 7th edn (London, Sweet & Maxwell, 2013) 599.
[60] ibid 600 ff.
[61] ibid.

In my view, it is at least primarily to the provisions of the legislation that one must look in order to decide whether a particular consideration is obligatory (relevant in the sense of mandatory), extraneous (irrelevant in the sense of prohibited), or a consideration which is of neither of those characters and which is therefore 'available'.[62] Considerations that are neither legally relevant nor legally irrelevant but are simply available would constitute the bulk of most primary exercises of administrative power.

Having cleared the ground, the aspect on which I wish to concentrate is the qualitative nature of the assessment by the court of the material which was before the person exercising the power, and his or her reasons, in order to decide whether or not an improper purpose (as that term is used in the AD(JR) Act 1977) is disclosed. Sometimes the express mandatory consideration can be at a high level of generality, such as a requirement to take into account the public interest or the national interest, and in other cases the statute may oblige the decision-maker to take into account representations or the results of consultations.

As to the first of these, whether or not an AD(JR) Act improper purpose is disclosed by the exercise of power by the administrative official or tribunal, let me assume that a mandatory relevant consideration is identified in the statute, whether by express statement or, commonly, by implication.[63] The exercise of power would therefore be a jurisdictional error or disclose an AD(JR) Act improper purpose if that consideration were not taken into account.

Where reasons are given for the exercise of the administrative power, those reasons may or may not refer expressly to the mandatory relevant consideration. But in either case that is not the end of the inquiry. This is because, first, even though the reasons refer expressly to the mandatory relevant consideration, the real question is not one of mere reference but of consideration or taking into account itself. No doubt an express reference to a mandatory relevant consideration may be a large step along the way to the conclusion that the mandatory relevant consideration has in fact been considered or taken into account. Conversely, it may be implicit although not express in the reasons that a mandatory relevant consideration has been taken into account. If there are no reasons then the assessment must be made by reference to the exercise of power itself and the materials which were before the person exercising the power.

Whatever language is used to describe taking into account, or having regard to, or considering a relevant consideration, and many adjectives have been offered in the cases, the fundamental point is that the court needs to assess the quality rather than the mere fact of the consideration in order to work out whether it has or has not been taken into account. In addition, the statute may be construed as involving a consideration of a particular factor to a particular standard.

[62] *NEAT Domestic Trading Pty Ltd v AWB Ltd* [2003] HCA 35, (2003) 216 CLR 277, [20] (Gleeson CJ). See also the equivalent analysis of the third category in *R v Somerset County Council, ex parte Fewings* [1995] 1 WLR 1037, 1049 (Simon Brown LJ). See also *Lo v Chief Commissioner of State Revenue* [2013] NSWCA 180, (2013) 85 NSWLR 86, [9] (Basten JA) and, more recently, *Duffy v Da Rin* [2014] NSWCA 270, (2014) 312 ALR 340, [53].

[63] *Minister for Aboriginal Affairs v Peko-Wallsend Ltd* [1986] HCA 40, (1986) 162 CLR 24, 40–41 (Mason J).

Again, whether and whatever descriptions are used, what needs to be avoided is merits review and what has to be borne in mind is the distinction, albeit elusive, between understanding the terms in which the power has been exercised and evaluating it for the purpose of seeing whether a matter has been taken into account, on the one hand, and, on the other hand, evaluating the decision in the sense of second-guessing *relative* weight.[64] But I see no alternative to assessing the nature of the consideration.[65] There is also a difference, depending on the statute, between a consideration which may be considered but given no weight[66] as opposed to a consideration which must be given weight as a fundamental element in making the decision.[67]

As to descriptions that have been used by the courts, in Australia these include: 'active intellectual process or engagement'; 'give weight to as a fundamental element in making the determination'; 'a process of evaluation, sufficient to warrant the description of the matters being taken into consideration';[68] 'focal points' and 'proper, genuine and realistic consideration', the last being taken out of its original context in *Khan v Minister for Immigration and Ethnic Affairs*.[69]

Wisely, in England the position seems to be that to have 'due regard' is the regard that is appropriate in all the circumstances.[70] This is perhaps akin to the formulation I have already set out from *Weal v Bathurst City Council*. 'But whether or not it can be judged that a matter has been considered is essentially an evaluative process based exclusively on what the decision-maker has said or written'.[71]

There is also the anterior task of determining the relevant level of particularity or abstraction at which these considerations are to be identified.[72] A related question arises whether the failure complained of is not a complete failure to address a certain subject, but a failure to make some inquiry about facts said to be relevant to that subject.

[64] As Mason J said in *Peko-Wallsend* (ibid) 41–42, in some circumstances a court may set aside an administrative decision which has failed to give adequate weight to a relevant factor of great importance, or has given excessive weight to a relevant factor of no great importance. The preferred ground on which this is done, however, is not the failure to take into account relevant considerations or the taking into account of irrelevant considerations, but that the decision is 'manifestly unreasonable'. Mason J added that a court should proceed with caution when reviewing an administrative decision on the ground that it does not give proper weight to relevant factors, lest it exceed its supervisory role by reviewing the decision on its merits.

[65] cf *Anderson v Director-General of the Department of Environmental and Climate Change* [2008] NSWCA 337, (2008) 251 ALR 633, [54]–[57], approving *Kindimindi Investments Pty Ltd v Lane Cove Council* [2006] NSWCA 23, (2006) 143 LGERA 277, [74]–[75].

[66] *Rathborne v Abel* (1964) 38 ALJR 293.

[67] *R v Toohey, ex parte Meneling Station Pty Ltd* (1982) 158 CLR 327, 333 and 338 (Mason J).

[68] *Weal v Bathurst City Council* [2000] NSWCA 88, (2000) 111 LGERA 181, [13] and [80].

[69] *Khan v Minister for Immigration and Ethnic Affairs* (1987) 14 ALD 291.

[70] See *R (Rotherham Metropolitan Borough Council) v Secretary of State for Business, Innovation and Skills* [2014] EWHC 232 (Admin), [87], citing *R (Baker) v Secretary of State for Communities and Local Government* [2008] EWCA Civ 141, [31]. See also *R (Domb) v London Borough of Hammersmith and Fulham* [2009] EWCA Civ 941, [52].

[71] *Anderson* (n 65), [58] (Tobias JA).

[72] *Foster v Minister for Customs and Justice* [2000] HCA 38, (2000) 200 CLR 442, [23].

If the statute identifies expressly what those considerations are then, of course, that is the level of particularity of the consideration which the person exercising the administrative power must take into account. If the statute does not identify expressly the relevant considerations the task can involve complex statutory construction.

This ground is more concerned with how a decision-maker has identified legal and factual issues which were required to be addressed when the relevant legislation was applied to the particular matter for decision, than with 'the process of making the particular findings of fact upon which the decision-maker acts'.[73]

Turning to whether the person exercising the power has taken into account an irrelevant (prohibited) consideration, in my view, the same analysis applies. It may well be necessary to analyse the reasons for, and the terms of, the exercise of the power and the material before the person exercising the power in order to reach a conclusion on whether the prohibited consideration has been taken into account.[74]

As with other categories of judicial review, where, following the court's decision, there is only one possible answer, the practical effect of a judicial review application may be to determine the substantive outcome of the exercise of administrative power.[75]

C. Unreasonableness

Next, I consider the legally unreasonable exercise of a discretion, classic *Wednesbury*. It has been said that *Wednesbury* involves substantive intervention in that:

> All tests of substantive judicial review entail the judiciary in taking some view of the merits of the contested action. This is so even in relation to the classic *Wednesbury* test. What distinguishes different tests for review is not whether they consider the merits or not, but the stringency of the judicial scrutiny.[76]

I proffer a different analysis.

First, in my opinion, judicial review of the exercise of a discretion for legal unreasonableness does not involve the court in the merits of the primary decision. As a matter of remedy, the usual course in Australia will be to remit the matter for determination according to law as the court will not determine the ultimate outcome where there remains a choice which is legally available. Of course the court must understand the substance of what has been decided but it is the legal context which must, but which does not always, dominate. Secondly, I do not see the *Wednesbury* ground as involving a view of the merits of the decision different in kind from the grounds of judicial review to which I have already referred. In my opinion, there is a

[73] *Yusuf* (n 4), [74] (McHugh, Gummow and Hayne JJ).

[74] The issues I have referred to under this subheading are fully explored in M Aronson and M Groves, *Judicial Review of Administrative Action*, 5th edn (Sydney, Lawbook Co, 2013) [5.20]–[5.190] and in R Lancaster and S Free, 'The Relevancy Grounds in Environmental and Administrative Law' in N Williams (ed), *Key Issues in Judicial Review* (Sydney, The Federation Press, 2014) 241.

[75] *Roberts v Hopwood* [1925] AC 578 provides an early well-known example in relation to the ultra vires exercise of a discretion.

[76] P Craig, *Administrative Law*, 7th edn (London, Sweet & Maxwell, 2012) [21-002].

real difference, as a matter of mental process, between taking a view of the merits in the sense of understanding the facts and taking a view of the merits in terms of what the judge thinks is the correct or preferable outcome.[77] The latter is impermissible. I accept that, consistently with this analysis, the court considers the outcome by reference to the standard of legal unreasonableness and, where satisfied that the outcome is not legally reasonable, remits the matter for further consideration. Thirdly, I would not describe the process as one of the stringency of judicial scrutiny, although I realise that is contrary to English authority. It seems to me that manifest unreasonableness or classic *Wednesbury* unreasonableness is a shorthand way of further describing the area of difference beyond which (reasonable) minds may not reasonably differ, as a matter of legal reasonableness.

It seems that the law in England and in Australia may now be drawing closer in this respect in that giving disproportionate weight to a relevant (lawful) consideration may establish a legally unreasonable exercise of discretion in both countries.[78]

Furthermore, the plurality in *Li* said that *Wednesbury* is no longer to be the yardstick of the legal standard of unreasonableness in relation to the exercise of discretion.[79] I take this to mean that what is no longer to have exclusive sway is the test 'so unreasonable that no reasonable person could have arrived at it' because the legal standard of reasonableness must be the standard indicated by the true construction of the statute,[80] unless there be an affirmative (statutory) basis for its exclusion or modification.[81] This, in my view, must have been at least implicit in *Wednesbury* itself since the Court of Appeal there referred to the subject matter or scope of the statute and the otherwise unqualified terms of the power to impose conditions.

It may also be that although Australia does not, expressly, have 'heightened scrutiny' or an 'anxious scrutiny' standard,[82] the same approach may be available by reference to the 'true construction of the statute', including the rights and interests to which the statute is directed.[83]

In *Minister for Immigration and Border Protection v Singh*[84] we said that *Li* did not create some kind of factual checklist to be followed in determining whether there had been a legally unreasonable exercise of a discretionary power: legal unreasonableness is invariably fact dependent, so that in any given case determining whether an exercise of power crosses the line into legal unreasonableness will require careful evaluation of the evidence before the court, including any inferences which may be drawn from that evidence.

[77] It is for this reason I questioned above whether *Wednesbury* unreasonableness is accurately described as substantive review.

[78] *Minister for Immigration and Citizenship v Li* [2013] HCA 18, (2013) 249 CLR 332.

[79] ibid [68] (Hayne, Kiefel and Bell JJ). See the fuller passage from the reasons which I have set out below.

[80] ibid [67].

[81] ibid [92] (Gageler J).

[82] *Bugdaycay v Secretary of State for the Home Department* [1987] AC 514.

[83] Compare *R v Secretary of State for Education and Employment, ex parte Begbie* [2000] 1 WLR 1115, 1130, where Laws LJ spoke of 'a sliding scale of review, more or less intrusive according to the nature and gravity of what is at stake'.

[84] *Minister for Immigration and Border Protection v Singh* [2014] FCAFC 1, (2014) 308 ALR 280, [42].

It seems clear that the still further heightened or restricted standard espoused by Lord Diplock in *Council of Civil Service Unions v Minister for the Civil Service*,[85] to which I return below, would be inconsistent with the reasoning in the plurality judgment in *Li*.[86] Perhaps it can now be seen as an unnecessary gloss on the approach in *Secretary of State for Education and Science v Tameside Metropolitan Borough Council*.[87]

As an aside, *Wednesbury* in its highest articulation may now be said to be a distracting influence. This may be what Lord Mance (with whom Lord Neuberger and Lord Clarke agreed) had in mind in *Kennedy v Charity Commission*[88] and it is more certainly what the authors of the plurality judgment in *Li* had in mind in saying:

> Lord Greene MR's oft-quoted formulation of unreasonableness in *Wednesbury* has been criticised for 'circularity and vagueness', as have subsequent attempts to clarify it. However, as has been noted, *Wednesbury* is not the starting point for the standard of reasonableness, nor should it be considered the end point. The legal standard of unreasonableness should not be considered as limited to what is in effect an irrational, if not bizarre, decision—which is to say one that is so unreasonable that no reasonable person could have arrived at it—nor should Lord Greene MR be taken to have limited unreasonableness in this way in his judgment in *Wednesbury*. This aspect of his Lordship's judgment may more sensibly be taken to recognise that an inference of unreasonableness may in some cases be objectively drawn even where a particular error in reasoning cannot be identified. This is recognised by the principles governing the review of a judicial discretion, which, it may be observed, were settled in Australia by *House v R* [(1936) 55 CLR 499], before *Wednesbury* was decided.[89]

It will be recalled that in *Wednesbury*, Lord Greene did not consider that he was creating new doctrine and indeed treated other 'grounds' of judicial review, such as taking into account irrelevant considerations, as one example of an unreasonable decision.[90] Lord Greene certainly did not envisage encouraging merits review and indeed the very thrust of the decision is that the courts should not engage in merits review. It is to be remembered that the underlying issue in *Wednesbury* was who was to be master: whether it could be said the discretion miscarried because the exercise of the discretion appeared unreasonable to the court or, as was held, whether the alleged miscarriage of the discretion should be tested from the perspective

[85] *Council of Civil Service Unions v Minister for the Civil Service* [1985] AC 374, 410–11.

[86] *Li* (n 78).

[87] *Secretary of State for Education and Science v Tameside Metropolitan Borough Council* [1977] AC 1014, 1051 (Lord Wilberforce), 1062 (Viscount Dilhorne), 1064 (Lord Diplock), 1070 (Lord Salmon), and 1075 (Lord Russell), who expressed himself somewhat differently. Of course, that case was primarily concerned with the word 'unreasonably' in the context of Education Act 1944, s 68. See also the formulation 'whether a reasonable Secretary of State, on the material before him, could reasonably conclude that the interference with freedom of expression which he determined to impose was justifiable' in *R v Secretary of State for the Home Department, ex parte Brind* [1991] 1 AC 696, 751 (Lord Templeman).

[88] *Kennedy v Charity Commission* [2014] UKSC 20, [2014] 2 WLR 808, especially [55].

[89] *Li* (n 78), [68].

[90] A comparable approach is to be found in *R v Boundary Commission; ex parte Foot* [1983] 1 QB 600 (CA), 626, citing HWR Wade's *Administrative Law*, 5th edn (Oxford, Oxford University Press, 1982) 362 ('[w]ithin the bounds of legal reasonableness is the area in which the deciding authority has genuinely free discretion. If it passes those bounds, it acts ultra vires') and then citing *Wednesbury* (n 17) 230.

of the authority and from the perspective of a hypothetical reasonable authority (the standard being set by the judges) and the discretion could only be said to have miscarried if 'no reasonable authority' could have so exercised the power.[91]

The dictum in *Wednesbury* is criticised as being tautological, but in my view the extent of the tautology is reduced if, in the phrase 'so unreasonable that no reasonable authority', emphasis is put on the word 'authority' so as to distinguish the decision-maker from the court.

It is unfortunate, in my opinion, that *Wednesbury* unreasonableness should have been rebadged as 'irrationality' as was famously done by Lord Diplock in *Council of Civil Service Unions v Minister for the Civil Service*.[92] That, in my opinion, is semantically different from unreasonableness.[93] Lord Diplock then went further and explained what he had in mind as 'so outrageous in its defiance of logic or of accepted moral standards that no sensible person who had applied his mind to the question to be decided could have arrived at it'. It is this, I think, which has had, in the past, a distracting influence on the development of the law of legal unreasonableness. In my opinion, 'accepted moral standards' is too diffuse and dangerous in so far as it suggests that those standards lie outside and are independent of the scope and purpose of the legislation as construed by the court.[94]

I add that there should be no difference in relation to the implication of reasonableness between the exercise of a discretion and the formation of an opinion or state of satisfaction as a prerequisite to the exercise of a statutory power.[95]

D. Irrational Fact-finding

I turn to fact-finding. There are real differences between England and Australia as to the availability on judicial review of challenges, as such, to findings of fact or fact-finding.

[91] The power to impose conditions was conferred by Sunday Entertainments Act 1932, s 1(1) and the condition imposed by the Wednesbury Corporation was: 'No children under the age of fifteen years shall be admitted to any entertainment, whether accompanied by an adult or not'.

[92] *Council of Civil Service Unions* (n 85), 410–11.

[93] See P Walker, 'What is Wrong with Irrationality?' [1995] *Public law* 556, 556–57; cf Airo-Farulla, 'Rationality and Judicial Review of Administrative Action' (n 20) 573–74 and P Sales, 'Rationality, Proportionality and the Development of the Law' (2013) 129 *Law Quarterly Review* 223 and see *Hayes v Willoughby* [2013] UKSC 17, [2013] 1 WLR 935, [14] (Lord Sumption, with whom Lord Neuberger and Lord Wilson agreed), [28] (Lord Reed). As Jason Varuhas points out in Chapter 4, 'The Public Interest Conception of Judicial Review: Its Procedural Origins and Substantive Implications', Lord Diplock did this to eliminate what he saw as 'confusion' because 'unreasonable' bears different meanings according to whether the context is that of private law or public law with the consequence that the word 'unreasonable' should be limited to private law and be 'best avoided' in public law. But, although logical, the influence of the rewording in judicial review has, in my view, been baneful.

[94] This may explain what appears to be the more ready acceptance by the courts in England, compared with Australia, of a lower threshold of legal unreasonableness: see n 18 above.

[95] *Li* (n 78), [90] (Gageler J).

In England it seems judicial review may be had for fundamental error of fact.[96] In addition it seems that *Wednesbury* unreasonableness is also applied to fact-finding. In England, as I understand it, fact-finding which is illogical or lacking a rational connection between the evidence and the decision or where the decision was made under a mistake or in ignorance of a material fact may found an order setting aside the administrative decision. In Australia there is a no evidence ground, with the emphasis on the word 'no',[97] but irrational or unreasonable fact-finding is not, as such, at least yet, a well-established ground of judicial review. I have not seen applied in Australia the approach of the Court of Appeal in *E*,[98] apparently now applied in *IA (Iran) v Secretary of State for the Home Department*.[99] For present purposes, it would seem that each of the paradigms in *E* involves a degree of evaluative judgement by the court. It also seems that, as in Australia, there are mistakes and mistakes.[100]

In Australia, the better view is that *Wednesbury* unreasonableness should be limited to its origins, that is, as a ground of review of the exercise of a discretion. But a similar principle may be emerging on which fact-finding may be judicially reviewed for serious irrationality.[101] It is to be noted, however, that in *SGLB* Gummow and Hayne JJ were making the point, with reference to *S20/2002*, that although the satisfaction of the criterion in question may include consideration of factual matters, 'the critical question is whether the *determination* was irrational, illogical and not based on findings or inferences of fact supported by logical grounds'.[102] This may mean that to look only at one instance or more than one instance of erroneous fact-finding may not of itself give rise to the conclusion that there has been a jurisdictional error. A wider enquiry is required and one which is founded in the statutory task vested in the person exercising the power.

It seems to be relatively uncontroversial that the absence of a reasonable or rational basis for a finding may found an inference that the decision-maker made a jurisdictional error on other grounds.[103]

Aronson and Groves say: 'There is a significant difference between supervising discretionary choices on the one hand (unreasonableness), and the care with which

[96] *E v Secretary of State for the Home Department* [2004] EWCA Civ 49, [2004] QB 1044; *Begum v Tower Hamlets London Borough Council* [2003] UKHL 5, [2003] 2 AC 430, 451 (Lord Hoffmann); cf *R (A) v London Borough of Croydon* [2009] UKSC 8, [2009] 1 WLR 2557.

[97] cf *Re Minister for Immigration and Multicultural and Indigenous Affairs, ex parte Palme* [2003] HCA 56, (2003) 216 CLR 212, [39] (Gleeson CJ, Gummow and Heydon JJ).

[98] *E* (n 96). This has been analysed by Craig, *Administrative Law* (n 76) 509–32.

[99] *IA (Iran) v Secretary of State for the Home Department* [2014] UKSC 6, [2014] 1 WLR 384, [54]–[57].

[100] *Ex parte Hebburn Ltd; Re Kearsley Shire Council* (1947) 47 SR (NSW) 416, 420, although Jordan CJ was there dealing with a mistake of law as to the proper construction of a statute investing a tribunal with jurisdiction.

[101] *Re Minister for Immigration and Multicultural Affairs, ex parte Applicant S20/2002* [2003] HCA 30, (2003) 198 ALR 59, [37] and [52] (McHugh and Gummow JJ), [173] (Callinan J); *Minister for Immigration and Multicultural and Indigenous Affairs v SGLB* [2004] HCA 32, (2004) 207 ALR 12, [38] (Gummow and Hayne JJ); *Minister for Immigration and Citizenship v SZMDS* [2010] HCA 16, (2010) 240 CLR 611.

[102] *SGLB* (ibid) (emphasis added).

[103] *R v Connell, ex parte Hetton Bellbird Collieries Ltd* (1944) 69 CLR 407, 430 (Latham CJ).

decision-makers have approached their tasks (irrationality)'.[104] However, in my opinion, this statement should not be taken as exhaustive of the available categories of judicial review in relation to fact-finding. As I have earlier written with reference to *SZRKT*,[105] what may be considered to be fact-finding is not universally immune from judicial review as it may fall within the question I have earlier suggested: having assessed the gravity of the error, is what has gone wrong of such significance to the statutory task that the person exercising the power has so departed from the task so that he or she has not carried out or completed the task. There may be some correspondence, even if non-conceptual, between that and 'the close link between judicial scrutiny of evidence [evidentiary review] and the general issue as to the reviewability of fact in judicial review proceedings' to which Paul Craig has referred.[106]

No doubt there is room for much debate here, but the point for present purposes is that any ground of serious irrationality in fact-finding must involve a close and qualitative evaluation of the fact-finding of the person exercising the primary power. As with all alleged unreasonableness, on judicial review it is necessary to precisely identify the 'nature and quality' of the error attributed to the administrative decision-maker and the legal principle that attracts a particular legal consequence.[107]

Although *R v Hillingdon London Borough Council, ex parte Puhlhofer*[108] and *Waterford v Commonwealth*[109] state that there is no error of law simply in making a wrong finding of fact, the emphasis should be on 'simply' and the question can be framed 'was the factual conclusion so badly formed as to reveal error to be characterised as legal error' going to jurisdiction?[110]

Where a ground of judicial review involves error of fact, the court must understand the facts and test, for example, whether there was any evidence for a finding or whether the finding has otherwise departed from the norm and, if so, to what extent. Relevant to this task is the often complex question of whether the alleged error is one of fact or one of law[111] but it is to be noted that justices of the High Court have

[104] M Aronson and M Groves, *Judicial Review of Administrative Action*, 5th edn (Sydney, Lawbook Co, 2013) 260.

[105] *SZRKT* (n 14).

[106] PP Craig, 'Substance and Procedure in Judicial Review' in M Andenas and D Fairgrieve (eds), *Tom Bingham and the Transformation of the Law* (Oxford, Oxford University Press, 2009) 73, 74.

[107] *Re Minister for Immigration and Multicultural Affairs, ex parte Applicant S20/2002* [2003] HCA 30, (2003) 198 ALR 59, [5] (Gleeson CJ).

[108] *R v Hillingdon London Borough Council, ex parte Puhlhofer* [1986] 1 AC 484, 518 (Lord Brightman).

[109] *Waterford* (n 32), 77 (Brennan J). Note that the word 'simply' must refer back to the opening sentence in Brennan J's paragraph: 'A finding by the AAT on a matter of fact cannot be reviewed on appeal *unless the finding is vitiated by an error of law*' (emphasis added).

[110] *Heffernan v Comcare* [2014] FCAFC 2; (2014) 218 FCR 1, [91] (Allsop CJ).

[111] See the analysis by T Endicott, 'Questions of Law' (1998) 114 *Law Quarterly Review* 292. In that respect, has the time come for the courts to jettison the presumption that a word or words in a statute have a meaning unaffected by the balance of the statutory context, with the resultant meaning being a question of fact only? See *Moyna v Secretary of State for Work and Pensions* [2003] UKHL 44, [2003] 1 WLR 1929, [23] (Lord Hoffmann), explaining *Cozens v Brutus* [1973] AC 854, 861 (Lord Reid), Lord Hoffmann's view being approved in *R (Jones) v First-tier Tribunal (Social Entitlement Chamber)* [2013] UKSC 19, [2013] 2 AC 48, [43] (Lord Carnwath); *OV and OW v Members of the Board of Wesley Mission Council* [2010] NSWCA 155, (2010) 79 NSWLR 606, (2010) 270 ALR 542, [32]; *Mainteck Services Pty Ltd v Stein Heurtey SA* [2014] NSWCA 184, (2014) 310 ALR 113, [73]–[77] (Leeming JA for the

rejected the argument that distinctions between legal and factual errors provide the decisive *discrimen* in claims under section 75(v) of the Australian Constitution.[112]

E. Other Grounds of Judicial Review

What about other commonly formulated grounds of judicial review (putting to one side for the moment my earlier strictures about the place of grounds)?

A question of statutory construction would not commonly (except perhaps in Canada or the United States) involve qualitative review of the primary exercise of the power.

However, *FTZK*[113] shows that error of law may also involve a detailed consideration and evaluation of the findings of fact made by the tribunal in the particular context of the structure of the reasoning. The High Court held unanimously that the tribunal misconstrued Article 1F of the Refugees Convention, which states that the provisions of the Convention 'shall not apply to any person with respect to whom there are *serious reasons for considering* that … he has committed a serious non-political crime outside the country of refuge prior to his admission to that country as a refugee'.[114] The statutory context was provided by section 36(2)(a) of the Migration Act 1958 (Commonwealth), which specified at the relevant time, as a criterion for a protection visa, that the applicant was a non-citizen in Australia to whom the Minister is satisfied Australia has protection obligations under the Refugees Convention as amended by the Refugees Protocol.[115]

Returning to the traditional categories or 'grounds', in my view, non-observance of procedures that were required by law to be observed in connection with the making of the decision would be approached in the same way as denial of natural justice or procedural fairness. An exercise of a power in such a way that the result of the exercise of the power is uncertain, a species of ultra vires, would also, I think, be approached in the same way as error of law.

Other grounds, that the decision was induced or affected by fraud, or an exercise of a power for a purpose other than a purpose for which the power is conferred, or an exercise of a discretionary power in bad faith, or an exercise of a personal discretionary power at the direction or behest of another person, or an exercise of a discretionary power in accordance with a rule or policy without regard to the merits

Court of Appeal). Plainly there is more scope for the conclusion that a word or phrase raises only a question of fact where the word or phrase has a trade or technical meaning or is a word or phrase of art and for that reason has been the subject of evidence.

[112] See *SZMDS* (n 101), [119] (Crennan and Bell JJ), citing *Re Minister for Immigration and Multicultural Affairs, ex parte Applicant S20/2002* [2003] HCA 30, (2003) 198 ALR 59, [54] (McHugh and Gummow JJ) who said that '[t]he introduction into this realm of discourse of a distinction between errors of fact and law, to supplant or exhaust the field of reference of jurisdictional error, is not to be supported'. Their Honours were not, I think, anticipating any resort to pragmatism as seen in *R (Jones) v First-tier Tribunal (Social Entitlement Chamber)* [2013] UKSC 19, [2013] 2 AC 48.

[113] *FTZK* (n 21): see above.

[114] Emphasis added.

[115] *FTZK* (n 21) [6], [16] (French CJ and Gageler J), [25], [31] (Hayne J), [97] (Crennan and Bell JJ).

of the particular case would each, I think, require a qualitative evaluation.[116] I have already referred to the ground of no evidence or other material to justify the making of the decision.

The courts must leave the merits to the person exercising the primary power and it seems reasonably clear that common law courts will stay away from a choice or policy at least where the statutory power has been exercised reasonably, not limiting the legal standard of unreasonableness to the irrational.[117] And a state of satisfaction by the person who has exercised the primary power must be reasonable in that it could be reached by a person understanding the statutory function being performed.

VI. CONCLUSION

To summarise, judicial review is largely qualitative in the areas I have primarily identified, natural justice, whether mandatory considerations have been taken into account or prohibited considerations have not been taken into account and unreasonableness/irrationality. Qualitative judicial review may be involved in an error of law case. I have sought to explain that judicial review of impugned fact-finding is also qualitative. I agree that 'the quality of the [administrative] decision made, both substantive and procedural, is the province of judicial review, whether or not the decision was "correct and preferable"'.[118]

This may be not far from what Lord Wilberforce had in mind in *Secretary of State for Education and Science v Tameside Metropolitan Borough Council*:

> The section is framed in a 'subjective' form—if the Secretary of State 'is satisfied'. This form of section is quite well known, and at first sight might seem to exclude judicial review. Sections in this form may, no doubt, exclude judicial review on what is or has become a matter of pure judgment. But I do not think that they go further than that. If a judgment requires, before it can be made, the existence of some facts, then, although the evaluation of those facts is for the Secretary of State alone, the court must inquire whether those facts exist, and have been taken into account, whether the judgment has been made upon a proper self-direction as to those facts, whether the judgment has not been made upon other facts which ought not to have been taken into account. If these requirements are not met, then the exercise of judgment, however bona fide it may be, becomes capable of challenge: see *Secretary of State for Employment v ASLEF (No 2)* [1972] 2 QB 455, per Lord Denning MR, at p 493.[119]

[116] As to fraud, see *SZFDE v Minister for Immigration and Citizenship* [2007] HCA 35, (2007) 232 CLR 189. As to acting under dictation, where it is necessary to show that the decision-maker gave no real independent attention to the exercise of the discretion to make the decision, see *Ansett Transport Industries (Operations) Pty Ltd v Commonwealth* (1977) 139 CLR 54 and *Telstra Corp Ltd v Kendall* (1995) 55 FCR 221. As to inflexible application of policy, see *British Oxygen Co Ltd v Minister of Technology* [1971] AC 610 and *NEAT* (n 62).

[117] *Li* (n 78).

[118] G Weeks, 'Litigating Questions of Quality' (2007) 14 *Australian Journal of Administrative Law* 76, 81.

[119] *Tameside* (n 87), 1047. It should, of course, be noted that Lord Wilberforce was there dealing with a state of satisfaction or opinion and, in terms, with jurisdictional facts.

But none of this is to say that judicial review tends to merits review as opposed to legality; or that it tends to policy rather than law. At the substantive end, understanding the quality of the exercise of the power is at its slightest when considering statutory construction and at its strongest when considering fact-finding. But even at its strongest, understanding the quality of the exercise of the power is not merits review in the sense that the court asks itself whether or not it agrees with the exercise or brings to the task the question of whether the exercise is right or wrong, albeit the court needs to understand the substance of what has been decided by the person who has exercised the power in order to rule on the lawfulness of what has occurred. This is not the same as judicial review being an appeal by way of a rehearing, nor is it the same as the court substituting its opinion for that of the administrator. Nor does the court, even in *Wednesbury* review, rule on the correctness of the decision. As the plurality recently said in *Li*: 'Properly applied, a standard of legal reasonableness does not involve substituting a court's view as to how a discretion should be exercised for that of a decision-maker'.[120]

It is possible to examine the substance without entering into the merits and the courts should so act. Where judicial review is qualitative it is not concerned with what the repository of the power should have done, where there were legally available choices. Instead the concern is with what the repository of the power should not have done.

The assessment of a legal error or the gravity of a legal error will often involve qualitative review.

[120] *Li* (n 78), [66]. See also *Boddington v British Transport Police* [1999] 2 AC 143, 175 (Lord Steyn).

12

Remedies for Laws that Violate Human Rights

KENT ROACH*

I. INTRODUCTION

REMEDIES SHAPE RIGHTS and crystallise relations between courts, legislatures and the executive. At the same time, they have rarely featured in modern theories of public law. This chapter is part of a larger project that attempts to fill that gap. It will examine the variety of remedies available for legislation that may infringe human rights with a focus on how such remedies help define the respective roles of courts and legislatures. It will take seriously the common expectation that courts will provide successful litigants with meaningful remedies. It will also try to respect the ability of legislatures to develop more comprehensive policies than the courts. These two goals—providing remedies while respecting the role of the legislature—are often at tension, but this chapter will examine ways of reconciling them.

Remedies will be defined in this chapter to include judicial rulings that interpret legislation to make it compatible with human rights and remedies for laws that clearly infringe human rights. These latter remedies range from declarations of invalidity in the United States, suspended declarations of invalidity in Canada and South Africa, and declarations of incompatibility under section 4 of the UK's Human Rights Act (HRA) 1998. Legislative responses to these latter remedies will also be considered as part of the remedial landscape. This is a broad and functional approach to remedies. It includes declarations under section 4 of the HRA 1998 even though in law they can be seen as 'purely exhortatory' and 'non-coercive'[1] and even though the Australian High Court has recently ruled that a similar remedy under one of Australia's statutory Bills of Rights is not a judicial function.[2]

* I thank the organisers and participants in the Public Law Conference 2014 at the University of Cambridge. I also thank the University of Victoria in Wellington for a Borrin Visiting Fellowship and the Gilbert and the Tobin Centre at the University of New South Wales where subsequent versions of the chapter were given as lectures and seminars. Special thanks to Petra Butler, Joel Colon-Rios, Fergal Davis, Rosalind Dixon, Robert Leckey, Philip Murray, Lynn Smith and Jason Varuhas for helpful comments.

[1] A Sathanapally, *Beyond Disagreement: Open Remedies in Human Rights Adjudication* (Oxford, Oxford University Press, 2012) 4, 23.

[2] *Momcilovic v The Queen* [2011] HCA 34.

This chapter will examine both positive and normative matters. Empirically it will suggest that the contrast that Mark Tushnet and others have drawn between 'strong' remedies associated with the ability of courts to strike down democratically enacted laws and 'weaker' remedies that allow for legislative formulation, pre-emption or even resistance to judicial rulings has been overstated. Although remedies are rightly critical to Professor Tushnet's distinction between strong and weak forms of judicial review,[3] detailed and contextual examination of the actual use of remedies and their legislative denouements undermine the utility of stark distinctions.

Professor Tushnet posits the American model of judicial review as the paradigmatic case of strong judicial review because courts can strike down democratically enacted legislation. This view of the American position has been widely and uncritically accepted. Many modern Bills of Rights have been deliberately tailored to afford the judiciary less power than it is perceived to have under the US Bill of Rights. Nevertheless, in the first part of this chapter I will suggest that the American experience is more nuanced than the simple story of strong form judicial review. US courts have often reserved facial declarations of invalidity to exceptional cases, often involving concerns that leaving overbroad laws on the books may chill free speech. Instead they often only invalidate laws as applied to the particular case or in as narrow a manner as possible.

The second part of this chapter will examine how Canadian and South African courts have softened so-called strong form judicial review under their constitutional Bills of Rights with suspended or delayed declarations of invalidity. This novel remedy, explicitly recognised in article 172 of the South African Constitution, fits well with a range of theories that seek to establish alternatives to stark choices between judicial or legislative supremacy.[4] It has been described as a 'dialogic'[5] or 'open'[6] remedy. They function as a form of legislative remand because they give Parliament an opportunity to address the larger policy implications of judicial rulings. Suspended declarations of invalidity are not, however, without their shortcomings or critics. For example, they often provide no effective or immediate remedy for the affected individuals.[7] Hence the tension that exists between providing effective remedies and respecting the role of the legislature.

The third part of this chapter will examine remedies under the HRA 1998. The UK courts have engaged in robust interpretations of laws under section 3 of the HRA 1998 in order to ensure that the rights of litigants are respected, especially

[3] 'Strong-form review itself has numerous variants. At its heart is the power of courts to declare statutes enacted by a nation's highest legislation unconstitutional, and to make that declaration practically effective': M Tushnet, *Weak Courts, Strong Rights* (Princeton, NJ, Princeton University Press, 2008) ix.

[4] S Gardbaum, *The New Commonwealth Model of Constitutionalism* (Cambridge, Cambridge University Press, 2013); K Roach, *The Supreme Court on Trial: Judicial Activism or Democratic Dialogue* (Toronto, Irwin Law, 2001).

[5] K Roach, 'Remedial Consensus and Challenge under the Charter' (2002) 35 *University of British Columbia Law Review* 211, 258.

[6] Sathanapally, *Beyond Disagreement* (n 1) 21–22.

[7] R Leckey, *Bills of Rights in the Common Law* (Cambridge, Cambridge University Press, 2015) 172; B Ryder, 'Suspending the Charter' (2003) 21 *Supreme Court Law Review* (2nd) 267.

in criminal cases.[8] An important example here is the courts' re-interpretation of a so-called rape shield law to make it compatible with fair trial rights.[9] Leaving aside the question of whether such an approach is justified by the HRA, it will be suggested that the interpretative remedy interfered with legislative policies to combat sexual violence as much as, and likely more than, the American approach of holding that similar laws were unconstitutional only on the facts of specific cases. Again, examining the neglected details of remedies undermines the utility of stark distinctions between strong and weak form judicial review.

The last part of the chapter will turn from positive analysis to normative matters of what the law ought to be. If the distinction between weak and strong form judicial review is not a helpful guide to understanding remedies for laws that violate human rights, then what can be a helpful guide? I will suggest that a distinction used by Abram Chayes in a seminal article on public law litigation between the traditional role of courts in resolving disputes between parties and their more tentative role in articulating public law or constitutional values may be a more useful guide.[10] I have drawn similar distinctions between the traditional compensatory/corrective functions of remedies as opposed to their newer regulatory/systemic functions in my own work.[11] In his recent book, Robert Leckey has drawn useful but non-watertight distinctions between judicial postures that orientate to 'dispute resolution' and 'constitutional enforcement' as opposed to those which focus on 'systemic improvements' and 'legislative engagement'.[12] These approaches all suggest that courts should both be concerned with providing remedies for those whose rights are violated and should engage more tentatively with larger systemic issues. Taken together they can be translated into a two-track remedial approach to devising remedies for laws that violate human rights. One track would provide affected litigants with meaningful remedies while a second systemic track would address broader issues, in collaboration with the legislature and the executive.

Although not fully embraced in any of the jurisdictions examined, my proposed two-track approach has been used in a few cases. One is a case from Northern Ireland where the court used a section 4 declaration of incompatibility with respect to an out-dated and discriminatory buggery offence, but also provided the accused with an effective remedy by refusing to convict him.[13] Another is a Canadian trial judgment that combined a suspended declaration of invalidity that remanded the issue of assisted suicide to Parliament while also contemplating that a successful litigant could obtain an exemption from the unconstitutional law while Parliament was

[8] R Dixon, 'A Minimalist Charter of Rights for Australia? The UK or Canada as a Model' (2009) 37 *Federal Law Review* 335, 343–51.

[9] *R v A* [2001] UKHL 25, [2002] 1 AC 45.

[10] A Chayes, 'The Role of the Judge in Public Law Litigation' (1976) 89 *Harvard Law Review* 1281.

[11] K Roach, *Constitutional Remedies in Canada*, 2nd edn (Toronto, Canada Law Book, 2013) ch 3.

[12] Leckey, *Bills of Rights in the Common Law* (n 7) 155 arguing that 'the notion is not of a choice between exclusive options but rather of relative responsiveness to different impulses ... attention to dispute resolution does not entail a corresponding reduction in attention to systemic engagement ... It is sometimes possible to fashion relief for the individual litigant as well as a systemic remedy for the future'.

[13] *Re McR's Application for Judicial Review* [2002] NIQB 58, [2003] NI 1.

given time to enact a better tailored law.[14] The Supreme Court of Canada did not follow the trial judge's two-track approach when it affirmed that the categorical ban on assisted suicide was unconstitutional, but only because the individual applicant had, unfortunately, died, making the case for the individual remedy moot. The Court remanded the issue to Parliament by suspending its declaration of invalidity for 12 months.[15] The UK Supreme Court in a recent similar case stopped short of issuing even a section 4 declaration of incompatibility. Nevertheless, the judges who had concerns with the existing law both sought to encourage Parliament to enact a better tailored law while also expressing some support for the idea that judges can and should make case-by-case decisions about when assisted suicide was warranted.[16] All of these cases provide some support for the idea that judges should be concerned both with fashioning effective remedies for litigants while also being aware of the need to allow other institutions, in this case the legislature, to help shape systemic remedies going forward.

A two-track approach that provides individual remedies can be criticised for infringing parliamentary supremacy.[17] Any incursion, however, stops short of the remedy most closely associated with strong form judicial review: namely, the immediate judicial declaration that legislation is of no force and effect because it infringes human rights. A two-track approach, consistent with its dialogic ambitions, attempts to avoid the extremes of both legislative and judicial supremacy. It contemplates an ongoing dialogue between courts and legislatures consistent with and nourished by the legal process origins of many dialogic theories. Specifically, it allows both legislatures and courts to enrich societal debates about justice by allowing both institutions to play concurrent and at times competing roles. It addresses the weaknesses of both suspended declarations of invalidity and declarations of incompatibility in not providing effective remedies for successful litigants.

Although Parliament has generally responded favourably to declarations under section 4 of the HRA 1998, in only a few cases has it provided litigants with effective remedies by making remedial legislation retroactive.[18] Similar results have been found in Canadian responses to suspended declarations of invalidity.[19] My proposed approach would allow courts do what they are best at, crafting remedies for individuals, while allowing them to remand policy issues to Parliament so that Parliament has an opportunity to do what it is best at, namely crafting policy and reconciling rights with social interests. Indeed, courts, Parliament and ultimately all of society

[14] *Carter v Canada* [2012] BSSC 886. The ruling was upheld on the merits but the Supreme Court only used a one-year suspended declaration of invalidity in part because the lead plaintiff had already died. *Carter v Canada* [2015] SCC 5.

[15] *Carter v Canada* [2015] SCC 5.

[16] *R (Nicklinson) v Ministry of Justice* [2014] UKSC 38, [2015] AC 657, [117].

[17] For a critical examination that argues that *Re McR's Application for Judicial Review* [2002] NIQB 57, [2003] NI 1, is inconsistent with the HRA 1998 and parliamentary supremacy, see F Davis and D Mead, 'Declarations of Incompatibility, Dialogue and the Criminal Law' (2014) 43 *Common Law World Review* 62.

[18] Sathanapally, *Beyond Disagreement* (n 1) 172–80.

[19] S Choudhry and K Roach, 'Putting the Past Behind Us?: Prospective Judicial and Legislative Constitutional Remedies' (2003) 21 *Supreme Court Law Review* (2nd) 205.

may benefit from the interplay of different remedial processes used by courts and legislatures.

II. STRONG JUDICIAL REVIEW? THE AMERICAN RELIANCE ON 'AS APPLIED' DECLARATIONS OF INVALIDITY

The United States' reputation as the home of strong judicial review depends on the idea that once the US Supreme Court has decided a constitutional matter, little can be done if the Constitution is not amended or the Court does not change its mind. To be sure, this type of judicial supremacy holds true in some contexts. It took the Civil War and subsequent constitutional amendments to overturn the Court's decision upholding slavery[20] and threats to pack the Court to have it abandon its opposition to the New Deal.[21] Nevertheless, the actual remedial practice of US courts is frequently more nuanced than the story of judicial supremacy suggests.

The US Supreme Court has long expressed a preference for narrow 'as applied' rulings of constitutional invalidity as opposed to broader rulings of facial invalidity. In other words, US courts generally do not strike down laws in their entirety but rather hold that they do not apply on the facts of the particular case presented to them. In 1912, the US Supreme Court upheld a challenged state law noting 'it suffices ... to hold that, as applied to cases like the present, the statute is valid'.[22] In 1987, the Court upheld this preference for narrow rulings by noting that the fact that a law authorising preventive detention 'might conceivably operate unconstitutionally under some conceivable set of circumstances is insufficient to render it wholly invalid'.[23] Facial declarations of invalidity that strike down laws in their entirety have often been reserved for cases involving freedom of expression issues. Mark Tushnet presents the United States as the paradigm of 'strong form' judicial review, but does not focus on the tendency of US courts to soften strike down powers through the use of narrow 'case-by-case' declarations of invalidity.[24]

Although the use of narrow 'as applied' remedies does not figure prominently in his analysis, the American preference for 'as applied' rulings is consistent with Cass Sunstein's defence of case-by-case constitutional minimalism as a basis for minimising the damage done by judicial 'mistakes' and maximising the space for legislative law-making.[25] It raises interesting questions, however, whether 'as applied' rulings themselves generate democratic debates and responses. Case-by-case 'as applied' rulings of invalidity suggest that the courts have taken care of the constitutional rights problem and that any other response may be inconsistent with human rights.

[20] *Dred Scott v Sandford*, 60 US 393 (1857).

[21] *West Coast Parish Hotel Co v Parrish*, 300 US 379 (1937).

[22] *Yazoo and Mississippi Valley RR v Jackson Vinegar*, 226 US 217, 219 (1912).

[23] *United States v Salerno*, 481 US 739, 745 (1987).

[24] In his book-length study of the issue, Professor Tushnet only mentions the distinction between 'as applied' and facial invalidity once: Tushnet, *Weak Courts, Strong Rights* (n 3) 144.

[25] C Sunstein, *One Case at a Time: Judicial Minimalism on the Supreme Court* (Cambridge, MA, Harvard University Press, 2001).

Such remedial responses implicitly invite legislatures to leave issues involving rights to the courts. In contrast, broader facial declarations of invalidity that strike down entire laws on First Amendment[26] or void for vagueness[27] grounds may attract more media and political attention because they intrude more deeply into the legislature's policies. Some of the US Supreme Court's most recent controversial rulings have involved broader facial declarations of invalidity. For example, the Court has used facial declarations of invalidity to strike down the Defence of Marriage Act limiting marriage to opposite sex couples and to strike down some gun and abortion laws.[28]

American commentators have cautioned against placing mechanical reliance on the preference for narrow 'as applied' rulings. They have argued that the choice between narrower and broader rulings is often a function of the particular right being protected.[29] Even in the First Amendment context, however, the US Supreme Court has upheld laws on the basis that the unconstitutional applications of such laws are so rare that the proper remedy is one limited to holding the law unconstitutional as applied in a particular case.[30] There remains much support in American jurisprudence for the idea that facial invalidation of laws is 'strong medicine that has been employed by the Court sparingly and only as a last resort'.[31] Although neglected by commentators, this remedial experience qualifies the idea that the United States is unequivocally the paradigm of strong judicial review.

A. Rape Shield Example

The continued importance of narrow rulings of invalidity is well demonstrated by how US courts have dealt with so-called rape shield laws that seek to protect complainants in sexual assault trials by placing limits on the admissibility of their prior sexual conduct. Such laws are designed to respond to a legacy of sexist discrimination and blaming the victim in the criminal justice system. They raise complex and difficult issues about the competing rights of the accused and victims. The courts have an important and traditional role in ensuring that the accused receives a fair trial. In turn, legislatures as elected institutions have an incentive to enact broad

[26] See, eg, *Thompson v Western States Medical Center*, 535 US 357 (2002) (striking down restrictions on commercial advertising); *Ashcroft v Free Speech Coalition*, 535 US 234 (2002) (striking down restrictions on laws against child pornography with respect to those who 'appear to be' minors); *United States v Playboy Entertainment Group Inc*, 529 US 803 (2000) (striking down provisions that limit the hours that adult programming can be shown).

[27] *City of Chicago v Morales*, 119 S Ct 1849 (1999) (loitering law struck down as excessively vague).

[28] See, eg, *District of Columbia v Heller*, 128 S Ct 2783 (2008) (striking down gun law); *Kennedy v Louisiana*, 128 S Ct 2641 (2008) (striking down death penalty for rape of a child); *Roper v Simmons*, 543 US 551 (2005) (striking down death penalty for crimes committed by minors).

[29] M Dorf, 'Facial Challenges to Federal and State Laws' (1994) 46 *Stanford Law Review* 235; R Fallon, 'As Applied and Facial Challenges and Third Party Standing' (2000) 113 *Harvard Law Review* 1321.

[30] The court stated that the petitioners' arguments that the law was overbroad should have been brought as 'as applied' challenges by an individual prosecuted for such conduct. Even if successful, such challenges would not have resulted in facial invalidation of the impugned law. See *Burson v Freeman*, 112 S Ct 1846, 1857 n 13 (2012).

[31] *National Endowment for the Arts v Finley*, 524 US 569, 580 (1998).

restrictions on the admission of evidence in order to protect women and children who are grossly overrepresented among the victims of sexual offences. Many US courts have dealt with the overly broad scope of rape shield laws not by striking the laws down, but by holding the law to be unconstitutional and of no force and effect only when the exclusion of particular evidence in a particular case will result in an unfair trial. In other words, the courts have issued constitutional exemptions for some accused based on the facts of their particular case while at the same time allowing the law to stand as enacted by the legislature.[32]

The American approach of relying on case specific declarations of invalidity or constitutional exemptions can be defended as the most practical response to the complex and fact-specific problems presented by rape shield laws. It has been endorsed in Rule 412 of the Federal Rules of Evidence which authorises judges to admit evidence of the complainant's prior sexual conduct when constitutionally required. Nevertheless, many state rape shield laws that remain on the books may be deceptive to some complainants who may find that the broad protections of privacy provided in the legislation will be inapplicable and that they may be cross-examined on prior sexual conduct in their particular case. At the same time, the American approach allows democratically enacted rape shield laws to remain in place even though they may not be applied in every case. As will be seen, the Canadian approach, though commonly thought to be less 'strong' than the American approach, forces courts to use either immediate or suspended declarations of invalidity for rape shield and other unconstitutionally overbroad laws.[33] This is another reminder of the importance of testing broad and theoretical categories such as strong and weak form of judicial review against the empirical details of particular remedies.

The American approach of case-by-case constitutional exemptions or 'as applied' declarations of invalidity can also be usefully compared to the British approach. In *R v A*,[34] the House of Lords interpreted a broad rape shield law under section 3 of the HRA 1998 so to expand the grounds for admission of the complainant's prior sexual conduct when necessary to ensure that the accused received a fair trial. This early 2001 case under the HRA 1998 was the start of a trend to strong and 'remedial' interpretations under section 3 that ensured that the applicant, in this case a criminal defendant facing prison, received a remedy. As Professor Rosalind Dixon has explained, judges were understandably reluctant in such cases to use a section 4 declaration of incompatibility and allow a defendant to face what they had effectively declared to be an unfair trial.[35] Nevertheless, the interpretation of the rape shield law adopted by the House of Lords in *R v A* was in tension to Parliament's intent to provide broad and categorical privacy protections to complainants in sexual assault trials. It produced at least as much uncertainty and distortion of legislative intent as the American approach. Indeed, the British approach arguably involved more distortion because it re-interpreted the law as it would be applied in all cases.

[32] See generally D Haxton, 'Rape Shield Statutes: Constitutional Despite Unconstitutional Exclusion of Evidence' [1985] *Wisconsin Law Review* 1219.

[33] *R v Ferguson* [2008] 1 SCR 96.

[34] *R v A* [2001] UKHL 25, [2002] 1 AC 45.

[35] Dixon, 'A Minimalist Charter of Rights for Australia?' (n 8) 344.

Following the doctrine of parliamentary supremacy still accepted in the United Kingdom, Parliament could have theoretically enacted legislation to repeal the judicial interpretation, but this might only have resulted in courts again reading down any new rape shield law to ensure that the accused receive a fair trial. In addition, the interpretative remedy adopted by the House of Lords was less controversial than a facial declaration of invalidity that the Canadian Supreme Court used with respect to a similar rape shield law.[36] As will be seen in the next section, the Canadian case provoked Parliament to engage in wide-ranging reform of sexual assault law to improve the protection of victims of sexual violence.

An important empirical point of this chapter is that the contrast between strong and weak form judicial review erodes in some remedial contexts. 'As applied' declarations of invalidity weaken strong form American judicial review. This feature of American constitutionalism is so taken for granted that it has not received much attention from influential American commentators, such as Professors Tushnet and Sunstein. Conversely, interpretative remedies under the HRA 1998 strengthen so-called weak form judicial review to give litigants effective remedies but sometimes at the expense of distorting Parliament's intent. Both the American and British approaches are consistent with the traditional judicial role of ensuring fair trials and providing effective remedies for individual litigants, but at some cost to both the role and intent of the legislature.

III. STRONG JUDICIAL REVIEW? THE CANADIAN AND SOUTH AFRICAN EXPERIENCES WITH SUSPENDED DECLARATIONS OF INVALIDITY

Commentators are increasingly categorising the Canadian Charter of Rights and Freedoms as a 'strong' form of judicial review because Canadian legislatures have been reluctant to use their power to override most Charter rights. To be sure, the Canadian courts have strike down powers under section 52(1) of the Constitution Act 1982 and have not hesitated to use them. Nevertheless, Canadian strike down powers are softened in a number of ways that are not generally appreciated. Similarly, South Africa's 1996 Constitution provides the Constitutional Court with strike down powers, but less attention has been paid to a specific provision that allows courts to suspend 'the declaration of invalidity for any period and on any conditions, to allow the competent authority to correct the defect'.[37]

The Canadian courts have avoided striking down laws by re-interpreting them to make them consistent with the Charter. For example, potentially overbroad obscenity and child pornography offences and correction of children defences have all been upheld through creative interpretative remedies.[38] As in *R v A*, such remedies run the danger of distorting parliamentary intent at least when the creatively interpreted law was originally enacted. Another danger is that Parliament has little

[36] *R v Seaboyer* [1991] 2 SCR 577.

[37] Constitution of the Republic of South Africa, 1996, s 172(1)(b).

[38] *R v Sharpe* [2001] 1 SCR 45; *Canadian Children's Foundation v Canada* [2004] 1 SCR 76.

incentive to revisit controversial issues once the courts have 'fixed' them. In the free speech context, Canadian courts have used interpretative remedies where US courts would have used facial declarations of invalidity to avoid any chill that a law that is facially overbroad might impose on free speech.[39] Strong interpretative remedies cannot be justified, as is done in the United Kingdom,[40] on the basis that they are necessary to provide effective remedies for litigants. In Canada, interpretative remedies are used as a less drastic and controversial alternative to a strike down.

Another way that strike down powers have been softened is through the use of suspended declarations of invalidity. This novel remedy has no textual basis in the Canadian Constitution. Indeed, it is at odds with section 52(1) which mandates that laws inconsistent with the Constitution are of no force and effect to the extent of their inconsistency. The suspended declaration of invalidity was first used in 1985 in a non-Charter case to avoid declaring all of Manitoba's laws unconstitutional because they were only enacted in English.[41] Since that time and despite some attempts to limit its use to cases that present dangers to the rule of law and public safety,[42] the suspended declaration of invalidity has become quite common and has been used in some of Canada's most controversial strike down cases. For example, the Supreme Court used it when striking down many of Canada's prostitution laws, laws prohibiting private medical insurance and laws that allowed the use of secret evidence in security cases without adversarial challenge.[43]

Despite dicta from the Supreme Court of Canada to the contrary,[44] it is difficult to dispute that one justification for the use of a suspended declaration of invalidity is that legislatures may have a greater institutional competence to devise a comprehensive remedial response. For example, in a case involving an unconstitutionally under-inclusive benefit scheme, a suspended declaration of invalidity would allow Parliament to extend the benefits to satisfy constitutional requirements of equality, but to reduce the magnitude of the extended benefits because of budgetary concerns.[45] Parliament can reduce benefits to save funds for other programmes in a way that the courts cannot. Indeed, this is a classic example of a multi-faceted or polycentric issue over which courts are at a disadvantage to legislatures.[46]

South African courts have recognised that one justification for the use of suspended declarations of invalidity is the legislature's superior ability to create policy

[39] C Rogerson, 'The Judicial Search for Appropriate Remedies under the Charter' in RJ Sharpe (ed), *Charter Litigation* (Toronto, Butterworths, 1987).

[40] A Kavanagh, *Constitutional Review under the Human Rights Act* (Cambridge, Cambridge University Press, 2009) ch 4.

[41] *Re Manitoba Language Rights* [1985] 1 SCR 721. The Court maintained jurisdiction in that case until all the unilingual laws were translated in 1992.

[42] *Schachter v Canada* [1992] 2 SCR 679.

[43] *Bedford v Canada* [2013] 3 SCR 110; *Chaoulli v Quebec* [2005] 1 SCR 791; *Charkaoui v Canada* [2007] 1 SCR 350.

[44] *Schachter v Canada* [1992] 2 SCR 679, 717, stating that the use of suspended declarations 'should not turn on considerations of the role of the court and the legislature' but on whether an immediate declaration of invalidity will harm the rule of law, public safety or deprive people of benefits.

[45] ibid. Parliament responded to the decision by accepting expanded paid parental leave benefits but lowering them from 15 to 10 weeks.

[46] L Fuller, 'The Forms and Limits of Adjudication' (1978) 92 *Harvard Law Review* 353.

and regulate complex matters going forward.[47] Writing in the South African context, Sandra Liebenberg has observed that a suspended declaration may be appropriate 'when there are a range of reasonable policy options to cure the constitutional defect and the particular choices are better made through democratic institutions and broad consultative processes'.[48] Aruna Sathanapally has similarly concluded that a 'specialised' division of labour between courts and legislatures has been the dominant justification for the use of declarations of incompatibility under section 4 of the HRA 1998.[49] The dialogic remedies of suspended declarations and declarations of incompatibility are designed to recognise that even if legislatures accept a rights decision by the court, they can often craft more comprehensive remedies than the courts or place the court's preferred remedy in a broader policy context.

The suspended declaration of invalidity is not without its critics and the new remedy can even be seen as something as a work in progress. Its use can be unpredictable, especially in Canada where courts are less than candid about how considerations of institutional capacity and competence influence their decision whether to use a suspended declaration of invalidity.[50] There are also practical issues with the appropriate timing of suspended declarations of invalidity. The shortest suspension in Canada has been four months,[51] likely reflecting the fact that the remedy related to medically required healthcare. This is likely too short a period to allow for an informed legislative reply. The typical period of a suspension is 12 months, but the Canadian government has already indicated that it will seek an extension of this time with respect to a suspended declaration of invalidity for an absolute ban on assisted suicide, in part because the 12-month period was disrupted by a scheduled election.[52] The longest suspension in Canada has been 18 months. This was justified on the basis that it would allow the government to consult with indigenous groups over the right of members to vote in Band elections, but the opportunity seemed to have been squandered by governmental delay and the eventual legislation that was enacted could have been enacted without such an extensive delay.[53] In other cases, however, legislatures have responded in a creative way that would not otherwise be open to the court. For example, a suspended declaration of invalidity was used in one early Charter case involving voting districts with unequal populations.

[47] *Mashavaka v President of the Republic of South Africa* 2005 (2) SA 476 (CC).

[48] S Liebenberg, *Socio-Economic Rights* (Claremont, Juta, 2009) 390.

[49] The alternative justification that legislatures will articulate and act on their own interpretation of human rights has only emerged as a factor in the prisoner voting response and even there Sathanapally and other commentators find Parliament's interpretative performance to be lacking: Sathanapally, *Beyond Disagreement* (n 1) ch 7.

[50] For arguments that courts tried without success to confine the use of suspended declarations in *Schachter v Canada* [1992] 2 SCR 679 into discrete categories and have yet to articulate the principles that should guide whether to use this remedy, see K Roach, 'Principled Remedial Discretion under the Charter' (2004) 25 *Supreme Court Law Review* (2nd) 101.

[51] *Canadian Doctors for Refugee Health Care v Canada* [2014] FC 65.

[52] 'Conservative government finally launches assisted dying consultation', *Toronto Star*, 17 July 2015. The 12-month suspension was provided in *Carter v Canada* [2015] SCC 5.

[53] *Corbiere v Canada* [1999] 2 SCR 203. For critical discussion of the legislative reply which simply extended the same voting rights to all Band members whether they were resident or non-resident on a reserve, see Roach, 'Remedial Consensus and Challenge under the Charter' (n 5).

The legislature responded with new legislation that expanded the number of ridings so as to ensure both that ridings had more equal populations, but also that ridings in northern and remote districts were kept to a manageable size to facilitate members being able to provide services for their constituents.[54]

The strongest principled argument against suspended declarations of invalidity is that they deprive the successful litigant of an immediate remedy.[55] This is a non-trivial weakness. There was a strong dissent when the South African Constitutional Court suspended a declaration of invalidity in a gay marriage case in part because this left the successful litigant without an immediate remedy.[56] In one case involving same-sex partners, the Supreme Court of Canada suspended a declaration of invalidity to allow the legislature to amend a large variety of laws to deal with the issue.[57] The legislature did so, but did not provide retroactive relief for the same-sex litigants in the case. The legislature also used the controversial category of 'same-sex partner' as distinct from 'spouse' in the new legislation. The legislative intent to distinguish same-sex partners from heterosexual partners was not admirable. Indeed, it was discriminatory, though it was subsequently unsuccessfully challenged under the Charter on that basis.[58] Nevertheless it was an expression of the considered views of a socially conservative government elected by the people of Ontario at a time before Canada recognised same-sex marriage and by a legislative dominated by a socially conservative government.

When it came to same-sex marriage, however, Canadian courts ordered an immediate remedy.[59] This provided an effective and immediate remedy for the successful applicants, but also created same-sex marriages that Parliament could not have retroactively undone had it been prepared to defend exclusions on marriage by explicitly and temporally overriding equality rights, as is possible under the Canadian Charter.[60] South Africa's use of a suspended declaration of invalidity in its same-sex marriage case could have easily led to the creation of a separate and discriminatory status for same-sex partners or even to the abolition of the civil institution of marriage altogether. Justice Albie Sachs who wrote the lead judgment noted that when Parliament held public hearings after the judgment 'there were many vociferous attacks on the idea of same-sex marriages—and only a few people defended it. Acutely homophobic statements were recorded'.[61] At the same time, the Constitutional Court made clear that should Parliament not act within the year, the appropriate remedy would have included same-sex couples in statutory and common law concepts of marriage. In other words, what matters is not simply the act of

[54] K Roach, 'Reapportionment in BC' (1990) 24 *University of British Columbia Law Review* 79.

[55] Leckey, *Bills of Rights in the Common Law* (n 7) 172; B Ryder, 'Suspending the Charter' (2003) 21 *Supreme Court Law Review* 267.

[56] *Minister of Home Affairs v Fourie* 2006 1 SA 524 (CC), [167]–[170] (O' Regan J in dissent).

[57] *M v H* [1999] 2 SCR 3.

[58] *Vincent v Ontario* (1999) 70 CRR (2nd) 365 (Ont SC).

[59] *Halpern v Canada* (2003) 225 DLR (4th) 529 (Ont CA).

[60] For criticism of the immediate remedy on this basis see K Roach, 'Dialogic Judicial Review and its Critics' (2004) 23 *Supreme Court Law Review* (2nd) 49, 83–85.

[61] A Sachs, *The Strange Alchemy of Life and the Law* (Oxford, Oxford University Press, 2009) 253.

suspension, but the hints that the courts provide and the form of the remedy that the court will order if Parliament does not act. The South African Constitutional Court suspended the declaration of invalidity but made it crystal clear that the exclusion of same-sex couples from marriage was not 'constitutionally sustainable. The defect must be remedied so as to ensure that same-sex couples are not subjected to marginalisation or exclusion by the law, either directly or indirectly'.[62]

One response to the shortcoming of suspended declarations of invalidity in not providing a successful litigant with an immediate remedy is to exempt that litigant from the suspension so that the litigant receives the benefit of an immediate remedy. Canadian courts have been less willing than South African courts both to exempt successful litigants from a suspension and to take responsibility to limit the damage of unconstitutional laws during the period of delay. Driven in large part by concerns for preserving a form of qualified immunity from damages for a validly enacted law later found to be unconstitutional, the Canadian courts have placed formalistic limits on combining remedies for individuals as an 'appropriate and just' remedy under section 24(1) of the Canadian Charter of Rights and Freedoms with more systemic remedies, including suspended declarations of invalidity, awarded under section 52 of the Constitution Act 1982 which simply provides that unconstitutional laws are of no force and effect.[63] The result is to make it difficult but not impossible for Canadian courts to both suspend a declaration of invalidity under section 52(1) and order an individual remedy for the litigant under section 24(1).

Another factor in explaining the reluctance of Canadian courts to order individual remedies while suspending a declaration of invalidity is that the Canadian Supreme Court has disapproved of case-by-case constitutional exemptions,[64] implicitly rejecting the American preference for narrow 'as applied' rulings as discussed in the last section. This approach has the effect of limiting the ability of courts to exempt successful litigants from the effects of a suspended declaration of invalidity and has also made courts reluctant to order remedies during the suspension. As in the United Kingdom, this has made the Canadian Court somewhat reluctant to use a suspended declaration in criminal cases where the effect of such a suspension might be to imprison a person under an unconstitutional law or after an unfair trial.[65] In contrast, the South African Constitutional Court appears more willing to order remedies during a suspension in an attempt to ensure some protection for litigants and to limit the damage to constitutional values during the suspension.[66]

[62] *Minister of Home Affairs v Fourie* 2006 1 SA 524, [147].

[63] *Guimond v Quebec* [1996] 3 SCR 347; *Mackin v New Brunswick* [2002] 1 SCR 405; *R v Demers* [2004] 2 SCR 489.

[64] *R v Ferguson* [2008] 1 SCR 96.

[65] For criticism of some exceptions to this trend on the basis that they could result in imprisonment or other severe consequences on the basis of an unconstitutional law, see Roach, *Constitutional Remedies in Canada* (n 11) [14.1860].

[66] *Zondi v Member of the Executive Council for Traditional and Local Government Affairs* 2005 3 SA 589 (CC), [129]–[134]; *Nyathi v MEC for the Department of Health, Gauteng* 2008 5 SA 94, [88] (CC). No exemption or interim remedy was granted in the South African gay marriage case because of concerns that it would have 'an impermanent or twilight character out of keeping with the stability usually associated with marriage': *Minister of Home Affairs v Fourie* 2006 1 SA 524, [154].

The South African approach in this regard is more consistent with the ideal approach that will be proposed in the final part of this chapter.

The suspended declaration of invalidity also has its virtues. As Mark Tushnet has suggested such a remedy may make it easier for courts to enforce socio-economic rights by allowing legislatures to enact positive measures and make distributive decisions about the allocation of scarce resources.[67] The Supreme Court eventually suspended a declaration of invalidity in the controversial *Chaoulli*[68] case which struck down Quebec's restriction on the purchase of private health insurance on the basis that long wait times for surgeries violated rights. Quebec used the 12-month suspension to stave off the potentially regressive effects of such a market approach by introducing a variety of new procedures to reduce wait times in Canada's universal public healthcare system.[69] The Court effectively drew the government's attention to those individuals harmed by long surgery wait times while also allowing the legislature to craft a variety of systemic remedies that even the most robust court could not devise on its own.

A. Rape Shield Example

The fact that the Canadian approach can be bolder than the American is underlined by the Supreme Court of Canada's 1991 decision in *Seaboyer*.[70] In that case, the Canadian Supreme Court struck down an overbroad rape shield law. It refused to follow the less drastic approach of lower courts, which like US courts, exempted defendants from the law on a case-by-case basis and only to the extent that the exclusion of evidence of prior sexual conduct would result in an unfair trial. The Court gave its facial declaration of invalidity immediate effect. One reason was that the case was decided in 1991 when suspended declarations were in their infancy. A better reason may be that the Court, like the House of Lords in *R v A*, was understandably reluctant to convict a defendant after an unfair trial.

The Court's facial declaration of invalidity unleashed a storm of public controversy. The federal government seriously considered using the override under section 33 of the Charter to restore the rape shield law. Nevertheless, after wide consultations, the government and Parliament opted for legislation, passed in 1992. The legislation enacted a less absolute rape shield law but also fundamentally reformed the law of sexual assault to underline that 'no means no' and to require an accused to make reasonable inquiries about consent to sexual activity. The result was the best example of constructive, respectful and creative dialogue between the Court and Parliament in the Charter's history. The new legislation respected the Court's

[67] Tushnet, *Weak Courts, Strong Rights* (n 3) ch 8.

[68] *Chaoulli v Quebec (Attorney-General)* [2005] 1 SCR 791.

[69] C Flood and B Chen, 'Charter of Rights and Health Care Funding: A Typology of Canadian Health Rights Litigation' (2010) 19 *Annals of Health Care Law* 479; K Roach, 'Polycentricity and Queue Jumping in Public Law Remedies: A Two Track Approach' (2016) 66(1) *University of Toronto Law Journal* (forthcoming).

[70] *R v Seaboyer* [1991] 2 SCR 577.

decision, but also re-affirmed and advanced the legislative goal of better protecting women and children from sexual violence in a manner that the courts could not achieve in a case narrowly focused on only the rape shield provisions.[71] Even though the Canadian Court engaged in strong form judicial review by striking down a recently enacted rape shield law in its entirety, the result was a vindication of Parliament's power to advance its objectives through comprehensive and creative legislative remedies that the courts could not devise.

Suspended declarations of invalidity have been used in some of the most controversial cases decided under the Charter. In 2012, the Court suspended a declaration of invalidity that three prostitution-related offences violated the Charter because they made sex work less safe. The Court provided no guidance on whether the unconstitutional laws should be enforced during the one year suspended declaration of invalidity.[72] Parliament responded with controversial new legislation that criminalised the purchase but generally not the sale of sex.[73] There is a danger that Parliament will use the opportunity provided by a suspended declaration of invalidity to enact an 'in your face' legislative reply that rejects the premises of the court's ruling about human rights. That said, a government that is not committed to human rights or the rule of law will enact unconstitutional legislation whether or not a suspended declaration of invalidity is employed. In any event, Canada's new law criminalising the purchase of sex will be challenged under the Charter and is the product of legislative choices made by Canada's most recent conservative government. The effect of the suspended declaration of invalidity was to force democracy in the sense of requiring Parliament to update laws in light of new evidence about the dangers faced by sex workers.

In 2015, the Court also employed a one-year suspended declaration of invalidity for the offence of assisted suicide.[74] The Court deferred to the ability of Parliament to consult and do research about the most effective way to regulate assisted dying. The one-year period to devise legislation will be challenging. Indeed, it is fraught in part because the government did not start its formal consultation until six months after the decision and within two months of a general election and then tasked the consultation to a three person panel that included two persons who the government had called as expert witnesses in its failed defence of the absolute ban on assisted suicide.[75] The Court in the assisted suicide case was able to avoid the dilemma of whether deferring to Parliament's role meant sacrificing its ability to ensure effective remedies for litigants because the litigant in this case had already passed away by the time that the Court decided the case. The trial judge in this case had suspended the declaration of invalidity but was also prepared to order an exemption from the law during the period of suspension for the successful applicant, something that is consistent with the preferred approach to remedies defended below.

[71] Roach, *The Supreme Court on Trial* (n 4) ch 14.

[72] *Bedford v Canada* [2013] 3 SCR 1101.

[73] Protection of Communities and Exploited Persons Act SC 2014 c 25.

[74] *Carter v Canada* [2015] SCC 5.

[75] 'Federal government appoints panel to review assisted dying but critics fear bias', *National Post*, 17 July 2015.

Suspended declarations of invalidity have emerged as a new remedy in Canada and South Africa, recognising Parliament's unique abilities to respond to rights concerns in a more comprehensive manner than the courts. This remedy softens strong form judicial review in both countries but in Canada especially has sometimes meant that successful litigants have not received immediate or effective remedies. The South African Constitutional Court also employs suspended declarations of invalidity, but seems to be more attentive to ordering interim remedies that minimise the damage of unconstitutional laws that are given temporary force in order to give the legislature an opportunity to craft a new law that better respects human rights. Again, the South African approach seems more consistent with the preferred approach outlined below.

IV. WEAK JUDICIAL REVIEW? THE BRITISH EXPERIENCE WITH REMEDIAL INTERPRETATIVE REMEDIES AND DECLARATIONS OF INCOMPATIBILITY

The HRA 1998 falls within Tushnet's model of weak form judicial review because a deliberate decision was made not to give courts the power either to strike down laws inconsistent with human rights or to follow the frequent American practice of refusing to apply them in the case at hand. Instead, courts were given the power under section 3 to read legislation 'where possible' as compatible with human rights. Where not possible, the court was to issue a declaration of incompatibility under section 4. Such a declaration has no effect in the case before it. Consistent with parliamentary supremacy, Parliament can reject or simply ignore a declaration of incompatibility. At the same time, section 10 of the HRA 1998 provides a fast-track procedure for remedial orders and legislation that is strikingly also available with respect to rulings of the European Court of Human Rights. Although this fast-track has seldom been used, Parliament has responded to most section 4 declarations.[76]

The declaration of incompatibility is a strange form of remedy in the common law tradition because in one breath it recognises that human rights have been infringed while in the next breath it indicates that the court will not provide a remedy for the litigant and indeed will enforce a law against the litigant that is incompatible with human rights. As Professor Dixon has suggested, the understandable unwillingness of courts to place themselves in such an awkward position helps explain why in criminal cases such as *R v A*, UK courts have tended to opt for interpretations under section 3 of the HRA 1998 that allow them to provide litigants with effective remedies.[77] The awkwardness of the declaration of incompatibility also may explain why the Australian High Court has characterised it as a non-judicial remedy that undermines the judicial function by offering gratuitous advice to Parliament.[78]

[76] Sathanapally, *Beyond Disagreement* (n 1) ch 6.
[77] Dixon, 'A Minimalist Charter of Rights for Australia?' (n 8).
[78] *Momcilovic v The Queen* [2011] HCA 34.

New Zealand courts have also been reluctant to make such declarations under their statutory Bill of Rights which, like the HRA 1998, denies courts the ability to strike legislation down. The New Zealand courts are especially reluctant to use such a weak remedy in a criminal case where it could result in a person being convicted under a law that nevertheless violates human rights.[79]

One possible explanation for why the United Kingdom has more willingly accepted the declaration of incompatibility than courts in Australia and New Zealand is the deeper integration of supra-national law in the United Kingdom. Baroness Hale has, for example, indicated that the purpose of a declaration of incompatibility 'is to warn Government and Parliament that, in our view, the United Kingdom is in breach of its international obligations' under the European Convention on Human Rights.[80] In addition, ten of the first 18 declarations of incompatibility have involved clear violation of Strasbourg jurisprudence.[81] Indeed, many suggest that the section 4 declarations have had a stronger impact than their merely persuasive force because of the availability of further appeals to the European Court of Human Rights.[82] In any event, the declaration of incompatibility, like most supra-national remedies, is more of a persuasive than a coercive command and control remedy. Nevertheless, even in the United Kingdom, the section 4 declaration remains an awkward and rarely used remedy. In a few recent cases, the UK Supreme Court has even resiled from issuing 'the firm words'[83] of a section 4 declaration. The Court instead relied simply on dicta or 'indications' that a law may infringe human rights.

The UK courts have issued about 20 declarations of incompatibility under section 4. Except in the prisoner voting case to be discussed in greater depth below, Parliament has chosen to respond to all the declarations. The most controversial case involved post 9/11 legislation authorising indefinite detention of non-citizens suspected of terrorism who could not be deported because of torture concerns.[84] Parliament enacted reply legislation that was creative in the sense of reaching a result that was not available to the courts.[85] The new control order legislation respected the findings that the previous legislation was discriminatory by applying control orders to all persons, not just non-citizens. Although the control orders enacted in response to the declaration of incompatibility were immensely controversial and

[79] There is no express power for such declarations of incompatibility in the New Zealand Bill of Rights and the courts have held that they lack jurisdiction to make such declarations in criminal cases: *Belcher v Chief Executive of the Department of Corrections* [2007] NZCA 54. See C Geiringer, 'On a Road to Nowhere: Implied Declarations of Incompatibility and the New Zealand Bill of Rights Act' (2009) 40 *Victoria University of Wellington Law Review* 613, 626 ff.

[80] *R (Animal Defenders International) v Secretary of State for Culture, Media and Sport* [2008] UKHL 15, [2008] 1 AC 1312, [53].

[81] Sathanapally, *Beyond Disagreement* (n 1) 123.

[82] ibid.

[83] *R (Nicklinson) v Ministry of Justice* [2014] UKSC 38, [2015] AC 657, [117]. See also *R v Gul* [2013] UKSC 64, [2014] AC 1260, indicating that Parliament should consider amending the definition of terrorism to allow a freedom fighter exemption.

[84] *A v Secretary of State for the Home Department* [2004] UKHL 56, [2005] 2 AC 68; affirmed in *Al-Khawaja and Tahery v United Kingdom* (2009) EHRR 1.

[85] Prevention of Terrorism Act 2005.

were eventually repealed by Parliament, they were a less drastic regime than the previous law which authorised indeterminate detention in prison.

Although section 4 declarations have been used and have resulted in remedial legislation, the main remedy under the HRA 1998 has been section 3 interpretations. The British courts have exercised their interpretative powers under the HRA in a fairly robust way. The 2004 decision of the House of Lords in *Ghaidan v Godin-Mendoza*,[86] in which the court read a reference to opposite-sex couples to include same-sex couples, was a more robust approach than the Canadian Supreme Court took to a similar issue in the 1999 *M v H* case discussed above.[87] The majority of the House of Lords justified their interpretation on the basis of the mandate that Parliament had given to courts under section 3. Lord Millett argued in dissent that the court's interpretative remedy in the case at hand precluded several different options before Parliament.[88] The UK courts have also read down reverse onuses to evidential burdens. The New Zealand courts, with a similar interpretative mandate under their Bill of Rights, have resisted such interpretations.[89] Such robust interpretations under section 3 are defended as remedial, but there are concerns that they can also distort legislative intent and interfere with the role of the legislature. Parliament could in theory legislate to displace a section 3 interpretation but this might only result in more problems. If the reply legislation was still ambiguous, the courts might simply re-assert their previous rights compliant interpretation. If it was not ambiguous, but the courts maintained their views on compatibility, Parliament might be faced with a section 4 declaration. Given this, it is not surprising that there is little evidence of parliamentary replies after section 3 interpretations.[90]

Aileen Kavanagh has defended robust use of interpretative powers by relying on Lord Steyn's understanding of section 3(1) as a 'remedial provision'. Section 3 is a remedial provision because it allows the court to give a successful litigant an immediate remedy. In contrast, section 4 declarations of incompatibility provide the successful litigant who has demonstrated an unjustified violation of rights with no immediate remedy. As such, it departs 'from the duty of the courts to do justice to the litigants before them'.[91] Professor Kavanagh's concerns that section 4 declarations leave successful litigants with no immediate remedy mirror the concerns expressed above about successful litigants receiving no immediate remedy under Canadian suspended declarations of invalidity. It thus appears that the HRA 1998 also contains a remedial dilemma. Section 3 remedies are effective for the litigant but may not always respect the role of the legislature, whereas section 4 declarations

[86] *Ghaidan v Godin-Mendoza* [2004] UKHL 30, [2004] 2 AC 557.

[87] *M v H* [1999] 2 SCR 3.

[88] *Ghaidan v Godin-Mendoza* [2004] UKHL 30, [2004] 2 AC 557, [96] ff.

[89] Compare *R v Lambert* [2001] UKHL 37, [2002] 2 AC 545 with *R v Hansen* [2007] NZSC 7.

[90] For recent findings that there is very little substantive dialogue after HRA 1998, s 3 interpretative remedies, see C Crawford, 'Dialogue and Rights-Compatible Interpretations under Section 3 of the Human Rights Act 1998' (2014) 25 *King's College Law Journal* 34. For findings of more substantive dialogue after s 4 declarations, see A Young, 'Is Dialogue Working under the Human Rights Act 1998?' [2011] *Public Law* 773.

[91] A Kavanagh, *Constitutional Review under the Human Rights Act* (Cambridge, Cambridge University Press, 2009) 130.

respect the role and indeed the supremacy of Parliament, but provide no immediate and effective remedy for the litigant.

A. Rape Shield Example

The re-interpretation of an overbroad rape shield adopted by the House of Lords in *R v A* was a more robust judicial decision[92] than the decisions made by various State courts in the United States to exempt specific defendants from the effects of rape shield laws because the House of Lords re-interpreted the law for all future cases. Moreover, in doing so the House of Lords rejected Parliament's intent that the complainant's prior sexual activity with the defendant would only be admissible if it happened close in time to the event that lead to charges. The broad nature of the section 3 interpretative remedy is underlined by Lord Hope's dissent which, consistent with the American approach, argued that any remedy should depend on the facts of particular cases. *R v A* is another example of the danger of simplistic contrasts between strong American judicial review and weak British judicial review. The American approach of limited case-by-case exemptions resulted in less 'policy distortion'[93] than the broader re-interpretation in *R v A*.

The Canadian approach resulted in the most 'policy distortion' by striking the entire rape shield law down, but Parliament quickly advanced its policies against sexual violence in several creative ways. The Canadian Supreme Court did not use a suspended declaration of invalidity in this case, but if it had, there would not even have been the temporary policy distortion caused by the immediate declaration of invalidity in the case and the court's insertion of more flexible common law rules to replace the overbroad statute. At the same time, suspended declarations of invalidity raise difficult issues in criminal cases because of the danger of convicting people under unfair laws. These might have been addressed had the Supreme Court of Canada imposed its more flexible common law approach as an interim remedy that would have ensured fair trials while Parliament used a year to consult and respond to a suspended declaration of invalidity, if one had been used in Canada's rape shield case.

In summary, the HRA 1998 creates several dilemmas. Judges may have to choose between strained remedial interpretations under section 3 to give affected individuals

[92] See *R v A* [2001] UKHL 25, [2002] 1 AC 45, [45]. Lord Slynn explained that it is 'therefore possible under s 3 to read s 41, and in particular s 41(3)(c), as subject to the implied provision that evidence or questioning which is required to ensure a fair trial under article 6 of the Convention should not be treated as inadmissible. The result of such a reading would be that sometimes logically relevant sexual experiences between a complainant and an accused may be admitted under s 41(3)(c). On the other hand, there will be cases where previous sexual experience between a complainant and an accused will be irrelevant, eg an isolated episode distant in time and circumstances. Where the line is to be drawn must be left to the judgment of trial judges. On this basis a declaration of incompatibility can be avoided'. The matter would be delegated to the trial judge but the trial judge would have to apply the law as newly interpreted by the House of Lords, with the majority of judges agreeing to the amendments the courts made to the law in a specific paragraph: ibid [46]–[47].

[93] M Tushnet, 'Policy Distortion and Democratic Debilitation' (1995) 94 *Michigan Law Review* 245.

meaningful remedies or deferring more to the role of the legislature with a section 4 declaration at the cost of providing no remedy for an individual who has succeeded in the litigation and established a rights violation. It can be argued that the litigants may eventually receive a remedy, but even when Parliament responds favourably to a declaration of incompatibility, it often does not provide a retroactive remedy. The cost of not providing a remedy to the successful litigant is a considerable one for courts in the common law tradition which has frequently celebrated the close connection between rights and remedies. We will now discuss whether these remedial dilemmas can be avoided in an ideal system.

V. AN IDEAL APPROACH TO REMEDIES FOR LAWS THAT VIOLATE HUMAN RIGHTS

An ideal system presented below attempts to accommodate both the traditional functions and strengths of courts in providing remedies to aggrieved individuals and the ability of legislatures to situate concerns about rights in a broader policy framework. It would draw on the traditions of the common law of ensuring that where there is a right, there is a remedy, but it would also recognise the legitimate role of legislatures and society to be involved in the broader issues raised by a particular claim of right.

A. Dilemma of Providing Remedies but Interfering with Legislation

Both suspended declarations of invalidity and declarations of incompatibility make room for creative legislative responses to rulings that existing laws violate human rights. Nevertheless, they can be criticised for depriving successful litigants of immediate and sometimes any effective remedy for the violation of their rights. If taken to the logical extreme, they would allow a person to be convicted after an unfair trial and imprisoned under a law that violates human rights.[94] Such an approach runs the risk of sacrificing the individual for the contingent benefit of a legislative reply.

Fortunately, some courts have pulled back from such potential injustices. A Canadian trial judge who found that absolute Criminal Code prohibition against assisted suicide violated the rights of the disabled issued a suspended declaration of invalidity to give Parliament an opportunity to regulate assisted suicide, but was prepared to provide a successful litigant an exemption from the law subject to appropriate safeguards.[95] This is a more robust approach than contemplated in the

[94] *R v Demers* [2004] 2 SCR 489. For criticisms, see K Roach, 'New and Problematic Restrictions on Constitutional Remedies' (2004) 49 *Criminal Law Quarterly* 253.

[95] *Carter v Canada* [2012] BSCC 886, affirmed on the merits in [2015] SCC 5 with a one-year suspended declaration of invalidity but not addressing the exemption issue. The trial judge's exemption-based approach provided safeguards against abuse of those requesting assistance with ending their lives without imposing those safeguards on Parliament as a matter of constitutional law. It also ensured that a person who was courageous and able to litigate this issue could receive its benefit. The consequences of

similar *Nicklinson* case where the UK Supreme Court did not even make a section 4 declaration despite the majority of the Court recognising that an offence against assisted suicide could be unjust in exceptional cases. The majority looked to the ability of judges to tailor just exemptions from the offence as the optimal remedy, but one that was simply not available given the absolute nature of the offence as drafted by Parliament and the limitations on their remedial powers under the HRA 1998. It remains to be seen whether this case heralds an even greater retreat from using declarations of incompatibility which sit uneasily with the traditional role of courts in providing remedies.

British courts have been understandably uncomfortable with convicting persons under laws that violate human rights and have often opted for robust remedial interpretative remedies. The problem with interpretative remedies, however, is that they can distort the intent of the legislature in enacting the law. Moreover such remedies often provide the legislature little incentive to re-assert or refine its intent through new legislation. For example, there has been little in the way of substantive legislative replies to the use of robust interpretative remedies in the United Kingdom or Canada.[96] All of this suggests that there is a danger that interpretative remedies can distort and usurp Parliament's function. The section 4 remedy is more respectful of Parliament's policy-making role, but as Sathanapally has recognised in her book-length treatment of the remedy, new legislation enacted after a section 4 declaration has generally been prospective and this has denied some litigants effective remedies.[97]

Is there any way out of the dilemma that either see courts renouncing their traditional functions of providing individual remedies for the sake of deferring to legislatures or that allow courts to interfere with the role of the legislature for the sake of providing individuals with effective remedies?

making a terminally ill person wait until Parliament enacted a new law following a suspended declaration of invalidity are considerable. The applicant would be forced either prematurely to end her life when she would not require assistance or else suffer an agonising death without assistance. For arguments that Canadian courts should consider exempting successful litigants from suspended declarations of invalidity see Roach, *Constitutional Remedies in Canada* (n 11) [14.1790] ff. Canadian courts have responded in other less effective ways to the problem that suspended declarations of invalidity can leave litigants without immediate remedies. In one recent case, a trial judge found that the denial of required healthcare to a refugee applicant violated the Charter but refused to order that such healthcare be provided until the government had four months to decide how it would respond to her ruling. The short period of the suspension arguably produced the worst of both worlds: a vulnerable person was denied needed medical care but, perhaps in recognition of this tragedy, the government was given an unrealistically short period of time to deliberate and consult about its response to the court's ruling: *Canadian Doctors for Refugee Care v Canada (Attorney General)* [2014] FC 651, [1114]–[1115].

[96] Crawford, 'Dialogue and Rights-Compatible Interpretations under Section 3 of the Human Rights Act 1998' (n 90). In Canada, Parliament has not even amended pornography or child correction laws to reflect the Court's new interpretation.

[97] Sathanapally, *Beyond Disagreement* (n 1) ch 7 finds that even when Parliament responded with the Gender Recognition Act 2004 to recognise the rights of transgendered persons, it did not do so in a retroactive manner. Parliament did, however, recognise the rights of deceased fathers retroactively in the Human Fertilisation (Deceased Fathers) Act 2003.

B. A Two-Track Approach to Individual and Systemic Remedies

The tension between the role of courts in providing effective remedies for individuals and their more tentative and collaborative role with respect to systemic remedies suggests that attention should still be paid to Abram Chayes's path-breaking work on public law remedies.

Writing in 1976, Professor Chayes contrasted a traditional model of bipolar litigation and retrospective remedies for individuals with an emerging public law model where relief was fashioned with an eye on the future and its impact on vulnerable groups. Contrary to the stereotype of judicial activism, Chayes accurately observed that broader systemic remedies in US cases involving school desegregation and prison reform were often the product of negotiations between multiple parties.[98] Although Chayes was writing about institutional reform litigation, his insights are relevant to a broader range of remedial issues. He was influenced by the legal process school which provided the intellectual foundations for dialogic, collaborative, Commonwealth or common law understandings of constitutionalism. Like Lon Fuller[99] and Alexander Bickel,[100] Chayes understood that the powers of courts ultimately depended on their ability to persuade. He contemplated justice as an ongoing process and 'the subject of a colloquy in which legislators, officials and ordinary people—not just lawyers and judges—take part'.[101] Hence he did not oppose public law litigation simply because it did not rely on coercive command and control remedies. Later in his career, Chayes extended his work to supra-national remedies and was comfortable with their persuasive and iterative nature.[102] This suggests that he might also have been comfortable with new remedies such as the declaration of incompatibility which some believe are designed 'to warn Government and Parliament' that 'the United Kingdom is in breach of its international obligations'.[103]

Chayes' work on outlining the differences between backward-looking personal remedies and more tentative and forward-looking systemic remedies can help in reformulating the range of remedies for laws that violate human rights. Chayes' landmark articles can be read as suggesting that public law litigation was eclipsing traditional litigation, but it is more realistic and helpful to see public law litigation as supplementing the traditional model. Indeed, the traditional model where courts hear arguments from the directly affected person and can provide that person with relief supports much of the legitimacy of the courts.[104] Judges who are not attentive

[98] A Chayes, 'The Role of the Judge in Public Law Litigation' (1976) 89 *Harvard Law Review* 1281, 1302.

[99] L Fuller, *The Morality of Law*, revised edn (New Haven, CT, Yale University Press, 1969).

[100] A Bickel, *The Least Dangerous Branch*, revised edn (New Haven, CT, Yale University Press, 1986).

[101] A Chayes, 'How Does the Constitution Establish Justice?' (1988) 101 *Harvard Law Review* 1026, 1039.

[102] A Chayes and A Handler, *The New Sovereignty* (Cambridge, MA, Harvard University Press, 1995). On the persuasive nature of international law, see J Brunnee and S Toope, *Legitimacy and Legality in International Law* (Cambridge, Cambridge University Press, 2010).

[103] *R (Animal Defenders International) v Secretary of State for Culture, Media and Sport* [2008] UKHL 15, [2008] 1 AC 1312, [53].

[104] Fuller, 'The Forms and Limits of Adjudication' (n 46).

to this remedial imperative risk both the parties and the public dismissing them as non-elected officials who are interfering in or offering gratuitous advice on policy matters. In other words, judicial contributions to ongoing dialogues about the treatment of rights may be strengthened by being grounded in the actual experience of litigants. In most cases, this may mean that the court will have to attempt to provide some effective remedy for the litigant.

With careful attention to the work of both Chayes and Fuller, Robert Leckey has recently suggested that judges should struggle to mediate between the tasks of enforcing the constitution through dispute resolution while also being concerned with systemic problems that may require legislative engagement. He raises concerns that remedies like suspended declarations and declarations of incompatibility may neglect the victim and may even diminish 'what constitutional supremacy means in rights cases'.[105] At the same time, Professor Leckey rightly warns against an either/or choice that is sometimes associated with Chayes work and recognises that 'it is sometimes possible to fashion relief for the individual litigant as well as a systemic remedy for the future'.[106]

The ideal system in my view would allow courts the freedom to do justice in individual cases while at the same time employing innovative remedies such as suspended declarations of invalidity or declarations of incompatibility to allow legislatures to play a role in devising systemic remedies. In the United Kingdom and other countries with similar statutory Bills of Rights this might mean that courts would have limited powers of 'as applied' invalidity that are presently denied to them. After tracing the general reluctance of Parliament to provide retroactive individual remedies when responding to section 4 HRA declarations, Sathanapally has similarly suggested that a better alternative may be to allow courts to exempt litigants from incompatible laws.[107] This approach has effectively already been done in the United Kingdom but in only one controversial case where a court in Northern Ireland declared a buggery offence to be incompatible with the HRA 1998, but also provided an effective remedy for the accused and found a way to avoid convicting him.[108] Such a result may appear revolutionary in the UK context, but less so when viewed in comparative perspective.

Defenders of parliamentary supremacy will argue that judicial remedies in individual cases should not ignore validly enacted laws. They might also suggest that the approach taken in the Northern Ireland case opens the door to weak form judicial review becoming strong form judicial review with its attendant dangers of judicial supremacy.[109] But the positive analysis in this chapter suggests that the distinction between strong and weak form judicial review is unstable. Moreover, the courts might have paid even less respect to Parliament if they had simply re-interpreted an offence in a rights compatible manner but in a way that Parliament had never

[105] Leckey, *Bills of Rights in the Common Law* (n 7) 172, 193.
[106] ibid 155.
[107] Sathanpally, *Beyond Disagreement* (n 1) 180.
[108] *Re McR's Application for Judicial Review* [2002] NIQB 58, [2003] NI 1.
[109] Davis and Mead, 'Declarations of Incompatibility, Dialogue and the Criminal Law' (n 17).

intended. In other words, section 3 HRA remedies can distort Parliament's role even more than a section 4 remedy or a suspended declaration of invalidity.

The argument that courts should only use declarations of incompatibility and provide no individual remedies (or provide no exemptions from suspended declarations of invalidity) too readily accepts injustices. These injustices will not be distributed evenly and fairly throughout society as some supporters of parliamentary supremacy imagine.[110] They will disproportionately be inflicted on those at a disadvantage in the legislative process: people like the accused in the Northern Ireland case, non-citizens and prisoners.

Defenders of parliamentary supremacy tend to suggest that any incursion on it will inevitably result in judicial supremacy. My proposed approach avoids judicial supremacy even in the short term because it would deny courts the ability to strike down laws in their entirety. Indeed, it would also make it less necessary for UK courts to engage in strained 'remedial' interpretations of statutes to make them consistent with human rights. Instead, courts could provide individuals before them with remedies while giving the legislature an opportunity to address the broader policy issue by using either a declaration of incompatibility or a suspended declaration of invalidity.

In Canada, South Africa and the United States, a two-track approach could mean that courts would no longer have the power to issue immediate declarations of facial invalidity. They would only have the power to issue suspended declarations of invalidity or perhaps only a declaration of incompatibility. They would remain free to fashion immediate remedies for the litigants. My proposed system would involve a modest increase in judicial power in the United Kingdom, Australia and New Zealand and a modest decease of judicial power in Canada, South Africa and the United States. It seeks to avoid the extremes of judicial or legislative supremacy and draw on the distinctive strengths of each institution.

To return to the rape shield example used throughout this chapter, UK courts under the two-track system could protect an accused from an overbroad rape shield law, without distorting parliamentary intent by re-interpreting the law as in *R v A*. Unlike in *Seaboyer*, a court could no longer strike down an overbroad rape shield law, but would have to issue a suspended declaration of invalidity or perhaps a declaration of incompatibility that would facilitate a parliamentary response. At the same time, Canadian courts would not be restrained, as they presently are now,[111] from issuing a constitutional exemption or an American style narrow 'as applied' declaration of invalidity to ensure that no accused was convicted after an unfair trial. They might also, borrowing from South African practice, issue interim remedies or temporary guidelines to mitigate the harm of an unconstitutional law during the year that Parliament had to enact a better-tailored and less absolute rape shield law. This interim remedy might even become more permanent should Parliament fail to enact a new rape shield law or where Parliament enacted one that defied the

[110] J Waldron, *Law and Disagreement* (Oxford, Oxford University Press, 1999).
[111] *R v Ferguson* [2008] 1 SCR 96 rejecting constitutional exemptions.

premises of the court's judgment holding that its previous absolute law was a disproportionate violation of human rights.

C. Systemic Remedies: Suspended Declarations of Invalidity and Declarations of Incompatibility?

An important design feature in the ideal system is whether the court can issue a suspended declaration of invalidity or only a non-binding declaration of incompatibility. In theory, this would seem to be a momentous decision. In the United Kingdom, New Zealand and some Australian States, deliberate decisions were made to deny courts strike down powers in large part because of a desire to maintain legislative supremacy and related fears of overreaching by an unelected judiciary. In practice, however, the distinction between non-binding declarations of incompatibility and suspended declarations of invalidity may not be quite as momentous. Both novel remedies give the legislature an opportunity to push back at the courts even by enacting hostile 'in your face' remedies that minimise or perhaps reject the right recognised by the court.[112] Both remedies also give legislatures an opportunity to take a more comprehensive approach than could be ordered by the courts.

The real difference between the two remedies is that the declaration of incompatibility assigns the burden of legislative inertia in favour of preserving a law that the courts have found to violate human rights whereas suspended declarations of invalidity give legislatures a time-limited period to enact new legislation before a law held by the courts to violate human rights is rendered null and void. The suspended declaration of invalidity can force legislatures to enact new legislation on an expedited timetable. Conversely, a declaration of incompatibility can allow a legislature to drag matters out and engage in 'passive resistance'[113] as the UK Parliament has done since the 2005 *Hirst* case[114] and a 2007 declaration of incompatibility with respect to the complete ban on prisoner voting.[115]

To be sure, there has been much discussion of and political posturing about prisoner voting in Parliament and even a backbench initiated vote, but Parliament has not responded to the courts' decisions with new legislation either affirming that all prisoners should continue to be denied the vote or with some less drastic alternative. The UK prisoner vote saga illustrates that while declarations of incompatibility and suspended declarations of invalidity may frequently have similar effects,

112 In both cases, such a hostile response might trigger attempts to obtain supra-national remedies. See *Moonen v Film and Literature Board* [2000] 2 NZLR 9, [20], noting that 'judicial indication' of incompatibility with human rights might be of value if the matter is considered by supra-national bodies such as the then UN Human Rights Committee. For a discussion of the role played by complaints under the International Covenant on Civil and Political Rights when Quebec used the override under the Charter, see K Roach, 'Constitutional International and Remedial Dialogues about Rights' (2005) 40 *Texas International Law Journal* 537.

113 Sathanpally, *Beyond Disagreement* (n 1) 180–85, 216–21.

114 *Hirst v United Kingdom (No 2)* (2006) 42 EHRR 41.

115 *Smith v Scott* [2007] CSIH 9.

the former allows a non-rights-compliant status quo to be maintained if Parliament avoids legislating.

In a democracy committed to human rights, there is much to be said for assigning the burden of legislative inertia to favour compliance with human rights and to encourage parliaments to engage in more, not less legislation. This is especially the case in a parliamentary system where a government with a majority in Parliament can usually legislate quickly to displace a court ruling on human rights that it considers erroneous or unacceptable. To be sure, the suspended declaration of invalidity can force democracy and require the enactment of legislation on an expedited timetable that may in some cases impair the quality of parliamentary deliberation. At the same time, the declaration of incompatibility allows rights to be violated if Parliament simply delays and can reward politicians for not taking a stand on difficult issues such as assisted suicide or same-sex marriage.

The ability of the UK Parliament to engage in 'passive resistance' to a declaration of incompatibility suggests that a suspended declaration of invalidity may be a superior remedy not because it necessarily allows the court's decision to prevail, but because it requires the legislature and society to grapple with issues that involve rights. Defenders of parliamentary supremacy and of denying prisoners the vote may rightly point out that Parliament has no obligation to respond to a section 4 declaration under the HRA 1998. Under my ideal system, however, it would. Again critics will argue that this stacks the deck in favour of the court's rulings and views on rights, but my response is that Parliament could simply re-affirm the complete ban on prisoner voting should it share and be prepared to put into writing the Prime Minister, David Cameron's emotional sense of 'disgust' at the thought of prisoners voting.[116]

At the same time, the courts have not been blameless in the lengthy prisoner voting rights saga in the United Kingdom. They have effectively rewarded Parliament for its delay in dealing with the matter. The UK courts have avoided their institutional obligation to consider claims of rights violations largely on the basis that it may disturb comity between the judiciary and Parliament.[117] The European Court of Human Rights has denied requests by prisoners for individual remedies such as damages during the long decade since *Hirst*.[118] It has also tried to impose deadlines in an attempt to induce the UK Parliament to introduce rights compliant legislation, but without success.[119]

[116] For my own argument that 'disgust' should not be accepted as an objective that can justify the infringement of a right to vote, see K Roach, 'The Varied Roles of Courts and Legislatures in Rights Protection' in M Hunt, H Hooper and P Yowell (eds), *Parliaments and Human Rights* (Oxford, Hart Publishing, 2015) 412–16.

[117] *R (Chester) v Secretary of State for Justice* [2009] EWHC 2293 (Admin), [34]; affirmed [2010] EWCA Civ 1439, [2011] 1 WLR 1436, [30]–[31].

[118] *Firth v United Kingdom* (47784/09) European Court of Human Rights, 12 August 2014 (denial of damages and legal costs).

[119] *Greens and MT v United Kingdom* (2011) 53 EHRR 21. (Six months until April 2011 given with subsequent extensions to September 2013 under the pilot judgment process to require countries to deal with structural roots of repetitive applications to the European Court of Human Rights. The Court is now considering over 2,000 applications from prisoners in the United Kingdom.)

Under my proposed two-track approach, disenfranchised prisoners who litigate should receive some remedy for being persistently denied the vote. Damage awards would have the advantage of publicising the continued violation of their rights. Awarding individual remedies to unpopular litigants such as prisoners is not without its risks. It reminds society that rights are continuing to be violated and makes those rights meaningful to prisoners who are still denied the vote. Granting damages to disenfranchised prisoners may provoke Parliament to react, and perhaps to over-react. But democracies run the risk of over-reactions.

D. Individual Remedies: 'As Applied' Declarations of Invalidity and Damages

An important part of my proposed two-track approach is the ability to give litigants some form of remedy, including damages, injunctions and 'as applied' declarations of invalidity. A significant part of a court's legitimacy and distinctiveness is its ability to give aggrieved individuals some tangible remedy.

As suggested above, the European Court of Human Rights has refused to give prisoners denied the vote in the United Kingdom any individual remedy, such as damages. In my view, this is regrettable both for the prisoners who have repeatedly been denied their rights to vote, but also for the Court which appears to be backing down from its initial ruling on prisoner voting rights. This does not mean that damages awards would be a panacea. There is a danger that low damages awards may trivialise human rights and even be seen as a weak tax on their violation.[120] Conversely there is a danger that even the award of modest damages to prisoners denied the right to vote might inflame public opinion and Parliament. Legislatures in the United States and New Zealand[121] have not hesitated to enact harsh laws restricting the damage awards available to prisoners, an unpopular group that is vulnerable in the legislative process.

A determined legislature might attempt to stop the award of robust individual remedies. Courts should protect themselves from such legislation on the basis of constitutional guarantees relating to the separation of powers and their inherent functions. The legislature should be able to resolve the systemic issue, but the core judicial function of providing remedies to individuals should not be curtailed by legislation in a democracy that respects the separation of powers.

Individual remedies such as damages are a tangible expression of respect for the humanity of those denied their basic rights and they help ensure that courts remain loyal to their institutional role. It is also possible that the award of individual remedies might promote a more informed political and social debate about the issue by publicising the fact that individuals continue to be denied their rights.

[120] For arguments that damages awards for human rights violations are often less robust than damages under the common law, see JNE Varuhas, *Damages for Violation of Human Rights* (Oxford, Hart Publishing, 2015).

[121] Prisoners' and Victims' Claim Act 2005, ss 3 and 14. Somewhat similar legislation was also enacted in the United States in the Prisoners Litigation Reform Act, 1996 110 Stat 1321; Title VII of Pub L 104–134.

More robust interim remedies than damages may be necessary to prevent a person from being convicted under a law that violates human rights during a suspended declaration of invalidity. The South African courts have been more active in this regard. Exemptions from laws or even more general interpretative remedies may be necessary to avoid convicting a person under a law that violates human rights. Strong individual or interim remedies bring the two-track approach closer to strong form judicial review. Nevertheless, they still avoid judicial supremacy because Parliament can still legislate in a way that limits or even overrides the interim measures that the court will enforce while it provides Parliament an opportunity to reconsider the matter.

E. Horizontal Equity Concerns

One objection to a two-track system is that it creates horizontal inequity between litigants who receive the benefit of a remedy from the court and other similarly situated individuals who may receive no remedy during a suspended declaration of invalidity. Non-litigants may receive no remedy even in cases where Parliament accepts the court's judgment. For example, legislatures in both the United Kingdom and Canada have rarely made new legislation retroactive when responding to suspended declarations or declarations of incompatibility and such a response can deprive people of a fully retroactive remedy or, in some cases, of any remedy at all.[122] Parliament's performance is disappointing given that section 10 of the HRA 1998 even contemplates retroactive legislation. Rather than encouraging the legislature to be more concerned about individuals receiving remedies by enacting retroactive legislation against legislative norms of prospectivity, it may be more practical to allow courts to engage in their traditional practice of awarding compensatory and effectively retroactive remedies for successful litigants.

In his recent warnings about suspended declarations of invalidity, Robert Leckey has argued that 'the idea of horizontal equality between the litigant and other members of her group differentiates constitutional law from private law'.[123] I agree with Professor Leckey that courts should do more to provide remedies to successful litigants in individual cases, but I am less convinced by his argument that constitutional law should be troubled by horizontal inequities, including those created when courts award individual remedies to successful litigants while others similarly situated might have to wait a year or so for new legislation.

In theory, whole classes and in some cases everyone enjoy constitutional rights equally, but the idea that courts should always enforce the rights of everyone in a uniform manner seems unrealistic. There is an element of inequity and queue jumping in any system of justice that stops short of the impossible world of full enforcement. For example, horizontal inequities are routinely condoned in cases

[122] S Choudhry and K Roach, 'Putting the Past Behind Us? Prospective Judicial and Legislative Constitutional Remedies' (2003) 21 *Supreme Court Law Review* (2d) 205; Gardbaum, *The New Commonwealth Model of Constitutionalism* (n 4) 198.

[123] Leckey, *Bills of Rights in the Common Law* (n 7) 99.

where victims of illegal searches have evidence (eg drugs, weapons) excluded if it is discovered and they are prosecuted, but often receive no remedy (or at most nominal damages) if the rights violation does not lead to the discovery of incriminating evidence. Judges often issue remedies in the former cases in an imperfect attempt to deter other similar rights violations in the latter cases. Another example can be taken from the prisoner voting case. The fact that only about 2,000 of 85,000 prisoners in the United Kingdom have sought remedies for being denied a vote is not a good reason to deny remedies such as damages to the minority of prisoners who have sought justice. The trial judge in the Canadian assisted suicide case only addressed the conditions on which the successful applicant in the case could obtain an exemption from the ban on assisted suicide during the 12 months given to Parliament to address the issue. She was silent on whether similar exemptions could be obtained for similarly situated litigants during that period, but nothing would prevent such litigation on behalf of the terminally ill who wish to expedite their death. The horizontal inequity created by the two-track remedial approach should in most cases be temporary. To be sure, the successful litigant will receive a remedy that others similarly situated do not receive, but the whole point of a suspended declaration of invalidity is to give Parliament a year or so to enact new legislation. Any continued horizontal inequities in the new legislation can be challenged to the extent that they violate human rights including equality rights. This approach contemplates a temporary period of injustice for some, but that is different from a permanent breach of a promise of horizontal equity in the enjoyment of rights.

Concerns about horizontal inequity are most pressing in the criminal context. A year in prison under an unconstitutional law while Parliament makes up its mind is simply unjust.[124] That said, horizontal inequities can be mitigated by courts developing interim remedies or guidelines concerning how people should be treated during that period. In the context of unconstitutional criminal offences, such interim guidelines might require a robust interpretative remedy that would apply during the suspension to ensure that a person is not convicted or imprisoned in violation of human rights.[125] At the same time, Parliament might be able to justify a departure from the court's interim remedies when enacting new legislation.

In summary, my proposed approach would have the benefit of ensuring that successful litigants before the court receive a meaningful remedy even while it allowed Parliament a year to enact a new constitutional law. The provision of an individual remedy accords with public expectations about how courts work. The remittance of controversial public policy issues to Parliament also accords with public expectations about how democracies work. The temporary horizontal inequity created by such an approach should be acknowledged and interim remedies can and should mitigate its harsher effects. Nevertheless, to reject a two-track remedial approach on the basis that it allows some horizontal inequities allows unattainable perfection to defeat a good system that avoids both judicial and legislative supremacy.

[124] See, eg, Roach, 'New and Problematic Restrictions on Constitutional Remedies' (n 94).

[125] *R v Swain* [1991] 1 SCR 933, as discussed in Roach, *Constitutional Remedies in Canada* (n 11) [14.1600]–[14.1620]. For the more robust South African experience with interim remedies that apply during a suspended declaration of invalidity see n 66 above.

VI. CONCLUSION

One point of this chapter has simply been to underline the neglected nature of remedies in public law. As Canada's Chief Justice McLachlin has argued, remedies often receive less attention than they deserve.[126] Mark Tushnet's influential distinction between strong and weak forms of judicial review seems to respond to this deficiency by tying the distinction to whether or not courts can declare legislation invalid. This highlights the importance of 'weak' remedies such as declarations of incompatibility. The positive analysis in this chapter, however, suggests that examining the details of remedies complicates this dichotomy. Professor Tushnet neglects the prevalence of narrow 'as applied' declarations of invalidity or constitutional exemptions in the United States as a means of preserving laws and softening 'strong form' judicial review. Suspended declarations of invalidity also soften strong form judicial review in Canada and South Africa, albeit in different ways than the American approach. Conversely, Parliament's willingness to respond to section 4 declarations of incompatibility, albeit with an eye on Strasbourg, conversely strengthens this so-called weak remedy. The empirical analysis in this chapter suggests that the polarised contest between weak and strong form judicial review often breaks down when held up to the actual practice of remedies. This should re-enforce the message that comparative lawyers and theorists of public law ignore remedies at their peril.

If Professor Tushnet's distinction between strong and weak form judicial review breaks down when viewed through the perspective of remedies (despite the centrality of remedies to the distinction), what can take its place? A distinction Abram Chayes drew long ago between individual remedies to resolve concrete disputes between parties and more contingent systemic remedies can be helpful. Chayes made this distinction in the course of his work on complex relief in institutional reform cases but it is also relevant to crafting remedies, including supra-national remedies, for legislation that violates human rights. Indeed Chayes' candid admission that systemic remedies are often the product of negotiation between interested parties can be applied to remedies such as the suspended declaration of invalidity or the declaration of incompatibility that invite a creative, political and negotiated legislative response.

Under the ideal approach proposed in this chapter, courts would be able to provide successful litigants with an effective and immediate remedy while at the same time giving the legislature a full opportunity to exercise their policy-making responsibilities when responding to and even authorising a violation of human rights. Such an ideal system might combine the American practice of narrow 'as applied' invalidity with the Canadian and South African practice of suspended declarations of invalidity, or perhaps the British practice of declarations of incompatibility. Such a system would increase judicial powers in the United Kingdom, but the increase in judicial power might be modest, especially if it was less necessary for courts to distort Parliament's intent by way of remedial interpretations under section 3 of the HRA 1998 so as to provide the accused and other litigants with effective remedies.

[126] B McLachlin, 'Rights and Remedies: Remarks' in R Sharpe and K Roach (eds), *Taking Remedies Seriously* (Ottawa, Canadian Institution of the Administration of Justice, 2010) 21.

None of the countries examined in this chapter fully embrace this ideal system, perhaps suggesting that it is too demanding. The demands of such a system are not so much on the judges, who simply would have to provide personal remedies and give Parliament an opportunity to address laws that violate human rights while indicating what remedy should apply should Parliament not be able to enact new legislation. That said, both the UK courts and the European Court of Human Rights have been criticised in this chapter for not providing remedies for continued violations of prisoners' right to vote.

Greater demands under this system would be placed on parliaments and by implication the polity. Parliaments would have to respond to declarations of incompatibility or suspended declarations of invalidity that would increase if courts could no longer engage in strong remedial interpretations of laws or immediate declarations of invalidity. A suspended declaration of invalidity can challenge the ability of parliaments to consult and deliberate about legislation. The prospect that parliaments may be more challenged than courts raises the deeper issue of whether the main problem with dialogic theories that aim to avoid both judicial and legislative supremacy is more with legislative than judicial capacity.[127]

The Canadian and South African systems are the closest of those examined in this chapter to the ideal two-track system. Nevertheless, the Supreme Court of Canada has hindered the ability of Canadian courts to provide strong individual remedies and more cautious systemic remedies by placing artificial restrictions on combining individual section 24(1) Charter remedies and systemic section 52(1) remedies and by preventing the use of constitutional exemptions for individual litigants even though these are widely used in the United States. The South African courts seem more willing to combine suspended declarations of invalidity with individual and interim remedies.

There are a few decisions that reveal that a two-track approach to remedies is possible, even practical. For example, a Canadian trial judge recognised that a one-year suspended declaration of invalidity of an assisted suicide offence would respect Parliament's role and its abilities to consult and devise comprehensive legislation to regulate assisted dying. Leaving aside the considerable challenges this will place on Parliament, the trial judge also recognised that she could not simply allow the successful litigant to suffer while Parliament deliberated and responded. She was prepared to fashion an exemption from the offence for the successful applicant provided that appropriate safeguards were satisfied.[128] This is the essence of the two-track approach advocated here: deference to Parliament on policy formation but recognition of a judicial duty to provide effective remedies to litigants.

[127] There is a small but growing literature, much of it critical, on the question of legislative capacity. See Hunt, Hooper and Yowell, *Parliaments and Human Rights* (n 116) and J Hiebert and J Kelly, *Parliamentary Bills of Rights: The Experiences of New Zealand and the United Kingdom* (Cambridge, Cambridge University Press, 2015). For an earlier and more optimistic take see M Tushnet, *Taking the Constitution Away from the Courts* (Princeton, NJ, Princeton University Press, 1999).

[128] *Carter v Canada* [2012] BSSC 886, affirmed, [2015] SCC 5. The Supreme Court did not address the individual remedy issue because the litigant had unfortunately passed away from natural causes by the time the case was decided on appeal. It did, however, use a one-year suspended declaration of invalidity to remand the issue to Parliament.

More attention needs to be paid to novel remedies such as the declaration of incompatibility and the suspended declaration of invalidity. These are promising new remedies. They should not be rejected simply because they involve remedial discretion or because they may create horizontal inequities. Nevertheless, these novel remedies are vulnerable to legitimate criticism to the extent that they fail to provide successful litigants with effective and meaningful remedies. This sacrifices a key judicial function, one unlikely to be replicated elsewhere. What is needed is a recognition that the courts have an important, unique and legitimate role in providing effective remedies for successful litigants while legislatures retain an ability to craft more comprehensive and creative systemic responses to rights rulings than courts.

Democracies can benefit from allowing courts to illustrate the effects of legislative policies on individuals who may be neglected or even disparaged in the legislative process. At the same time, courts cannot provide all the answers. Legislatures have an important role in establishing policies, including policies that involve rights.

New remedies such as declarations of incompatibility and suspended declarations of invalidity can force Parliament and ultimately all of us to resolve important and difficult issues involving rights without dictating how these difficult issues will be resolved. The challenges of such an approach may ultimately be greater for Parliament and societies than courts.

The choice between courts and legislatures is a false one: we have and we need both institutions. The two-track remedial approach proposed in this chapter allows the public to benefit from the distinctive ability of courts to focus on the plight of individuals and the distinctive ability of legislatures to focus on the big picture, including legislative goals and trade-offs in the formation of policies.

13

'Striking Back' and 'Clamping Down': An Alternative Perspective on Judicial Review

CAROL HARLOW AND RICHARD RAWLINGS

> A judge? You don't want to make a *judge* a doctor of laws! Politicians are the ones who make the laws, and pass the laws!
> Jim Hacker, MP in 'Yes Minister' (1981)

I. INTRODUCTION

THIS CHAPTER DEALS with a practice that we have called 'striking back', a phenomenon all too often glossed over in the literature of judicial review. By 'striking back' we mean official responses to court rulings that are deliberately negative in the sense that government or administration sets out to rid itself of a judicial decision that it finds inconvenient or otherwise dislikes. Striking back is essentially a backward-looking or 'fire-fighting' activity designed to remove or minimise the effects of a specific decision. In its impact it may nonetheless be purely forward-looking, eg regulations may be redrafted or a new statutory definition substituted with prospective effect. Occasionally, however, the action taken is retrospective—a dubious practice that we shall nonetheless encounter on several occasions in this chapter. Also, government may adopt a 'fire-watching' stance, taking steps to protect itself against the threat of future judicial 'interference' by changing the rules of the game in restrictive fashion, a variant on striking back that we call 'clamping down'. There are many forms of pre-emptive action, ranging from structural or procedural changes to the judicial review process with a view to blunting substantive legal action, to changes made to the general funding regime with a view to inhibiting it. At this pragmatic level, striking back is to be read as an element in a broader literature of impact theory, though this is typically more concerned with evaluating the positive effects of judicial review on bureaucratic decision-making and its impact on officialdom.[1]

[1] See, eg, D Feldman, 'Judicial Review: A Way of Controlling Government?' (1988) 66 *Public Administration* 21; M Hertogh and S Halliday (eds), *Judicial Review and Bureaucratic Impact* (Cambridge, Cambridge University Press, 2004).

At a higher, constitutional level, striking back forms an intrinsic part of the 'law and democracy' debate, challenging the complacent assumption that courts 'control' government or 'secure' the rights of citizens.[2] Courts in the UK constitution are classically seen as exercising the twin functions of protecting individuals and controlling misuse of power by the executive. The ability to secure compliance with judicial rulings is therefore inevitably a measure of 'how effective judicial review is at protecting individual rights and reducing government lawlessness'.[3] For a period of almost 40 years, the Application for Judicial Review (AJR)—the procedural machinery of judicial review—has been refined and there has been steady expansion of its ambit. At every stage of the process it is infused with considerable judicial discretion.[4] Predicated at one level on vibrant common law principles, at another on many applications of EU law and Convention rights, judicial review has been transformed.[5] A court-centred literature has mushroomed. By looking at judicial review other than through judicial eyes this chapter is a modest attempt to redress the balance.

Striking back is hardly new, nor is it confined to the Westminster model of parliamentary government (though this obviously offers great potential). We need only look back to Paris in the 1960s to find that the highly prestigious French Conseil d'Etat, at that time considered the acme of administrative jurisdictions, was experiencing considerable difficulty in implementing its rulings and had installed a special section, the Commission du Rapport, dedicated to tackling the problem. Guy Braibant, then *commissaire du gouvernenement*, highlighted three main tactics whereby recalcitrant public authorities could avoid implementing bothersome judgments: (i) they could utilise delaying tactics, involving appeals, judicial delays and the jurisdictional complexities of the dual French jurisdictions; (ii) they could retake annulled decisions by proper procedures; or (iii) they could resort to validatory legislation.[6] Harlow, in a follow-up article,[7] added the possibility (iv) that 'government would simply disobey'. Citing as exceptional the case of *Madzimbamuto v Lardner-Burke*,[8] where the Privy Council had to proceed to judgment in the face of a clear statement that the Rhodesian regime would not respect it, the author felt justified in remarking that it was 'assumed in England that administrative law judgments will be implemented'.[9] There is indeed a general perception that domestic judges operate within a mandatory model of judicial review in which powerful mandatory public law orders, injunctions and interdicts can be directed at all public authorities.[10]

Our interest in striking back arose in an era when UK Ministers could count on the powerful weapon of parliamentary sovereignty. Section II of this chapter, which looks more closely at the tools and techniques at the disposal of central government

[2] See P Cane, 'Understanding Judicial Review and its Impact' in M Hertogh and S Halliday (eds), *Judicial Review and Bureaucratic Impact* (Cambridge, Cambridge University Press, 2004) 16–17.
[3] ibid 30.
[4] C Harlow and R Rawlings, *Law and Administration*, 3rd edn (Cambridge, Cambridge University Press, 2009) ch 15.
[5] R Rawlings, 'Modelling Judicial Review' (2008) 61 *Current Legal Problems* 95.
[6] G Braibant, 'Remarques sur L'efficacité des Annulations pour Excès de Pouvoir' [1961] *EDCE* 53.
[7] C Harlow, 'Administrative Reaction to Judicial Review' [1976] *PL* 116.
[8] [1969] 1 AC 645.
[9] Harlow, 'Administrative Reaction' (n 7) 117.
[10] See *M v Home Office* [1994] AC 377 (Lord Woolf).

to achieve its ends,[11] is 'domestic' in the sense that it focuses on examples in which this historic constitutional model is directly in play. But ratification of the European Convention on Human Rights (ECHR) in 1951 and concession of the right of individual petition to the Court of Human Rights (ECtHR) in 1966, accession to the then European Communities in 1973 and passage of the Human Rights Act (HRA) 1998, set in motion changes to the constitutional framework with consequential displacement in the balance of power between legislature, executive and judiciary.[12] More prosaically, each in its own way changed the rules of the litigation game in expansive fashion. Thus, section III considers the limitations on striking back after the introduction into the legal order of the two powerful European Courts sitting in Luxembourg and Strasbourg. Under these regimes, striking back has in some ways become harder and the steps taken to counter judicial decisions may have to be different: in terms of Braibant's classification, there is less scope for validatory legislation but more room for delaying tactics. Nonetheless, a recurring theme of the chapter is continuity; the objectives of striking back and often the tactics (though not always the targets) remain, we shall suggest, broadly the same.

Our research for *Pressure Through Law* (1992),[13] where we set out to evaluate the 'success' of litigation strategies by interest groups, taught us that pre-emptive action is not always a question of government versus judiciary. The aim may be to stack the cards against (classes of) individual litigants and/or to target strategic forms of litigation or even particular campaigning groups. We ventured to prophesy that the UK government might one day take major steps to clamp down on judicial review. We identified various possibilities. Government might (v) take direct and drastic steps, for example, by inserting an ouster clause into a statute governing a substantial area of government activity. It might restrict the competence of the courts or render justice less effective, for example, by moving all immigration cases out of courts into immigration tribunals without giving them power to order injunctive relief. Appeal rights might be curtailed or very short time limits for legal action imposed. Less directly, government might (vi) take action to undercut the judicial review process itself. One option was stricter rules of standing—something of a temptation at a time when the statutory test of 'sufficient interest' had been opened up in a way that would greatly facilitate public interest litigation.[14] Funding was an obvious target: (vii) the cost of judicial review could be made prohibitive by changing the right to legal aid or ramping up court fees. These tactics are the subject of extended discussion in section II of the chapter where two such general forays by UK governments are documented: the first when in 2003–2004 Labour Home Secretary David Blunkett led retaliatory action against the judges in immigration and asylum cases; the second, when under the 2010–2015 Coalition Government of Conservatives and Liberal Democrats, a raft of restrictions on the judicial review process was launched.

[11] The positions of the devolved governments lie beyond the scope of the chapter.

[12] V Bogdanor, *The New British Constitution* (Oxford, Hart Publishing, 2009).

[13] C Harlow and R Rawlings, *Pressure Through Law* (London, Routledge, 1992) ch 7.

[14] *R v IRC, ex parte National Federation of Self-Employed and Small Businesses* [1982] AC 617.

We pick up a second theme from *Pressure Through Law* in section III of the chapter. In 1992, we documented the start at domestic level of the use of arguments based on European law and of the growth of public interest litigation at Strasbourg and Luxembourg. Here we note the rise of a movement for thoroughgoing retaliatory action against these two Courts in response to events described briefly in section III of the chapter. At the time of writing, threats are being made of recourse to (viii) the 'nuclear option' of legislating against international legal obligations. As we shall see, the suggestion has openly been made in the House of Commons of introducing a Canadian-style 'notwithstanding clause' into legislation,[15] while the Manifesto on which the Conservatives won the 2015 election promised to 'scrap Labour's Human Rights Act and introduce a British Bill of Rights'.[16]

II. WESTMINSTER AT HOME

A. Flying High

In the uncodified UK constitution, where Parliament is legally sovereign, compliance with judicial rulings must ultimately be a matter of expectation—but an expectation strongly underpinned by appeal to the rule of law.[17] Although it may theoretically always be open to government to legislate, even retrospectively, to reverse a judicial decision, Ministers may be subject to criticism and pressed to play fair. If a government departs too far from the expectation, judicial retaliation and a breakdown of the usually harmonious relations between executive and judiciary may be provoked. A game of legislative and adjudicative 'ping pong' between judges and Ministers may ensue.

The sequels to particular cases illustrate the different ways in which government may choose to strike back. The first edition of our textbook, *Law and Administration* in 1984,[18] included a trio of examples from the domestic pantheon of great cases. In *Burmah Oil*,[19] a paradigm case of striking back, the government used legislation both retrospectively to annul a House of Lords decision so as to deprive Burmah Oil of any damages that might be awarded and prospectively to clamp down on future claims. Professor HWR Wade excoriated the 'unusual measure of retaliation' as a demonstration that Parliament 'can, when it wishes, expropriate without compensation and in violation of existing legal right, in a manner not permitted in some other countries which enjoy the protection of written constitutions and bills of rights'.[20]

[15] A 'notwithstanding clause' takes its name from s 33 of the Canadian Charter of Rights, under which legislation may provide that it shall operate notwithstanding the provisions of the Charter.

[16] See Conservative Party, *Conservative Party Manifesto 2015* (2015) and Conservative Party, *Protecting Human Rights in the UK: The Conservatives' Proposals for Changing Britain's Human Rights Laws* (2014).

[17] Perhaps increasingly so: T Bingham, *The Rule of Law* (London, Allen Lane, 2010).

[18] C Harlow and R Rawlings, *Law and Administration*, 1st edn (London, Weidenfeld and Nicolson, 1984).

[19] *Burmah Oil v Lord Advocate* [1965] AC 75 was annulled by the War Damage Act 1965.

[20] See latterly, HWR Wade and C Forsyth, *Administrative Law*, 11th edn (Oxford, Oxford University Press, 2014) 681.

Our case study presented both sides of the argument, remaining studiously neutral. On the one hand, retrospective legislation was dangerous because it overstepped the essential boundary between executive and judiciary; on the other hand, it was justifiable in this case to restore parity between the many victims of war damage who had accepted limited compensation and the few able to claim redress through the courts on a (supposedly) preferential scale.[21]

Our second illustration was *Padfield*,[22] the archetypal example of striking back by taking the same decision twice (Braibant's second category). The House of Lords having moved decisively to control ministerial discretionary power, the Minister implemented the judgment by referring the impugned decision to an investigatory committee for consideration; he then declined to follow its advice. This outcome illustrates the 'halfway-house' nature of quashing orders (formerly certiorari), which allow the administration to revisit a matter following correct procedures. Today, this is a well-established and usually lawful practice, as illustrated in *R (Greenpeace) v Secretary of State for Trade and Industry*,[23] where a consultation exercise concerning government policy on 'nuclear new build' was quashed as 'very seriously flawed'. Having 'reviewed the evidence' and 'carefully re-examined the impact of excluding nuclear power from our future energy mix', the government maintained its position and policy.

Anisminic,[24] arguably the most significant of all twentieth-century judicial review cases in England, was our third example. It concerned that emblematic device of 'striking back' and/or 'clamping down', a preclusive clause. The statute plainly stated that a 'determination' of the Foreign Compensation Commission 'shall not be called in question in any court of law'. The Commission duly made an error of law in making a decision; in the face of the ouster, the House of Lords duly ruled the decision a nullity. Lord Reid's famous speech listing the many factors that might render a decision a nullity (bad faith, jurisdictional error, breach of natural justice, irrelevant considerations, etc) was sufficient to render preclusive clauses virtually ineffective. Yet the immediate effects of *Anisminic* were quickly mitigated by new legislation, which introduced limited appeal rights but otherwise expanded the statutory formula such that a Commission determination including 'anything which purports to be a determination' was protected. We suggested that 'control' models of administrative law, in which courts controlled abuse of power and successfully defended citizens' rights against erosion by the state, needed 'some modification'.[25]

Though obviously atypical when viewed in terms of the great bulk of routine or 'bureaucratic' judicial review, striking back had thus been identified as a significant feature of the working constitution. Later high profile examples of government manoeuvring would confirm the element of continuity. Take the subterfuge by

[21] Harlow and Rawlings, *Law and Administration*, 1st edn (n 18) 377–82.

[22] *Padfield v Minister of Agriculture, Fisheries and Food* [1968] AC 997; Harlow and Rawlings, *Law and Administration*, 1st edn (n 18) 327–29.

[23] [2007] EWHC 311, [116–20] (Sullivan J). See also *Meeting the Energy Challenge: A White Paper on Energy*, Cm 7124 (2007); *Meeting the Energy Challenge: A White Paper on Nuclear Power*, Cm 7296 (2008).

[24] *Anisminic v Foreign Compensation Commission* [1969] 2 AC 147.

[25] Harlow and Rawlings, *Law and Administration*, 1st edn (n 18) 102–7, 282.

which Whitehall tried to by-pass the provisions of the Criminal Justice Act 1988, which unexpectedly and against the wishes of the government placed on a statutory basis the existing *ex gratia* criminal injuries compensation scheme. In *Fire Brigades Union*,[26] a much cited authority on separation of powers, the Law Lords narrowly upheld a challenge to the Home Secretary's decision to substitute a new, less generous, tariff scheme on the ground of inconsistency with the continuing power to bring the statutory scheme into force. The victory was quickly reversed when the Criminal Compensation Act 1995 introduced the tariff system, albeit with some concessions. Or take the executive machinations surrounding the shocking affair of the Chagos Islanders, expelled from their homeland in the interests of establishing an American air base. When the High Court quashed the expulsion orders,[27] the UK government indicated that the Islanders would be allowed to return. Instead, it invoked an antiquated prerogative power to legislate by Order in Council in colonial territories to reverse the decision and make unauthorised presence on the Islands a criminal offence. Game, set and match went to the government in the domestic courts when in *Bancoult (No 2)*[28] the House of Lords by a 3–2 majority upheld this course of action.

B. Ground Level

At the time of *Pressure Through Law*, studies of the impact of judicial review on British administration were rare and we had to depend on American studies, mainly authored by sociologists and political scientists and aimed at evaluating (as we ourselves were doing) the contribution of public interest litigation. The American literature taught us that striking back was not always a high-visibility activity involving Ministers and legislation. We recorded the discouragement of a leading American welfare lawyer as he realised that 'victory for one class of welfare client leads inevitably to losses for another, less privileged, section of the community'.[29]

Law and Administration presented an analysis of *Malloch v Aberdeen Corporation*,[30] a largely-forgotten affair where the individual's rights were expunged by the validating statutory formula that the Minister's power to make regulations 'shall be deemed always to have included power' to prescribe the employment only of registered teachers. We observed that 'recognised techniques exist for the circumvention of court orders' and that judicial decisions often 'entailed no genuine reconsideration of policy', though we stressed the need to 'beware generalisation'.[31]

[26] *R v Secretary of State for the Home Department, ex parte Fire Brigades Union* [1995] 2 AC 513.

[27] *R (Bancoult) v Secretary of State for Foreign and Commonwealth Affairs (No 1)* [2001] QB 1067.

[28] *R (Bancoult) v Secretary of State for Foreign and Commonwealth Affairs (No 2)* [2009] 1 AC 453. Following an unsuccessful application by the islanders to the ECtHR (*Chagos Islanders v United Kingdom*, App no 35622/04 (11 December 2012)), the saga has reached the Permanent Court of Arbitration under the name, *Republic of Mauritius v United Kingdom*, Award made 18 March 2015, available at www.pca-cpa.org/MU-UK%2020150318%20Awardd4b1.pdf?fil_id=2899.

[29] E Sparer, 'Gordian Knots: The Situation of Health Care Advocacy for the Poor Today' (1981) *Clearinghouse Review* (May) 1.

[30] *Malloch v Aberdeen Corporation* [1971] 1 WLR 1578; Education (Scotland) Act 1973.

[31] Harlow and Rawlings, *Law and Administration*, 1st edn (n 18) 274–82.

Tony Prosser's impact study of the fate of welfare test cases (the first of its kind in the United Kingdom)[32] took matters a step further. His conclusion was stark: 'successful test cases which threaten established policy, especially by increasing expenditure, will meet with quick nullification by legislative or administrative action'.[33] Prosser noted three main categories of negative response: action through primary legislation, sometimes retrospective in character; action through regulations, which given the cursory nature of the parliamentary procedures lessened the opportunity for open debate; and informal administrative practices, including furtive and underhand activity or deliberate disobedience. A celebrated Child Poverty Action Group victory in *Simper*[34] was, for example, virtually expunged by means of a secret circular that refused to implement some elements of the decision and unlawfully modified others. The justification given was that it would be 'administratively impracticable' to implement the decision, which failed to explain why the government did not proceed to legislation, as ultimately it was forced to do.[35] Prosser also noted a dubious new trend to use legislative technique to anticipate or interrupt the judicial decision-making process. The touchstone is *Atkinson*,[36] a case about student rights to welfare benefits, where the government pushed through retrospective statutory provision ahead of the relevant appeal, arguing that, were the Department to lose, it would result in a substantial burden on public funds, serious administrative disruption and widespread abuse. Noting these practices in *Pressure Through Law*, the authors were forceful, claiming that departmental technique was improving all the time in 'heartlessly depriving' claimants of the fruits of litigation and 'cynically expunging' court victories.[37]

This early case law introduces a persistent phenomenon. Two decades after *Simper*, the House of Lords was faced in *Bate*[38] with a complex statutory provision specifically designed to bar the re-opening of social security claims affected by subsequent contrary rulings: the so-called 'anti-test case' clause.[39] By the time the House of Lords overturned it, the Court of Appeal judgment circumventing the restriction had already been obliterated by the rapid use of delegated legislation. Providing against unfavourable judicial rulings had become a standard part of social security administration that we shall meet again in section III.

This is not to deny that government action to counter the effects of judicial rulings is often legitimate or even necessary. As well as being expensive and time-consuming, the litigation process is classically two-dimensional; issues of resources are not primarily the affair of judges.[40] The test of legitimacy is not only what is done but

[32] T Prosser, *Test Cases for the Poor* (London, CPAG, 1983).

[33] ibid 74.

[34] *R v Greater Birmingham Appeal Tribunal, ex parte Simper* [1974] QB 543.

[35] Prosser, *Test Cases* (n 32) 61–62; National Insurance and Supplementary Benefit Act 1973.

[36] *R v Barnsley SBAT, ex parte Atkinson* [1976] 1 WLR 1047 (DC), [1977] 1 WLR 917 (CA); Supplementary Benefits (Miscellaneous Provisions) Act 1977; Prosser, *Test Cases* (n 32) 45–46, 63–65.

[37] Harlow and Rawlings, *Pressure Through Law* (n 13) 301.

[38] *Bate v Chief Adjudication Officer* [1996] 1 WLR 814; Income Related Benefits Schemes (Miscellaneous Amendments) (No 6) Regulations 1994 (SI 1994/3061).

[39] Latterly, Social Security Act 1998, s 27.

[40] But see Harlow and Rawlings, *Law and Administration*, 3rd edn (n 4) 717–22.

how it is done. Prefiguring the voluminous contemporary debate over constitutional 'dialogue' between the legislature and executive and the judiciary,[41] Prosser suggested three basic criteria: (i) the response must be made publicly; (ii) there should be opportunity for adequate informed debate; (iii) a properly reasoned justification must be presented by government. Tested against these standards, many routine administrative practices must surely fail. The vices inherent in secret administrative instructions are neatly underscored in *Anufrijeva*,[42] where the Home Office sought to justify a policy of not notifying asylum seekers of withdrawal of income support under the regulations on grounds of expense and administrative inconvenience. By a majority, the House of Lords outlawed this way of proceeding as a violation of the fundamental right of access to justice and the rule of law. It was a 'peep into contemporary standards of public administration' of which transparency was not a hallmark.[43]

C. Shifting Sands

By 2009 we were sufficiently confident to say that 'transforming judicial review … has a dual effect: not only biting more deeply on the policy-making sinews of government, but also limiting its capacity for a muscular response'.[44] Beyond the protective cloak of parliamentary sovereignty, regulation-making looked increasingly vulnerable to legal challenge. In the period immediately prior to the HRA 1998, the judicial review context was changing. Well-known cases such as *Witham*,[45] where the 'constitutional right' of access to court was used to block increased court fees for poor persons other than through specific statutory provision, and *Simms*,[46] where the judges' interpretative power in protection of 'the basic rights of the individual'[47] was underlined as an aspect of the principle of legality, marked a growth in rights-based jurisprudence at common law. Today, these developments also appear as precursor to a new wave of constitutional case law in the Supreme Court premised on the common law's vibrant potential.[48]

As the recent case of *R (Public Law Project) v Secretary of State for Justice*[49] reminds us, different judicial review methodologies can produce a similar effect. An attempt to introduce a residence test for civil legal aid, a forerunner of the Coalition Government's more general attack on judicial review, was held unlawful on the

[41] For a recent overview, see M Cohn, 'Sovereignty, Constitutional Dialogues, and Political Networks: A Comparative and Conceptual Study' in R Rawlings, P Leyland and A Young (eds), *Sovereignty and the Law* (Oxford, Oxford University Press, 2013).

[42] *R v Secretary of State for the Home Department, ex parte Anufrijeva* [2004] 1 AC 604.

[43] ibid [24] (Lord Steyn).

[44] Harlow and Rawlings, *Law and Administration*, 3rd edn (n 4) 730.

[45] *R v Lord Chancellor, ex parte Witham* [1998] QB 575.

[46] *R v Secretary of State for the Home Department, ex parte Simms* [2000] 2 AC 115.

[47] ibid 131 (Lord Hoffmann).

[48] Exemplified by *Osborn v Parole Board* [2014] AC 1115; *Kennedy v Charity Commission* [2014] UKSC 20; *R (Evans) v Attorney General* [2015] UKSC 21.

[49] [2014] EWHC 2365. The case, which is one of a slew of recent challenges to restrictions on legal aid, is currently under appeal.

standard basis that regulations must be consistent with the policy and object of the empowering statute. The High Court read Parliament's intention in the Legal Aid, Sentencing and Punishment of Offenders Act (LASPO) 2012 as being to allocate civil legal aid to those in greatest need.[50] For good measure, the Court held that, in light of the overarching constitutional principle that all are equally subject to the law and entitled to its protection, the residence test as formulated involved discrimination that could not be justified.[51] Since Parliament was still in the process of approving the regulations, this avowedly public interest challenge constituted an effective pre-emptive strike. Business had to be hastily re-arranged to avoid the unhappy prospect of the House of Lords debating the merits of provisions already declared unlawful!

With a view to minimising legal risk, an extra premium has been placed on the use of statute, leading directly to 'fast-track legislation', another significant feature of the working constitution that is currently proliferating as a means of minimising the extra work, disruption and delay for government associated with the standard primary legislative process. Indeed, a successful call by the House of Lords Constitution Committee for reasoned justification of reductions of the primary legislative process to a matter of days has arguably had the perverse effect of normalising the technique by the establishment of guidelines.[52]

Read against a background of increasing judicial resistance, the evident propensity for striking back translates into elongated forms of 'ping pong'. Take the case of welfare support for asylum seekers. Regulations designed to exclude many asylum seekers from benefit were ruled ultra vires on the basis that condemning people to 'a life so destitute that no civilised nation could tolerate it' needed clear statutory authorisation.[53] But primary legislation in the guise of the Asylum and Immigration Act 1996 promptly reinstated the regulations from the date of the statute and removed the right to assistance in respect of homelessness. The Court of Appeal found a way round via the National Assistance Act 1948[54] but Ministers struck back again with the Immigration and Asylum Act 1999, which excluded the operation of the 1948 Act in similar cases. The later Nationality, Immigration and Asylum Act 2002 removed support for those making 'late' asylum claims save where it was necessary to avoid a breach of Convention rights. After further twists and turns, judicial guidance on a modicum of entitlement was eventually forthcoming in *Limbuela*.[55] 'Far from the happy idea of "partnership"', we noted 'sharp conflict between the executive and the judiciary in the context of draconian legislation directed at a vulnerable group'.[56]

As Lord Steyn was once at pains to emphasise, never say never in judicial review. Posed as the proverbial 'nuclear deterrent', and so redolent of a period of heightened

[50] ibid [45].
[51] ibid [84].
[52] Constitution Committee, *Fast-track Legislation: Constitutional Implications and Safeguards*, HL 116 (2009).
[53] *R v Secretary of State for Social Security, ex parte Joint Council for the Welfare of Immigrants* [1997] 1 WLR 275 (Simon Brown LJ).
[54] *R v Westminster City Council, ex parte M* (1997) 1 CCLR 85.
[55] *R (Limbuela) v Secretary of State for the Home Department* [2006] 1 AC 396.
[56] Harlow and Rawlings, *Law and Administration*, 3rd edn (n 4) 738–47.

constitutional tensions, the remarkable obiter dicta in *Jackson*[57] are today just about visible on the Westminster radar screen. According to Lord Steyn, Ministers should understand that if Parliament were to introduce 'oppressive and wholly undemocratic legislation'—as, for example, by moving to abolish judicial review—then the judges, who (according to Lord Steyn) had created the principle of parliamentary sovereignty, might have to qualify it. In other words, faced with an attempt to clamp down by statute, they might have to consider whether judicial review 'is a constitutional fundamental which even a sovereign Parliament acting at the behest of a complaisant House of Commons cannot abolish'.[58]

D. First Foray

Judicial review is too important to be the exclusive concern of the judges. In particular, we disagree with the view, expressed by an ex Law Lord,[59] that judicial review is not a matter for Parliament. After all, in the long view, Parliament has not only flanked the inherent common law jurisdiction with major roles for the national courts in respect of the ECHR and European Union, but also helped free the courts from their own historical legacy of arcane and restrictive procedural rules by grounding in section 31 of the Senior Courts Act 1981 the more generous and holistic modalities of AJR procedure. Given the twin-hatted position of the executive as chief defendant and chief legislative architect, however, a healthy scepticism is in order when considering government proposals to clamp down on judicial review.

The conflict over benefits culminating in *Limbuela* was part of a wider political and legal struggle over decision-making in immigration and asylum taking place under the Labour Government and later extending, as we shall see, under the subsequent Coalition. Glossing over glaring defects in the quality of departmental administration, Prime Minister Tony Blair spoke of cutting back a 'ludicrously complicated appeal process' and of removing failed applicants 'without further judicial interference'. Giving vent to populist ideas of majoritarian democracy, the Home Secretary, David Blunkett, bluntly declared that it was 'time for judges to learn their place'. Through the Bill which eventually became the Asylum and Immigration (Treatment of Claimants, etc) Act 2004, the government looked to the three techniques of squeezing legal services, reducing appeal rights, and ousting Dicey's prized 'ordinary courts'. For Rawlings, this was nothing less than 'a revenge package' designed 'to pre-empt or drastically reduce a whole activity of formal legal challenge' and thus 'neuter the judicial role in the constitution'.[60]

The proposed ouster clause was designed to turn Lord Reid's speech in *Anisminic*[61] on its head, so knocking out his listed grounds of review one by one.

[57] *Jackson v Attorney General* [2006] 1 AC 262. For similar dicta, see *AXA General Insurance v Lord Advocate* [2012] 1 AC 868 (Lord Hope) and *Moohan v Lord Advocate* [2014] UKSC 67, [35] (Lord Hodge).

[58] ibid [102].

[59] HL Deb vol 755 col 1440 (28 July 2014), Lord Brown of Eaton-under-Heywood.

[60] R Rawlings, 'Review, Revenge and Retreat' (2005) 68 *MLR* 378, 379.

[61] *Anisminic* (n 24).

Referencing the aftermath of that iconic case, this was the language of 'prevent[ing] a court, in particular, from entertaining proceedings to determine whether a purported determination … was a nullity' by reason of lack of jurisdiction, etc. The clause aimed to immunise both the administrative tribunal (responsible for adjudicating status determination decisions) and Home Office enforcement measures.[62] Claims under the HRA 1998 were likewise attacked; linkage to the ordinary courts would essentially be confined to requests from the tribunal president for non-binding opinions on points of law. Using the informal and time-honoured 'usual channels', senior judges had naturally tried to stop the clause at an early stage; perversely, however, their technical analysis was used to tighten the drafting.[63]

Armed with a huge majority, the government had reason to be confident of definitively changing the rules of the game. Yet paradoxically, the resulting imbroglio highlights the key role of Parliament—or more precisely, the House of Lords—in reinforcing expectations over judicial review. Despite much rhetoric along the lines of 'unnecessary, vexatious and useless judicial reviews', a failure publicly to document the scale and incidence of 'abuse' put Ministers on the back foot in an increasingly forensic examination.[64] The policy became messy as Ministers were pressurised into making concessions or 'clarifications', for example over the continued availability of that common law hallmark, *habeas corpus*. Ministers could not wish away the prospect of successful challenge in Strasbourg[65] or Luxembourg[66] even though there would be an administrative tribunal in operation. However, the government's eventual withdrawal of the ouster clause most clearly points up how domestic (common law) developments can not only produce a whiplash effect but also strengthen the judicial lines of defence in the political and legal processes. Confronted by the threat of such a radical departure from constitutional expectation, a line of senior legal figures summoned up, first, model precepts of government under law, equal protection and access to the established legal system; and, secondly, the spectre of head-on constitutional conflict. In Lord Woolf's terms, prefiguring *Jackson*, the courts might be 'required to act in a manner which would be without precedent' if Parliament 'did the unthinkable'.[67]

Though it was Ministers who blinked first, they were not completely routed. The 2004 Act contained some additional restrictions on funding, made structural reforms to the tribunal system, and grounded a streamlined form of statutory review. Not, it must be said, that this did much to stem the tide of asylum and immigration litigation, which continued to dominate the caseload of the Administrative Court into the next decade.[68]

[62] Contemporary developments in Australia provided a source of inspiration: see M Aronson, B Dyer and M Groves, *Judicial Review of Administrative Action*, 3rd edn (Pyrmont, Lawbook, 2004) ch 17.

[63] Lord Woolf, *The Rule of Law and a Change in the Constitution*, Squire Centenary Lecture (Cambridge University, 2004) 8. See also A Le Sueur, 'Three Strikes and It's Out? The UK Government's Strategy to Oust Judicial Review from Immigration and Asylum Decision-making' [2004] *PL* 225.

[64] For an informed view, see R Thomas, 'The Impact of Judicial Review on Asylum' [2003] *PL* 479.

[65] Notwithstanding a restrictive jurisprudence in asylum: *Maaouia v France* [2000] 33 EHRR 42.

[66] Especially in view of cases like *Johnston* on access to judicial process (see below).

[67] Lord Woolf, 'Droit Public—English Style' [1995] *PL* 57, 69.

[68] For the later history, see R Thomas, 'Immigration Judicial Reviews', UK Const L Blog, 12 September 2013.

E. Second Foray

In seeking to clamp down, the Coalition Government approached matters somewhat differently to their Labour counterparts. The policy involved a rebalancing of the internal dynamics of the judicial review process in favour of public authorities. It can also be read as attempting to turn the clock back towards a narrower conception of judicial review historically associated with a more restrained constitutional role for the courts and centred on individual redress of grievance and defence of private interest.[69] Perhaps some element of institutional memory was in play. As against the hammer blow suggested by Labour's ouster clause, a whole series of screws would be tightened—harder to mobilise against.[70] Unlike Mr Blunkett, Chris Grayling, the Secretary of State for Justice and Lord Chancellor, avoided ruffling feathers by direct criticism of the domestic judiciary. The official documentation suitably rehearsed the theme of judicial review as 'the rule of law in action'.[71]

The Coalition Government gave numerous reasons for clamping down. Some are classic concerns about the scale and nature of the caseload, as in the opening salvo that judicial review has 'expanded massively' and is 'open to abuse'.[72] Others speak to broader impacts on government and people—for which read negative effects of expensive and time-consuming litigation on schemes for economic growth and on the taxpayers' purse in a period of austerity. Others again provide glimpses of constitutional theory, to the effect of buttressing the 'separate identity' of the judicial process from the normal rough-and-tumble of the political process. The evident concern that, in the words of the House of Lords Constitution Committee, 'judicial review has become too much of a political tool of opposition to government policy',[73] also shows a revengeful element: witness Mr Grayling's declared interest in restricting 'a promotional tool for countless Left-wing campaigners'.[74]

As under Labour, the scale of the rhetoric is in inverse proportion to the strength of the evidence base. In blunting government claims of sharp growth[75] and few tangible results, critics had a field day in the statistics,[76] underlining the important role of settlement, limited growth outside asylum and immigration, and of course infinitesimal numbers of cases when compared with the scale of government decision-making. Likewise, when considering the caseload pressures on the Administrative Court, a recent transfer of most immigration reviews to the Upper Tribunal by the Lord Chief Justice[77] can scarcely be ignored.

[69] Associated with what we call the 'drainpipe model' of judicial review: Harlow and Rawlings, *Pressure Through Law* (n 13) 310–14.

[70] For the attempted spoiler, see M Fordham *et al*, *Streamlining Judicial Review in a Manner Consistent with the Rule of Law* (London, Bingham Centre, 2014).

[71] Ministry of Justice, *Judicial Review: Proposals for Reform*, Cm 8515 (2012) [11].

[72] Ministry of Justice, *Proposals for Further Reform*, Cm 8703 (2013) Foreword.

[73] Constitution Committee, *Criminal Justice and Courts Bill*, HL 18 (2014) [6].

[74] C Grayling, 'The Judicial Review System is not a promotional tool for countless Left-wing campaigners', *Daily* Mail, 6 September 2013.

[75] From over 4,500 applications for permission in 1998 to 12,400 in 2012: *Proposals for Further Reform* (n 72) [9].

[76] V Bondy and M Sunkin, 'Who is Afraid of Judicial Review? Debunking the Myths of Growth and Abuse', UK Const L Blog, 10 January 2013.

[77] Practice Direction given in accordance with Constitutional Reform Act 2005, sch 2, Pt 1 and Tribunals, Courts and Enforcement Act 2007, s 18 (21 August 2013).

The policy was rolled out in successive rounds of law-making. Published in December 2012, the consultation paper *Judicial Review: Proposals for Reform* zeroed in on procedural changes that could be quickly introduced. Given that only a small minority of cases proceed beyond the distinctive permission ('leave') stage of AJR procedure to full hearing,[78] this was the natural target. The government proposed a package consisting of shorter time limits for bringing claims, most notably in planning cases, a new court fee and restriction of the right to renew a claim dismissed on the papers, duly implemented via changes to the Civil Procedure Rules operative from July 2013.[79] In an important flanking development, regulations were used to make the payment of legal aid fees conditional on success at the permission stage, with only limited exception for 'meritorious cases' settled by public authorities.[80]

Published in September 2013, a second consultation paper, *Judicial Review: Proposals for Further Reform*, outlined a series of possible statutory reforms. One major piece in the jigsaw was, however, quickly lost in the pre-legislative process. The idea of rationing judicial review and hitting at strategic forms of litigation by rewinding the test of standing towards 'direct interest'[81] was effectively vetoed by the senior judiciary. Having at first stood on the key principle from representative democracy that 'Parliament and the elected Government are best placed to determine what is in the public interest',[82] Ministers seemingly had no answer to the liberal judicial orthodoxy that 'unlawful use of executive power should not persist because of the absence of an available challenger with a sufficient interest'.[83] By corroborating this key constitutional expectation grounded in the rule of law, their own evidence of relatively high rates of success for public interest litigants[84] hardly helped the government.

Other restrictive proposals eventually made it to the statute book in Part 4 of the Criminal Justice and Courts Act 2015. Relevant sections deal with such matters as permission (leave) and third party intervention, costs orders[85] and information about financial backing[86] (an historical echo surely of the extinct common law torts of maintenance and champerty).[87] Two overlapping features command attention. First, there is repeated use of financial disincentives to litigate, a redeployment of risk. A chief target is public interest litigation as commonly practised by expert 'repeat players'; and, more particularly, procedural techniques like protective

[78] In 2011, there were 11,360 applications for, and 1,276 grants of, permission to proceed: *Proposals for Further Reform* (n 72) 9.

[79] Civil Procedure (Amendment No 4) Rules 2013 (SI 2013/1412).

[80] Civil Legal Aid (Remuneration) (Amendment) (No 3) Regulations 2014 (SI 2014/607). The subject of 'a regret motion': see HL Deb vol 753 cols 1540–68 (7 May 2014).

[81] Closer that is to the 'victim test' for Convention rights claims: Human Rights Act 1998, s 7.

[82] *Proposals for Further Reform* (n 72) [80].

[83] Senior Judiciary, *Response to the Consultation Entitled 'Judicial Review: Proposals for Further Reform'* (2014) [15].

[84] *Proposals for Further Reform* (n 72) [78].

[85] Criminal Justice and Courts Act 2015, ss 88–90. There is, however, special provision for environmental cases in light of the Aarhus Convention on Access to Information, Public Participation in Decision-making and Access to Justice in Environmental Matters.

[86] Criminal Justice and Courts Act 2015, ss 85–86.

[87] Harlow and Rawlings, *Pressure Through Law* (n 13) 48–50.

costs orders[88] which have been developed in recent years to facilitate the activity. Secondly, judicial discretion, which we identified earlier as a key ingredient in the domestic process of 'transforming judicial review', is targeted. In seeking to codify existing judicial powers to craft and discipline the shape of judicial review proceedings, Mr Grayling has preferred 'must' to the 'may' word. Not that Ministers had it all their own way in the formal legislative process; some limited concessions were extracted by the House of Lords via the process of parliamentary 'ping pong' with (the executive seat of power in) the Commons.[89] Neatly demonstrating the sense of continuity, senior legal figures headed by Lord Woolf once again took a leading role against the government, trumpeting the rule of law in Ministers' ears.

Two provisions serve for illustration. The first[90] hits directly at public interest intervention, which became established as a means of bolstering judicial decision-making in the 1990s[91] and has seen a step change in usage in the wake of the HRA 1998.[92] It imposes a duty on the High Court and Court of Appeal to levy the consequential costs on those choosing to intervene if any one of four conditions is met: the intervener acts 'in substance' as a principal party; their intervention is not of 'significant assistance'; a 'significant part' of it is 'not necessary' for resolution of the issues; 'the intervener has behaved unreasonably'. Since intervention has been pre-eminently a matter of permission on terms, lack of trust in the judges is the not-so-subliminal message.

Bearing directly on the exercise of the supervisory jurisdiction, the second provision[93] takes the process of instructing the judges to another level. It expands on the so-called 'no difference' doctrine, whereby the court exercises discretion to refuse permission or a final remedy because the public authority would surely have made the same decision if it had acted lawfully.[94] The Act substitutes the (somewhat arcane) test of 'highly likely that the outcome for the applicant would not have been substantially different' and is drafted in mandatory terms: if the court considers the test made out, it 'must refuse' to grant permission or relief. Viewed through Ministerial spectacles, the formula has the considerable attraction of reducing the scope for administrative disruption, not least in view of the recently burgeoning common law jurisprudence on consultation requirements.[95] The approach is rightly criticised, however, as being a get out card for unlawful conduct and a likely driver of argument at the permission—supposedly filter—stage.[96] Only thanks to the House of Lords is

[88] *R (Corner House Research) v Secretary of State for Trade and* Industry [2005] 1 WLR 2600.

[89] For the twists and turns, see HC Deb vol 589 cols 70–100 (1 December 2014); HL Deb vol 757 cols 1737–85 (9 December 2014); HC Deb vol 590 cols 808–33 (13 January 2015); HL Deb vol 759 cols 1341–51 (21 January 2015).

[90] Criminal Justice and Courts Act 2015, s 87.

[91] See R Rawlings, 'Courts and Interests' in I Loveland (ed), *A Special Relationship? American Influences on Public Law in the UK* (Oxford, Clarendon Press, 1995).

[92] S Shah, T Poole and M Blackwell, 'Rights, Interveners and the Law Lords' (2014) 34 *OJLS* 295.

[93] Criminal Justice and Courts Act 2015, s 84.

[94] *R (Core Issues Trust) v Transport for London* [2014] EWCA Civ 34, [42]–[44] (Lord Dyson MR). See further, *R (Champion) v North Norfolk District Council* [2015] UKSC 52.

[95] *R (Plantagenet Alliance Ltd) v Secretary of State for Justice* [2014] EWHC 1662.

[96] Joint Committee on Human Rights, *The Implications for Access to Justice of the Government's Proposals to Reform Judicial Review*, HC 868 (2014) [38]–[56].

there now a special judicial trump whereby the restriction may be disregarded if the court considers and certifies that 'it is appropriate to do so for reasons of exceptional public interest'. We recall the firm words of *The Judge Over Your Shoulder*, the guidance for civil servants issued by the Treasury Solicitor's Department: 'the principle is that only a fair procedure will enable the merits to be determined with confidence'.[97] Time will tell how the serving judiciary responds.

III. WESTMINSTER IN EUROPE

A. Belated Realisation

Although this was not well understood at the time, the constitutional situation changed radically with passage of the European Communities Act 1972, which limited the freedom of the UK Parliament to legislate in a manner contrary to EC law. Westminster, which under Dicey's classic theory of parliamentary sovereignty could make or unmake any law, was no longer in that comfortable position.[98] A significant factor in the new dispensation was section 3 of the 1972 Act, which rendered British courts effectively subservient to the European Court of Justice (ECJ, now Court of Justice of the European Union, CJEU) by providing that all questions as to the meaning or effect of EC law must be determined in accordance with its jurisprudence. As this jurisprudence developed, it transpired that national legislation must be interpreted so far as possible to comply with EC law or, if clearly non-compliant, must be 'disapplied'.[99] Moreover, the EC institutions gradually acquired sanctions. The Commission power to bring infringement proceedings was reinforced at Maastricht by the possibility of substantial fines,[100] while the concept of Member State liability in damages was introduced by the CJEU in its controversial *Francovich* decision.[101] The power in section 2(2) of the 1972 Act to implement an obligation under EC law by Order in Council and the thoroughgoing 'Henry VIII clause' in section 2(4) also contributed to an erosion of parliamentary power since they greatly reduced the opportunity for parliamentary debate. It took some time for the House of Commons,[102] and latterly the courts,[103] to claw back the position by stages.

It was not until the *Factortame* affair that Parliament and public became aware of the magnitude of constitutional change.[104] The United Kingdom had sailed too close to the wind in the Merchant Shipping Act 1988 which, while purporting to

[97] Treasury Solicitor's Department, *The Judge Over Your Shoulder*, 4th edn (2006) [2.46].

[98] See D Nicol, *EC Membership and the Judicialization of British Politics* (Oxford, Oxford University Press, 2001) ch 6.

[99] See respectively C-106/89 *Marleasing SA v La Comercial International de Alimentacion SA* [1990] ECR I-4135; *R v Secretary of State for Transport, ex parte Equal Opportunities Commission* [1995] 1 AC 1.

[100] TFEU, Art 260 (ex TEC, Art 228). The United Kingdom has not in practice been subject to fines.

[101] C-6/90 and C-9/90 *Francovich and Bonafaci v Italy* [1991] ECR I-5357.

[102] See notably European Assembly Elections Act 1978, s 6 and the European Union Act 2011.

[103] See *Thoburn v Sunderland City Council* [2002] EWHC 195 and, for the position of the Supreme Court, *R (HS2 Action Alliance Ltd) v Secretary of State for Transport* [2014] 1 WLR 324.

[104] Nicol, *EC Membership* (n 98) ch 7.

implement Community fisheries policy, effectively limited ownership of fishing vessels to UK nationals for purposes of national fisheries quotas. When the Act was ruled incompatible with EC law,[105] the United Kingdom faced actions in damages for losses caused to fishing companies[106] said to be settled by payments in the region of £55 million. The high costs of non-compliance with EU law had become very apparent and the 'shock of the new' led the UK government to attempt a strike-back. It took steps (though these were ultimately unsuccessful) to gain support at the next Intergovernmental Conference for action to curb the expansive interpretations of the CJEU and provide a limited appeals procedure,[107] a defeat that further underscored the realities of the constitutional framework. Pointing to future reactions, a Private Member's Bill introduced in the House of Commons but defeated at second reading would have allowed the House to 'disapply' specific CJEU judgments where Parliament decided they were not in the national interest.[108]

From our limited perspective, a warning bell had been rung when the CJEU ruled in *Johnston v Royal Ulster Constabulary*[109] that a ministerial certificate (effectively an ouster) could not under EC law bar review for legality by an employment tribunal. The reasoning was significant: first, the procedure inhibited the effectiveness of an EC Directive; secondly, access to judicial process was a 'general principle of law' reflecting the common constitutional traditions of the Member States and recognised by ECHR, Articles 6(1) and 13. This left ouster clauses in an ambiguous position; we inferred in *Pressure Through Law* that they might be precluded by both EC law and the ECHR.[110] There is equal uncertainty over retrospectivity, an issue that arose in a set of cases concerning changes to the law of unjust enrichment based on EC law.[111] To deal with the problem, the government enacted legislation that curtailed the limitation period for certain tax claims. Unsure about the validity of this retrospective element, the Supreme Court asked the CJEU whether it was 'compatible with the principles of effectiveness, legal certainty and legitimate expectations' to bar claims in this manner 'without notice and retrospectively'? The reply from the CJEU was conditional: retroactive change to the limitation period was permissible provided that adequate transitional arrangements were made; otherwise national legislation retroactively curtailing the period within which repayment could be claimed 'infringes the principles of legal certainty and the protection of legitimate expectations'.[112] This left the wider question open.

[105] C-221/89 *R v Secretary of State for Transport, ex parte Factortame* [1991] ECR I-3905.

[106] C-46/93 and C-48/93 *Brasserie du Pêcheur SA v Germany, R v Secretary of State for Transport, ex parte Factortame* [1996] ECR I-1029; *R v Secretary of State for Transport, ex parte Factortame (No 5)* [2000] 1 AC 524.

[107] See *A Partnership of Nations: The British Approach to the European Union Intergovernmental Conference 1996*, Cm 3181 (1996); J Tallberg, 'Supranational Influence in EU Enforcement: The ECJ and the Principle of State Liability' (2000) 7 *JEPP* 104, 114–15.

[108] HC Deb vol 276, col 198 (23 April 1996), Mr Iain Duncan Smith.

[109] C-222/84 *Johnston v Royal Ulster Constabulary* [1986] ECR 1651, [13].

[110] Harlow and Rawlings, *Pressure Through Law* (n 13) 318.

[111] *Woolwich Equitable Building Society v IRC* [1993] AC 70; *Kleinwort Benson v Lincoln City Council* [1999] 2 AC 349; *Deutsche Morgan Grenfell Group Plc v IRC* [2006] 3 WLR 781. The foundational case was C-199/82 *Amministrazione delle Finanze dello Stato v San Giorgio* [1983] ECR 3595; C-446/04 *Test Claimants in the F11 Group Litigation v IRC* [2006] ECR I-11753.

[112] C-362/12 *Test Claimants in the F11 Group Litigation v IRC* [2014] AC 1161, [44]–[49].

Whether government reaction to the CJEU decision in *Digital Rights Ireland*[113] was a case of striking back is largely a matter of opinion. The Court had invalidated the EU Data Retention Directive, which imposed on electronic communications businesses an obligation to retain and make available certain data for purposes of 'investigation, detection and prosecution of serious crime and terrorism'. In the United Kingdom, where the Directive had been implemented by codes of practice reinforced by Order in Council in terms of the European Communities Act,[114] the legal situation was unclear; the Order was based on an invalid Directive, which could hardly create an 'EU obligation' for the purposes of section 2(2). Purportedly to give effect to the three-month old judgment, the government suddenly announced the Data Retention and Investigatory Powers Bill, emergency legislation to be 'fast-tracked' through Parliament in four days.

Introducing the Bill, the Home Secretary expressed confidence that the regulations remained in force but emphasised the need 'to act now to remove any doubt about their legal basis and give effect to the COJ judgment'.[115] Similarly, the Minister of State asserted that the regulations remained 'extant and in full force and effect' but because they had been questioned, it was essential 'to deal with the risk and put the matter beyond doubt'.[116] More robustly, the Chairman of the EU Scrutiny Committee said:

> The only way in which we can avoid running into difficulties with European Court judgments that we do not want—which, clearly, is what the Bill is about—is by using primary legislation, such as this Bill, to disapply the provisions of European law that come through sections 2 and 3 of the European Communities Act, and that it has to be notwithstanding those provisions.[117]

Yet the use of fast-track procedure points to ulterior motives. It was suggested, for example, that the Data Retention and Investigatory Powers Act (DRIPA) 2014 was 'far more than an administrative necessity; it [was] a serious expansion of the British surveillance state' requiring 'full and proper parliamentary scrutiny'.[118] Equally, the aim may have been a wish to 'clamp down' on a pending judicial review application that challenged the regulations in terms of EU law.[119] If so, this was simply to postpone the evil. Liberty, acting in the names of two MPs, set down a judicial review

[113] C-293/12 and C-594/12 *Digital Rights Ireland Ltd v Minister for Communications, Marine and Natural Resources* [2015] QB 127; Directive 2006/24/EC [2006] OJ L105/54.

[114] Retention of Communications (Code of Practice) Order 2003 (SI 2003/3175); Data Retention (EC Directive) Regulations 2007 (SI 2007/2199), superseded by the Data Retention (EC Directive) Regulations 2009 (SI 2009/859).

[115] HC Deb vol 584 col 456 (10 July 2014), Mrs Theresa May. The Bill is now the Data Retention and Investigatory Powers Act 2014. And see for later amendment by further fast-track legislation, the Counter-Terrorism and Security Bill 2014 and Joint Committee on Human Rights, *Legislative Scrutiny: The Counter-Terrorism and Security Bill*, HC 859 (2015) [5.4]–[5.6].

[116] HC Deb vol 584 col 763 (15 July 2014), Mr James Brokenshire.

[117] HC Deb vol 584 col 765 (15 July 2014), Sir William Cash.

[118] Open letter from 15 technology-law academics, *Guardian*, 15 July 2014.

[119] *R (Cosgrove) v Secretary of State for the Home Department* CO/7701/2011 had been stayed pending the judgment of the CJEU.

application questioning the compatibility of DRIPA 2014 with Articles 7 and 8 of the EU Charter of Fundamental Rights and with *Digital Rights Ireland.*[120]

Without referring to Luxembourg, the High Court interpreted *Digital Rights Ireland* generously to mean that legislation (such as DRIPA 2014) that establishes a general retention regime for communications data must include an access regime (laid down at national level), which provides adequate safeguards for those rights. Applying this principle to DRIPA, the Court granted a declaration that it infringed EU legal requirements because it neither laid down clear and precise rules providing for access to and use of retained communications data nor did it provide for prior review by a court or independent administrative body to set the conditions of the access.[121] Returning the ball hard to the baseline, the Court made an order disapplying section 1 of DRIPA 2014 in respect of the inconsistencies, while suspending it for eight months to allow the government to pass new legislation.[122] It added the rider:[123]

> The courts do not presume to tell Parliament for how long and in what detail Bills should be scrutinised, but it is right to say (to put it no higher) that legislation enacted in haste is more prone to error, and it would be highly desirable to allow the opportunity of thorough scrutiny in both Houses.

Other less final ways to strike back effectively at the European Courts exist through appeals, judicial delays and the jurisdictional complexities (Braibant's category (i)) that afford multiple opportunities for manoeuvre in transnational jurisdictions. Delay has become an endemic problem in both European Courts: the epic *Factortame* saga, for example, took more than a decade to resolve, while the backlog of cases awaiting decision by the ECtHR is notorious.[124] The convoluted nature of EU decision-making procedures also lends itself to relentless 'cat-and-mouse' games played by governments at the expense of individuals. When, for example, the Iranian Organisation des Modjahedines (OMPI) was proscribed as a terrorist organisation in the United Kingdom and its assets frozen in 2001, it appealed successfully to the appropriate security tribunal (POAC). When this decision was upheld by the Court of Appeal in May 2008[125] the Home Secretary duly made a delisting order, approved

[120] *R (Davis) v Home Secretary* [2015] EWHC 2092. In *Digital Rights* the applicants pleaded their right of privacy under ECHR, Art 8 but the CoJ virtually ignored the point, prioritising the Charter, as seems to be becoming customary: see further G de Búrca, 'After the EU Charter of Fundamental Rights: The Court of Justice as a Human Rights Adjudicator?' (2013) 20 *Maastricht Journal* 2.

[121] ibid [89]–[90].

[122] ibid [121]–[122]. The Data Retention and Investigatory Powers Act 2014, s 8 contained a 'sunset clause' providing for the operative provisions to expire at the end of 2016. In the meantime the Independent Reviewer of Terrorism Legislation had considered the legality of DRIPA 2014 and recommended amending legislation: see D Anderson, *Question of Trust: Report of The Investigatory Powers Review* (2015) ch 5.

[123] *Davis* (n 120) [122].

[124] In 2013, a direct action in the CJEU averaged 20 months and, more significantly, a reference for a preliminary ruling added 15 months on average to the duration of proceedings in a national court: *Court of Justice of the European Union Annual Report 2014* (2015) 9. Efforts to reduce the backlog led to the Council of Europe High Level Conference on the Future of the European Court of Human Rights and the 'Brighton Declaration', adopted in April 2012.

[125] *Home Secretary v Lord Alton of Liverpool* [2008] EWCA Civ 443; POAC Appeal No PC/02/2006 (30 November 2007).

by Parliament in June. But OMPI was immediately re-listed by the Council of Ministers,[126] necessitating renewed applications to the EU Courts and it took six judicial hearings over 10 years to get OMPI delisted in the European Union.[127] Again, after the assets of Sheikh Kadi were frozen in late 2001, the freeze was annulled by the General Court in 2010[128] and the appeal against the decision was finally heard in 2013—in all, 12 costly and fruitless years of litigation.[129]

B. Bringing Rights Home

The impact of the ECHR and its Court of Human Rights (ECtHR) was gradual. The ECHR was never legally enforceable within the United Kingdom and the domestic courts held back from judicial incorporation of what successive governments chose not to incorporate.[130] Although the United Kingdom had also ratified the ECHR, Article 46, under which it is obliged to comply with any judgment of the Court in any case to which it is party, ECtHR judgments are not technically binding in the United Kingdom, and the only external control over implementation is through the highly political Committee of Ministers, whose resolutions (as we shall see) lack legal force. Nonetheless, in *Pressure Through Law*, we recorded a steady drip of public interest litigation by pressure groups based on the Convention and looked in detail at the 38 UK violations found by the ECtHR to 1989.[131] Our conclusion was that implementation by the UK government was usually forthcoming but not always in a whole-hearted fashion. There was the notorious 'Asian wives case', involving the right of immigrant Asian women to bring their husbands into the country. When the ECtHR found a discriminatory violation of the Article 8 right to family life, the Conservative Government 'levelled down' by administrative instruction, reducing men's rights to bring in their wives, a response that the Joint Council for the Welfare of Immigrants, which had sponsored the case, called 'negative, grudging, cynical and opportunist'.[132] Again, after *Campbell and Cosans*,[133] a key victory in the ECtHR for the campaign to stop corporal punishment in schools, the United Kingdom took only minimum steps to implement the decision by administrative direction, applying it to Scottish but not English or Welsh schools and then only if parents actively refused consent to corporal punishment.

[126] Council Decision 2008/583/EC [2008] OJ L188/21.

[127] The last being C-27/09P *French Republic v People's Mojahedin Organization of Iran* [2011] ECR I-13427.

[128] T-85/09 *Yassin Abdullah Kadi v Commission* [2010] ECR II-5177.

[129] C-584/10, C-593/10 and C-595/10, *Council, Commission and United Kingdom v Kadi* [2013] ECR I-518. Kadi was in fact delisted at UN level prior to this hearing after the intervention of the UN Ombudsperson.

[130] *R v Home Secretary, ex parte Brind* [1991] 1 AC 696. See also T Bingham, 'The European Convention on Human Rights, Time to Incorporate' (1993) 109 *LQR* 390.

[131] Harlow and Rawlings, *Pressure Through Law* (n 13) 254–55. By 1989, 52 complaints against the United Kingdom had reached the ECtHR.

[132] *Abdulaziz, Cabales and Balkandali v United Kingdom* (1985) 7 EHRR 471; *Joint Council for the Welfare of Immigrants Annual Review 1984–85* (1985) 3.

[133] *Campbell and Cosans v United Kingdom* (1982) 4 EHRR 293; Harlow and Rawlings, *Pressure Through Law* (n 13) 262–63.

The changes introduced by the HRA 1998 were substantial and are the subject of a rich though often legalistic literature. All that is necessary for our purposes is to know that, in stark contrast to the CJEU, ECtHR jurisprudence does not bind the domestic courts. Section 2(1) of the HRA 1998 requires the UK courts simply to 'take account' of decisions of the ECtHR insofar as they are relevant; section 3 requires the courts 'so far as possible' to interpret and apply domestic legislation in a manner compatible with the Convention rights; and, where this is impossible, section 4 enables the court to make a declaration of incompatibility, the effect of which is not to invalidate the statutory provision but to invite Parliament to reconsider the issue. In this way, the principle of parliamentary sovereignty is said to be preserved.

Responsibility for ensuring compatibility of statute law with human rights law is actually shared: section 10 of the HRA 1998 allows a Minister where necessary to amend statute by means of statutory instrument but Schedule 2 subjects such orders to affirmative resolution of both Houses. Section 19 obliges a Minister when introducing a Bill into Parliament to make a declaration as to its compatibility with the ECHR or, if unable to do so, to explain why action is necessary, leaving the final decision to Parliament and its committees. Implementation of ECtHR judgments is a government responsibility but is systematically monitored by the Joint Committee on Human Rights, which is often highly critical. From the standpoint of the domestic courts, the effect of the HRA was to shift responsibility to them for 'form[ing] a judgment whether a ECHR right has been breached and, so far as permissible under the Act, grant[ing] an effective remedy',[134] thus making them a potential target for striking back. This may help to explain the adoption of the so-called 'mirror principle' enunciated by Lord Bingham in *Ullah*,[135] which transferred responsibility to the ECtHR by providing that the domestic courts would go as far as but no farther than Strasbourg in interpreting the ECHR. It may also help to explain why, as hostility to Strasbourg has grown, the domestic courts are keen to increase their room for manoeuvre and are cautiously beginning to draw back.[136]

C. A Rising Crescendo

In *Pressure Through Law* we noted the start of long-lasting struggles with Strasbourg over prisoners' rights. *Golder v United Kingdom*,[137] which concerned the right of prisoners to correspond with a lawyer, saw the start of problems with Articles 6(1) and 8, while the conformity of procedures in mandatory life and indeterminate sentences with ECHR, Article 5 was initiated by *Weeks v United Kingdom*.[138] Prisoners' rights cases were defended with spirit; along the way indefensible cases were fought

[134] *R (Daly) v Secretary of State for the Home Department* [2001] 2 AC 532, [23] (Lord Bingham).

[135] *R (Ullah) v Special Adjudicator* [2004] 2 AC 976, [20] (Lord Bingham).

[136] See *R v Horncastle* [2010] 2 AC 373; *Manchester City Council v Pinnock* [2011] 2 AC 104; *Osborn* (n 48); *R (Robinson) v Justice Secretary* [2014] UKSC 66, [17]–[21]; *Moohan* (n 57) [104]–[105].

[137] (1975) 1 EHRR 524.

[138] (1987) 10 EHRR 293; *Thynne, Wilson and Gunnell v United Kingdom* (1991) 13 EHRR 666; *Stafford v United Kingdom* (2002) 35 EHRR 32. See latterly, *Hutchinson v United Kingdom* App no 57592/08 (3 February 2015).

and predictably lost in Strasbourg and were implemented according to the letter and not the spirit of the rulings. The flames of resentment were stoked by *Hirst*,[139] where the Grand Chamber held that the automatic disenfranchisement of prisoners at parliamentary or local government elections as mandated by section 3 of the Representation of the People Act 1983 was disproportionate and violated ECHR, Protocol 1, Article 3. The margin of appreciation accorded to states under the ECHR was wide but not all-embracing and this 'blanket restriction' fell outside any acceptable margin of appreciation, 'however wide that margin might be'.[140] The majority judgment took Westminster on directly, remarking that there was no evidence that Parliament had, since 1968, 'ever sought to weigh the competing interests or to assess the proportionality of a blanket ban on the right of a convicted prisoner to vote'.[141]

The House of Commons struck back with a Westminster Hall debate set down by a Eurosceptic backbencher, who called for a 'proper parliamentary debate on the issue, so that colleagues can debate the pros and cons and be given the opportunity to vote to maintain the status quo'; the *Hirst* affair was 'a golden opportunity' for the then Coalition Government 'to put Britain first' and consider 'pulling out of the Convention'.[142] There was no government response. A more moderate, cross-party, backbench motion followed asserting that 'legislative decisions of this nature should be a matter for democratically-elected lawmakers' and supporting 'the current situation in which no prisoner is able to vote except those imprisoned for contempt, default or on remand'. It passed by 234 to 22 votes.[143]

Initially, the ECtHR had asked for legislation within six months. The previous Labour Government had made gestures at compliance with a two-stage consultation on policy options, which remained unimplemented at the time of the UK General Election in 2010. Left to clear up the mess, the Coalition announced legislation which would provide for offenders sentenced to a custodial sentence of less than four years to vote in UK Westminster parliamentary and European Parliament elections, unless the judge considered this inappropriate when making the sentence.[144] In the same year, the Court, treating *Greens and MT* as a 'pilot case' imposed a further six-month deadline.[145] By 2013, when no timetable had been announced for legislation, the government intervened in the *Scoppola* case[146] to ask the ECtHR to reconsider *Hirst*. The Court firmly declined. Caught between the ECtHR and Parliament, the Supreme Court manoeuvred skilfully in *Chester*, holding itself bound to follow the law as repeatedly confirmed by Strasbourg but declining to grant a further declaration of invalidity.[147] Perhaps thankfully, Lord Mance declared that

[139] *Hirst v United Kingdom (No 2)* (2006) 42 EHRR 41. There was a 12–5 majority. For a detailed account of the voting rights affair, see I White and A Horne, *Prisoners' Voting Rights*, HC Library Standard Note SN/PC/01764 (2015).

[140] *Hirst* (n 139) [83].

[141] ibid [79].

[142] HC Deb vol 521 cols 5–6WH (11 January 2011), Mr Philip Hollobone.

[143] HC Deb vol 523 col 493 (10 February 2011).

[144] HC Deb vol 520 col 151WS (20 December 2010), Mr Mark Harper.

[145] *Greens and MT v United Kingdom* (2010) ECHR 1826, [97]. A further extension was negotiated with the Committee of Ministers in 2014.

[146] *Scoppola v Italy (No 3)* (2013) 56 EHRR 19.

[147] *R (Chester) v Secretary of State for Justice* [2014] AC 271. See also *Moohan* (n 57). A declaration of invalidity was granted by the Scottish Election Appeal Court in *Smith v Scott* (2007) SC 345.

it was 'now for Parliament as the democratically elected legislature to complete its consideration of the position'.[148]

In fact, the Ministry of Justice had in November 2012 submitted to a Committee of both Houses a draft Bill with three options: a ban on prisoners sentenced to four or more years; a ban on prisoners sentenced to six months or more; a restatement of the existing ban. The Committee recommended that prisoners serving sentences of 12 months or less should have the vote.[149] No mention was made of the Bill in the government legislative programme for 2014 or indeed in the 2015 legislative programme of the newly elected Conservative Government and no legislation has been forthcoming.[150]

If prisoners' voting is (as Lady Hale remarked in *Chester*) an emotive subject on which people seem to hold strong views, then immigration is a high-visibility political issue on which the outcome of elections may turn. As the ECtHR began to interpret the ECHR as a 'living instrument', to expand its ambit by opening up the area of security that government tends to regard as peculiarly its own territory, and extend its protection to immigrants, hostility to the Strasbourg Court began to grow. Less than 10 years after the HRA 1998 had been adopted, Tony Blair had called for possible amendments to the HRA to compel judges to balance the rights of the individual with public safety, which they 'do not always do'; David Cameron, then in Opposition, was promising to 'reform or repeal' the Act.[151] Events came to a head in the case of Abu Qatada, a radical Muslim cleric. Lawfully in the country as a refugee, Abu Qatada was arrested in October 2002, detained under the governing anti-terrorism legislation and served with notice of intention to deport while his appeal against his control order was still pending. It took nearly a decade of litigation before Abu Qatada was finally deported,[152] fuelling resentment at the Strasbourg case law, which limited the power to deport or extradite suspected terrorists if they were likely to be tortured. It is, however, noteworthy that the government made no attempt to strike back.

Tensions have undoubtedly been rising, with the target of animosity shifting to the use (or misuse according to one's viewpoint) of ECHR, Article 8 to protect convicted criminals against deportation for family reasons, an area now attracting a multiplicity of immigration appeals. Until recently, the question whether deportation was in the public interest was very much a matter of discretion, in the first instance for the Home Secretary who made the deportation order, afterwards for the courts who reviewed the decision. The factors to be taken into consideration were later incorporated into non-statutory Immigration Rules, which were laid before Parliament.[153] It was the effect of the 'mirror principle' that changed the rules of the game by substituting for the ministerial view of the public interest a two-stage test to be applied by the courts with reference to the Strasbourg jurisprudence and the

[148] *Chester* (n 147) [42].

[149] *Joint Committee on the Draft Voting Eligibility (Prisoners) Bill: Report*, HC 924 (2013).

[150] The position is now complicated by the decision of the CJEU in Case C-650/13 *Delvigne* (Judgment of 6 October 2015) based on EU law and the ECFR.

[151] See *Guardian*, 15 May 2006.

[152] *Othman (Abu Qatada) v United Kingdom* (2012) 55 EHRR 1; HC Deb vol 565 col 23 (8 July 2014).

[153] Rules 398 and 399 of the Immigration Rules, HC 395 (as amended in 2012).

proportionality principle that this enjoined.[154] By 2010, the impact on deportation of suspected terrorists and convicted criminals was so considerable[155] as to persuade the Home Secretary, Theresa May, into announcing changes to the rules 'to ensure that the misinterpretation of Article 8 of the ECHR—the right to a family life—no longer prevents the deportation of people who shouldn't be here'.[156] It now fell to the courts to consider whether the 'new Rules' created a 'complete code' as the government argued, rolling up Article 8 proportionality testing into a single determination conducted in the framework of the Rules. Both the Upper Tribunal and Court of Appeal disagreed. The primary decision-makers were as much bound by section 6 of the HRA 1998 as the judges and the new rules 'maintain[ed] the obligation on primary decision-makers to act "in compliance with" all the provisions of the Convention'.[157]

Up to this point, the government had stopped short at attempting draconian measures such as ouster, thought likely to violate the ECHR or international law. Now it struck back with legislation that hit at Article 8 adjudication in two slightly different ways. First, it allowed the Secretary of State to prevent a person bringing an appeal from the United Kingdom when the Secretary of State certified that removal would be in the interests of national security—a technique redolent of that outlawed by the CJEU in *Johnston*.[158] Secondly, it gave the force of primary legislation to the Rules by 'requiring a court or tribunal, when determining whether a decision is in breach of Article 8 ECHR, to have regard to the public interest considerations as set out in the Act'.[159] The Act specifies in very considerable detail the criteria to be applied by judges when determining the public interest and the weight that should be given to them. This provision, which sought to guide courts and tribunals in their determination of Article 8 claims in immigration cases, was drawn to the attention of the House of Lords by its Constitution Committee, which called it 'a significant innovation'.[160] The JCHR concern was greater; it saw the provision as a significant legislative trespass into the judicial function[161] and recommended amendment, which was not conceded. The tenor of some of the speeches in the legislative debates hinted at a changing climate of opinion. Critics targeted both the Strasbourg Court for 'steadily eroding' UK powers of deportation and the UK courts, responsible for tightening the fetters as a consequence 'rightly or wrongly' of the HRA 1998. Parliament, it was argued, must 'make it clear which, ultimately, is the supreme court for British law'; 'the final word should stay in this country'.[162]

[154] *R (Razgar) v Secretary of State for the Home Department (No 2)* [2004] 2 AC 368.

[155] See *MF (Nigeria) v Secretary of State for the Home Department* [2013] EWCA Civ 1192, where it is stated that of 602 appeals allowed by the immigration tribunals in 2013, 324 involved convicted criminals who succeeded under ECHR, Art 8.

[156] Speech to the Conservative Party Conference (4 October 2011).

[157] *MF* (n 154) [46]; *MF (Article 8—New Rules) Nigeria* [2012] UKUT 00393; *Izuazu (Article 8—New Rules) Nigeria* [2013] UKUT 45.

[158] *Johnston* (n 109).

[159] Explanatory notes to Immigration Act 2014, s 15.

[160] Constitution Committee, *Immigration Bill*, HL 148 (2014) [9]–[18]. Clause 14 became s 19 of the Immigration Act 2014.

[161] Joint Committee on Human Rights, *Legislative Scrutiny: Immigration Bill*, HC 935 (2013) Recommendation 9. See similarly Constitution Committee (n 159).

[162] HC Deb vol 574 col 1092 (30 January 2014), Mr Julian Brazier.

In the different policy area of benefits entitlement, *Reilly and Wilson*[163] bit more deeply into political autonomy. The case concerned a package of welfare reforms supposedly designed to assist the unemployed in finding employment. As an element in this package, certain jobseekers were required to participate when instructed to do so in a specified, work-related scheme; further, a claimant who refused unreasonably to do so could be sanctioned by loss of benefit. In *Reilly and Wilson*, the package was challenged on the ground that the Regulations made under the Act[164] were insufficiently specific; that the general notice required by the statute was inadequate; and that, in the case of one of the claimants, no notification had been given. The Court of Appeal ruled the Regulations ultra vires; they did not contain an appropriate description of the scheme and the notices sent to claimants did not comply with the statutory requirements.[165] The government struck back immediately, using the package tried and tested in social security cases, as described in section II. The 2011 Regulations were revoked and replaced by new prospective Regulations, which came into effect on the date of the Court of Appeal judgment.[166] This was followed up with retrospective legislation. The Jobseekers (Back to Work Schemes) Bill introduced into the Commons on 14 March 2013 under 'fast-track procedure',[167] provided that notices served under the 2011 Regulations informing claimants about participation requirements and the consequences of failing to meet them, were effective. The Bill was in short designed to strike back at the Court of Appeal judgment and to provide against future appeals.

The Bill did not escape parliamentary censure. There were two main accusations: there was an abuse of emergency procedures to fix the consequences of losing an appeal and the Bill was suspect on the grounds of retrospectivity. The government response to the Commons was unconvincing: the judgments had been 'about a technicality'; the system was robust and would stand up to scrutiny by the courts, as the government hoped to show by continuing an appeal before the Supreme Court; emergency legislation was the only way to insure against substantial sums in sanction repayments if the appeal were to succeed.[168] The House of Lords Constitution Committee took up both points; in particular, the Bill offended:[169]

> the cardinal rule of law principle that individuals may be punished or penalised only for contravening what was at the time a valid legal requirement. According to the doctrine of the sovereignty of Parliament, retrospective legislation is lawful. Nonetheless, from a constitutional point of view it should wherever possible be avoided, since the law should so far as possible be clear, accessible and predictable.

[163] *R (Reilly) v Work and Pensions Secretary* [2012] EWHC 2292.

[164] Jobseeker's Allowance (Employment, Skills and Enterprise Scheme) Regulations 2011 (SI 2011/917). The draft Regulations had been severely criticised by the House of Lords Select Committee on the Merits of Statutory Instruments: HL 137 (2011) [10], [11].

[165] *R (Reilly) v Work and Pensions Secretary* [2013] EWCA Civ 66.

[166] Jobseeker's Allowance (Schemes for Assisting Persons to Obtain Employment) Regulations 2013 (SI 2013/276).

[167] See for explanation, Constitution Committee (n 52).

[168] HC Deb vol 560 cols 827–28 (19 March 2013), Mr Mark Hoban. The cost of refunding sanctions unlawfully imposed for refusal to comply with an administrative direction was said to be around £130 million, a sum challenged in the litigation.

[169] Constitution Committee, *Jobseekers (Back to Work Schemes) Bill*, HL 155 (2013) [22].

Unusually, despite the fact that their judgment would be hypothetical, the Supreme Court chose to press on. It was, they explained, 'rather unattractive for the executive to be taking up court time and public money to establish that a regulation is valid, when it has already taken up Parliamentary time to enact legislation which retrospectively validates the regulation'; nonetheless the issue could be of some significance to the drafting of regulations generally.[170] It confirmed the Court of Appeal reasoning while allowing the appeal by reason of the 2013 Act.

But the HRA 1998 had provided the claimants with further arguments. In *Reilly and Hewstone*,[171] aggrieved claimants returned to the High Court to challenge the 2013 Act on the ground that the claimants' right to a fair trial under ECHR, Article 6(1) had been violated. This brought the Strasbourg jurisprudence squarely into the frame. The Convention argument was that retrospective legislation when used to affect the outcome of a judicial determination where the state itself was a party was justifiable only on 'compelling grounds of the public interest'. Perhaps surprisingly, the judge granted a declaration that the 2013 Act was incompatible with the principle of the rule of law and the notion of a fair trial protected by ECHR, Article 6(1). This ruling reworks the constitutional position. As correctly stated by the Constitution Committee, retrospective legislation is lawful subject to an understanding in the nature of convention that it is highly undesirable; *Reilly and Hewstone* elevates this to a serious legal obstacle to the practice. Moreover the judge carried the war on to parliamentary territory, raking through the parliamentary proceedings with a nit-comb, discovering a number of 'misconceptions' and 'inaccuracies'.[172] This type of approach strengthens the argument for 'notwithstanding' clauses and heightens the danger that government may strike back with a more general attack on the HRA 1998.

IV. CONCLUSION

Our objective in this chapter has been to examine negative responses from government to unfavourable judicial decisions and the techniques available for striking back at the judiciary and clamping down on judicial review. We have considered two classes of case: retrospective, where government expunges the effects of a particular decision, and prospective, where it seeks to prevent or inhibit unwanted challenges or decisions, often by changing the rules of the game. We have looked at these practices in two different constitutional contexts: first, in the framework of the classical British constitution, where Parliament is sovereign, and secondly, in the more restrictive framework of the post-European constitution. And, with a wish to avoid the court-centred literature that is a particular feature of the law and democracy debate, we have deliberately side-stepped the question of judicial techniques used to respond

[170] *R (Reilly) v Secretary of State for Work and Pensions* [2014] AC 453, [40]–[41].

[171] *R (Reilly (No 2) and Hewstone) v Secretary of State for Work and Pensions* [2014] EWHC 2182. The case is currently under appeal.

[172] ibid [92]–[114].

in kind. This chapter is, as we remarked in our Introduction, a modest attempt to redress the balance.

We have in fact uncovered a considerable degree of continuity. Section II of the chapter dealt with striking back in the domestic context; in other words, in a modified framework of Westminster government predicated on the day-to-day working of parliamentary sovereignty. Here, we saw in the context of social security law a regular practice of retrospective legislation coupled with pre-emptive strikes. It was somewhat surprising to find identical techniques used in the jobseekers' affair, nearly 15 years after the HRA 1998 became law. In both cases, the legitimacy of this type of activity is in issue and, although we have chosen not to dwell at length on these questions, we have quoted instances where there is a clear violation of the rule of law. In our view, retrospective legislation striking down an unpopular decision in the course of the appeal process is—though emphatically not illegal—a dubious practice, especially when it is carried out by regulations or 'fast-track' procedure that escape proper debate in Parliament. We support in this context Prosser's suggestion that retrospective legislation should, if it is to be legitimate, measure up to the three basic good governance principles of openness, participation and accountability, which requires that government must publicly present a properly reasoned justification for its actions and provide the opportunity for adequate informed debate.

It is generally supposed that the United Kingdom's latter-day relationships with Europe, and more particularly the establishment of powerful transnational courts in Strasbourg and Luxembourg, have brought about a fundamental shift in power away from Parliament and the doctrine of parliamentary sovereignty as propounded by Dicey. Our case studies in section III suggest that this is not entirely true. Yes, limitations have in principle been imposed on government action and we may think that the restrictions are likely to tighten. Yet, as indicated earlier, we have registered a considerable degree of consistency. All the main techniques for striking back, whether directly through ouster, validatory legislation, delaying tactics or the retaking of annulled decisions by proper procedures, are still in play. Recently too, there has been resort to indirect measures, such as changing the rules of judicial review procedure and upping its cost so as to undercut the judicial review process and clamp down on targeted litigants. In short, traditional techniques are still in use, though their weight and value may have changed. Perhaps more importantly, there is little evidence of a decisive change in the mindset of successive governments. At the time of writing indeed a Conservative Government is in power with a manifesto commitment to support a general strike-back at judicial power through replacement of the HRA 1998 and perhaps, in the event of a No vote in the promised referendum, to engineer a 'Brexit' from the European Union. But these 'nuclear options' raise questions better left for discussion in the context of a full-scale law and democracy debate that we prefer to reserve for another occasion.

14

The Use and Effects of Judicial Review: Assumptions and the Empirical Evidence

MAURICE SUNKIN AND VARDA BONDY*

I. INTRODUCTION

THERE IS GROWING interest amongst academics in obtaining an empirically based understanding of judicial review's contribution to social and policy change, its influence on the quality of public administration, and its effectiveness as a means of redress. However, the relevance of empirically based evidence relating to the use and effects of judicial review extends beyond the academic community, including to practitioners seeking to support legal argument; to judges seeking to assess the likely implications of their decisions; and to policy-makers and reformers concerned to ground their decisions on robust empirically based evidence. Having access to such evidence is, of course, also important to stakeholders when seeking to respond to reform proposals and hold public decision makers accountable.

The significance of these matters was highlighted in the United Kingdom by the Coalition Government's reforms to judicial review in 2013–15 and their accompanying restrictions to the availability of legal aid. The judicial review reforms were introduced with the aim of curtailing people's ability to challenge government and thereby reduce burdens on public bodies and impediments to public decision-making in the interests of economic recovery.[1] There is no need here to deal in

* This chapter is based on that delivered by Maurice Sunkin to the Public Law Conference at Cambridge in September 2014. It draws principally on three research projects: V Bondy and M Sunkin, *The Dynamics of Judicial Review Litigation* (Public Law Project, 2009); V Bondy, L Platt and M Sunkin, *The Value and Effects of Judicial Review* (Public Law Project, 2015), both funded by the Nuffield Foundation, and *The Impacts of Judicial Review on the Quality of Local Authority Performance*, funded by the ESRC. Both Nuffield-funded projects were undertaken by the Public Law Project (PLP) and the University of Essex. At the time Varda Bondy was Research Director of the PLP and we acknowledge the PLP's involvement and support. We owe a debt of thanks to Lucinda Platt, Professor of Social Policy and Sociology, LSE., who was Co-Researcher on both the Value and Effects of Judicial Review project and the ESRC funded research. We are also very grateful to Christopher Luff, Senior Research Officer on the Value and Effects project. We also thank the editors of this volume for their comments and suggestions.

[1] The reform programme was announced by the Prime Minister in a speech to the Confederation of British Industries in November 2012, available at www.cbi.org.uk/media-centre/news-articles/2012/11/david-cameron-sets-out-plans-to-slash-red-tape-at-cbi-annual-conference/.

detail with the specific reforms.[2] Suffice to say that the reforms drew on three widely held assumptions concerning the use and effects of judicial review: first, that there has been considerable growth in the use of judicial review over the past few decades largely driven by claimants abusing the process; secondly, that judicial review hinders government and exerts overwhelmingly negative impacts on the quality of public administration, not least because it causes delay and absorbs resources which would otherwise be better deployed; and thirdly, that judicial review tends often to concern technical matters of process rather than substance so that even when claimants succeed in court they rarely, if ever, obtain tangible benefits as a result. Typical of such attitudes to judicial review, the Ministry of Justice asserted that:

> [J]udicial review can too often be used to delay perfectly reasonable decisions or actions. Often this will be part of a campaign or other public relations activity and the judicial review will be founded on a procedural defect rather than a substantive illegality. The Government is considering strengthening the law and practice to enable the Courts to deal more swiftly with applications where the alleged flaw complained of would have made 'no difference'.[3]

An implication is that because judicial review litigation disrupts good government and is rarely worth the fuss and bother it can be curtailed without substantial loss or injustice. This chapter questions each of the above assumptions in turn. It seeks to show that it is misleading to assume: (a) that there has been a significant growth in the use of judicial review driven by claimants abusing the system; (b) that judicial review necessarily impedes good administration; and (c) that judicial review litigation is unlikely to provide effective redress to claimants. However, before turning to these matters we offer some general comments about the evidence relating to the use and effects of judicial review in England and Wales.

II. EVIDENCE BASE FOR REFORMING JUDICIAL REVIEW

A. General Approach to Use of Evidence

It has been a *leitmotif* of government decision-making since at least the 1990s that public decision-making and policy be based on the best available evidence.[4] It is now widely acknowledged that this is conducive to ensuring the quality of decisions as

[2] See A Mills,'Reforms to Judicial Review in the Criminal Justice and Courts Act 2015' [2015] *Public Law* 583.

[3] Ministry of Justice, *Judicial Review: Proposals for Further Reforms Consultation*, Cm 8703 (2013) [99].

[4] It was a core philosophy of New Labour's White Paper *Modernising Government*, Cm 4310 (1999). See also Performance and Innovation Unit, *Better Policy Delivery and Design: A Discussion Paper* (London, Cabinet Office, 2001). The philosophy stimulated the establishment of the ESRC's UK Centre for Evidence Based Policy and a substantial literature. See, eg, W Solesbury, *Evidence Based Policy: Whence it Came and Where it's Going* (London, ESRC UK Centre for Evidence Based Policy and Practice, 2001), available at www.lgsp.uz/old/publications/option_paper_training/ebp_when_it_came_and_where_it_is_going_eng.pdf. More recently, see also the Campaign for Social Science's report, *Business of People* (London, SAGE Publications, 2015), available at http://campaignforsocialscience.org.uk/wp-content/uploads/2015/02/Business-of-People-Full-Report.pdf.

well as enabling accountability and effective participation, since it informs interested parties of the evidence relied on. On the other hand, it is also widely acknowledged that rational evidence is unlikely to deter government from pursuing its policy preferences. The reforms to judicial review provide an illustration of this. This is not to say that the government wholly discounted the need to base its case for reform on empirical data. On the contrary, a feature of the reforms was the degree to which the government sought to rely on a combination of statistics and more anecdotal evidence to show the need for reform.[5] However, rather than bolster the case for reform, how the government employed data came to be seen as one of the major weaknesses of the reform programme. Instead of assisting and smoothing the path to reform, the manner in which 'evidence' was presented by the government was often patently unconvincing and this fanned concerns that the reforms were unnecessary and based on political hostility and populist assumptions rather than on real need. More specifically worrying, the approach of the government to evidence also suggested that it had embarked on its reforms without a full understanding of the relevant evidence base and was learning on the hoof.

The following exchange between Lord Hart and Chris Grayling in the House of Lords Constitution Committee, for example, shows the Lord Chancellor struggling to identify to what extent the reforms were likely to achieve their core objective, namely, to limit the use of judicial review:

> Lord Hart of Chilton: By what proportion do you think that your proposals are going to lead to a decline in the number of judicial reviews? …
>
> Chris Grayling MP: I do not know the answer to that.[6]

B. Use of Official Statistics

A striking feature of the reform programme was the degree to which the government relied on official statistics relating to judicial review. The basic purpose of these statistics is to provide an annual indication of the overall scale of the Administrative Court's caseload by showing the number of decisions taken and their outcome at the main stages of the process. Given this narrow purpose it is unsurprising that the official statistics can provide only very limited insight into the way judicial review is used and no indication of its broader effects.[7] For example, the statistics say nothing

[5] The government cited 'case studies' illustrating the adverse effects of judicial review. In one, a series of challenges to the grant of planning permission for 360 homes which would have created 45 construction jobs per year delayed the project by two years. Another concerned the establishment of a Free School. Here there was 'inappropriate use of judicial review as a campaign tactic' when a legal challenge to planning permission allowing the school to use what was previously a nursery led the local authority to retake its decision to grant planning permission. See Ministry of Justice, *Judicial Review: Proposals for Further Reform*, Cm 8703 (2013) 6–7, available at www.gov.uk/government/uploads/system/uploads/attachment_data/file/264091/8703.pdf.

[6] Unrevised transcript of evidence given by the Lord Chancellor to the House of Lords Constitution Committee on 26 March 2014, available at www.parliament.uk/documents/lords-committees/constitution/annual%20oral%20evidence%20sessions%202013-2014/ucCONST260314ev1Grayling.pdf.

[7] The limitations of the official statistics have been known for many years. See M Sunkin, 'What is Happening to Applications for Judicial Review?' (1987) 50 *Modern Law Review* 432.

about such matters as why claims are made, whether claimants are bringing cases on behalf of themselves, or others, or for wider public interest reasons; the demographic characteristics of claimants or their geographical location; what, if any steps, were taken prior to litigation to resolve the dispute; the nature of settlements and when and why these occur. Nor do the statistics show what happens following litigation and whether and how public bodies comply with judgments; or what, if any, benefits claimants obtain from their litigation; or how the litigation may have affected public bodies.

Moreover, until recently the statistics gave no indication of how particular cases or groups of cases progressed through the process, or which government departments are challenged.[8] For instance, they could not have been used to show what proportion of claims issued in (say) January 2012 obtained permission and went to a final hearing and were successful or unsuccessful at that hearing. Recent changes to the way the official statistics are presented, perhaps in response to criticism made by researchers, have enabled some indication of the progress of cohorts. Unfortunately, from the outset the figures on the way cohorts progress have been analysed by the Ministry of Justice to produce a misleading image of the process. For example, the Ministry of Justice produced sensational headlines to the effect that only 1 per cent of judicial review claims were successful. In this context it has been observed that:

> It is interesting that the MOJ chooses to highlight that only 1% of cases lodged have been won at a final hearing rather than that public authorities have prevailed at final hearings in only about 2% of cases lodged. The latter is perhaps the more revealing statistic given the very high number of cases that settle in favour of claimants before trial. The true significance of the 1% statistic ... is in indicating how few cases lodged actually make it to a final hearing. The vast majority of cases are either withdrawn before reaching this stage or refused permission.[9]

III. FIRST ASSUMPTION: GROWTH IN THE USE OF JUDICIAL REVIEW HAS BEEN DRIVEN BY ABUSE

A. Growth, What Growth?

There can be little doubt that the qualitative importance of public law litigation has grown in the decades since the 1960s. Whether there has been a quantitative growth in the number of judicial review claims is another matter altogether. When the government embarked on their reforms they perhaps understandably assumed that the official statistics showed there to have been a significant growth in the numbers of legal challenges. Certainly the official statistics, on the face of it, show for example that in 1974 there were only 160 applications for judicial review, that by 2000 this

[8] Eg in 2001 the official statistics showed there to be more permission decisions recorded than there had been claims issued in that year.

[9] T Hickman and M Sunkin, 'Success in Judicial Review: The Current Position' (2015) *UK Constitutional Law Blog*, available at http://ukconstitutionallaw.org/2015/03/20/tom-hickman-and-maurice-sunkin-success-in-judicial-review-the-current-position/.

number had grown to nearly 4,250 and by 2011 to over 11,000.[10] However, as was very quickly recognised by many commentators, the statistics relied upon by government did not in fact show what the government claimed they showed. The headline figures obscured the true picture because they did not distinguish between the number of immigration and asylum claims and the number of claims that were not concerned with immigration or asylum.[11] As Sunkin put it in his evidence to the Joint Committee on Human Rights:

> If one leaves aside the immigration case load, the evidence does not show that there has been a substantial increase in the use of judicial review. In fact, the official statistics ... reveal that, in non-immigration civil judicial reviews over the last 15 years or so, case numbers have remained fairly constant at just over 2,000 a year ... By any measure, that is not a large number compared with the number of decisions taken by Government annually.[12]

In the summary to its report the Joint Committee on Human Rights said that:

> We ... do not consider the Government to have demonstrated by clear evidence that non-immigration related judicial review has 'expanded massively' in recent years as the Lord Chancellor claims, that there are real abuses of the process taking place, or that the current powers of the courts to deal with such abuse are inadequate.[13]

Given the relatively steady level of use of judicial review in non-immigration matters it is perhaps surprising that the use of judicial review had not grown more over this period given developments such as the enactment of the Human Rights Act 1998.

That the government was aware that their repeated insistence that judicial review in general has expanded massively was inaccurate is evident from their own citation of the official statistics relating to the volume of non-immigration/asylum claims.[14]

B. Quality of Claims

The assertion that there has been large-scale abuse of judicial review has two limbs to it. One is that a high proportion of challenges have been without merit and have been brought by claimants knowingly issuing unmeritorious claims for a variety of inappropriate reasons such as to cause a delay in their deportation. That assertion is based on both anecdotal evidence and an (unreliable) interpretation of official statistics. There can be no doubt that abuse of judicial review and of public funding does occur, but judges are well placed to identify such cases and deal with them appropriately, not only by refusing permission, but also in extreme cases by

[10] Ministry of Justice, *Judicial Review: Proposals for Reform*, Cm 8515 (2012) [28], citing Ministry of Justice, *Judicial and Court Statistics 2011* (London, 2012) table 7.12.

[11] See R Thomas, 'Mapping Immigration Judicial Review Litigation: An Empirical Legal Analysis' [2015] *Public Law* 652.

[12] Joint Committee on Human Rights, *The Implications for Access to Justice of the Government's Proposals to Reform Judicial Review*, HL 174/HC 868 (2013–14) [27].

[13] ibid 3.

[14] *Judicial Review: Proposals for Further Reforms* (n 3) [10]. While the government recognised that significant growth in the use of judicial review had not occurred beyond immigration, the mantra of growth was repeated in the consultation documents. See, eg, *Judicial Review: Proposals for Further Reform* (n 3) 3, 5.

imposing personal costs penalties on errant lawyers and even reporting them to their respective professional bodies.[15] The claim that abuse is pervasive, however, has been primarily based on interpretation of the official statistics which show that only a small, and declining, percentage of claimants are granted permission to seek judicial review. The Ministry of Justice, for example, said that:

> In the majority of applications considered by the courts, permission to bring Judicial Review proceedings is refused. Of the 7,600 applications for permission considered by the Court in 2011, only around one in six (or 1,200) was granted.[16]

There has been an historical decline in the proportion of claims granted permission. However, as we have shown elsewhere, the reasons for this do not necessarily lie in an increase in the overall level of abuse or a decline in the quality of claims.[17] Factors such as changes in the way the judiciary interpret and apply the permission criteria, as well as an increase in settlement prior to the permission stage have also played a part in the longer term trends. Moreover, figures based on single years also need to be carefully interpreted.

For instance, the figures cited by the government relating to 2011 took no account of 3,600 claims which appeared to have been lost to the statistics between having been issued and the permission stage (11,200 less 7,600). This proportion is consistent with research findings showing that 34 per cent of judicial review claims are withdrawn after being issued but prior to being considered by a judge for permission, often after being settled in favour of the claimant.[18] In other words, there is a significantly higher rate of success than that suggested by the permission grant rate figures alone. We have already referred to the government's further misleading claim that only 1 per cent of judicial reviews are successful.

C. It's the Left ...

The other, more specific claim about abuse, was that the process had been increasingly used by pressure groups (specifically on the Left) to challenge and frustrate government decisions. Indeed, the then Justice Secretary, Chris Grayling, took the unusual step of publishing an article in the *Daily Mail* in September 2013, in which he presented the reform of judicial review as a war on campaigning groups:

> One essential part of the campaigner's armoury is the judicial review, through which it is possible for them to challenge decisions of government and public bodies in the courts ... In proposing these changes, I will no doubt be accused of killing justice and destroying Magna Carta.[19]

[15] Eg in *R (Hamid) v Secretary of State for the Home Department* [2012] EWHC 3070 (Admin), the court warned lawyers of the consequences of failing to complete the requirements in Form N463 regarding urgency where applications appear aimed merely at delaying removal.

[16] *Judicial Review: Proposals for Further Reform* (n 3) [31].

[17] V Bondy and M Sunkin, 'Accessing Judicial Review' [1987] *Public Law* 647.

[18] V Bondy and M Sunkin, *The Dynamics of Judicial Review Litigation* (London, Public Law Project, 2009) 39–41.

[19] C Grayling, 'The judicial review system is not a promotional tool for countless left-wing campaigners', *Daily Mail*, 6 September 2013.

He then made it clear that this was a political battle against 'the Left':

> Britain cannot afford to allow a culture of Left-wing-dominated, single-issue activism to hold back our country from investing in infrastructure and new sources of energy and from bringing down the cost of our welfare state … The Left does not understand this, and believes that our society can do everything for everyone, and that those who work hard to get on in life should pick up the tab. They want more money for public services, but at the same time to be able to halt the investments which can deliver the wealth that pays for those services.[20]

Such inflammatory language does not add credibility to any assertion concerning abuse of process, and as already mentioned, disregards the fact that the procedure enables judges at the permission stage to filter out cases which are not sufficiently arguable or which are brought by claimants without a sufficient interest. Moreover, as will be seen below, there is no empirical justification for associating 'the Left' with excessive use of judicial review, let alone abuse of the system. The empirical evidence cited below shows that pressures groups comprise a tiny proportion of claimants and, incidentally, that commercial corporations bring a similar proportion of claims.[21]

IV. SECOND ASSUMPTION: JUDICIAL REVIEW HAS A NEGATIVE EFFECT ON PUBLIC ADMINISTRATION

A. Normative and Practical Considerations

A second widely held assumption, and one which clearly motivated the reform programme, is that judicial review litigation has an overwhelmingly negative impact on public administration which justifies curtailing its use. There is an obvious public interest in ensuring that government is not unduly hampered by unjustified legal challenges. This public interest has also been recognised in the characteristics of the judicial review procedure and in particular the short limitation period, the permission requirement, and the discretionary nature of the remedies.[22] Although the reforms were premised on the view that the existing protections for public administration were inadequate and required strengthening, as with the prevention of abuse judges have always been able to exercise their discretion in individual cases to balance the interests of justice and the needs of good administration. It is understandable that government might want to maximise the degree to which public administration is protected from legal challenge, but is there a genuine issue for government to be concerned about here? Does judicial review threaten to impede the process of government in any real sense?

[20] ibid.

[21] See V Bondy, L Platt and M Sunkin 'The Value and Effects of Judicial Review: the nature of claims, their outcomes and consequences' (Public Law Project, 2015).

[22] Features of substantive law also strike a balance between public and claimant interest. See further Jason NE Varuhas, Chapter 4, 'The Public Interest Conception of Public Law: Its Procedural Origins and Substantive Implications'.

The first point to make is that from a normative perspective, arguably no fundamental tension exists between the goals of judicial review and those of public administration. The importance of judicial review is grounded in the rule of law and the constitutional need to ensure both that government is legally accountable and that when public bodies exceed or abuse their legal powers, those adversely affected have effective legal redress. These requirements are fundamental to our system and are an aspect of good government. As Sir John Donaldson MR famously said, there is a partnership between judges and public authorities 'based on a common aim, namely the maintenance of the highest standards of public administration'.[23] The requirements cannot be dispensed with by government, even if at times their achievement causes inconvenience or may appear unpopular. In this sense, far from being a threat to good government, judicial review is fundamentally concerned with securing its achievement.

But if we put the normative position on one side for the moment, what about actual practice? What, if anything, does the empirical research tell us about the way judicial review affects public administration? There is now much work exploring whether judicial review does lead to the highest standards of public administration; whether it does encourage public bodies to adhere to the standards of legality, fairness and justice implicit in the principles of judicial review; and if so, whether such standards are conducive to good administration. The prevailing message of the research is that we should not expect too much from judicial review; it has only 'limited ability ... to influence administrative decision-making'.[24] The research findings appear to show, as Genevra Richardson has summarised them, 'that there is nothing particularly significant about judicial review; it is likely to be simply one of a number of factors influencing decision makers'.[25]

Moreover, work on routine decision-making has found that where judicial review does exert an influence, this tends to be 'negative' when viewed from the perspective of the standards of administrative law. For example, based on his study of local housing authority decision-making in the context of homelessness, Simon Halliday found evidence that increased exposure to legal challenge reduces the extent to which organisations scrutinise themselves and, where they do, the scrutiny does not 'reflect the values of judicial review'.[26] Ian Loveland's research, also on homelessness, similarly found that moves on the part of local authorities to comply with legal requirements were essentially defensive, being designed 'to safeguard decisions from legal challenge, not to improve routine decision-making in any real sense'.[27] The thrust of this work seems, then, to suggest that judicial review has little to contribute to routine decision-making and may well lead to results that undermine rather than

[23] *R v Lancashire County Council, ex parte Huddleston* [1986] 2 All ER 941, 945.

[24] G Richardson, 'Impact Studies in the UK' in M Hertogh and S Halliday (eds), *Judicial Review and Bureaucratic Impact: International and Interdisciplinary Perspectives* (Cambridge, Cambridge University Press, 2004) 112.

[25] ibid 114–15.

[26] S Halliday, 'The Influence of Judicial Review on Bureaucratic Decision-Making' [2000] *Public Law* 110.

[27] Richardson, 'Impact Studies in the UK' (n 24) 114, citing I Loveland, *Housing Homeless Persons: Administrative Law and the Administrative Process* (Oxford, Clarendon Press, 1995) ch 11. See also M Sunkin and K Pick, 'The Changing Impact of Judicial Review: The Independent Review Service of the Social Fund' [2001] *Public Law* 753.

improve the legal quality of government. At best these studies seem to suggest that curtailing the use of judicial review is unlikely to have significant adverse effects on the quality of government. The findings indicating that judicial review is unlikely to exert significant impacts on routine decision-making may be unsurprising bearing in mind the context within in which such decisions are made. Front-line officials tend to work in accordance with internal guidance. If their decisions are questioned, the matter is much more likely to be dealt with by internal reviews or appeals to a tribunal than by judicial review. If judicial review is used at all, this will normally only be as a last resort when all other opportunities to challenge decisions have failed. Consequently, very few officials will have any direct contact with judicial review. For most it is likely to be a rather distant consideration, even if they are required to adopt processes which are rooted in concepts such as the need to act fairly.

B. A Rosier Picture of the Effects of Judicial Review

However, not all the available research is so dismissive of judicial review's ability to make a positive contribution. Jeff King, for example, has more recently presented a rather 'rosier picture'.[28] He makes five points. First, he says that work of the type undertaken by Halliday and Loveland on areas such as homelessness 'might not be representative of the administrative justice field as a whole'.[29] He cites research on other aspects of welfare rights adjudication, including on social security and on reform of mental health law, which indicates that judicial review has been an influential driver of positive change.[30] Secondly, he doubts 'whether these studies … take adequate note of how practitioners themselves view the role of law'.[31] Thirdly, he contrasts the 'downbeat' findings of British research with 'more mixed' findings of research in Australia, Canada and the United States.[32] Fourthly, he notes that the studies 'do not for the most part consider the value of individual redress'.[33] Fifthly, he comments that the work is predominantly qualitative in nature and that in the absence of 'more quantitative data it is difficult to draw any conclusions about whether judicial review and legal accountability are marginal'.[34]

C. Judicial Review and the Quality of Local Government Services

With King's comments in mind we now turn to the findings of a study concerned with the impact of judicial review on the quality of local government services in

[28] J King, *Judging Social Rights* (Cambridge, Cambridge University Press, 2012) 70–76.

[29] ibid 72.

[30] Including T Buck, 'Judicial Review and the Discretionary Social Fund: Impact on the Respondent Organisation' in T Buck (ed), *Judicial Review and Social Welfare* (London, Pinter, 1998) and J Peay, *Tribunals on Trial: A Study of Decision-making under the Mental Health Act 1983* (Oxford, Clarendon Press, 1989).

[31] King, *Judging Social Rights* (n 28) 74.

[32] ibid 74–75.

[33] ibid 75.

[34] ibid 75.

England and Wales which suggests a more nuanced view of judicial review's influence on public administration.[35] This study used qualitative and quantitative techniques. The qualitative dimension included case studies based on judicial review decisions that were identified by officials as having had significant impacts on local authorities. The research examined why these cases were considered to be so important and how they impacted on local authorities. It is worth noting that the cases were identified by officials precisely because they were not typical or routine. We cannot therefore assume that these were representative of the way judicial review normally affects local authorities, rather they are indications of how local authorities responded to decisions which posed particularly difficult problems for them. In other words, they illustrate what happens when judicial review exerts its greatest impacts. Two cases illustrate some of the issues revealed by this aspect of the research.

In *R (Behre) v London Borough of Hillingdon*,[36] Hillingdon was held to have mistaken the scope of its duties to former unaccompanied asylum-seeking children who had been 'looked after' by the local authority. They had to do more than provide general support under section 17 of the Children Act 1989. They also had to provide accommodation and after-care services until the claimants were 21 years old or beyond if they stayed in full-time education. The judgment clarified the law and officials now knew what was required of them. But the real impact of the judgment was that it required the council to spend money it believed it could not afford and to rethink its budget priorities.[37] With other affected London Boroughs, Hillingdon also relied on the judgment to successfully campaign for extra funding from central government.[38]

In *R (J) v Caerphilly County Borough Council*,[39] the Council was held to have failed in its duties to a minor who had left a young offender institution. The judge, Munby J (as he then was), was highly critical of the 'mindset' and 'culture' of local authorities who exclude families when decisions are taken about establishing care plans for their children and in his judgment Munby J set out ways in which local authorities should approach such care plans.[40] Officials said that the decision was 'a shock' that 'came out of the blue' for them.[41] One spoke of the judgment's 'harshness'.[42] Other officials doubted that the judge understood the problems they

[35] L Platt, M Sunkin and K Calvo, 'Judicial Review Litigation as an Incentive to Change in Local Authority Services in England and Wales' (2010) 20 *Journal of Public Administration Research and Theory* i243.

[36] [2003] EWHC 2075.

[37] E Free, *Local Authority Support to Unaccompanied Asylum-seeking Young People: Changes Since the Hillingdon Judgment* (London, Save the Children, 2005); *Ringing the Changes: the Impact of Guidance on the Use of Sections 17 and 20 of the Children Act 1989 to Support Unaccompanied Asylum-seeking Children* (London, Refugee Council, 2005); *Safeguarding Children: The Second Joint Chief Inspectors' Report on Arrangements to Safeguard Children* (London, Commission for Social Care Inspection, 2005) 16.

[38] Following the decision, councils continued to push for better funding and Hillingdon brought unsuccessful judicial review proceedings against central government: *Hillingdon London Borough Council v Secretary of State for Education and Skills* [2007] EWHC 514.

[39] [2005] EWHC 586.

[40] ibid [34].

[41] Platt, Sunkin and Calvo, 'Judicial Review Litigation as an Incentive to Change' (n 35) i253.

[42] ibid i253.

faced when dealing with difficult young people. From the point of view of the officials the decision had clear negative effects both for them and the wider reputation of the authority.

While Caerphilly Borough Council initially found it difficult to respond to the judgment, it eventually revisited its approach and altered its practice. Over time, the judgment came to be viewed more positively as having helped the authority improve its services. Indeed, the Council became a model for others to emulate.

D. We should not Generalise About the Effects of Judicial Review

These cases illustrate the difficulties of generalising about the impacts of judicial review. They each called for major changes, in *Hillingdon* principally affecting budget and service priorities, and in *Caerphilly* affecting professional practice and cultural attitudes within social services. They illustrate how judicial decisions concerned with the legality of particular decisions may come to have impacts beyond the individual case and beyond matters of law. They illustrate how the implications of court decisions may vary across departments within the same authority, with street level officials benefiting from the clarity and guidance they provide and budget holders and senior managers confronting the more complex challenges posed. And they illustrate the difficulty of generalising about whether the effects of judicial review are negative or positive. Whether a decision is positive or negative is largely a matter of perspective and context, not least because the implications of judgments may change over time. Decisions which initially shock and threaten may become resources stimulating and enabling authorities to improve the quality of their decision-making. This might include encouraging them to find ways to reconcile the tensions between satisfying general demands, driven perhaps by populist policies (such as the view that money should not be spent on asylum-seekers or criminals), while meeting the needs of individuals and less popular groups. Such tensions lie at the heart of administrative justice.

E. Judgments Do not Tell the Whole Story

As indicated earlier, research by Halliday and Loveland suggests that the influence of judicial review may be linked to the extent to which bodies are exposed to legal challenge. The research suggests that as judicial review becomes more common, public bodies may develop strategies to cope which may be incompatible with the aims of administrative law. In short, with familiarity judicial review loses its ability to provide external accountability. This may indicate that judicial review exerts its greatest influence in relation to matters where it is used infrequently or against bodies which are rarely challenged. Perhaps, contrary to impressions, there are many of these. Indeed, the vast majority of public bodies in England and Wales only experience a very small number of challenges a year: in the six years 2000–2005 inclusive, the period covered by the research, 85 per cent of local authorities in England

and Wales had fewer than two challenges annually.[43] As we shall see below, most departments of central government also experience relatively few judicial review cases.

The quantitative aspects of the study explored these issues by examining the relationship between levels of challenge and quality of local authority services. Two questions were asked: first, did poorly performing authorities attract higher levels of challenge than better performing ones? Secondly, did challenges lead to improvements in the quality of local authority performance? For the purposes of the research official indicators of 'quality' were employed, namely, Comprehensive Performance Assessment (CPA) scores used by government to judge the quality of local authorities.[44]

The research found there to be a statistically significant negative association between levels of challenge and CPA scores, controlling for type of authority and a range of other characteristics of the authorities that might be thought to influence their quality, such as levels of deprivation. In other words, authorities with lower scores for quality were challenged more often than authorities with higher scores, all other things being equal. It is perhaps unsurprising that poorly performing authorities attract more challenges than better performing ones. But the findings could reflect an element of reverse causation. That is to say, they could be showing not that poor performance causes legal challenge, but that legal challenge causes poor performance, perhaps by obliging authorities to divert resources from core service provision to defending litigation. This, of course, would be compatible with the assumption that judicial review impedes good government.

In fact, the findings do not support this conclusion. In particular, they showed a link between increases in judicial review litigation and improvements in the quality of local authority performance. They also showed that where local authorities experienced an increase in the incidence of judicial review challenge from the level they had normally experienced, the quality of their services improved as measured by their CPA quality scores.

These intriguing findings suggest that legal challenges have the potential to drive improvements in local authority performance.[45] That increases in challenge were associated with improvements in the ability of local authorities to deliver quality, as defined by government indicators, is significant. It certainly presents a more positive view of the effects of judicial review than is often seen. Moreover, these findings also challenge the assumption that judicial review leads to a decline in the quality of public administration, since if judicial review did have an adverse effect, an increase in challenge could only make things worse: the increase would lead to a reduction in quality not an improvement. It should be noted that because the CPA quality indicators do not identify whether local authorities comply with the principles of judicial

[43] M Sunkin, K Calvo, L Platt and T Landman, 'Mapping the Use of Judicial Review to Challenge Local Authorities in England and Wales' [2007] *Public Law* 545.

[44] The CPA was replaced by the Comprehensive Area Assessment in April 2009.

[45] The estimate is likely to be a conservative one, since there may be aspects of service improvement affected by judicial review that are not reflected in the CPA, including compliance with law.

review, these findings do not tell us whether the legal challenges led to improvements in legal compliance or to more 'just' administration.

There is, of course, a need for caution when interpreting these findings. That a causal link exists between changes in the rate of challenge and later improvements in quality cannot be assumed. It is, for example, possible that the association between litigation and CPA scores is a spurious one in the sense that we may be seeing the impact of separate factors that are simultaneously driving the increase in litigation and the improvement in CPA score.

Nevertheless, these findings are highly suggestive and consistent with the view that public law litigation contributes over time to achieving improvements in the quality of local authority performance. They therefore challenge the assumption that judicial review litigation tends to impede good public administration.

V. THIRD ASSUMPTION: JUDICIAL REVIEW DOES NOT PROVIDE EFFECTIVE REDRESS

A third assumption is that judicial review is not an effective means of redress and tends not to be worth the fuss and cost involved. There are a number of reasons why this assumption may appear justified. At first sight judicial review, as it operates in England and Wales, appears ill equipped to provide effective remedies for claimants dissatisfied with decisions or actions of public bodies. The shortcomings flow partly from factors we have already mentioned which are intended to prevent abuse of the process and protect public administration, such as the very short limitation period and the permission stage. They are also partly due to the fact that the procedure is unsuitable for questioning issues of fact; the discretionary nature of the remedies; the limited availability of damages, and perhaps most importantly, the nature of the review jurisdiction which gives judges very limited ability to alter decisions taken by public authorities. In reality, however, judicial review may have more effect on the outcome of disputes, beyond the legal remedy granted by courts, than might be expected.

In the following sections we consider the ability of the judicial review process to deliver meaningful outcomes for claimants.

A. Settlements

We have already seen that a significant proportion of claims settle in favour claimants and that the process enables claimants to obtain positive outcomes without the need for a final court hearing. However, several observations may be offered regarding the settlement process. That so many cases settle raises a number of issues, not least whether matters could have been resolved at an earlier stage thereby saving the claimant from having to start legal proceedings in the first place. They also highlight the importance of early dialogue between lawyers on both sides in securing timely settlements. While we found widespread concern amongst representatives of both claimants and defendants to resolve disputes as quickly as possible, the research revealed significant obstacles to dialogue and communication that hinder and delay settlement. One is what interviewed practitioners called the 'wait and see' attitude to litigation that persists in some public authorities. In other words, there is a tendency in some authorities to do little in response to an issued claim in the hope that the claim may be withdrawn, perhaps due to lack of funds, a change of circumstances, or failure at the permission stage. Some public bodies only involved their legal department once permission had been granted in circumstances when, had lawyers been involved earlier, they would have advised against defending the case, thereby saving costs to the public purse, especially where the claimant is publicly funded.

A common theme, then, was that settlement often depends on effective communication between expert lawyers on both sides who understand the process and are able to assess the strengths and weaknesses of their respective arguments. This may be an important factor when cutbacks in legal aid lead to more claimants representing themselves. While there may be reductions in the costs of legal aid in the short term, such savings may be at the expense of reductions in the incidence of early settlement, or at least of good quality settlement in which claimants obtain a proper early resolution of their case. In short, reducing legal aid may prolong litigation, with all the costs this involves, and lower the quality of settled outcomes.

B. What Do Successful Claimants Achieve Following a Court Hearing?

One of the most interesting and important questions is what, if anything, do claimants who have been successful in court achieve as a result of their success? When the claimant is successful and the court decides that a decision of the public body should not stand, judges only very rarely go a stage further to substitute the unlawful decision with their own.[46] Normally, the matter is referred back to the body so that it can be reconsidered in accordance with the judgment. It has been widely assumed that 'a successful judicial review ... would most likely be followed by an agency remaking the same decision, though taking care to avoid the earlier legal error';[47] or, in similar vein, that 'administrators usually can and do find some way to reach the same conclusion again despite the defects found by the court in the original decision'.[48] If public bodies did routinely react in this way it would seriously undermine the value of judicial review as an effective remedy and would lend weight to concerns that judicial review litigation tends to be an unnecessary and costly detour to a known and expected outcome.[49]

[46] When a quashing order is made the court may, if statute permits, substitute its own decision for the decision to which the claim relates: Civil Procedure Rules, Part 54, Rule 19.2(b).

[47] R Creyke and J McMillan, 'The Operation of Judicial Review in Australia' in M Hertogh and S Halliday (eds), *Judicial Review and Bureaucratic Impact: International and Interdisciplinary Perspectives* (Cambridge, Cambridge University Press, 2004) 186.

[48] P Cane, 'Understanding Judicial Review and its Impact' in M Hertogh and S Halliday (eds), *Judicial Review and Bureaucratic Impact: International and Interdisciplinary Perspectives* (Cambridge, Cambridge University Press, 2004) 31.

[49] See comments below on Criminal Justice and Court Act 2015, s 84.

C. Nuffield Study on the Value and Effects of Judicial Review: Redress

In a further study we investigated the effect and value of judicial review litigation and explored what happened following judgments of the Administrative Court over the 20-month period from July 2010 to February 2012, inclusive. During this period judgments were delivered in 502 cases.[50] Unsurprisingly, the vast majority (77 per cent) of these cases were brought by individuals. More surprising perhaps, given the Coalition Government's concerns regarding abuse of judicial review by campaigning groups, is the fact that only 14 of the 502 cases (less than 3 per cent) were brought by interest groups.[51]

(i) Types of Claim: Scope of the Issues Involved

Claimants resort to judicial review for a range of reasons. We distinguished between three types of claim according to the scope of the issues which appeared to be raised: 'own fact' cases, 'procedure or policy' cases, and 'wider public interest' cases.[52]

'Own fact' cases were those in which the claimant challenged how law, policy or procedure had been applied to their particular circumstances (rather than the legality of policies or procedures themselves). Here, claimants typically sought redress in a matter directly concerning them in order to secure a service or benefit which a public authority had failed or refused to provide. While they concerned particular decisions, such cases may have broader ramifications, for instance by establishing a precedent or revealing a pattern of error. For example, there were 14 cases in our sample brought by prisoners challenging refusals to allow oral hearings before the Parole Board.[53] A barrister who acted for defendants in several of these told us that in one of the cases the judge had stressed that granting an oral hearing was exceptional; nonetheless, the barrister suggested that in his experience, such challenges 'are not, in fact, all that rare; cases such as this one are likely to lead to more oral hearings as prisons see the way the courts are leaning'. Indeed, not long after that the UK Supreme Court subsequently established that oral hearings should normally be held.[54]

While 'own fact cases' only question the way procedure or policy was applied to a particular claimant, in 'policy or practice' cases the claimant directly challenged the legality of procedures and/or policies themselves. Here too, claimants will typically have been seeking individual redress. However, judicial decisions in such cases are

[50] The information on the judgments was obtained from BAILII, supplemented from other sources, including Westlaw and information from solicitors where cases were unreported. In addition, we received questionnaire responses from claimant solicitors in respect of 198 cases in our sample; from defendant solicitors in respect to 52 cases; and we conducted interviews in respect of 56 cases.

[51] Of these, one was an environmental challenge and one was brought by the Equality and Human Rights Commission; neither of these fell within the scope of the reforms.

[52] We are unaware of any official classification of cases similar to that we have adopted. Classification was primarily based on our reading of the judgments coupled with the questionnaire responses and interviews. Deciding in which category a case fell was not always straightforward and was ultimately a matter of judgement.

[53] Eight of these challenges were allowed and six were dismissed.

[54] *Osborn v Parole Board* [2013] UKSC 61, [2014] AC 1115.

likely to have ramifications beyond the individual case in addition to their potential value as precedents. 'Wider public interest' cases were brought by claimants for wider public interest reasons without seeking remedies for themselves. The ramifications of such cases would typically extend beyond individual decisions.

Of the 502 judgments we considered 374 (75 per cent) to be 'own fact' cases, 88 (18 per cent) to be 'policy or practice' cases, and 40 (8 per cent) to be 'wider public interest' cases (see Table 14.1).

Table 14.1: The scope of the issue*

	Number	%
Turns on facts	374	75
Policy and practice	88	18
Wider public interest	40	8
Total	502	101

* All percentages rounded to nearest percentage point.

It is often said that much judicial review litigation concerns disputes about the way individuals are treated. Peter Cane has referred to such cases as bureaucratic judicial reviews.[55] With this in mind it is perhaps unsurprising, but nonetheless revealing, that the vast majority of the judgments were primarily concerned with redress in relation to particular decisions affecting the claimants. It is also noteworthy, especially in the context of recent government concerns that judicial review is widely abused by pressure groups, that only a relatively small number judgments concerned explicitly public interest cases, where obtaining individual redress appeared unlikely be a principal consideration.

Table 14.2: Outcome by interest*

	Turns on facts		Policy and practice		Wider public interest		Total	
	N	%	N	%	N	%	N	%
Allowed	159	43	44	50	18	46	221	44
Dismissed	215	58	43	49	22	55	280	56
Total	374	100	88	100	40	101	502	100

* All percentages rounded to nearest percentage point.

As can be seen in Table 14.2, the highest success rate (50 per cent) was achieved by claimants who challenged the lawfulness of policy and practice, but the differences as between the three types of claim are not great. That claimants in 'policy or practice'

[55] Cane, 'Understanding Judicial Review and its Impact' (n 48).

cases fared marginally better overall than did claimants in 'own fact' cases may suggest judicial reluctance to become embroiled in particular decisions. The slightly lower claimant success rate in the 'wider public interest' category is consistent with the view that courts are likely to be more cautious when asked to intervene where wider public interests are engaged, but the small differences in the figures do not suggest that claims in this category are significantly less meritorious than those in the other categories.

(ii) Scope of the Issue and the Nature of the Claimant

Table 14.3 shows how the three categories of case were distributed across different claimant types.

Table 14.3: Claimant type by interest, column percentages[*]

	Own facts		Policy practice		Wider public interest		Total	
	N	%	N	%	N	%	N	%
Individual	312	83	64	73	12	33	388	78
Interest groups	1	0.3	0	0	13	36	14	3
Corporation/ legal person	53	14	18	21	7	19	78	16
Public authority (not local or central government)	3	1	1	1	0	0	4	1
Central government	0	0	0	0	1	3	1	0.2
Local government	5	1	5	6	3	8	13	3
Total	374	100	88	100	36	100	498[**]	100

[*] All percentages rounded to nearest percentage point, unless below 1.
[**] Note the total is 498 as four cases were building schools cases and do not fit straightforwardly into the classification. This also explains why the total for wider public interest has reduced from 40 to 36. In the final report of the study these four cases are included as local government 'wider public interest' cases, see V Bondy, L Platt and M Sunkin, *The Value and Effects of Judicial Review*, above cited, at p 25.

Table 14.3 shows that the vast majority of 'own fact' cases (83 per cent) were brought by individuals[56] and 14 per cent were brought by corporations.[57] Three of the four cases brought by public authorities, other than central or local government, were 'own fact' cases: a Commissioner of Police challenged a tribunal's consideration of

[56] 80% of the claims by individuals were in this category (312 of the 388 such cases).
[57] Typically to protect their financial or other interests, eg a college challenged a decision to suspend it from the list of licensed sponsoring organisations for migrant students. 68% of the cases brought by corporations were 'own fact' cases (53 of the 78 cases in this category).

allegations of gross-misconduct; a chief constable challenged a decision to reduce punishment for serious misconduct; and a school challenged the legality of a time limit for compliance attached to a planning enforcement notice.

Individuals also brought the vast majority (73 per cent) of the 'policy or practice' challenges.[58] In such cases claimants may be bringing proceedings as representatives of a group or jointly with a group, but it is not always easy to ascertain whether or not such a relationship exists. An example of a case in which a link can be clearly seen is *Djangoly v Westminster City Council*,[59] where the claimant was the chairman of a campaign group formed to oppose charges for motorcycle parking in the city of Westminster. By contrast, in a case such as *R (Griffin) v Newham London Borough Council*,[60] which was an application to quash the London Borough of Newham's decision to permit variation of conditions to planning permission for operations at London City Airport, there is no evident link between the claimant, a local resident and an organised interest group.

Only 12 'wider public interest' challenges were brought by individuals and only 13 were brought by interest groups. Three of the 'wider public interest' cases were claims by local authorities, and one was by central government.

(iii) What Claimants Achieved

We explored what happened following the judgments and whether claimants gained tangible benefits or whether there were intangible consequences, positive or negative, for them. Examples of tangible benefits would be having a decision made when previously a public authority had refused to decide; obtaining or retaining a service or benefit; obtaining an apology; being released from detention. Intangible consequences included a sense of disempowerment or reduced confidence in the system (examples of negative intangible consequences); a sense of empowerment; or improved confidence in the legal system (positive intangible consequences). Since we were also interested in effects beyond the claimants, we also explored wider effects, such as how the case was thought to have affected policy, procedures or human rights protection.

(iv) Intangible Consequences

While here we shall focus on tangible benefits, the importance of intangible consequences should not be underestimated, not least because they bear on whether claimants consider the system to have delivered procedural justice.[61] As Lord Reed has stressed in the context of the need for the Parole Board to adopt fair procedures,

[58] 17% of the claims by individuals were in this category.

[59] [2010] EWHC 1825 (Admin).

[60] [2011] EWHC 53 (Admin).

[61] There is a huge literature on procedural justice; the work of Tom Tyler is of particular pertinence: see, eg, TR Tyler, *Why People Obey the Law*, 2nd edn (Princeton, NJ, Princeton University Press, 2006).

fairness may be important aside from whether it affects the substantive quality of decisions:

> There is no doubt that one of the virtues of procedurally fair decision-making is that it is liable to result in better decisions … however[62] … [a]t least two other important values are also engaged. The first was described by Lord Hoffmann … as the avoidance of the sense of injustice which the person who is the subject of the decision will otherwise feel … This aspect of fairness in decision-making has practical consequences … In the present context … research reveals the frustration, anger and despair felt by prisoners who perceive the board's procedures as unfair, and the impact of those feelings upon their motivation and respect for authority[63] … The potential implications for the prospects of rehabilitation, and ultimately for public safety, are evident. The second value is the rule of law.[64]

We identified a range of intangible positive and negative consequences for claimants, both in cases where the claimants were successful and where they were unsuccessful. Amongst successful and unsuccessful claimants the most often expressed positive intangible consequences were a sense of empowerment and confidence in the legal system, and improved communication between the parties. The most commonly mentioned negative intangible consequences were a sense of disempowerment; a decline in confidence in the system; and stress and frustration. The following quotations reflect the spectrum of ways claimants perceived their experience of the judicial review process.

A claimant who was part of a group of parents who challenged the reduction in the level of care for their disabled children articulated a range of positive intangible consequences arising from her participation (and success) in the litigation:

> As a result of the case my son got back the level of care and respite that he had before the changes … I quite enjoyed going to court. I … found it very interesting. We didn't know what would happen until the judge said it. It was quite emotional. It was quite amazing that we've done it … There were four of us involved in the case … We felt we were dealing with the same problems, and we became a support group for each other.

A solicitor described his client's experience following the dismissal of his challenge to a recategorisation as follows:

> He felt that the JR, despite losing, was a positive experience and gave him a sense of empowerment. He was very down, feeling that he is never going to be released, and the case gave him the feeling of being listened to; the judge's comments, especially, gave him hope and increased confidence on the basis of that reasoning.

A claimant solicitor who acted for a group of minors seeking asylum referred to their mixed feelings:

> [The claimants experienced] empowerment as well as frustration with the process: on the one hand, they couldn't believe how they were able to challenge that the way they were treated was wrong. One of them said that he assumed that the Home Office could do

[62] Citing Lord Hoffmann in *Secretary of State for the Home Department v AF (No 3)* [2009] UKHL 28, [2010] 2 AC 269, [72].

[63] Citing N Padfield, *Understanding Recall 2011*, University of Cambridge Faculty of Law Research Paper No 2/2013 (2013), available at http://ssrn.com/abstract=2201039.

[64] *Osborn* (n 54) [67]–[71] (Lord Reed).

> whatever they wanted. They felt empowered by being able to voice their experiences and challenge and to make a difference to the way that all children were treated on arrival. But there was also frustration due to the length of the process, the ongoing changes in the position of the Secretary of State, the RMJ going into administration.

Other reactions were more negative:

> The frustration with the process was that the claimant had won but was no closer to the situation being resolved for a long time.

(v) Tangible Benefits: Winning and Losing in Court

While claimants are more likely to gain tangible benefits (the nature of benefits gained will be discussed below) when they win in court than when they lose, it cannot be assumed that successful claimants will always gain such outcomes or that unsuccessful claimants will never do so. We received completed claimant solicitor questionnaires relating to 198 cases and in 95 of these the claimant had been fully or partially successful in court (excluding any further appeals). Table 14.4 shows that in 75 of these 95 cases, claimants obtained one or more tangible benefits. In over half the cases they obtained two or three such benefits, and in 3 per cent of cases, four or five such benefits. However, there were 20 cases in which the claimant was at least partially successful in court in which there appears to have been no tangible benefit.

Table 14.4: One or more tangible benefits by judicial outcome*

	Allowed		Dismissed		Total	
	N	%	N	%	N	%
No tangible benefits	20	21	62	60	82	41
1 or more tangible benefits	75	79	41	40	116	59
Total	95	100	103	100	198	100

* All percentages rounded to nearest percentage point.

At first sight, it was striking that in such a high proportion of cases (20 out of 95) where claimants had succeeded in court no tangible benefits had been obtained. This may reflect the ability of the public bodies to reach the same substantive decisions when revisiting the matter following defeat in the courts, an issue to which we return in a moment. Also, not all cases are brought in order to achieve tangible benefits. For instance, in a successful case against the Commissioner for Police, we were told that the claimant had not sought damages but wanted and 'achieved vindication and "closure"'. There were also several cases in which solicitors had not mentioned beneficial outcomes because the benefit was considered not to have been the direct consequence of the judicial review decision. For example, in one case the court quashed a decision to return a vulnerable individual to Turkey where they might face an interrogation. The judgment halted the removal but it was a later tribunal that allowed the appeal against the removal. Finally, it is worth noting that in all but seven of these cases, the claimant was said to have experienced positive intangible consequences.

As indicated, claimants may also obtain tangible benefits despite losing in court. In 40 per cent of the cases where claimants failed in court (41 cases) we were told that claimants obtained at least one tangible benefit and in four of the cases they were said to have secured more than one such benefit. Even allowing for the possibility of bias on the part of claimant solicitors, this is a striking indication that tangible benefits may be achieved despite failure in the court. The following are examples:

— In a challenge to a consultation into a planning decision, the flaw in the consultation process was insufficient to justify impugning the process and the claim was dismissed. However, the judge noted that 'in due course the claimant's objection did cause the defendant to change its mind'.[65]
— In another case, there had been an unsuccessful challenge to a local authority's decision that the claimant was not entitled to accommodation under section 21 of the National Assistance Act 1948. However, we were told that the claimant benefited from having secured accommodation for a considerable period of time pending and during the course of proceedings. From the defendant's perspective, this could be seen as an unfair financial burden caused by failed litigation, although the local authority's solicitor considered the case to have been of benefit in that it clarified the law and reduced the potential for future challenges.
— A third example is a failed challenge by a learning-disabled adult to the manner in which the prison handled his complaint that he had been sexually assaulted. As a result of the challenge it was discovered that the prison authorities had not correctly recorded the claimant's disability. His needs were then properly reviewed and a plan to meet them proposed.

While we were primarily concerned with their consequences, it is worth recognising that judgments, and even judicial comments and observations, may benefit the parties independently of what is formally decided or what follows the decision. In one case, for example, we were told that 'although the judge did not grant a declaration ... [his judgment] ... made clear that the ... policy was unlawful'. In other cases, claimant solicitors stressed the importance of obtaining a favourable judgment in order to exonerate the claimant, or as a potential resource to assist with possible future proceedings. One solicitor explained:

> The claimant took the judicial review proceedings for the limited but very important purpose of obtaining the declaration of unlawfulness: he wanted to avoid any suggestion that he had financial or other extraneous motives for the judicial review.

Another solicitor indicated that the finding of liability for false imprisonment was a tangible benefit that would open the way for separate proceedings for damages.

(vi) What were the Tangible Benefits?

Table 14.5 summarises the principal tangible benefits that were obtained both when claims were allowed and when they were dismissed.

[65] *JL & AT Baird v Environment Agency* [2011] EWHC 939 (Admin), [20].

Table 14.5: Type of tangible benefit by outcome*

	Allowed (N = 95)		Dismissed (N = 103)	
	Number	%	Number	%
Provision/retention of service	23	24	10	10
Grant/retention of licence	7	7	3	3
Conferment/retention of status	8	8	4	4
Conferment/retention of state benefit	2	2	1	1
Compensation	20	23	1	1
Getting decision	21	22	7	7
Preventing closure of facility	1	1	1	1
Apology	2	2	3	3
Other**	33	35	24	23
No benefit	20	21	62	60

* NB percentages sum to more than 100 as multiple responses can apply (apart from 'no benefit' which is exclusive). All percentage points rounded to nearest percentage point.

** 'Other' benefits specified in completed questionnaires included: being released from detention; being released with damages to be agreed; ending of a deduction from a welfare benefit; having bail curfew reduced; members of the Law Society retaining contracts that they had lost pursuant to an unlawful tender exercise, and a new exercise put in place; a case being reopened to a social worker and assessments remitted; employment being continued. As one respondent put it: 'All the client gained in the end was a (protracted) period of around two and a half years before being evicted—however that must be a good thing in itself'.

(vii) Tangible Benefits When Public Bodies are Required to Reconsider their Decisions or Actions

A successful legal challenge often means that public bodies are required to reconsider the challenged decision. Arguably this represents judicial review at its strongest and most coercive, especially when a quashing order reflects the court's emphatic view that the illegality warrants quashing of the decision. On the other hand, the situation may also display the profound weakness of judicial review as a provider of effective redress. As we have already seen, it is widely assumed that when public bodies are required to reconsider their decision following a successful challenge they will tend to remake 'the same decision, though taking care to avoid the earlier legal error'.[66]

Research both in the United States and Australia has suggested that the value of judicial review in this context is greater than may be assumed. In the United States, Peter Schuck and Donald Elliott found that remand of decisions back to US agencies resulted in 'major changes' in the petitioner's favour in 40 per cent of cases.[67]

[66] R Creyke and J McMillan, 'The Operation of Judicial Review in Australia' in M Hertogh and S Halliday (eds), *Judicial Review and Bureaucratic Impact: International and Interdisciplinary Perspectives* (Cambridge, Cambridge University Press, 2004) 186.

[67] PH Schuck and ED Elliott, 'To the Chevron Station: An Empirical Study of Federal Administrative Law' [1990] *Duke Law Journal* 984, 1059–60.

In Australia, Robin Creyke and John McMillan found that in about 60 per cent of the cases in which the Australian Federal Court set aside an agency's decision, the applicant ultimately obtained a favourable outcome. Creyke and McMillan conclude that the belief that after being successfully challenged administrative bodies will routinely seek to re-make their original decision 'has been disproved'. They say that: 'If theories are built upon facts, then the value of judicial review in producing a favourable outcome to an applicant has been demonstrated'.[68]

The factors explaining these finding are no doubt complex and as Cane warns we should not assume that studies of judicial review in one jurisdictional context help to understand its influence in other jurisdictional contexts.[69] Our work, nonetheless, provided an opportunity to look at the issue across the spectrum of judicial review cases in England and Wales. The findings are consistent with those summarised above.

In our study there were 43 cases in which we were told that a decision of a public authority had been quashed.[70] In nine of these no fresh decision had been made by the authority by the date the questionnaire had been completed. There were therefore known outcomes in 34 of the cases.

In only four of these 34 cases were we told that the public body had made the same decision on the substance as it had originally made. Interestingly, despite the authority reaching another decision that was unfavourable, in each of these cases the claimant was said to have obtained either tangible or intangible benefits. In two of the four cases, the fresh decisions were retaken in a manner that complied with the equality duties; in a third case, concerning adoption, although the fresh decision was substantively the same as that which had been quashed, the judgment was said to have improved policy and clarified the law; and in the fourth case there was a second unfavourable asylum decision, but here too the claimant solicitor said that the judgment improved human rights protection and provided a helpful precedent,[71] and the claimant's experience of judicial review was said to have given a sense of empowerment and led to increased confidence in the system.

In the remaining 30 cases the public body made a fresh decision that differed from the original decision and favoured the claimant. The outcomes included the following: continuation of statutory care including the purchase of needed equipment; a fresh care plan with appropriate placement and increased budget; fresh assessment of needs with appropriate provisions and a dedicated social worker; retention of appropriate level of respite care; increase in budget for residential care and accommodation services for the elderly; entitlement to police injury pension; grant of

[68] Creyke and McMillan, 'The Operation of Judicial Review in Australia' (n 66) 186.

[69] Cane, 'Understanding Judicial Review and its Impact' (n 48) 31.

[70] From the 100 in which we were told that claimants achieved a successful court outcome. This included two cases that were initially dismissed but reversed on appeal and four allowed cases that were subsequently reversed on appeal. The largest single subject area of the cases was immigration/asylum (13). There were also seven community care and seven prisons cases.

[71] In that case the new decision treated the further submissions as fresh human rights claims, and included an unusual element concerning the impact of interrogation at the Turkish airport on return, and possible implications in relation to Art 3 of the European Convention on Human Rights in light of the claimant's mental state. The claim had subsequently been allowed on appeal.

humanitarian protection and social services support; release from detention pending deportation and grant of damages; a statutory plan and a personal adviser provided in an age assessment case; fresh inquest into death in custody; continuation of a Legal Services Corporation contract; retention of licence by a language school; environmental impact assessment carried out; removal of days wrongly added to prison sentence for disobeying rules; access to education in prison; and release from prison following fresh parole review.

The range of situations in the above list is clearly diverse and the factors leading to the particular outcomes are likely to have been dependent on the case. In some, the authorities will have reconsidered the matter in the light of the court's decision; in others, the fresh decision will have followed changes in the circumstances, or the existence of new information; in some, authorities may have decided to concede the matter in order to avoid future litigation or cost; and in some they may have simply accepted that their initial decision was wrong. Whatever the precise factors, it seems reasonable to argue that in these cases judicial review litigation made a significant and substantive contribution to the outcome and that the process was more than purely formal or symbolic. Certainly, the public authorities appear to have genuinely engaged with the consequences of the litigation and we found no apparent evidence that in these cases they responded in ways that were wholly negative or ritualistic. Bearing in mind that in such cases judicial review is likely to have been used as a last resort when no other mechanism of redress was available, these findings reinforce the importance of access to the High Court's inherent supervisory jurisdiction. They also show that judicial review does provide effective redress and that it cannot be assumed to be an expensive and time-consuming detour to a known and predictable outcome. The findings also indicate that it may be far from easy to establish whether 'it is highly likely that the outcome for the applicant would not have been substantially different if the conduct complained of had not occurred'.[72]

VI. CONCLUSIONS

We have drawn on empirical research to question three widely held and influential assumptions about the use and effects of judicial review in England and Wales. In so doing we have shown that it is misleading to assume that there has been a significant growth in the use of judicial review driven by claimants abusing the system; that judicial review necessarily impedes good administration; and that judicial review litigation is unlikely to provide effective redress to claimants. The Coalition Government's claim that their reforms to judicial review were rooted in sound evidence was unconvincing. This was partly because they appeared to embark on their programme of reforms without a complete understanding of the evidence that was available, and partly because they relied too heavily on a narrow body of statistical data that they insisted on interpreting in a way that was evidently misleading. The overall impression is that the Coalition Government paid lip service to the need to base its reforms

[72] Criminal Justice and Courts Act 2015, s 84.

on sound evidence and that it was willing to drive its reforms forward whatever the evidence said.

It is to be hoped that future reforms to this or any other aspect of the legal system will be based on the best evidence available. To this end, improving opportunities for dialogue between government and researchers is an important priority. Researchers must also do their utmost to ensure that their work is effectively disseminated not only to government but also to the wider stakeholder community so that the evidence can be understood and marshalled, including to challenge reform proposals, especially when these may have serious adverse effects on access to justice and the enforcement of the rule of law.

15

Common Law Public Law: Some Comparative Reflections

CHERYL SAUNDERS

I. INTRODUCTION

THE ESSAYS IN this volume are based on a selection of presentations to the Public Law Conference held at Cambridge in 2014. The theme of the conference, process and substance in public law, gave participants considerable licence to explore contemporary problems in relation to either or both of these broad dimensions of public law, including changes in emphasis between them. While the conference was attended by a few hardy public lawyers from civil law jurisdictions, its explicit focus was on public law in common law systems. For this purpose, public law was tacitly assumed to be confined to those aspects of domestic law that are otherwise described as constitutional law, administrative law and human rights law, insofar as these now can be disentangled from supra-national and international influences. In the event, as the title of the volume suggests, the essays finally selected for publication here deal, in one way or another, with aspects of public law adjudication. With only a few outliers, most are concerned with judicial review of executive action taken pursuant to statute, from a theoretical, doctrinal or comparative point of view.[1]

The contributors to this volume come from Australia, Canada, the United Kingdom and the United States, and their essays deal with aspects of public law in at least these four jurisdictions. The design of the collection is not explicitly comparative. Nevertheless, it lends itself to comparison in several ways.

Most obviously, this range of contributions provides the opportunity to draw insights from differences in law and practice between jurisdictions that have enough in common to minimise the possibility of error in the comparative conclusions that are drawn. Insights might be directed to any of the many purposes of comparative law, including its use to assist in the formulation of explanatory theories, a more accurate understanding of the legal arrangements of others, a greater degree of self-knowledge and development of possible options for change. The first two substantive sections of this chapter attempt this comparative exercise, first, by identifying

[1] The obvious exceptions are Jerry L Mashaw, Chapter 2, 'Public Reason and Administrative Legitimacy' and Kent Roach, Chapter 12, 'Remedies for Laws that Violate Human Rights'.

the shared dimensions of the public law foundations of these jurisdictions, and secondly, by examining some of the many ways in which their public law now has diverged. Here and elsewhere, the primary focus of much of the comparative analysis is the legal experience of the three states in the British public law tradition, from which the United States is more sharply differentiated and with which most of the chapters deal. This section of the present chapter also considers how divergence might be explained and the conclusions that might be drawn from it, using the tools of comparative law.

In an application of comparative law of a different kind, the essays in this volume also encourage reflection on the dynamics of the common law, or at least the public law aspects of it, as one of the great transnational legal traditions in the early twenty-first century. Neither the common substratum of the public law of common law states nor the divergence of national legal systems is particularly surprising, interesting although they may be. On the evidence of this volume, however, the common law remains more cohesive, and its family members more interdependent, than might have been supposed. This phenomenon, the reasons for it and the significance of it are explored in the last substantive section of the chapter.

By way of conclusion, a final section of the chapter points to the potential for future gatherings that bring together public law scholars from across the common law world. This exercise has been so fruitful that the editors should feel encouraged to try it again. On the next occasion, however, there is a case for being more ambitious, in terms of both jurisdictions and the range of issues covered. Ambitions of this kind bring more methodological problems in their wake, but the ground has now been laid on which to begin to resolve them.

II. SHARED FOUNDATIONS

Jurisdictions in which public law is shaped broadly by reference to the common law share an almost infinite range of features, from terminology to tools of analysis to an inductive and often discursive style of legal reasoning. Highly technical terms, of which 'mandamus' is an example, spark instant recognition. Common law public lawyers assume, without question, that there is a hierarchical relationship between legislation and judge-made law; accept that *Wednesbury* unreasonableness hovers on the border of permissible judicial intervention; and understand the historical rationale for the different properties of the prerogative and equitable remedies, despite its limited relevance in contemporary conditions. Despite some differences that have evolved in the presentation of judicial decisions, a common law case follows a sufficiently recognisable form for it to be comprehended readily enough in all common law jurisdictions. The streak of pragmatism to which Christopher Forsyth draws critical attention in this volume, with particular reference to the Supreme Court of the United Kingdom, is present in attitudes to public law in common law jurisdictions everywhere, albeit in varying degrees.[2]

[2] Christopher Forsyth, Chapter 7, '"Blasphemy Against Basics": Doctrine, Conceptual Reasoning and Certain Decisions of the UK Supreme Court'.

Some shared assumptions of the common law approach to public law go to the very nature of a common law legal system and may be clearly perceived only through comparison with others. These lie so deep that they shape the way in which problems are understood and the parameters within which they are resolved. At least three, which also are interconnected, cut across many of the essays in this volume and help to explain why trans-jurisdictional dialogue of this kind is so productive.

The first is the distinction or, to be more accurate, the relative lack of distinction, between public law and private law in common law systems. This theme is taken up directly in Jason Varuhas' analysis of the public interest aims of public law but is an unexpressed subtext in other chapters as well.[3] The tensions in the role of public law and the values to which it gives effect, to which Varuhas points, is endemic in common law systems, not only in the twenty-first century, but over time. There have always been distinctive public elements of common law public law: in the origins and use of the prerogative writs; in the limited availability of damages; in the potential for a finding of non-justiciability; in the standards effectively imposed on public as opposed to private actors. In recent decades, the distinctiveness of public law has been further enhanced through, for example, innovations in the procedure for seeking judicial review, relaxation of the rules of standing and greater explicit emphasis on the public interest, at least in some jurisdictions, in the way that Varuhas describes. But the boundaries between public and private law in common law systems have always been and remain porous. There is no fixed understanding of the bodies against which actions lie in public law. There is no definitive view of the extent to which public law standards are applicable to governments when exercising power that might otherwise be described as private. Adjudication typically takes place in generalist courts, capable of applying principles of both public and private law to resolve the case at hand.

Reliance on generalist courts to resolve legal disputes involving government is another shared characteristic of common law systems, with a range of consequences that are reflected in the essays in this volume. Courts applying legal rules against institutions able to claim democratic legitimacy have the most sensitive of tasks. Their task is rendered more challenging still by the attitudes and practices associated with parliamentary sovereignty (whether it is a legal reality or not), which do not necessarily respect the values protected by courts in the name of the rule of law. The tension thus created between the executive and the judiciary, with the Parliament sometimes an unwitting bystander, are explored explicitly in this volume in relation to the United Kingdom in the essays by Maurice Sunkin and Varda Bondy[4] and by Carol Harlow and Richard Rawlings.[5] As the essays by, for example, Paul Daly,[6]

[3] Jason NE Varuhas, Chapter 4, 'The Public Interest Conception of Public Law: Its Procedural Origins and Substantive Implications'.

[4] Maurice Sunkin and Varda Bondy, Chapter 14, 'The Use and Effects of Judicial Review: Assumptions and the Empirical Evidence'.

[5] Carol Harlow and Richard Rawlings, Chapter 13, '"Striking Back" and "Clamping Down": An Alternative Perspective on Judicial Review'.

[6] Paul Daly, Chapter 3, 'Administrative Law: A Values-based Approach'.

Alan Robertson[7] and Mark Aronson[8] suggest, however, relations between the executive branch and the judiciary are often uneasy in Canada and Australia as well. The dynamics of this relationship account for judicial self-restraint in all jurisdictions, whether or not described explicitly in terms of deference. It underpins the tug-of-war over privative clauses, which is a recurring feature of common law public law. It also feeds into the compromises over remedies for rights violations, analysed so effectively in the essay by Kent Roach.[9]

The necessarily limited role of powerful courts in resolving disputes in the field of public law in common law democracies plays out through what may be regarded as a third group of shared characteristics, in which judicial authority is claimed over process rather than substance and questions of law rather than merits, including facts. An earlier version of this dichotomy prioritised remedies over grounds in a manner that, as Philip Murray's chapter argues, has some continuing relevance still.[10] The evidence of this collection is that, at particular times, courts in different common law jurisdictions vary in their willingness to engage explicitly with substance or merits or both. Exactly where the acceptable limits lie is a constant preoccupation, however. Whatever their domestic solutions, it is an issue with which all common lawyers in the public law tradition can engage and in relation to which jurisdictions continue to influence each other in a process of systemic evolution that is by no means linear.

Shared foundations of this kind ease, without eliminating, the challenges of comparative public law. They make simple misunderstanding of terms, concepts and institutional dynamics less likely. They ensure some familiarity with the legal context in which public law applies. They should minimise the potential for error commonly associated with the functional approach, of misunderstanding the purposes that a particular phenomenon is intended to serve.[11] They by no means preclude comparative error altogether, however. There is an obvious danger that superficial similarity may cause underlying difference to be overlooked. In this as in other comparative contexts, it is easy to fall into the subjective trap of assuming the similarity of all systems, on the basis of familiarity with one. As diversity increases, identical terms may assume different meanings, as the varying usages of the principle of legality now show.[12]

Comparison between the United Kingdom, Canada and Australia is further assisted by other contextual similarities: shared legal foundations in pre-settlement common law; parliamentary systems broadly along Westminster lines; and comparable levels of economic development. The independence of Canada and Australia,

[7] Alan Robertson, Chapter 11, 'Is Judicial Review Qualitative'.

[8] Mark Aronson, Chapter 6, 'The Growth of Substantive Review: The Changes, their Causes and their Consequences'.

[9] Kent Roach, Chapter 12, 'Remedies for Laws that Violate Human Rights'.

[10] Philip Murray, Chapter 5, 'Process, Substance and the History of Error of Law Review'.

[11] R Michaels, 'The Functional Method of Comparative Law' in M Reimann and R Zimmermann (eds), *The Oxford Handbook of Comparative Law* (Oxford, Oxford University Press, 2006) 339.

[12] Compare, eg, usage in South Africa, as explained in *Fedshure Life Assurance Ltd v Greater Johannesburg Metropolitan Council* 1999 (1) SA 374 (CC) [58] and in the United Kingdom, as in *HM Treasury v Ahmed* [2010] UKSC 2.

which created the conditions for the divergence of national legal systems, is still relatively recent, leaving a great deal in common, including habits of cross-references to each other's law. The degree of comparative difficulty is increased once the United States is added to the mix. The United States lies within the common law tradition and shares, at a general level, at least some of the characteristics claimed as foundational here. Jerry Mashaw's plea in this volume for a richer understanding of public reason strikes a common chord because it resonates with a commitment to public reasoning that all jurisdictions share, with similar, concomitant, disappointments of the kind to which Mashaw refers.[13] But the period of time since the legal system of the United States began its own, long, national evolutionary process, the diversity of law and practice within the United States and the distinctiveness of the constitutional and institutional setting for public law in the United States can complicate doctrinal comparison of a more detailed kind. To take one, somewhat obvious example: reliance on the *Chevron* decision of the Supreme Court of the United States[14] to support judicial deference in statutory interpretation elsewhere in the common law world must surely consider the differences in institutional dynamics between legislature, executive and administration generated by a presidential system, in significant contrast to the comparable relationships in conditions of parliamentary government.

III. DIVERGENCE

While similarity eases the task of comparison, difference makes it intriguing and potentially productive. Even amongst the relatively small catchment of common law jurisdictions that are analysed in some detail in this collection, myriad points of divergence have emerged over time. This is an unsurprising consequence of different national and sub-national institutions responding to the needs and preferences of polities operating in different national contexts, generally and as particular issues arise. Context for this purpose includes the constitutional, institutional and political settings with which public law is interdependent, but also extends to a wide range of other phenomena capable of having a bearing on the form and operation of public law, including legal and political culture.

This section seeks to bring some order to the differences between national systems of public law revealed by this collection by considering them in three categories: doctrinal, institutional and conceptual. The categories are by no means watertight, however. Rather, doctrine, institutional arrangements and supporting intellectual constructs exist in a symbiotic relationship in which each influences the other, constituting a critical dimension of context. This phenomenon tends to become increasingly pronounced as systems mature.

Doctrinal difference suggests divergence of the common law itself, albeit with the stimulus of context, and has particular interest for present purposes. Specific issues on which the common law of these jurisdictions has, to some extent, parted ways

[13] Jerry L Mashaw, Chapter 2, 'Public Reason and Administrative Legitimacy'.
[14] *Chevron USA v Natural Resources Defence Council*, 467 US 837 (1984).

range from the principles that govern standing;[15] to the recognition of a common law right to reasons;[16] to standards for the review of delegated legislation.[17] Four more general points of divergence recur throughout the collection, however, and merit closer attention. They are the use of jurisdictional error as an analytical tool; the relevance of legitimate expectations in determining breach of procedural fairness; the scope of review on the ground of reasonableness; and acceptance of deference as an appropriate consideration in resolving questions in the course of judicial review.

Australia is something of an outlier in comparison to Canada and the United Kingdom although these jurisdictions also differ from each other, in significant ways. Jurisdictional error now is a critical step in determining the validity of challenged action in Australia.[18] By contrast, it has long since been abandoned in the United Kingdom[19] and has been tightly confined in Canada, where it is equated with correctness review.[20] Jurisdictional error in Australia has followed a trajectory apparently similar to that followed earlier in the United Kingdom, in the sense that it is no longer confined to flaws at the threshold of a decision-making process, has expanded over time to encompass the more specific grounds of review, and remains ambivalent about the extent to which errors go to jurisdiction when made by inferior courts.[21] Nevertheless, the High Court of Australia has been undeterred by the concerns expressed elsewhere that the borderline between jurisdictional and non-jurisdictional error is too difficult to determine objectively, retaining it as an important symbol of the limits of judicial authority.

Similarly, unlike Canada and the United Kingdom, Australian jurisprudence has effectively abandoned legitimate expectations as a consideration in determining an entitlement to procedural fairness and has repudiated any notion of substantive legitimate expectations along the lines accepted by the Court of Appeal in *Coughlan*.[22] Until relatively recently, also, Australia adhered literally to the *Wednesbury* standard of unreasonableness as it softened in Canada and the United Kingdom, raising questions about proportionality as an alternative ground of review.[23] There is change

[15] Compare *Walton v Scottish Ministers* [2012] UKSC 44, [82]–[96]; *Kuczborski v Queensland* [2014] HCA 46; *Canada (Attorney-General) v Downtown Eastside Sex Workers Against Violence Society* 2012 SCC 45.

[16] Compare the discussion in this volume by Paul Daly, Chapter 3, 'Administrative Law: A Values-based Approach' and by Mark Aronson, Chapter 6, 'The Growth of Substantive Review: The Changes, their Causes and their Consequences', on the still more restrictive Australian position.

[17] See the claim by Andrew Edgar, Chapter 9, 'Judicial Review of Delegated Legislation: Why Favour Substantive Review over Procedural Review?', citing cases from Australia, the United Kingdom, Canada and New Zealand: 'The major difference ... is that substantive review has been extended in Australian law to proportionality review for delegated legislation without the support of human rights law'.

[18] *Plaintiff S157/2002 v Commonwealth* (2003) 211 CLR 476; *Kirk v Industrial Relations Commission* (2010) HCA 1.

[19] *R v Lord President of the Privy Council, ex parte Page* [1993] AC 682; although see Philip Murray, Chapter 5, 'Process, Substance and the History of Error of Law Review'.

[20] *Alberta (Information and Privacy Commissioner) v Alberta Teachers' Association* [2011] SCC 61, [33]–[34].

[21] *Kirk v Industrial Relations Commission* (n 18); *R (Cart) v Upper Tribunal* [2011] UKSC 28.

[22] *Re Minister for Immigration and Multicultural Affairs; Ex parte Lam* (2003) 214 CLR 1; *CUPE v Ontario (Minister of Labour)* [2003] I SCR 539; *R v North and East Devon Health Authority, ex parte Coughlan* [2001] QB 213.

[23] *Dunsmuir v New Brunswick* [2008] 1 SCR 190; *Pham v Secretary of State for the Home Department* [2015] UKSC 19.

here too: Australian decisions over the last few years have opened the door wider to claims of unreasonableness of various kinds, moving Australia closer to the position of other jurisdictions to this extent while they continue to move, at varying speeds, in the direction of proportionality.[24] And while the new Australian jurisprudence on unreasonableness is still inchoate, it is already possible to tell that its contours are likely to be distinctive.[25] Finally, in contrast to Canada, the Australian High Court has eschewed a general doctrine of explicit deference to the administration in the course of judicial review, in company for the moment with the UK Supreme Court.[26]

Bare doctrinal differences are misleading if taken in isolation. Typically, the public law of a particular jurisdiction is a coherent whole, the elements of which complement each other. Thus, in the examples just given, explicit deference offers a counterpart to relatively broad grounds of review, as in Canada, but is less relevant in jurisdictions, such as Australia, where the bases for judicial intervention arguably are more narrow, restraining the judiciary in another way. Doctrinal difference also should be understood in the light of its institutional setting, which may provide a moving cause or a source of justification.

Institutional arrangements in any event are another point on which common law systems of public law have diverged. They may be set by the terms of a Constitution, as interpreted over time, or by various forms of legislation, including orders of a court. In this collection, both are shown to be significant. The constitutional framework necessarily is a starting point. The absence of a formal, entrenched Constitution in the United Kingdom leaves judicial review more exposed, accounting, in part, for the intellectual gymnastics associated with privative clauses, which began the long decline of jurisdictional error.[27] By contrast, in Canada and Australia, an entrenched Constitution, as interpreted by the courts, provides the ultimate backstop for judicial review, although on the basis of different reasoning and sparking different doctrinal dynamics. In Australia, entrenchment of the jurisdiction to issue named remedies against an 'officer of the Commonwealth' in section 75(v) not only protects judicial review in the Commonwealth sphere but is understood to reinforce jurisdictional error.[28] In Canada, the rule of law precludes a privative clause being given effect according to its terms but instead is an indicator of reasonableness as the appropriate standard of review.[29] Constitutional substance has implications for judicial review as well. The systemic protection of rights in both Canada and the United Kingdom affects the perception of the purpose of judicial review and the tools that might be available to achieve it, accounting for the flirtation with the

[24] *Minister for Immigration and Citizenship v SZMDS* (2010) 240 CLR 611; *Minister for Immigration v Li* [2013] HCA 18.

[25] See Alan Robertson, Chapter 11, 'Is Judicial Review Qualitative?'; Mark Aronson, Chapter 6, 'The Growth of Substantive Review: The Changes, their Causes and their Consequences'; Matthew Groves and Greg Weeks, Chapter 8, 'The Legitimacy of Expectations About Fairness: Can Process and Substance be Untangled?'.

[26] *City of Enfield v Development Assessment Commission* (2000) 199 CLR 135; *Dunsmuir v New Brunswick* [2008] 1 SCR 190; *R v British Broadcasting Corporation, ex parte Pro-Life Alliance* [2003] UKHL 23.

[27] *Anisminic v Foreign Compensation Commission* [1969] 2 AC 147.

[28] *Plaintiff S157/2002 v Commonwealth* (n 18); *Kirk v Industrial Relations Commission* (n 18).

[29] *Dunsmuir v New Brunswick* (n 26) [52].

principle of proportionality, which in the United Kingdom receives further impetus from the approach of European institutions. In Australia, on the other hand, the virtual absence of systemic rights protection has augmented the significance of the constitutional organisation of power, including the separation of judicial power. It also provides at least a partial explanation for the technical style of judicial reasoning and for the functionalist focus to which Groves and Weeks refer.[30]

Legislation is an obvious means by which doctrine and practice diverge in common law jurisdictions. Even function-specific legislation can cause doctrinal change that is system-wide. To take one example: the irrationality ground of review emerged in Australia after amendments to the Migration Act restricted reliance on the ground of unreasonableness in proceedings before the Federal Court, setting a precedent for confining unreasonableness to the exercise of discretion alone.[31] More generally, however, legislative initiatives contributing to divergence between common law jurisdictions might be divided between those designed to restructure judicial review itself and those dealing with the organisation of tribunals. The former include the Civil Procedure Rules (UK) Part 54, the Federal Courts Act (RSC 1985 c.F-7) in Canada and the Administrative Decisions (Judicial Review) Act 1977 of the Commonwealth of Australia. These measures variously offer formulations that affect access to judicial review, the grounds of judicial review, the remedies that are available and the procedures that must be followed. Even where the changes made appear relatively marginal, some effect on the common law is inevitable.

The organisation of tribunals also has proceeded down quite different lines. In Australia, the consolidation of tribunals at the Commonwealth level in a single Administrative Appeals Tribunal that structurally is outside the judiciary and that exercises 'merits' review is largely responsible for the distinction between 'law' and 'merits' that plays such a role in Australian doctrine.[32] By contrast, in the United Kingdom, the incorporation of tribunals within the judicial branch throws up a different set of questions for the scope of review of tribunal decisions of the kind that presented the doctrinal dilemma in *Cart*.[33] In yet another variation, in Canada, the reliance on large numbers of specialised tribunals across the regulatory state has fuelled a rationale for the doctrine of deference that has lesser force elsewhere.[34]

Relatively tangible variations of this kind stimulate and are stimulated by the legal conceptual approaches that provide the intellectual underpinning for public law and that, also, may differ between states, despite the free flow of ideas in conditions of globalisation. This more subtle form of variation may be the product of legal or political culture. Equally, however, in addition or instead, it may be attributable to coincidence, of timing or personnel. The phenomenon is reflected in many

[30] See Matthew Groves and Greg Weeks, Chapter 8, 'The Legitimacy of Expectations About Fairness: Can Process and Substance be Untangled?'.

[31] *Re Minister for Immigration and Multicultural Affairs; Ex parte Applicant S20/2002* (2003) 198 ALR 59.

[32] Administrative Appeals Tribunal Act 1975 (Cth).

[33] *Cart* (n 21).

[34] B McLachlin, 'Administrative Tribunals and the Courts: An Evolutionary Relationship', Lecture at Sixth Annual Conference of the Council of Canadian Administrative Tribunals, Toronto, Ontario, 27 May 2013, available at www.scc-csc.gc.ca/court-cour/judges-juges/spe-dis/bm-2013-05-27-eng.aspx.

of the chapters in this collection, of which the following are examples. The public interest focus of judicial review in the United Kingdom, which Varuhas ascribes to the response of particular far-sighted jurists to the opportunities presented by procedural reforms from the late 1970s, has no clear equivalent in Australia, although public interest considerations can be discerned in some aspects of Australian public law. Conversely, the developed understanding of the separation of powers in Australia, which informs so much of Australian public law, is a product of the reliance of the Australian Constitution on the organisation of public power and has no immediate counterpart in other common law jurisdictions. In yet a third example, Daly's analysis in this volume of the values of the rule of law, good administration, democracy and separation of powers that, in his view, underlie public law resonates with the approach of the Canadian Supreme Court to constitutional understanding by reference to 'underlying principles'[35] and to that extent is distinctively Canadian. This observation may, in fact, be pressed further, noting not merely the role played by values in Daly's analysis but also his explanation of the values themselves, none of which are understood in precisely the same way in pragmatic, functionalist Australia.

This survey of some of the points of divergence between these common law systems of public law provides a platform on which the purposes of comparison can be revisited. Most obviously, it assists to understand not only the doctrine and practice of public law elsewhere but also the reasons why they take a particular form. The examples in this collection are legion: the significance of a privative clause in Canada; the meaning of a legitimate expectation in the United Kingdom; the scope of the ground of unreasonableness in Australia. Equally significantly, however, comparison promotes the self-understanding that comes from knowledge of other, workable approaches in broadly similar contexts, prompting reflection on the reasons for one's own. From the standpoint of an Australian, for example, a collection of this kind inevitably provokes some introspection about reliance on jurisdictional error or the absence of a doctrine of deference without, at least necessarily, prompting a desire for change. Finally, but by no means least, comparison offers a tool for the development of public law, drawing on the experience of others in a manner that minimises the risk of surprises. This is a familiar dynamic in common law public law, which casts some light on its character as a transnational tradition of public law, to which I turn in the next section.

IV. UNITY IN DIVERSITY

In the early decades of the twenty-first century, the common law has necessarily shed some of the coherence that characterised it in the immediate aftermath of empire. What is striking, however, is the extent to which coherence has been retained, reinforcing the character of the common law as a distinctive legal tradition,[36] albeit

[35] For example, in *Reference re Secession of Quebec* [1998] 2 SCR 217.

[36] In the sense in which the term is used by H Patrick Glenn, *Legal Traditions of the World*, 3rd edn (Oxford, Oxford University Press, 2007) ch 1.

now of a transnational kind. This observation does not depend only on the shared foundations discussed earlier, significant though these may be. It draws also on some features of the dynamics of the common law, or at least that part of it that can be described as public law, as it operates over time in its various national settings. Three themes that run throughout this collection illustrate the point: the trajectories of legal and political developments in relation to public law; the cross-fertilisation of legal experience between common law jurisdictions; and what I will describe as the equilibrium of common law doctrine, in which, despite often apparently dramatic developments, a broadly similar state is often maintained.

The chapters in this volume touch on similar stories of political action and judicial reaction in all jurisdictions, which repeat themselves over the latter part of the twentieth century and into the twenty-first. Thus, the expansion of the administrative state in the aftermath of two World Wars was met everywhere by developments in judicial review that responded to the new challenges for the rule of law. These included elaboration of the grounds of review, a broadening of the availability of remedies and an early articulation of the significance of reasons. Within a few decades, in all jurisdictions, initiatives of a legislative kind responded further to the changing context for public law by simplifying or at least clarifying the procedure for making an application for review and removing unnecessary legal technicalities. The greater accessibility of judicial review inevitably increased its incidence, heightening the potential for tension between the courts and the other branches of government. In all jurisdictions this tension has played out from time to time in the legislative imposition of privative clauses, which in turn have encountered judicial resistance in one form or another. In each jurisdiction, equally, a network of administrative tribunals developed over time, often as an alternative to judicial review. In each, also, judicial review adapted by according the new bodies a measure of the respect due to statutory institutions, while contributing to their judicialisation and retaining ultimate authority to review their procedures and decisions, at least by reference to law. Most recently, in all jurisdictions, relations between courts and the executive in Parliament have been exacerbated further still by policy initiatives in relation to immigration and anti-terrorism, setting in train new attempts to restrain review and new techniques by courts to ensure that, as far as possible, the executive remains subject to law.[37]

The broad similarities between common law jurisdictions in these patterns of executive and judicial action at broadly similar points in time reflect the creative tension between the branches of government in the common law tradition as the elected branches respond to local and global pressures and judges seek to maintain the rule of law. The tension has been heightened in recent years as the pressures increase and politics become more challenging, weakening political commitment to the rule of law. Attacks on the very institution of judicial review have become more familiar, through claims of overuse and detrimental consequences. In this volume, the empirical study by Sunkin and Bondy largely refutes these claims in their application to

[37] The detail of this latest round of interaction in the United Kingdom is the subject of Carol Harlow and Richard Rawlings, Chapter 13, '"Striking Back" and "Clamping Down": An Alternative Perspective on Judicial Review' but a broadly similar story could be told elsewhere.

the United Kingdom. The similarities in institutional behaviour across common law jurisdictions suggest that comparable findings would be likely to be made elsewhere as well.

These same similarities further underpin the utility of cross-fertilisation between common law jurisdictions in the field of public law. One of the characteristic features of most common law courts is their willingness to draw on the legal experience of other jurisdictions and, in particular, of those with which they are most familiar, elsewhere in the common law world.[38] The prevalence of the practice might be explained in a variety of ways, ranging from the perpetuation of old habits formed under the umbrella of the Privy Council to the open nature of the common law tradition and the processes of reasoning that it employs.[39] It is sustained by a dense network of contacts between common law judges and jurists of which the Commonwealth Law Association, with its biennial conference is only one of the most formal. It is fuelled by the ready and immediate availability of decisions of most jurisdictions through information technology and social media.

An anecdotal impression of recent public law cases in all jurisdictions suggests that explicit reference to foreign law may have diminished to a degree. If this is correct, it may be due to two quite different forces that are inducing greater caution. One is a growing consciousness of the reality of the doctrinal divergence of national systems of common law, demanding some sophistication in comparative method if substantial reliance is placed on legal experience elsewhere. The other is the greater prominence given both to the practice and to potential nationalist objections to it by the furore over references to foreign and international law by Justices of the US Supreme Court in a string of cases at the turn of the present century.[40] Whether explicit or not, however, the reality of cross-fertilisation cannot be doubted in the face of the coincidence of broad lines of doctrinal development, whatever their deviation in matters of detail. Examples canvassed in the chapters in this volume include the use of the nullity of a decision as a shield against privative clauses; the ongoing exploration of the interface between reasonableness and proportionality; the extension of judicial review to non-statutory decisions; the ubiquity of the requirement to provide procedural fairness; and the spread of the principle of legality. Not all of these developments need be explained as the consequence of direct interaction between the judges of different jurisdictions. Ideas of these kinds are disseminated also through the writings of public law scholars, who have dense and developed transnational networks of their own.

The phenomenon of equilibrium is more subtle and impressionistic. On the evidence of this collection, it has at least two dimensions. One is that, despite doctrinal divergence, each jurisdiction, in its own way, maintains a balance between the authority of the elected branches and that of the courts that respects the democratic

[38] C Saunders, 'Judicial Engagement' in R Dixon and T Ginsburg (eds), *Comparative Constitutional Law in Asia* (Cheltenham, Edward Elgar, 2014) 80

[39] H Patrick Glenn, 'Professional Traditions: The Reciprocating Ethics of Jurist and Judge' in J Erauw, V Tomljenovic and P Volken, *Liber Memorialis Petar Sarcevic* (Munich, Sellier, 2006) 641–42.

[40] The cases included *Atkins v Virginia*, 536 US 304 (2002), *Lawrence v Texas*, 539 US 558 (2003) and *Roper v Simmons*, 543 US 551 (2005).

credentials of the former while preserving the capacity of the latter to carry out sensitive tasks that lie in their domain. The tipping point is not fixed but varies between jurisdictions and over time. Maintenance of the balance broadly within acceptable limits is secured through self-correcting mechanisms embedded within the dynamics of the system itself. A second dimension of the equilibrium that typifies the common law legal tradition is that no doctrine is ever definitively settled and no useful doctrinal tool is ever finally abandoned. Rather, consistently with the common law method and assisted by the possibilities of cross-fertilisation, doctrines are adapted, reinterpreted and refashioned as circumstances change and needs arise. The recent history of jurisdictional error provides some insight into how this works. It enjoyed desultory use in Australia for much of the twentieth century as an indicator of the circumstances in which prerogative remedies would lie against tribunals and inferior courts.[41] It was revived in the 1980s[42] and gradually adapted to meet the purpose it presently serves, as an increasingly generous marker of the borders of constitutionally protected judicial review.[43] It has long since been abandoned in the United Kingdom. It might nevertheless have been useful in *Cart*, for something akin to its original purpose.[44] And while, ultimately, *Cart* was decided on another ground, the analyses in this volume by both Murray and Forsyth suggest that the cause may not yet be entirely dead.

V. CONCLUSIONS

The essays collected in this book make a valuable contribution to comparative public law. They analyse and theorise some of the latest and most significant issues for public law in a range of common law states. In doing so, they identify and explain similarities and differences in public law doctrine and practice. They throw some light on the nature of the common law itself, as a transnational legal tradition that retains a surprising degree of unity despite the pressures for diversification. They offer an understanding of the context in which the public law of each jurisdiction has developed on which other comparative projects also may draw. Both the essays and the public law conference that preceded them are welcome and structured additions to the myriad ways in which ideas about public law are disseminated within and between common law states.

The range of jurisdictions on which these essays focus is relatively small. Australia, Canada, the United Kingdom and the United States have rich and dynamic systems of public law but they are only four of around 60 states that, for this purpose, comprise the common law world.[45] In a sense, however, this more restricted

[41] In, eg, *Parisienne Basket Shoes Pty Ltd v Whyte* (1938) 59 CLR 369.

[42] *R v Coldham, ex parte Australian Workers' Union* (1983) 153 CLR 415 is an early usage, although still in relation to tribunal review.

[43] The usage is exemplified in, but was well underway by, *Plaintiff S157/2002 v Commonwealth* (n 18).

[44] *Cart* (n 21).

[45] 'World Map: Legal Systems of the World', Notarius International 1-2/2009, available at www.notarius-international.uinl.org/DataBase/2009/Notarius_2009_01_02_worldmaps.pdf.

focus is a strength of this initial collection. Albeit at the expense of breadth, it has encouraged depth, not only in knowledge of public law developments but also in understanding of the reasons for them. This is the level at which the real interest in public law lies, without which comparative public law offers no reliable insights at all. The approach taken here sets an important precedent for the conceptualisation of future public law conferences.

In the future, there are at least three ways in which the ambit of inquiry might usefully be extended.

First, and most obviously, a future conference might expand the range of common law jurisdictions that are covered at some depth. Contributions from, for example, South Africa, New Zealand, India and Singapore would introduce a more complex set of variables into the endeavour to understand the current state of common law public law: more diverse constitutional settings; other mixed legal systems; new social, economic, political and cultural conditions. Significantly greater variation in the contexts in which public law develops and is given effect would present a significantly greater challenge, but with corresponding benefits for the insights that might be obtained.

Secondly, a future conference might tackle a different range of problems in common law public law. The focus of the present collection is on the areas that comprise much of the public law judicial caseload: executive action taken pursuant to statute and public action that affects human rights. There are many other, difficult, public law problems, however, which are conceptually significant although numerically less prominent and which would benefit from comparative analysis in this way. These include, for example, review of decisions in the exercise of inherent executive power, including pursuant to contract; the more general interface of public law with private law; the complications of judicial review of extra-territorial action; judicial review of actions by non-state actors; the implications of soft law for the principles and practices of public law.

Finally, a future gathering of common law public lawyers might be designed to examine claims about the globalisation of public law. Even if this avoids the quite distinct question of the application of public law principles and practices to global institutions, it could have several dimensions. It might examine claims of the horizontal convergence of public law, encouraging consideration of the similarities and differences between public law in common law and civil law jurisdictions, and of whether the pattern is changing in conditions of globalisation. Alternatively or in addition, it might explore the relationship between public international law and common law public law, including the causes and extent of growing interdependence. The avoidance of both in the present collection facilitated concentration on the modalities of common law public law in a way that was useful for deep engagement with the present range of topics. But common law public law is susceptible also to external influences of various kinds, the nature and extent of which also varies between jurisdictions. This aspect of the discipline is another that could usefully be examined through the lens of comparative public law.

16

Comparison, Realism and Theory in Public Law

DAVID FELDMAN*

I. THE JOB OF PUBLIC LAW

THE CONFERENCE FROM which the chapters in this volume are drawn revealed what a very broad church we public lawyers are. This reflects the protean character of the term 'public law'. It engages with at least five problematic, contested issues, solutions to which vary widely between places and times: (1) the notions of government and the state; (2) the place of the state and public law in the world at large; (3) relationships between institutions and officials within the state; (4) the legitimacy of institutions; (5) the identity and worth of public law in relation to politics. These are not solely the concern of public lawyers.[1] Political theorists, political scientists, psychologists and sociologists make their own distinctive contributions, and we can all learn from each other. Public lawyers' distinctive contributions seem to me to presuppose the existence of state institutions with the distinctive function of exercising power—economic as well as physical and moral—over people for what is conceived to be the good of the public, conceived as a collective body which is more than the sum of goods of its individual members. Public lawyers are not utopian. We recognise that good intentions can produce bad effects. Our role is to find ways of ensuring, so far as possible, that institutions' capacity for good is maximised while limiting their capacity to do serious harm, whether intentionally or inadvertently. We do this by requiring institutions to justify their actions by reference to legal norms which are, we hope, sufficiently determinate to allow institutions to organise their activities to comply with them. To this end we look for ways of distinguishing systematically between the public and private realms of social life and between legal and non-legal means of regulating the public realm.[2]

* I am very grateful to Mark Elliott and Jason Varuhas for thought-provoking comments and suggestions on an earlier draft of this chapter, which helped me to clarify my ideas and improve the arguments. Remaining errors and eccentricities are my own.

[1] M Elliott and D Feldman, 'Introduction' in M Elliott and D Feldman (eds), *The Cambridge Companion to Public Law* (Cambridge, Cambridge University Press, 2015).

[2] D Feldman, 'The Distinctiveness of Public Law' in M Elliott and D Feldman (eds), *The Cambridge Companion to Public Law* (Cambridge, Cambridge University Press, 2015).

In terms of scholarly and practical focus, the class of public lawyers includes people who are interested mainly in the public sphere within which public law operates, concentrating on 'public' and not being too worried about 'law' as a distinct mode of regulating the public sphere (although these people were not strongly represented at the conference). At the other end of this axis are people who are lawyers, and concern themselves less with the operation of the public sphere as a whole than with finding sensible answers to specifically legal problems arising in that sphere.

On another spectrum, parallel to the first, we range from philosophers looking at law, and particularly public law, out of concern for the nature and legitimacy of systems for managing public power, to trial lawyers whose main concern is to persuade tribunals and advise clients, and whose need for philosophy depends on its utility in providing weapons and a degree of predictability.

Less well represented at the conference, but extremely important to the health of systems of public law, were practising lawyers in the public sector whose work helps to make states function effectively while respecting the rule of law. These professionals are legal engineers working at the interface between politics and law. Their work allows government to operate in accordance with legal and constitutional rules and principles. Their presence helps to imbue public institutions with that respect for lawfulness which confers legitimacy and makes democracy possible. These legal engineers work in ways which outsiders rarely see, and even more rarely appreciate; but they are vital if the rule of law, which Professor Jeffrey Jowell illuminatingly describes as an 'institutional morality',[3] is to survive in the public sphere. Their task is to persuade bureaucrats (who have a natural predisposition towards order, consistency, and principled pragmatism) and politicians to pursue their goals through, rather than outside, a framework of law.[4] They are the unsung (and sometimes conflicted) heroes and heroines of the story of the rule of law.

The papers at the conference and the chapters in this volume have prompted three general reflections about the directions in which public law scholarship seems to be moving in the common law world. The first relates to a concern about a tendency to flee from legal analysis towards inchoate political values. The second is a tendency to shift attention away from the important question of what state institutions should be allowed to do and towards the less important, second-order question of who should decide what institutions should be allowed to do. The third is a general concern about the use to which public lawyers are putting theory.

II. VALUES

There is a clear trend among public lawyers towards restricting the evils which state institutions can bring about, tolerating for that purpose a narrowing of the good which

[3] J Jowell, 'The Rule of Law' in J Jowell, D Oliver and C O'Cinneide (eds), *The Changing Constitution*, 8th edn (Oxford, Oxford University Press, 2015) 27.

[4] See the papers in Part III of D Feldman (ed), *Law in Politics, Politics in Law* (Oxford, Hart Publishing, 2013): S Laws, 'Legislation and Politics', especially at 93–98; D Seymour, 'Whitehall, Transparency, and the Law'; M Wood, 'The Role of International Lawyers in Government'; M Windsor, 'Government Legal Advisers through the Ethics Looking Glass'.

they can achieve. This is reflected in the rise and rise of 'liberal constitutionalism' to the point where it has come to be regarded as the dominant theoretical framework from which to view public law. To scholars in the United States, as Jerry Mashaw observes at the opening of his chapter in this volume, the idea that constitutional structures are designed to limit governmental action in order to preserve the greatest possible space for individual freedom can appear to be 'the only game in town'. In the United States, liberalism dominates economic and political discourse, so its position in the forefront of constitutional scholarship is not surprising. The challenges from the critical legal studies movement and civic republicanism, which seemed to be gaining ground in the 1970s and 1980s, appear to have receded somewhat.

Problems arise, however, when one tries to use liberal constitutionalism as a global metwand for constitutional and political systems. In Europe, Africa and Asia, society and the state tend to be viewed from a more collectivist, if not communitarian, perspective. Attempts to impose ideal-form liberal-constitutionalist arrangements in eastern European states after the break-up of the Soviet bloc in the late 1980s and 1990s have not produced reliably long-lasting constitutions, as developments in Hungary, Russia and elsewhere illustrate. Where social mores are not predominantly liberal and democratic, and even more where there is no tradition of state institutions operating throughout the territory claimed by a state's government, liberal constitutionalism suffers a lack of fit with social expectations and arrangements, weakening the pulling-power of a constitution, as experience in Iraq, Afghanistan, Bosnia and Herzegovina, Libya, Somalia, East Timor and elsewhere demonstrates. Even in countries which one might expect to have well established social and economic traditions of liberalism, such as the United Kingdom, legal and political traditions may make it impossible to fit the constitution within a paradigm of liberal constitutionalism.[5] Nevertheless, even in the United Kingdom the effort to limit the evils a state may do has led to the development of fascinating conceptual tools; an expansive and, it seems, ever-expanding notion of error of law encompassing (in certain jurisdictions) errors of fact, defective procedures, and failing to give effect to fundamental (or constitutional, or human) rights, is among the most prominent. In the course of this, some of us have gone beyond rules, beyond rights, beyond even principles, and either claimed that officials give effect to 'values' or exhort them to do so.

This tendency worries me. What are values? For Paul Daly, they encompass principles and policies, which are metaphysical but relatively comprehensible. But some would have lawyers give effect to values of a less defined type. Francesca Klug, for example, is a long-standing advocate of using human rights not as a category of legally defined concepts but as emanations of background values which should be given effect without being restricted by legal forms and formalities.[6] This is acceptable if we give up the idea that human rights should be capable of legal analysis and,

[5] I have explored some of these matters in D Feldman, '"Which in Your Case You Have Not Got": Constitutionalism at Home and Abroad' (2011) 64 *Current Legal Problems* 117.

[6] See, eg, F Klug, *Values for a Godless Age: The Story of the United Kingdom's New Bill of Rights* (London, Penguin, 2000). Compare: P Sales, 'Judges and Legislature: Values into Law' (2012) 71 *CLJ* 287.

in the last resort, enforcement. Values are the common currency of politics and some morality, offering both suggestions as to the justification for giving effect to harder-edged norms and aspirations for people to pursue through social and political channels. But for lawyers, an appeal to values is either part of an argument about the proper scope or application of a legal right or obligation or it is a cry of desperation from an advocate who knows that the law is against him. If law and lawyers attempt to give effect directly to values, it is a recipe for unconstrained moralism and a threat to the legal predictability which forms an important part of the rule of law. It endangers sound political institutions, because values are normatively subjective but are usually presented as being immanent in a legal or constitutional regime. In this form, advocates for values can cover them with a cloak of what appears to be descriptive objectivity, which is as insubstantial as gossamer once one realises that one person's objectively real constitutional values are invisible to someone else.

Values tend to make public law (and private law, but that is not our focus here) transform itself into public morality. Now public morality is important, and public law should try not to make it impossible to achieve public morality. But it is a mistake to try to use public *law* as if its role were a perfectionist one. When law seeks to achieve moral perfection, it becomes tyrannical, because (as Sir John Laws said in the opening session of the conference) it tries to stop people thinking for themselves and experimenting. This is as true of public law as it is of private law. It can be controlled when we stick to fairly clear rules (and bear in mind that a rule may be tolerably clear even if the effect of applying it in particular circumstances is highly contested). When we move to values, the result is a lack of clarity which makes rigorous analysis impossible, and puts at risk the ability of public law to achieve its important goal of limiting the capacity of state institutions to do serious harm by unlawful means.

If public law has, and public lawyers have, anything to offer the management of state institutions, it is their distinctive talent for deploying analytical rigour and principled consistency to find resolutions for intractable disputes, both in dealing with individual cases and in designing systems. When we try to use tools which make analytical rigour and principled consistency more difficult, we make it less likely that our talents and labours will produce anything which non-lawyers consider to be useful. My view of the role of public law is that it works best and is most useful when it concentrates on upholding minimum standards, and leaves aspirations to the politicians and moral philosophers.

III. WHO DECIDES?

A great deal of 'public law scholarship' today seems to be devoted to questions about who should make certain kinds of decisions. Such questions are of interest to a political theorist, but seem relatively unimportant for a public *lawyer*. How should we decide who should decide? Who would be acting 'legitimately' when deciding? For public lawyers, these questions seem to be a distraction from our core task of limiting the potential for state institutions to do serious harm without lawful justification. Consider the forms which those questions typically take in legal discourse: justiciability; deference; varying intensity of review; democratic accountability for decisions; political responsibility, and so on. Such considerations are, it is true, connected to the task of assessing justifications for harmful activity of state institutions, but the connection is procedural, not ethical or normative. Notions of deference and variable standards or intensity of review, for example, seem to be concerned with how courts should assess evidence and competing arguments, or evaluate assessments (empirical or policy-related) made by others. As the Appellate Committee of the House of Lords wrote in its joint opinion in *Huang v Secretary of State for the Home Department*, giving weight to different factors 'is performance of the ordinary judicial task of weighing up the competing considerations on each side and according appropriate weight to the judgment of a person with responsibility for a given subject matter and access to special sources of knowledge and advice'.[7] This does, of course, affect the assessment of legality. We might not be able to say positively that the challenged decision or conduct was justified, but we can at least say authoritatively that it has not been shown, to a judge's satisfaction, to be unlawful. The substantial effect is to change or exclude the burden of justification which would otherwise lie on a state institution. Sometimes (as in Canada) this can directly challenge the separation of powers: where a court is prepared to defer to a non-judicial institution's interpretation of law or assessment of lawfulness, as seems to happen in Canadian administrative law, it deprives both judiciary and other institutions of distinct constitutional functions. Such a system operates on the basis of a different conception of the rule of law from those, such as Australia and the United Kingdom, in which Dicey's influence is more central.

A defender of the Canadian approach might say that one has a legal outcome, even if it can be expressed only negatively, in terms of 'not shown to have been unlawful' rather than 'shown to have been lawful'. On that view, we do not face the abrogation of the rule of law, but only a local version of the rule of law linked to a distinctive balance of power between judicial and executive institutions which is appropriate for Canada. The Australian version of that balance, with its insistence on judicial officers being the final authority on questions of law and, in Commonwealth constitutional law at least, a very clear separation of powers, could be seen as better for Australia but not better for all places and all times. But it is hard to acquit Canadian public lawyers of surrendering something of general importance to good governance when they allow their judiciary to push away responsibility for making its own assessment of matters of law, even if inter-institutional conflict may result.

Non-justiciability is analytically different, but its effect is to distance the judiciary even more completely from responsibility for assessing lawfulness. If, after much agonising, we decide that it is not proper for us to decide a question as a matter of law, it leaves a legal black hole. It is not a situation where a legal decision has been made that the decision or conduct in question is lawful, nor even that it has not been shown to be unlawful. The only decision is that the law is unable to say whether or not the decision or conduct has been shown to be lawful or unlawful. There is no legal decision at all, beyond a decision not to decide. This does not mean that there will inevitably never be scope for a judicial assessment of the merits of a case.

[7] [2007] 2 AC 167, [16].

A national court may apply conflict-of-law rules to leave the issue to a national court in another jurisdiction. If that is impossible, an international tribunal may be able to provide an assessment by reference to international or supra-national law. But the state's own judicial system will have judged itself to be incompetent. Within the state, the task of assessing of legality, as well as other criteria of desirability, passes to the challenged institutions themselves, perhaps (depending on the political and bureaucratic structures of the state) in consultation or negotiation with other political or bureaucratic institutions.

Judiciaries are not the only institutions which are tempted to concentrate on who should decide a question, or how the decision-maker should be chosen, rather than what the decision should be. Governments and legislatures like to duck controversial decisions, especially on moral questions on which society is divided. In a democracy particularly, politicians may feel that they are likely to lose more votes than they gain by taking a position. Focusing on who should decide, or how they should decide, avoids the need to make unpopular decisions. This is not new. In his Introduction to the eighth edition of his *Introduction to the Study of the Law of Constitution* in 1914, AV Dicey, surveying the development of political and constitutional ideas in the 30 years since he had completed the first edition, identified four key areas: what Dicey called 'woman suffrage'; proportional representation; federalism; and the referendum.[8] He noted first that little of the inventiveness which people had displayed in other fields, such as engineering and commerce, had been evident in political thinking. The 'new' ideas were not novel; they had merely come to command new interest. Secondly, attention had been devoted almost exclusively to ensuring, so far as possible, 'that no law should be passed or maintained … which is condemned by the public opinion of the … people'.[9] This, Dicey noted, was only one aim of a good political system. The other is that laws should be good, or wise. These two aims cannot always be achieved at the same time:

> Indeed the wisdom of legislation has little to do with its popularity. Now all the ideas which are most dear to constitutional reformers or innovators in 1914 lead to schemes of more or less merit for giving full expression in the matter of legislation to public opinion. But these schemes make in general little provision for increasing the chance that legislation shall also be wise, or in other words that it shall increase the real welfare of the country.[10]

The same could be said today of much of public law scholarship.

Could public lawyers grasp the nettle of assessing the justification offered by public institutions for their harmful acts and decisions without going beyond the bounds of law into moralism? We can, as long as we remember that our important, though minimalist, goal is to limit the capacity of state institutions to do serious harm by unlawful means. We can apply established legal tests to justifications without falling into moralism. Public lawyers can make legal assessments and leave to others the task of deciding what is wise and good. This is, of course, an over-simplification.

[8] AV Dicey, *Introduction to the Study of the Law of the Constitution*, 8th edn (London, Macmillan, 1914) lviii ff.

[9] ibid lx.

[10] ibid lxi–lxii.

We need to work out what the relevant legal norms are. Some of them stem from legislation, others from judicial development. The content of the norms might be contested. For example, in a particular jurisdiction is 'proportionality' a free-standing test for legality of some public acts or decisions? If it is, to what acts or decisions does it apply, and what obligations do public actors have as part of the duty to act proportionately? Do such obligations operate alongside an obligation not to act unreasonably, or does the former subsume the latter? These questions about doctrine have to be answered by the judiciary, sometimes with contributions from other institutions, including the legislature or executive branches of the state. Why, then, should judges not take the view that there is a judicially enforceable legal norm requiring public actors to behave wisely, virtuously or kindly?

My answer, outlined in the previous section of this chapter, is that such a norm would be too indeterminate to be a subject of rigorous legal analysis using legal techniques. It would be a bad legal norm because it would displace legal methods in favour of moral reasoning. Such a contest of the desirable content of legal norms does not, however, give rise to the sort of 'who decides?' question with which this section of the chapter is concerned. Here, we are confronting arguments about who should decide on the meaning of something which (perhaps unwisely) is acknowledged to be a legal norm, and whether there has been a breach of that legal norm. The Canadian approach to errors of law concentrates on the question of a court's worthiness to decide what is, on any view, a legal question. If public lawyers allow that to be a live issue, we not only lose some of our ability to limit the capacity of public actors to cause harm by unlawfully using state power, but we also lose some of whatever small opportunity we may have to make 'public law', whatever that means, an instrument of good and wisdom in the exercise and regulation of state power.

IV. THEORY AND COMPARISON?

Oliver Wendell Holmes considered that the proper role of comparison and theory in law is to help lawyers to reach robust decisions when developing the law. Their contribution to this is to illuminate the significance of a local problem by placing it in a more universal perspective.[11] Most of the chapters in this volume are mainly about administrative law, especially judicial review of administrative action. They examine a number of controversial issues, and raise technical, but important, questions about the grounds on which courts review administrative decisions and rules and the methods they use. For example, when courts review for 'error of law', what kinds of error does that term encompass? Are grounds of review such as natural justice, fairness and unreasonableness creatures of common law alone or do they depend on an interpretation of relevant legislation? Where courts review for error of fact, is that because they are a kind of error of law (because they cause the decision-maker to do something other than that required by applicable legislation) or as an aspect of fairness?

[11] OW Holmes, 'The Path of the Law' (1897) 10 *Harvard Law Review* 457.

Discussions of these matters in depth, focusing on single jurisdictions, show that differences between systems of administrative law are at least as significant as similarities. There is a superficial similarity between the structures of judicial review in England and Wales, Scotland, Canada, Australia, and other parts of the world which came under the sway of English common law. They share concepts such as jurisdictional error, natural justice and unreasonableness. On the other hand, there is a difference between concepts, which are general, and conceptions, which are a particular person's or system's articulation or instantiation of the concept. Contributors to the volume show how varied are different systems' conceptions of shared concepts.

The reasons for these differences are usually related to differing constitutional principles. In the conclusion to their chapter, Matthew Groves and Greg Weeks make this point powerfully in respect of differing conceptions of the concept of 'fairness' in Australia and the United Kingdom. Australian Commonwealth constitutional law is very different from that of the United Kingdom. The two systems deploy similar concepts—parliamentary sovereignty, representative and responsible government, separation of powers—but the words mean different things because of the contexts. In Australia, the Commonwealth Constitution is shaped by the differences from the United Kingdom's constitution. The separation of powers is far more pronounced than in the United Kingdom, reinforced by judicial decisions driving a constitutional wedge between judicial and ministerial functions and, to a lesser extent, between legislative and other functions. Allocation of powers is a key factor in Australian constitutional law. The picture is further complicated by differences between parliamentary sovereignty in the United Kingdom and in Australia, themselves given added complexity by Australia's federal structure. The Commonwealth Parliament is not sovereign in the UK sense, having only enumerated legislative powers and being subject to judicial review of its legislation for constitutional competence. State Parliaments are closer to the sovereignty of the UK Parliament, but their legislation is subject to constraints imposed by valid Commonwealth legislation and, where state institutions exercise functions conferred by Commonwealth law, to the Commonwealth doctrine of separation of powers. The Commonwealth government is responsible to the Commonwealth Parliament, but within the Parliament the two Houses have equal weight, because the Commonwealth Parliament operates no convention similar to that which governs relations between the two Houses of the UK Parliament. Nor is there any Australian equivalent of the United Kingdom's Parliament Act 1911. An Australian government can fail if either the House of Representatives or the Senate blocks supply.

For Australians, these constitutional differences predispose courts to approach problems of administrative law in ways which diverge from their English equivalents. For example, the separation of powers between the legislature and the executive makes courts readier than their English counterparts to review the exercise by executive agencies of delegated legislative power. Such delegated legislation is constitutionally suspect, because legislation delegating such power seems to breach the constitutional doctrine of the separation of powers. This, as Andrew Edgar argues, makes Australian courts more prepared than English courts to review delegated legislation made by central government for unreasonableness. Where English courts use unreasonableness and cognate grounds of review to invalidate delegated legislation, it is nearly always in relation to local authority bye-laws or regulatory rules. When regulations made by central government are invalidated in England, it is nearly always on the ground of excess of power (the maker of the regulations made regulations outside the scope authorised by the parent legislation) rather than unreasonableness.

This is connected to another difference between Australia and England. In Australia, courts are usually less willing than in England to supplement the procedural requirements laid down in a statute with judicial glosses drawing on common law principles of fairness. Where a statute lays down procedural prerequisites to the making of delegated legislation, Australian courts tend to give full scope to broad statutory discretion conferred on makers of delegated legislation regarding the pre-legislative procedure to be followed.

As a final example, the concept of 'jurisdictional error of law' is narrower in Australia than it is usually said to be in England and Wales. Since *Anisminic Ltd v Foreign Compensation Commission*,[12] courts and commentators in England have gradually come to regard virtually any failure by a decision-maker to meet a legal standard as being an error of law which removes the decision-maker from its jurisdiction. In Australia, the bounds of an error of law for this purpose are more tightly drawn. There is a jurisdictional error where a decision-maker mis-identifies the issue, ignores relevant material, and sometimes where it makes an erroneous finding or reaches a mistaken conclusion, but only if the error affects the exercise of the statutory power so significantly that the decision-maker has either not embarked on or has failed to complete its statutorily defined task. Unreasonableness, too, is assessed in relation to the requirements of the statute.[13] Australian courts, it seems, approach such questions primarily as being about the interpretation of the power-conferring or duty-imposing statute.

If we broaden the comparative focus to include Canada, the differences are multiplied. Like both Australia and England and Wales, the scope of judicial review in Canadian administrative law is influenced by ideas about the separation of powers. Unlike the other jurisdictions (though more like the United States), Canada regards separation of powers as justifying, or even requiring, judges to defer to other decision-makers on the scope of the latter's statutory powers. As Mary Liston explains in her chapter, instead of saying firmly that questions of law are the province of courts, Canadian judges relegate their protection against error of law to a review of the process of reasoning which leads a decision-maker to think that it is acting lawfully. Liston argues that the effect is to replace legal rules with principles which carry weight according to the application of a list of relevant considerations and so determine the degree of judicial deference to the original decision-maker.

Whatever the merits of these different conceptions of jurisdictional error, they are shaped by the historically determined particularities and peculiarities of each constitutional system. This makes it dangerous to try to compare them, or assess their merits, with a view to borrowing or transplantation between them. Is there an

12 [1969] 2 AC 139.

13 See Alan Robertson, Chapter 11, 'Is Judicial Review Qualitative?', including his discussion of *FTZK v Minister of Immigration and Border Protection* [2014] HCA 26.

international, or at least common law, community of systems of administrative law? On the evidence of the chapters in this volume, the answer seems to me to be 'No'. We can use other systems of administrative law to help to understand our own by way of contrast, or by using other systems as Weberian 'ideal types' by reference to which we can position our own system. Alternatively, we can seek to understand the concepts themselves by looking at conceptions of them as manifested in other systems. But if we do that, we must be aware of the true significance of the concepts and their conceptions in each jurisdiction as shaped by the varied constitutional and political matrices in which they operate.[14]

This prompts a reflection on the nature of the key concepts. If we take a concept such as 'jurisdictional error', it is tempting to assume (under the influence of HLA Hart) that there is a core meaning which is clear and well understood, surrounded by a penumbra of uncertainty.[15] We may find, however, that there is no 'core of certainty' to such concepts. Far from being fixed points surrounded by areas of greater or lesser contestation, they may merely mark out fields of contestation. In a different context, Christopher McCrudden has suggested that the concept of 'human dignity' may be of this kind, a 'place-holder' in an unending disagreement between moral, religious, political and legal theories about what the core, fundamental characteristics of or justification for human dignity are.[16] Such concepts help to frame the disagreement by providing a common linguistic armoury, but do nothing to determine the outcomes.

If there are at least as many deep differences between systems of administrative law in Australia, Canada and England and Wales as there are similarities, the most important function of shared concepts such as 'jurisdictional error' may be to provide a linguistic device which lawyers in each system can use to cloak whatever political and constitutional assumptions and principles seem to them to fit their own system best. The shared concepts allow players within each jurisdiction to aspire to something bigger or better than their own jurisdiction can generate, without limiting the range of arrangements which can be adopted. On this view, generalisations about concepts are useful not because they identify truths about any system or systems, but because they offer measuring posts with which to describe and understand better the features of particular systems. Such general conceptual categories are neither prescriptive nor explanatory, but purely descriptive instruments, in the way that a ruler provides a way of describing the height of individuals without either explaining people's different heights or justifying them. This is one of the lessons to be drawn from the very different chapters by Kent Roach on the classification of different forms of judicial review of legislation and Jason Varuhas on the extent to

[14] See JWF Allison, *A Continental Distinction in the Common Law: A Historical and Comparative Perspective on English Public Law* (Oxford, Clarendon Press, 1996) 4–41; J Bell, 'Mechanisms for Cross-fertilisation of Administrative Law in Europe' in J Beatson and T Tridimas (eds), *New Directions in European Public Law* (Oxford, Hart, 1998); JWF Allison, 'Transplantation and Cross-fertilisation' in J Beatson and T Tridimas (eds), *New Directions in European Public Law* (Oxford, Hart, 1998).

[15] HLA Hart, *The Concept of Law* (Oxford, Clarendon Press, 1961) 4, 121–32 on the 'open texture' of law.

[16] C McCrudden, 'Human Dignity and Judicial Interpretation of Human Rights' (2008) 19 *EJIL* 655.

which different systems use the idea of 'public interest' as a guide to delimiting their conceptions of 'public law'.

These ideas about the potentiality and purposes of comparative administrative law play into a wider debate within political theory more generally. It is often presented as being either between moralism and realism or between universalism and localism (both territorial and chronological). In the former form, the question is normative. Are there any moral standards which inform, or should inform, all political systems, or are all systems of politics ultimately about the structures of real power in a society or societies generally? The latter form of the debate is more descriptive, although part of what is described may be concerned with norms. Is it possible to generalise about political systems, or are all systems so different, and so conditioned by local and contemporary factors, that all one can do is to point to differences, either between places or between times? There is enough shared ground between the camps to give rise to a danger of becoming fixated on matters of degree rather than of kind. Is the glass half full or half empty? Nevertheless, it is instructive to realise that debates about the purposes and even the possibility of comparative public law are part of a much wider debate among those who study many different aspects of states.

In this light, several of the chapters dealing with administrative law in its various forms can be seen as adopting different positions on both the moralism/realism and the universalism/localism spectra. A question concerning the possibility of a general justifying theory for public law takes its place on the intersection of both spectra. A question concerning the existence of a general organising framework for administrative law lies, in its descriptive manifestation, on the universalism/localism framework, and, in its normative manifestation, on the moralism/realism spectrum. The spectra might not be as distinct in practice as they appear to be in theory. This should not surprise us. Practical lawyers (or politicians) understand that a normative proposition might work adequately as a basis for practical adjudication or law-making despite being unsatisfactory from a theoretical point of view because of a lack of internal coherence or normative fit. The conception or proposition is good enough as a day-to-day guide to workmanlike professionalism in judicial review, but could not found a general normative theory or, perhaps, be useful descriptively or prescriptively in other settings. Jerry Mashaw, in his chapter, makes this point powerfully in respect of the operation of 'public reason' as a value of public institutions: it is in practice essential to the practice of democracy, but is not strongly conceptualised in political theory; on the other hand, it is regarded in theory as a key to the legitimacy of administrative regimes, but does not operate well there in practice.

We can understand the chapters by Jason Varuhas (on the public interest element in definitions of public law) and Philip Murray (on the history of error of law) as arguments for localism over universalism and, perhaps, for realism over moralism. Another example of the same kind is found in the chapter by Alan Robertson on the scope of judicial review, where he suggests that courts may review exercises of the same statutory power in different ways at different times without any change in the words of the statute, because judicial review is rooted in the common law which may change over time (often in response to altered weight being allocated to competing principles). Maurice Sunkin and Varda Bondy's chapter, showing how big a gap there may be between political assumptions or rhetoric concerning judicial review and its actual effect on administrative organisations, uses local and realistic analysis as a basis for evaluating a particular, local critique of judicial review, while prompting one to consider whether the argument has implications for more universal and moralist theories concerning judicial review in particular and public law more generally.

In all this, we see a constant struggle to hold together justifying theories for exercising coercive power in the name of the state with the ordinary practice of administrative and judicial institutions. It may be correct, in theory, to say of England and Wales and Australia, respectively, that jurisdictional error of law is the primary organising concept for judicial review. But one then has to grapple with the fact that this is not how courts actually seem to work, as Paul Daly points out (although perhaps Daly's own values-based approach reflects Canadian ideas which do not travel well). Some mediating principles are needed in order to bridge the gap between theoretical tidiness and practical complexity; where public lawyers resist that kind of middle-range theory, as Mark Aronson's chapter shows to be a tendency in Australia, it is hard to develop a sense of a direction of travel in the development of the law. The matter is still more complicated where courts and legislatures are engaged in a cat-and-mouse game (without being sure which is the cat and which is the mouse) as courts try to uphold what they regard as theoretically or practically important principles in the face of a legislature seeking to secure what politicians regard as practically important, if short-term, political goals (such as the control of immigration). The resulting ping-pong, or what Carol Harlow and Richard Rawlings in their chapter call 'striking back' and 'clamping down', is characteristic of many jurisdictions, including Malaysia and India, as well as Australia and England and Wales. As Mark Aronson shows in his analysis of the High Court of Australia's doctrinal innovations in response to legislative attempts to strike back against and clamp down on judicial review of immigration decisions, the results may sometimes be unexpected, in that a legislative strike-back in the context of immigration may leave unexpected new grounds of review operative in relation to other fields of decision-making.

V. CONCLUSION

These reflections suggest two conclusions. First, we can usefully employ comparison to show how many different ways there are of doing things and what factors tend to make one way more useful or successful than another. In that way we can break down presumptions and remove blinkers. If we use it to do more than that, we risk either obscuring reality by wrongly eliminating an appreciation of differences and the reasons for them, or pretending that our preferred normative structure has some illusory universal normative force. We need to ensure that we are honest in our use of comparative law, and do not allow our liking for a particular norm, structure or outcome to weaken our commitment as scholars to understanding and making clear, rather than obscuring, the range of conclusions which our comparative studies reasonably and logically support.

Secondly, we need to ensure that we are clear about the aim and capacity of any theory we develop. We should not slide from empirical findings to normative claims without clearly signalling that we are doing so. Even more importantly, we must not allow a normative claim to shape our approach to empirical analysis; we must not read our data in the light of our preferred norms. If the analysis leads to normatively uncomfortable results, we should acknowledge it, not fudge the argument by reading back our normative preferences into our analysis. A desire to support a particular line of normative advocacy must not lead us to ignore empirical differences or to ignore or gloss over inconvenient truths.

Index

www.ingramcontent.com/pod-product-compliance
Lightning Source LLC
LaVergne TN
LVHW080008210926
848481LV00011B/2969